Poets Reading

Poets Reading

The **FIELD** Symposia

Edited by David Walker

Oberlin College Press

http://www.oberlin.edu/~ocpress

Publication of this book was made possible in part by a grant from the National Endowment for the Arts.

LIBRARY OF CONGRESS CATALOGING-IN-PUBLICATION DATA

Main entry under title:

Poets Reading: The FIELD Symposia / edited by David Walker.
    A collection of essays which originally appeared in FIELD magazine.
    1. Poetics—Addresses, essays, lectures. 2. Poetry—study and teaching.
I. Walker, David, 1950-.

LC: 99-60376

ISBN: 0-932440-84-3 (pbk.)

CONTENTS

Preface   xi

Emily Dickinson (1830-1886)   1
   NANCY WILLARD: Questioning the Pilgrim   2
   CHARLES SIMIC: Ambiguity's Wedding   5
   DAVID WALKER: Stinging Work   6
   STANLEY PLUMLY: Doors Ajar   11
   MARTHA COLLINS: The Outer from the Inner   17
   DAVID YOUNG: Electric Moccasins   20

Gerard Manley Hopkins (1844-1889)   27
   CHARLES WRIGHT: Improvisations: With
      Father Hopkins on Lake Como   28
   GERALD STERN: Some Thoughts   35
   DAVID YOUNG: Surprised by Grief   38
   LEE UPTON: "Disremembering, Dismembering"   44
   DENNIS SCHMITZ: On "Carrion Comfort"   47
   STANLEY PLUMLY: "Hear What I Do"   51
   MARIANNE BORUCH: Becoming "Epithalamion"   56

Wallace Stevens (1879-1955)   61
   DENNIS SCHMITZ: On "Peter Quince at the Clavier"   62
   PHILIP BOOTH: On "Domination of Black"   66
   ALBERTA TURNER: Astonished   69
   LAURA JENSEN: Why I Like "The Snow Man"   73
   MAXINE KUMIN: On "A Postcard from the Volcano"   74
   DAVID YOUNG: Gaiety of Language   76
   SHIRLEY KAUFMAN: On "A Rabbit as King of the Ghosts"   79
   WILLIAM STAFFORD: On "Poetry Is a Destructive Force"   81
   ALBERT GOLDBARTH: On "The Glass of Water"   83
   STANLEY PLUMLY: "The Glass of Water": A Footnote   84
   PAMELA STEWART: On Stevens' "Yellow Afternoon"   86
   MARVIN BELL: On "Arrival at the Waldorf"   88
   DAVID WALKER: On "Puella Parvula"   91

William Carlos Williams (1883-1963)   95
   DONALD JUSTICE: On Purity of Style   96
   MARVIN BELL: Williams and "Dedication..."   100

MARCIA SOUTHWICK: On "Dedication for a Plot of Ground"   104
DONALD HALL: William Carlos Williams and the Visual   106
DAVID WALKER: On "The Polar Bear"   111
MIROSLAV HOLUB: W. C. Williams on Death   113
CHARLES SIMIC: Streets Strewn with Garbage   118
GERALD STERN: On "Canthara"   120
STANLEY PLUMLY: Reading Williams   123
PAUL MARIANI: An April of Small Waves   126

Ezra Pound (1885-1972)   **133**
DONALD HALL: Pound's Sounds   134
WILLIAM MATTHEWS: Young Ezra   138
STANLEY PLUMLY: Pound's Garden   141
JAMES LAUGHLIN: Rambling Around Pound's Propertius   144
NORMAN DUBIE: Some Notes: Into the Sere and Yellow   154
CAROL MUSKE: Alba LXXIX   161
CHARLES WRIGHT: Improvisations on Pound   172

Marianne Moore (1887-1972)   **181**
LYNNE MCMAHON: On "The Steeple-Jack"   182
DAVID WALKER: Imperial Happiness   186
BARBARA MOLLOY-OLUND: Man—Sea—Silence   193
STANLEY PLUMLY: Absent Things   198
LEE UPTON: An Invitation to Wonder   201
DAVID YOUNG: Clipped Wings   204

Anna Akhmatova (1889-1966)   **213**
LENORE MAYHEW: Images from a Life   214
ALBERTA TURNER: Translating the Translations   217
MARCIA SOUTHWICK: A Slab of Clay, a Handful of Dust   221
JUDITH HEMSCHEMEYER: A Poet and Her Country   224
DEBORAH DIGGES: Translation and the Egg   227
DAVID YOUNG: Mending What Can't Be Mended   232
MARILYN KRYSL: The Leper's Battle   238

Osip Mandelstam (1892-1941)   **241**
FRANZ WRIGHT: Persephone's Bees: Thoughts on Mandelstam   242
AGHA SHAHID ALI: The Blessed Word   248
DAVID YOUNG: Stars Versus Salt   253
SYLVA FISCHEROVÁ: The Time vs. the Age   259
MARTHA COLLINS: The Speech of Silence Laboring   263
ROBERT BLY: The Beauty of Sound   266

Eugenio Montale (1896-1981)   269
   SANDRA MCPHERSON: On "In the Greenhouse"   270
   JEROME MAZZARO: "The Custom-House" and "Lemons"   272
   DAVID ST. JOHN: Eugenio Montale's "Two in Twilight"   278
   DANA GIOIA: From Pastoral to Apocalypse in Mid-Sentence   282
   JAMES MERRILL: On "Mottetti VII"   285
   SONIA RAIZISS: Montale's "Dream" Poem   286
   DAVID YOUNG: The Poem That Took the Place of a Mountain   291
   REG SANER: Montale and the Outsider   296
   CHARLES WRIGHT: Improvisations on Montale   300

Robert Francis (1901-1987)   307
   DAVID YOUNG: Robert Francis and the Bluejay   308
   DONALD HALL: On "His Running My Running"   311
   ROBERT WALLACE: The Excellence of "Excellence"   313
   ALBERTA TURNER: Permitting Craft   316
   RICHARD WILBUR: On Robert Francis' "Sheep"   319
   DAVID WALKER: Francis Reading and Reading Francis   321

Pablo Neruda (1904-1973)   325
   MARIANNE BORUCH: The Shape of His Melancholy   326
   DAVID YOUNG: The Wave That Does Not Die   330
   DAVID ST. JOHN: Pablo Neruda's "Walking Around"   337
   ROBERT BLY: Walking Around with Pablo Neruda   340
   WILLIAM O'DALY: To the Earth and Its Winter   346

Theodore Roethke (1908-1963)   359
   MARIANNE BORUCH: Three Spirits   360
   THOMAS LUX: The Secret Joinery of Song   364
   ALBERTA TURNER: A Second Reading   369
   MARTHA COLLINS: Word-Work   371
   GERALD STERN: More Major   375
   BECKIAN FRITZ GOLDBERG: The Case of "The Tree, the Bird"   378

Elizabeth Bishop (1911-1979)   385
   SANDRA MCPHERSON: "The Armadillo": A Commentary   386
   DAVID WALKER: Elizabeth Bishop and the Ordinary   389
   ELIZABETH SPIRES: Questions of Knowledge   393
   MARIANNE BORUCH: Original Shell   398
   SHEROD SANTOS: A Connoisseur of Loneliness   402
   J. D. MCCLATCHY: Some Notes on "One Art"   406
   ALBERTA TURNER: On "First Death in Nova Scotia"   412
   JEAN VALENTINE: On "Sonnet"   415

Robert Hayden (1913-1980)   **417**
    ALBERTA TURNER: On "Those Winter Sundays"   418
    NICCOLÒ N. DONZELLA: Elegy for an American   420
    W. D. SNODGRASS: Robert Hayden: The Man in the Middle   423
    CALVIN HERNTON: Shining   437
    ANTHONY WALTON: The Eye of Faith   445
    YUSEF KOMUNYAKAA: Journey into "(American Journal)"   448

Randall Jarrell (1914-1965)   **455**
    LAURA JENSEN: Potential for Whole Totem   456
    BRUCE WEIGL: An Autobiography of Nightmare   460
    C. D. WRIGHT: Mission of the Surviving Gunner   462
    FRED CHAPPELL: The Longing to Belong   465
    DAVID ST. JOHN: Randall Jarrell's "Seele im Raum"   472
    RALPH BURNS: The Plain Truth in "The Truth"   478
    DAVID YOUNG: Day for Night   482
    NANCY WILLARD: Radiant Facts   487
    MARIANNE BORUCH: Rhetoric and Mystery   491
    DAVID WALKER: The Shape on the Bed   496

William Stafford (1914-1993)   **501**
    CHARLES SIMIC: On "At the Bomb Testing Site"   502
    HENRY TAYLOR: Millions of Intricate Moves   504
    JONATHAN HOLDEN: On "With Kit, Age 7, at the Beach"   514
    MARGARET ATWOOD: On "Waking at 3 A.M."   517
    LINDA PASTAN: On "Ask Me"   521
    TOM ANDREWS: Glimpses into Something Ever Larger   523
    ALBERTA TURNER: On "Things I Learned Last Week"   526
    DAVID YOUNG: Shivers of Summer Wind   528

Miroslav Holub (1923-1998)   **535**
    EDWARD HIRSCH: Surveyor of Worlds   536
    LARRY LEVIS: So That: On Holub's "Meeting Ezra Pound"   538
    DENNIS SCHMITZ: Distancing   542
    SYLVA FISCHEROVÁ: A Game with Faces   547
    TOM ANDREWS: Lives of a Cell   551

W. S. Merwin (b. 1927)   **557**
    BRUCE BEASLEY: The Anti-Catechism of W. S. Merwin   558
    DAVID WALKER: W. S. Merwin as Dramatist   563
    C. D. WRIGHT: Echo Rising   569
    JAMES BAKER HALL: If There Is a Place
        Where This Is the Language   571

DAVID YOUNG: Caught Breath   581
CHRISTOPHER MERRILL: In Search of the Genuine   587
WILLIAM MATTHEWS: Layered Vision   591
CAROL MUSKE: The Transparent Mask   594

Notes on Contributors   597

Acknowledgments   605

Index   613

PREFACE

In 1979, in honor of the one hundredth anniversary of the birth of Wallace Stevens, *FIELD* magazine invited a number of American poets to choose a favorite Stevens poem and write a short essay on what it meant to them. The response was immediate and enthusiastic: thirteen poets responded, including William Stafford on "Poetry Is a Destructive Force," Dennis Schmitz on "Peter Quince at the Clavier," Maxine Kumin on "A Postcard from the Volcano," Stanley Plumly and Albert Goldbarth on "The Glass of Water," Laura Jensen on "The Snow Man," Philip Booth on "Domination of Black," Pamela Stewart on "Yellow Afternoon," Shirley Kaufman on "A Rabbit as King of the Ghosts," and Marvin Bell on "Arrival at the Waldorf." The essays testified to the variety and richness of Stevens' work, the extraordinary regard in which successive generations of poets hold him, and the kinds of influence he may have had on them. Equally compelling was the light the essays shed on how poets *read* and the interplay of analysis and intuition that produces their responses. In describing the qualities they celebrate in Stevens' work, the poets cut through the conventions of literary criticism and reasserted poetry as a living art, charged with immediacy and excitement. Readers of *FIELD* responded with equal enthusiasm.

Almost every year since that time, *FIELD* has published a symposium on the work of another major poet, and these conversations—among poets reading poetry—have become one of the most popular features of the magazine. Often the occasion has been a significant milestone: William Carlos Williams', Ezra Pound's, and Anna Akhmatova's hundredth birthdays, Robert Francis's eightieth, William Stafford's seventy-fifth, Eugenio Montale's death. Sometimes our goal was simply to invite renewed attention to poets who seemed to us insufficiently understood or appreciated through more conventional analysis, and about whom we thought current poets might have especially interesting things to say: Elizabeth Bishop, Marianne Moore, Theodore Roethke, Robert Hayden, Osip Mandelstam. The first eighteen featured poets include central American modernists (Stevens, Williams, Pound, Moore), the next two generations (Francis, Roethke, Bishop, Hayden, Jarrell, Stafford, W. S. Merwin), two nineteenth-century forerunners of modernism (Emily Dickinson and Gerard Manley Hopkins), and a number of European (Akhmatova, Mandelstam, Montale, Miroslav Holub) and South American (Pablo Neruda) counterparts. While we have not attempted to provide a comprehensive survey, this group of poets clearly represents modern literature at its finest, in all its richness, complexity, and considerable variety.

The list of contributors to the symposia is a virtual *Who's Who* of contemporary poetry. Some of the poet-essayists are trained as literary critics, others are not, but something about the medium of the *FIELD* symposium seems to encourage lively responses and genuinely illuminating insights from them all. A few examples will suggest the range of approaches and voices represented:

> One of the marvelous things about "Canthara" is that it needs no explanation, and that it was written without an explanation in mind. It is a poem about an old man remembering the wild days of his youth; it is a poem celebrating the simple joy, and the humor, of sexuality; it is a poem that honors energy, and faith, and ecstasy; it is a "small" poem, touching a brief moment in time; it is a slightly pedantic poem, teaching the value of sensuality, in all its wholesome and unwholesome forms, in producing "lasting happiness"....
>
> (Gerald Stern on Williams)

> I think Pound to be the most American of poets, especially of his time, including Williams. American of a certain, unflagging sort: more European than the Europeans, more concerned about their heritage than they were. Like Berenson. But with such a Twainian "innocence abroad." His poetic line ends up a broken Whitmanian line and he remains totally American to the end: paranoid, in a white study.
>
> (Charles Wright on Pound)

> Some poems are profoundly, willfully plain. Like efficient but passionate hosts bored by the party, they usher us *out*, past the church, past the large showy houses that look like cakes, into the blank countryside of a listless month, November maybe. Little is said really, and what's said is repeated, moving with reserve and overlap toward the secret of the trip. No digression, that brief glad accident against purpose. Nothing ornate, airy, playful. Wonder is carefully distilled into weight, not a gift but a given.
>
> (Marianne Boruch on Jarrell)

> The poem's irregularity, its sometime awkwardness, its commitment to scenic action further underscore its reality, once the reader is ushered into its world. The speaker asks us to "hear what I do," to "make believe," to trust, on location, where he is going, inventing as he goes. The unfinished "Epithalamion" is, therefore, a poem off-balance, tilted toward its verticality, its longitude, toward some distant center of gravity, rather joyously lost in the pleasure of its own company.
>
> (Stanley Plumly on Hopkins)

Whether incisively analytical or extravagantly metaphorical or reflectively autobiographical—or all three at once—these essays all share a passionate attention to the *process* of poetry. "It isn't what [a poet] *says* that counts as a work of art, it's what he makes," Williams said, and most of these essays are written in the same pragmatic spirit. Clarity and precision, rather than obfuscation and mystification, reign here. There's a good deal of attention to matters of craft, of line-by-line and even word-by-word strategy; the reader has the sense of investigating the writing process from a particularly privileged position, sharing the informed, canny insights of one poet settling down to enter imaginatively into the world of another.

At the same time, this is not simply a book about technique; it's equally a testament to why poetry matters. Generously and often movingly, the essays explore the ways in which reading—and writing—poetry is a fundamental source of knowledge, insight, and pleasure. Especially striking are the ways some contributors find to speak about the importance of particular poets in their lives as well as in their writing. Nancy Willard says that "it was Emily Dickinson who taught me to love questions more than answers." Sandra McPherson remembers that "at age 21 or 22, I felt that I needed to read Elizabeth Bishop to learn how to use *anything* as the subject of the poem or as an object in the poem. Her work said, if you like things enough they'll stay alive even in a poem, whatever their nature. And another thing: her work *didn't* say 'I am a poet.' In fact, the *I* was omitted from her work for pages on end, the better to show her affection for her subjects." David St. John acknowledges that "I have always been reluctant to discuss in print the work of Eugenio Montale. This is not because of any ambivalence I feel about his poetry, but because it has, for many years, been for me a place of sanctuary, a world of privacy I find consoling. Montale's work has always existed for me in a realm beyond the daily literary clatter of my life as a poet and teacher." The poets' willingness to discuss what they value in poetry helps to make sometimes quite challenging material feel more immediate and human. In speaking not only as writers but as *readers*, acknowledging their uncertainties as well as their insights, they have produced a uniquely valuable form of literary discussion.

Some of these essays have been reprinted in collections and anthologies, but most have not, so it is a distinct pleasure to bring them all back into print. I have arranged the symposia chronologically by poet rather than in the order in which they first appeared in the magazine, and one or two contributors asked to make slight revisions, but otherwise they appear as they first did. The individual essays within a symposium always bear interesting relations to each other, and setting the various symposia cheek-by-jowl together turns out to produce all sorts of additional cross-pollination. My thanks to the contributors for permission to reprint the essays, and to the National Endowment for the Arts for generous publication support. I'm especially indebted to the founding editors of *FIELD*—Stuart Friebert, Alberta Turner, and David Young—who helped inspire and generate the symposia in the first place. This book would not exist without them.

David Walker
Oberlin, Ohio

EMILY DICKINSON
(1830-86)

T hwarted in her attempts to publish during her lifetime, and later consigned to the role of eccentric, unschooled spinster and composer of decorative verse, Emily Dickinson is now widely credited, along with her fellow pioneer Walt Whitman, with having invented American poetry. In a life lived largely in the seclusion of her father's house in Amherst, Massachusetts, she published only seven poems, but she left over 1700 in her bedroom for posterity to discover, many carefully bound into 43 separate collections she called "fascicles." Her work demonstrates extraordinary psychological subtlety, especially in rendering states of ambivalence, instability, loss, and ironic detachment. Its disconcerting leaps and mysteriously associative logic were far ahead of the poetics of her time, prefiguring Imagism's discovery of what Ezra Pound was to call the luminous image. Only after the formal experiments of the early Modernists could her unconventional prosody, syntax, and punctuation be allowed as conscious, deliberate innovation. Similarly, her fiercely uncompromising exploration of the nature of spiritual experience, frequently at odds with the orthodoxies of her day, could only be fully appreciated in the more skeptical and less sentimental light of modernism. Perhaps more vigorously than ever, Dickinson remains our contemporary, illuminating the deepest possibilities of language, identity, and poetic voice.

BOOKS: The standard text remains *The Poems of Emily Dickinson*, ed. Thomas H. Johnson (3 vols., 1955); the best selection of the poems is *Final Harvest*, ed. Johnson (1961). The fullest biography is Richard B. Sewall, *The Life of Emily Dickinson* (1974). See also *The Letters of Emily Dickinson*, ed. Thomas H. Johnson and Theodora Ward (1958).

101

Will there really be a "Morning"?
Is there such a thing as "Day"?
Could I see it from the mountains
If I were as tall as they?

Has it feet like Water lilies?
Has it feathers like a Bird?
Is it brought from famous countries
Of which I have never heard?

Oh some Scholar! Oh some Sailor!
Oh some Wise Man from the skies!
Please to tell a little Pilgrim
Where the place called "Morning" lies!

Nancy Willard

QUESTIONING THE PILGRIM

It was Emily Dickinson who taught me to love questions more than answers the summer I turned sixteen and found myself on the cusp of the question that pricks all travelers who hear the gates clang shut on the gardens of childhood: *what will become of me?* School was out, I stopped wearing my watch and set myself the task of memorizing a poem a day, an ambition which soon shrank to a poem a week. I chose the poems from two books I loved and trusted. One was a beat-up copy of the songs from Shakespeare's plays. The other was a Modern Library edition of Emily Dickinson's selected poems.

"Will there really be a 'Morning'?" was the first poem I memorized, and what attracted me was its apparent lack of subject. When I puzzled over the question, What is the poem about?, I could only answer by quoting the poem itself. Yet what could be more artless? There was nothing here I couldn't actually say if I were a traveler asking directions.

But of course I, for whom morning was a time and not a place, wouldn't ask those questions. Where was the speaker and what circumstances had kept her in the dark about so simple a matter? Under that guileless opening question, wasn't the speaker asking a more urgent one? The only way into the poem was the method of the poem itself: questions leading to questions, which changed and refined themselves as I read more of Dickinson's poetry and discovered she was a riddle-maker, and therefore a poet after my own heart.

Long before I could recognize a metaphor, I loved riddles for giving me what I have always valued in poetry: a way of looking at the commonplace in an uncommon way. The riddle Dickinson wrote to accompany the gift of a cocoon to her young nephew requires no answer, only the reader's close scrutiny of her subject through a catalogue of metaphors:

> Drab Habitation of Whom?
> Tabernacle or Tomb—
> Or Dome of Worm—
> Or Porch of Gnome—
> Or some Elf's Catacomb?

The poems of Dickinson's that have taught me the most are those in which she does not name her subject, though every metaphor reveals it and every verb in her succinct narratives dramatizes it. The following two stanzas (the first and last in a five-stanza poem) are rooted in the reticence of riddles, but I know of no riddle about snow that surprises the reader the way Dickinson does throughout this poem.

> It sifts from Leaden Sieves—
> It powders all the Wood.
> It fills with Alabaster Wool
> The Wrinkles of the Road—
> . . . .
> It Ruffles Wrists of Posts
> As Ankles of a Queen—
> Then stills its Artisans—like Ghosts—
> Denying they have been—

Behind the face of the familiar lies the deeper question: *who are you?* Many years after I committed "Will there ever be a 'Morning'?" to memory, I discovered a poem similar in form, yet different in voice, that had not snagged my attention that summer, though I must surely have read it. This poem, too, consists of questions, but their context is narrative and therefore more specific—and more sinister.

> What Inn is this
> Where for the night
> Peculiar Traveller comes?
> Who is the Landlord?
> Where the maids?
> Behold, what curious rooms!
> No ruddy fires on the hearth—
> No brimming Tankards flow—

Necromancer! Landlord!
Who are these below?

A traveler who does not know she is moving from life to death looks at the grave and sees an inn—and an ill-furnished one at that. Because an inn is what travelers might expect to see, her questions describe not what is, but what is not. Only in the ninth line does she call her landlord by the name that suits him, acknowledging that he works his wonders by communicating with the dead. But she does not count herself among them. The final question shows the speaker has been taken by surprise and tricked by her own ignorance. She has not yet surmised that when death kindly stopped for her, the destination was eternity.

In a letter written fifteen years before she died, Dickinson's questions suggest she has not only found the place where morning lies, she is one of its keepers: "Dare you dwell in the East where we dwell? Are you afraid of the sun?—When you hear the new violet sucking her way among the sods, shall you be *resolute?* All we are *strangers*—dear—The world is not acquainted with us, because we are not acquainted with her. And pilgrims!"[1]

---

[1] From a letter to Catherine Scott Turner (Anthon), written about March 1859. *The Letters of Emily Dickinson*, ed. Thomas H. Johnson (Harvard University Press, 1958), II: 349.

Charles Simic

AMBIGUITY'S WEDDING

after E. D.

Bride of Awe, all that's left for us
Are vestiges of a feast table,
Levitating champagne glasses
In the hands of the erased millions.

Mr. So and So, the bridegroom
Of absent looks, lost looks,
The pale reporter from the awful doors
Before identity was leased

At night's delicious close,
A few denizens of insignificance about,
The spider at his trade,
The print of his vermilion foot.

A faded boy in sallow clothes
Badly smudged, his shadow on the wall
Still visible, a wintry shadow
Quieter than sleep.

Soul, take thy risk,
There where your words and thoughts
Come to a stop,
Abbreviate me thus, in marriage.

443

I tie my hat—I crease my Shawl—
Life's little duties do—precisely—
As the very least
Were infinite—to me—

I put new Blossoms in the Glass—
And throw the old—away—
I push a petal from my Gown
That anchored there—I weigh
The time 'twill be till six o'clock
I have so much to do—
And yet—Existence—some way back—
Stopped—struck—my ticking—through—
We cannot put Ourself away
As a completed Man
Or Woman—When the Errand's done
We came to Flesh—upon—
There may be—Miles on Miles of Naught—
Of Action—sicker far—
To simulate—is stinging work—
To cover what we are
From Science—and from Surgery—
Too Telescopic Eyes
To bear on us unshaded—
For their—sake—not for Ours—
'Twould start them—
We—could tremble—
But since we got a Bomb—
And held it in our Bosom—
Nay—Hold it—it is calm—

Therefore—we do life's labor—
Though life's Reward—be done—
With scrupulous exactness—
To hold our Senses—on—

David Walker

STINGING WORK

Perhaps it's the portrait. That solemn, rather plain photograph of the young woman in the dark dress, reprinted in countless critical and biographical studies, is the one physical link most of us have to the poet. Formally posed so as not to blur the daguerreotype, she gazes out at the camera, nearly expressionless, giving very little away. Along with the mythology of the spinster in the white dress, the recluse in her father's garret, the cookies in the basket, the portrait allows us to project our own version of who Dickinson was and what she means. Even once we've set aside the most patently false images—the greeting-card Dickinson, the lovelorn Dickinson, the one who was so hapless at punctuation that she needed to be corrected— there remains the enormous riddle of seeing beyond the images to the self they teasingly refuse to locate.

Riddles were of course deeply congenial to Dickinson, and comprise a central strategy of many of the poems. There are the poems such as "It sifts from Leaden Sieves" (#311) and "I like to see it lap the Miles" (#585), which leave it to the reader to puzzle out the "it" ("snow" and "a train," respectively). More challenging are poems that also refuse to specify the "it," but which, we gradually recognize, *have* no single, precisely identifiable referent. A poem like the exuberantly Gothic "'Twas like a Maelstrom, with a notch" (#414) may look like a riddle poem, but its power depends on the reader's eventual realization that the simile points to nothing specific beyond itself; the speaker refers to a psychological state so complex and terrifying that she cannot name or know it except indirectly, by analogy. I sometimes think of the self in Dickinson's work as represented in much the same way: elusive, protean, and finally unknowable. In the work taken as a whole, and sometimes within an individual poem, Dickinson can seem at once intensely, self-flayingly personal and thrillingly, acrobatically self-creating, making herself over into a boy, a corpse, a "wife." This is one of the most daunting challenges of the work. It is also, of course, one of its greatest rewards.

What does all this have to do with the poem I've singled out? At first glance, anyway, "I tie my hat—I crease my Shawl" seems to confirm the persona we read in the photograph. Simple, modest, scrupulous: the diction of the opening appears to define her as exactly as the activities she describes. What sort of person actually takes the trouble to crease a shawl? Well, one for whom such trivial, even banal details "do"—meaning "suffice." Hers is a life lived within narrow horizons, like Jane Austen's "little bit (two Inches wide) of Ivory on which I work with so fine a Brush, as produces little effect after much labour." Despite the air of calm and habituated self-sufficiency, there's a hint of unrest in that "As" that starts the third line; here it means "as if"—by implication, the speaker recognizes the actual chasm between the "little duties" of her own life and the infinite beyond, even though the *tone*, like the gaze in the photograph, says nothing overtly.

The beginning of the long central stanza returns with determination to the mundane, yet the complacency of the portrait soon falters. She moves from the familiar task of replacing faded flowers with fresh ones, to a much odder gesture: "I push a petal from my Gown/That anchored there" expresses considerable weight, as though she scarcely has the energy or even the will to "push" away the petal. The little pun that gets her from "anchor" to "weigh" serves also to emphasize how heavily time weighs on her. Despite all the emphasis on activity, this is clearly a life which seems like suspended animation, consisting of long stretches of time in which one watches a petal fall on one's dress and then summons the effort to push it away. Read in this way, the commonplace "I have so much to do" becomes deeply poignant, desperately evoking housework as wish-fulfillment.

Even if we've been alert to the underlying ironies—and I suspect most readers are not, on first encountering the poem—what follows comes as a real shock. In mid-quatrain, the speaker rips off the mask and confronts the existential crisis directly, in so many words. The narrative widens disconcertingly suddenly to become the metaphysical:

> And yet—Existence—some way back—
> Stopped—struck—my ticking—through—

What may have seemed oblivious self-deception is revealed as wholly deliberate stratagem. This couplet, by the way, is a wonderful example of the effect of Dickinson's unorthodox punctuation. The voice halts, stutters, as the speaker struggles to find language adequate to her experience, just as the reader must struggle to read the syntax coherently. The notion that existence itself has "stopped" at some indeterminate point is fairly clear, especially if we are familiar with Dickinson's other death-in-life poems. And "my ticking—through" seems to echo other poems in which the debilitated self is figured as a stopped clock (e.g., "A Clock stopped—/Not the Mantel's" [#287]). But "struck" points both backward to "stopped" and forward (as in "struck...through," as though she's been physically pierced by existence), an effect that more regularized punctuation simply couldn't achieve.

At this point the personal pronouns shift from singular to plural, throwing the net of implication over the reader; what seemed the experience of an isolated and rather pathetic individual becomes an icy rendering of the human condition. The voice takes on a note of resolution, even revelation, though the theology evoked here promises no redemption, only suffering:

> We cannot put Ourself away
> As a completed Man

> Or Woman—When the Errand's done
> We came to Flesh—upon—
> There may be—Miles on Miles of Naught—
> Of Action—sicker far.

Has any twentieth-century writer taken this idea any farther? Even if the putting-away of the self for which she longs isn't literally suicide, the image of existence as "Miles on Miles of Naught" and the notion of action as simply a kind of pathology anticipate the work of, say, Beckett to a striking degree. And yet I would argue that, as in Beckett, the confrontation with pain here embodies not simply a masochistic impulse, but also a facing-up to experience that is bracing, even exhilarating. That impulse is defined more precisely in what follows:

> To simulate—is stinging work—
> To cover what we are
> From Science—and from Surgery—
> Too Telescopic Eyes
> To bear on us unshaded.

The act of simulation, of putting on the face in the portrait, is here defined not as play but as itself painful; the "little duties" which at the beginning of the poem seemed to afford such pleasure—or at least comfort—are acknowledged as "stinging work." They are necessary protection from the even greater threat of vulnerability, which is presented metaphorically as the result of invasive technology: the microscope, the scalpel, the telescope of prying eyes bearing down "unshaded." The voice now is at its most neurotic, as paranoid about the menace of other people as Dickinson ever got.

Yet here the poem takes its final and, I think, most surprising turn. The threat, she tells us, is not finally to oneself; rather, we disguise what we are from others "for their—sake—not for Ours." For others to be forced to face the naked truth about us would be too disruptive: "'twould start them." The stanza turns inside out, presenting the gestures of concealment not as cowardice but as a sort of heroism. "We—could tremble," she tells us, "But since we got a Bomb—/And held it in our Bosom...." It's a powerful, multilayered metaphor; as in Conrad's terrorist fantasia *The Secret Agent*, the one who carries the bomb is both in mortal danger and possessed of enormous power. And in a wonderful moment, the poem enacts our reaction to this startling and volatile image: "Nay—Hold it," she exclaims, as though we'd nearly dropped that bomb. "It is calm": the explosiveness and the ennui, inside and outside, are held in perfect symbiotic suspension.

After a tiny pause for breath, the poem sums up in a quatrain neat as a sampler; only because we've had the self-revelation can we intuit the terrible cost implicit in that neatness. The gap between the meaning of "*do* [perform] life's labor" and "life's Reward—be *done* [finished]" is indeed infinite. Once we've had a glimpse of the bomb carried around as part of the daily routine, the scrupulous exactness necessary "to hold our Senses—on" seems less than simply metaphorical. And yet, as I've said, the poem is not merely an expression of pain. As in many of Dickinson's poems about concealment, there's the irony that it is in fact a self-portrait, a deliberate gesture of revelation. One of the experiences the poem evokes is that of being in the closet; reading the poem, forced to confront the implications of the gaze, we witness Dickinson's coming out.

640

I cannot live with You—
It would be Life—
And Life is over there—
Behind the Shelf

The Sexton keeps the Key to—
Putting up
Our Life—His Porcelain—
Like a Cup—

Discarded of the Housewife—
Quaint—or Broke—
A newer Sevres pleases—
Old Ones crack—

I could not die—with You—
For One must wait
To shut the Other's Gaze down—
You—could not—

And I—Could I stand by
And see You—freeze—
Without my Right of Frost—
Death's privilege?

Nor could I rise—with You—
Because Your Face
Would put out Jesus'—
That New Grace

Glow plain—and foreign
On my homesick Eye—
Except that You than He
Shone closer by—

They'd judge Us—How—
For You—served Heaven—You know,
Or sought to—
I could not—

Because You saturated Sight—
And I had no more Eyes
For sordid excellence
As Paradise

And were You lost, I would be—
Though My Name
Rang loudest
On the Heavenly fame—

And were You—saved—
And I—condemned to be
Where You were not—
That self—were Hell to Me—

So We must meet apart—
You there—I—here—
With just the Door ajar
That Oceans are—and Prayer—
And that White Sustenance—
Despair—

Stanley Plumly

DOORS AJAR

"Tell all the truth but tell it slant," like the slant of light on winter afternoons. Angles of vision, angles of light, angles of insight: Emily Dickinson is the master of indirection, implication, rich ambiguity; and her poems are the mastery of—to quote Keats, one of her heroes—loading every rift with ore. We think of her symmetrical brilliance, in which the lines and rhymes balance the silences as perfectly as "syllable from sound" and the epigrams of thought act out their meanings "as imperceptibly as grief" as they speak to us at just the moment, it seems, of their inscription. I can think of no other poet who seems so imperatively to speak and write at once (see the *Letters*), to "tell all" yet understate at the same time. Her most famous poems—#s 258, 280, 465, 712, etc.—vary only slightly the hymnal quatrains of her obsessive music and vary no more than a few lines from her happy twenty. But when I think of Dickinson's exponential power I think of those poems that frustrate her perfections and worry her

formalities to something closer to the nerve of the experience, where the angles and slantings are more severe and exposed, where the duration is extended, and where the emotion meets its edge, as in her longest poem, #640.

"I cannot live with you" is fifty lines of tight quatrains, in which not only
the trimeter/dimeter base of the rhythm widely varies but the 2/4 rhymes
range from pure to slant to not at all (stanza eight). The length of the poem
has a lot to do with this "opening" of the form, just as the abbreviation of the
line (compared to her standard tetrameter/trimeter) quickens the pace of the
sentences down the page. Dickinson obviously has a deal on her mind; you
feel the pressure of what it is at every turn and image—at every angle and
slanting. And the longer the poem goes the quicker (and more densely) it
seems to move, acquiring specific gravity and momentum as it accumulates
its dramatic information. This is one of Dickinson's most personal poems—
if that is a fair term for the excruciating reticence she brings to bear on all of
her material, a reticence she struggles with in this poem as she tries on one
analogy (strategy) after another, trying, it seems at first, to say enough, to
find what will articulate the apparent contradiction that "I cannot live with
you—/It would be Life."

There is, of course, a plotted structure to what she is working out—a
cause-and-effect sequence of comparisons, figures, and conflict (the conflict
is the passion here)—particularly since one cannot write fifty lines of quatrains. The final stanza adds, or discovers, the two more lines ("And that
White Sustenance—/Despair—") that in themselves summarize the way
open closure operates as a principle throughout the poem. The intensity of
her intensely private experience is such that the poet cannot hold the form to
shape—nor clearly does she want to—and she cannot hold it back. The intensity increases the longer she sustains her "inadequacy." This is angular
form at its best, slanting as needs be in order to test the emotion against the
images of the thought. And by the time we arrive at the single theme-haunted
pure and impure rhymes of the final, elongated moment of the poem, "there-
here-Door-ajar-are-Prayer-Despair" add up, in their little space, to something
just short of an explosion.

If I had to choose a Rosetta-Stone word to serve as a signature for the
poem as a whole it would have to be one of Dickinson's favorites, "ajar,"
which suggests dissonance (jarring) as much as partialness (part-opened),
discordance (grating) as much as variance (unclosed). "Ajar" speaks naturally to the metrical outline of the poem's music (disharmony) but also to the
internal dissonance of its syntax where the speed of disclosure ("For One
must wait/To shut the Other's Gaze down—/You—could not —") and complexity ("That New Grace//Glow plain—and foreign/On my homesick
Eye—/Except that You than He/Shone closer by—") become so elliptical as
to sound almost like code. By stanza eight, the opposition and parsing out of
the "Us" has become so squeezed—"They-Us-You-You-I"—that its passage

alone narrows the rhythmic size. "Ajar" is the condition of things in this
poem, and their dimension: both the oceans of separation that a slightly
opened door might represent and the white sustenance (more terrifying because it is white, the color of absence) that is despair. "Ajar" is the condition
of love, the condition in which life—*which is over there*—might be lived.

Dickinson builds her "narrative" on the ride of a religious-mythic trope—
to "live-die-rise" in "Heaven-Hell-despair"—linked in its parts by her growing sense of inadequacy when compared to her antagonist, who in the course
of things appears to have numinous presence beyond that of a would-be
lover. (The "you" is commonly considered to be Rev. Charles Wadsworth,
Dickinson's second "preceptor" and "kindly spiritual counsel," and probably
the one man [married] she ever imagined she was in love with. Wadsworth's
move to California in 1862—an "ajar" of three thousand miles—likely accounts for her most poetically productive, painful year.) This trope, which
presides in any number of her poems though never so prolonged, moves
along a line of development that ultimately describes a circle, so that the idea
of "living" at the beginning of the poem undergoes its transformations only
to return to its reprised and fully defined state of "living in despair." The leit-
motifs of home-references echo this reprising as we advance from quaint or
broken porcelain, "Discarded of the Housewife" (which wife, we wonder—
Wadsworth's literal wife or the wife Dickinson would be), to "my homesick
Eye," to the awful "Door," with its partialness and partitioning (two sides).
The domestic touches help keep the ironic (ajar) resurrection allegory from
becoming too righteous, of course; but even more they underscore the reality
of what is at stake: homemaking, housekeeping, homesickness.

Typical of the contrariness in Dickinson's tone, the poem is stratified in
negatives, except the darkest and last moment when the terminal stanza
makes the one rhetorically positive assertion that "We must meet apart...." So
we proceed through a series of I-cannots, I-could-nots and had-no-mores, in
order for the speaker to reiterate her unworthiness for the lived life, the community of love. The degree of her self-rejection is formidable in that it so depends on the superiority of the other: life is over there, you are over there,
while I am here, and the ajarring distance—though it may look like a crack in
the door—is an abyss as intimidating as it is non-negotiable. In fact, it is
Hell, and closer to Dante than to Edward Taylor. There is no more naked moment in Dickinson than the penultimate stanza when she declares that "were
you—saved—/And I—condemned to be/Where you were not—/That self—
were Hell to Me—." The abyss suddenly moves inside and "here" (the dominant slanting rhyme with "ajar" and "despair") becomes the existential position of one who has realized the truth of her separation, alienation, and
isolation. It is the condition of white, the shade of nothing.

Still, all in all, Dickinson's great poem does not in itself feel as empty as
the emptiness it protects. Quite the contrary, it feels full, replete and articu-

late in the teeth of its denials. Perhaps this is so because the poem's details and configurations are so well worked through; perhaps because the phrasing is so stone-cutter brilliant; perhaps because the epigrammatic impulse has submitted to the generous process of the experience, pressure point by pressure point. The poem is richest to me, however, because of the sacred honesty it achieves at no sacrifice to its beauty. #640 is a masterpiece of sustained yet suspended voice. It draws no conclusions, supports no moral, wins no philosophy. Each aspect of its nature carries forward; each image yields to and opens, inevitably, on the next; each phase motivates its length; each negative is answered, until, in the "saturation" at the end, where all the rhymes ring true, the poem closes with just its door ajar. There is a strange resignation in "I cannot live with you," a reconciliation at best understood at the outset and at the least consummated at the finish. The poem is confident with knowledge and the acceptance of that knowledge but in no way smug. The pain, like the tone of the writing, is transparent.

The year before #640, Dickinson wrote a kind of prequel, a comic mask to its tragic face. #289, "I know some lonely Houses off the Road" (one of several pentameter lines in the poem), is, at forty lines, her second longest piece; it toys with the same core ending image of a door ajar ("Fancy the Sunrise— left the door ajar!"), while reversing the build-up by making the final stanza the shortest, though it plays with a similar rhyme (Sneer/'Where'/astir/ajar). The conceit of the poem is thievery in the middle of the night ("I know some lonely Houses off the Road/A Robber'd like the look of—"), in which the interior of the house is violated yet nothing is stolen. There are two characters (one to hand the tools, the other to peep), whose act as robbers makes them subversives to the aging social order, rather like a spinster loving a married man in nineteenth-century Amherst, Massachusetts. But there is no harm done. With wit and devilment, the poem becomes an inventory of curiosity about other people's small "plunder"—tankard, spoon, earring, watch, an ancient brooch—and about how the moonlight—and ultimately the morning sunlight—illuminates the intimacy of privacy. It is a poem about the house of an "old Couple," so trusting in their habits they leave the "Windows hanging low."

On the other hand, where poems really live, #289 is about secrecy and the subversive nature of the imagination and about how fantasy foreshadows a world we come to live in. However playful its tone, its essential images of the night, the robbers (lovers in the moonlight), and the door ajar anticipate the terms that define the lament and requirement of #640, where this time the lonely house is not off the road but right on Main Street (Dickinson's real address) and where this time the warm intimacy of the old searched house—as if one were antiquing—becomes the enormous distance (Wadsworth is leaving) within walls. The door ajar in #289 leads out and lets in the sunrise; the door in #640 is within the domestic spaces of the house, which in themselves are so vast they can contain oceans, prayer, and "that White Sustenance—/ Despair—." Even the sequence of the passing night, with the ticking clock, the sliding moon, the rattle of the first daylight, the third sycamore, and Chanticleer at sunrise—even this sequence looks forward to the Christian cycle rewritten later. But since emotion is a narrative, Dickinson will not, cannot let the matter rest with sunrise and resurrection. #640's extra length derives from its need to satisfy its despair, to turn its afterlife into a living hell that she can live with, in which she is "condemned to be" where the other isn't. It is as if in trying out her terms of engagement in the lighter poem—intimacy, subversion, escape—Dickinson finds a language to deal with and transform the emotional crisis in the darker poem: a language she can fall back on, a language familiar and domestic enough that she can risk the intensity of an extreme that leaves her no exit.

280

I felt a Funeral, in my Brain,
And Mourners to and fro
Kept treading—treading—till it seemed
That Sense was breaking through—

And when they all were seated,
A Service, like a Drum—
Kept beating—beating—till I thought
My Mind was going numb—

And then I heard them lift a Box
And creak across my Soul
With those same Boots of Lead, again,
Then Space—began to toll,

As all the Heavens were a Bell,
And Being, but an Ear,
And I, and Silence, some strange Race
Wrecked, solitary, here—

And then a Plank in Reason, broke,
And I dropped down, and down—
And hit a World, at every plunge,
And Finished knowing—then—

Martha Collins

The Outer from the Inner

"The Outer—from the Inner/Derives its Magnitude," she wrote (#451), but the metaphorical traffic is two-way. The outer world comes in: "One need not be a Chamber—to be Haunted" (#670). But the poet also goes out, even beyond the world, drunkenly "Leaning against the—Sun" (#214), or uncannily touching "the Universe," "Beyond the Dip of Bell" (#378).

"I felt a Funeral, in my Brain" (#280) travels in both directions, not only embodying both movements, but also conflating their terms. The distance between inner and outer is often an issue for Dickinson, a situation that

metaphor seeks to overcome. It succeeds in this poem, and does something
more besides: the poem's astonishing reversal of inner and outer is so powerful that it ends up producing something like the aesthetic opposite of the terrifying experience it sets out to describe.

The first two stanzas are neatly metaphorical, but emotionally cramped:
though a narrative structure moves us systematically through the stages of a
funeral, with ritualistic repetition of syntax and sound, the location of the funeral "in my Brain" both compresses and intensifies the ordeal. The third
stanza promises a change of both syntax and scene, as the service ends; but
the intensity of the internalized experience is increased, as the mourners'
"treading—treading" is replaced by the pallbearers' "Boots of Lead" creak-
ing "across my Soul," presumably on the way out of the church, on the way
to the metaphorical cemetery.

At this point, though, both narrative and metaphorical expectations are defeated, and the terms of the metaphor, the "inner" and "outer" of the poem,
are suddenly reversed. "Then," at the end of the third stanza, appears to introduce a continuation of the story, but is actually a break from it: just when
we can imagine the church door opening, what's been inside the speaker's
mind is suddenly thrust outside it altogether. We're still in the metaphorical
mode; but now, though the funeral sounds continue, bell replacing boots and
drum, it's space, everything outside the speaker, that contains the sound.
What had been so uncomfortably proscribed within the brain is now in opposition to it, while "Being" is what we might expect space to be, merely receptive of sound. The speaker joins "Silence" and perhaps "Being" as well to
create a "Race" on a metaphorical island where they're "wrecked," as from a
shipwreck; but the status of being "solitary" and even "here" is in marked
contrast to the crowded state of the brain produced by the mourners. Though
frightening and nightmarishly surreal, the reversal offers some aesthetic release from the colossal headache suggested by the first two stanzas.

But the resolution isn't complete. The funeral story resumes in the final
stanza, the metaphorical procession having arrived at the graveyard in the interval. A "Plank in Reason" returns us to the mind as well as the narrative;
but when it breaks it takes the initial metaphor with it, for the speaker falls
not into the grave but rather into the space of the fourth stanza, thereby fus-
ing the two metaphorical structures of the poem: the speaker who had circumscribed a funeral in her brain has entered the magnitude of space, hitting
"a World, at every plunge."

This space travel is of course terrifying: the speaker has, after all, "Finished knowing." What this end of consciousness may "refer to" has been
much debated: is Dickinson describing despair, a nervous breakdown, a spiritual crisis, the onset of madness, the repression of thought, a fainting spell,
or merely a migraine headache? Or is she, in fact, imagining what it's like to
be dead? If the poem's otherworldly ending is more astronomical than theo-

logical, it's nonetheless possible to sense that the speaker has so thoroughly absorbed the metaphor that vehicle has become tenor by the end of the poem, bringing her into the ranks of the posthumous who speak in poems like "I heard a Fly buzz—when I died."

But then there's the final "then." Much like the "Then" that introduces the metaphorical shift in line 12, the word at the end opens up the poem. It's of course possible to read "then" as a final narrative marker, but that leaves us with the tension of wondering how one so finished with knowing can speak so knowingly of the process of finishing. In fact, "then" necessarily suggests its opposite, a possibility that's underscored by the punctuation surrounding it: setting it off from "knowing" and following it with a dash leave the reader with an intonational uncertainty that's ultimately liberating. And once the inflection of "then" begins to shift, "Finished knowing" may begin to shimmer a little too: the words are primarily and inarguably final, but isn't it possible to put an inflectional spin on "knowing," so that the emphasis shifts to the positive, as in "finished in a state of knowing"? Perhaps there's a glimmer of this even in the first stanza, where "Sense was breaking through."

"'Tis so appalling—it exhilarates": the line that begins the next poem in the 1955 *Poems*, and in Dickinson's own arrangement, may serve as a commentary on this one. And while the identity of the "it" in both poems may be beyond determination, that's certainly part of the strength of "I felt a Funeral," which is, like so many of Dickinson's poems of extremity, a linguistic and aesthetic triumph over the psychological terror it so boldly confronts and conveys.

1593

There came a Wind like a Bugle—
It quivered through the Grass
And a Green Chill upon the Heat
So ominous did pass
We barred the Windows and the Doors
As from an Emerald Ghost—
The Doom's electric Moccasin
That very instant passed—
On a strange Mob of panting Trees
And Fences fled away
And Rivers where the Houses ran
Those looked that lived—that Day—
The Bell within the steeple wild
The flying tidings told—
How much can come
And much can go,
And yet abide the World!

David Young

ELECTRIC MOCCASINS

We think of Emily Dickinson as a poet of human moments, documenting states of crisis, loss, bewilderment and elation. She is also, we know, a genius of metaphor, reifying and particularizing elusive aspects of spiritual and psychic experience, giving to belief and mystery forms and shapes and stories that we had not thought they could attain. She writes with confidence about the realm of the dead. Putting herself in their place, she turns and speaks to us from beyond life. And as she reports on her wrestlings with the giant angels of depression and despair, we marvel at her wit, her wry quickness and spareness, her pokerfaced ability to turn tonal corners sharply, skidding into glee or horror without warning or preparation.

Less often, it seems to me, do we speak of her as a nature poet. A certain nervousness accompanies such discussions, almost as if we feared to discover that her nature is too cute—pretty flowers, busy bees and decorative sunrises—a lessening of that bold originality that makes her so much our model and mentor. Yet a little reflection will remind us that Dickinson was superb on the sheer otherness of animals—the snakes of "A narrow fellow in the grass" and "Sweet is the swamp with its secrets," the robin of "A bird came down the walk," the hummingbirds of "Within my Garden, rides a Bird" and "A Route of Evanescence," and all the other bees, rats, and flies that populate her poems.

Her feeling for trees, meanwhile, is comparable to Thoreau's:

> Four Trees—upon a solitary Acre—
> Without Design
> Or Order, or Apparent Action—
> Maintain—
>
> The Sun—upon a Morning meets them—
> The Wind—
> No nearer Neighbor—have they—
> But God—
>
> The Acre gives them—Place—
> They—Him—Attention of Passer by—
> Of Shadow, or of Squirrel, haply—
> Or Boy—
>
> What Deed is Theirs unto the General Nature—
> What Plan
> They severally—retard—or further—
> Unknown—

I disagree with what Susan Howe (*My Emily Dickinson*) says about this poem: "This is the *process* of viewing Emptiness without design or plan, neighborless in winter blank, or blaze of summer. This is waste wilderness." How anthropocentric to assume that when the human factor is dropped out of the picture we have "Emptiness" and "waste [*waste!*] wilderness." A moment later, Howe brings up Nature as annihilation. Other critics have followed a similar pattern of response, assuming that the trees' existence outside a perceivable order or plan signals some kind of existential crisis for the speaker. But the speaker is calm and approving. It is the critics who have brought their weird equation of "waste" with "wilderness" to the poem. This kind of reading is one good reason why we need ecocriticism.

Much more to the point is what Guy Davenport says about this poem in his book *Burchfield's Seasons*, where he is comparing it to Burchfield's wonderful painting, *The Three Trees*. "It is the raw fact of the trees' existence that Dickinson focuses on," he argues, "making a piercing riddle of that fact." What he says about the painting applies equally well to the poem: "Burchfield's trees are beings, presences, silent and majestic cohabitants of the earth with the lion and the robin. They are alive in a different way, secretly in public view."

So Dickinson takes her place, I believe, in the long line of poets who have reconnected us with nature, with Neolithic and Paleolithic understandings of the sacredness and majesty of our environment, our natural home, resisting the hierarchic, hegemonic view of nature that is inadvertently reflected in Howe's assumption that if we can't own and understand the trees we somehow face existential terror.

We need to honor Dickinson for her sense of the meaning, texture and innate value of nature, including its ultimate independence from human manipulation and control. In "A Bird came down the Walk" the speaker gains confidence by noting likenesses—the eyes are like beads, the head is like velvet—until the moment when the bird takes flight. That moment, charged with revelation, while it notes more likenesses, nevertheless kicks the props of human control out from under the poem, opening a vista of wonder and mystery. Her sense of nature's size and intricacy is everywhere evident in Dickinson's work, supporting her other insights and interlocking with them, early and late.

****

I've chosen the late (1883) summer thunderstorm poem, "There came a Wind like a Bugle," for two main reasons. First, it illustrates, having had earlier treatments, how Dickinson liked to come back to certain subjects and treat them again, Cézanne-like, building on previous achievement but unsatisfied, restless, pushing her own envelope. And it shows her accessing the natural sublime, finding a way—since she could seldom visit the sea, walk in the forest, climb high mountains, camp in the wilderness—to confront the awesome and destructive side of nature that romantic poets had made a favorite location for reconsidering the human place in the universe, and that American literature and painting were revisiting on the new terms dictated by a New World.

Around 1864 Dickinson had done a version (#894) of a thunderstorm poem, one that she shortly revised to good effect. She had begun, for instance, in what must have seemed to her too domestic a fashion:

> The Wind begun to knead the Grass—
> As Women do a Dough—
> He flung a Hand full at the Plain—
> A Hand full at the Sky—

In revision, this became more somber, with the wind as a kind of master musician and demonic giant:

> The Wind begun to rock the Grass
> With threatening Tunes and low—

> He threw a Menace at the Earth—
> A Menace at the Sky

The following stanza needed little reworking. Now that the earlier hands image had been removed, the hands of the dust were new to the poem, and rather startling:

> The leaves unhooked themselves from Trees—
> And started all abroad
> The Dust did scoop itself like Hands
> And threw away the Road.

The next stanza substitutes "hurried slow" where she had first written "gossiped low," exchanging another domestic image for an oxymoron, and alters "Yellow Head" and "livid Toe" to "Yellow Beak" and "livid Claw," making a blond giant (with a sore toe?) into a gigantic bird of prey:

> The Wagons quickened on the Streets
> The Thunder hurried slow—
> The Lightning showed a Yellow Beak
> And then a livid Claw.

The new version, thereafter, pretty much follows the first:

> The Birds put up the Bars to Nests—
> The Cattle fled to Barns—
> There came one drop of Giant Rain
> And then as if the Hands
>
> That held the Dams had parted hold
> The Waters Wrecked the Sky,
> But overlooked my Father's House—
> Just quartering a Tree—

I should also note that the first version doesn't use stanza breaks. In general, the poem shows Dickinson's expertise at quick-sketch evocation: not only of the details of a violent summer storm, but of the psychology of response in humans, who combine fear, awe and wonder in their confrontation with forces beyond their control. The "Father's House" echoes the Bible and makes the storm a force that is separate from, and even threatening to, God himself. It could have hurt a sky-god when it wrecked the sky, but it contented itself with the torture and execution of a single tree. A tree in the Garden of Eden? The blasted tree that shows up in so many romantic paintings? We hesitate to go too far afield, and our imaginations settle back into Amherst and the house where Dickinson spent her life.

Her decision, in revising, to make the poem a little less domestic and a little less anthropomorphic shows her urge to take us to the edge of what we can comprehend and identify with. The otherness of the storm, its tendency to have more identities and features than we can easily assimilate, is more fully rendered in the second version. But that Dickinson was still not satisfied with what she had accomplished is demonstrated by her return to the subject, almost twenty years later, in "There came a Wind like a Bugle."

****

This late poem takes some of her stylistic characteristics, her signature as a poet, a step or two further:

1. A more difficult syntax, especially in the sentence that begins "On a strange Mob of panting Trees" and doesn't arrive at its verb ("Those looked") for several more lines. We are very likely to imagine the moccasin treading on the trees until we have worked out the periodic sentence and realized that a full break exists between the images.
2. An ambiguous placement of adjectives—is the steeple wild or is it the bell?—and of verbs: does "lived" mean "happened to be alive" or "survived"?; and what exactly does "abide" at the end? At first we are likely to think of ourselves, trying to be at home in a world of such unpredictable meteorological destruction; then we are apt to move to the insight that it is the world that abides while we come and go, all too briefly.
3. Detail that requires pondering—in what sense are the "Fences fled away"?—and questions about precisely how severe the storm finally was: was there, for instance, a flood? Did it move among and around houses or did it actually destroy and carry some away?
4. A superb economy in the chain of evocations, each image giving rise to the next. The bugle suggests the Last Judgment for a moment, and then, as we pick up the distinction between bugle and trumpet, the army or cavalry, a marching column which the quivering grass then metamorphoses into a snake, the snake in turn (zero at the bone) becoming a "green chill" that calls up the experience of fever, so much more feared (because so much less treatable) in the poet's day, while the Emerald Ghost transforms that green chill's color to precious stone and its quivering presence, now a held musical note, a sliding serpent, and an invasive fever, all resonating together like a chord, into an eerie spirit that can next be identified as "Doom," wearing an "electric Moccasin."

I want to dwell a moment, finally, on that last detail, as a way of exploring Dickinson's experiments with an American sublime. The issue is partly one of diction. No British poet would be likely to use the Algonquin/Narragansett word for wilderness footgear that had long been associated with Native

Americans and adopted by the backwoodsmen and trappers who had borrowed so freely from the indigenous cultures. Moccasins can also, we might note, be deadly snakes and harmless flowers. One critic, in hot pursuit of the phallic, would have the moccasin in this poem be only a snake.

Doom would not wear a moccasin, surely, in the English Lake District or on the moors or across the Alps. Whether its footgear would ever be "electric" in a European poem is also an interesting question. Is an electric moccasin simply the manifestation of energy typical of a thunderstorm, or are we encountering once again the machine in the garden, to borrow Leo Marx's phrase, that crossing and clashing of technology and pastoral that have been so characteristic of our literature? Rather than settle these speculations, I offer them as evidence that Dickinson's poem takes its place in the long-standing dialogue between English and American poetry on such issues as the meaning of wilderness, the nature of the sublime, the place of other cultures in the dominant culture, and the precariousness of settlements and settlers—issues that we also find Whitman, Frost, Stevens, Moore and Williams engaged with, both implicitly and overtly.

Our sublime, the tacit argument runs, is different, and we need different images, different diction and a different response to articulate it. Those who came here found a wilderness far vaster and less "humanized" than anything European humanity had known for many thousands of years. They also found peoples living amongst that wilderness who had never felt separate from it or driven to subdue and control it. They were very much like the Paleolithic and Neolithic peoples who preceded the European civilizations and lived in harmony with their environment for some 200,000 years of prehistory. It was as though humankind turned a corner and found itself facing its own deep past, encountering its own beginnings and recovering its lost mode of understanding nature. Of course civilization was *officially* better, but both pastoral and Christianity carried implicit messages about the corrupting effects of culture and the fall of humanity from a better, earlier state that made the alternative humanity of native American peoples a powerful attractant and implicit challenge.

The world is full of change and mystery. Yet the world abides. And as it does that, it is our world, a unique one. An American summer thunderstorm is a singular experience. It has much in common with the storms of other literatures and cultures, but possesses distinctive details, moments and meanings of its own. Our poets try to show us how this is true, insofar as language is capable of such demonstration. When Americans read Dickinson they have an opportunity to compare their own experiences to her evocations, a bond of shared existence that gives them a sense of privilege and empathy. Jingoism and nationalism are not at issue here. It is more the question of how we come to understand our place in our own environment. Surely we do it more fully when there is a poetry of that environment to guide and enlighten us. Such a poetry, and such an understanding, were necessary in Paleolithic times, and our need for them is even greater now.

Next time you are in a summer thunderstorm, listen carefully for Doom's electric moccasin. It will be both thunderous and inaudible, familiar and strange, the footgear of an emerald ghost. Nature will be unleashing some of its mysteries. Not for your benefit, though you are privileged to witness. A mob of trees will gather, panting. Fences, our way of ordering place and marking ownership, will disappear in the face of what we can't control, becoming irrelevant. Where there were houses, rivers may come again.

We come and go. The world abides. The idea that Dickinson was not a nature poet seems absurd, just as the idea that nature poets are simply admiring birds and scenery falls far short of their true function and value. But that is another lesson, for another time and place.

GERARD MANLEY HOPKINS
(1844-89)

T he arc of the literary career of Gerard Manley Hopkins is strikingly parallel to that of his contemporary, Emily Dickinson: his best poems were not accepted for publication during his lifetime, and his achievement as one of the three or four greatest Victorian poets was not widely acknowledged until after World War I. More than any of his English peers, Hopkins may be considered a precursor of Modernism: his thrilling formal and musical experiments, and his commitment to forging a language that would do justice to his vision, have been widely admired by later generations of poets. His early drawings and journal entries reveal the obsession with minute detail that would preoccupy him throughout his life. They also illuminate his quest to discover through those details the distinctively unifying pattern (which he called "inscape") that gives an object its identity, and the presence of divine force ("instress") that produces those patterns throughout the natural world. Hopkins converted to Catholicism as a student at Oxford and spent the rest of his life as a Jesuit priest, often serving as a teacher and curate in the bleakly industrial cities of Wales, the English Midlands, and Ireland. He also suffered considerable anguish at the conflict between his vocation as a priest and his calling as a poet, a difficulty often reflected in poems of spiritual struggle, especially the late sequence referred to as the "terrible sonnets." Despite these anxieties, Hopkins became one of the great nature poets: his sensuous, passionate, highly detailed renderings of the landscape are among the most beautiful in the language.

BOOKS: *The Poems of Gerard Manley Hopkins*, ed. W. H. Gardner and N. H. MacKenzie (1970); a good selection is *Poems and Prose*, ed. Gardner (1985). See also *The Notebooks and Papers of Gerard Manley Hopkins* (1959) and *The Letters of Gerard Manley Hopkins to Robert Bridges* (1955).

GOD'S GRANDEUR

The world is charged with the grandeur of God.
   It will flame out, like shining from shook foil;
   It gathers to a greatness, like the ooze of oil
Crushed. Why do men then now not reck his rod?
Generations have trod, have trod, have trod;
   And all is seared with trade; bleared, smeared with toil;
   And wears man's smudge and shares man's smell: the soil
Is bare now, nor can foot feel, being shod.

And for all this, nature is never spent;
   There lives the dearest freshness deep down things;
And though the last lights off the black West went
   Oh, morning, at the brown brink eastward, springs—
Because the Holy Ghost over the bent
   World broods with warm breast and with ah! bright wings.

Charles Wright

IMPROVISATIONS: WITH FATHER HOPKINS ON LAKE COMO

4 June/ Rereading in Hopkins' *Journals* yesterday: it's his reverence that strikes you, reverence for the minutiae as well as the miraculous, in their combinations as well as their separateness. Description, exactitude: a photo-realism from the insect to infinity. The spiritual eye that sees God's fingerprint and face on everything. And to look on something hard enough, that hard, is to change it.

Rain today, little apocalypses in the water beads mirroring the white, blank sky on broad leaves circling the goldfish pond. Downlake, cloud-curtain and mist-curtain obscure the mountains. White ferries appear and disappear like messengers far below from another country. The water beads explode and re-form. How easily worlds come and go.

After you've been here long enough, Jim Barnes says, the black birds begin to whistle, in their ubiquitous but intermittent song, "prego," "prego."

They've cut the long grass in the olive orchard that spills down the deep slope below the main building, the Villa Serbelloni, to the lake. From above, the trees themselves appear shorn and reduced, as if their limbs, too, had been cut back. The trees in the adjoining, uncut field seem still full and olivesque; the ones in the field I just walked through, on the other hand, seem flattened, like hair wet from rain.

I was walking to the abandoned monastery, called locally "I Frati," The Monks, or The Brothers, where I have a room in the afternoons to work in. The monastery was built in the early 1600s by one of the Sfondrati, early owners of the property: when one of his sons wanted to become a priest, rather than have him leave home, the Duke built him a monastery of his own. Outside the window in front of my desk, a corner of the faded red tile and red plaster building cuts wedge-shaped, like a Giorgio Morandi painting, across the view. Beyond it are some cherry trees and olive trees and five rows of grape vines. Beyond that is a pine tree and then the lake. Beyond that the mountain above Varenna across the water, mist-bothered today and unfocused. Seagulls, crows, hawks, pigeons, sparrows, blackbirds and various other feathered fellows rip in and out of the painting from time to time. Higher up, swallows free-lance among the thermals. Here's one (a blackbird) on the roof tile saying "dunque," "dunque."

—6 June/ Rain again. Steady rain. Uninterruptible strings. If we had a woof to cross with this warp, we would have a crystal curtain endlessly falling across the landscape, rain cloth collapsing in huge, invisible folds beneath the olive trees and the hemlocks. In the frog pond outside the window (this window in my other studio—I have two, one in the old monastery down the hill, in the afternoons, the other up the hill, in the mornings, a converted gazebo where the woods begin), the drops bulls-eye and blister the surface. The blisters form along the waterskin, drift momentarily toward the lilies, then break and vanish in tiny circles.[1] The lilies, open and yellow two days ago, stay half-closed and hunched beneath the incessant pressure from the head-taps of the rain beads.

Suddenly, after lunch, the rain stopped. Fifteen minutes later the sun was out and we all stepped onto the terrace, after three continuous days of downpour, as though we were stepping off the Ark. That branch of Lake Como that runs back toward Lecco was cleansed and accessible as I had never seen it in almost two weeks—small towns began to pile up on the shoresides and moun-

---

[1] There has to be a certain rhyme to the rainfall, a certain velocity, before the blisters can form—too little rain and the force isn't enough to bubble the surface, too much and they're destroyed, either before or during formation. Like everything else in this world, they have their own metrics, their own rhythms of being.

tainsides, red roof after red roof until the lake bent under the stern stone of the mountain, blue sky like a Chinese glaze seeped at all the corners of things.

Below, in the cloister yard, 5:30 sunshine fierce and finite pushing down on the eyelids, coating the skin, ^{2}/$_3$rds of the yard in shadow, shadow that gives the walls their color back, a yellowish Tuscan dun-orange. The part in sun is lighter, as though rinsed over and over to rid it of something. In the church, Peter is playing the oboe, winding North African sounds that circle and loop. Warrior ants forage and circulate over the flat stones in the courtyard, singly, each on his own mission. One never sees them in groups or pairs. If they are centaurs, the dragon hangs on the sunny walls, or crouches in the sunny corners, or rises immobile and enormous on the hard, rocky plain of the paving stones, waiting for some invisible thing. The ants let him loom as they scurry under the towering overgrowth of the yellow-topped flower weeds and the dandelion groves and the understory of clover and mustard grass. Dog soldiers, lone wolfscouts ceaselessly on the move. They meet and exchange a word or two, then break and are off again. The stone-plain and weed-forest are both alive with them. And here's a lizard down from the wall. In jerks and false starts he spurts and halts. Ants go over his tail and under his nose. Green as a piece of water, his body rises and falls then streaks in one motion back toward the ivy and out of sight. The ants keep checking the territory.

Back upstairs, the windows open, afternoon sun on the lake and grey stone mountains, lake green as a lizard, light clear as water through glass. Surely the world is charged with the grandeur of God. At least from time to time.

—7 June/ In the cloister courtyard, 11 o'clock in the morning. Each wall surrounding the inner yard is slightly different: west wall has six arches into the passageway that runs along all four sides of the cloister. There are two cells on the west side. The south has five arches and three cells, the east no arches but a door and two windows and thus has walled in the passageway—four cells. The north wall has five arches and no cells as it is the south side of the church. There is, of course, an upper passageway that's windowed, not arched, above the ground floor. In the courtyard itself, four cedar topiaries, one at each corner, four little boxwood diamonds enclosing them. In the center of the yard, a circle of boxwood containing a large stone urn, chipped and shaped by hand, very crude, very functional and very beautiful. Red poppies grow in the circle. Yellow button-top weeds and yellow dandelions grow in the spaces between the paving stones, somewhat lighter in color than the walls, but not incompatible. Generations have walked to the urn, and walked back, have walked the quadrangle under the arches, the stone steps and paving stones. But none does now. Only the maintenance supervisor, whose office is in the east wing, unbalances the solitude now and then. Down here, where the heart of the order tapped out its daily routine, every door is locked but one. Just now, a hawk sailed over toward the lake, mewling and meowing like a cat. The swallows shrieked and subsided, their shadows descending and climbing the walls as they drag the air for food. A truck pulls up the hill, a Weed-Eater coughs and stops in the adjoining field. Quietness.... Stillness.... Cheep of baby swallows somewhere out of sight. Weeds bow in the small breeze. Poppies, hooded and cowled, nod in their noontime doze. Lisp and swish of a swallow's wing. Have trod, have trod....

The only unlocked door leads to the crypt. Twenty walled-in burial slots in the walls, nine each on two sides and two in the north wall. On the south wall, the only window has a painting, very faded, of a monk holding the Baby Jesus on his lap over it. Under the window, a small stone altar, just large enough to hold the bodies that were lowered from the church above through the hole— now sealed over—in the ceiling a short while before entombment. Each of the twenty tombs is sealed by a slab of hand-hewn, grey stone, the same stone the mountains around here are made of, the same stone the stairs, the lintels, the door jambs, the window sills and archway sills are made of. At the top of each slab, a skull and crossbones looks out, a cross on top of the skull, each painted there, not enfrescoed. Most of the information painted below the skulls has eroded from dampness, but several dates can still be read—1761, 1790, 18 something—and a name or two—Giovanni da Bellano is one—and one anonymous tomb is legible: Un Pellegrino da Lecco (A Pilgrim from Lecco). One tomb, on the right in the north wall, differs from all the rest—it has a skeleton painted on the slab. And that's all. They recked his rod.

—8 June/ Deluge. Whitecaps like ocean waves breaking on a beach ride down the lake under a north wind. Rain almost solid in its intent and descent. Lightning behind the cloud and shifting mist-mass like klieg lights shot on and off behind gauze draperies. Tremendous and rolling claps from the thunder-throne. One hour south of here the World Cup soccer tournament begins today. Right where the storm rolls, down the lake, the battle, as Miss Bishop said, now in another part of the field. Justin Kaplan left this morning. Big rip in the social fabric. Yesterday at lunch he told the story of two tanks, one Israeli, one Egyptian, that collided during a battle in the desert during the Six Day War. The Egyptian driver climbed out with his hands over his head repeating, "I surrender, I surrender." The Israeli climbed out of his tank at the same time, rubbing the back of his neck and muttering, "Oi, whiplash."

Intense green stretch-marks over the lakeskin where the tide currents slide just under the surface after a storm. One of a series of storms that has tumbled and fulminated out of the Alps behind us. A black pigeon is strolling in the rain along the roof tiles outside the window, now scruffily getting wetter on the ridge line of the building, jerking and bobbing his head as though the sun were out. Here comes the hard stuff again. And there he goes. GMH's death day, 101 years ago.

—12 June/ False neon of afternoon, crow in the Chinese pine bare-branched at lake's edge, seagull and pigeon skim over greencap and whitecap. Inside, in the cloister yard, three sundials shadow the hour against the church wall's south side. The hour shadows me. I shadow a lizard upside-down on the same wall. His shadow shadows the world.

Along the grey stone walls going down to the village, tiny young ferns have appeared, growing out of the moss and concrete, like clusters of tangled, miniature green starfish arms jutting from the stones.

— 14 June/ Reading through the journals, one is constantly struck by the faith GMH has, and the absolute certainty of that faith: that when he decides to describe something—a leaf, a wave or series of waves, a bird, a landscape sweep—minutely or particularly, he is able to transcend it, through language, and enter whatever it is he is describing; that the inscape is knowable and tactile through language. That the heart of the mystery, the pulse at the very unspeakable center of being, is apprehensible through writing about it. Thus the lovingly, intricately laid down musical strings of language. One no longer believes this is possible. One more often now knows that the only answer to inscape is silence. How marvellous, however, to see how the world once seemed, how Adamic it all was before the word and the world became separate. And the Word and the world became separate.

Crow shadows climb the evergreens outside the window, tiny, quick black crosses up, up and dissolve as the birds circle and plane above the spruce and pine woods. Like moving imprints of the Unholy Ghost, they rise and vanish so rapidly one is tempted to think one didn't see them. But one did. One always has....

—15 June/ GMH has style, style to burn, onto-theological style. It is one of the several reasons he continues to haunt us, both in his poems and in his prose. He has, in fact, great style. Great style is transcendence and flash. It is that moment of exscalation, that moment when the light of recognition and understanding, the phosphorous-flare of perception renatures a thing. You find the burn and you feed it. There is, as Hopkins said, the dearest freshness deep down things. True style exfoliates this into the sudden glare of awareness. GMH's inscape, Joyce's epiphany, Cezanne's simultaneous presentation are all moments of exscalation. Great style is like that, linked moments of exscalation down the page—fluid, not static and insular, the after-aura of rediscovery flooding the thing in question. I'm talking about poems here—the after-aura spreading and interlocking, a retreating radiance highlighting language and its excavations of new combinations and new geographies.

—16 June/ Going down to the monastery from the Villa, you go through the olive orchard. A path of flat stones, approximately two feet square each (although they aren't square), paving stones, is set in the ground from the top to the bottom of the orchard. At the beginning of the descent, as though an offering stone among the more pedestrian and utilitarian ones, is a small dark grey, grainy rectangular stone. It has a carving—more precisely, a bas-relief—engraved in it, now worn almost smooth. Still visible, however. Probably part of a frieze on some building or even a cemetery decoration. It resembles—the figure—something, I fancy, of Gwan Yin, the Chinese goddess often depicted with flowing drapery falling away from her. Her body in the Italian sunlight and rain, sentinel of the track through the sacred olive grove, each season growing smaller and less defined, her amphora-like figure so still, so still this morning in the first summer day-haze. Our Lady of the Olives.

Interesting to me that GMH set, or said he set, only two of his own poems to music—"Hurrahing in Harvest" and "Spring and Fall"—from a total of some twenty-seven settings there are either music for or mention of, given the aggressive "musical" base he advertised as grounding his poems. Perhaps they were written for instruments that don't exist yet. Or have been forgotten. I would love to have heard Billie Holiday sing "Spelt From Sibyl's Leaves." Uh huh....

As for poetry and speech and meaning: one knew this already, but it's interesting to see it in writing (in a little piece entitled "Poetry and Verse")—"Poetry is...speech framed to be heard for its own sake and interest even over and above its interest of meaning.... (Poetry is in fact speech only employed to carry the inscape of speech for the inscape's sake—and therefore the inscape must be dwelt on.)"

Seagulls drifting over, backlit by the sun—their wings translucent, or wing back-feathers translucent, as they balance and right themselves over the hemlocks and evergreen topiary. Strangely unplaced, their black wing-centers trailed by pinions flamed out like a shining, they circle, lazy boomerangs, in their fiery gyres.

—17 June/ I've watched a lizard patrol the sunny edge of a boxwood hedge for about 45 minutes now. Back and forth, never venturing into the shadow, occasionally stopping suddenly to rub, vigorously, his forelegs against the ground. Is he hunting? He never, that I could see, found anything. Is he ranging his territory? What is it that lizards do, little sticks, little swift sticks, belly to the ground, taking the sun this Sunday? They hold the world together, that's what.

—18 June/ Excursion yesterday to the upper end of the lake to see two churches, one the Abbazia at Piona and the other S. Maria del Tiglio in Gravedona. The Abbazia—a seminary abbey—is 11th century, but modernized into indiscrimination. On the grounds, behind the church, the Cistercian brothers have built a miniature replica of the grotto at Lourdes. On Sunday, as yesterday was, crowds come to sit in the shade of the giant cypress in front of the shrine—a shrine, in fact, that consists of a bank of electric candles inside the fake grotto: insert a coin and a candle is turned on—all day. Families with the physically unfortunate member—a Downs Syndrome child, a legless and armless brother, a disturbed daughter—sit quietly, hoping, I suppose, for some magic radiation out of the mortar and stone. For the afflicted. Or, more probably, for themselves, to lighten the load. Has it come to this? Of course it has—it has always come to this.... S. Maria del Tiglio was more authentically preserved. Also 11th century, they solved the modernization problem by building a new church next door in the 1800s, thus avoiding the layering that has bastardized the Abbazia. In all, a disappointing trip; even the ice cream was mediocre as we waited for the hydrofoil to take us back down the lake.

Outside the window, in a fern clump, an almost perfect replica of the Janus face in the leaves' configuration. Or the Devil's visage. At the right time, in the right circumstances, I could declare vision, etc., and set up shop. As it is, it is only the physical world, as it always does, trying to jump-start the imagination. The morning begins to settle itself across the lake, warm breast, bright wings.

—June, 1990 / Bellagio

Gerald Stern

SOME THOUGHTS

One of the things I love best in poetry is the earnest argument. In it, the poet offers a position, and makes a claim, as if his life depended on the truth of his discovery, as if, really, he wasn't truly interested in such an absurd thing as the sweetness or beauty of language, as if, indeed, that were the farthest thing from his mind, as if he only wanted to be heard for the logic of his statement. There are hundreds of poems like this and, in a sense, every poem "presents an argument." But certain poets—and certain poems—possess that "earnestness" more than others.

Stevens is an example of an earnest poet. I think, in him, the argument is nominal, even though it presents itself as real, and the music counts most. Williams, on the other hand, takes his ideas seriously—I mean at the first level. It is not a question of him indulging in earnest arguments—it is worse—or better—than that—he is *earnest*. Pound is earnest too, and Ginsberg, mostly, and Levertov. Creeley, on the other hand, and Levine, for example, engage in earnest argument. Merwin is earnest. In no way is it a question of music vs. content. Not this argument.

I have an idea that I am partly talking about irony and the metaphysical. And I have an idea that the sonnet, of all forms, most aptly conducts the earnest argument, as I describe it. That is because the sonnet, probably more than any other form, carries another music with it. It is the supreme lyric. There were attempts, of course, to use the sonnet—and the lyric—as dramatic and political vehicles, but the form itself then didn't work. Who could imagine Neruda attacking the United Fruit Company or Pound attacking the Jews in sonnet form?

It is in this connection that Hopkins' sonnets must be considered. I don't mean to say that they are not vital, or critically important, or alive with belief. They are as vital and important now as when they were written. But they are earnest arguments. "God's Grandeur" is simultaneously an argument for the constant presence, power, perhaps aloofness, of God, and an argument albeit awkwardly put, for the identity of God with nature. It is awkward, mostly, because it is not a pantheistic argument. Hopkins merely replaces the name of God with the name of Nature and lets it go at that. It is as if, thinking of the unending forgiveness of God, or the unending energy, what he calls "grandeur," he translates that into the exhaustless power and resources of nature, as a late nineteenth-century observer, a good "modern" reader, would see nature. Although sometimes, when I read the poem, I think it is more gnostic in intent, and what he calls "nature" is the forgiving aspect of God, the "Christ" aspect, only in Hopkins the forgiving aspect is feminine; it is motherly and inexhaustible, and it is inexhaustible—or endlessly forgiving—because it is motherly, and it is, finally, the holy ghost that is that for-giving—and giving—mother.

On a technical level, it is the *sestet* that redeems and transforms the *oc-tave*, just as it always does in the sonnet, only in this case the redemption and transformation is not just literary and linguistic. It is a life-and-death matter. The generations that are stuck, as it were in the *octave*, that have "trod and trod and trod," whose feet are "shod," are liberated by "the dearest freshness deep down things." There is, I think, a little originality in the the-ology even if the physics is conventional. What is wonderful about the poem is his earnestness coupled with his naiveté. Thus his earnestness, though it resembles Yeats and Shakespeare in its ability to *regain* the obvious and even the primitive, to make statements about things as if no one had ever been there before, has the additional quality of encountering his own most powerful beliefs, even if they are quirky, through the very earnestness of his language. Thus the purpose of his argument is not only poetry, or not just po-etry, it is prayer.

I would like to suggest, therefore, that this poem—and others like it—sur-vives, and is held in such awe, because of the earnestness of his belief. That is an odd and ridiculously Victorian term to apply to belief, but it is perfectly appropriate to Hopkins. His isolation, his innocence, perhaps his neurosis, made it possible for him to be unselfconsciously "earnest." I am sorry for his unhappiness, but we are lucky to have the poetry, for it is unstintingly great.

Most lovers of this poem—and they are all lovers rather than admirers—are excited, indeed overwhelmed, by the last two lines, coming as they sud-denly do to both change and regain the subject. They seem an unexpected gift; or, on second thought, it's not the last two lines but the last eight words, or the last three words or—truly—the third from the last word, the word "ah," that in its personalization of the experience, even its interruption of the action, simultaneously detached and passionate and deeply human, so moves the reader. At any rate, God's grandeur, that which can only be powerful and distant, is suddenly converted to the nurturing, kind, half-mammalian, half-angelic holy ghost. Theologically they are the same, of course, but logically, if I may presume, and, more importantly, poetically, they are quite different. They are, at the very least, masculine vs. feminine.

I have always deeply loved Hopkins' sonnets. I read them so much in my early twenties that I discover now—in my sixties—that I know most of the main ones by heart, though I err a little bit here and there in the rendering. For one reason or another, I have never, as a Jew, felt any distance from them, or any skepticism or disbelief. That may be because Hopkins is making de-mands only on himself, or because he does not exclude others, or because I am persuaded by the honesty, the authenticity—and the lack of politics, or because I am so moved by the beauty of the language and the efficiency of the argument that I overlook the theology, though I don't think that's the case. When I read "God's Grandeur," I believe in the warm breast and the bright wings. How different this is from the religious poetry of T. S. Eliot. How excluded I feel from that. How tiny is the world he admits and under what preposterous conditions. How courageous and universal and holy is the spirit of Hopkins.

FELIX RANDAL

Felix Randal the farrier, O is he dead then? my duty all ended,
Who have watched his mould of man, big-boned and hardy-handsome
Pining, pining, till time when reason rambled in it and some
Fatal four disorders, fleshed there, all contended?

Sickness broke him. Impatient he cursed at first, but mended
Being anointed and all; though a heavenlier heart began some
Months earlier, since I had our sweet reprieve and ransom
Tendered to him. Ah well, God rest him all road ever he offended!

This seeing the sick endears them to us, us too it endears.
My tongue had taught thee comfort, touch had quenched thy tears,
Thy tears that touched my heart, child, Felix, poor Felix Randal;

How far from then forethought of, all thy more boisterous years,
When thou at the random grim forge, powerful amidst peers,
Didst fettle for the great grey drayhorse his bright and battering sandal!

David Young

SURPRISED BY GRIEF

There are many characteristics of Hopkins that still put readers off, I suspect. He is uncompromising in his demands on us, resolute in his distinctiveness. It seems sometimes that he cannot resist yet another alliteration, yet another internal rhyme, until he appears to be a kind of poetic over-achiever, parading his own talent from under the burden of his religiosity, which certainly comes in a form—high Victorian Roman Catholicism—that many readers no longer find sympathetic or interesting. And yet the spell of his language and the power of his experiments with lyric form and design remain fresh and daring a century after. No serious working poet can afford ignorance of the way in which Hopkins expanded the expressive possibilities of English. He taught us to see more closely and clearly, and to translate that observation into poetic imagery, and he taught us to hear more acutely, both the sounds of the natural world and the inherent music of speech. That he had gifts as a visual artist and as a composer comes as no surprise. That he also had a unique command of what we might call historical poetics is worth noting too.

Just when you think you have glimpsed the scope—I might say "scape"—of Hopkins' achievement, he will surprise you. You will suddenly have a breakthrough with the movement or design of that most remarkable of mature debuts, "The Wreck of the Deutschland." Or you will discover, as I recently did, a previously unglimpsed psychological acuity. This is an authority we assign to Browning or Eliot or Dickinson, while we think of Hopkins as mainly concerned with landscapes and religious ecstasy. But I can use the sonnet "Felix Randal," a relatively late poem, to demonstrate just how penetrating Hopkins' command of human experience and emotion became.

It is especially important to distinguish poet from speaker in this instance. It is true that the poem's speaker is a priest, one whose experience rather closely matches Hopkins' own. But the poem is clearly intended to be a portrait of the priest's discovery of his own feelings. It contains a degree of objectification that self-portraiture does not possess. Drawing on his own insights and experiences, Hopkins depicts a man whose profession has distanced him from his own emotions in a way that makes their sudden manifestation a surprise. The result is masterful, and not a little problematic: the reader must decide, in effect, how much the poem is about the farrier and how much about the priest, and precisely where its complex sequence can be said to take us.

We come in on the thoughts and speech of the priest at the precise moment when he hears of his parishioner's death. His reactions are first a bit perfunctory—"O is he dead then?"—and then self-referential—"my duty all ended." Both responses can put us off. The first may strike a reader as callous, the second may seem egotistical. But it takes only a little sympathy, or a little familiarity with the psychology of those who minister to the dying, to recognize the necessity and humanity of the response. If the priest (or the doctor or the nurse, for that matter) responded rawly to the death of each visited parishioner or patient, he would never get through his day, his week, his year. He must insulate himself emotionally in order to survive, and he must shoulder and discard his responsibilities ("my duty all ended") as necessity and the changing situation dictate. Hopkins would of course have fully understood this from his own parish work in Liverpool, work he found hard to inure himself to, especially in light of the poverty, illness and despair it brought him into daily contact with.

The phrase that ends the first line turns out not to be a self-contained statement but part of a second and much longer question that takes the priest through a brief history of Randal's protracted suffering: the humiliating destruction of his strength and vigor, his delirium and the multiple nature of his illness (how literally we are meant to take "fatal four disorders" is something I haven't been able to work out). The relief of concluded duty is mingled, it turns out, with relief at the conclusion of a suffering that involved a long-drawn dwindling—the repetition of "pining" is among the poem's simplest strong effects—and became a kind of horrible feast by sickness: the disorders were "fleshed" in the man, glutting themselves. The full quatrain reduces and softens the apparent egotism of the priest's response.

The mental review of Randal's illness, apparently a kind of involuntary checking of facts triggered by the news of the death, continues in the second half of the octave. The priest takes considerable satisfaction in the role he was able to play. His professional familiarity, even overfamiliarity, with the last rites he so often administers is reflected in the "and all" that is tacked on to "being anointed." The detailed remembrance of his spiritual counseling of the farrier, a process that was by no means steady and consistent, gives the priest a sense of professional pride, almost a complacency, as he recalls it. He closes the second quatrain with another perfunctory response, cast in vernacular speech. The idiom reflects Hopkins' great interest in language, including dialects and slang, but we are meant, I think, to understand that this "God rest him" comes as much out of the priest's own cultural background and upbringing as out of any theological doctrine.

Perhaps this is too fanciful, but I hear this whole octave spoken by a quiet, musing voice, rather like that of James Mason or Cyril Cusack, and I imagine the priest crossing himself as he utters its closing sentiment.

It is part of the beauty of all this psychological portraiture that Hopkins makes the contours of poetic form embody his insights into human behavior. An Italian sonnet has two large parts that can also be subdivided, so that four distinct movements can emerge. The poet has used that possibility to create four separate attempts at conclusion by the priest. Because he doesn't know he's uttering a sonnet, he keeps trying to put a lid on his response to a death and go on to something else. We know, of course, that he won't be able to do that until the form has fulfilled itself; the demands of traditional structure become a means of demonstrating how our own responses can distract us, how questions resurface until we have fully dealt with them. The first of the priest's attempts at closure is the full question that completes the first quatrain. Its rhetorical answer is supposed to be "yes," but the continuation of the poem undermines the completeness and adequacy implied both by the death and by the "duty all ended." The second closure, a more emphatic one, comes as the second quatrain rounds out the octave. By his "God rest him all road ever he offended," the priest really does seem to be trying to put an end to the matter. All the more fascinating, then, to discover in the sestet that there is much more to think about, reflect on, discover.

As the sestet opens, the priest is trying to move in the direction of generalization, "seeing the sick," and away from the individual and the particularities of his death. But he fails to remain at such a theoretical level. The question of who bonds to whom takes him right back to his relationship with Felix and to the discovery that a spiritual link was formed between the two men that had considerable power for both of them. Men don't—or certainly didn't then—like to cry in front of each other. All the more reason, then, for Felix's tears and his priest's wiping away of them, to be the key that unlocks the muffled emotions of love and friendship and brings the priest to his second, and much more tender, naming of the man. The final line of this tercet is choppy with the gathering emotion and full acknowledgment of grief that culminates in two single words—"child" and "Felix"—and then, like a full release, the whole name and the adjective that has in effect been suspended since the poem opened. If I read this line out loud, with full attention to its emotional impact, I find that my voice tends to break, and that breaking feels natural to the movement and the power of the utterance.

That second naming makes for the most satisfactory conclusion so far, but there is one more turn for the poem to take. Every line ending has rhymed except "Randal"; there must be a rhyme for that word too. What Hopkins has his priest do is attempt to recreate an earlier Felix Randal, before the priest even knew him, imagining him not just in his pitiable state but in his days of strength, his physical prime. That attempt to reconstitute Felix as a healthy farrier becomes, given the fact that this is a poem, something mythic and legendary. The means, as so often with Hopkins, is a heightened attention to the archaic meanings that still inhere in the language. They can invoke an ancient, heroic world for us, a world of archetypes and magical utterances that is still present under the surface if we attend to etymologies. Thus "random," which used to mean "violent," and which derives ultimately from an Old High German word for a shield, or a shield's edge, invokes the first forgers of weapons even as it carries its more modern sense of "haphazard" and its relatively rare sense of "neglected." The second adjective for the forge, "grim," is no less carefully chosen; its origins stretch back through Old Norse words for grief, hostility and enmity, and perhaps on back to Greek and Slavic words for crashing, neighing and thunder. Its cousins include words like "chagrin," "grimace," and "grumble." Knowing how deeply interested Hopkins was in his language's history and etymologies, it is not fanciful to assume that these considerations were factors in his choice of diction.

I don't know whether Hopkins knew the Middle English alliterative poem about blacksmiths that begins: "Swarte smeked smethes, smattered with smoke,/Drive me to deth with den of here dintes!" Probably he did. In any case, he certainly knew that alliteration was another means he could use to invoke the sense of a lost, heroic past. The final tercet increases alliteration's already significant role in the poem. "Powerful amidst peers" and "How far from then forethought of," not to mention "bright and battering," sound as though they might have come straight out of Middle English or Old English poems about heroes and warriors. They add to our sense that the final three lines intensify the mythic and archetypal meanings of the poem.

Around the middle of the eighteenth century, considerably predating Wordsworth and other romantics, various artists, especially visual artists, began to give a new meaning to the value of rural life and everyday labor through depictions of harvesting, smithing, and similar activities that were at once realistic and eulogizing. One thinks of painters like Wright of Derby or Joseph Stubbs when looking for a precedent for Hopkins' chiaroscuro portrait of a working blacksmith. I say chiaroscuro because I think the total effect is of a dark space with the gray horse dimly lighting it and a point or ray of light emanating from the picture's very center, the newly forged and glittering horseshoe being hammered into place on the great creature's patient, doubled-up leg. There's a secondary association, perhaps, with the way that the drayhorses' shoes must have struck sparks on the Liverpool cobblestones as they went about their business of freight and delivery.

These sudden manifestations of light are central to Hopkins' poetry. They stand for epiphany, theophany, divinity making itself known in this world. He makes them the thrilling centers and climaxes of his lyrics and they carry a formidable charge of meaning and emotion. Here the sparking and glittering horseshoe corresponds imagistically to the priest's discovery of his own tenderness and love for his lost parishioner and friend. As that human emotion shows him at his most godlike, a kind of moral and spiritual glory, so the visual world has its equivalent moments of thrilling beauty when we witness, Hopkins felt, the presence of the creator. Thus the priest's essential being, his inscape, is realized in his piercing emotion, while Randal's is recalled in the way beauty and its underlying meaning, divinity, suddenly emerge from his grim, random, unlovely occupation. The two revelations bring the poem finally to a state of realization and completion. Two men have been celebrated, twinned, rhymed, through their relation in life and death, and through the imagination that has designed the sequence of the poem. It isn't just that the word "Randal" must rhyme with the priestly word "sandal." It's that the farrier Randal must rhyme with the priest who is trying to remember and fully understand him.

A good friend, whose judgment I admire, says he can never fully love a poem in which a horseshoe is characterized as a sandal. I understand his objection. Hopkins is given to such risky maneuvers, and they sometimes fail to persuade us. For me, "sandal" not a problem. It seems to come both from the heroic world of myth and from the biblical literature the priest would be most comfortable with. Its etymology may be Persian, a word for a skiff, and I don't think a shoe that is mainly a sole is an extravagant way of thinking about a horseshoe. If my friend reads the poem only through the first tercet of the sestet, he has a very satisfying and largely complete portrait of a priest's mental sequence, discovering his love and surprised by his grief. What he lacks, of course, is the moment when work, as embodied in the occupations of priest and blacksmith, finds its full justification and celebration. There's a sense, I think, in which the priest is enabled to go on with his life and work by rhyming himself with the dead man as faithful laborer.

Or call it a three-way rhyme, involving the horse as well. Having been shod, the workhorse can go on with its mundane but mysterious existence. Like the horse, the priest can continue his journey. The way is mythic, but it is also ordinary, like a sandal, like a horseshoe. Unlike my friend, I find that the poem's final move is the one that I can least resist. That bright and battering image, that moment at the forge, leaves me thrilled and helpless. It concentrates the poem's meanings in a single gleam of brilliance, transcending ordinary limitations of life and language. It is Felix's reward, and the priest's, and the reader's.

SPELT FROM SIBYL'S LEAVES

Earnest, earthless, equal, attuneable, | vaulty, voluminous, . . . stupendous
Evening strains to be time's vást, | womb-of-all, home-of-all, hearse-of-all
    night.
Her fond yellow hornlight wound to the west, | her wild hollow hoarlight
    hung to the height
Waste; her earliest stars, earl-stars, | stárs principal, overbend us,
Fíre-féaturing heaven. For earth | her being has unbound, her dapple is at an
    end, as-
stray or aswarm, all throughther, in throngs; | self ín self steepèd and
    páshed—quíte
Disremembering, dísmémbering | áll now. Heart, you round me right
With: Our évening is over us; óur night | whélms, whélms, ánd will end us.
Only the beak-leaved boughs dragonish | damask the tool-smooth bleak
    light; black,
Ever so black on it. Our tale, O óur oracle! | Lét life, wáned, ah lét life wind
Off hér once skéined stained véined variety | upon, áll on twó spools; párt,
    pen, páck
Now her áll in twó flocks, twó folds—black, white; | right, wrong; reckon
    but, reck but, mind
But thése two; wáre of a wórld where bút these | twó tell, each off the óther;
    of a rack
Where, selfwrung, selfstrung, sheathe- and shelterless, | thóughts agaínst
    thoughts ín groans grínd.

Lee Upton

"DISREMEMBERING, DISMEMBERING"

In "Spelt from Sibyl's Leaves" Gerard Manley Hopkins sees the night as
cancelling the variety of the world and prefiguring God's final judgment.
The very stars in the "Fire-featuring heaven" foretell ultimate destruction. With the onset of night, Hopkins is thrust into contemplation of the
most torturous aspects of his theology, for the night that "will end us," the
night of God's final judgment, must be rehearsed each evening.

In the poem's opening—a form of eloquently slowed stutter work
("Earnest, earthless, equal, attuneable")—the evening strains to overcome
the multiplicitous world that Hopkins so often celebrates. A stone-like and
deathly mother, the night would prove "womb-of-all, home-of-all, hearse-of-

all." Like the pagan sibyl or Eve, this vast night introduces self-consciousness. This mad mother, overwhelming the sense of sight, threatens to absorb all being, just as light itself has been absorbed and the earth's "being has unbound."

Like the sibyl, Hopkins reads a prophecy in nature. As the evening forecloses visibility, so too all physical and spiritual properties appear reduced, prefiguring the terrifying judgment of God. What can matter more than morality when the "dapple" of nature will be shattered and perdition awaits the immoral? "The beakleaved boughs dragonish" suggest the actual leaves of nature as frighteningly transformed, indeed, rendered diabolical. The poem progresses as nightfall itself progresses, evoking a gradually more oppressive spiritual darkening. Hopkins' images of blackness then make way for an image of two spools separating "black, white" and "right, wrong." All variety is reduced, wound as threads upon these two spools dividing the saved from the damned. "Selfwrung, selfstrung, sheathe- and shelterless," the mind agonizes in its hell, separated from God. As such, the poem is poised treacherously between Hopkins' most compelling desires and his most agonizing beliefs—his attachment to the plenitudinous natural world and his theology in which a wrathful God punishes sinners and destroys earth itself.

Significantly, reading "Spelt from Sibyl's Leaves" is an experience of repetition, each word recalling us to a previous word marking off our frustration, our exhilaration, and finally our acknowledgment of Hopkins' very despair. The mind presented at the poem's conclusion must repetitively strain against itself, "thoughts against thoughts in groans grind." As readers we must laboriously and slowly "spell out" the poem's meaning. The fragmentary language itself resembles the leaves that we, like the ancient oracle of Cumae, must read. Spawning variants, compound words reveal a mind anxiously compounded upon itself. The poem, then, is a confrontation for Hopkins with "Our tale"—not only the tale of single mortality and the punishment of individual sinners but the ultimate mortality of all living things.

"Spelt from Sibyl's Leaves" could hardly differ more from "Hurrahing in Harvest"—the earlier poem exultant, its speaker engaged in seeking Christ in the natural world. Amid "the lovely behavior/of silk-sack clouds," a freshening beauty prompts courage: "The heart rears wings bold and bolder/And hurls for him, O half hurls earth for him off under his feet." The loss of bearings is partial and only momentary. And yet Hopkins reveals a joy that is so bodily that it uproots both the earth of the savior and of the speaker's body.

It is this moment of nearly airborne freedom that I wish to summon in contrast to the earthbound despair encased in "Spelt from Sibyl's Leaves." In the later poem Hopkins reverses his exultant movements—as if his sustained work in language must call for a reversal of tone and approach, a "Disremembering, dismembering." By negating the former direction of his processes he would, however painfully and laboriously, refresh his sources in language.

In a letter to Robert Bridges in 1886, Hopkins describes "Spelt from Sibyl's Leaves" as "the longest sonnet ever made and no doubt the longest making." In another letter to Bridges he advises that the poem be read with "loud, leisurely, poetical (not rhetorical) recitation, with long rests, long dwells on the rhyme and other marked syllables and so on." Each line of eight feet is a mark of will, a will that echoes the final harnessing of the mind, for this consciousness in despair must focus upon its own processes. The poet is like a man who labors to close a particularly difficult lid. Nevertheless, the sonnet may not be sealed; a strained groan issues from the poem, the plates of the unrelieved mind grating upon one another. Hopkins presents warring tensions between grace and perdition, day and night, and between his rapturous attachment to the beauties of the world and his torturous belief in the ultimate wrath of his God. The mind on "a rack" in hell after death or on "a rack" in hell within life is restricted to feeding upon its own limited and frustrated energies. God does not appear at the sonnet's conclusion; instead we are met with the agonized and isolated mind—an image that may seem ultimately modern to us.

That Hopkins anticipates later literature is a critical commonplace. His sinewy delineations of despair, his obsessive attention to words, his muscular tonal difficulty, his persistent efforts to contend with an ideology—these effects are more than ever compelling in the midst of some of the placidity and shapelessness that periodically threaten our poetry. Hopkins would revive the withered poetic line and rupture the facile equation through "skeined stained veined variety." And that he would both exult and despair with such violence makes him more than ever a provocative poet.

(CARRION COMFORT)

Not, I'll not, carrion comfort, Despair, not feast on thee;
Not untwist—slack they may be—these last strands of man
In me ór, most weary, cry *I can no more*. I can;
Can something, hope, wish day come, not choose not to be.
But ah, but O thou terrible, why wouldst thou rude on me
Thy wring-world right foot rock? lay a lionlimb against me? scan
With darksome devouring eyes my bruisèd bones? and fan,
O in turns of tempest, me heaped there; me frantic to avoid thee and flee?

   Why? That my chaff might fly; my grain lie, sheer and clear.
Nay in all that toil, that coil, since (seems) I kissed the rod,
Hand rather, my heart lo! lapped strength, stole joy, would laugh, chéer.
Cheer whom though? The hero whose heaven-handling flung me, fóot tród
Me? or me that fought him? O which one? is it each one? That night, that
    year
Of now done darkness I wretch lay wrestling with (my God!) my God.

Dennis Schmitz

ON "CARRION COMFORT"

Hopkins was part of my Catholic education—not only his poems specifically but also the contradictory nature of the spiritual development. The "terrible sonnets" ("Carrion Comfort" is one of them) are the perfection of his art and his humanity. He seems as resolute in his sacrifice for order as Rimbaud, his contemporary, was for disorder—affinities by opposition—he seems as rarefied and alone as another contemporary, Emily Dickinson.

How and where are humans to find God, and in finding God, become worthy to address God? Catholic ascetic practice for some centuries seemed based on programmatic self-negation—admitting to unworthiness. This practice could lead to the self-abandonment of Jesus' paradox: "He who loses his life shall find it," or it could lead to self-hatred and spiritual automatism, in effect making one work harder and harder at being unworthy. It was a religious method that often became a point of view, making the Catholic's burden an oppressive but undefined sense of guilt.

Hopkins converted from the official religion of his class, Anglicanism, to a minority religion, became a Jesuit priest, a position of exclusion, isolated except with reference to the difficult ideals of the strict priestly order (the Jesuits, for example, had vows of poverty, chastity and obedience and required a fifteen-year period of spiritual testing, education and service before ordination). If sanctity can be reached by labors of the will, Hopkins would've been a saint. But will had little to do with his ministrations—he spent a few years in parish work and didn't seem very good at it; his teaching often was a burden because of his scrupulosity in reading papers and in preparing lectures. Hopkins was too brilliant for the jobs he had but too devoted to them to redirect his energy entirely to poetry. He also thought his religious ideal forbade the puffery and self-aggrandizement of publication. The friendship with Robert Bridges merely gave him the permission to write. He never questioned that he should be a priest (at least in any form as public as a letter); he didn't seem able to frame a question of any sort without reference to his spiritual concerns. His despair too is religious, and his answer to it is religious as well.

"Let all consider this," Hopkins wrote in his "Meditations on Hell," a series of notes using the models for meditation suggested by Ignatius Loyola, the founder of the Jesuits, in his *Spiritual Exercises*, "we are our own tormentors, for every sin we then shall have remorse and with remorse torment and the torment fire." This is the way he might refer to the flames of his own scrupulosity.

Hopkins wrote extensive notes for a commentary on *Spiritual Exercises* itself; the "terrible sonnets" written near the end of his life repeat some of concerns of the commentary. Ignatius encourages the person who is meditating to experience the matter of the meditation through the senses—each of the senses is evoked in a running commentary the person makes, almost a self-hypnosis, a series of little dramas. This process is similar to the initial stages of writing, imaging, which has two functions: *deriving*, describing the thing itself as present, and *attributing*, which uses figures, metaphor. Hopkins the priest could apply the method to the advantage of Hopkins the poet, though metaphor is not mere substitution. Maybe meditative practices helped—in any case, the poetry came. Trusting the world required a mental reservation—thus, his small production in his later life (he denied the notion of career) as writer.

"Carrion Comfort" has all the drama of Hopkins' religious despair. It is also one of my favorite sonnets for the way it questions the form. The passion, the fear of self-betrayal is in the word "not" used three times in the first line—the first "not" announces, the second is the emphatic (the contraction "I'll" prepares for the emphasis), the third "not" is the least emphatic because "feast" is the self-reviling emphasis here. Obviously, the speaker has done more than nibble at despair. "Carrion" and "feast" are cruel in tandem—the line has balance because of the situation of these complementary terms. Part of the urgency of delivery in Hopkins' poems, and this one in particular, is the asymmetry, the hesitations, interruptions, the second thoughts of idiomatic speech as knotty, flagrant and full of self as Shakespearean dialogue. It's impossible not to *say* the accumulating feelings of the poem, impossible not to be pulled on to finish the thought.

The sonnet format (how elastic it seems here) allows for the orderly, progressive presentation—what the order is we discover as we go. The "not" repeated four times sets up a defensive, a reluctant, negative stance in the first two lines. What an intuitively right line-break from the first to the second line—and an odd pun ("not untwist") before the parenthetical "slack they may be," which is another of those interruptions which will prepare for the emphasis ("strands" in this case). Hopkins also varies the length of his syntactic units to slow or speed up the delivery in a kind of counterpoint to the pattern of alliteration. Read aloud from "these last strands..." in line two to the end of line three—notice the pace. The three repetitions of "can" in lines three and four are an attempt at the positive, at self-motivation. Notice how the headlong urgency of the fourth line is stopped by the double negative "not choose not to be"—still a defensive stance.

The pattern of "not" and "can" is paralleled by the strategic series of questions (stanzas two and four) that come in spurts of realization, ending with a triumphant "...I wretch lay wrestling with (my God!) my God." The whole of the last stanza is a series of gaspings, realizations, shouts ("that year") culminating in the emotional, breath-depleting double-alliterations of the final line. What power in the parenthetical "(my God!)" to stop the run of the line, the power of the echo in underlining the realization.

Christ (the "hero") has put Hopkins through feats of despair worse than those undergraduate regimens of fasting and minor heroics some twenty years before at Oxford when he wrote to his father to explain his conversion to Catholicism: "those who do not pray to Him in His Passion pray to God but scarcely to Christ." The whole of his adult life, not just "That night, that year," was wrestling.

The process of winnowing that is the central image of the poem incorporates both the notion of beating and the notion of fanning (to free grain from chaff). When the process is done, the run of verbs ("Lapped strength, stole joy, would laugh, cheer") ending the stanza makes the reader breathless with relief.

I like the use of questions to set up the separate movements of the two stanzas of the sestet. I like the use of introductory "buzz words" at the beginning of each stanza ("Not," "But," "Why," "Cheer") as another framing device. When Hopkins is unsuccessful, he works too hard, as in the abandoned religious poems he mentions to Bridges or in other poems as overwrought and artificial as mechanical nightingales. Comments on religious orientation—"We are our own tormentors..." or "for God punishing him through his own guilty thoughts made him seem to suffer in the part that had offended"

("Meditations on Hell")—might very well be about writing and be added to his remark to Bridges on his poetic fatigue: "...I have of myself made verse laborious."

No poet drew more from language—each poem is a workshop in the writing process. One sees Hopkins making choices based mostly on syntactic and aural cues he gives himself, cues at patterning, echoes at the periphery of meaning. "My verse is less to be read than heard," he writes to Bridges, "...it is oratorical, that is the rhythm is so." Hearing his poems, being astonished by the rightness of the patterning, at the rhetorical chances he takes, is the particular pleasure of Hopkins' work. The joy for the reader is to be raised to speak-as-a-great-speaker—*cri de coeur*, generosity of soul, eloquence.

EPITHALAMION

Hark, hearer, hear what I do; lend a thought now, make believe
We are leafwhelmed somewhere with the hood
Of some branchy bunchy bushybowered wood,
Southern dene or Lancashire clough or Devon cleave,
That leans along the loins of hills, where a candycoloured, where a glue-
     gold-brown
Marbled river, boisterously beautiful, between
Roots and rocks is danced and dandled, all in froth and waterblowballs,
     down.
We are there, when we hear a shout
That the hanging honeysuck, the dogeared hazels in the cover
Makes dither, makes hover
And the riot of a rout
Of, it must be, boys from the town
Bathing: it is summer's sovereign good.

By there comes a listless stranger: beckoned by the noise
He drops towards the river: unseen
Sees the bevy of them, how the boys
With dare and with downdolphinry and bellbright bodies huddling out,
Are earthworld, airworld, waterworld thorough hurled, all by turn and turn
     about.

This garland of their gambols flashes in his breast
Into such a sudden zest
Of summertime joys
That he hies to a pool neighbouring; sees it is the best
There; sweetest, freshest, shadowiest;
Fairyland; silk-beech, scrolled ash, packed sycamore, wild wychelm, horn-
     beam fretty overstood
By. Rafts and rafts of flake-leaves light, dealt so, painted on the air,
Hang as still as hawk or hawkmoth, as the stars or as the angles there,
Like the thing that never knew the earth, never off roots
Rose. Here he feasts: lovely all is! No more: off with—down he dings
His bleachèd both and woolwoven wear:
Careless these in coloured wisp
All lie tumbled-to; then with loop-locks
Forward falling, forehead frowning, lips crisp
Over finger-teasing task, his twiny boots
Fast he opens, last he offwrings
Till walk the world he can with bare his feet

And come where lies a coffer, burly all of blocks
Built of chancequarrièd, selfquainèd rocks
And the water warbles over into, filleted with glassy grassy quicksilvery
    shivès and shoots
And with heavenfallen freshness down from moorland still brims,
Dark or daylight on and on. Here he will then, here he will the fleet
Flinty kindcold element let break across his limbs
Long. Where we leave him, froliclavish, while he looks about him, laughs,
    swims.

Enough now; since the sacred matter that I mean
I should be wronging longer leaving it to float
Upon this only gambolling and echoing-of-earth note—
What is . . . the delightful dene?
Wedlock. What is water? Spousal love.

   . . . .
   . . . .
Father, mother, brothers, sisters, friends
Into fairy trees, wild flowers, wood ferns
Rankèd round the bower

   . . . .

Stanley Plumly

"HEAR WHAT I DO"

Of the sixty-five poems of his that survive, the first four are catego-
rized as "early poems," though they are, not surprisingly, remarkably accomplished, while the final dozen are separated as unfinished
or fragmentary, though in many ways—as in the last poems of Shelley and
Keats—the best of them (#s 60, 62, 65) point to greater openness and modernity of form, certainly more so than such achieved classics as "The Wind-
hover" and the abrupt "Pied Beauty" or the darker "I Wake to Feel" and
"Spring & Fall." "Epithalamion" is Hopkins' last numbered poem, and what
his friend Robert Bridges says about it is revealing:

> Four sides of pencilled rough sketches, and five sides of quarto first draft,
> on 'Royal University of Ireland' candidates' paper, as if G.M.H. had written
> it while supervising an examination. Fragments in disorder with erasures
> and corrections; undated.... The text, which omits only two disconnected

> lines, is my arrangement of the fragments, and embodies the latest correc-
> tions. It was to have been an Ode on the occasion of his brother's marriage,
> which fixes the date as 1888.

Several things appeal to me in this description. First, the fact that the poem
was written, as is much of Wallace Stevens, on the job—Hopkins' Jesuitical
assignment of "supervising an examination." Second, that, therefore, as per
the distraction of the moment, the poem is "fragments in disorder with erasures and corrections." Third, that the poem was meant to be that potentially
most open and enlarging of lyric texts, an ode, a philosophic poem. And
fourth, that Bridges had to "arrange" the poem, when in truth by the arrangement of its own narrative it is already a sequence and within itself whole. The
poem has other and obvious properties and qualities as well, distinctions that
suggest a poet struggling with his established venue.

To me, the distinctions—or perhaps, to put it more precisely, the exten-
sions and corruptions of earlier successes—are what make "Epithalamion"
valuable. Traditionally, Hopkins' claim on modern attention has largely had
to do with his applied prosodic brilliance in concert with his platonic perception of an ulterior, interior, and holistic reality he called inscape: or, to reverse the formula: that sense of a tentative inward fusion of thought and feeling manifested in an outward harmony of "sprung" rhythm and sound
texture—the artful carnal word as the signature of the wholeness of the spirit.
The busy, brilliant compounding of effects within a Hopkins word or line virtually announces itself to the reader, as if a kind of salesmanship were involved. The special modernist intensity of Hopkins' prosody is that it is not
only self-fulfilling, it is—both Jesuitically and personally—self-abnegating.
Readers who admired, in the 1950s, the Metaphysical poets found in Hopkins yet another anachronism to rescue into Modernism. They still do.

For Hopkins, though, perfection of the poem became an expression of his
inherent imperfectibility as a religious being. Which makes the fragmentary
imperfect work placed at the end of his collection of poems all the more interesting. Hopkins, for many of us, is often a difficult poet to get close to—
not because of any organic poetical difficulty but almost in spite of it. His
theoretical comments on rhythm, for example, serve as a bridge between
Wordsworth and Pound: "Rhythm is the most natural of things...of common
speech and written prose." His insights concerning inscape and instress anticipate the emotive images of both the Symbolists and the Imagists. And as
a poet preoccupied with visual and vocal texture he provides an agreeable
link between the gorgeousness of Keats and the concentration of Yeats. Yet
the poems themselves enact an extremity that occasionally comes close—for
this reader—to parody, especially when the accents and image-clusters seem
to instruct the experience ("Spelt from Sibyl's Leaves," "That Nature is a
Heraclitean Fire"). Which, again, makes the last, "unfinished" efforts inter-

esting: perhaps most of all as examples of the way poets break out of the
cloister-perfections of their self-absorption and success. How right, then, that
"Epithalamion," written in 1888, should celebrate a wedding, the shared
imagination, the specific capacities of the natural world, and its own failure
to complete or perfect its form.

As an experiment, it should also be no surprise that this "Epithalamion" is
less a wedding song than a wedding space, less a chant or dance or "eccho
ring," as Spenser calls his, than an imitative structure, a built but natural
bower as wedding chamber. Its dene-as-bower, that is its invented natural
public setting becoming, in the course of the poem, a more intimate private
enclosure, is a wholly imagined event, a stated construct of words, a fiction
with characters. The poem overall acts, as we find out at its "conclusion," as
a sort of emblem-allegory of the transformation of the flesh of language into
the word of the spirit: at the center of the poem is the understanding that,
once articulated, nature becomes the word as both feast and ceremony. Hopkins' dialectic may be paraphrastically familiar theology, but the energy and
velocity of the writing, the assumption of the bower-conceit of the poem, and
the willingness of the poem to delay its subject all help to give the piece its
openness, its newness, its inventiveness. Its chief tension, in fact, lies in its
"fragmentation." What is unusual here, for Hopkins, is that the eyes of the
poem depend less on a lyric mode—a vital, shimmering, single moment—
than on narrative, on the speaker's sense of discovery of his own make-believe, and of time as a series of moments within a larger continuum. The
poem's irregularity, its sometime awkwardness, its commitment to scenic action further underscore its reality, once the reader is ushered into its world.
The speaker asks us to "hear what I do," to "make believe," to trust, on location, where he is going, inventing as he goes.

The unfinished "Epithalamion" is, therefore, a poem off-balance, tilted toward its verticality, its longitude, toward some distant center of gravity,
rather joyously lost in the pleasure of its own company. It is an ode fragment
built on the allegorical secret of its destination (not unlike Frost's "Direc-
tive"), even though it will not half-arrive. "We are leafwhelmed somewhere,"
says the speaker, "lend a thought now," as if he were a storyteller asking us to
suspend disbelief and follow. This could be, he continues, any dene in England, north, south or west. And so we are ushered into an artifice of nature.
What is basic to the vision that is developing, and basic to its sexual/nuptial
implications, basic, in a word, to its believability, is that the two bathing
scenes occur in sequence, in a cause-and-effect rather than a static order, and
that we, as readers and witnesses, become complicit in the plot...trusting nar-
ration over lyric assertion. Hopkins' "storyline" is also a way of narrowing
the scale of the dene down to something like the intimacy of a bower—the
boys from the town evoked in their larger space, the listless stranger in a
neighboring, shadowier, sweeter, smaller space. Thus, having established

one imaginary cleave, "along the loins of hills," with its "gluegold-brown/Marbled river," with its "hanging honeysuck" and "dogeared hazels," the poet is able to focus on his true bower, the sexual enclosure of "scrolled ash, packed sycamore, wild wychelm, hornbeam fretty overstood/By." In each of these instances he has asked us to be corroborators, as if to confirm the natural and parallel world the details of the imagined one come from (which may account for the particularity of naming actual places). "We are there" first with the "riot of a rout," only to be with the listless stranger, brought suddenly more awake—do I wake or sleep ?—to some deeper dream "beckoned by the noise." The device of the use of a sublunary protagonist is interesting in that it further saturates the text in its fiction, its invention-code. The stranger is, of course, a stand-in, but is required because Hopkins cannot, in his make-believe, break his authorial contract with the witness-reader. The complexity of the play of point-of-view is, I suspect, part of the reason Hopkins never finished this poem: his elaboration of the fiction drew him farther and farther away from his perceived epithalamion mission. The didactic issues involve—as we are informed at the "end" of the poem —the symbology of a wedding; but the narrative, which has taken over the poem, involves the simple fiction of an innocent stranger inspired by his own eyes ("This garland of their gambols in his breast") to find his own bower-pool in which to "feast" his body and spirit. Unlike the boys', though, his immersion will be relatively quiet and reflective—once he gets his clothes off.

At which point, remembering his mission, exhausting his story-scenes, Hopkins declares "Enough now," time to turn to the "sacred matter that I mean." So he leaves his stranger "froliclavish," happy, treading water. In a sense he suspends one strategy, one kind of poem, a kind of accident, for another kind of poem, a strategy of sacrament, a statement of ritual meaning. His two baptismal bathing scenes are locked inside the inscape of consciousness, locked inside his verbal layering and "bowering," his own signature "downdolphinry and bellbright" language. The two concluding short stanzas—the first an explanation of the terms of his illustrating story, the second a figural, family-tree post-script—abruptly unlock the secret of the example, turn it outside, and represent the author-priest emerging from the camouflage of the bower in order to give his pagan nature frolic the seriousness and defining purpose he thinks it deserves. Bridges, in his note, would like to take the blame for the arrangement of "Epithalamion," but once the poem is set with its invitation to the reader to "Hark, hearer," there is no turning back on what becomes an inevitable sequence. For the modern, purist reader, this poem truly ends treading water, at the evocative moment of the stranger-Hopkins lavish in the "heavenfallen freshness." The tacked-on explanations and apologies stick the poem with Victorian, let alone religious, piety. They turn it back in time. Hopkins' worry that "I should be wronging longer leaving it to float" is exactly the level of insight that will generate the discussion of form that will obsess the Modernists. "Floating" is exactly the metaphor for the supreme fictions of the Symbolists and after. Hopkins, at his best, knows this, since so many of his poems burst on the air. But they are, in their sonnet-lengths, perfected forms, and in the long run, limited forms. In the career of the maturing poet such perfections can become circumventions. The life of every important poet is an illustration of a writer struggling to enlarge his or her text, to narrate the lyric. One wonders what Hopkins' work would have looked like had he written and saved, say, a hundred poems—or what it would have become had its reception not been posthumous.

Marianne Boruch

BECOMING "EPITHALAMION"

First off, there's its fragmenthood to cherish, watching this poem, this epithalamion rise and float and fail, not yet—never—caught in any final certainty. "It has some bright lines in it," Hopkins admitted in a rare show of pleasure to his friend and first editor Robert Bridges, "but I could not get it down." Of course the longing's there, as in all of Hopkins, that stretch toward the largest mystery. But "Epithalamion" is a curiously secular piece. It's incomplete, a thing hurried and left; its stall and starts are mortal. Like our human grasp of anything, the poem goes as far as exhaustion goes, or confusion or boredom, until the fine simple nerve it takes to write at all balks, then stops unto the stubborn ellipsis.

Meanwhile, we have the giant lucky mess of it. Bridges, naturally, complained: full of "disorder" and "erasures" and "corrections," this draft scribbled on "Royal University of Ireland" candidates' paper, written, he suggests, while Hopkins sat in some dim light administering an exam. One of the last poems he would write, it followed the "terrible sonnets" their "fell of dark," their "cliffs of fall" by three years, a kind of gift, a cool relief, this thing that would be itself a gift to Hopkins' brother Everard and his bride Amy Sichel. Two things: trance and timidity. These cross angles keep the poem buoyed up, and turning on itself like music, like the water it describes.

The sweet thing is trance, though we enter distantly, through rhetoric, and only by miming the poet's own deep wish to imagine. "Hark, hearer, hear what I do; lend a thought now, make believe/We are leafwhelmed somewhere...." And before us opens the "branchy bunchy bushybowered wood," its river "gluegold-brown" and "boisterously beautiful," and so much more, the long layering line after line—one sentence!—of it. Writing richly, so richly in fact it nearly parodies his own high ecstatic style elsewhere, Hop-

kins seems to cut nothing of the vision. Perhaps this counts: he had just taken
up sketching seriously again—mostly woods, and running brooks—after a
lapse of several years. Still, this is a draft. Which is to say we are some 100
years later, quite possibly close to the moment of initial *seeing*, that first necessary excess. In this breathless expanse—the view flashing aerial (this dene
that "leans along the loins of hills") and close up (this river that "is danced
and candled, all in froth and water-blowballs")—Hopkins is all courage, his
tentative "make believe" of the start swamped, made true by the triumphant
declarative "We are there...." And we are. Proof: "we hear a shout" in the
woods, and can do nothing but follow it.

This is an odd moment, and itself mimics the mind clicking out of its natural blur, into focus. Boys there in "the hanging honeysuck, the dogeared
hazels," boys, a dizzy human wealth. Hopkins' double take is in the syntax itself—something he apparently borrowed from Welsh verse, the *tor
ymadrodd*, the so-called "interjected absolute." "And the riot of a rout/Of, it
must be, boys from town/Bathing..." he writes, seems to find again, suddenly,
even as we read it. *...it must be....* I love that stepping back, that consciousness of treasure. Much has been said about movement in Hopkins' poems,
their free fall feel, their high wire muscle. But against such rapid turn and
counterturn is dramatic stillness, a kind of urgent languor; here, it's through
that stillness—*it must be*—that wonder enters.

Then abruptly, another level to this reverie. A character, a "listless
stranger" comes unseen upon the boys exactly as we have. We who've
watched the boys now watch him. It's a commanding shift, and through it,
the silence, the attention of that silence, deepens and grows complex. Of
course, the boys only get louder, more specific and radiant in their antics, full
of "dare" and "downdolphinry," their "bellbright bodies hurdling out/Are
earthworld, airworld, waterworld thorough hurled, all by turn and turn
about." In another mood, Hopkins might have stopped the piece right here,
this high split-second the thing that ends and overwhelms, his favorite way of
closure. But the boys are mere trigger; the real heat is yet to come. We're in
that far; we're lost, enchanted maybe—to be 19th century about it—and the
stranger, not so listless now, is fully changed, and charged by the sight of
such joy.

What stops me is the trees in this transition. The stranger, in finding his
own separate "neighbouring" pool, finds the "sweetest, freshest, shadowiest"
ringed around, as it is, with "silk beech, scrolled ash, packed sycamore, wild
wychelm, hornbeam...." Here the privacy—more, the solitude—is eternal
and inhuman; the depth of shade measures the intensity of the vision. "Here,
he feasts," Hopkins tells us, "lovely all is!" And in the dazzle of such happiness, the most peculiar happens, peculiar that is, for Hopkins, good Jesuit: *a
man takes off his clothes.* Now it's our turn at the *tor ymadrodd*, stepping
back, *it must be.* But how precise the poet is—no timidity, no hesitation now.

"...down he dings/His bleached both and woolwoven wear...." Hopkins is careful to give us the final fumbling at the "twiny boots," the "lips crisp/Over finger-teasing task" until the stranger can "walk the world" toward water, its "glassy grassy quicksilver strives and shoots...."

It's as if we sleepwalk though, summoned by the "heavenfallen freshness" of the pool. So deep is this dream that some might say Hopkins has in fact gotten it wrong, the shoes going last, a funny inverse of the million times we've taken off our clothes. But around us, woods, their danger a large measure of their flickering beauty. For generations, we've been this careful—"the soil/Is bare now, nor can foot feel, being shod," Hopkins wrote in lament years earlier. All's so precariously made, so vulnerable, but in the final spellbound rush—boots coming off at last, everything exposed—we have that crucial slip into being, the shift from watcher to the one watched, to the one who no longer gives a damn but simply (simply!) jumps in. It is, I think, an extraordinary moment in a whole lifetime of work. And the water that draws the stranger, that "flinty kindcold element" breaks through all reserve. "...we leave him," Hopkins tells us, almost back to his rhetorical overvoice, "froli-clavish, while he looks about him, laughs, swims."

How the poet wakes then, stunned, maybe shaking his head—it's right in the text. "Enough now;" Hopkins says as though to an unruly child, "since the sacred matter that I mean/I should be wronging longer leaving it to float/Upon the only gambolling and echoing-of-earth note—" In the long nay-saying beauty of that sentence, he's nearly set adrift again, purpose waylaid by the charm of recollection.

"An epithalamion on my brother's wedding," he called this painterly fragment—fitting for this brother who actually was a professional artist—and the last section is Hopkins' visible struggle back to that clear-eyed thesis. He hesitates, though all business now. "What is...the delightful dene?/Wedlock," he intones as though, finally, we've reached the point. "What is water? Spousal love." One feels the drop and press of duty in these questions; howbeit awkward, it's endearing, this turning back deliberately, away from dream. But is such an equation really so much the point? Two lines are missing. Bridges called them "disconnected" and simply trashed them. We stare instead at two rows of ellipsis, as if their pause could tell us something. Elsewhere, the poet is busy, locking himself into overdrive. Wedding? Of course, the wedding. And now the silliest scene unfolds, the entire family set to glitter "ranked round the bower," parents, siblings, friends transformed into "fairy trees, wild flowers, wood ferns...."

I don't doubt Hopkins' earnestness; it's just that I've never known what to make of this shift to Victorian pop, this leap into the warm nubbies of another age. Are we to believe then, that the whole brilliantly wrought vision of boys and whatever listless stranger, this epiphany really, is merely conceit, a device to shoulder up one side of metaphor? "I could not get it done," Hopkins

wrote to Bridges, giving up. His reluctance to work these two strands together is itself revealing.

But of what? Surely in Hopkins' standstill, one remembers things too
bone-close, too strange for words at all. It's in that depth of shade, those
trees, that stranger's rare lovely fever that would have us strip down every
trace of the human-made world to be engulfed and buoyed up by water. For a
poem supposedly about union, the central mystery and heat is solitude, less
about the self than about its letting go. For Hopkins is not reacting, not making sense of circumstance. Nor is he the poet simply pleased to watch his
own starry mind at work. He's made something, and put it over there, and he
can't explain. Imagination here is more than palpable; it is place. That's the
poetry in this poem. That's its lucid, sea-green light.

WALLACE STEVENS
(1879-1955)

"Poetry is a response to the daily necessity of getting the world right," Wallace Stevens wrote in his notebooks, and the whole of his work throughout a long and productive career may be seen as an exploration of that idea. Grounded in the values of a skeptical age, when faith in the existence of absolute values and a divinely-inspired cosmic order has been lost, his poems work to discover value and meaning in the world itself, through the redemptive power of perception and imagination. Early a poet of extravagant wordplay ("Personally, I like words to sound wrong"), he matured into one of the most eloquent and subtly musical poets in our language. As a lawyer for the Hartford Accident and Indemnity Company, rising eventually to the position of vice-president, Stevens lived a comfortable middle-class life, and in formal terms his poetry may seem to reflect a bourgeois conventionality. American poets, though, have long understood his remarkably innovative role in the development of twentieth-century poetry. Influenced variously by French symbolist poetry, impressionist and post-impressionist painting, and the arts of China and Japan, Stevens created meditative poetry of a haunting delicacy, poignancy, wit, and power. He is our great poet of the vital imagination, of "the poem of the act of the mind."

BOOKS: *The Collected Poems of Wallace Stevens* (1954); *Opus Posthumous*, ed. Samuel French Morse (1957); *The Necessary Angel: Essays on Reality and the Imagination* (1951); *The Letters of Wallace Stevens* (1966). The standard selection of Stevens' poems is *The Palm at the End of the Mind*, ed. Holly Stevens (1971).

PETER QUINCE AT THE CLAVIER

I

Just as my fingers on these keys
Make music, so the selfsame sounds
On my spirit make a music, too.

Music is feeling, then, not sound;
And thus it is that what I feel,
Here in this room, desiring you,

Thinking of your blue-shadowed silk,
Is music. It is like the strain
Waked in the elders by Susanna.

Of a green evening, clear and warm,
She bathed in her still garden, while
The red-eyed elders watching, felt

The basses of their beings throb
In witching chords, and their thin blood
Pulse pizzicati of Hosanna.

II

In the green water, clear and warm,
Susanna lay.
She searched
The touch of springs,
And found
Concealed imaginings.
She sighed,
For so much melody.

Upon the bank, she stood
In the cool
Of spent emotions.
She felt, among the leaves,
The dew
Of old devotions.

She walked upon the grass,
Still quavering.
The winds were like her maids,
On timid feet,
Fetching her woven scarves,
Yet wavering.

A breath upon her hand
Muted the night.
She turned—
A cymbal crashed,
And roaring horns.

III

Soon, with a noise like tambourines,
Came her attendant Byzantines.

They wondered why Susanna cried
Against the elders by her side;

And as they whispered, the refrain
Was like a willow swept by rain.

Anon, their lamps' uplifted flame
Revealed Susanna and her shame.

And then, the simpering Byzantines
Fled, with a noise like tambourines.

IV

Beauty is momentary in the mind—
The fitful tracing of a portal;
But in the flesh it is immortal.

The body dies; the body's beauty lives.
So evenings die, in their green going,
A wave, interminably flowing.
So gardens die, their meek breath scenting

The cowl of winter, done repenting.
So maidens die, to the auroral
Celebration of a maiden's choral.

Susanna's music touched the bawdy strings
Of those white elders; but, escaping,
Left only Death's ironic scraping.
Now, in its immortality, it plays
On the clear viol of her memory,
And makes a constant sacrament of praise.

Dennis Schmitz

ON "PETER QUINCE AT THE CLAVIER"

Perhaps more fugue than improvisation—how much that notion appealed to me twenty years ago when I came to poetry and to Stevens the hard way, through an Oscar Williams anthology: that a poem uttered its own predicate, that a self-consistent pattern of sounds, phrase to phrase, was the body of poetry. What I found in Stevens was that the testing and application of virtuosity is joyful, is a natural celebration of the thing loved; though irony loves itself most of all, at last it achieves courteous distance.

The subject statement in the first half-dozen lines of the poem is immutable, clean, as are so many Stevens beginnings, from "Sunday Morning" to some of the last short poems. Does it sound curiously like an answer to Orsino's petition at the opening of *Twelfth Night*? Note the balance of the first line, the line-break ("make music" is picked up in the eighth line with "Is music": the exact half-way mark in Part I, at which point the counter-subject is introduced). The vowel development in lines 10-11 leads into the alliterative motif of lines 12-15. The repetition of "green" (water, this time), and of "clear and warm" in the first line of Part II anticipate a tonal change.

Accepting the musical terms Stevens proposes—why does the episode (illustration), Susanna, become more important than the subject-statement of Part I? What is Stevens saying about himself as poet—is the implied irony that narcissism is a function of virtuosity? Is the strength of chastity a self-involvement that concentrates on the music within, rather than discontinuous noise ("Bawdy string," "roaring horns")? The string of verbs modulates the pace of the short lines in Part II; the couplet rhyme, the second, third and

fourth couplets framed by the end couplets to contain the rapid pace and resolution of Part III—the action of the poem is the development of the music.

Part IV is a paradoxical answer. How does the act of the mind find embodiment, even permanence? The elders' (an audience's) enjoyment of Susanna's body is an event parallel to Susanna's enjoyment of the limits of sensation—ironically, she is no longer chaste, though she has not been
violated—what is thought, is so. Does that sound like Jesus' observation that
the act of desire is the act of commission?

DOMINATION OF BLACK

At night, by the fire,
The colors of the bushes
And of the fallen leaves,
Repeating themselves,
Turned in the room,
Like the leaves themselves
Turning in the wind.
Yes: but the color of the heavy hemlocks
Came striding.
And I remembered the cry of the peacocks.

The colors of their tails
Were like the leaves themselves
Turning in the wind,
In the twilight wind.
They swept the room,
Just as they flew from the boughs of the hemlocks
Down to the ground.
I heard them cry—the peacocks.
Was it a cry against the twilight
Or against the leaves themselves
Turning in the wind,
Turning as the flames
Turned in the fire,
Turning as the tails of the peacocks
Turned in the loud fire,
Loud as the hemlocks
Full of the cry of the peacocks?
Or was it a cry against the hemlocks?

Out of the window,
I saw how the planets gathered
Like the leaves themselves
Turning in the wind.
I saw how the night came,
Came striding like the color of the heavy hemlocks.
I felt afraid.
And I remembered the cry of the peacocks.

Philip Booth

ON "DOMINATION OF BLACK"

Except when Stevens invents fancy variations on his basic dialectic, he's a marvel. Given the neatly free-floating qualifier in his prose adage, "In poetry at least the imagination must not detach itself from reality," I'm willing to forgive a lot of what he elsewhere belabors. I like nothing better in Stevens than how his ambivalences balance. I like the Thurber-comedy of "A Rabbit as King of the Ghosts" almost as much as I admire that most demanding of all single-sentence poems, "The Snow Man." I have long fondness for Stevens' "...Ordinary Evening...," and for the extraordinary gray day of "No Possum, No Sop, No Taters." Over and over, in Stevens, I am touched by the minimal that refuses to be reductive.

Of all the "balances that happen" in Stevens, whether abundant or bleak, none has moved me longer than "Domination of Black." I woke late to what Frost called the "design of darkness"; I was maybe twenty when "Domination of Black" first appalled me. I've half grown used, now, to such dark as the poem involves, but I've never outgrown the questions the poem asks, or the design of Stevens' asking. The ways in which the poem turns in on itself, combining what he would later call "the philosopher's search// For an interior made exterior/ And the poet's search for the same exterior made/ Interior....," continue to stun me. For years I was stunned into blind misreading: I wanted every aspect of the peacocks, not only "the colors of their tails," to counter the night and its "heavy hemlocks." I wanted the last line of the first strophe, emphatically repeated as the last line of the full poem, to begin with "But...." But Stevens, twice, wrote his own clear sentence, "And I remembered the cry of the peacocks."

Since my imagination had so demonstrably detached itself from the reality of the poem, it took some extraordinary actuality to make me understand how deeply Stevens' imagination was dominated by emptiness. Maybe ten years ago, my youngest daughter and I, flashlights in hand, searched into the March woods near our house for the source of a cry-of-distress she was sure she'd heard. I was skeptical until I heard, too: a voice, almost strangulated with fear, crying "Help!" But the sound moved toward us as we moved into the woods, and it turned out to be no more or less than the cry of the apparently lonely peacock just acquired by a doctor who lived down the road. The doctor knew, of course, when we told him how close the peacock's cry came to the cry of a human voice.

Stevens knew, and wrote "And...." He had just written in "Domination..." what is, perhaps, his most emotionally revelatory line: "I felt afraid." He wasn't about to say more; he let the peacocks confirm his fear and climax the poem, a poem that is truly "the cry of its occasion,/ Part of the res itself and not about it." It is the poem I remember now, not the house we used to live in, or the woods my daughter and I tried to search. The bird and the doctor are dead. It is the poem I think of when I see out the window how the planets gather, when I feel in myself the color of the heavy hemlocks.

THIRTEEN WAYS OF LOOKING
AT A BLACKBIRD

I

Among twenty snowy mountains,
The only moving thing
Was the eye of the blackbird.

II

I was of three minds,
Like a tree
In which there are three blackbirds.

III

The blackbird whirled in the autumn winds.
It was a small part of the pantomime.

IV

A man and a woman
Are one.
A man and a woman and a blackbird
Are one.

V

I do not know which to prefer,
The beauty of inflections
Or the beauty of innuendoes,
The blackbird whistling
Or just after.

VI

Icicles filled the long window
With barbaric glass.
The shadow of the blackbird
Crossed it, to and fro.
The mood
Traced in the shadow
An indecipherable cause.

VII

O thin men of Haddam,
Why do you imagine golden birds?
Do you not see how the blackbird
Walks around the feet
Of the women about you?

VIII

I know noble accents
And lucid, inescapable rhythms;
But I know, too,
That the blackbird is involved
In what I know.

IX

When the blackbird flew out of sight,
It marked the edge
Of one of many circles.

X

At the sight of blackbirds
Flying in a green light,
Even the bawds of euphony
Would cry out sharply.

XI

He rode over Connecticut
In a glass coach.
Once, a fear pierced him,
In that he mistook
The shadow of his equipage
For blackbirds.

XII

The river is moving.
The blackbird must be flying.

XIII

It was evening all afternoon.
It was snowing
And it was going to snow.
The blackbird sat
In the cedar-limbs.

Alberta Turner

ASTONISHED

I ask poems to astonish me. I had long been astonished by Donne's ir-
refutable argument that God must rape him, by Pope's serene ratiocina-
tion that all that is is right, by Arnold's desolate sound of human hope
rattling down the steep pebbles of Dover, and by Frost's deliberately flattened demonstration that the range of humankind is so insignificant that it's
out of range. All these were stated or implied by good logic and illustrated by
images that rang like good bells. I could agree or disagree. So imagine my
astonishment when, much later, I came upon Stevens' "Thirteen Ways of
Looking at a Blackbird," a sequence of thirteen separate poems that he
seemed to be daring me to thread on a string of my own providing. Or was he
teasing me with actual discreteness? Realizing that he was capable of either
and would be amused by my struggle, I struggled—long enough to tire even
him.

What a teacher! By the time I climbed out of the poem, he had showed me
(not told me) the relation between perceiver and perceived so that I should
not only understand it but should *have* it—for my own manipulation and delight—always.

Blackbird: it could have been any creature with perception, movement,
commonness, and connotations that would not cancel the dignity of humankind's effort, fear of the unknown, and exposure to seasonal change and
death. Try dolphin, fox, rabbit, crab—none of them quite right, none with
quite the alertness, speed, flocking habit, commonness, and iridescence of
blackbird, but living things that might both comprise and examine an otherwise static and sterile landscape. Stanza I makes this blackbird both perceiver and perceived. Being perceived, it focuses, assembles, proportions,
and determines values—much like the jar in Tennessee. Perceiving and con-
sequently doing, it will act on the perceiver's perception so that the perceiver

must give up the confidence of sure expectation, the power to manipulate stasis, in favor of change, chance, and even the unperceivable—thus both challenging and extending his power. Stanza II multiples and diversifies both perceiver and perceived. In III the separate eye of the perceiver is not mentioned. Self is submerged in the act of perceiving. In IV both are specifically fused. In V act becomes after-act or meaning. In VI it moves beyond perceived meaning into emotional or subconscious meaning, into mystery.

Then (in VII and VIII) comes a typical Stevens shift in tone. Instead of following the previous ascending arc into space or to the gate of heaven, he brings the blackbird to ground and reminds us that mystery is also mundane. The perceiver I, who has been implicitly the poet in II and V, becomes more obviously so and taunts those other poets ("thin men of Haddam," Connecticut) who expect Byzantine birds, "noble accents," and "inescapable rhythms," when a common blackbird can provide the most jolting perceptions: the demarcation of the limits of perception, that by just being noted as limits incite us to exceed them (IX), the shock of beauty (X), the terror of death (XI), the seasonal surge of aliveness (XII). Then back full circle (XIII) to a scene of deathlike stasis, a blackbird in snow and an implied invitation to Nos. XIV, XV, etc.

Stevens has said to me, "Take it. It's yours." And I have it—an eye, my I— that can design and redesign the whole snowy landscape. Stevens has been generous. He has handed me the power and the danger. I'm astonished.

THE SNOW MAN

One must have a mind of winter
To regard the frost and the boughs
Of the pine-trees crusted with snow;

And have been cold a long time
To behold the junipers shagged with ice,
The spruces rough in the distant glitter

Of the January sun; and not to think
Of misery in the sound of the wind,
In the sound of a few leaves,

Which is the sound of the land
Full of the same wind
That is blowing in the same bare place

For the listener, who listens in the snow,
And, nothing himself, beholds
Nothing that is not there and the nothing that is.

Laura Jensen

WHY I LIKE "THE SNOW MAN"

First of all—the poem is one sentence, a unit of grammar; this gives the poem a special crystal aspect, like a snowflake. Snow is our first image of winter. It is winter given presence. Here that image is given presence—a mind and senses. The presence beholds, yet is said to be nothing; at the center of this nothing is the word "misery." Be it the misery of the image itself or the misery of others in winter—the small animals and birds which are not there in the cedars, or the derelicts, or the poor, or the old—misery is not a part of the image's presence.

I like the poem for its drawing forth of the image of winter. And for the good ambiguity of its title: for as children we rolled a ball out of snow, put the middle and the head on, and there—we had a creation. It had structure, it was immobile. Despite the suggested mountain or country atmosphere of "The Snow Man," I can see that snowman, wrapped in maybe an old scarf, deserted in a cold yard at twilight.

A POSTCARD FROM THE VOLCANO

Children picking up our bones
Will never know that these were once
As quick as foxes on the hill;

And that in autumn, when the grapes
Made sharp air sharper by their smell
These had a being, breathing frost;

And least will guess that with our bones
We left much more, left what still is
The look of things, left what we felt

At what we saw. The spring clouds blow
Above the shuttered mansion-house,
Beyond our gate and the windy sky

Cries out a literate despair.
We knew for long the mansion's look
And what we said of it became

A part of what it is . . . Children,
Still weaving budded aureoles,
Will speak our speech and never know,

Will say of the mansion that it seems
As if he that lived there left behind
A spirit storming in blank walls,

A dirty house in a gutted world,
A tatter of shadows peaked to white,
Smeared with the gold of the opulent sun.

Maxine Kumin

ON "A POSTCARD FROM THE VOLCANO"

" **A** Postcard from the Volcano," published in 1935, is not widely anthologized, although it reflects Stevens' ongoing preoccupation
with weighing the ominous present against an ever more forbidding future. "I believe that, in any society, the poet should be the exponent of
the imagination of that society," the poet said, introducing *Ideas of Order.*
Here, he projects a modern Vesuvius or Mt. Pelee (or, heaven forfend, a second Hiroshima), a site of future devastation through which survivors and
their descendants roam, sifting the rubble for remnants of our present culture. In this Pompeii brought up to date, children wander innocently over the
hill, come upon the chips and shards of human bones and artifacts, and are
unaware of their meaning.

Whatever the setting, the poignancy of stopped time conveyed by the
poem is vivid and convincing. The two opening stanzas never fail to cause
my neck hairs to stand up, however often I read them. I am in awe of the fast
breakaway of the first line, an effect carried in part by the trochaic "children"
and augmented by the short "i" sounds that echo, along with consonance,
through "picking," "will," "quick," ("foxes"), and "hill." Transported by
these initial sound effects, all my defenses fall away in the second stanza,
where long and short "a" sounds are played off with the rolling consonantal
"r" sounds. Moreover, the base line, iambic tetrameter, is just tight enough to
control the diction without imposing stringencies on it.

Of course none of these devices—if we are to call largely unconsciously
arrived-at juxtapositions of sounds and meter devices—would be enough to
carry the poem without the hard sensibility of the poet informing it. How the
newly dead Stevens has created regret all that is left behind them unfinished,
treasured, yet stamped with their human imperfection! Looking backward
from a destroyed future "cries out for a literate despair" indeed.

Even if I never know surely whether "budded aureoles" signify the haloes
of innocence or the early garlands of flowers, I will always see civilization's
ruins haloed in this strongly rhetorical last stanza. The spirit of the creative
artist is condemned to storm romantically through the ruins, railing against
destruction, while, well outside human concern or influence, the sun paints
the desolation a rich gold. How gracefully we go on bending the indifference
of nature to human uses, and how insistently Stevens makes us aware of our
self-deception.

David Young

GAIETY OF LANGUAGE

A lovely and majestic poem. Rather somber. But watch out. Stevens is like Bugs Bunny, moving with lightning speed and changing identity constantly, while thick-witted critics fumble with their blunderbusses, so many Elmer Fudds. Look at that title. Can a volcano send you a postcard? More to the point, can a volcano—"Greetings From Mount Vesuvius"—be adequately represented on a postcard? An air of comic futility hangs over the proceedings already. The juxtaposition of postcard and volcano should send us into the poem delighted and intrigued, wary of taking it too seriously.

Then there is the marvelously arresting first line. Did any postcard message ever venture such an image? We catapult miraculously forward in time, to contemplate our own oblivion. And we were quick as foxes! The adjective glances at the famous typesetter's sentence, with fox sailing gracefully over lazy dog. And while we know that the hill is just part of a comparison characterizing our living (the other sense of "quick") bones, don't we try to associate it with the slope of the volcano? Straining to bring the title to bear on the poem—e.g., are our bones being found in some Pompeii?—is something Stevens knows we can't help doing. He leaves room for us to interject relationships where he has been content to suggest, even to deflect. This trick of making the reader help construct the poem, even overconstruct it, is perhaps his most notable rhetorical habit.

The grapes do not go with the fox, but their conjunction gives us a little whiff of Aesop. What the second stanza, with its heady music and pungent imagery, mainly accomplishes is the greater involvement of the reader's body. We have all experienced that sharp air and have vivid physical recollections of seeing our own breath on frosty days. It's important to bring the whole of our physical beings to bear on a poem; by the time Stevens has had our bones picked up and has stirred our memory of breathing frosty air, he has us more fully engaged than we realize.

The rhetoric grows more formal in the third stanza, though no less playful, with its overlapping repetitions of "left," the last of them facing its anagram, "felt," as the sentence prepares to topple over into the next stanza. "What we saw" is now vividly illustrated by the little scene of clouds, shuttered mansion, gate and windy sky. It's spring, suddenly, instead of the autumn of a moment earlier, and the tense has subsided into the present. Still nervous about getting geography straight, the reader is wondering whether to situate the mansion near a volcano, but the poem is busy arguing that the visible world is permeated with our feelings—"literate despair," for instance—and will remain that way long after we disappear, leaving the world a shuttered mansion that bears the stamp of its former owner's character when his name and ways have been forgotten. What proof of this? The behavior of succeeding generations, and, more specifically, their language. Children will make wreaths of flowers in spring, half-conscious rituals to make sense of the season and their relation to it, gestures that echo our own. What's more important, they'll use the language we use, our heritage and theirs, a way of seeing the world and saturating it with "what we felt//At what we saw." What Stevens has the children say might well be classified under some heading such as "Things We Doubt Children Weaving Budded Aureoles Ever Spoke," but it's *our* speech—formal utterance as well as native tongue—that they speak because they *are* us, our imaginative projections, our hypothesis about the future, a trick of language and metaphor. Their ignorance—which the ending suggests is by no means as complete as the rest of the poem has claimed—duplicates ours. If we knew for long that mansion's look and what we said of it became a part of what it is, the same thing will happen with the children. What they will say is in fact what we say, and they in turn will probably muse about children picking up *their* bones. Finally, the poem contradicts its own assertions about oblivion and time.

What the children say, incidentally, makes the mansion sound a little bit like an extinct or dormant volcano, as regarded by superstitious natives. That multiplies the perspectives of the ending still further. Squint at the next-to-last line and you get a glimpse of Kilimanjaro or Fuji. Or am I succumbing to that trick of overinterpretation I said Stevens loves to play on us? At any rate, the last line undermines the self-pity the poem has been experimenting with, as the "gutted" world renews itself through spring and children and the vitality of language (how wonderful to have thought of calling the sun "opulent"!) and sunlight. This poem is elegiac, wonderfully so, at the same time that it teases and dismisses the elegiac. It is both a volcano (the Sublime) and a postcard (the Ridiculous).

The point about multiple tone deserves reiterating. In order to read this poem well, a reader has to keep all sorts of options open. Whether it's Fujiyama at the end or a Hopper painting matters less than it might with another poet. But the fullness of the experience will arise in great part from the uncertainty and relativity produced by the combinations of image, rhetorical mannerism, allusion, wordplay, tense shift, and syntax, so that reducing the poem to its message or its philosophical content will be as fruitless as that "irritable reaching after fact" that poetry means to wean us from. Haven't we all the potential to be quickchange artists too, to receive postcards from volcanoes and to send them as well, little eruptions of the imagination?

Finally, am I too hard on the critics? The paucity of good discussion on Stevens is a little alarming. Even as good a critic as Helen Vendler tries to make a romantic of him, bent on self-expression, so that the fantastic and wonderful "Le Monocle de Mon Oncle" is really about the failure of his marriage! The absence of effective commentary means that this great poet still remains largely inaccessible to most teachers and students. Poets, on the other hand, have recognized for some time the degree of playfulness and rhetorical legerdemain in Stevens' work, and have borrowed freely from his repertoire to leaven their own efforts. It's time they shared their findings.

A RABBIT AS KING OF THE GHOSTS

The difficulty to think at the end of day,
When the shapeless shadow covers the sun
And nothing is left except light on your fur—

There was the cat slopping its milk all day,
Fat cat, red tongue, green mind, white milk
And August the most peaceful month.

To be, in the grass, in the peacefullest time,
Without that monument of cat,
The cat forgotten in the moon;

And to feel that the light is a rabbit-light,
In which everything is meant for you
And nothing need be explained;

Then there is nothing to think of. It comes of itself;
And east rushes west and west rushes down,
No matter. The grass is full

And full of yourself. The trees around are for you,
The whole of the wideness of night is for you,
A self that touches all edges,

You become a self that fills the four corners of night.
The red cat hides away in the fur-light
And there you are humped high, humped up,

You are humped higher and higher, black as stone—
You sit with your head like a carving in space
And the little green cat is a bug in the grass.

Shirley Kaufman

On "A Rabbit as King of the Ghosts"

I n the Palaz of Hoon he was "not less" at sunset. King Hoon. He is the
world in which he walks, and what he sees or hears or feels comes only
from himself. And in that world he finds himself "more truly and more
strange."

Now there's this fat cat who's been driving him crazy all day. It probably
sells insurance, in fact it gets to be vice-president of the company. And here's
this rabbit at sunset in his own Palaz—"the grass, in the peacefullest time"—
poet, king of the ghosts. And "then there is nothing to think of." Nothing but
light on his fur. Nothing to be explained. How sublime is that nothing! With
the liberated imagination acting on it. The cat hasn't changed. But you—the
rabbit/poet—have. "A self that touches all edges...." And as you are transformed, you transform the perceived object. That "monument of cat" gets
smaller and smaller.

The cat has been a threat. Its domesticity is too blatant, too tame, "slopping its milk all day." You can't cope with it. You have to resist, to forget, and
when the moon comes up and "nothing is left except light on your fur—,"
you begin to know your own freedom. You begin to "feel that the light is a
rabbit-light." You make of the night an acceptable fiction, your own special
kingdom. It's a matter of perception, all the way to the end. After all, your
head is only like a carving in space. But the perception is so intense, the new
awareness of self is so delicious, that you really see the cat as a bug in the
grass. Should we feel sorry for the cat? The cat has its daytime life. But the
rabbit owns "the whole of the wideness of night."

"In the long run the truth does not matter," Stevens said.

"The final belief is to believe in a fiction which you know to be a fiction.
There is nothing else." (Camus: "I want to know if I can live with what I
know and only with that.")

For Stevens the world did not exist except as he ordered it. In the part of
the world where I live now, the Middle East, where almost everyone possesses the TRUTH, divine or political or both, I need Stevens again. Whether
it's a bomb exploding in the market at Mahane Yehuda, or a piece of the Sky-
lab falling while we hold our breath to see where it will land, or a stony
mountain in the Sinai desert, or a crippled old woman who rings my doorbell
in Jerusalem begging for money so she can marry off her daughter, I want to
believe with Stevens there is nothing in life except the human imagination
shaping and filling it. That the human imagination is precious. That finally
we must take the sense-data of our lives, and recognizing them, arrange and
re-imagine them.

POETRY IS A DESTRUCTIVE FORCE

That's what misery is,
Nothing to have at heart.
It is to have or nothing.

It is a thing to have,
A lion, an ox in his breast,
To feel it breathing there.

Corazon, stout dog,
Young ox, bow-legged bear,
He tastes its blood, not spit.

He is like a man
In the body of a violent beast.
Its muscles are his own . . .

The lion sleeps in the sun.
Its nose is on its paws.
It can kill a man.

William Stafford

ON "POETRY IS A DESTRUCTIVE FORCE"

When I first encountered Stevens' "Poetry Is a Destructive Force" I was sitting in an office at the University of Washington. I got up and went and looked out the window; from high up I looked out over space, a few people walking the paths, a far vista of water. Then I went back and looked at the poem again. It hit me:—

Anguish, misery, the self-canceling obligations and impulses that life sometimes loads onto a person—these were like a load ready for recognition—and Stevens went straight for the charge. I couldn't then, and I can't now, sort out a definitive prose rendering of the poem. It was only later that I found some defense of my combination of allegiance to the poem and haziness about its paraphrase. I was reading in Whitehead: "...the essential distinctive between operation of Reason governed by the purposes of some external dominant interest, and operation of Reason governed by the immediate satisfactions arising from themselves...." This poem gives me that second kind of satisfaction.

Further, the separate sentences are abrupt, focused, emphatic—but the whole world outside those clear, individual sentences is wildly mysterious—the way the world is. And the ending of the poem comes down so inevitably through three, rolling-forward simple statements—and they reach back so scarily for the title of the poem: delicious! Poetry, the world, Stevens—everything—is irradiated by power. I ricochet to the window every time I read this poem.

THE GLASS OF WATER

That the glass would melt in heat,
That the water would freeze in cold,
Shows that this object is merely a state,
One of many, between two poles. So,
In the metaphysical, there are these poles.

Here in the centre stands the glass. Light
Is the lion that comes down to drink. There
And in that state, the glass is a pool.
Ruddy are his eyes and ruddy are his claws
When light comes down to wet his frothy jaws

And in the water winding weeds move round.
And there and in another state—the refractions,
The *metaphysica,* the plastic parts of poems
Crash in the mind—But, fat Jocundus, worrying
About what stands here in the centre, not the glass,

But in the centre of our lives, this time, this day,
It is a state, this spring among the politicians
Playing cards. In a village of the indigenes,
One would have still to discover. Among the dogs and dung,
One would continue to contend with one's ideas.

Albert Goldbarth

ON "THE GLASS OF WATER"

Ancient knowledge of the Dogon, an African tribe in what was once the French Sudan, places primary importance upon a star their cosmology claims circles Sirius—it is an important generative figure in this cosmology, thought of as the smallest and heaviest star in the sky, and so named *po* after the smallest but most important seed from the day-to-day soil-smudged world of Dogon agriculture. Every 50 years this star is celebrated, and has been for centuries past. 20th-century science shakes its head yes: there is such a star circling Sirius, and Dogon lore *re* its movements is exact. But this star is invisible to the human eye without sensitive telescopic equipment unknown to the Dogon—in fact its discovery through even West-

ern machinery is very recent. At the time of its discovery it was, indeed, of
the type of star known to Western astronomy as the smallest and heaviest in
the heavens.

Not surprising. The reptile/mammal/neocortex brains, or the brain's
left/right shuffle; the microscopic dance of sperm and egg; the polygraphic
registering of floral sentience—poets and seers have known it always, the
workings of the sweep of pulsing macrocosmos, the place in there of one
specific itchy cigar-smoking human skin. The sciences, hard and soft, at their
truest amplify and validate and feed back into the reaches of meditation.

"The Glass of Water" asks clearly *to be about* such poles. And is—that is,
holds within itself—the poles themselves. Here, pure Idea in one stanza becomes supple carnivore Flesh in the next. The unworldliness of Metaphysical
Speculation overlaps increasingly, stanza by stanza, with World: jungle pool,
political boundary. The force that drives through the airiest and most abstract
of fuses, here also powers the calendar day at its most mundane. That space
which both links and separates Mind and Matter: hums here. I admire the
poem's embrace, yes; and the grace with which the embraced is then carried.
Really the stanzas themselves stack into a glass of water. Water ubiquitous,
primeval, life-engendering; while at this pole Jocundus sits in his office, sips
it to clear some phlegm, and writes three paragraphs for *FIELD*. Calls it a
day.

Stanley Plumly

"THE GLASS OF WATER": A FOOTNOTE

One of the things we have loved about Wallace Stevens is his genius
for playing serious games, for allowing the mind to disclose as it
discovers the motives for metaphor. The game may preoccupy the
logic as much as it does the language of a Stevens poem; the game may even,
and usually does, promote good sense, reasonableness, and a willing embrace of the improbable. Nevertheless, the underline and bottom line in
Stevens is an honesty almost pure in its clarity—as in "where was it one first
heard of the truth? The the."

"The Glass of Water," for instance, proceeds through four propositions to
come to its "simple" point. The fun is only half in getting there. The logic of
the poem is deductive insofar as we move from a kind of generalization to a
kind of particular. Argument, with examples. As the line of that logic develops through its several states we are made aware that, typically, *state* itself is
a metaphor: hence physical/metaphysical state, symbolic state, imaginative

state, and, oddly (and Stevens lives in that *oddly*), national or native state, as in state of the nation. Not to mention state of being, Stevens' inevitable source of gravity.

That last, the ontological issue, is also his abiding *center* of gravity, center being the position between the poles. So that the glass of water stands *for* as it stands at the center. If the light coming down to drink can be a lion, as regal as a Rousseau, all claws and jaws, it can also be refractory or plastic, as in kinesis, the plastic parts of poems, this poem, for example—*metaphysica*—"crashing" in the mind. Cubist. And if the light, the active agent, can transform to illustrate, it can transform to illuminate. That is, at the center of our lives, in the most alien and insouciant of circumstances, this time, this day, one must still deal with the state of one's mind. A state perpetually at the center, betwixt and between, says the poem.

What saves Stevens' mock seriousness from sententiousness is his tone: the way in which the contending voice of the poem participates in and is a part—no, is at the center—of what is revealed—becomes, indeed, the ultimate subject. Subject, as in the subjective.

We have been taught for so long that poetry's real subject is itself that we often forget why we write it. The tone of "The Glass of Water" has less to do with ideas about various central states than about one central idea: that we must not only contend with the celestial ennui of our ideas, regardless of the dirt at the doorstep, but that we are alone with our ideas, regardless. We are alone to the degree that we can and must make metaphor speak for the center of our lives. Stevens is addressing needs rather than notions. The trouble is that ideas are metaphors too. Therefore, even fat Jocundus is a worrier. One might as well depend on versions of the light in the water in a glass as depend on the truth, which is also a metaphor.

If *claws* and *jaws* are the easy, allegorical terms of the argument, then *indigenes, dogs,* and *dung,* not to mention *ideas* and *discover,* are the hard terms, the hard words to rhyme, to mix through metaphor. The humanity of Stevens, here and elsewhere, is that the discovery, the contention with ideas, goes on after the poem. And it is this leftover quality, once the object, the poem itself, is complete, that makes the subject, subjective, come clear.

YELLOW AFTERNOON

It was in the earth only
That he was at the bottom of things
And of himself. There he could say
Of this I am, this is the patriarch.
This it is that answers when I ask,
This is the mute, the final sculpture
Around which silence lies on silence.
This reposes alike in springtime
And, arbored and bronzed, in autumn.

He said I had this that I could love,
As one loves visible and responsive peace,
As one loves one's own being,
As one loves that which is the end
And must be loved, as one loves that
Of which one is a part as in a unity,
A unity that is the life one loves,
So that one lives all the lives that comprise it
As the life of the fatal unity of war.

Everything comes to him
From the middle of his field. The odor
Of earth penetrates more deeply than any word.
There he touches his being. There as he is
He is. The thought that he had found all this
Among men, in a woman—she caught his breath—
But he came back as one comes back from the sun
To lie on one's bed in the dark, close to a face
Without eyes or mouth, that looks at one and speaks.

Pamela Stewart

ON STEVENS' "YELLOW AFTERNOON"

I discovered this poem when it had just turned from a yellow into a purple thunderstorming afternoon, and I became totally entranced with storm and poem simultaneously as if the poem were the still center of all elemental experience. A multi-faceted, stony, and serene-beyond-expression omphalos. As Leonard Michaels suggests, it is that deflection off concrete articulation in Stevens' diction that allows the reader to take it all in—to eat the cake without having to have it.

At the bottom of *things.* What things? All things that *are,* that resist being named. They do so because they are mute and sculptured; we see all they are within and without at once. *So that one lives all the lives that comprise it—* the unity of one lifetime in time and space. But what is that? Whatever! Those intense and passionate moments are lived as in disastrous times, for this is a love poem, or a poem speaking of such matters obliquely. Stevens, ever shy, desirous of decorum and safekeeping, sees that and says to himself "look, this is a metaphor for what is not expected—for what is unnerving and not on my schedule!"

The third stanza of "Yellow Afternoon" is where I love arriving after meandering through the considerations of the first two. *The middle of his field—* the visual, limited field of an individual life where the earth, as being-ness, allows him to be touched and to know it! *All this/Among men, in a woman— she caught his breath.* (His soul because she is its ex-pression? I'd love to have been her!) And if it is his "soul," he is suddenly noticing how it suffered for him an urgent experience, strong treasure. But he must return to the requirements of his field, his circumscribed life, to lie down *in the dark, close to a face*—featureless—that regards him, judges and speaks its judgment without speaking out loud. That is all the more frightening, aspects of self at war. Familiar? What has been touched so deeply must now be put in place and ordered for the next time he will realize and describe the world. If he were to speak directly about this, all would be violated and his vulnerability would show through. Afternoon—pulling toward sleep, rewinds the birth-string and while it is not the dark night of the soul at 3 a.m., it is perhaps all the more relentless as it is night encroaching, not the dawn.

ARRIVAL AT THE WALDORF

Home from Guatemala, back at the Waldorf.
This arrival in the wild country of the soul,
All approaches gone, being completely there,

Where the wild poem is a substitute
For the woman one loves or ought to love,
One wild rhapsody a fake for another.

You touch the hotel the way you touch moonlight
Or sunlight and you hum and the orchestra
Hums and you say "The world in a verse,

A generation sealed, men remoter than mountains,
Women invisible in music and motion and color,"
After that alien, point-blank, green and actual Guatemala.

Marvin Bell

ON "ARRIVAL AT THE WALDORF"

I have had to choose again and again among Stevens' poems because they do not matter to me in the same way that they once did, and as, I think, they may first matter to many young poets—for their fresh language, their oddness, the singularity of their style, their sense of the precious. Nor do I need to pretend, like a young fan, that Stevens' distinctive, hard-thinking body of poetry is not in some parts precious and prejudiced and only interesting. Nor have I a wish to puff for Stevens by noting his influence in the work of living poets. In fact, despite the talk, there aren't many to name. I'll name three: John Ashbery, in whose work the influence is seen most clearly in *Some Trees;* Donald Justice, a poet of singular purity and precision; and Robert Funt, a young poet who could write more like Stevens than anyone, who changed styles and went to live for a time in a waterfront hotel in California, and whose whereabouts are now unknown to me.

So much preface. I still like some of the old favorites for old, and sometimes personal, reasons. "The Snow Man" accomplishes what only poetry can accomplish. "The Emperor of Ice-Cream" was taught to me by one of my favorite undergraduate teachers shortly before his death. "The American

Sublime" is a special accomplishment of tone. "Gubbinal" is disarming. "Thirteen Ways of Looking at a Blackbird" is fun. "Sunday Morning" is rich. Most of his titles sparkle. "Of Modern Poetry" has the virtue of being right. "Connoisseur of Chaos." "The Sense of the Sleight-of-Hand Man." "Mozart, 1935" can get one up out of one's chair. One would have to be insensitive (or a fast reader) not to like almost everything by Stevens at one time or another.

The poem I like today (looking about for one to remark on, on Tuesday, the 29th of May, 1979) is "Arrival at the Waldorf," written in 1940. I like it partly because it is pretty, though Gertrude Stein is right to note that great art often seems ugly to us at first. And I like it because its content interests me. (Those dummies who hate all poems which are in part or wholly about poetry or art have little to read in Stevens, but that is all right because they can hardly read anyway.)

In it, the speaker sees, and sees through, the uses art makes of love and, in addition, witnesses his personal circumstance. He is one of a "sealed generation." It will be the Waldorf most of his days and nights, not Guatemala and "the woman one loves or ought to love." He is a man "remoter than mountains," for whom the object of his love will now exist only "in music and motion and color," invisibly. If he is more at home at the Waldorf than in Guatemala, and if he is the sort of man who can touch a hotel in the same way that he "touches" moonlight,—to say so is a kind of confession. If he cannot be at home with the "point-blank" and the "actual," still he does not claim to be better off.

The line nearing judgment is line six—hopelessly and, I suspect, deliberately ambiguous. Is the rhapsody that of the poem or of the woman? (If one is a fake, the other may be genuine, but which?) Can "another" be taken to mean the woman rather than one-or-another rhapsody?

Beneath this poem, there follows in Samuel French Morse's selection of Stevens the poem, "Mrs. Alfred Uruguay." There, to a donkey's ear, a lady says, "I fear that elegance/Must struggle like the rest."

Stevens' poems are not "about" his struggles. Well-intentioned attempts to infuse his poems with his biography will not work. His accomplishment is not in the use of his life in his art but, perhaps, the other way around. His art may even have saved him from too much life.

On the other hand, Stevens, like anyone else, could not do otherwise than to write his obsessions. It is no disrespect to credit his shaping of them to cold mastery, for he is sparing rather than stingy. Hence, his wit has room to do fine work. In turn, he can spare (and we can spare him) a phrase and notion like "the wild country of the soul," a phrase sure to be stricken within the semester (wrongly?) from the poems of three young Romantics.

And if Stevens needs any fleshing out behind what his "Connoisseur of Chaos" calls his "Pages of illustrations," we have only to consider how wild the "wild country of the soul" must have been to surround one so, back at the tacky Waldorf. Or, if you recall the Waldorf for its elegance, think how thick a mental jungle it must have been that could recreate the romance of a lush country, given only the word "Guatemala." Mrs. Uruguay would have understood.

(1979)

PUELLA PARVULA

Every thread of summer is at last unwoven.
By one caterpillar is great Africa devoured
And Gibraltar is dissolved like spit in the wind.

But over the wind, over the legends of its roaring,
The elephant on the roof and its elephantine blaring,
The bloody lion in the yard at night or ready to spring

From the clouds in the midst of trembling trees
Making a great gnashing, over the water wallows
Of a vacant sea declaiming with wide throat,

Over all these the mighty imagination triumphs
Like a trumpet and says, in this season of memory,
When the leaves fall like things mournful of the past,

Keep quiet in the heart, O wild bitch. O mind
Gone wild, be what he tells you to be: *Puella.*
Write *pax* across the window pane. And then

Be still. The *summarium in excelsis* begins . . .
Flame, sound, fury composed . . . Hear what he says,
The dauntless master, as he starts the human tale.

David Walker

ON "PUELLA PARVULA"

One of the persistent myths about Stevens is that in his late poems he sacrificed the lyric intensity of *Harmonium* for the dreary articulation of ideas. "Puella Parvula" effortlessly dispels this notion. True, it explores a familiar preoccupation of the late work, reality seen as a condition of absence or blankness, and its subject is abstract—the subduing of wild grief by the imagination, which shapes from it the powerful composure of art. Yet any paraphrase is entirely inadequate. The poem's meaning consists not of ideas but of immediate experience, experience which is lyric and dramatic and narrative at once. It is one of the most exuberant and expressive in the whole body of Stevens' late work, and understanding it is not simply a matter of following what it says, but of seeing the world in terms of what the poem does.

Key words like "unwoven," "devoured," "dissolved," and "vacant" suggest a landscape encroached on by nothingness. But if we anticipate the cold blankness of "The Snow Man," we are forced to do a double-take: here the tone has a distinctly comic edge. The threat of oblivion is offset in the first stanza by the disparity between "great Africa" and Gibraltar on the one hand and the monster caterpillar and the colloquial "spit in the wind" on the other. The great impact of Stevens' "nothingness" is felt when it is internalized as spiritual desolation; here, externalized and exaggerated, it feels considerably less ominous.

The next two stanzas continue this ironic distancing. To express the imma-nence of destruction, the poem adopts the image of a vast, roaring wind. But the metaphors that describe the wind are so lively and inventive that the im-pression the lines make is not essentially destructive but creative and expan-sive. The extended sentence, with its clauses strung out in apposition and its emphatic gerunds and participles, becomes a celebration of variety and mul-tiplicity. The real wind is immediately transformed into its own "legends." The savage beasts of Armageddon are deflated: the elephant is perched on the roof like a cartoon figure, and since the lion is *either* in the yard *or* about to spring from the clouds, it loses any pretense to bloody realism. When, in the fourth stanza, we are told that "over all these the mighty imagination tri-umphs," it is only to describe what we have already seen in practice: the movement toward destruction has indeed been transfigured by the imagina-tion.

The long sentence comes to an end in a startling way. The direct address of "O wild bitch. O mind/Gone wild" seems designed to bring us up short, and the metaphoric distance between tenor and vehicle is dissolved. Since there is no obvious figure for the poem to be addressing, and since our hearts and minds have presumably been excited by the imaginative action of the first half of the poem, we might guess that *we* are being addressed. But if the imagination is deeply involved in the description of the chaos, how is it sud-denly detached from and opposed to it? Who is the "he" who is suddenly in command of the mind? *"Puella"* reminds us of the title, but how can the "very little girl" be the same as the wild bitch? In fact a wonderfully mysteri-ous dissociation has taken place. The imagination is both acting in the poem and controlling its movement from outside, the reader is both involved par-ticipant and detached observer, the mind is both wild bitch and little girl in turn. Then, through a powerful tonal resolution, both confusion and despair are calmed; the prominent use of Latin, and the command to "write *pax* across the window pane," suggest that language is the key to controlling the chaos and to achieving a resolution of the self. The sound and fury of inhuman destruction are composed by the imagination into "the human tale" that begins as the poem ends. Humanized and pacified even in the face of winter's approach, the mind is ready to turn from nature's chaotic noise and listen to the heroic tale of art. And of course in reading the poem that is precisely what we have done.

WILLIAM CARLOS WILLIAMS
(1883-1963)

William Carlos Williams is the foremost American poet of the concrete and the particular, of immediate contact with one's own time and place. Unlike his contemporaries Ezra Pound and T. S. Eliot, he rejected the appeal of expatriation, choosing to spend virtually his entire life in his birthplace, Rutherford, New Jersey. Under the early influence of Pound, whom he met as an undergraduate at the University of Pennsylvania, Williams resolved to use unsentimental, idiomatic diction, precise images, and a stripped-down, intuitive free-verse line to embody the dynamics of a mind in contact with experience. The international scope and grand mythologizing of Eliot's *The Waste Land* seemed to Williams "the great catastrophe," and the rest of his career may be seen as a response in defense of a distinctively *American* voice and perspective, of "no ideas but in things." Like Wallace Stevens, he had a full-time occupation outside poetry: he practiced as an obstetrician and pediatrician for nearly 50 years. The alternation in his daily life between poetry and medicine is a useful analogy for the nature of his writing, drawing as it always does on the material of the everyday. Sometimes crystalline and lucid, sometime jarringly chaotic, Williams' work provides a complex, dissonant, extraordinarily lively portrait of the American landscape and psyche.

BOOKS: *Collected Poems*, ed. A. Walton Litz and Christopher MacGowan (2 vols., 1986-88); *Paterson* (rev. ed., 1992); *Imaginations* (1970); *Selected Essays* (1954). The best available selection of Williams' poems is *Selected Poems*, ed. Charles Tomlinson (1985).

BETWEEN WALLS

the back wings
of the

hospital where
nothing

will grow lie
cinders

in which shine
the broken

pieces of a green
bottle

Donald Justice

ON PURITY OF STYLE

*And where a man may say that Pindar
many times praiseth highly victories
of small moment, matters rather of
sport than of virtue...so indeed the
chief fault was in the time and custom
of the Greeks, who set those toys at so
high a price.*

—Sir Philip Sidney

This is a small, painterly poem by the doctor who had wanted perhaps to be a painter, whom the Armory Show of 1913 greatly excited, whether or not he actually saw it, one of the early champions of the Cubists, a companion of artists. A painting in words and, like some of the new painting, it seems to occupy a shallow, severely delimited space, flat, one-dimensional. The objects are sparse, mostly drab.[1] They seem disposed

---

[1] Williams in the fifties: "We were writing poems from the dungheap—the Ashcan School."

on the page in part as a composition for the eye rather than the ear, yet rhythmically still, for the ear, by way of a syntactical arrangement requiring constant alertness. (The impression that this is an easy prose sentence is an illusion.) The climax comes about largely because the one touch of vivid color has been saved for the end—those broken pieces of green bottle—a final appeal to the visual sense. One of Williams' anthology pieces, it is so definitive an instance of the art of limited means that it seems still to mark off, fifty or so years later, one possible extreme of verbal expression. Doubtless the ground had been prepared by "In a Station of the Metro" and other Imagist pieces, but the first effect, two generations ago, can perhaps be imagined as mildly breathtaking, for those able to respond at all. That so much, esthetically speaking, could be claimed for so little!—the little gasp of astonishment remains a part of the intended effect, however matter-of-fact the delivery.

"Between Walls" is not of course a found object, not like Duchamp's pickax, praised by Williams, though it does come comfortably close. Newspaper clippings, transactions of the proceedings of historical societies, letters from friends: only perhaps items such as these could come closer to being truly found verbal objects, and it would be years yet before Williams was to paste such matter up into the large context of *Paterson*. Without some larger context into which it might be seen as fitting, this small early landscape suggests something like the art of the photograph. The artist, Williams, frequent visitor at Stieglitz' old gallery 291, intervenes only so far as to select what the eye of the camera is to record. The objects as they are caught remain totally static, though in some other poems belonging more or less to the same genre, the well-known cat poem among them, we would find movement. Here, however, the camera is a still camera. What moves is the eye of the beholder, down the page, led by the syntax, towards the visual climax: as the eye might trace the composition of photograph or painting. The shortness of the lines presumably is to ease, even to speed, this progress of the eye downwards, aided by the preponderance of unsyntactical line breaks. American, Williams thought it.

The complaint Sidney mentions is just such a complaint as might be lodged against much of Williams, that the victories he praises are of small moment; and the defense might well be, like Sidney's of Pindar, a cultural excuse. We Americans value our material objects, and Williams gives them back to us in words. Beyond that was the drive to purify the dialect of the tribe; and in the main American poetry was, when Williams started out, in need of some purification, as periodically it has been ever since, not taking purification to signify anything like genteel uplift. To purify "American" was no mean cultural motive. Yet there is more to be said, even of such small toys as Williams', to justify the price we set on them.

Happened upon though their objects seem to be, they have clearly been selected. The rhetorical stance may be to pretend that the selection is random, but in "Between Walls" it is not. The air of the casual is reassuring, but we are aware that the objects have been rescued from our habit of neglect by the noticing eye of an observer superior to ourselves. The eye finds not only the objects but a relation between them: it is at that instant that the shutter clicks. To fix these things and their relation in a language so transparent as Williams' stays here makes available to others the interest and importance locked away till now in the "found." And yet—and yet the act of choosing is a clue that points through, or beyond, the objects themselves to the one who chose, to the character of the perceiver and recorder, to his attitudes, his values. Williams was, from all accounts, a solid egotist. In other poems, early and late, he appears front-stage center, unabashedly, the happy genius of his household and townfull of objects. Amazing that he should have managed in such poems as "Between Walls" the illusion of having withheld, even withdrawn, himself; and more decisively than the enemy, Eliot, espouser of the very doctrine of self-effacement, ever managed, or so it may seem to us now.

In the face of such neglect as has surely been exaggerated—by Williams himself as well as by his recent biographer—he held confidently, even arrogantly, and certainly with good cause to his own path, which was for him the right track, while persuading himself and others that it was the only right track for everyone. In the face of such suffering as he saw, being a doctor, and of such ugliness, being a citizen of New Jersey, he remained, with understandable qualifications, an optimist, one who could go on for years finding a certain joy and beauty practically anywhere, almost by inadvertence, one who did often praise victories of small moment. This seems to me neither good nor bad in itself. It is simply how he was. But the point is that this attitude, far from being hidden in the bareness of the Imagist or Objectivist[2] poems, is in fact revealed by them. Stevens, the surfaces of whose poems are much more opulent, finds cause, as a rule, only for the stoic resolution of a determined pessimist before the American scene: "The empty spirit/In vacant space." His acquaintance Williams, even between walls, where "nothing will grow," among cinders, though it is in broken fragments, discovers a green that actually shines. This object on which he focuses, without being put through any of the usual rhetorical transformations of the verbal art, becomes, as placed, an image or emblem. And the glass reflects the man. It affirms, brightly.

****

The notes above were set down for a lecture in 1967, and I find myself now making a few changes to bring them up to date, none of much conse-

---

[2] "Between Walls" has been called both.

quence. As I see the case now, there is one point these old notes seem to be driving at which never quite gets articulated but which counts a lot for me these days. It seems crucial, in fact; and especially so perhaps in view of the present condition of American poetry. Far more than the reality of the scene, which I nonetheless highly prize, I would call attention now to the absolute purity of style achieved in this little masterpiece, and effortlessly achieved, rarely to be equalled even by Williams. Other poems by Williams—certainly poems by other poets—are much richer in what they encompass, their vision is deeper, the character of the poet stands as a more affecting human presence. Often enough the language is more brilliant. But this poem is perfectly said. Lean, streamlined: and there is nothing extra, no excrescence, no excess, no showing off; nor indeed any shortcoming whatever. We have what we see; we have it exactly. Art can aspire higher and no doubt, at times, should. But not always. I think of Wang Wei, the Chinese effect in general, here naturalized. I begin to understand how a critic like Winters can argue that the brief lyric may be greater than a complete tragedy, since the lyric can hope for perfection, an unflawed wholeness and unity. One of Williams' many admirers has written of "Between Walls" that since "there is no living thing in the poem—just a mockery of the color of growing plants—the feeling of the poem is...sterile and airless." But this is the result of an absurd prejudice, probably got up out of some all too simple understanding of the organic and the natural. There is no mockery in this green: imitation, yes, and, one might even suggest, a certain pathos and bravery in the imitation. There is more to it than that, but there is, just glintingly, that. Meanwhile we do have also, thanking the muse of reality, pieces of a broken bottle, the real thing, as good as any green leaf here. Like Breughel, the poet saw it and with "grim/humor faithfully/recorded/it," confident that that was, if anything was, enough.

DEDICATION FOR A PLOT OF GROUND

This plot of ground
facing the waters of this inlet
is dedicated to the living presence of
Emily Dickinson Wellcome
who was born in England, married,
lost her husband and with
her five year old son
sailed for New York in a two-master,
was driven to the Azores;
ran adrift on Fire Island shoal,
met her second husband
in a Brooklyn boarding house,
went with him to Puerto Rico
bore three more children, lost
her second husband, lived hard
for eight years in St. Thomas,
Puerto Rico, San Domingo, followed
the oldest son to New York,
lost her daughter, lost her "baby,"
seized the two boys of
the oldest son by the second marriage
mothered them—they being
motherless—fought for them
against the other grandmother
and the aunts, brought them here
summer after summer, defended
herself here against thieves,
storms, sun, fire,
against flies, against girls
that came smelling about, against
drought, against weeds, storm-tides,
neighbors, weasels that stole her chickens,
against the weakness of her own hands,
against the growing strength of
the boys, against wind, against
the stones, against trespassers,
against rents, against her own mind.

She grubbed this earth with her own hands,
domineered over this grass plot,

blackguarded her oldest son
into buying it, lived here fifteen years,
attained a final loneliness and—

If you can bring nothing to this place
but your carcass, keep out.

Marvin Bell

WILLIAMS AND "DEDICATION..."

W illiam Carlos Williams is, arguably, our most American-American
poet—as distinguished from such hybrids as Stevens (French-
American), Eliot (British-American) and Pound (Italian-Ameri-
can). "Americanism," for Williams, meant that the circumstances of poetry
are local, the tone of poetry is personal, the process of poetry is improvisational, and the subject of poetry is reality.

"Dedication for a Plot of Ground" is one of those one-of-a-kind poems, almost a "found" poem, a poem that is notable for its strategy and organization
and one or two key "moves" amidst content that insists on its preeminence. I
would understand if the reader were to think it artless. For its artistry resides,
in large measure, in such seemingly unartistic "skills" and "talents" as personal energy, a belief that reality may be the content of a poem, feeling
deeply without blurry eyes or fuzzy thoughts, and (above all!) strong values—local in origin, stated without irony.

Williams' writing stands in evidence against what most poetry is and even
against what most people say *his* work is. Amidst the merely fanciful that
dominates the poetry of any age, it stands out still for its sense of worthy content. By example, Williams' poems oppose the mind-set of literary convention in general, and the notion, in particular, that the naming of objects, the
accomplishment of literary forms, or the geometries of the imagination are
the actual subjects of poetry. Their method tilts toward improvisation: an
abandonment of the daily, reasonable and restrained self to force, need, momentum and invention. In *Book Three*, part III, of *Paterson*, Williams (over-)
states his method: "Only one answer: write carelessly so that nothing that is
not green will survive."

Because of such ideas and methods, Williams is sometimes carried by his
writing to a moment when words fail. That is, it takes him to the point where
poems accomplish what is most rare and most worthy: they enlarge the si-

lence. Hence, his work stands in forceful opposition to that poetry of any time which consists of lies, playful or weighty, which is based on theory, guesswork or manners, which is essentially entertainment, and which only fills up the silence. Who was that Frenchman who called artists "the elite of the servant class"?

Williams' work is badly misunderstood—of course. From those poems of his we can only consider to have been finger exercises, many readers have decided that his is a poetry of cadence and object. Didn't he say, in *Book One* of *Paterson*, "Say it! No ideas but in things"? Yes, but by *Book Two*, he has already amended it to read: "No ideas but/in the facts"; and in *Book Five*, he writes: "You can learn from poems/that an empty head tapped on/sounds hollow/in any language!"; and one has only to read such poems as "These" and "The Descent" to see that he is a poet of intelligence and ideas. His poems, graphs of a mind, are as good as they are because his mind is as good as it is.

As for the "variable foot," the "triadic stanza" and the "American idiom"—these were all ways to beat the conventional poetic modes of his age and certain prevailing assumptions (still with us) about the nature of poetry. The foot, he said, not being fixed, must be variable. That was a way of using the vocabulary of the other guys to get away with something, since the foot, not being fixed, is not a foot. The triadic stanza—that was genius!—derives, I believe, from Williams' sense of his strength in writing—improvisation, taking the form of wildly various syntax—and his need to use the poetic line with and against whatever sentences energy, rapid association and "impure" diction might throw up. His genius lay in having sensed so definitely that prose can be poetry; that, indeed, it may be the prose of one's time that furnishes the language and strategies for what emerges later as the new poetry.

As for the American idiom, on the surface that means using the language as it is, where you live. Underneath, however, it signals a fundamental position on the nature of content. For if the common lingo is fit for poetry, so is the common man and woman. We are what we say.

Williams' "Dedication..." is so simple, so crude, that, were the essential terms of it given to us for imitation, we might disdain the assignment as unpromising. "Write a poem," we would be told, "to be said over a piece of property. Catalog the life of its owner. Keep going until you can't."

Ah, but how could one "assign" the emotion, or the values that create it? Williams feels something from the start. In line three, he dedicates the ground to the living presence of Emily Dickinson Wellcome. (Yes, his father's mother was actually named E. D. Wellcome.)

It is the actual, the thing or event which is its own best image and metaphor, which engages Williams. And so he begins to take stock of his grandmother's life. Just the *outer* events, you might notice. She was born,

married, widowed, transported, remarried, and a second time widowed. She
lost children, raised motherless grandchildren, and tended her lawn here for
fifteen years.

Sure, when the facts by themselves begin to lose their distinction in the
general welter of a life, he adds a little something to them: for example,
"lived *hard*/for eight years in St. Thomas," or "*defended* herself," which are
the additions of language; or "against flies, against girls/that came smelling
about," which are the additions, also, of imagination; or "against the growing
strength of the boys," which is the addition, *in addition*, of feeling and
thought.

And so Williams arrives, by means of memory, association, momentum
and improvisation, near to that silence where no more can be said because
everything which needed to be said has been. What can he do, then, but return to the physical circumstances of the poem—the ground where somewhere she lies buried, the ground right here which still bears her life. He begins again from the plot of ground, and says what little is needed to conclude
the story. When the end is in sight—*before*, that is, it has been stated—he
merely interrupts the long litany of facts to say what he has thought all along:
that this plot of ground is dedicated, not to a corpse, not to knowledge of
death, not to fear, not to lush wonder or pained beseeching of the infinite, but
to the *living presence* of one who lived, lived hard, and fought for her values.
She was not just a carcass. Hence, if you can bring nothing but your carcass
to this place (without bringing, say, intelligence, values and feelings), you
might as well stay away. She was better than that.

It is worth noticing the free verse of this poem. Lines three, twenty and
thirty-four end with the preposition "of," line seven with "with," lines thirty
and thirty-five with "against." Line twenty-two is nothing more than the
words "mothered them—they being." Stanza one is seven times as long as
stanza two, and each stanza consists of only one sentence. Everyone knows
why these things are unacceptable, right? What everyone knows, no one
knows. Truisms are false. People are wrong. Williams is alive. If you can
bring nothing to his work but your carcass, never mind.

(1983)

Marcia Southwick

ON "DEDICATION FOR A PLOT OF GROUND"

I would call the poem "a small (or large) machine made of words" if it weren't for the absolute humanity of the perceptions. Somehow Williams is both there and not there! In his prose he says: "The trick is never to touch the world anywhere, leave yourself at the door, walk in...."

Whenever I read Williams, I always have the sense that the poem is an object distinct from the poet. Williams himself would agree: "It is a popular superstition that a house is somehow the possession of the man who lives in it. But a house has no relation whatever to anything but itself." And yet, even though the poet is only the architect of the poem, which upon completion is entirely *other*, the connection between the man and what he makes isn't completely broken. Williams also says: "The architect feels the rhythm of the house drawing his mind into opaque partitions in which doors appear, then windows and so on until out of the vague or clearcut mind of the architect the ill-built or deftly-built house has been empowered to draw stone and timbers into a foreappointed focus."

Perhaps the poet has entered the poem, but in a way that causes him to be opaque. I love that notion because it explains why the poem can be so utterly simple—the poet doesn't intrude by making intellectualized statements—and also why his intelligence is nevertheless deeply *there*—camouflaged, enclosed in the words, which instead of serving to reveal the poet's thoughts in motion, serve to reveal physical objects in motion. As a result, the words *are* things, and they almost seem to be writing themselves! Or the poem itself seems to be drawing the words into a "foreappointed focus."

In "Dedication for a Plot of Ground," Williams uses his mind in a very particularized way to resist the onrush of words, to hold them back, to let only some of the words fall through. Towards the end of the poem, especially, the reader can begin to feel pressure exerted against the descending flow of the words, and the result is a sudden widening of the distance between the details. And here, if I list the things and people Emily Dickinson Wellcome defended herself against, I can't help but see the gaps between them: thieves, storms, sun, fire, flies, girls, drought, weeds, storm-tides, neighbors, weasels, hands, boys, wind, stones, trespassers, rents, and "her own mind."

The details are suddenly held apart, as if the intelligence, under the pressure of emotion, were leaving things out. The emotion itself, however, also seems to be causing the details to coexist, to arrange themselves in exactly the right order. And, finally, since the emotion of the poet has entered, he can fully emerge to say those wonderful last two lines. Even so, he doesn't call attention to himself, but to the reader. And that's what I love about the poem. The poet doesn't *bring* his carcass here. Instead, he leaves himself at the door, and walks in.

NANTUCKET

Flowers through the window
lavender and yellow

changed by white curtains—
Smell of cleanliness—

Sunshine of late afternoon—
On the glass tray

a glass pitcher, the tumbler
turned down, by which

a key is lying—And the
immaculate white bed

Donald Hall

WILLIAM CARLOS WILLIAMS AND THE VISUAL

When I began reading poetry, early in the 1940s, William Carlos Williams was old news. At a bookstore, I picked up a copy of *New Directions 1937*: with Henry Miller, John Wheelwright, Gertrude Stein, E. E. Cummings, William Saroyan, Richard Eberhart, Delmore Schwartz, Kenneth Rexroth—and WCW's "Paterson: Episode 17," the marvelous "Beautiful Thing" poem. But by the end of the decade I was studying at college under new critics, reading Blackmur and Empson, doing *explication de texte* with enthusiasm. We practiced on the well-surveyed countries of John Donne and T. S. Eliot; we talked Eliot all day and wrote Eliot all night. Whitman was off-bounds, impossible, an embarrassment, the crazy cousin at the dinner party.

But what did we do with William Carlos Williams?

When I say "we," of course, I exclude Robert Creeley, Charles Olson, Cid Corman, Louis Zukofsky, and others who knew what to do with him—who attended not only to his poems but to his theory. "We" is the rest, who swam with the new critical tide and found it exhilarating. Like Thomas Hardy, WCW wrote poems which made it hard for us to explicate intellectual complexity. We knew poems about a red wheelbarrow, the road to the contagious hospital, and yachts, from anthologies like Untermeyer's and Williams's. A teacher loaned me a copy of *The Wedge*. I bought *The Pink Church*. I *liked* him; everybody claimed to like him—but I don't think we read him very well.

It was the convention then to praise Williams for his *eye*. Out of recollections of Imagism, or what Imagism might have been, we praised him and pigeonholed him. We condescended by admiring him—and we ignored his inventions. Book One of *Paterson* made some of us take notice: later books of *Paterson* rewarded attention less. When he wrote the late, triadic poems, many readers responded with more enthusiasm. It is still the late poetry—the excellent Wisdom Literature which Williams turned to in his age—by which he is best known, and not by the characteristic early work. For me, his early work remains the most shocking and the most useful. "Nantucket" is typical of the early work—short, stark, clear, relentless, ecstatic, with purity of speech and great delicacy of sound.

Put "Nantucket" up against "A Valediction: Forbidding Mourning" or "Lycidas" or "Ode to a Nightingale" or "Dover Beach." Or put it against "The Love Song of J. Alfred Prufrock," for that matter, with its honeyed Tennysonian conclusion; put it against "Sunday Morning." If we measure a centipede against a Japanese beetle, both are tolerably insects. But how are "Nantucket" and "Epithalamion" both *poems*? These other poems assemble lines and images into an order of thinking, appropriately complex, pendulum-arcs along the true path of ambivalence. But "Nantucket" does not perform on this path. If you come to it out of literary history (as opposed to reading with the naked eye, which is always in short supply) it looks like something you might call Imagism, and you start talking about "eye."

In reality, "Nantucket" has little to do with the movement which Hulme and Flint cooked up in London before the Great War; nor does it resemble HD's early lyrics, nor Pound's from the time of *Des Imagistes*. In early WCW, maybe because of his rejection of his English father, his emphasis falls not on visual description but on the gestures of American speech, on the poem's visual shape which enforces rhythm, and on something which we might call a painterly stasis.

"Nantucket" has eye enough. But the visual adjectives are general: "yellow," "white," "white" again; also the nouns: "curtains," "sunshine," "tumbler," "a key...." WCW does not write about an oblong-ended, brass, Yale key; the curtains are white but they are neither lace nor linen nor printed nor wrinkled nor ironed. When he writes of "yellow/changed by...," the past participle is indirectly visual; the word asks recollection to color the curtain, and the reader to alter the tints of flowers as white curtains alter them. He does the same, in another area of sense, with "Smell of cleanliness," giving us no sense-image or metaphor, speaking in general or abstract language. WCW is master of abstract language; "no ideas but in things" has no things in it, only ideas.

It is by his absences that we know a poet. WCW's absence of striking particularities, and of unusual word-combinations and metaphors, make a gesture of simplicity and naturalness in diction, speech-likeness. This is the true
shock of WCW; he writes plain talk. He writes nouns and adjectives, no
verbs except "is lying" and the past participles of "changed" and "turned";
not much action here: the vision is breathless with nouns. Egalitarian diction—no word better than its neighbor!—sets up "immaculate" to crash like
a thunderball. Of course this violates egalitarianism. Why use egalitarianism
unless you violate it?

Although a tradition of English and American poets—like Crabbe,
Wordsworth, and Frost, Whitman to a degree—uses the demotic, WCW in
the twenties and thirties was the most shocking. And he used it in connection
with his other absence—of ideas. Now idea-less-ness is not unprecedented,
but critics and professors teach and write about ideas rather than poems,
which leaves idealess poems off the agenda. Of course ideas are perfectly
fine objects to stuff into the container of the poem: one may add old shoes,
emotions, industrial waste.... Poems contain everything like (in the words of
the poet) the stomach of the shark. Mother Goose is a wonderful poet not notable for ideas. The academic neglect of Thomas Hardy's great poems derives from the difficulty teachers find in discussing poems that lack difficulty. Even Keats, in "To Autumn," writes a poem almost immaculate of
idea. Of course Keats's ode is not without suggestions of value; it makes
statement by shape—a quality we find in music, in Greek vases, in architectural design, in painting and sculpture, and for that matter in poems of intellectual content.

"To Autumn," of course, does not share "Nantucket's" other absence—of
unusual or unusually arranged language; for a poem that shares both absences we need another American. Look at Whitman, not always, but here:

A FARM PICTURE

Through the ample open door of the peaceful country barn,
A sunlit pasture field with cattle and horses feeding,
And haze and vista, and the far horizon fading away.

What a lovely small poem. One must qualify with a word like "small" and
one must be sure that the qualification is not condescension.... Or let me con-
descend to "A Farm Picture" and to "Nantucket" only by acknowledging that
they are not so ambitious as "Out of the Cradle Endlessly Rocking" nor "Paterson Book One." We may love Herrick without calling "Upon Julia's
Clothes" as great a poem as "The Garden." And in poems like "Nantucket,"
"Upon Julia's Clothes," and "Bah-bah Black Sheep" we begin to isolate poetry; it is more difficult to isolate the *poetry* of "Church Monuments" because ideas and theology distract us.

WCW makes me think of Herrick in other ways. Both give us models of joyous world-love. In "Nantucket" and in many other poems, WCW enacts a joy—unpretentious, accomplished in action not in reflection—like Herrick's double pleasure in Julia's motions and in the language by which he embodies her motions. Now WCW takes delight in his words also; no one is so scrupulous in movement of line-break and rhyme: "yell*ow*" picks up "wind*ow*" and harks back to "fl*ow*ers"; consonants from "curtains" return in "cleanliness"; the bang-bang percussive "glass tray" is followed with "glass pitch-," "turned down," and "white bed"....

In "Nantucket" *ear* does ten times what eye does. If we try a portion in paragraph form—saying it aloud as if we were reading from the newspaper—we have: "On the glass tray a glass pitcher, the tumbler turned down, by which a key is lying...." Nothing. The line on the page does the thing, providing we hear it according to its visual shape, the lines controlling rhythm and enforcing speech-likeness. In the next to last line, he places a neat pause between "the..." and the thunderball "immaculate"—then swiftly bang-bangs his coda: "white bed." Sound is scored by WCW's re-invention of the page.

The re-invention of the page. In *this* sense—a visual method for capturing speech—maybe WCW's eye was as important as we said, forty years ago. Let me try setting Whitman's "A Farm Picture" into lines that imitate WCW's spacing. (My version is arbitrary; other breaks might do just as well or better.) I omit capitals, respell "thru," omit two copulas, and come up with:

> thru the ample
> open door of
>
> the peaceful country
> barn, a sunlit
>
> pasture field
> with cattle and
>
> horses feeding,
> haze, vista, and the
>
> far horizon
> fading away

If it does not seem to resemble WCW, I mistake my point—which is double: first, the absences of Whitman's poem anticipate WCW (so does its emphatic stasis, which I will mention in a moment); second, the characteristic visual arrangement of WCW's early work—with all its pausing—provides a considerable part of the stylistic signature. Of course this Whitman poem, mistreated, lacks WCW's characteristic intimacies of sound, especially his frequent rhyming.

We need say one more thing about "Nantucket." Like many poems by WCW, it takes pleasure in stasis. Meister Eckhart among other mystics tells us what the soul longs for: repose. It is worth noticing the relationship to still-life, and recollecting WCW's closeness to his painter-friends. It is also worth remarking that for many poets painting is the second art. The perspective of painting-values, as it were misapplied to the time-art of poetry, suggests or necessitates a useful conflict, as words-in-motion command stillness.

"A Farm Picture" and "Nantucket" provide repose. I compared "Nantucket" to "To Autumn" for its absence of ideas; WCW's poem also resembles Keats's in the value it suggests for the experience it embodies. This WCW poem does not begin by saying "so much depends/upon" but such insistence is implicit: an intense, even ecstatic value placed upon the act of total attention, stasis becomes ecstasis, and soul flies out of body in astonished, acute notation of experience.

THE POLAR BEAR

his coat resembles the snow
deep snow
the male snow
which attacks and kills

silently as it falls muffling
the world
to sleep that
the interrupted quiet return

to lie down with us
its arms
about our necks
murderously a little while

David Walker

ON "THE POLAR BEAR"

The great achievement of Williams' late poetry is the lyric structures he found to merge openly personal feeling with the techniques of objectivism. Despite critical emphasis on discursiveness and didacticism in the late poems, at his best Williams never surrendered to the excesses of Romantic subjectivism. He found ways of measuring and controlling subjective experience, not by translating it into metaphysical or symbolic structures, but by objectifying it. Like Wallace Stevens, Williams sought not to stress the poet's anonymity by adopting fictional masks, and thus enforcing the division between writer and work, but in essence to construct a self *within* the poem by centering it on a process of consciousness or act of vision.

"The Polar Bear" is a good example. At first it seems to represent one of the most common romantic forms, a discursive meditation on an object in nature. But to read the poem is an experience altogether different from reading Frost's "The Oven Bird" or Lawrence's "Snake," which attempt to communicate the poets' subjective impressions as though to an auditor. The movement of Williams' poem is so internalized, so intuitive, that it is difficult to say precisely even what its subject is. But as it forces us to adopt its perspective, it provides a vision that is powerfully evocative and mysterious.

The poem opens conventionally, even banally, with a descriptive analogy

intended to express the appearance of its ostensible subject. But immediately
the syntax loosens and the rhythm breaks: the sentence loops back on itself to
explore the image so obsessively that by the end of the stanza the snow has
replaced the polar bear as the focus of attention. Or rather, the bear becomes
a sort of submerged metaphor expressing itself through the murderous violence of the snow. Normal logic in the form of descriptive simile gives way to
irrational vision. Nothing about the bear's coat *requires* the associations that
emerge.

The second stanza pursues these developments farther. Rather than returning to the description of the bear, it continues within the same sentence to
shift the perspective again: the violence of the snow is muffled and merged
with sleep. By this point the reader must abandon all expectations about
where the poem will lead; in fact, the illusion is that it is not leading at all,
but following the unpremeditated course of mind in reverie or dream. In the
seventh line, "that" is an extremely ambiguous connective—presumably
meaning "in order that," but the syntax here is very loose—and in the next
line it is unclear whether "quiet" is an adjective or a noun, and whether "return" is a noun or a verb. To stop and attempt to puzzle these questions out is
to assume there is a clear statement one is not "getting." This is precisely the
wrong response. The poem works to establish a powerfully imaginative perspective, a vision in which cold and violence and sleep and death are inextri-
cably tied, and the purpose of its stylistic eccentricities is to force us into the
world.

Thus drawn in, we are apt to find the last stanza both chilling and exhilarating. It is at the same time simple and enormously mysterious, given what
precedes it: the "it" whose arms encircle our necks is the quiet, the snow, and
even the bear at once, and the death with which it threatens us is also a kind
of love and a kind of sleep. By proceeding intuitively and suggestively,
Williams involves us in the experience even if we only dimly understand it;
indeed, the sense that it can only be evoked indirectly seems crucial to the
paralysis, the hibernation, that gradually emerges as the poem's subject.

DEATH

He's dead
the dog won't have to
sleep on his potatoes
any more to keep them
from freezing

he's dead
the old bastard—
He's a bastard because

there's nothing
legitimate in him any
more
          he's dead
He's sick-dead

                    he's
a godforsaken curio
without
any breath in it

He's nothing at all
          he's dead
shrunken up to skin

          Put his head on
one chair and his
feet on another and
he'll lie there
like an acrobat—

Love's beaten. He
beat it. That's why
he's insufferable—

          because
he's here needing a
shave and making love
an inside howl
of anguish and defeat—

He's come out of the man
and he's let
the man go—
                    the liar

Dead
          his eyes
rolled up out of
the light—a mockery

                              which
love cannot touch—

just bury it
and hide its face
for shame.

Miroslav Holub

W. C. WILLIAMS ON DEATH

Every author absorbs a certain number of his contemporaries or ancestors into himself. It is a rather accidental process, something like the
choice of one's lifelong companion: one takes what turns up on the
way. Poets do not undertake exhaustive research to become themselves.
Some national literatures are nearly saturated with the quality and quantity of
domestic production, and a foreign, usually translated, more or less important author is regarded as a rarity, as some above-the-usual-standard information from somewhere else. However, there are literatures—and Czech serves
as a good example—that move constantly in the atmosphere of both their
own and translated production; and a certain percentage of authors can speak
one or two foreign languages to be able to read original poetry. Foreign authors are then received as an integral developmental component, either initi-
ating or confirmatory; they become not only a part of one's erudition, but
they are a subject that is even less of a taboo than the domestic writer in
terms of adopting his field of action.

The foreign author, particularly the author we find on our own and can
read in his or her language, is sometimes regarded as one's personal invention; because we often meet authors just once, in one book or one poem, we
do not share their evolution, lights and shadows; they are more of a literary

source than an interfering person. Their source is received and somewhat changed by the local literary context. They get permanent credit for the transfer, for possible faults in translation and mistakes in understanding. It can be said that William Carlos Williams is quite markedly present in Czech poetry. The sixties generation of poets was familiar with him—*Desert Music* was published in Czech in 1964, as well as a selection from the earlier and later poems, *Pictures from Brueghel* and *Paterson*, Part I; but I was surprised to discover that at least one of the young poets knew him well.

For me Williams was a personal invention. I think somebody must have told me—I'm sure you know him, he's a doctor like you. So I felt an *a priori* liking for him and I got his *Selected Poems* from New Directions. I found he was my kind of man, in fact my pediatrician, although pediatrics is not my line. He certainly healed the children's diseases of my own production, he was there as I progressed from rhyme and meter to free verse and dissected lines, or enjambment, and he delighted me by the poetic use of a thing as itself. For me he was the world blessing of a statement by Vítezslav Nezval, a Czech poet: "Poetry in which the word *garlic* doesn't fit is somewhat alienated from man." In 1961, I quoted as a motto, in Czech, a whole poem by Williams: "We have/a microscopic/anatomy/of the whale./This/is/reassuring." Because the translator of my poem with this motto could not find Williams's original, a wrong version in English appears in the Penguin edition of my *Selected Poems* (p. 23): see how much I took possession of Williams.

Only my shyness in the use of mottoes and dedications prevented me from quoting some twenty other Williams poems. I would have certainly quoted his poem "Death." It is one of those poems one feels one missed, perhaps by the skin of one's teeth.

The poem is based on a steep and shocking statement about death as the dead person's fault and shame. That's how I see it, I don't know about you. I know no other poem about death like this one. It is shocking in its logic. But this logic is not so much autoptic as it is humanly consequential. If survival until a very old age and a high degree of dementia is regarded as worthy of respect, then the loss of life is without honor.... He's let the man go.

In the generally customary approach, the dead person is the victim of a demon, a painful transformation, a loser in an uneven fight, a permanent memento of the innocent sufferer, a return into something, for instance decomposition, a lesson for a clinical doctor, a relic of merit. Here the dead person is a clown and it's all his fault anyway. That, I think, is a hell of a subject.

The poem "Death" begins with a direct statement, and in the second line it jumps suddenly to the unpredictable image of a dog who doesn't have to keep his potatoes from freezing anymore, no doubt an abandoned dog and poor potatoes. It is a strange jump, maybe a little comical, and certainly slightly irreverent. For me it even implies some social sympathy. It is in fact the only more extensive and specifying image in the whole poem. But instead of sympathy you get the direct blow, direct curse, "old bastard," and a direct accusation of the loss of legitimacy. The repetition of "he's dead" in the twelfth line could almost end the poem, the argument and the image are finished, and nothing new and radical will be said now. It is a poem of a single idea.

The essential feature of this poem is the decision to maintain the initial high level of consternation and to accumulate without a noticeable construction more and more depraving denotations: sick-dead, curio, acrobat, he who beat love, not shaven, insufferable, defeated one, liar with eyes rolled up out of the light.... The deepest accusation—"He's nothing at all"—comes in fact in the 18th line and there is no further gradation until the last stanza but one; individual stanzas give the impression of being incidental rather than intentional. Due to this the poem assumes an authenticity of a verbal expression of high emotional tension, it becomes a series of randomly shouted pejoratives, a stream of argument of the speaker with the person who is now only an inside howl.

The dead person is illuminated from various aspects by the lightnings of accusation—accusation in a hurry—and he takes on a peculiar tangible and obvious character, which could hardly be achieved by a string of great metaphors and which would be impossible in a gentle description. In the weak light of panic, the memory registers the outlines of this embarrassing object: somebody who assumed human appearance, a parasite of human relationships, such as love, neither man nor no-man, but a body snatcher with all the anatomical details. And in the end—a hint of gradation after all, conclusive gradation—not even *he*, but *it*.

In Lorca's enormously suggestive poem "Death," published as it happens in *FIELD* 28, one cannot forget the image, "What a strain/for the dog to become the swallow!" Maybe I'll forget all the words and metaphors from Williams's poem, all except the dog on the potatoes, but I'll not forget the dead man. I don't know any more unforgettable dead person, although I once had to do autopsy on a few hundred dead.

In this aspect, the poem "Death" very accurately documents a method: things uncovered by ornamental words remain engrams more often than things treated verbally in the whole extent and power of poetic gifts. This dead man is just as unforgettable as Williams's whale, old woman, red wheelbarrow and waterfall. And the poem springing from a specific decision, maybe a so-called dryly intellectual decision, produces a highly emotional impact. It is an emotional poem against routine emotion, a cynical—to curse a dead man cannot be called by another word in a civil context—film against the cynicism of sentiment.

I read this poem with a bias because I agree with its central argument, but I think that even without this agreement its provocative force will not be hurt.

In fact, if it were introduced in our official literary medium—which has not happened yet—it would bring about many readers' letters because of vulgarity and inhumanity—and the author is a doctor! Perhaps even a discussion, and the poem would become a small, not quite literary whirlwind. That would also be an interesting aspect of transfer, reading and impact.

It might seem strange to Doctor Williams, but he would soon realize he got to the place where poetry is still regarded as a very serious matter.

translated by Dana Hábová

THE TERM

A rumpled sheet
of brown paper
about the length

and apparent bulk
of a man was
rolling with the

wind slowly over
and over in
the street as

a car drove down
upon it and
crushed it to

the ground. Unlike
a man it rose
again rolling

with the wind over
and over to be as
it was before.

Charles Simic

STREETS STREWN WITH GARBAGE

It is the ordinary, the overlooked, the quotidian, the supposedly familiar
and commonplace that is the place of the miraculous, the numinous.
Williams made it his life-task to show that, and he did it with a rigor of a
Euclid or a Galileo. Consider the simple and not so simple little poem at
hand.

Poetry is made out of words and time. That's what the title reminds me of.
It refers to a time or period through which something lasts and to which limits have been set. In other words, a limited, definite extent of time during
which something exists, lasts, or is in progress. Truth, for example.

We also say, "the two were on terms of great intimacy," or we say, "they fought on equal terms." This is how one speaks of love and drama. Even a short poem must have a bit of both.

"The Term" is an example of Williams at his best. Nothing happens in the poem; everything happens.

Williams knew that anything clearly seen and severely framed can be a poem providing one glimpses in it a polarity. I mean, something needs to occur and you can't have an occurrence without dialectics. The genius of Williams is that he realized that even the littlest event has the whole world in it, providing one pays close attention.

The issue here is identity and difference. We think, to every being as such there belongs an identity unique to itself. We know things by their difference. We claim, something is unlike anything else in the world.

I suppose this is the way in which representational thinking usually works until the old demon of analogy begins to take interest. In his domain, resemblance is the only law. Things resemble each other. No point denying that. But—there's always that but—one is tempted (via resemblance) into *identity* only to eventually remember *difference*.

> ...to be as
> it was before.

Says Williams and puts a period at the end. Not true. There's no end. The whole process will begin again and again, but in other terms. In the meantime, we are left with this paper which rises unlike a man to go on being forever suspended between the thing itself and what it resembles. A kind of "indeterminate immediacy"—which happens to be Hegel's definition of Being. The truth is that something simultaneously *is* and *is not*, that it is not just one or the other but both together that matter. A seeming self-contradiction in the manner of that supremely metaphysical figure of speech, the oxymoron. "The uncertain certainty" is what Emily Dickinson called it, and it has been a source of everlasting delight to poets and philosophers.

Williams' imagist poems teach monastic virtues: attention and selflessness. That they also teach how to think is what I've just learned.

CANTHARA

The old black-man showed me
how he had been shocked
in his youth
by six women, dancing
a set-dance, stark naked below
the skirts raised round
their breasts:
                    bellies flung forward
knees flying!
                    —while
his gestures, against the
tiled wall of the dingy bath-room,
swished with ecstasy to
the familiar music of
                    his old emotion.

Gerald Stern

ON "CANTHARA"

One of the marvelous things about "Canthara" is that it needs no explanation, and that it was written without an explanation in mind. It is a poem about an old man remembering the wild days of his youth; it is a poem celebrating the simple joy, and the humor, of sexuality; it is a poem that honors energy, and faith, and ecstasy; it is a "small" poem, touching a brief moment in time; it is a slightly pedantic poem, teaching the value of sensuality, in all its wholesome and unwholesome forms, in producing "lasting happiness"; it is a poem of mimicry, and therefore it is the expression of a neglected or abused person or class; it is a poem touching on dancing, the one art form that Williams revered, because of its primitiveness, because of its expressiveness, perhaps because of its wordlessness; it is a happy poem, without one sad or miserable thought to it; it is a poem celebrating the poor and the neglected—even the abandoned—and one showing the virtues and values in that overlooked life; it is a poem, like dozens of others that Williams wrote, about Blacks, and their secret knowledge and their suffering and their joy and their wisdom and their final joyous affirmation (whatever it's worth, his view); and it is a poem where the speaker, as always, is a lonely observer, and in exile, and in longing. A longing that Williams would express many years later in "Asphodel" as he encounters an "ambassador" in outrageous garb—his father, an angel from the other world, his own blurred and confused image in the subway window—but again a mysterious agent, again full of power and dignity and strangeness. And again black.

There are many poems like "Canthara" in Williams' work, small set pieces, moments in time, sketches and observations. They reflect, or seem to reflect, a passing mood. They are jottings in a notebook, journal entries. They are written quickly, not labored over. They are spontaneous. Yet they reveal, in their accumulation, a coherent aesthetic and philosophic position, albeit a "position" arrived at by passionate and obedient listening, the poet's method. Williams, in a loose and general way, can be identified with the race of anti-Victorians who, in their thousands, thought life could be renewed and enjoyed and understood by turning away from the prurience and repression of the late nineteenth century in Europe and America; and he could as well be identified with the race of anti-colonialists, domestic and foreign, who thought life could be remade, and transformed, through new modes of political organization, and changes of heart, and renewals of lost wisdom. He is a brother to Henry Miller and a brother to Eugene Debs, even if the two of them would be most uncomfortable with each other on their respective front porches. Or privies. And he taps both sources. In this kind of thinking, and feeling, he is almost alone in his generation, and he anticipates by many years the visions of later artists and revolutionaries, who finally saw the connection between the two modes. Every single poem does not contain all the elements. "Canthara" is a sexual poem, not a political poem, and there are some that are strictly political. Although a case could be made, in the manner of Freud or Marcuse, that the concentration, and the intense memory, of sexual joy is a peasant, or working class, or at least "lower" class passion, a kind of "monstrous" response to idleness or exclusion from busy-ness, just as such passion and concentration prevent the "appropriate" commitment to work, and therefore the poem has economic and political overtones. Or tones. Here Freud and Carnegie and Stalin were all in agreement, although things have become a little mixed and confused in the twentieth century's second part, particularly in the non-socialist and exhausted west.

Certain poems come to mind. "To a Poor Old Woman," "The Return to Work," "The Girl with the Honey-colored Hair," "A Negro Woman," "Trees," "Drink," "Impromptu, the Suckers," "Franklin Square," "A Rosebush in an Unlikely Garden," "Approach to a City," "The Hard Core of Beauty," "The Men," "To a Dog Injured in the Street," "Proletarian Portrait." Poems about sooty sparrows and locust trees and blessed idiots. "Elsie." Without Wordsworth's measure, and distance. What was Williams doing? He was, as he says in the terrifyingly beautiful chapter from his autobiography called

"The Practice," listening to the "underground currents," the "secret springs."
In the lives of the sick and the neglected. His patients. His bias is immense.
*Truth comes from ordinary people. There is only one poem, to which we all
attest. The "presence" cannot be captured and exploited by the academy.*
Something enormous stood between the ego and the poem. What it was gave
him his energy and his vision. It was his work, in both places. It was his love.
His belief.

THE HORSE SHOW

Constantly near you, I never in my entire
sixty-four years knew you so well as yesterday
or half so well. We talked. You were never
so lucid, so disengaged from all exigencies
of place and time. We talked of ourselves,
intimately, a thing never heard of between us.
How long have we waited? almost a hundred years.

You said, Unless there is some spark, some
spirit we keep within ourselves, life, a
continuing life's impossible—and it is all
we have. There is no other life, only the one.
The world of the spirits that comes afterward
is the same as our own, just like you sitting
there they come and talk to me, just the same.

They come to bother us. Why? I said. I don't
know. Perhaps to find out what we are doing.
Jealous, do you think? I don't know. I
don't know why they should want to come back.
I was reading about some men who had been
buried under a mountain, I said to her, and
one of them came back after two months,

digging himself out. It was in Switzerland,
you remember? Of course I remember. The
villagers tho't it was a ghost coming down
to complain. They were frightened. They
do come, she said, what you call
my "visions." I talk to them just as I
am talking to you. I see them plainly.

Oh if I could only read! You don't know
what adjustments I have made. All
I can do is to try to live over again
what I knew when your brother and you
were children—but I can't always succeed.
Tell me about the horse show. I have
been waiting all week to hear about it.

Mother darling, I wasn't able to get away.

Oh that's too bad. It was just a show;
they make the horses walk up and down
to judge them by their form. Oh is that
all? I tho't it was something else. Oh
they jump and run too. I wish you had been
there, I was so interested to hear about it.

Stanley Plumly

READING WILLIAMS

William Carlos Williams' great poem "The Horse Show" is of that personal range in his work that includes "A Unison" and "At Kenneth Burke's Place" and "Burning the Christmas Greens" and the poems to D. H. Lawrence and Ford Madox Ford and the wonderful poem to the asphodel, that greeny flower. The cooler, authority poems, like "Tract" and "Spring and All" and "To Elsie" and "The Yachts," speak from a harder, flintier, more elliptical part of his idiom. Perhaps the difference is age; his poems warm up, soften at the edges, yield to the narrative as he gets older. It's as if the famous plum poem, the one in which he's sorry, had found, in later life, its fuller emotional expression. He's no longer, like Yeats in his sixties, preoccupied with form, either as counterculture or experiment. He is *of form*. That may be why the later poems offer the invitation and generosity of richness, confidence, and embrace. But I don't mean to imply that he became Uncle Santa; he could still look out his window in Rutherford, New Jersey, at seventy-three, and say that there's a lot of bastards out there.

"The Horse Show" is a love poem, and it's also an elegy—actually it's a poem about lost opportunities. Yet the son and mother are reconciled by the end, if not with each other exactly then reconciled to the idea of what is past, passing, and to come. The son is sixty-four, the mother in her nineties. Part of the power of the poem's argument is the age of both contestants and the fact that only now, only this late in their lives, have they begun to reach an understanding, though they may be understanding different things. After a lifetime, it seems, Williams and his mother have finally talked, "of ourselves,/intimately, a thing never heard of between us." And it's just happened, yesterday. The mother's realization is absolute, like the discovery of honesty: "There is no other life," she says, "only the one." It is all we have. So she speaks of the world of spirits and how they come, just like her son now, to visit and talk. She is almost a century old. She wants to know why the spirits come to bother her, if they are jealous. Williams doesn't know. Instead he tells her a story, a ghost story, about a man who survives an avalanche and after two months comes back to his village. The villagers think he's a ghost come back to complain. At which point the mother complains about not being able to read—ghost stories or otherwise. She is practically a ghost herself, her body in her bones; and half blind. All she has is memory. "All/I can do is to try to live over again/what I knew...." Memory, though, is fallible. She wants to hear something new and has been waiting all week to hear about the horse show. But Williams fails her—"I wasn't able to get away." No matter, it was only the horses put through their paces. "Oh is that/all? I tho't it was something else."

> Oh
> they run and jump too. I wish you had been
> there, I was so interested to hear about it.

The poignancy of the exchange is dramatized, of course, through Williams' marvelous submersion of the dialogue into the text of the encounter—an afternoon's visit, "disengaged from all exigencies/of place and time." Although the poet takes pains to differentiate who is speaking, the intimacy, the immediacy of the exchange is directly the result of the blurring of such distinctions. The capacities of Williams' use of dialogue in this poem are obvious on the first reading. The block form of the stanzas helps to further, to intensify the power of the blurring of the dialogue. The exchange is real, formal. The greatness of the poem, however, transcends the apparent technique. Williams has told a story, truly a ghost story, and he is one of the ghosts. The pleasure of his poem is practically Jamesian, insofar as the speaker participates in an event its author better comprehends. The horse show of the week before is an experience neither mother nor son has had, yet it's one of the reasons they are together this day, yesterday. It may be the single most, superficial reason. By the time it comes up in the poem, at the end, it cannot help but take on the gravity of the world of spirits, the world, as William Gass once called it, within the word. It's their mutual acceptance of the reality of the word over the exigencies of time that reconciles the complaints, the worries in this poem. And Williams sitting there, his mother still wondering what a horse show is, is, like her, of the word. The word written, yes; but even more, the word spoken, from the spirit into the silence. In the course of words here Williams comes to love his mother's spirit, that which is passed to sons.

THE BIRTH OF VENUS

Today small waves are rippling, crystal clear, upon the pebbles
at Villefranche whence from the wall, at the Parade Grounds of
the Chasseurs Alpins, we stood and watched them; or passing along
the cliff on the ledge between the sea and the old fortress, heard
the long swell stir without cost among the rock's teeth. But we

are not there!—as in the Crimea the Black Sea is blue with waves
under a smiling sky, or be it the Labrador North Shore, or wherever
else in the world you will, the world of indolence and April; as,
November next, spring will enliven the African coast southward
and we not there, not there, not there!

Why not believe that we shall be young again? Surely nothing
could be more to our desire, more pebble-plain under a hand's breath
wavelet, a jeweled thing, a Sapphic bracelet, than this. Murder
staining the small waves crimson is not more moving—though we strain
in our minds to make it so, and stare.

Cordite, heavy shells falling on the fortifications of Sebastopol,
fired by the Germans first, then by the Russians, are indifferent to
our agony—as are small waves in the sunlight. But we need not elect
what we do not desire. Torment, in the daisied fields before Troy
or at Amiens or the Manchurian plain is not

of itself the dearest desired of our world. We do not have to die,
in bitterness and the most excruciating torture, to feel! We can
lean on the wall and experience an ecstasy of pain, if pain it must
be, but a pain of love, of dismemberment if you will, but a pain
of almond blossoms, an agony of mimosa trees in bloom, a

scented cloud! Even, as old Ford would say, an exquisite sense of
viands. Would there be no sculpture, no painting, no Pinturicchio, no
Botticelli—or frescos on the jungle temples of Burma (that the jungles
have reclaimed) or Picasso at Cannes but for war? Would there be
no voyages starting from the dunes at Huelva

over the windy harbor? No Seville cathedral? Possibly so. Even
the quietness of flowers is perhaps deceptive. But why must we suffer
ourselves to be so torn to sense our world? Or believe we must so
suffer to be born again? Let the homosexuals seduce whom they will
under what bushes along the coasts of the Middle Sea

rather than have us insist on murder. Governments are defeats, distortions. I wish (and so I fail). Notwithstanding, I wish we might learn of an April of small waves—deadly as all slaughter, that we shall die soon enough, to dream of April, not knowing why we have been struck down, heedless of what greater violence.

Paul Mariani

AN APRIL OF SMALL WAVES

"The Birth of Venus" was published in the Rome-based magazine, *Botteghe Oscure*, in 1948. On the surface of it, this is another of Williams's spring poems celebrating once more the return of the goddess into the poet's world. The goddess—or the Godhead, as he calls her in another poem—is nothing less than the feminine principle of regenerativity (to phrase it more abstractly than Williams himself might have liked) figured doubly as Persephone and Venus. Does not the title itself point to Botticelli's painting of that name in the Uffizi, before which Williams had twice stood: first in March of 1910 when he toured Italy with his brother Ed in his twenty-seventh year, and again with his wife fourteen years later during another March, this one in 1924. It is a world of springtime Williams evokes in this poem, a world stirred into realization by the memory itself. The rhythms of the poem underscore this meditation. What Williams uses here is a five-line stanza with an uncharacteristically long line which can expand or contract to anywhere between four and seven stress units of what appears to be quantitative measure. And if it were not for the forward momentum of the poem's meaning, the need to get said what must be said, one would read the rhythm as slow, stately, meditative, the phrasal units creating at least two medial caesurae within each line. The effect of this is that the poem's tensions work against themselves, so that in one sense the poem reads like a hurried and pained reflection on a world quickly going to hell and in another level reads as a rehearsal for the long poem Williams would begin composing in the step-down triadic foot (that long, maxi-Alexandrine line with its own two pronounced caesurae) four years later in "Of Asphodel, That Greeny Flower." In both poems it is the Keats of the odes which informs if not the pace then certainly the strategy of the meditation on absence and desire.

Consider how Williams begins "The Birth of Venus" by making vivid to the mind's eye what the second stanza will take away. It is an evocation, this opening, of that February springtime Williams and Floss had experienced together a quarter of a century before, the play of waves on the Mediterranean

at Villefranche in southern France, whether in sunny, calm weather or in
storm. We know from the diary Williams kept at the time how intensely he
watched the waves for some sign. And the speaker of this poem knows that
today, even as he thinks about them, the waves again

>   are rippling, crystal clear, upon the pebbles
> at Villefranche whence from the wall, at the Parade Grounds of
> the Chasseurs Alpins, we stood and watched them; or passing along
> the cliff on the ledge between the sea and the old fortress, heard
> the long swell stir without cost among the rock's teeth. But we
>
> are not there!

Here the seaswell phrasing and the connective tissue of the syntax itself draw
us forward from line to line in growing expectation until, in near despair, the
speaker (and we) are pulled up short. Now, at 65, Williams has seen the
world altered by the cataclysm of the Second World War. In a letter written a
few years earlier, he had confessed that he had no desire to return to France
since the France he had known in the mid-1920s had been altered by the war
beyond what he was ready to accept. But at least the changing and unchang-
ing waves would not have altered. How beautiful to stand before those waves
and to listen.

But we are not there, he cries, not there this April to see the waves lapping
the shore and not there—even more importantly—in our imaginations, even
though, he has reminded us, it would be money in our pockets to value such
things. But this is the world of the new cold war which has swept over our
world so soon after the end of the war itself. And yet, Williams risks, is not
the Black Sea this April also "blue with waves/under a smiling sky"? As
(again) with the North American coast—the Labrador North Shore, for example, up which he and Floss had sailed in the summer of '31, when
Williams, drawn to those icy waters, had been—he tells us—the only one on
their cruise ship to strip and dive into those icy waters, slicing his stomach in
the process on those Venusian shells lining the water's shallow bottom.

Spring is here, Williams cries, here in Russia and France and in America,
a spring indifferent to national boundaries and doing all it can to thaw the
Cold War, just as, when the world has turned to bask its other side half a year
hence, spring will begin again to "enliven the African coast southward." And
again, Williams repeats with growing alarm, "we not there, not there!" And
we understand now with that refrain-like lament that that is the plight exactly
of the dead: not to be there.

"Why not believe that we shall be young again?," Williams asks with a
rhetorical directness and urgency characteristic of this new, late strain in his
work. It is a rhetoric which goes beyond, simply, the earlier phrasing of "so
much depends upon" or the mandarin wryness of "rather notice, mon cher."

We will see this newer strain of address in "Asphodel" and in "For Daphne and Virginia," something brought on by the sense of time running out and the need to say what has to be said, as directly as the poet can. Is it not what we desire, Williams asks, this persistence of springtime in our lives, the possibility of holding onto our youth, the Sapphic bracelet spotted under the waves in the mind's eye as new now as when it was first made those thousands of years ago. It is an artifact as replete with nostalgias as any Grecian urn.

And yet it is death we keep hearing about, the deaths of soldiers on beaches like Villefranche with its once-sleepy French garrison, only now those beaches have names more familiar to Williams's first audience: Omaha Beach and Juno, Iwo Jima, Okinawa. For is it not death which colors the "small waves crimson"? It is an image which seems to have obsessed Williams's imagination in these late years: the bodies of young men lying face down or half buried in the sands or bobbing face up at sea, and it may owe something—this preoccupation—to Williams's daily worry about his two Navy sons: Bill serving with the Navy Seabees in the far Pacific, Paul on destroyer duty in the North Atlantic. We will see this drift out into the crimson sea again and again in the last pages of *Paterson IV*, even as another war was beginning in Asia, this one in a place called Korea. Do we not believe that war is inevitable, Williams suggests, and so consume our daily drafts of poison from the news Mithradates-like, preparing for the final catastrophe?

But about life and eros and springtime, about the gentleness of eternal spring we are less certain. The shells which ripped Sebastopol, for example, a fortress-city "fired by the Germans first, then by the Russians," remain indifferent to our agony. Not, of course, Williams is quick to add, that sunlight playing on the waves is any less indifferent to our cries. The difference, therefore, is in us. But at least we need not choose to fix our imaginations on death. It is a crucial observation for the poet approaching his own end. We do not have to dwell on the human torment that informs so much of the *Iliad*, for example, or the various battlefields of Amiens, or the reported atrocities during the Japanese invasion of Manchuria in the 1930s, even now with China, like Russia, becoming the new enemy to be feared.

Nor do we need to sacrifice our lives in skirmishes with death (our own or—vicariously—the deaths of others) to appease the gods within us in order to *feel*, Williams insists. Life is gentler than that, ready to share its pleasures, if only we would let it. Thus Williams, in his own version of the Paterian esthetic. Let us rather experience the exquisite pain of "almond blossoms" or "an agony of mimosa trees in bloom," he offers instead, even the "sense of viands," as his friend, dear Fordie—Ford Madox Ford—dead now and buried in Provence, had time and again reminded him. The poem is constructed on this double-edged principle of the death-like things Williams would reject and the absence of the beautiful thing he would make present to the imagination. "I see a schoolboy when I think of him," Ille says to Hic in Yeats's "Ego Dominus Tuus," "With face and nose pressed to a sweet-shop window...Shut out from all the luxury of the world [to make] luxuriant song." Keats. There is much of Keats in this most American of poets and surely loss is a large part of their likeness to each other.

The argument goes that art and beauty must have their blood sacrifice, that the flowering of a culture is based on the bone meal of thousands of victims who served to make that flower bloom. Williams knew the arguments and he even knew their validity. "And yet ...would there be no Pinturicchio, no Picasso, no Botticelli," he asks, "no frescos on the jungle temples of Burma," no cathedrals even, no Columbus starting out from Huelva to discover the beautiful thing over the wide waters, but for the exorbitant costs of death and war? Perhaps, Williams realizes, perhaps he is a fool. Perhaps the world of flowers is itself filled with its own internecine strife, as one flower crowds out or succumbs finally to another, so that the quietude such a pastoral world evokes is merely a lie. Perhaps. But must we, Williams asks again, imitating the very polarities of the poem itself, must we fill our imaginations with images of death before we can feel we have earned the right to enjoy the world? Must we constantly undergo a physical or imaginative death in order "to be born again"? That last phrase resonates, of course, with traditional religious significance. For what the poem asks during this particular April is if indeed we need Good Friday before we can again experience a new eastering.

The tension bonding this poem together suggests that Williams's answer to this question is yes, even though the answer Williams provides in terms of the poem's rhetoric is otherwise. For what the poem's structure tells us is that spring is made sweeter because we know that soon enough death will take it and eventually the perceiving I with it. What is there to do, then? Forget restrictions, forget taboos, sanctions, punishments, and let Eros—even in its culturally forbidden manifestations—flourish where and as they will. "Let the homosexuals seduce whom they will," Williams nearly shouts in his poem. Let them seduce whomever they will "under what bushes along the coast of the Middle Sea//rather than have us insist on murder." For are not all governments, he adds, by the fact that they are governments, an acknowledgment that the human dream of eternal spring has been defeated? Why do we check our impulses with something far worse, Williams asks? Why do we allow a pornography of violence and death to flourish, shells exploding everywhere, while we shun the lovely shell of the body?

What then is there to do? One can *wish*, which is, the poem's logic tells us, already to fail, because by wishing we admit that we do not yet possess what we so desire. In other words, it is truly an absence only which we possess. And yet and yet, Williams ends his poem, in a sentence whose characteristic ambiguities of syntax keep cutting back and forth:

                                                                    ...I wish we might
learn of an April of small waves—deadly as all slaughter, that we
shall die soon enough, to dream of April, not knowing why we have been
struck down, heedless of what greater violence.

That is, if I read these lines correctly, with an eye on that dash, that infinitive, and those particles, what Williams asks here is why we cannot learn that death is there for all of us regardless of what we would wish otherwise. Moreover, the very idea of resolution in death, the way we comfort ourselves, is by way of an image of an unending dream of springtime itself. And here the infinitive is crucial—*to dream of April*—for the very thing we wish for in death is what death itself may deprive us of forever. Nor is death the answer, for we shall never understand why the greater violence of our own deaths (more final than any imagining of it) had to be at all. In short, instead of rehearsing our own deaths in the rumors of war and violence we are daily fed, Williams suggests, why not read in the sea the eternal return of spring? For if death is as real as eros, it follows that, conversely, eros must be as real as death, and sweeter to dwell on.

If "The Birth of Venus" looks half forward to the later, meditative cadences of a poem like "Asphodel," the Williams so many like because that Williams seems at least accessible, as if—after a lifetime of fighting—the old revolutionary had stopped long enough to sip a glass of orangeade and to dwell on his world—the other half of the equation is to remember just how urgent-sounding this poem really is. Ironically, the long lines themselves do not slow the poem down, for there is a forward momentum to them which works against the meditative form. It would take two strokes, finally, to slow Williams's poetic metabolism down.

EZRA POUND
(1885-1970)

E zra Pound's influence on the development of twentieth-century poetry has unquestionably been greater than that of any other poet. The list of writers for whom he was both friend and champion includes Yeats, Williams, Moore, Joyce, Eliot, H.D., and Frost. With astonishingly single-minded energy he took on the task of remaking literature for the modern age; assimilating influences as various as French *Symbolisme*, classical Chinese poetry, and ancient Greek fragments, he forged a notion of poetry that would be "harder and saner...'nearer the bone'...austere, direct, free from emotional slither." The Imagist movement he founded in London in 1912 was short-lived, but it constituted a revolutionary moment whose impact is still being felt today. His translations, his articles on art and aesthetics, his work as an editor all served to disseminate these ideas widely. Pound's own poetry developed from short evocative lyrics, through longer, more knotty and allusive sequences exploring the meaning of history (such as "Homage to Sextus Propertius" and *Hugh Selwyn Mauberley*), to the gigantic, autobiographical, unfinished (and unfinishable) epic he called the *Cantos*, which occupied him from 1915 on. Judgment of his work is inevitably complicated by knowledge of the last phase of his life: in the period leading up to the Second World War, Pound, who had lived for many years in Italy, became increasingly caught up in the rise of Italian Fascism. During the war he made strident radio broadcasts protesting American involvement in the war; in 1945 he was accused of treason, imprisoned, judged mentally unfit to stand trial, and committed to a mental hospital for 13 years before returning to Italy to spend his final decade.

BOOKS: *Collected Early Poems*, ed. Michael John King (1976); *The Cantos of Ezra Pound* (rev. ed., 1995); *Translations of Ezra Pound*, ed. Hugh Kenner (1970); *Selected Prose 1909-1965*, ed. William Cookson (1973). The standard selection is *Selected Poems* (1949).

Donald Hall

POUND'S SOUNDS

In his life as a poet, which *The Cantos* extends and replicates, Ezra Pound discovered a thousand ways to make a noise. Although he was not innovative as an iambic poet, on the whole Pound's ear is the most inventive in modern literature. With "Cathay" he invented the lyrical flatness developed by Rexroth, Snyder, Bly and Wright; powered by an illusion of simplicity, this sound (which is also a diction) erects itself as plain, clear, lucid; and stylelessness is always a style. Along with "Cathay" Pound developed the related note of imagism, and the free-verse epigram-noise of the *Blast* poems; his flat sarcasm can contain or transmit social notes, literary judgments, cultural observations, moral outrage, and erotic feelings.... In his "Propertius" Pound invented a discursive narrative noise which can fly to lyric touchstone-lines and accommodate narrative or reflective passages together. Useful to *The Cantos*, this sound accommodates and includes, can turn ironic *or* ecstatic, lyric *or* narrative without altering itself to the point of indecorum. By the time of "Propertius" and "Mauberley," Pound's sounds can move with swift sureness from tones at one end of the scale to the other.

But there is one special Poundian sound-figure, starting in *Personae* earlier than "Cathay" and running through *The Cantos*, which I find most breath-taking. It bunches adjacent loud syllables, as in Canto VII:

> Ear, ear, for the sea-surge; murmur of old men's voices.

(In Canto VII, "rattle" is substituted for "murmur," and the line broken after the semi-colon.) The beat is slow: percussive monosyllables, often hyphenated compounds, caesuras pronounced, loud syllables usually long as well as loud. This frequently-percussive figure softens to a falling rhythm, often for its coda, and it runs all through the Cantos. Here it is again in Canto II:

> Seal sports in the spray-whited circles of cliff-wash,
> Sleek head, daughter of Lir,
>   eyes of Picasso
> Under black fur-hood, lithe daughter of Ocean...

From LXXIV (Pisa):

> and olive tree blown white in the wind
> washed in the Kiang and Han
> what whiteness will you add to this whiteness,
>   what candor?

Here it is in a line from LXII, a patch where such examples are fewer:

> Ice, broken ice, icy water

The middle Cantos for long stretches use a documentary flatness, rarely attempting this sound-figure, but it returns in the Pisan Cantos accompanied by the most Shakespearean blank verse since John Keats's. This sound-figure shows again in the wonderful bits and pieces Pound assembled towards his unreachable Paradiso in *Drafts and Fragments*:

> A blown husk that is finished
> > but the light sings eternal
> a pale flare over marshes
> > where the salt hay whispers to tide's change.

My examples assemble a small variation of tunes, Pound's sounds at their most erotic. These quotations refer to nothing in common; they exist in the mouth, then outward to muscle and skin in bodily sensuousness.

The sensuousness belongs to the real sound, not to idea or to the visual image or (sometimes) sound referred to. Anybody knows that the word "food" fills no bellies, but the word "food" is for chewing on all the same: *ef* that sets lip to tooth, *ou* that rounds the lips as if for kissing, *deh* that smacks tongue onto mouth-top. The word carries no calories but in a receptive mouth the juices flow.... In this sound-figure the syllables are often long in the saying and delicious in the chewing, either through length of vowel or of vowel in combination with extended consonants, long sounds adjacent and percussive: *ear, ear; sea-surge; old men's voice-; Seal sports; spray white-; cliff-wash; Sleek head daught-; Lir,/eyes; black fur-hood; lithe daught-; tree blown white; wind/washed; ice, broke-; ice, ic-.... Green time; blown husk; light sings; pale flare; salt hay whisp-; tide's change....* The mouth holds (chews, sucks on) those long syllables, and the adjacent bang-bang-bang slows rhythm down and concentrates mouth-sensations.

Other devices enforce more connections. Alliteration links these clusters: see the first, second, and fourth examples above. Assonance or near-assonance makes further linkage in "green time" the consonants resemble each other but also the dipthong in "time," held onto, becomes the vowel of "green." Caesura's slowness enforces the thud of adjacent monosyllables. Like Ben Jonson, Pound experiments with the multiple caesura. If we reset these lines by dropping the line down the page at the caesura (as Pound sometimes does) we have:

> sleek head,
> > daughter of Lir,
> > > eyes of Picasso

or:

                    where the salt hay
                                    whispers
                                            to tide's change

or:

            icy,
                broken ice,
                            icy water

Surely this rhythm resembles the triadic foot of late William Carlos Williams.

When Pound in this figure moves away from adjacent stress, he tends (daughter of Lir, eyes of Picasso) toward something like the trisyllable foot of English meter. I avoid reference to the dactyl, as I avoid saying spondee for adjacent stress, for Pound is not making classical meter—or meter at all. Meter is measure; meter is what we count. Prosody is the larger subject or study: rhythm, euphony, pitch—what we count as well as what exists uncounted. In Greek meter, we count the length of time syllables take to pronounce, and by convention syllables are either short or long, a short syllable just half the duration of a long one. Variations in pitch and volume of course occur, and they may be controlled and beautiful—but the poet does not *count* them.

This sound-figure of Ezra Pound's makes the happiest mouth-occasion since "Ode to Autumn" but it does not derive from anything in the iambic tradition. The few words above try to describe some of its characteristics. Another way to talk about this figure is to speculate on its sources. What in Pound's eclectic reading allowed him to invent this tune? Breaking the pentameter, we were told, was the first thing. If Pound's sounds broke the pentameter by a dozen innovations, most of them derive from his study of the alien—from reading Anglo-Saxon, Greek, Chinese, Provençal. I suggest that this sound-figure is Pound's fortuitous combination of two different, one might think unassimilable, sources.

Let me quote some pre-Canto Poundian chestnuts from *Ripostes* (1912). For one thing, there is the alliterative, percussive, falling-rhythm'd, becaesura'd "Seafarer," translated from the Anglo-Saxon and mimicking its rhythm:

            May I for my own self song's truth reckon,
            Journey's jargon, how I in harsh days
            Hardship endured oft.
            Bitter breast-cares have I abided....

Repetition of sound is rhythmic and consonantal, drumbeats of loudness separated by pronounced caesura, muscle or dance rhythms. And on the other hand there is "Apparuit," in which Pound tried writing Sapphics in English, imitating Greek prosody with its longs and shorts, with its emphasis on the connections of repeated vowels and consonants—mouth-sound rather than leg's pounding beat. Surely "Apparuit" fails as quantitative meter: in the English tradition loud is more noticeable than long because by tradition it is what we count, and Pound makes long and loud coincide. But in its concentration on long vowels and mouth-connections, "Apparuit" moves toward the later sound figure: "Golden rose the house," it begins, and goes on to speak of "a marvel, carven...."

Later, Pound wrote that "progress lies rather in an attempt to approximate classical quantitative meter (NOT to copy them)...." I think the approximation was not to classical meter but to a Greek or classical notion of euphony. This approximation shows itself in "The Return," also from *Ripostes*:

> Haie! Haie!
> These were the swift to harry;
> These the keen-scented;
> These were the souls of blood.
>
> Slow on the leash,
> pallid the leash-men!

There are eight long e's here, and the last broken line is characteristic of the cadence of the later sound-figure.

Now Anglo-Saxon metric and Greek metric do not resemble each other, and neither of them resembles traditional English meter. Anglo-Saxon verse counts the presence of caesura and the number and placement of loud sounds. It does not count relatively-louder sounds, as in the relative-stress-verse which is traditional from Chaucer's pentameter to Stevens's, nor does it count quantity like the Greeks nor court Greek euphony.

The most mouth-luscious, limb-erotic of Pound's sounds derive from the weird combination of Sappho's euphony and a Viking drumbeat. To the Greek sweetness of assonance (the first line of the Iliad includes six variations of the *ay* dipthong) Pound adds the bang-bang of north-sea alliteration and warrior drum pounding. From the quantitative dactyl (in our misreading of long for loud) he takes his falling-rhythm. In his percussive repetition of long vowels he brings the northern drum-beat of alliterative accents together with the southern mouth-hold of two, three, four, and even five *long* syllables together—the true quantitative spondee, sometimes two spondees in a row followed by the initial long-syllable of the quantitative dactyl. North is muscle, south is mouth, and the combination is "Ear, ear, for the sea-surge; murmur of old men's voices."

THE GARDEN

En robe de parade.
                          Samain

Like a skein of loose silk blown against a wall
She walks by the railing of a path in Kensington Gardens,
And she is dying piece-meal
                of a sort of emotional anaemia.

And round about there is a rabble
Of the filthy, sturdy, unkillable infants of the very poor.
They shall inherit the earth.

In her is the end of breeding.
Her boredom is exquisite and excessive.
She would like some one to speak to her,
And is almost afraid that I
                will commit that indiscretion.

William Matthews

Young Ezra

Pound's earliest poems—those published, let's say, before *Cathay*—compelled and puzzled me when I first read them. I couldn't then say why. It was in 1959 and I was in high school, ferally ignorant of almost everything.

But I could hear something remarkable in the poems: they sounded like poetry as it was taught in school, and yet they sounded like someone talking—it was a heightened, shapely and passionate sort of talk such as I had scarcely heard or could only dimly imagine, but it was indisputably like talk. Sometimes the two verisimilitudes alternated and sometimes they were concurrent. The effect was magnetizing.

Jostling each other without apology in the first pages of the recently released *Selected Poems of Ezra Pound* (1957) were first lines like

What hast thou, O my soul, with Paradise?

or

> Towards the Noel that morte saison

or

> Cydonian Spring with her attendant train,

and first lines like

> Come let us pity those who are better off than we are

or

> "Thank you, whatever comes." And then she turned

or

> Your mind and you are our Sargasso Sea.

And both tones cohabit peacefully in a first line like

> Damn it all! all this our South stinks peace.

Of course the combination of what sounds complex, acculturated, learned and exotic with what sounds direct, colloquial and dramatic is like catnip to a young reader. For it embodies the yearned-for and distrusted complexities of adult and communal life, and it embodies equally the brash, self-dramatizing resistance youth needs to stave off inundation by adult and communal life.

****

The young Pound was up to a similar struggle, albeit on a far more complex and fully furnished stage. Literary apprenticeship shares certain things with adolescence, after all, even if the literary apprenticeship is painstaking, learned, largely self-administered and in Pound's case will lead to the brave making of a great poet. But there is an important difference between the two, for all the obvious similarities. We all have to age and die, even if we should resist that inevitability horse, foot, and artillery. But Pound *chose* quite deliberately the apprenticeship that might make him a great poet.

It was great literature the young Pound hoped to join and from which he had sense enough to know he had much to learn. In his role as frenetic and prescient apostle of the new, Pound opposed the *worship* of great literature, which led to passive imitation, but never the *use* of great literature. Or I should say *uses*, for they include active imitation, pillaging, parody, quotations and misquotation, ventriloquism and any other means that Pound (and,

most prominently among his literary cronies, Eliot) could find to put tradition to use.

That the tradition came to be more and more idiosyncratically defined
only served to raise the ante for Pound's powers of discrimination. For the
more he could recast the tradition in the image of his needs, the more likely
that he would someday speak to Poetry or Literature the way he speaks in "A
Pact" (the poem, written when Pound was quite young, serving him as a kind
of promissory note to himself) to Walt Whitman:

> I have detested you long enough.
> I come to you as a grown child
> Who has had a pig-headed father;
> I am old enough now to make friends.

****

For all his chip-off-the-old-block pigheadedness (some pig! some head!)
Pound began humbly enough, with finger exercises. *Understand the form*
and *get the tone right* seem to have been the two rules. And like the pedagog-
ical pieces of Bach (though Bach wrote them primarily to enlighten others),
they bear among them wonderful melodies and flashes prefiguring mature
brilliance.

Like many of Pound's best lines from this period, the first line of "The
Garden" is, except for "against," all monosyllables:

> Like a skein of loose silk blown against a wall

At first glance the image seems related to the famous "petals on a wet, black
bough": a beautiful and evanescent object brought forward from the blurry
urban ground to be made figure. But there's also an argument in the line. The
woman is ravelled and blown loose; what was coiled or wound, as a skein is,
is now without form or tension. And as the first stanza goes on we see that the
woman is ill, growing weightless and blowable.

Not sticking to the rail, like the woman, but "round about" are the children
of the very poor. There may be a lapse of tact in this second stanza, but then
maybe not; it's easier to see from 85 years into Pound's century than it was
when he wrote this poem how killable the infants of the very poor can be. In
any case, they are in the poem unkillable in contrast to her. There is a bumpy,
durable, discursive rhythm to "filthy, sturdy, unkillable infants," by contrast
to the more languid and liquid measures describing the woman, that gives the
infants a future, however drab. As to the woman, her reappearance in the final
stanza may well be a last sighting.

The poem seems to have travelled a long way from its first lyrical line to
the abrupt and summary rhetoric of "They shall inherit the earth" and "In her

is the end of breeding." But it is headed toward two final lines that recapitulate the tone and rhythms that end the first stanza. Just before those final lines will come a line, flatly declarative this time, composed wholly of monosyllables:

> She would like some one to speak to her.

What's "in her," what she's "dying piece-meal/of," *is* the end of breeding, now understood to be the full name of her disease. Her boredom is not only a poor response to the world, but also a defense, insufficient though it may prove, against the etiolation of illness. She *would* like someone to speak to her, we realize. That line is spoken by the-poet-in-sympathy-to-the-character. It is only in the last two lines that Pound shifts his tone to the poet-who-knows-who-shall-inherit-the-earth.

For all its American bluster at mannerly Britain and for all its alert interest in class and social life, the poem is swift, delicate, precisely modulated, and demonstrates both Pound's love of the large view and of shimmering detail.

****

Pound was to go on to bigger, more important and certainly gnarlier poems. But I continue to find these earliest poems moving and enduring, and not only—though of course that would be enough—for themselves. In them we see the invention of a style, and so by extension the invention of an artist. To think that the young man sat down to teach himself how to write verse, and to work out at the same time his ambivalent attitudes toward tradition and the new, toward American and Europe, toward colloquial and oratorical uses of English, and wrought for himself in the process a style so muscular and so lucid!

Stanley Plumly

POUND'S GARDEN

I like to think there is a pure phase in Pound's career, a phase parallel to, if entirely different from, another kind of beauty in his exilic, resolute, rich life, a phase, like that of *The Pisan Cantos*, when the technique truly was the test of the man's sincerity. It is a time between his discovery, in 1912, of the image and the hard "constatation of fact" and the discovery, two years later, of the vortex; a time between—perhaps no more than a moment—his association with H. D. and Aldington and Hulme and Flint and Ford and Yeats and the long list of poets he helped or would help and his association with artists Wyndham Lewis and Henri Gaudier-Brzeska and other contributors to *Blast*; a time between Harriet Monroe and Mrs. Mary Fenollosa; between the troubadours and the *Canzoni* and the Chinese written character; between the station of the Metro and *Cathay*; between the low and the "high Modernist mode"; between economic innocence and the coming of the Great War.

I guess I'm using *pure* because in so many ways the relatively small poems that come out of this brief period—among those written in 1912 and published in *Poetry* in April, 1913, under the title "Contemporania"—rejoice in the transition between Pound's brilliant translations of the Provençal and his imitations-into-English of the Chinese and Japanese; poems that anticipate the cool, "Latin tone" of *Sextus Propertius*. These poems, these "Contemporania," though, are not conversions, whatever Latinate or Imagistic influences they may show, and they are certainly not of the epical, multiple, historical, magical voice attempted in the *Cantos*. They are the least personal of his poetry—they are really his first Pound rather than Poundian poems—and bear about the same relationship to the poet's major work as do the stories in *Dubliners* to *Ulysses*. They are strict and clean, personal and direct, "free of emotional slither," yet passionate; their intensity comes from concentration and juxtaposition; their power, I think, from the autobiography of the moment, not unlike those moments of memory and humanity in the cantos written from the cage.

"In a Station of the Metro" and "A Pact" are probably the best known of the "Contemporania" poems, but the best, in my view, is "The Garden," coming as it does, in this early portion of Pound's career, between "Portrait d'une Femme" and the incomparable "The River Merchant's Wife: A Letter," both of which begin in aesthetic rather than actual sources. "The Garden" is no imaginary garden, and the fact that Pound makes obvious the variance between the blatant symbol of his title and the reality of the place—Garden versus Gardens—suggests how uninterested he is in the issue. And he is just as uninterested in the New as he is in the Old Testament—hence the parody, again obvious, of who shall inherit. The question is what shall they inherit. By raising these blunt issues so plainly he dismisses them. As the garden is real, the central figure, the woman, is real. Her "portrait" is like a photographic blur against a background of neutrality, "a skein of loose silk blown against a wall." This opening, resonant, remarkable simile—the warmest image in the poem—will be immediately adjusted by the literalness of the second line, and from then on the poem becomes completely an act of transformation, comprehension, and empathy—even, in hindsight, didactic. Pound, however, brings it off because like the good naturalist (i.e. Zola) he is he is making an analysis, out of care for the particular and out of passion for the type.

The tension here between the specific case and the anonymity of the general helps rescue the encounter from both sentimentality and condescension (attitudes of high purchase among Georgians). In those days Pound lived a short distance from Kensington Gardens, at 10 Church Walk, so he must have run into his subject, or others like her, more than once. "The Garden" has the feel of felt experience backed up behind it, the feel of Pound inside the poem, as an actor as well as speaker. Its language is ironic, of course; more importantly its language is beautifully precise, beautifully realized in the terms of what we would later call the correlative. Rather than Imagist, it seems to me a poem of pointed rhetoric; its impulse is to interpret, its tone to understate. We witness the woman, essentially, in stages, or frames, through a process of growing substantiation. The more we see the more, says the speaker, we know. The romantic yet poignant skein image of the first line will become, by the end, an image of boredom, both exquisite and excessive. As the poem develops it qualifies: she is dying *piecemeal*, and she is dying *of a sort of* emotional anemia; around her there is a rabble, wonderfully extended, as vers libre, as *the filthy, sturdy, unkillable infants of the very poor*, who shall inherit, like beggar Christians, the earth, this garden; her boredom is as much her problem as it is her signature; she would like to talk and is *almost* afraid the speaker will, which, given the circumstances, would be an indiscretion.

En robe de parade, the epigraph for the poem, is taken from the French of Albert Samain ("The Infanta"), and is part of the poem's incisive vocabulary. "Dressed as for a state occasion" is on line with the sublimity of the sequence of the other "exquisite" understatements, which Pound needs to achieve the distance that will allow him insight. The distance is finally the poem's vision. Some readers have found that distance to be "excessive," and they quote Pound's reference that "in her is the end of breeding," as his judgment. I can agree that the lady does seem to act, according to report, superior to the situation. But that same report surrenders to considerable compassion—the speaker would like to speak to, not simply for, the woman—and renders serious anger—the speaker understands, with some bitterness, that all of them, man, woman, unkillable child, live in a world of determinism.... They are in this garden together, if at arm's length. I find this poem, therefore, to be less a portrait of Pre-Raphaelite pallor or a "study in aesthetics" than a severe and responsive reading of the "luminous detail"—Pound's phrase—inherent in a moment, in the autumn of 1912. Pound's sympathy is saved by his disgust, his disgust redeemed by the absolute clarity of his perception. The woman is exactly killable, and she is as caught up in the encounter in the garden as is the rabble who will inherit it, as caught up as the poet himself. Pound has more than identified and identified with his subject—he has imagined it, knowing full well that the filthy, sturdy infants are the future, while he and the woman are part of the twilight, before the interregnum.

from HOMAGE TO SEXTUS PROPERTIUS

I

Shades of Callimachus, Coan ghosts of Philetas
It is in your grove I would walk,
I who come first from the clear font
Bringing the Grecian orgies into Italy,
                              and the dance into Italy.
Who hath taught you so subtle a measure,
                    in what hall have you heard it;
What foot beat out your time-bar,
          what water has mellowed your whistles?

Out-weariers of Apollo will, as we know, continue their Martian generalities,
          We have kept our erasers in order.
A new-fangled chariot follows the flower-hung horses;
A young Muse with young loves clustered about her
                    ascends with me into the aether, . . .
And there is no high-road to the Muses.

Annalists will continue to record Roman reputations,
Celebrities from the Trans-Caucasus will belaud Roman celebrities
And expound the distentions of Empire,
But for something to read in normal circumstances?
For a few pages brought down from the forked hill unsullied?
I ask a wreath which will not crush my head.
                    And there is no hurry about it;
I shall have, doubtless, a boom after my funeral,
Seeing that long standing increases all things
                              regardless of quality.

And who would have known the towers
                    pulled down by a deal-wood horse;
Or of Achilles withstaying waters by Simois
Or of Hector spattering wheel-rims,
Or of Polydmantus, by Scamander, or Helenus and Deiphoibos?
Their door-yards would scarcely know them, or Paris.
Small talk O Ilion, and O Troad
                              twice taken by Oetian gods,
If Homer had not stated your case!

And I also among the later nephews of this city

shall have my dog's day,
With no stone upon my contemptible sepulchre;
My vote coming from the temple of Phoebus in Lycia, at Patara,
And in the meantime my songs will travel,
And the devirginated young ladies will enjoy them
            when they have got over the strangeness,
For Orpheus tamed the wild beasts—
                    and held up the Threician river;
And Citharaon shook up the rocks by Thebes
    and danced them into a bulwark at his pleasure,
And you, O Polyphemus? Did harsh Galatea almost
Turn to your dripping horses, because of a tune, under Aetna?
We must look into the matter.
Bacchus and Apollo in favour of it,
There will be a crowd of young women doing homage to my palaver,
Though my house is not propped up by Taenarian columns
    from Laconia (associated with Neptune and Cerberus),
Though it is not stretched upon gilded beams;
My orchards do not lie level and wide
                    as the forests of Phaecia,
                    the luxurious and Ionian,
Nor are my caverns stuffed stiff with a Marcian vintage,
My cellar does not date from Numa Pompilius,
Nor bristle with wine jars,
Nor is it equipped with a frigidaire patent;
Yet the companions of the Muses
            will keep their collective nose in my books,
And weary with historical data, they will turn to my dance tune.

Happy who are mentioned in my pamphlets,
        the songs shall be a fine tomb-stone over their beauty.
            But against this?
Neither expensive pyramids scraping the stars in their route,
Nor houses modelled upon that of Jove in East Elis,
Nor the monumental effigies of Mausolus,
                are a complete elucidation of death.

Flame burns, rain sinks into the cracks
And they all go to rack ruin beneath the thud of the years
Stands genius a deathless adornment,
            a name not to be worn out with the years.

James Laughlin

RAMBLING AROUND POUND'S PROPERTIUS

Propertius Comes to Harvard Yard

At Choate, in 1931, it was not H.P. ("Hup-Hup") Arnold, the classics master, but the poet Dudley Fitts who started me on Propertius. "Hup," who skipped the part about Dido & Aeneas in the cave in the *Aeneid*, knew that "Integer Vitae" built character in boys but that the Elegiac Poets would not sit with the Head, whose great sermon on the Honest Sailor who reported an errant master was repeated annually to a cheering audience in chapel.

S.P.'s name came up a few days after I enrolled at the Ezuversity in Rapallo in 1934, and was loaned a marked-up copy of the Mueller edition. But I didn't get deep into what Pound had done with him until I was reading the Elegiac Poets with E.K. Rand—what a charming and learned man! And those were still the days when doctors made house calls and great professors invited students to dinner and served port.

Professor Rand was not a noddy like Prof. William Hale who reviewed the *Propertius* as a *translation* in *Poetry* magazine. His favorite work of modern poetry was Robert Bridges' *Testament of Beauty*. But he was willing to talk about Eliot and Pound, unlike his colleague the Boylston Professor of Rhetoric, Robert Hillyer, who was known to eject students from his classroom for mentioning their names. So I ventured to offer Rand a paper on the *Propertius*, this about 1937. With him I had no worry that the visits to his study where I could examine his classic texts printed by Aldus and Estienne and Didot would cease. I defined the *Homage* immediately as a transcription, but hedged with some comments about "egregious errors": "sitiens" as "sitting," "vota" as "vote"—and the "distortions" of the collage structure. Then I let fly with praise for Pound's "verbal valence" (we had our innocuous terminologies in those days too) in the "Nox mihi candida." Professor Rand was advised (as if he didn't know) that in the *Propertius* he could watch "the metamorphosis of observation into imagination," that Pound favored "terminal syzygies," but that (take care!) "Propertius seems to have been an ill-disciplined person subject to rapid and violent changes of mood." However I went too far when I suggested that Augustus was Propertius' Sir Basil Zaharoff (Metevsky). That line was crossed out in red with no comment.

The comment at the end of my paper was: "A judicious evaluation. But a little more care with your syntax, please." And below that, "Cur tua praescripto sevecta est pagina gyro."?

Those Welsh Mines

According to Gallup, the *Propertius* first appeared in Pound's 1919 book *Quia Pauper Amavi,* which also contained "Langue d'Oc," "Moeurs Contemporaines," and three ur-cantos. When Pound translated the Latin phrase (from Ovid) for me as "love on the dole," I saw to what the title applied. Propertius was well-born but he lost his family estates when they were given to veterans, and he wrote "sollicitate tu causa pecunia vitae." In their London days the Pounds were living on Ezra's small literary jobs, Dorothy's allowance and an occasional $10 bill (that bought a lot then) in Homer's letters from Wyncote. Can not their situation support the thesis that Pound made *his* Propertius more anti-establishment than Propertius really was because of his own growing dislike of the banking system? "The bank makes it *ex nihil*" (233.46.75). Sullivan records that the *Homage* was completed in 1918. Pound did not meet Major Douglas in the office of the *New Age* until 1918, but he had been researching the causes of war since shortly after Gaudier's death.

I suspect that the "Welsh mines" passage may prove my point. "Cimbrorumque minas et benefacta Mari" means, more or less: "the threat of Cimbrian invasion (wild men from Wales pillaging the Roman settlements in Britain) and Marius's public service and the profit in defeating them." But Pound makes it "...Welsh mines and the profit Marus had out of them." "Minas" cannot mean "mines." No way. "Mines" would be "metalla." But the line rang a bell with Ezra and he saw how he could use it to get at his enemies, the bankers and their military stooges. This sort of thing goes on constantly in the *Homage*—it is part of the mask mechanism—but it is seldom so clear-cut. Usually it is done in the service of one of the several kinds of irony and humor which give the poem its marvelous flavor.

In our correspondence Ezra teased me a good deal, usually referring to my "Haavud iggurance," and I sometimes teased him back. I wrote him in 1935 that those mines were really a bit too much, and had this reply: "The Homage is on a list of mine somewhere as a persona [which means he was writing under the guise or mask of another person]. D/n suppose S propertius hadn'd died/or had Ripvan Winkled. and come to and wrote a poem/In yanqui. I NEVER said the Homage was a translation. Some of it coincides/as if I rewrote a poem I had done twenty years ago/The Hardy [Thomas Hardy] prob/Hit it when he said it wd/ have helped the boob reader if I had called it 'S.P. soliloquizes.' 'boob'/is not textual. Mr. Hardy's langwidg waz choicer. Continuin'/My contribution to classical scholarship if any/wd. consist in blasting the idea that Propertius wd. have been an editor of the New Republic/or that he was a moon-headed decorator/smaragdos chrysolithosve. As thesis it wd be that he had a bean/plus a bit of humor and irony which the desiccated do not see.... Perhaps 'nowhere seeking to make or to avoid translation' wd. answer query."

On The Palatine Hill

Atra dies. One of my blackest. All during the shooting of Lawrence Pitkethly's documentary on Pound (as an old friend of Ezra's I was supposed to be the continuity figure, but the film editor left most of my continuations on the cutting room floor) as we traipsed in a van from troubadour country, through the Sacred Places and finally to Rome, I was dreaming of my Great Event. I had been promised that I could do the "Nox mihi candida" on the Palatine Hill. The day came. I had rented a toga in the Via della Scrofula. The shooting went on. I waited. The light was fading. Lawrence was making more and more useless shots of memorial arches. (I think he is queer for arches.) "Lawrence," I pleaded, "you promised." The cameraman took a light reading. "It's too late for that now." "You can at least do it on tape," Lawrence said. I gave a magnificent declamation. And only then noticed that the tape was not running. I wasn't worth even a bit of tape. The film will be on PBS in 1986, but I don't care if you watch it. I was betrayed.

Die Stimme hinter dem Vorhang

I have a great admiration for Donald Davie. With R.P. Blackmur and John Espey he was one of the first critics to make high claims for Pound. In our present climate that sounds simple enough; but Espey told me the story of how his professors, when he announced that he would do his dissertation on Pound, begged him not to destroy his academic career before it had even begun.

My admiration for Davie recently increased when I heard him do a superb hatchet job, so elegant and so witty, on some neo-Marxists and post-structuralists whom Terry had imported to the Pound Conference at Orono. I felt, as Davie punctured those gaseous balloons of non-signification, that he was speaking for Ez, who was muttering "Cat-piss and porcupines!!" It was a bravura performance. Davie is also a fine poet; the master always told me that good poets were the ones qualified to explain poetry.

But there have been moments when D.D. puzzled me. First at Noel Stock's conference at Toledo in 1971 when he remarked that Lawrence and Williams—two of my heroes—were a pernicious influence on his writer-students. And I was puzzled when I read in his books on Pound that the *Propertius* was composed in "Babu English," or "translatorese." I had spent some time working in India, doing cultural Boy Scout jobs for the Ford Foundation. This had meant a lot of time in the offices of minor functionaries of the Ministry of Education, tedious hours while the punkahs whined and barefoot but turbaned peons were sent scurrying after file folders. I had those bureaucratic intonations pretty well fixed in my head; they were indeed curious, but I could not relate them to what I heard in the *Homage*. There was a correspondence of idiom in the "political" passages, where Pound is using the "Latinate polysyllables" to deride the Establishment, but that seemed to me a matter of vocabulary not of poetic cadence. Who or what was it that I was hearing? Or was it only Pound's lines of prose in the *Cantos*?

I put the problem on hold. And it wasn't until 1983 when we went to Hexham in Northumbria to interview that grand old man Basil Bunting (R.I.P.) for Pitkethly's documentary that I found what seemed a satisfactory answer. That was for me an historic day. We had set up the lights and the camera in the living room of the cottage. "The Bas" sparkled his eyes at us and talked away, as only he could talk, while he nipped at the Scotch we had brought him.

There were some remarkable stories about his life in Persia, as a seaman on the Murmansk run and in the RAF in Italy, good tales about Pound, but most of the talk was on poetry, particularly melopoeia. He told us that when Pound came to London in 1908 "he was forty years behind" and that "his father—and his mother—were Rossetti." But he knew that Yeats was "the great living poet to go after." Some ten years later Yeats would tell Bunting that the *Propertius*, and especially the "Nox mihi candida," had the best *vers libre* structure yet done in English. It was, Bunting said, "in the *Homage* that Pound discovered how to organize a poem on the model of music so that every line grows out of the line before by modification. The effect is very much like the sonata form." "Was there," I asked, "a basic rhythm?" There was indeed and it turned out to be—Whitman. I was amazed. Pound had never mentioned Whitman that I can recall so I had never made that connection. Bunting went on to recite the beginning of "Out of the cradle endlessly rocking," beating time with his finger; then he did part of the "Nox mihi candida." The echo was clear to all of us. What clinches the argument for me was his telling us that once, years before, he had gotten stuck reciting the Whitman to Ezra; then Pound had picked up and carried through to the end without a pause. The poem was permanently in his head.

That was a great day in Hexham. We had lunch in the village pub, then continued the shooting. At about three the bottle of Scotch was empty; "The Bas's" chin declined to his chest and he slipped softly into slumber. We had had a course in the bond between poetry and music, and what Pound had made with it. Only a fraction of the interview found its way into the film, but the out-takes are safe and I hope to have a video cassette edited from them.

The Sounds of the Old Words

I ask whether some of the beaneries may be paddling the young up shit creek? Is poking a computer as conducive to the formation of style as reading Plato or Vergil? (And by style I don't mean this parody of E.P. at the lunch table; I mean the way Leon Edel or Harry Levin writes prose.) I submit that style is heard in the head as it is put down, and that those sounds come from reading the right texts in youth: the classics in the originals, the King James Version, even the Gettysburg Address.

When I was invited to do Pound & Williams at Brown I warned the students that I would not turn in a grade until I had heard them recite 4 lines of Latin. (My wife said this reminded her of Radcliffe when the girls had to swim across the pool to be graduated.) I let the students choose anything that pleased them, even Catullus 80 if they liked that sort of thing. I simply wanted them to have in their heads the sound of some good Latin words and how the words move in the line, "rubbing themselves" on each other forwards and backwards.

Since we were doing the *Propertius*, most chose from him, and the favorite turned out to be the "dum nos fata sinunt," lines that echo in my own head though I suppose they are sentimental.

> "dum nos fata sinunt, oculos satiemus amore
>   nox tibi longa venit, nec reditura dies"

> "While our fates twine together, sate we our eyes with love;
>   For a long night comes upon you and a day when no day returns."

Not long afterward I was Loebing my way through Tibullus and was startled to come on exactly the same line. I even found one in Catullus that isn't far from it. What does this tell us about the literary life in Rome? Were the boys cribbing from each other? Or paying compliments by imitation? Or was this a poetic convention of the time? John Speirs points out that many scholars believe that much of Propertius was drawn from Callimachus—hard to prove since so little Callimachus survives. And could it have been Kenner who remarked that what the Elegiac Poets say is not extremely profound; what they do with the words gives their poetry its charge.

A Backward Glance

Not everyone has seen Pound's 1911 (*Canzoni*) translation of Propertius, III, 26, because it was dropped from *Personae* though it is now in the *Collected Early Poems*. It bears looking at to see how much Pound improved in six years.

PRAYER FOR HIS LADY'S LIFE

Here let thy clemency, Persephone, hold firm,
Do thou, Pluto, bring here no greater harshness.
So many thousand beauties are gone down to Avernus
Ye might let one remain above with us.

With you is Iope, with you the white-gleaming Tyro,
With you is Europa and the shameless Pasiphae,
And all the fair from Troy and all from Achaia,
From the sundered realms, of Thebes and of aged Priamus;
And all the maidens of Rome, as many as they were,
They died and the greed of your flame consumes them.

> *Here let thy clemency, Persephone, hold firm,*
> *Do thou, Pluto, bring here no greater harshness.*
> *So many thousand beauties are gone down to Avernus,*
> *Ye might let one remain above with us.*

Look at IX, 2 (page 223 of *Personae*) to see what happened. Some of the mythological fustian has been cut, to advantage, but the great change is this: the tame and trite "So many thousand beauties are gone down to Avernus" has become the superb "There are enough women in hell,/quite enough beautiful women" for "sunt apud infernos tot milia formosarum." It's like going from Sully Prudhomme to Laforgue.

Nuggets

T.S. Eliot (1919):

"The *Homage* is a new *persona*, a creation of a new character, recreating Propertius in himself, and himself in Propertius."

Prof. W. G. Hale (1919):

"Mr Pound is incredibly ignorant of Latin. He has of course a perfect right to be, but not if he translates from it. The result of his ignorance is that much of what he makes his author say is unintelligible.... If Mr Pound were a professor of Latin, there would be nothing left for him but suicide."

E.P. (in a letter to Orage, 1919):

"Hale pretends to read Latin, but has apparently never *understood* anything but syntax and never seen the irony of Propertius.... Re decadence: We all know that Propertius went to midweek prayer meeting.... If I were, however, a professor of Latin in Chicago, I should probably have to resign on divulging the fact that Propertius occasionally copulavit, i.e. rogered the lady to whom he was not legally wedded."

Robert Nichols (1920):

"In place of the quiet and tender irony we are accustomed to see upon the face of Thomas Campion's favourite Latin poet we behold a mask of gaiety and elegiac irony, sometimes almost saturnine.... The voice is not that of the professional gramophone, being at least a live voice. That is, however, I fear, all that can be said for the version.... Mr Pound is not, never has been and almost, I might hazard, never will be, a poet. He is too hard, too clever; he has yet to learn that poetry does not so much glitter as shine."

Wyndham Lewis (in reply to the Nichols review, 1920):

"Mr. Pound, without being a pedant, may conceivably know that Chaucer, Landor, Ben Jonson, and many contemporaries of Rowlandson, found other uses for classic texts than that of making literal English versions of them. Or, again, that the parody of Yeats...and the mention of Wordsworth...would have indicated to a sensitive or less biassed critic than Mr Pound...had some other aim than that of providing a crib for schoolboys or undergraduates."

Ford Madox Ford (1926):

"What is the *Homage* but a prolonged satire upon our own day, as if Propertius should come to New York or London...."

R.P. Blackmur (1933):

"What is characteristic of this poem more than its attitudes toward love and toward the poet's profession, is the elegance of the language in which these attitudes are expressed. By elegance is meant...a consistent choice of words and their arrangement such as to exemplify a single taste...."

"...the element of conversational, colloquial ease used formally, almost rhetorically to heighten the seriousness of the verse."

Hugh Kenner (1951):

"By 1917 Pound had forged a new language; not only the expression, but the sensibility brought to the Latin, is liberated from Victorian emotional cliché...a block of speech and perception new to the English poetic tradition, and a use of language that responds to the pressures of perception with (Ching Ming) accuracy and adequacy."

"Pound...brought to Propertius' Elegies a sensibility alert to elegant cynicism, informed by Laforgue's dealings with pretentious sentiment and pretentious bombast alike."

"The deliberate *collage* of poker-faced misreadings performed by Pound in certain portions of this poem should perhaps be connected with the exploration of these zones of consciousness initiated by Joyce five years later."

"...the enormous freedom and range of tone, the ironic weight, the multiple levels of tongue-in-cheek self-deprecation everywhere present in the *Propertius*."

(1971)

"The *Homage*...was achieved by a mind filled with James's prose.... Not only the ghost of the Latin elegiac couplet presides over its way of dividing discourse, but the great ghost also, 'phantom with weighted motion,' that drank (he wrote thenabouts) 'the tone of things,' and spaced its discourse with suspenseful deliberateness."

(1983, from the documentary interview transcript)

JL: Why was Pound attracted to Propertius?
HK: A lot of things came together...the fascination with the poet whom the establishment has missed...Maecenas, the Ford Foundation of his time, didn't give him a fellowship...the wars and rumors of wars in Rome which rhymes with the British imperial propaganda of 1917...and then finally there was the opportunity presented by the enormous number of Latin words embedded in the English language that he could use in the poem...from which he got a strange tone of abstract supercilious...just what he wanted.

CANTO XLIX

For the seven lakes, and by no man these verses:
Rain; empty river; a voyage,
Fire from frozen cloud, heavy rain in the twilight
Under the cabin roof was one lantern.
The reeds are heavy; bent;
and the bamboos speak as if weeping.

Autumn moon; hills rise about lakes
against sunset
Evening is like a curtain of cloud,
a blurr above ripples: and through it
sharp long spikes of the cinnamon,
a cold tune amid reeds.
Behind hill the monk's bell
borne on the wind.
Sail passed here in April; may return in October
Boat fades in silver; slowly;
Sun blaze alone on the river.

Where wine flag catches the sunset
Sparse chimneys smoke in the cross light

Comes then snow scur on the river
 And a world is covered with jade
Small boat floats like a lanthorn,
The flowing water clots as with cold. And at San Yin
they are a people of leisure.

Wild geese swoop to the sand-bar,
Clouds gather about the hole of the window
Broad water; geese line out with the autumn
Rooks clatter over the fishermen's lanthorns,

A light moves on the north sky line;
where the young boys prod stones for shrimp.
In seventeen hundred came Tsing to these hill lakes.
A light moves on the south sky line.

State by creating riches shd. thereby get into debt?
This is infamy; this is Geryon.
This canal goes still to TenShi

though the old king built it for pleasure

```
K E I     M E N     R A N     K E I
K I U     M A N     M A N     K E I
JITSU     GETSU     K   O     K W A
T A N     F U K U   T A N     K A I
```

Sun up; work
sundown; to rest
dig well and drink of the water
dig field; eat of the grain
Imperial power is? and to us what is it?

The fourth; the dimension of stillness.
And the power over wild beasts.

Norman Dubie

SOME NOTES: INTO THE SERE AND YELLOW

While an undergraduate I memorized from the *Selected Poems* the first six stanzas of this canto and its concluding two lines. In later years, I would repeat them aloud for they were pacifying like some of the psalms I learned as a boy. For all the description here, there was, nevertheless, a satisfying otherworldly melody and emptiness to the landscape. There was also a mystery.

The late autumn, late evening and wintry village scene that accounts for the first six stanzas of the Seven Lakes Canto *was* my mystery! I wanted to know where I was in time and space. The Pound scholars didn't know. Some said it was the province of Hunan, a rich lake district in China. Some said it was a Taoist fancy, an imaginary place outside of time. The first notion is reasonable, for the original six stanzas of the canto are involved very perversely, with poems, anonymous poems ("and by no man these verses"), that Pound and a friend, Pao-sun Tseng, translated in spring 1928, in Rapallo. The anonymous poems are from a Chinese picture book that had long been in the possession of Pound's father. The picture book contained Chinese and Japanese poems adjoined by painted scenes of Hunan Province.

But are we in the Hunan? This province in China enjoys mild winters; once every five years or so, tea bushes might be singed with the cold. But in the Seven Lakes Canto, our village is suffering a blanketing frost, ice in the canals, and snow. The seven lakes ought to be a clue but the literature says there is no configuration of seven lakes anywhere in Hunan. The answer is in the last of the first six stanzas:

> A light moves on the north sky line;
> where the young boys prod stones for shrimp.
> In seventeen hundred came Tsing to these hill lakes.
> A light moves on the south sky line.

In seventeen hundred came Tsing to these hill lakes. Tsing is the 22nd Dynasty; its ruler in 1700 is K'ang-hsi, a benevolent emperor who reminds one of a cross between Augustine and Thomas Jefferson. K'ang-hsi was born at a critical time in the history of the Manchu regime; the fallen Ming loyalists, a bad crowd, were still hiding in small numbers in the Hunan and the Ming eunuchs of the Office of Household were still, sadly, influential. K'ang-hsi was born in the Forbidden City of Peking, was passed to the Imperial throne in 1661, and was not yet seven years old. The government was not in the hands of this boy but rather was trusted to some villainous Manchu courtiers, the most powerful of whom was Oboi, the dictator. At fifteen, K'ang-hsi with the aid of the Grand Dowager Empress and a roomful of boy wrestlers succeeded in arresting the monster Oboi. K'ang-hsi now set about radical tax reforms, becoming a much loved figure in the eyes of the peasants. K'ang-hsi respected the Confucianists, had an interest in many religions, and adored the arts and education. He was a revered figure in Pound's early personal mythology, a representative of imperial enlightenment—it is K'ang-hsi and not Mussolini, as has been argued, who is the adored personage of this canto.

But what of my mystery? What brought K'ang-hsi to the landscape of this canto in 1700? It was K'ang-hsi who took the huge province of Hu-kuang and broke it ("A light moves on the north sky line./...A light moves on the south sky line"); he broke Hu-Kuang into two smaller provinces, the Hupeh (north of the lakes and the Yang-tze) and the Hunan (south of the lakes and the Yang-tze). The Hupeh is several hundred miles to the north of the scenes from our Chinese picture book. It has short but very rigorous winters. It has a hilly lake district. After dividing the Hu-kuang the Emperor, K'ang-hsi, visited (circa 1700) numerous remote towns in the Hupeh. The demarcation was solemnized and the Tsing had come to these hill lakes.

The ancient historian Ssu-ma Ch'ien wrote of the people of the Hupeh region: their children collect crayfish, the land is tilled by fire and hoed with rain—they are self-sufficient with the wild cinnamon. These are the ancestors of the people of my mystery village. They lived on either side of the river Han Shui, the second largest river in the Hupeh. And, friends, on either side of this river is a constellation of seven lakes.

****

But why do I insist on a reality of place for this poem? I believe Pound scholarship continues in its indulgence of this canto by ignoring the value of stanzas seven through nine. The reality of place is important because this is a poem of harsh realities raised only by the beauty of a very cold season. The Pound scholars find the arrival of Tsing a shattering moment in the next to the last line of the sixth stanza—most say it is a sobering moment that breaks the charm of the poem's pastoral imagery while returning us to the Twentieth Century—in fact, it is the beginning of a wild, eccentric exordium. Now, that moment of the poem was so difficult for me in my youth that I stopped learning the canto in consecutive stanzas and jumped to the orphic benediction that closes the poem. But as troubling as the sixth stanza is for people, it is only so because we failed to go on to the seventh stanza while knowing what Pound knew. The sixth stanza opens or passes logically to the seventh stanza of public works:

> State by creating riches shd. thereby get into debt?
> This is infamy; this is Geryon.
> This canal goes still to TenShi
> though the old king built it for pleasure.

Here we have the familiar usury obsession. Geryon is the monster who symbolizes fraud in the eighth circle of Dante's Hell. He is also a double for the old king who builds for mere pleasure. The old king is not a benevolent figure, though some scholars have taken him for just that. The last of the Sui Dynasty emperors, he reached the throne by assassinating his father and brother. He set about ornamental public works that left the people starvelings. He began a building program that would have exhausted the combined talents of Moses and Albert Speer. He weighed property taxes against landless peasants; some of this money was diverted to Taoist alchemists to create an elixir to extend his life. Pound knew this, and had little use for the Emperor, Sui Yang Ti, and even less use for the slither of his Taozers. (It is silly by the way to study this canto simply in terms of Taoist contentment—this is a poem of opposing yet reconciled beliefs, a poem of synizesis.) Anyway, the spendthrift ruler, Sui Yang Ti, built canals in the Hupeh region; they were poorly constructed and would only support vessels of three feet draft. But a future emperor dredged these canals, making them a renewed source of pleasure while making them a profound conveyance for commerce. This new king was none other than the Emperor K'ang-hsi, our paradigm of imperial function who is introduced in the previous stanza. Mere beauty is not enough for this canto—Pound scholars rightly suggest that this poem carries the notion that the best things in life are both free and aesthetically pleasing, but the poem is weighted equally with another familiar and sobering Confucianist notion: the necessary things of life are rarely free and are obtained only through a difficult and ennobling struggle with the natural world.

Once K'ang-hsi has been introduced to the poem at the end of the sixth stanza, we must only wait for the second shoe to drop. This sounds like a mistake in protocol, for we are in Pound's world of juxtaposition without copula, floating with a broken fantasia of tetrameter lines. But there is no mistake—the new king enters the poem of lights with an escort of major cardinal lights; the old king enters the poem already shamed in the procession by who precedes him, the disgusting three-bodied monster Geryon who had his cattle seized by the Greek wonder, Heracles. The old king, Sui Yang Ti, was similarly undone by an unlucky but large-hearted Korean prince in the last year of his reign.

****

Stanzas eight and nine are interesting similarly and are also misunderstood. The eighth stanza is a romanization of the Japanese pronunciations for a poem by the ancient Chinese Emperor Shun (2254-05 B.C.) who belongs to the exquisite, painted pottery culture. He is a benign shadow of K'ang-hsi. Why is his poem, which Pound found in the Fenollosa notebooks, left untranslated? It is suggested that this is done to estrange us, in the Twentieth Century, from the harmonious pastoralisms of a lost, now conjured time. Almost the same mistake we made about the difficult *came Tsing to these hill lakes.* Neither moment is meant to alienate the reader; just the opposite, they beckon. To explain I must go on to the ninth stanza which is a peasant song Pound found translated, once again in the Fenollosa notebooks.

> Sun up; work
> sundown; to rest
> dig well and drink of the water
> dig field; eat of the grain
> Imperial power is? and to us what is it?

Again, why is the previous stanza, Emperor Shun's poem, left untranslated? Because it stands for divine wisdom, for breeding archetypes of imperial ministry that combine with the mysterious movements of sun and moon, things we can never understand. But, yet, the eighth stanza *is* translated to a vulgar plane where we can understand joyfully, quietly through the peasant song of the ninth stanza with its simple ordeals and its sunset and inevitable moonrise. What is imperial power to us, the whole canto makes it clear: it is accords of humility, surrender and peace, orderliness, hard work and value.

Most epiphanies are concealed in grim or mundane realities. The confucianist notion of the imperial is after all an emperor who is not divine himself; his divinity depends on the proper performance of his duties. This translates to our plane of existence in the two material forces (Yin/Yang) and in the five agents (metal, wood, fire, water and earth). Principle or value are the laws of nature, nature is, well...just the fact, nature.

I have left Pound's irascibility out of my discussion, for gratefully I find little of it here, only perhaps the fantasy of the two stray sparks of geography: *Sai Yin* which is a revery for a southern county in coastal China and *TenShi* which refers to the old western lake that represents the exhaustion of the Yang-tze. They are not important. What is important, and one of the more astonishing things about this canto, is the leap from the 1928 translations of the poems in the picture book to the 1937 fragments that cohere making the first six stanzas. With some ambitious tinkering great reversals are achieved: we go from images of spring to images threatening winter, from a prosperous region south of the lakes to an unlikely region north of the lakes, from a bucolic Tao to a sober Neo-confucianism, to utter stillness. The unflinching artistry of these translations, or reversals, is part of the experience and knowledge of the poem though it is not at all a weight borne by the text.

****

But now we come to the benediction: we come into the *sere and yellow* of the last lines of the canto.

> The fourth; the dimension of stillness.
> And the power over wild beasts.

What about the fourth dimension and its still point and is it resonant with the seven lakes in Chinese philosophy? The septenary *is* resonant, is known through the directions of space of which there are seven: two opposite directions for each dimension, plus the still center which is often accepted as a dimension in and of itself—*it is therefore, the fourth and transcendent.* Seven is sacred to the Chinese for there are seven colors; seven foods to be gathered in the field; there are seven possible landscapes; the seven planets; and the most desirable of amulets is the lotus with its seven leaves. Also, seven is empty in the contemplative sense, as with the river of this canto's opening two lines.

K'ang-hsi once remarked that it is impossible not to find the world evil, but that it is a waste of time to do so. Pound came to the dimension of stillness in his self-enforced silence of the later years. In the Chinese picture books the seasons run most often from spring to winter but winter is not just the fourth season. It is also, I believe, the fourth dimension of stillness, where the beasts sleep and man sleeps or is unhurried. And for the Chinese, especially for the people of a poor region like Hupeh, it was a time for stillbirths, madness and famine. But it was not to be feared if you were in accord with it. And its overture was the lovely minimal music of this canto's first six stanzas: the music of bamboo, cinnamon spikes, and the dark rooks taking flight.

CANTO LXXIX

M oon, cloud, tower, a patch of the battistero
                                all of a whiteness,
        dirt pile as per the Del Cossa inset
think not that you wd/ gain if their least caress
were faded from my mind
I had not loved thee half so well
Loved I not womankind"
                        So Salzburg reopens
        lit a flame in my thought that the years
                Amari—li   Am—ar—i—li!
and her hair gone white   from the loss of him
        and she not yet thirty.
On her wedding day and then thus, for the next time,
        at the Spielhaus,
        . . . might have been two years later.
Or Astafieva inside the street doors of the Wigmore
                        and wd/ not have known her
        undoubtedly wd/ have put in the cart)
present Mr G. Scott whistling Lili Marlene
        with positively less musical talent
        than that of any other man of colour
                whom I have ever encountered
but with bonhomie and good humour
                (to Goedel in memoriam)
Sleek head that saved me out of one chaos
and I hear that G. P. has salmoned thru all of it.
Où sont? and who will come to the surface?
And Pétain not to be murdered   14 to 13
                after six hours' discussion
Indubitably, indubitably re/ Scott
                I like a certain number of shades in my landscape
as per/ "doan' tell no one I made you that table"
or Whiteside:
                "ah certainly dew lak dawgs,
                ah goin' tuh wash you"
(no, not to the author, to the canine unwilling in question)
                with 8 birds on a wire
or rather on 3 wires, Mr Allingham
The new Bechstein is electric
and the lark squawk has passed out of season
whereas the sight of a good nigger is cheering

the bad'uns wont look you straight
Guard's cap quattrocento passes *a cavallo*
   on horseback thru landscape Cosimo Tura
      or, as some think, Del Cossa;
up stream to delouse and down stream for the same purpose
seaward
different lice live in different waters
some minds take pleasure in counterpoint
      pleasure in counterpoint
and the later Beethoven on the new Bechstein,
or in the Piazza S. Marco for example
finds a certain concordance of size
      not in the concert hall;
can that be the papal major sweatin' it out to the bumm drum?
what castrum romanum, what
      "went into winter quarters"
is under us?
as the young horse whinnies against the tubas
      in contending for certain values
(Janequin per esempio, and Orazio Vechii or Bronzino)
Greek rascality against Hagoromo
    Kumasaka vs/ vulgarity
       no sooner out of Troas
than the damn fools attacked Ismarus of the Cicones
    4 birds on 3 wires, one bird on one
the imprint of the intaglio depends
    in part on what is pressed under it
the mould must hold what is poured into it
        in

       discourse
          what matters is
to get it across e poi basta
    5 of 'em now on 2;
    on 3; 7 on 4

       thus what's his name
and the change in writing the song books
    5 on 3   aulentissima rosa fresca
so they have left the upper church at Assisi
    but the Goncourt shed certain light on the
french revolution
    "paak you djeep oveh there"
the bacon-rind banner alias the Washington arms
    floats over against Ugolino

in San Stefano dei Cavalieri
        God bless the Constitution
and *save* it
        "the value thereof"
        that is the crux of the matter
and god damn the perverters
        and if Attlee attempts a Ramsey
"Leave the Duke, go for the gold"
        "in less than a geological epoch"
and the Fleet that triumphed at Salamis
and Wilkes's fixed the price per loaf
ἦθος
        Athene cd/ have done with more sex appeal
caesia oculi
"Pardon me, γλαύξ"
                ("Leave it, I'm not a fool")
mah?
        "The price is three altars, multa."
        "paak you djeep oveh there."
                                2 on 2
what's the name of that bastard? D'Arezzo, Gui d'Arezzo
notation
                3 on 3
                chiacchierona   the yellow bird
        to rest   3 months in bottle
                                (auctor)
by the two breasts of Tellus
        Bless my buttons, a staff car/
si come avesse l'inferno in gran dispitto
Capanaeus
        with 6 on 3, swallow-tails
as from the breasts of Helen, a cup of white gold
2 cups for three altars. Tellus γέα feconda
        "each one in the name of its god"
        mint, thyme and basilicum,
the young horse whinnies against the sound of the bumm band;
to that 'gadgett,' and to the production and the slaughter
(on both sides) in memoriam
"Hell! don't they get a break for the whistle?"
        and if the court be not the centre of learning . . .
in short the snot of pejorocracy . . .
                tinsel gilded
of fat fussy old woman

and fat snorty old stallions
    "half dead at the top"
My dear William B. Y. your ½ was too moderate
"pragmatic pig" (if goyim) will serve for 2 thirds of it
to say nothing of the investment of funds in the Yu-en-mi
and similar ventures
    small arms 'n' chemicals
whereas Mr Keith comes nearest to Donatello's
            O Lynx, my love, my lovely lynx,
            Keep watch over my wine pot,
            Guard close my mountain still
            Till the god come into this whiskey.
        Manitou, god of lynxes, remember our corn.
        Khardas, god of camels
            what the deuce are you doing here?
        I beg your pardon . . .
        "Prepare to go on a journey."
            "I . . ."

            "Prepare to go on a journey."
or to count sheep in Phoenician,
            How is it far if you think of it?
So they said to Lidya: no, your body-guard is not the
                town executioner
the executioner is not here for the moment
the fellow who rides beside your coachman
            is just a cossak who executes . . .
        Which being the case, her holding dear H. J.
        (Mr. James, Henry) literally by the button-hole . . .
    in those so consecrated surroundings
                    (a garden in the Temple, no less)
                    and saying, *for once*, the right thing
namely: "Cher maître"
to his chequed waistcoat, the Princess Bariatinsky,
as the fish-tails said to Odysseus, ἐνὶ Τ ροίῃ,

        The moon has a swollen cheek
and when the morning sun lit up the shelves and battalions
of the West, cloud over cloud
                    Old Ez folded his blankets
Neither Eos nor Hesperus has suffered wrong at my hands

        O Lynx, wake Silenus and Casey

<pre>
                    shake the castagnettes of the bassarids,
     the mountain forest is full of light
               the tree-comb red-gilded
     Who sleeps in the field of lynxes
                    in the orchard of Maelids?
     (with great blue marble eyes
               "because he likes to," the cossak)
     Salazar, Scott, Dawley on sick call
                    Polk, Tyler, half the presidents and Calhoun
     "Retaliate on the capitalists" sd/ Calhoun "of the North"
     ah yes, when the ideas were clearer
               debts to people in N. Y. city
               and on the hill of the Maelids
     in the close garden of Venus
                         asleep amid serried lynxes
     set wreathes on Priapus Ιακχος, Io! Κύθηρα, Io!
                         having root in the equities
     Io!
               and you can make 5000 dollars a year
     all you have to do is to make one trip up country
     then come back to Shanghai
                         and send in an annual report
     as to the number of converts
                         Sweetland on sick call
                    ἐλέησον   Kyrie eleison
               each under his fig tree
               or with the smell of fig leaves burning
     so shd/ be fire in winter
     with fig wood, with cedar, and pine burrs

               O Lynx keep watch on my fire.

     So Astafieva had conserved the tradition
     From Byzance and before then
                    Manitou remember this fire
     O lynx, keep the phylloxera from my grape vines
     Ιακχε, Ιακχε, Χαῖρε, AOI
                    "Eat of it not in the under world"
                    See that the sun or the moon bless thy eating
     Κόρη, Κόρη, for the six seeds of an error
     or that the stars bless thy eating
                    O Lynx, guard this orchard,
                    Keep from Demeter's furrow
</pre>

This fruit has a fire within it,
                    Pomona, Pomona
No glass is clearer than are the globes of this flame
what sea is clearer than the pomegranate body
            holding the flame?
                    Pomona, Pomona,

            Lynx, keep watch on this orchard
            That is named Melagrana
or the Pomegranate field
            The sea is not clearer in azure
            Nor the Heliads bringing light

            Here are lynxes   Here are lynxes,
            Is there a sound in the forest
                        of pard or of bassarid
      or crotale   or of leaves moving?

                    Cythera, here are lynxes
Will the scrub-oak burst into flower?
            There is a rose vine in this underbrush
Red? white? No, but a colour between them
            When the pomegranate is open and the light falls
half thru it

            Lynx, beware of these vine-thorns
            O Lynx, γλαυκῶπις coming up from the olive yards,
            Kuthera, here are Lynxes and the clicking of crotales
There is a stir of dust from old leaves
            Will you trade roses for acorns
            Will lynxes eat thorn leaves?
            What have you in that wine jar?
                    ιχώρ, for lynxes?

Maelid and bassarid among lynxes;
            how many? There are more under the oak trees,
We are here waiting the sun-rise
            and the next sunrise
for three nights amid lynxes. For three nights
            of the oak-wood
and the vines are thick in their branches
            no vine lacking flower,
no lynx lacking a flower rope

no Maelid minus a wine jar
this forest is named Melagrana

O lynx, keep the edge on my cider
Keep it clear without cloud

We have lain here amid kalicanthus and sword-flower
        The heliads are caught in wild rose vine
The smell of pine mingles with rose leaves
        O lynx, be many
        of spotted fur and sharp ears.
        O lynx, have your eyes gone yellow,
        with spotted fur and sharp ears?

Therein is the dance of the bassarids
        Therein are centaurs
And now Priapus with Faunus
        The Graces have brought Ἀφροδίτην
        Her cell is drawn by ten leopards
                O lynx, guard my vineyard
                As the grape swells under vine leaf
                "Ἤλιος is come to our mountain
                there is a red glow in the carpet of pine spikes

                O lynx, guard my vineyard
                As the grape swells under vine leaf

                This Goddess was born of sea-foam
                She is lighter than air under Hesperus
                    δεινὰ εἶ, Κύθηρα
                terrible in resistance
                    Κόρη καὶ Δήλια καὶ Μαῖα
                trine as praeludio
                    Κύπρις Ἀφρόδιτη
                a petal lighter than sea-foam
                    Κύθηρα
                                aram
                                nemus
                                vult

O puma, sacred to Hermes, Cimbica servant of Helios.

Carol Muske

ALBA LXXIX

Hilda Doolittle, who was always Pound-foolish, liked to think that the Pisan canto, LXXIX, which begins, "Moon, cloud, tower...," was written for her. The image of the lynx, which Pound employs in the poem, suggested herself to H.D. She bore, as her biographer Barbara Guest points out, a discernable physical resemblance to the cat. She coupled this, as evidence, with the fact that Pound's lifelong nickname for her was "Dryad." Dryads aren't lynxes, after all, but both possess *sagesse*, the natural smarts of beast and nymph. Somehow, sagesse did not prevent H.D. from reading herself unbidden into the text. Her sense of the mythic differed from Pound's in one crucial aspect. Her sense of deific determinism was personal, her private pantheon peopled with gods who were a lot like herself and her friends. Pound's mythos flowed from the opposite sense of the sacred: divine standards absorbed the personal and exacted homage of it—and Pound was nothing if not a worshipper.

In LXXIX, in fact, Pound *is* on the trail of a woman, but not, I believe, a personal memory of a mortal woman. Instead, he courts his familiar Provençal Lady, the Lady who was an idea, a metaphor: light-as-wisdom. It is poignant to the reader of the cantos to observe that as Pound lost personal and public power, as his morality was questioned in a national court, he clung to, in fact intensified, his belief in the pure salvation of this metaphor.

And as his swashbuckling joy in his personae of the past diminished, The Lady stood by him—and even as he spoke finally of "an old bitch gone in the teeth, a botched civilization"—he stood by The Lady.

In the canto in question, he is "Ez," as close as he comes to a public "self-voice." He is no longer Bertran de Born, Arnaut Daniel, Odysseus, Sextus Propertius or the Seafarer Bard. In this one, he is Ezra Pound, traitor, in a tiger cage, on view like an animal in the U.S. Army Detention Center in the village of Metato, north of Pisa. He could smell the sea. His concrete-floored cell was open to the sky.

What is most amazing to me about LXXIX is that it consists entirely of *counterpoint*. The major "harmony" is (necessarily) only implied and it is a grim sound, or lack of: the unrelenting silence of enforced solitude. He got the tone precisely right—the thoughts of all prisoners are contrapuntal. In prison, the present is stuck in the present, like a needle stuck in a groove. To "hear" it unremittingly is madness.

And "Ez" is not mad, he clings to sanity by establishing the poem emphatically in the temporal. (Though not the temporal of clocks and watches, he has neither—he is acutely aware of skytime.) It is night-coming-on-morning (moon, cloud, tower), he busily compares a camp obstacle fence to a

Francesco del Cossa inset panel, he paraphrases Lovelace, he "sings" a song composed by one of the inventors of opera, he thinks of Mozart's wife, of Serafina Astafieva, of William Carlos Williams, he provides an ugly bit of blackface—then a guard's cap "quattrocento passes *a cavallo*."

Then he says it outright: *some minds take pleasure in counterpoint.* Then, with irresistible, other-shoe-falling irony, he repeats it: "pleasure in counterpoint."

He notices the birds on the wires above. His observations of their lightings forms a visual contrapuntal. They flock and disperse like notes on a staff. "Lark squawk out of season" is a sad nod to Provençal and also calls up his thoughts in 1911 on Arnaut's realism, oddly apt now: "no gardens where three birds sing on every bough." A young horse whinnies against the off-key tuning of a band: "4 birds on 3 wires, one bird on one...," it goes on. The mind forcing itself to compose its silent music, like the shifting background of birds against sky—*in the sequence of the musical phrase, not the metronome.* The metronome insists on the present, its mindless tock emptying the universe of import. No. A form must be found that will *hold*, will suffice to enclose this experience in meaning. "The mould must hold what is poured in it." And as Cavalcanti: "Thought cuts through thought with a clean edge. "

The birds group and re-group and Pound reflects that the Americans, bombing their way through Italy, have "left the upper church at Assisi." The sense of upper church, rose windows, rose light, gives us the first hint that this canto is an aubade. As a staff car pulls up by "the two breasts of Tellus" (Helen), as he calls the mountains in his view, the sky opens majestically behind the jostling assemblage of his thoughts. And then the poem turns toward a great dawn-song (the section H.D. wished most to claim), the litany-invocation of the Muse that begins, "O Lynx, my love, my lovely lynx...."

Pound counted on a lynx being a lynx in the poem and a manifestation of a divine presence in nature. It mattered that the light-colored cat with the pale blinking eyes evokes both the Greek "leukos" and ηειδδεξυ, "to see." "To see," any reference at all to eyes in the cantos is a segue to the Lady. Usually to Aphrodite, who is known by the emblem of her eyes in the cantos. But then there are the eyes of Athena, flashing through the leaves. As Pound said in a letter (quoting Allen Upward):

> ...she was the owl-eyed goddess,
> the lightning that blinks like an owl.

The "lightning" is here in the blinking eyes, the counterpoint of darkness, then sudden blinding light, or as the olive leaves, showing their dark side, then their light, then, as Donald Davie has pointed out, *Paradisio* itself, which is jagged, fragmented, *spezzato*:

            but is jagged
For a flash,
                    for an hour.
Then agony,
                    then an hour.
                            (from "Rock Drill," Canto LXXXXII)

When Pound says "Prepare to go on a journey," he is not just being funny,
flip Ulysses. He is saying goodbye to himself, knowing he will never be the
same again. "Ez" will be taken back to the U.S., the country he fled and
which obsessed him through forty years of expatriation—to stand trial for
treason. And then, most certainly, he will be someone else.

The chilling effect of these lines ("Keep watch over my wine pot,/Guard
close my mountain still"), despite the lulling beauty of the language, goes
straight to the bone. He uses the image of the mountain still (a filling vat of
moonshine *and* his life's work) which he begs the lynx to guard, "till the god
come into this whiskey."

When will the god come into this whiskey? Pound clearly believed that the
Lady, whose white light stands at the center of the cantos, that the cantos
themselves, would, if not exonerate, explain him. A canto like LXXIX could
certainly have clarified his position, for it shows everything haywire and de-
spicable about his "misunderstandings" (his "misdemeanor" as he called
it)—coupled with his vision of absolute perfection. The desire for divine in-
tervention vibrates through this poem, it goes beyond a prayer, he is confronting the altar boldly. What has he done wrong that the gods cannot make
cohere?

It is not surprising (though certainly disturbing) to next meet Henry James,
and the exiled Princess Bariatinsky, like a mismatched vaudeville team, cast
up in a net of Homeric phrases from a thirty-year-old memory of a garden
party. The half-mad Princess and her terribly polite (heroic) captive share a
truth Pound seizes on in the present. He identifies for one odd second with
the princess. She knows too, what it is to be surrounded by "escorts," "cos-
saks"—by riders, one of whom is not the official executioner, just a soldier
"who executes." Hadn't Pound had a foretaste of his country's style of hands-
on justice? Hadn't he seen it in the camp, inmates shot by "mistake," exoner-
ated in the post-war atmosphere of opprobrium?

Now the moon has a "swollen cheek" (like his own, perhaps, from sleeping on concrete) and when the morning sun begins to light things up, Old Ez
folds his blankets. The prayers to the Lynx go on. The birds on the wire are
no longer setting the rhythm; there is another, rising beat, the momentum of
invocation. As the sun rises and the figwood fires burn, the eyes of the imagination stay on what needs to be guarded, to be "kept" sacred. And as prayer
articulates our dread, Pound's mind worries each vision, refuses to relinquish
it to equivocal language. The litany is ecstasy and it is despair. Much like

Alba, Pound's longtime dream of the dawn of a new American renaissance, the return of the earthly Paradise.)

Now the canto is visually very beautiful. The white of the lynxes and the pomegranate red of the rising sun fill the sky. ("Red? White? No, but a color between them/When the pomegranate is open and light falls half through it.") The underworld, where Persephone may not eat of the pomegranate, is abandoned. The night has seemed half a year long ("we are here waiting the sunrise/and the next sunrise") as nights do among lynxes. And more to come.

One has to imagine the aging panther—scraggly, blood-colored-and-grey beard, green cat eyes (the way he once described Arnaut) standing in his cage-cell, alone, half-mad, with an invisible mental baton. The great cloud orchestra before him, the Heliads before him ("Neither Eos nor Hesperus has suffered wrong at my hands")....

And then Aphrodite steps from the sea-foam, the Goddess arrived, full daylight, negating his presence entirely, what he wanted in the first place. The reader too is left alone with the echoes, left in the simple fact of the physical world, sun up, private trouble.

No H.D. or any other mortal woman, no matter how loyal, can get the sun up. Only the Goddess, the perfect one, his *liaison blanc*—whose eyes on his blinded him, made him bestial, but made him also a demi-god. Paradisio *spezzato*—slipped through the net again, who was he? Standing there for a thousand years in the wink of an eye: old man in a cage, conducting the sunrise.

CANTO CXVI

Came Neptunus
                his mind leaping
                        like dolphins,
These concepts the human mind has attained.
To make Cosmos—
To achieve the possible—
Muss., wrecked for an error,
But the record
                the palimpsest—
a little light
                in great darkness—
cuniculi—
An old "crank" dead in Virginia.
Unprepared young burdened with records,
The vision of the Madonna
                above the cigar butts
                        and over the portal.
"Have made a mass of laws"
                        (muccchio di leggi)
Litterae nihil sanantes
                Justinian's,
a tangle of works unfinished.

I have brought the great ball of crystal;
                who can lift it?
Can you enter the great acorn of light?
                But the beauty is not the madness
Tho' my errors and wrecks lie about me.
And I am not a demigod,
I cannot make it cohere.
If love be not in the house there is nothing.
The voice of famine unheard.
How came beauty against this blackness,
Twice beauty under the elms—
                To be saved by squirrels and bluejays?
                        "plus j'aime le chien"
Ariadne.
        Disney against the metaphysicals,
and Laforgue more than they thought in him,
Spire thanked me in proposito
And I have learned more from Jules

                        (Jules Laforgue) since then
deeps in him,
             and Linnaeus.
                        chi crescerà i nostri—
but about that terzo
             third heaven,
                        that Venere,
again is all "paradiso"
             a nice quiet paradise
                        over the shambles,
and some climbing
             before the take-off
to "see again,"
the verb is "see," not "walk on"
i.e. it coheres all right
             even if my notes do not cohere.
Many errors,
             a little rightness.
to excuse his hell
             and my paradiso.
And as to why they go wrong,
                        thinking of rightness
And as to who will copy this palimpsest?
             al poco giorno
                        ed al gran cerchio d'ombra
But to affirm the gold thread in the pattern
                        (Torcello)
al Vicolo d'oro
             (Tigullio).
To confess wrong without losing rightness:
             Charity I have had sometimes,
                        I cannot make it flow thru.
             A little light, like a rushlight
                        to lead back to splendour.

Charles Wright

IMPROVISATIONS ON POUND

Frankly, I'm not sure it's such a good thing for writers to write "about" other writers, especially those whose work they admire. Such work should be endlessly variable, offering something new with each rereading. Once you write "on" another writer, a certain solidification must necessarily take place, or at the least a necessary narrowing of vision. And at once a certain stratification sets in: you've had your say, you've made your mind up: it's this way, it's read this way. As I say, I resist this. And having said so, I'd like to talk a minute or two about Ezra Pound, who certainly believed the opposite.

****

The world is divided into those who like Pound up to *Mauberley* and those who think his best work comes afterward. *The Cantos* is the landshed—if you like him, he starts there. If you don't, that's where he stops. It's a bit like going to the circus and leaving before the animal acts and the trapeze high flyers come on. The first Cantos I read were *The Pisan Cantos,* in a huge green and white Guandi paperback of poor quality which I loved and have to this day. Before that I had read the Faber *Selected Poems*, which was big medicine for me—the first poet I'd actually read on my own and hadn't been assigned. And one who talked about places I was walking around in, Sirmione, Verona and the others I'd subsequently go to and look at more closely.

****

I remember how it began for me with *The Cantos*. It was one word, *dodici* in *The Pisan Cantos*. The line was *Trattoria degli Apostoli (dodici)*. It referred to a restaurant in Verona, the town I lived in. It came at the end of Canto 74, the first Pisan canto, and the first canto I had ever read. It was a reference I fully understood—it was the most famous restaurant in town—and I think I thought, "If I can understand this one, maybe the others can be tracked down too." And so I began to read them for what they were saying as well as for the music of the lines, the only thing I had responded to before, when he would put on his "poetry" mask and take off his "message" one. From that day I read much farther in it.

****

At Coltano, on the flat Pisan plain at the edge of the great Maremma swamp (disfecemi Maremma), the man swung his arm to the left, pointing out from under the pine trees toward a wide, empty field, golden in the June sun: *I re-pubblicanini* (meaning Fascists, the holdover believers, members of the Republic of Salo) *erano li*. "The Republicans were there." Nothing, of course, remained of 40 years before, nothing was out there but the fierce sunlight. We were standing in front of the building which had served as the headquarters for the American forces, in the shade of the Tuscan pines. "And over there," he gestured, "were the others, officers on one side, soldiers on the other." And that was all. Later, on the pine-bordered road that ran alongside the field where the *repubblicanini* had been kept, I stopped and looked back toward Pisa. Off to the left an Alitalia jet undulated through the heat waves as it moved slowly into take-off position on the new jetway of the Pisa airport. And over the town, the calibrated, steadily symmetrical mass of Monte Pisano (Taishan) rose through the haze, still keeping Lucca from seeing Pisa, as Dante has said, and over which, as Pound repeatedly asserted, were clouds as fine as any in Italy. But not today: not a cloud, not a smudge: only the malarial, faded blue of a scorched June day when one could feel, out in the noon sun, the top of one's head begin to loosen. Later still, of course, we found we had gone to the wrong place. An American prison camp, yes, but Pound had been farther north, near Metato. But the heat was the same, the emptiness was the same, and the sense of everything having come to a bad end was surely the same.

****

It has often been said—and with some truth—that Pound spoke best through another's mask. It is a fact that *The Cantos* has many personae and many voices. It is also interesting that the one section which has little, if any, ventriloquism is *The Pisan Cantos*, written during the time when he was effectively without books (He was translating Confucius, true, at the same time, and had Legge's Chinese-English dictionary, but that was a different project altogether; and he did have a Bible and an anthology of English verse). This remains my favorite section, where he speaks with his own voice and about things that are around him in the natural world and about those things he remembers. Always as EP, however, always as Old Ez out of his own despair and affirmation and not out of anyone else's mouth.

****

The Cantos is essentially mystic/religious: Greek/Roman, Troubadour/Condottiere influence giving way to a strange Confucian/Dantescan (both "reflectors" of light) orthodoxy. (No Dualism in Confucius: the arrow doesn't have two heads. Nor in Dante.) They are laced with The Mysteries ("The gods have not returned, they never left." "Eternal states of mind," he called

them) and American Transcendental ethics. Confucius becomes the main religious thread—the good man, the good state, the man standing by his word.
Mencius quotes Tsang as saying after Confucius' death: "Washed in the
Kang and the Han, bleached in the autumn's sun's slope, what whiteness can
one add to that whiteness, what candor?" A Confucian when he died, apparently still a believer in the Greek gods, he was buried in a Catholic cemetery
(*Reparto Evangelici*) by an Anglican priest after an ecumenical service. Layers within layers past the end.

****

I think Pound to be the most American of poets, especially of his time, including Williams. American of a certain, unflagging sort: more European
than the Europeans, more concerned about their heritage than they were.
Like Berenson. But with such a Twainian "innocence abroad." His poetic line
ends up a broken Whitmanian line and he remains totally American to the
end: paranoid, in a "white study."

****

As in the Mysteries of Eleusis, not too much should be revealed—wonder
and awe must reside always in partial obscurity. Thus the core of *The Cantos*
remains: unresolved, unexplainable. Unfinished, hardly ever revised, the
parts trailed along for almost 50 years until a comprehensive revision, even
had they ever been finished, was out of the question. Analogies to music,
painting, ancient and medieval story lines, associational blocks of information, etc., all exist but do not satisfy completely. The poem was never finished, thus it has no Final Form. Which is all right as far as I'm concerned,
the sum of the parts adding up to more than the whole. Since the *Metamorphoses*, the book of changing forms, was one of the formal icons of *The Cantos*, how can one be surprised that the poem keeps shifting under our very
eyes and resists all efforts at formal declension?: seen from this angle, it's
this, seen from another it's that? Its *only* constant seems its inconstancy. The
gods are capricious: we do the best we can with what we've got to wrestle
some order out of a large and overwhelming body of chaos. He never finished the poem, it was abandoned. All his models suited a world-view and
world-order that no longer applied in the 20th century. His final structure
ended up not so much changing and shiftable (as in the *Metamorphoses* and
Divine Comedy) as liquid and uncontainable. If it remains a voyage of discovery to the end, then the emphasis is on *voyage* and not *discovery*. The attempt to make everything coalesce, time and space, to include everything,
past and present and future in one suspended, eternal state, never stopped. Interruptions were there, but probably not in the writer's vision, more likely in

the material itself. If it is an overall "failure," as it probably is, it is the most interesting failure of the century and, to my mind, the most aesthetically pleasing poem, either failed or realized, of the century. Its ultimate formlessness becomes its Ultimate Form. This, as well, is part of the Process: if one of the primary urges of a work of art is to become circular and come to a completion, then one of the real jobs of the artist is to keep this closure from happening so he can work in the synapse, the spark before the end. Surely *The Cantos* accomplished this and continues to be Process and part of The Way (Confucius) even after it has stopped. Heracleitean to the end. His Paradiso is a collection of notes, in shorthand, elliptical. One of the few "sustained" fragments is Canto CXVI.

****

If the overriding poetic consideration is one of form, then one of the great thrusts of *The Cantos* is the search—unsuccessful—for Major Form. CXVI is the admission that it has not succeeded, at least not on the page. It is the broken shadow, *spezzata*, of the ideal form he saw in the air, or thought he saw, for 50 years. He foundered on his own Paradiso: in periplum, where the winds took him, not an orderly Dantescan rising. And they did not take him to Dioce, the city whose terraces were the color of stars, ideal city, though he thought he knew where it was.

****

Canto CXVI, lines 23-26: light, order and beauty: main threads being pulled together: *attempt* to pull them together by naming them. Some considerations: the great ball of crystal and the acorn of light are the two symbolic points toward which the poem has been leading us. Crystal is the image of paradisal clarity. He calls on the meanings of crystal as structural mineral formed through the evaporation of water, as highly transparent cut glass and as synonym for eyes. The succession of fire/light/crystal suggests how crystal synthesizes the aspects of the sun and moon, the total light process, the intelligence. The Chinese ideogram for the intelligence: "the sun and the moon, the total light process, the radiation, reflection and reception of light," though not in this canto, is alluded to throughout the poem. Some further considerations: the acorn of light and Grosseteste, one of the medieval, Generation of Light philosophers Pound had been interested in since his Cavalcanti days: "Light shines in all directions so that a point of light will at once become a sphere of light of any size unless curbed by some opaque object." Also, in Paradiso 28, Dante sees the point of pure light which is God reflected in Beatrice's eyes—it shines from the Empyrean through the Crystalline Heaven of the Primum Mobile. In lines 53-54, Dante and light come in again with the explanation of the verb "to see": i.e., you see Paradise, you don't walk on it (Also "see again" may allude to the last words of the *Inferno, reveder le stelle.* Or it could be when Dante is blinded in Paradise when he looks at St John to see if he has been taken up in the body: his sight is restored and he sees Adam...). And then the final allusion in the last two lines of the canto: "A little light, like a rush light/to lead back to splendour." (Splendour has been tangentially alluded to before in line 29—"I cannot make it cohere"—which reference may be to *Women of Trachis* where Pound has Herakles say: "Splendour, it all coheres.") In lines 8-11, Pound has talked of "the record/the palimpsest—/a little light/in great darkness—": is this then it, the record, the poem, his palimpsest of history, a small light, etc.? Is splendour Pound's imagination? Paradise? Is it the Manichean splendor of the One Light? Scotus Eregina's light? Grossteste's? Dante's? The divine spark in man where everything is one and everything is fire/Heraclitus at the beginning of all things (and at the end)?

A last consideration: this is Pound's gloss on a passage from Richard of St Victor: "They are ineffable and innumerable and no man having beheld them can fittingly narrate them or even remember them exactly. Nevertheless, by naming over all the most beautiful things we know we may draw back upon the mind some vestige of the heavenly splendour."

****

There are, of course, references to other continuing preoccupations throughout the poem in this last finished canto (the last if one discounts 120, as one is often tempted to do since it seems an addendum rather than a culmination): the unwillingness to release Mussolini, his chosen figurehead for the new state and ideal system, wrecked because of a bunch of laws (*mucchio di leggi*)—the error of not bringing order to himself, thus not being able to create order about him (Confucius, Canto 13); the wreckage of his own poem, his own errors, out of which he continually hands forth his "notes," as he calls his work; the continued insistence on love as the guiding principle in all things; his assertion that there is a coherence in history, in the flow of civilization, even if his poem doesn't cohere, that there is a gold thread in the pattern, that he is right to have tried to follow it wherever it led him, even if he did not get back to the splendor of total order and beauty and harmony inherent in the universe.

****

As postscript: 8 August, 1985, I drove to the Padua train station and caught the 9:54 Milan-Venice train. On arrival in Venice, I took the vaporetto to Rialto, got off and walked in the direction of the Fondamente Nuove, where one catches the boat to Murano, Torcello and San Michele, the cemetery island. Along the way I stopped at the church of S. Maria dei Miracoli, a Renaissance church built in the 1480s and much admired by Pound, especially its marble carvings, up near the apse, by Pietro Lombardo, and especially still, several of their delicate mermaids and putti. I admire them myself, and a toothed dolphin around one corner as well. Later, on the boat, the sky was that summer blue-white of washed-out denim, the green swells like marble in their sheen. The grave was easily found and is obviously visited often, though I was alone during my entire visit. A circular plot of ivy and grass with a small tree at the back (laurel?): a simple marble slab reads EZRA POUND. Section XV, mostly foreigners—English and German. The most interesting inscription belonged to one Archibald Campbell, master of the SY Minerva, who died on board in 1891 at the age of 56: "The heart knoweth its own bitterness and the Stranger intermeddleth not therewith." I walked back to the Pound grave, wanting to leave something, and at last took a eucalyptus pip I had carried in my jacket pocket for years and placed it flat side down in the middle of the O in POUND, a coin for a closed eye, and left.

As addendum to the postscript: Later, sitting on the Zattere, I had lunch (close to the Rio S. Trovaso) with the critic David Kalstone. He told me a little story about the only time he had met Pound. They had been sitting outside having coffee after supper, he and Pound and Olga Rudge and the sculptor Joan Fitzgerald. The only light seemed to gather on Pound's hands, he said, everything else and everyone else in a kind of elusive, watery darkness, and throughout the time they sat there—while Pound apparently spoke, but inaudibly, his comments being repeated each time by Olga Rudge—Pound kept scratching at the back of one hand with the nails of the other, clawing almost, over and over, as though to rid himself of something: only the hands obsessively scratching in the artificial light, the voice inaudible and sibylline.

MARIANNE MOORE
(1887-1972)

One of the most original and idiosyncratic poets of her age, Marianne Moore has always been more respectfully regarded than widely read. An exceptionally private individual, she nevertheless became well-known in her later decades as an eccentric in a tricorn hat who wrote about animals and cheered for the Brooklyn Dodgers. In the 1920s she was associated with other young writers and artists in avant-garde New York, and began to produce highly experimental, often satirical, densely allusive poems. Having majored in biology at Bryn Mawr, Moore brought a scientific precision and detachment to her writing; the overwhelming impression is of her indomitable curiosity about the world and its multiplicity, and of her scrupulous accuracy in presenting it. A magpie who collected quotations from a wide variety of sources from the erudite to the frivolous, she then assembled them into collages highly unstable in their opposing voices and elusive points of view. Her 1935 *Selected Poems* probably represents the high point of her achievement; while she was to go on to write other fine poems, a moral earnestness and conventionality began to dilute the fierce experiments of her earlier work. More alarmingly, Moore obsessively cut and revised her early poems for subsequent editions, so that at present the original, and in most cases superior, versions are no longer in print. In Moore's best work, the playful, beautifully articulated attention to the surfaces of things becomes the way to moral sense; the exercise of peculiarity signals a keenly individuated human presence.

BOOKS: *Complete Poems*, ed. Clive E. Driver (1967, 1981); *Complete Prose*, ed. Patricia C. Willis (1986); *Selected Letters of Marianne Moore*, ed. Bonnie Costello et al. (1997).

THE STEEPLE-JACK

Dürer would have seen a reason for living
        in a town like this, with eight stranded whales
to look at; with the sweet sea air coming into your house
on a fine day, from water etched
        with waves as formal as the scales
on a fish.

One by one in two's and three's, the seagulls keep
        flying back and forth over the town clock,
or sailing around the lighthouse without moving their wings—
rising steadily with a slight
        quiver of the body—or flock
mewing where

a sea the purple of the peacock's neck is
        paled to greenish azure as Dürer changed
the pine green of the Tyrol to peacock blue and guinea
gray. You can see a twenty-five-
        pound lobster; and fish nets arranged
to dry. The

whirlwind fife-and-drum of the storm bends the salt
        marsh grass, disturbs stars in the sky and the
star on the steeple; it is a privilege to see so
much confusion. Disguised by what
        might seem the opposite, the sea-
side flowers and

trees are favored by the fog so that you have
        the tropics at first hand: the trumpet-vine,
fox-glove, giant snap-dragon, a salpiglossis that has
spots and stripes; morning-glories, gourds,
        or moon-vines trained on fishing-twine
at the back door;

cat-tails, flags, blueberries and spiderwort,
        striped grass, lichens, sunflowers, asters, daisies—
yellow and crab-claw ragged sailors with green bracts—toad-plant,
petunias, ferns; pink lilies, blue
        ones, tigers; poppies; black sweet-peas.
The climate

is not right for the banyan, frangipani,
      or jack-fruit trees; or for exotic serpent
life. Ring lizard and snake-skin for the foot, if you see fit;
but here they've cats, not cobras, to
      keep down the rats. The diffident
little newt

with white pin-dots on black horizontal spaced-
      out bands lives here; yet there is nothing that
ambition can buy or take away. The college student
named Ambrose sits on the hillside
      with his not-native books and hat
and sees boats

at sea progress white and rigid as if in
      a groove. Liking an elegance of which
the source is not bravado, he knows by heart the antique
sugar-bowl shaped summer-house of
      interlacing slats, and the pitch
of the church

spire, not true, from which a man in scarlet lets
      down a rope as a spider spins a thread;
he might be part of a novel, but on the sidewalk a
sign says C. J. Poole, Steeple-Jack,
      in black and white; and one in red
and white says

Danger. The church portico has four fluted
      columns, each a single piece of stone, made
modester by white-wash. This would be a fit haven for
waifs, children, animals, prisoners,
      and presidents who have repaid
sin-driven

senators by not thinking about them. The
      place has a school-house, a post-office in a
store, fish-houses, hen-houses, a three-masted
      schooner on
the stocks. The hero, the student,
      the steeple-jack, each in his way,
is at home.

It could not be dangerous to be living
in a town like this, of simple people,
who have a steeple-jack placing danger-signs by the church
while he is gilding the solid-
pointed star, which on a steeple
stands for hope.

Lynne McMahon

On "The Steeple-Jack"

"The Steeple-Jack" has few of the signature elements we associate with Marianne Moore's poetry. There are no words we need to look up (the animals and plants are to some degree familiar); there are no arcane facts from engineering manuals or quotations from the National Museum's Curator of Reptiles. That we know Dürer made a trip to see a beached whale is perhaps less important than our recognition that Dürer's paintings detail a "fascination with the strange in the real" (Bonnie Costello) that is very like the poet's own. That she multiplied the stranded whales by eight makes that vision at once more and less apocalyptic: more because eight whales is a phenomenon that bespeaks a deep disturbance in the sea; less because their being there is noted so casually the scene is almost a cartoon.

And there are other cartoon-like images. The sea, as in a child's drawing, is scalloped with waves "as formal as the scales on a fish." The seagulls fly without moving their wings. Even the storm is only a harmless animated "whirlwind fife-and-drum." And certainly the steeple-jack is something akin to those toy acrobats whose wooden stilts, when pressed, make the tiny figures flip up and over. This toy village cannot be dangerous. And yet something dreadful seems about to happen. Something is gathering itself just outside the margin of the sketch-pad, of the poem, and only the creator can keep it out. Fortunately, that creator is Marianne Moore.

This poem was originally envisioned as the novel portion of a three-tiered poem, "Part of a Novel, Part of a Poem, Part of a Play," and the elements of fiction are evident: the setting, picture-postcard pretty, deceptively serene; the (possible) protagonist, a college student named Ambrose; and the action, a steeple-jack gilding a church star. (This is minimal action, to be sure, but there is a storm brewing, and he could lose his footing.) But these remain only elements, contained in a suspension; these are not novel events and characters carried through time to a climax. In fact, climax is to be avoided at

all costs. There is a fiction being created here, but it's not the one we anticipate. This is the fiction of perfect, even perverse, calm.

A novel in which nothing happens.... Yet in the poem there is a whirl of
images which is itself activity. And "it is a privilege to see so/much confusion"—a privilege because from our vantage point (from above, like the
gods), we see both the things and "what/might seem the opposite." What is
"favored by the fog"—another term for imagination?—has become transformed. We are in New England falling headlong into the tropics, a glory of
flora whose abundance is too much to take in all at once—"cat-tails, flags,
blueberries and spiderwort,/striped grass, lichens, sunflowers, asters,
daisies—." This catalogue is very like the one Keats employs in the middle of
the nightingale ode, the stanza which begins "I cannot see what flowers are at
my feet." Keats lets us see them, however, a mix of trees and flowers which
is an impossibility, for the grass, thicket, fruit-tree wild, white hawthorn,
eglantine, violets and musk roses don't share the same growing season. Keats
collapses time, allows everything to bloom at once, and the cadences of their
names, as well as their various perfumes, sends the poet into a swoon. That's
what happens to us in Marianne Moore's catalogue. As if "yellow and crab-
claw ragged sailors with green bracts" is not enough, we get also "toad-
plant,/petunias, ferns; pink lilies, blue/ones, tigers"; all the way to banyan
and frangipani. This is the action inconceivable in a novel—riotous vegeta-
tion.

But, abruptly, this avalanche is checked. We return to the facts: "here
they've cats, not cobras, to/keep down the rats." What was, for a breathless
three stanzas, a teeming roil, ends in "boats//at sea...white and rigid as if in/a
groove." Why the sudden halt, the stiffened sea, and then description of the
village buildings? Is it perhaps because Ambrose is safer looking at the summer-house he knows by heart ("antique sugar-bowl shaped"), and C. J. Poole
safer atop the spire (though it's tilted, "not true")? The buildings are mundane, after all—school house, post-office, fish-houses, hen-houses—not like
the sea, about to break its rigid delineations; not like the flowers, a carpet of
uncertain magic. The church is a "fit haven for/waifs, children, animals, prisoners,/and presidents who have repaid/sin-driven//senators by not thinking
about them," fit, in short, for all of us. Civilization is salvation, at least for
"simple people,/who have a steeple-jack placing danger-signs by the
church." In this perfect place, perfection is maintained by buildings and by
rigorous distancings. It is ironic, yes, but beneath the irony is the author's serious insistence that it must be so. The sea and its whales must be kept a
child's sketch. The trumpet-vines must not overrun the church. Nature red in
tooth and claw has no place in the town square. And above all the church
must keep its star gilded, that we may not be overwhelmed.

NINE NECTARINES AND OTHER PORCELAIN

Arranged by two's as peaches are,
at intervals that all may live—
    eight and a single one, on twigs that
    grew the year before—they look like
a derivative;
    although not uncommonly
the opposite is seen—
nine peaches on a nectarine.
    Fuzzless through slender crescent leaves
        of green or blue—or both,
        in the Chinese style—the four

    pairs' half-moon leaf-mosaic turns
out to the sun the sprinkled blush
    of puce-American-Beauty pink
    applied to beeswax gray by the
unenquiring brush
    of mercantile bookbinding.
Like the peach *Yu*, the red-
cheeked peach which cannot aid the dead,
    but eaten in time prevents death,
        the Italian peach-
        nut, Persian plum, Ispahan

    secluded wall-grown nectarine,
as wild spontaneous fruit was
    found in China first. But was it wild?
    Prudent de Candolle would not say.
We cannot find flaws
    in this emblematic group
of nine, with leaf window
unquilted by curculio—
    which someone once depicted on
        this much-mended plate; or
        in the also accurate

    unantlered moose, or Iceland horse,
or ass, asleep against the old
    thick, low-leaning nectarine that is the
    colour of the shrub-tree's brownish
flower. From manifold

small boughs, productive as the
magic willow that grew
   above the mother's grave and threw
     on Cinderella what she wished,
       a bat is winging. It
        is a moonlight scene, bringing

     the animal so near, its eyes
are separate from the face—mere
   delicately drawn gray discs, out from
   itself in space. Imperial
happiness lives here
   on the peaches of long life
that make it permanent.
A fungus could have meant
   long life; a crane, a stork, a dove.
     China, with flowers and birds
     and half-beasts, became the land

   of the best china-making first.
Hunts and domestic scenes occur
   in France on dinner-plates, signed on the
   back with a two-finned fish; England
has an officer
   in jack-boots seated in a
bosquet, the cow, the flock
of sheep, the pheasant, the peacock
   sweeping near with lifted claw; the
     skilled peonian rose
     and the rosebud that began

   with William Billingsley (once poor,
like a monkey on a dolphin, tossed
   by Ocean, mighty monster) until
   Josiah Spode adopted him.
Yet with the gold-glossed
   serpent handles, are there green
cocks with 'brown beaks and cheeks
and dark blue combs' and mammal freaks
   that, like the Chinese Certainties
     and sets of Precious Things,
     dare to be conspicuous?

Theirs is a race that 'understands
the spirit of the wilderness'
and the nectarine-loving kylin
of pony appearance—the long-
tailed or the tailless
small cinnamon-brown common
camel-haired unicorn
with antelope feet and no horn,
here enamelled on porcelain.
It was a Chinese who
imagined this masterpiece.

David Walker

IMPERIAL HAPPINESS

> *Their eyes mid many wrinkles, their eyes,*
> *Their ancient, glittering eyes, are gay.*
> Yeats, "Lapis Lazuli"

A reader of "Nine Nectarines" in Marianne Moore's 1967 *Complete Poems* might well be confused, on consulting the explanatory notes in the back of the volume, to be provided the origin of a phrase ("brown beaks and cheeks") that does not appear in the poem. In fact, the notes were written for the poem's appearance in the 1935 *Selected Poems*, where—under the title "Nine Nectarines and Other Porcelain"—the poem is nearly twice as long. The later version includes only the first three and a half stanzas and the final one. "Omissions are not accidents," Moore says pointedly, but in this case (as, I would argue, in many others) her omissions do not serve her well: the revised version is a sadly truncated and, to my mind, much less interesting poem. The original, on the other hand, marvelously exemplifies Moore's difficulties and satisfactions.

Surely the difficulties should not be minimized. The poem is in rhymed syllabics (three pairs of rhymes per stanza, and you have to hunt to find the third), and the intricacy of the form is mirrored in its movement. Restoring the missing forty lines helps clarify the poem's sense of shape; nonetheless, its apparently meandering movement, its skillful use of feint and diversion, the peculiarities of its voice, and its blending of the scrupulously precise and the bewilderingly obtuse—all combine to make the poem puzzling on first reading and then increasingly multilayered on further acquaintance. The fierce, focused attention and patient curiosity that are so clearly present in the poem must be mirrored in the reader if the whole is to mean more than the delicate, fascinating parts. The measure of the poem's modernity is that it cannot be identified as anything other than itself, a playfully unpredictable verbal performance; certainly, for instance, it is not the "description of a painted plate" that at least one critic has taken it for. For one thing, the plate doesn't appear until the end of the third stanza: to read the poem as literal description would be to read Moore as manipulative or simply inept. It's the *words* that matter here, not the plate: the poem is an enacted meditation for which the plate is merely the catalyst.

Like most of Moore's poems of the period, this one begins without a clear sense of dramatic context. The title seems to indicate a still-life, though the questions it raises ("other" porcelain? are these nectarines real or manufactured?) suspend comfortable assumptions, and in fact will reverberate throughout the poem. Moore begins in description, all right, but what exactly is being described, despite the tone of cool, scrupulous precision, is never named directly. The bough of nectarines we are peering at seems an emblem of natural perfection ("at intervals that all may live") and at the same time vaguely unreal ("they look like/a derivative")—and since we soon discover that they are in fact an artistic representation, the ironic play is entirely appropriate. The second half of the first sentence, with its epigrammatic turn (nectarines are to peaches as peaches are to nectarines), is Moore at her most slyly subversive. It's the sort of gesture that sounds merely fussy, overmeticulous (the *live/derivative, seen/nectarine* rhymes enhance the effect), but surely the vaguely Edward-Learish quality (what does it *mean* to claim that nine peaches are not uncommonly seen on a nectarine?) is meant to arouse our suspicion. And the next sentence nudges us further from the realm of horticulture into that of imagination, first as the leaves are described as "green or blue—or both,/in the Chinese style" (does this indicate the observer's uncertainty, her inability to name the color exactly, or have we moved from consideration of the particular to that of the whole genre of nectarine-painting and the options it allows?), and then in that terrific analogy of the fruits' "sprinkled blush" to the pink-and-gray mottle of endpapers.

"Unenquiring" is a striking word for the bookbinder's brush, of course, and it demonstrates how far we are from simple description. The focus of attention here is less the object itself than the act of attention to and representation of that object, as reflected both in the artist who painted the nectarines (still, at this point in the poem, a covert presence) and in the voice that in turn reveals that image to us. As opposed to the "unenquiring brush" of the bookbinder, the artist's brush and the speaker's eye are both highly inquisitive, probing, imaginative. If the voice at first seems almost selflessly precise, it soon reveals itself as actually playful, eccentric, highly intuitive. The poem's aesthetic values have already begun to reveal themselves.

The following passage extends Moore's metaphysical concerns further. Braced by her reading of Alphonse de Candolle's 1886 *Origin of Cultivated Plants* ("According to the word of Chin-noug-king, the peach *Yu* prevents death. If it is not eaten in time it at least preserves the body from decay until the end of the world"), she plays the helpful natural historian while evoking the nature/nurture conundrum that has underscored the poem since the title. This is another of her characteristic strategies: her quotations and elaborate footnotes often make her seem—and this is much like the Eliot of *The Waste Land*—a bit of an obsessive packrat, while in fact nothing is even slightly irrelevant, and every trinket contributes significantly to the design. The question of the relation between the object in nature and its representation in art, between wildness and cultivation, emerges overtly here, as the plate is finally named:

> But was it wild?
> Prudent de Candolle would not say.
> We cannot find flaws
>   in this emblematic group
> of nine, with leaf window
> unquilted by curculio—
>   which someone once depicted on
>   this much-mended plate....

We have moved farther toward the flawless world of artifice ("emblematic," "depicted") here, and given the proximity of "unquilted," we might take "curculio" for a kind of Italian dropstitch. But the poem continues to maintain its curious, complicated balance: curculio is in fact "any of various weevils, especially one that injures fruit," and even though it is absent from the painting, it is very much present in the poem. Even more striking, the plate itself has been damaged and "much-mended"; the fact that the representation of perfection is itself subject to the vagaries of accident gets us very close to the poem's thematic center. Like "the peach *Yu*" whose magical properties depend on its being eaten "in time," the meaning of the poised perfection of the nectarines depends on their being seen in relation to the natural world.

The next passage widens the lens; what before seemed a detached bough now appears as a detail in a landscape that also includes...well, what exactly is that animal?..."the also accurate/unantlered moose, or Iceland horse,/or ass, asleep against the old/thick, low-leaning nectarine that is the/colour of the shrub-tree's brownish/flower." The moose/horse/ass uncertainty mirrors the earlier green/blue/both question, and points up the importance of the speaker's position as observer rather than creator: her knowledge may seem encyclopedic, but it is not magisterial. And yet the gently blurred, multiple possibilities indicate a further irony: if the observer can't be sure whether the animal is moose, horse, or ass, how can she claim that its depiction is "accurate"? The earlier meditation on the relation between reality and representation may have suggested an answer, but we must wait for the end of the poem for it to emerge fully.

The extension of the scene is so haunting that one wonders how Moore could have omitted it in her revision:

> From manifold
>   small boughs, productive as the
>   magic willow that grew
> above the mother's grave and threw
>   on Cinderella what she wished,
>   a bat is winging. It
>   is a moonlight scene, bringing
>
>   the animal so near, its eyes
>   are separate from the face—mere
>   delicately drawn gray discs, out from
>   itself in space. Imperial
>   happiness lives here
>   on the peaches of long life
>   that make it permanent.

The reference to Cinderella might at first seem intrusive, yet surely the magic power that fulfills wishes by transcending the grave is a reflection of the same force as the peaches of eternal life. The image itself, it seems, has undergone a transformation: while in the second stanza the nectarines turned "out to the sun," now they are "peaches," and the scene is moonlit. And in that moonlight, the animal that only a stanza earlier seemed sleepy and passive is now spectral, alert, its eyes open and floating out in space. (Grammatically this sentence might seem to refer to the bat, but I tend to think it makes more sense to read it in relation to the still-unidentified animal that is more central to the poem as a whole. In either case, it is the sense of mystery and depth that is important.) The static depicted image has become animated in time and space under the observer's inquiring gaze; its meaning is "imperial/happiness," but only in the moment when it is fully perceived. "A fungus could have meant/long life; a crane, a stork, a dove," we are told: the representation is arbitrary, the symbolic possibilities multiple—and yet under the controlling authority of the artist's imagination, the painting becomes not simply a representation but an image with its own inherent mythic truth.

In an apparent shift of focus, the next two stanzas return us to the "other porcelain" of the title, comparing Chinese ware to that of France and England. This might be taken by the unwary as a digression, but in fact Moore is pursuing her theme relentlessly. The survey of national characteristics becomes a meditation on aesthetics: while France and England present nature in domesticated, codified forms ("the cow, the flock/of sheep, the pheasant, the peacock"), the Chinese indulge in drama, peculiarity, mystery. As in the landscape we have been minutely observing, to "dare to be conspicuous," to cross-breed nature with imagination, is risky, but it is also the source of enormous vitality. The contrast is simply presented without comment, and certainly the English scene is detailed with affectionate humor, but the cumulative weight of the poem leaves no doubt about which tradition Moore chooses to ally herself with. The poem has become a covert manifesto, justifying its own "conspicuous" eccentricities for the peculiar pleasures they may inspire.

And thus the last stanza, whose language seems resolutely objective, may be read as intensely personal. Having indirectly established her affinity with the Chinese, she can maintain her focus while apparently giving herself entirely up to contemplation. The Chinese are "a race that 'understands/the spirit of the wilderness'"—and that spirit is precisely what cannot be captured by literal representation, and what brought the painting mysteriously to life. (Interestingly, "understands/the spirit of the wilderness" is unattributed in the notes: could Moore in fact have invented the quotation in order to further "objectify" her argument?) In mid-sentence the perceiver returns to the painting and effortlessly establishes her total authority: the animal that earlier was only vaguely defined is here precisely named, neither moose or horse but kylin, a Chinese unicorn. Having emerged out of a meditation on the representation of reality, the spectral animal is in fact the representation of the fabulous, "here enamelled on porcelain." The link back to the title emphasizes the poem's central paradox: in capturing "the spirit of the wilderness" as figured by the kylin, the porcelain plate is an emblem of permanence; at the same time, it is enormously fragile ("much-mended") and entirely dependent on perceivers who can "understand" that spirit sympathetically. The final sentence—"It was a Chinese who/imagined this masterpiece"—might seem anticlimactically flat, unless we recognize the weight of "imagined" in this context. As in Yeats's exactly contemporaneous "Lapis Lazuli," which provides a striking parallel, the meaning of works of art depends on two acts of imagination, that of the artist and that of the audience. To read Moore's poem, we must become conspicuously "Chinese."

A GRAVE

Man looking into the sea,
taking the view from those who have as much right to it as
                                                you have to it yourself,
it is human nature to stand in the middle of a thing,
but you cannot stand in the middle of this;
the sea has nothing to give but a well excavated grave.
The firs stand in a procession, each with an emerald turkey-
                                                foot at the top,

reserved as their contours, saying nothing;
repression, however, is not the most obvious characteristic of
                                                the sea;
the sea is a collector, quick to return a rapacious look.
There are others besides you who have worn that look—
whose expression is no longer a protest; the fish no longer
                                                investigate them
for their bones have not lasted:
men lower nets, unconscious of the fact that they are
                                                desecrating a grave,
and row quickly away—the blades of the oars
moving together like the feet of water-spiders as if there were
                                                no such thing as death.
The wrinkles progress among themselves in a phalanx—
                                beautiful under networks of foam,
and fade breathlessly while the sea rustles in and out of the
                                                seaweed;
the birds swim through the air at top speed, emitting cat-calls
                                                as heretofore—
the tortoise-shell scourges about the feet of the cliffs, in motion
                                                beneath them;
and the ocean, under the pulsation of lighthouses and noise of
                                                bell-buoys,
advances as usual, looking as if it were not that ocean in which
                                dropped things are bound to sink—
in which if they turn and twist, it is neither with volition nor
                                                consciousness.

Barbara Molloy-Olund

MAN—SEA—SILENCE

I've gone everywhere with my speculation on the man of this poem's first line. At a first reading, and after several readings, I still want to know, what is he to the speaker? It seems natural to suppose that his mysterious position at the receiving end of the address in "A Grave," once cracked, would lead things calmly into the lap of some narrative conclusion. If the speaker would only interpret him for us—if she would look down at him maternally, or up at him religiously, or at him squarely as through a memory—then wouldn't the poem's vast metaphor crystallize?

Not really. One problem is that the speaker's tone, like her poem, is not that simple. In the breadth of its subject matter, "A Grave" is capable of living among contradictions without exactly tackling them, and without really resting among them either. The relationship between the man and the speaker might include all or none of the above possibilities. In fact, the poem pushes off from the man immediately, as if to leave me with my speculation, while it proceeds in its unusual and passionate one-sided discussion. However the man moved this speaker at first—a stranger, a tourist, a concept, a God—he is in a poem whose vision is broader than identity (even the sea cannot be named). The identities of man and sea are eschewed rather conspicuously, so that I begin to think I have asked both a wrong and an integral question, the kind a child might ask, such as "what is the sky" or "why do dogs bark"— one whose answer seemed implicit until the question was asked. Finally, I can only know that this man's silence is brazen and impressive, that he stands there increasing the poem's point of view, agitating its narrator, without so much as breathing a word.

There is another interesting silence in this poem, a stillness that separates lines from one another, and which often seems so definite as to be deliberate. It effectively inserts itself in the midst of ongoing thoughts, at the brink of and in the afterward, and sometimes in the middle of them (the enjambments begin to sound like stanzas). Full stops pick up that silence, meticulously punctuated. And yet, sentences seem as fiercely begun in this poem as they are fiercely concluded, as if the breath and space detaining the speaker had as substantial a voice as her own:

> The firs stand in a procession, each with an emerald turkey-
> foot at the top,
> reserved as their contours, saying nothing;
> repression, however, is not the most obvious characteristic of the sea.

I am startled by how tangible the interim is in that shift between the firs and the quick, abstract characterization of the sea. It makes me think of the physical distance between one thought and the next. I feel as though I can hear the writer's mind, there after the semi-colon, clearing a palpable impasse and coming to the other side with as much ambivalence as lights clicking back on after an electrical outage. Like the man's silence, the silence between image, conception and recognition in this poem seems a death of a kind, and concrete in its own right.

If the poem is about death, it is a death that does not prefer human mortality, I think. The fish are not bothered by it or attracted to it, although they could easily be included in its progress. It is a death that moves the poet, and that in her eye, lives back to back with continuity. To her the firs on the water's face are seen as "in a procession," so that even if a funeral likeness is what she imagines, her eye is with the advancement of it all. I am intrigued by the obvious contradictions she perceives as mutual in the grave, our most tangible representation of human death it would seem, and the sea whose surface pictures motion almost exclusively. I am especially attracted to the metaphor this becomes for the way it shifts and progresses within the definitions or "contours" of metaphor, as if the sea were something splitting inside a cocoon.

But, overall, I am moved by the predicament of this poem's speaker, who by the fourth line of the poem is talking more or less to herself. The relationship between the speaker and the man appears clear in one sense at least; she is the speaker and he is the all too silent receiver. She can insist:

> but you cannot stand in the middle of this;

She can know and admonish:

> the sea is a collector, quick to return a rapacious look.

She can say "this is this and that is that. You have taken the view but I know better." In fact, she can circumvent, detour, all but escape this man's silence, which much like the sea to the fishermen in the latter half of the poem, offers not only no resistance, but nothing in return.

The queer thing about "A Grave," for me, is the lack of provocation. The intensity of the speaker, her vision of the sea (the darkness in it), and the lack of alternative they present, the lack of echo therein, are not easily explained. The context of this poem finds the speaker at once superior and humbled, or awed, and it never changes. It would be like talking to one's hands or a mirror, I imagine. And, at what point would all that silence begin to sound like an accomplice? Suddenly, the words printed on the page begin to look like cool shoals of fish brushing up, in their traffic, against utter neutrality. Sadly, there is no version of the sea to lend spark to this one, no version of the sea that comes to interrupt the speaker's own.

Perhaps she would merely be risking righteousness if she weren't so vigorous in her awareness, everywhere, of that as man's original and flawed position. Then too, by observing the man's situation from the ironic distance of her own, she has turned the table, so to speak, on herself. At the same time, she appears to be unable to resist her own urge to speak and the great freedom the man's silence offers. As she exercises the ability to perceive, order, and analyze, she recognizes that these are the acts of volition and consciousness not existing in the depths and processes of the universe:

> ...looking as if it were not that ocean in which
>   dropped things are bound to sink—
>   in which if they turn and twist, it is neither with volition nor
>   consciousness.

Her poem suggests that hers is an explicit authority and that that authority is all but meaningless.

I am reminded as I read "A Grave" of the strange contexts poems and fictions are, and of the question of how much distance permits them. The answer, for me, which is not an answer, is sound enough—a poem begins to work its way out of real life tension into some other order that resembles the original only in ways I hadn't dreamed of. I used to believe the two things, the experience of the poem and the experience of real life, were not all that distant from one another. Lately, I've come to think that the distance is practically colossal. Imagination seems to prefer only so much of real gravity. I've never understood this. I don't know how far a thing can slant before it becomes deceptive. I don't often think of such questions while writing, but on the other hand, such questions are immediate and real. I think of the triangles of geometry which allow us to conceive of the spaces we inhabit, but which are not at all those spaces. I suppose I think of this because in Moore's poem, the poetic refinement that places the speaker at one point, the man at another, and the sea at yet another, works. It seems false in a way that makes the poem beautiful, and makes the poem sound unlike any other. She has stretched things a bit, I think, but I find myself fascinated by the results, and fascinated by how much she seems to be, within her own angle, by her own angle, deeply challenged.

I can't help but think of how small a stretch it probably is between imagination and manipulation, or between speech and oppression, "repression." There ought to be whole unknowable landscapes between death and desecration. But, like the sometimes small ground between discovery and repetition, often there is little. In place of an original struggle between man and survival, one finds organizations and hierarchies apparent in even the smallest systematic killings. Soon enough "men lower nets, unconscious of the fact that they are desecrating a grave/and row quickly away—the blades of the oars/moving together like the feet of water-spiders as if there were no such thing as death."

Of course, there *is* such a thing as death. The speaker knows this. She knows it like a blood relative. Her frankness, her urge to speak, her intelligence increase the poignancy of that fact, until what was obvious at first, is not in the least obvious. It isn't only that her voice is attached to the same human consciousness that drives the fisherman, but that a silence precedes it as well as them. There's the inclination always to say something into it, to say something to it, which is not the problem until one stands in the middle of it as in a boat, letting effort dim. The problem is that the little silences, the little deaths which might at one time have interfered, have been novel and slippery, can arrive all too easily.

Fortunately, in Marianne Moore's case, a real character speaks. Her effort is alive as her voice is alive, and full of contradiction: fearful, wise, despairing at times, resilient, urgent, nearly righteous, almost prophetic, it places its strange convictions between the ear and consciousness. She speaks and hears herself. She orders and sees order for what it is. It is both difficult and delightful, I think, that in the end, as she observes the man, and he observes the sea, the sea, whose foremost conditions are mystery, movement, and silence, is not and never was observing anybody.

SILENCE

My father used to say,
"Superior people never make long visits,
have to be shown Longfellow's grave
or the glass flowers at Harvard.
Self-reliant like the cat—
that takes its prey to privacy,
the mouse's limp tail hanging like a shoelace from its mouth—
they sometimes enjoy solitude,
and can be robbed of speech
by speech which has delighted them.
The deepest feeling always shows itself in silence;
not in silence, but restraint."
Nor was he insincere in saying, "Make my house your inn."
Inns are not residences.

Stanley Plumly

ABSENT THINGS

For the last edition of her *Collected Poems*, Marianne Moore edits her famous "Poetry" from twenty-nine lines down to three. The severity of the reduction suggests several possibilities, ranging from issues of the literalist imagination (" 'imaginary gardens with real toads in them' ") to issues of rhythm vs. cadence (is it poetry or is it prose?). It could also be a case of modesty or irony. I prefer to think of the revision in terms of an understanding of and commitment to the uses of silence, reluctance—or what Elizabeth Bishop, in her moving essay "Efforts of Affection," calls Moore's "grace" and "reticence." We might even refer to it as the art of the absence of a certain kind of noise. *The Norton Anthology of Modern Poetry* reprints the earlier version of "Poetry" with the note that ultimately "Miss Moore omitted all the poem following the first three lines." The footnote is incomplete. I want to make a little fuss about the oversight because, in light of her notions of poetry, I think it is significant what else Moore left out of her poem, in the very first line: "there are things that are more important beyond all this fiddle."

The fiddle can, of course, cover all sorts of fiddling. One of the values I'd like to assign it relates to those advertisements of originality so often cited in Moore's writing, those appearances of style—for which exclusive attention is itself reductive—such as the preoccupation with her syllabics, the emphasis on her playfulness and eccentricity, the fixation on the entertainment of her information, and the relegation to rhetoric of her powerful intuition concerning what Whitman called the tally ("Elizabeth, don't speak to me about that man!"), the tiering, the simultaneity of particulars. I don't put these concerns down; I mean only, for a moment, to put them in their place. It may be true that like Williams and Stevens—but without their considerable commentary—Moore is a revolutionary—or is she a reactionary?—of the individual lyric form, of how a poem can sound and what it can look like, line and image and shape. It may be true that her unique contribution is the admixture of media interaction—prose to verse—she manages to alloy with both intensity and ease, as if her poems were antique findings as well as elaborately invented constructs, and as if she were both shopper and scientist. Yet it's possible that her greatest insight has to do with content rather than technique—with contents, with the meaning and nature of the found; with not only what poems consist of but where they come from, in the world and in her own distancing presence.

Moore, for one thing, is a genius of scale, of letting the air out of the large and of giving a touch of the grand to the small: glaciers that are octopi, snails that make modesty a virtue. She does this primarily by analogy, as in "An Octopus" and "The Grave" (perhaps her two best poems), by juxtaposition, as in "The Plumet Basilisk" and "Critics and Connoisseurs," and by focus on the funny fact, as in "Elephants" and "The Pangolin." Likely these methods come out in the wash more or less the same—to compare is to juxtapose is to focus on the evocative, ironic particular. The point is the quality of the extra-literary information and what the observer wills. Moore reverses D. H. Lawrence, for example, and instead of treating the animal as the passional subject, sees it wholly as the inspiring object, and in doing so denies the figure in the narrative for the figure in the round. Lawrence is an expressionist with a story to tell, Moore a cubist with an object (objet d'art?) to see—her buffalo—"black in blazonry"—is structured for the eye and ear, the wit and thought, a kind of exemplary statuary. The norms of time and landscape are suspended in Moore, in just the ways that the outside, found information seems to float from zoo or library, neighborhood or newspaper into the text, like water ouzels and *anastasis* and ponies named Blue Bug. At her best Moore is a magical realist, a fabulist, a combiner of worlds, a maker of hybrids, a dramatist of detail.

At the level of voice, of tone, however, for all her multiple verbal dexterity and fluent imaginative layering, for all her observational and intellectual skills—the whole poetry noise—Moore is a rather quiet poet. She is certainly reluctant to speak "personally," even to the extent that she would escape personality. She is utterly shy as to asserting her place in a poem: the performance of the specialty act speaks for her. She is the poet off-stage, in the wings, running the show. Witness rather than first cause. Indeed, Moore is unique—notably in her own generation—in the pressure and purity she brings to bear on this essential modern poetic problem: how to create the authenticity of the emotion without compelling the close proximity of the self. Moore is not a cold poet, yet how seldom even the first-person personal pronoun even pops up. "Silence," as an instance, is an *ars poetica* in the pose of personal homily. The reference "My father," as if Moore were passing on actual parental advice, is just another distancing device, part of a larger quotation she has borrowed from Miss A. M. Homans. Its use is really no different from the Edmund Burke quote that ends the poem, "Make my house your inn," which is also "misassigned." Quotations, like other data in Moore's work, are objects too. This doesn't mean that Moore is being ironic or appositional to the advice offered in the poem—the last "didactic" line is clearly hers—but it does mean that she wishes to disguise a strong and cool aesthetic statement within a familiar, and familial, setting. Even a warm setting, by New England standards. The poem is about restraint, not silence exactly—about the talents of reticence, about the power of the mouthpiece, all of which is magnified through the tension of denial, distance.

Self-restraint, privacy, solitude—these are themes of silence all right. The speech of silence, though, is the speech of theft, the speech that through delight robs silence; and that moment, both still and fluent, is the moment of reticence, power, restraint, of silence-into-speech and—in order to achieve self-deniability—speech back into silence. Moore's objectifications, through the use of the found and/or the exotic, the borrowed or the quoted, are the perfect methodology of saying without speaking, of building without showing her hand. I find a certain poignancy in Moore's method, and admiration. Even the thievery is brick by brick, perhaps because the sources are so common, close-at-hand. Moore is always the blackbird lining the nest with brightness and use. Enlarging by the little. Keats described the perfect poetic stance as disinterestedness, Stevens as disappearance into the text. They may be positing the same thing. For Moore the world is the self and through it she is confirmed: it is her collateral. That is why for her a language of absences is no abstraction: it is her tongue. One never senses even a purchase on the drifty narrative of things. One sees Moore standing perfectly still in the middle of the commotion. The real irony is that usually her longer poems are her most restrained, reticent, such as "An Octopus," which builds on the principle of silences to be filled, of image or fact generating the need for the next, the way a glacier is finally snow. The longer the form the less the presence of the poet is called for.

BY DISPOSITION OF ANGELS

Messengers much like ourselves? Explain it.
Steadfastness the darkness makes explicit?
Something heard most clearly when not near it?
          Above particularities,
these unparticularities praise cannot violate.
      One has seen, in such steadiness never deflected,
      how by darkness a star is perfected.

Star that does not ask me if I see it?
Fir that would not wish me to uproot it?
Speech that does not ask me if I hear it?
          Mysteries expound mysteries.
Steadier than steady, star dazzling me, live and elate,
      no need to say, how like some we have known; too like her,
      too like him, and a-quiver forever.

Lee Upton
AN INVITATION TO WONDER

Among her poems, Marianne Moore's "By Disposition of Angels" is
a little like a dikdik, an ibex or a jerboa, that "small desert rat,/and
not famous." Less inclusive than much of her work, less imagistic,
the poem receives comparably little attention. Yet "By Disposition of Angels" is recognizably Moore's, marked by her multidirectional intelligence,
her mix of humility and effrontery. The poem proceeds by merging, however
tentatively, the earthly and the celestial, the human and the divine. The
poem's six questions enact urgent, exuberant inquiry, for Moore pays
homage to the hypothetical, inviting us to practice her strategies without violating the wondrous or ourselves. Here our wonder creates our questions.
    Moore's title, "By Disposition of Angels," immediately alerts us. Are we
to consider the temperament of angels, their inclinations and powers? Or are
we to think of their placement or distribution? While the poem may take part
in each of these possibilities, it primarily adopts a drama of position: What is
the perspective we may take toward the absolute, "the genuine"? The angels,
like the absolute poem, may exist in contradiction, fixed and in motion, exact
and strict—and yet out of bounds, "a-quiver forever."
    Moore opens with a question, "Messengers much like ourselves?," fol-
lowed by a command that is part rebuke, part challenge: "Explain it." Moore

thrived, I should think, on a good question. While her question tentatively
identifies us with angels and the angels, as messengers, with language, her
following two-word command places upon the poem the burden of proof.
What follows are chains of paradoxes. The dark allows us to see the star. In
absence those we love may appear clarified to us as never before. "Mysteries
expound mysteries."

The poem is a performance of "too like," of repetitions in structure and
language overlapping until the poem might seem as curiously watertight as
the feathers of certain birds. Repetitions accumulate, accrete: *steadfastness,
steadiness, steadier, steady, particularities, unparticularities, mysteries,
mysteries, too like her, too like him.* Defining by negation, Moore repeats *not*
five times; she repeats *like* four times, defining by resemblance. At terminal
position, the first three lines of these structurally duplicate stanzas, each like
the cut wing of a sonnet, repeat *it,* that most ambiguous of pronouns. The
poem then moves from the abstract to the concrete, from the generalized to
the particular, from angels and star to the human. Moore takes us from the element of air to earth to speech itself, our particular "element." Each stanza's
indented fourth line—"above particularities" in the first and "mysteries expound mysteries" in the second—suggest the angels must remain as distant
as stars. The poem's self-compoundings perform like the winged and doubly
embracive power we may associate with angels.

"By Disposition of Angels" first appeared in 1948, a year after the death of
Moore's mother, a woman who was perhaps the most intimate presence in
her daughter's life. Moore added a postscript to her *Selected Poems* that exemplifies her sense of indebtedness to her mother as a source, an originary
mind:

> Dedications imply giving, and we do not care to make a gift of what is in-
> sufficient; but in my immediate family there is one "who thinks in a partic-
> ular way;" and I should like to add that where there is an effect of thought
> or pith in these pages, the thinking and often the actual phrases are hers.

Apparently written at a time when Moore was preoccupied with her mother's
long illness and death, "By Disposition of Angels" may be the most private
of a species of love poem, alluding to the mother as much as the mother
tongue and mother wit. The woman "who thinks in a particular way" recalls
us, paradoxically, to "these unparticularities praise cannot violate." Moore
reminds us elsewhere that "efforts of affection—/attain integration too tough
for infraction." The poem's weight of feeling is almost implosive in its privacy and tenacious double-mindedness:

> Steadier than steady, star dazzling me, live and elate,
>   no need to say, how like some we have known; too like her,
>   too like him, and a-quiver forever.

The quills of the poem seem to rise. Angel, star, the spirit, the poem must for Moore be "a-quiver forever," resonantly in movement.

Moore's repetition of the prefix *ex* (out) in *explain, explicit,* and *expound* directs us to the letter *x*, not as a cancellation but as a marker, an intersection, the power of the double, the chromosome and the chiasmus, the unknown element, a sign for our crossed position—the x as the minimalist's star. The poem performs as an intersection in which qualities of sensibility and aesthetics ("steadfastness," an absolute integrity) meet. Dickinson's "Tell all the Truth but tell it slant—" may be a prescription for Moore's truths amid both these x's and her curious syllabics that verge on a kind of skeptic's numerology. For Moore, a truth does not require that we take one short dive but that we make our approach on the "slant."

"Too like," a certain power of excess, signals curious affinities, kinships. Reflections drift over reflections, for Moore's angels emerge as doubly human, our higher powers. The poem, then, offers us both a measure of heightened possibility and a tonic against easy presumption.

THE FRIGATE PELICAN

Rapidly cruising or lying on the air there is a bird
    that realizes Rasselas's friend's project
    of wings uniting levity with strength. This
        hell-diver, frigate-bird, hurricane-
bird; unless swift is the proper word
      for him, the storm omen when
    he flies close to the waves, should be seen
        fishing, although oftener
        he appears to prefer

    to take, on the wing, from industrious cruder-winged species
    the fish they have caught, and is seldom successless.
    A marvel of grace, no matter how fast his
        victim may fly or how often may
turn, *the dishonest pelican's ease*
      in pursuit, bears him away
    with the fish that the badgered bird drops.
        A kind of superlative
        swallow, that likes to live

on food caught while flying, he is not a pelican. The toe
    with slight web, air-boned body, and very long wings
    with the spread of a swan's—duplicating a
        bow-string as he floats overhead—feel
the changing V-shaped scissor swallow-
      tail direct the rigid keel.
    And steering beak to windward always,
        the fleetest foremost fairy
        among birds, outflies the

aeroplane which cannot flap its wings nor alter any quill-
    tip. For him, the feeling in a hand, in fins, is
    in his unbent downbent crafty oar. With him
        other pelicans aimlessly soar
as he does; separating, until
      not flapping they rise once more
    closing in without looking and move
        outward again to the top
        of the circle and stop

and blow back, allowing the wind to reverse their direction.

This is not the stalwart swan that can ferry the
woodcutter's two children home; no. Make hay; keep
the shop; I have one sheep; were a less
limber animal's mottoes. This one
finds sticks for the swan's-down dress
of his child to rest upon and would
not know Gretel from Hänsel.
As impassioned Handel—

meant for a lawyer and a masculine German domestic
career—clandestinely studied the harpsichord
and never was known to have fallen in love,
the unconfiding frigate-bird hides
in the height and in the majestic
display of his art. He glides
a hundred feet or quivers about
as charred paper behaves—full
of feints; and an eagle

of vigilance, *earns the term aquiline; keeping at a height*
so great the feathers look black and the beak does not
show. It is not retreat but exclusion from
which he looks down and observes what went
secretly, as it thought, out of sight
among dense jungle plants. Sent
ahead of the rest, there goes the true
knight in his jointed coat that
covers all but his bat

ears; a-trot, with stiff pig gait—our tame armadillo, loosed by
his master and as pleased as a dog. Beside the
spattered blood—that orchid which the native fears—
the fer-de-lance lies sleeping; centaur-
like, this harmful couple's amity
is apropos. A jaguar
and crocodile are fighting. Sharp-shinned
hawks and peacock-freckled small
cats, like the literal

merry-go-round, come wandering within the circular view
of the high bird for whom from the air they are ants
keeping house all their lives in the crack of a
crag with no view from the top. And here,

unlikely animals learning to
    dance, crouch on two steeds that rear
  behind a leopard with a frantic
    face, tamed by an Artemis
    who wears a dress like his,

and hampering haymaker's hat. "Festina lente." Be gay
  civilly. How so? 'If I do well I am blessed
  whether any bless me or not, and if I do
    ill I am cursed'. We watch the moon rise
on the Susquehanna. In his way
    this most romantic bird flies
  to a more mundane place, the mangrove
    swamp, to sleep. He wastes the moon.
    But he, and others, soon

rise from the bough, and though flying are able to foil the tired
  moment of danger, that lays on heart and lungs the
  weight of the python that crushes to powder.
    The tune's illiterate footsteps fail;
the steam hacks are not to be admired.
    These, unturbulent, avail
  themselves of turbulence to fly—pleased
    with the faint wind's varyings,
    on which to spread fixed wings.

The reticent lugubrious ragged immense minuet
  descending to leeward, ascending to windward
  again without flapping, in what seems to be
    a way of resting, are now nearer,
but as seemingly bodiless yet
    as they were. Theirs are sombre
  quills for so wide and lightboned a bird
    as the frigate pelican
    of the Caribbean.

David Young

CLIPPED WINGS

W hen I was growing up and starting to take an interest in poetry I became aware of certain spinster-poets who dressed eccentrically and inspired a mixture of affection and contempt in the media and the public. England had Edith Sitwell and we had Marianne Moore. They were different, to be sure, but somehow one lumped them together. I found them supremely uninteresting.

I mention these early impressions of Moore only because I suspect that they are typical. They helped prevent me from becoming a serious and sympathetic reader of her poems for quite a long time. No doubt they reflect my own ignorance and poor judgment, as well as our cultural disposition to make poets, especially women poets, tame or safe or a bit ridiculous. But they may also tell us something about the shape and character of Moore's career.

Without having studied the matter closely, I have come to suspect that Moore collaborated somewhat in her own diminution from a fiercely experimental modernist to a quaint little old lady interested in baseball and rodents, a purveyor, at her worst, of dessicated whimsy. My suspicion stems from my gradual discovery that the texts in her *Collected Poems* (1951) and her *Complete Poems* (1956, 1958, 1967—billed on its current Penguin cover as "The Definitive Edition...") are quite often drastically reduced and appallingly "safe" versions of her best early works. For whatever reasons, Moore came to distrust her early, experimental tendencies, and she could not leave her own work alone. The tart headnote to the *Complete Poems*—"Omissions are not accidents"— emphasizes her right to second-guess herself artistically, but it does not resolve the issue of what a reduced version of this wonderful poet we have in her final version of her own canon. If we are to learn to read her well we must be willing to search out earlier versions of her poems and to exercise our own judgments in comparing revised versions to their predecessors.

This is not a matter of not letting Moore have the last word. It is a matter of choosing among her artistic impulses. If Picasso had decided to paint later, safer versions of his cubist masterpieces we would not object, though we might not care much for them. But if the artist tried to destroy or paint over those masterpieces, or if they were carried off to museum basements through a conspiracy of neglect in the art establishment, then we would want to intervene. Marianne Moore needs to be rescued from her own late timidity about her work, and from the tendency of the critics, with the exception of John Slatin and, to a lesser extent, Bonnie Costello, to accept that timidity as canonical.

The poem I've chosen to discuss, "The Frigate Pelican," is a dramatic example of Moore's drastic overrevising of her work. I have asked the printer to

set it with the excised passages in italics, to aid readers in following this discussion. The original version, first printed in T. S. Eliot's magazine, *The Cri-
terion*, in July 1935, and then in the *Selected Poems* of 1935 (still the one
book by Moore to own if you could have only one), consists of twelve nine-
line stanzas. The stanzas are cast in a syllabic pattern of 15-12-11-9-7-9-7-6.
Lines 1 and 5 rhyme, as do 6 and 7, 8 and 9. This formal commitment, most
of us would agree, is an extremely demanding one. Yet Moore cut her hundred and eight lines to forty-seven, reducing the poem by over sixty per cent.
In the process, she produced two variant stanzas, one of eight lines and one
of three, marring her own beautiful and careful patterning in the original. We
presume this was not done lightly. And in some respects that "revised" version may be said to be a tighter and more orderly poem. But its ending makes
no real sense as it stands, and some of the finest moments have been excised
along the way. Whatever the problems of the first version, they are not eradi-
cated by the "solution" of turning a vigorous and sizable original into a kind
of *Reader's Digest* abridgement of itself. This has to be said emphatically,
since reverence for Moore's editorial eye and revisionist practices seems to
be the prevailing sentiment among her commentators.

It's probably wise to be candid about this poet's shortcomings from the outset. She has a comparatively bad ear. She is capable of triviality and irrele-
vance. She often risks incoherence and disorder, following private associations too far or letting her taste for arcane detail and verbal gymnastics get the
better of her. When we have acknowledged these problems we can get on to
the business of appreciating her strengths. It is no accident that her modernist
contemporaries—Williams, Stevens, Pound and Eliot—had enormous respect
for her. She was a virtuoso of experimentation, willing to risk much. She
broke up received ideas about how poems should behave, what they should
include, and what kinds of challenges they could offer their readers. Her
poems attack traditional notions of unity and decorum. They shift without
warning from one topic to another. They are brilliant, unpredictable collages
and assemblages, full of driving energy and imaginative somersaults. Her
syntax is capacious and intricate, appropriate to poems so inclusive that they
threaten to grow enormous in the interests of demonstrating the unifying and
synthesizing powers of the imagination. Form is always a hard-won triumph
in these circumstances, and the poet has her own special forms of control: the
calming syllabics, the intricately patterned stanzas, the special uses of rhyme.
She's as free-ranging as Whitman and as rigorous as Dickinson. She reminds
us of seventeenth-century figures like Vaughan and Traherne, with their ecstatic, charged poems in complex, replicating, anisometric stanzas. Surely she is
our great modern practitioner of the ode, the elaborate formal poem of praise
and celebration that comes down to us all the way from Pindar and has some
of our language's greatest examples in the Romantic period.

Probably her best poem is the early "An Octopus," a headlong avalanche of language about a mountain—Mt. Rainier or a composite of such peaks and their glaciers. It manages to destroy the prim cautions of Imagism and re-define the American Sublime all in one burst of precariously controlled energy. Thank goodness she left it intact. It is the poem with which to begin any study of her work. It teaches you to accept her overloaded sentences and ap-parent detours. Having been swept away by it, you are ready to allow her her style and to stop worrying unduly about length and coherence. Then her best poems, while they will still ask a great deal from you, will reward you might-ily for your attention.

"The Frigate Pelican" typifies her excitement about animals. There's no doubt that the bird is partly chosen for its capacity to reflect her own values and temperament. The frigate pelican is of course misnamed. Its character comes not from any pelican-like ability to store fish in its beak but from its astonishing maneuverability in flight. It steals from other fishing birds, but playfully and expertly, by outflying them. If we think about Moore's own reputation as a kind of literary pillager, filling her poems with other people's phrases and thoughts, we can see why she might have been attracted to this thievish and misnamed aerial acrobat. I have watched them fly, in the Gala-pagos, and can testify to the absolute accuracy with which she describes them.

The original poem's first four stanzas were devoted to careful description of the bird's names, characteristics, and flight behavior. In cutting the four down to two, Moore performed a fairly arbitrary kind of surgery, losing help-ful clarifications like "he is not a pelican" and the anticipation of the fifth and sixth stanzas in the comparison to the wingspread of the swan. She sacrificed some extremely exact language, both metaphoric and literal, in excising the third and fourth stanzas. And she lost some highly expressive poetry. I sug-gested earlier that Moore often has a tin ear, but I would praise this poem for the musical legerity with which it celebrates flight. The cut stanzas have a consistency of effect in their alliteration and consonance, as well as their light touch with vowels, that does a great deal to sustain the mood of excite-ment.

Moore's cut version retains the next two stanzas, in which she teases the swan of romantic and symbolist poetry as a bird that by comparison reflects a stolid, bourgeois anthropomorphism, making animals into moral emblems by de-emphasizing their otherness. The rhyme that leads us from Hänsel to Handel allows Moore to introduce music into the poem, not through the bird's song but by analogy to an artist who began in the safe and burgherly mode and ended by defying it, swan into frigate bird. There are some inter-esting tensions in the three-way comparison that involves Moore, Handel and the frigate pelican. All can be said to hide "in the height and in the majes-tic/display" of their art. Reproduction and love are another matter. The bird builds nests for its offspring, a caricature of the swan, while Handel, like

Moore, "never was known to have fallen in love." In any case, the alignment
of the composer's exuberant melodies, the bird's effortless mastery of the air
and the poet's own soaring by means of her intricate, patterned stanzas is an
exciting one. That Moore should later have clipped her own wings seems a
shame.

The largest cut, of three stanzas, follows. It is true that this passage is difficult for a reader, but it is also surely the most far-ranging and inventive part
of the original poem, one that opens it up not merely to the kind of analogy
represented by Handel but to an entire animal kingdom, partly natural and
partly fanciful, that reaches finally into the realm of myth. Moore's own
notes about the giant armadillo and the blood-spotted orchid survive in the
Complete Poems to baffle readers, a last trace of the excised original. May
they tempt others, as they did me, to investigate and discover the poem in all
its bewildering and fascinating entirety.

The three cut stanzas give us the frigate pelican's bird's-eye view, an exclusive vantage but not an escapist one, of a world that includes what a real
frigate bird might see—Latin American flora and fauna—as well as a mythic
merry-go-round of possibilities within the privileged purview of the artist.
Did Moore feel she had gone too far by reaching all the way to an Artemis
taming leopards? Perhaps. But the stretch is appropriate to her characterization of the frigate pelican's flight capacities and her own amazing instincts as
an artist. Such connections are not for everybody, but they constitute Moore's
real strength as a working poet and they did not deserve to be treated as superfluous. They validate her celebration of the bird. It is not simply that it
flies so well but that it flies so high and far. Since there's an implicit defense
of the artistic imagination here, it deserves to be as full as possible and not to
be retracted, either as argument or as a stunning list of details.

We come next to the matter of the ending. The unit I'm considering now
was originally three stanzas, subsequently cut to less than two. There are
some undeniable difficulties—I'm still unsure what "steam hacks" are,
though I think they may be the organs that accompany merry-go-rounds, losing the tune as the carousel slows down—but I think the earlier version is
much to be preferred, both as closure and as a psychological and aesthetic
extension of what has gone before.

One way to get at this is to compare this ending with Keats's "Ode to a
Nightingale," the prototype, perhaps, for any ode-like poem centered on a
bird. Keats, or his speaker, it will be recalled, after an ecstatic sense of union
with the bird, suffers at the end a sense of separation as he falls back into his
own humanity and the bird disappears into a transcendent realm where we
mortals cannot follow. Something like this happens, I think, in the final stanzas of "The Frigate Pelican." Our humanity begins to separate us from this
wonderful flyer. We struggle with the paradoxes of how to make haste
swiftly or be gay civilly, while the bird lives out a Hindu motto without hav-

ing to think about it. We watch (having returned to North America and a river Moore knew well) the rising of the moon, passive and bemused. The bird "wastes the moon" but manages to sleep briefly and to fly all night if necessary, without fatigue. Somehow human beings are much more subject to entropy. Our merry-go-rounds run down and stop. Even our Handel melodies must end. But the frigate pelican, by flying so effortlessly, using turbulence to remain unturbulent, seems to have solved the problems of gravity and exhaustion. It lives on the giant, endless minuet of the wind, as if it could go on forever and ever. It appears to be "bodiless." And yet—and now we now fall back once again into our own realm of paradox and puzzlement—how somber its quills are, given its lightboned and soaring propensities. Thinking about the satisfactions and frustrations that close the "Ode to a Nightingale" helps me understand how Moore is resolving her own ode.

Bonnie Costello, in her thoughtful study of Moore, is cautiously noncommittal about the two versions of this poem. She quotes and praises the earlier one, but she also has good words for the "final version" and its three-line coda, which closes the poem by characterizing "the tired/moment of danger" in terms of "the/weight of the python that crushes to powder." Having taught that version, quite innocently, I can testify that students find it bewildering and abrupt. Having tried to defend it—I even suggested that "though" was a misprint for "through"—I can also testify to my relief at discovering that it was not the true ending at all, merely the result of some rather arbitrary cutting.

If we look back now at the original in its entirety, I think we can say it was by far the stronger of the two versions. Admittedly, it had some obscurities. By the time Moore gets to Artemis in the ninth stanza, she has come a long way and included a great deal. But this imaginative range is what makes her so exciting. She does not merely describe—Costello treats this poem in a chapter titled "Descriptive Poems"—but instead lets language enact transformations that are only possible in the kind of highly experimental poetic context she is capable of creating. Artemis is a good case in point. If you try to find, as I did, the painting which is the probable source for this passage, you will discover that painters do not show Artemis taming leopards while wearing a dress or a haymaker's hat. Perhaps she is really Circe. More likely the "painting" is an imaginary conflation of several paintings Moore liked, with a carousel thrown in for good measure.

I would admit too that "steam hacks" is extremely obscure, and that my reading of it is precariously conjectural. But surely the answer to these difficulties, if that is what they are, was not the revised version that Moore came up with. It's like amputating limbs as a way of dealing with warts. Someday we may have a better idea of why Moore did what she did to her poems. Until then, we owe it to her and to the poems and to ourselves as attentive readers to look behind and beyond the confines of her "Definitive Edition" just as often as we like.

ANNA AKHMATOVA
(1889-1966)

A nna Akhmatova, along with her fellow Russians Nikolai Gumilev and Osip Mandelstam, was a major proponent of Acmeism, a reaction in the 1910s and 1920s against the dreamy mysticism of the Symbolist movement. Like the contemporaneous Imagists in England, the Acmeists used simple diction and concrete imagery, and emphasized the immediacy of human experience. Akhmatova's work is generally divided into two major periods: the intimate short lyrics mainly about love written in 1909-22, and the longer poems on public and political themes from 1935-66. The lengthy silence in between reflects the period when she found herself at odds with the Soviet regime and unable to publish. The early poems treat love in a terse, highly psychological way, in which usually unrequited or tragic relationships are suggested through precise external details and an almost icy control. By her early thirties, Akhmatova had published five books and become widely celebrated, but then she fell out of favor with the increasingly repressive Stalinist state: publication of her work was banned between 1925 and 1952, and many of those closest to her, including her first husband and her son, were imprisoned or executed. Out of these experiences came her two masterpieces, "Requiem" and *Poem without a Hero*, in which she synthesizes her own personal tragedies with those of her country. Through bold formal experiments in voice, and through her own personal courage and integrity, Akhmatova regained enormous esteem both in Russia and internationally, and is now regarded as an essential modern Russian poet.

BOOKS IN ENGLISH TRANSLATION: *Collected Poems of Anna Akhmatova*, ed. Roberta Reeder, trans. Judith Hemschemeyer (2 vols., 1990). A good selection is *Poem Without a Hero and Selected Poems*, trans. Lenore Mayhew and William McNaughton (1989).

EVENING

In the garden there were snatches of music
Wordless, melancholy.
The sharp fresh odors of the sea
Rose from oysters on cracked ice.

He said to me,
                    "I am your faithful friend,"
And touched my dress:
Unlike an embrace
The touch of that hand.

So one pets a cat or a bird
So one looks
                    at well-built circus riders.
And in his tranquil eyes there was laughter
Under lashes of light gold.

And behind the drifting smoke
The voices of nostalgic violins sang
"Give thanks, thanks to the Gods—
For the first time
You are alone
                    with your love."

translated by Lenore Mayhew

Lenore Mayhew

IMAGES FROM A LIFE

When Anna Akhmatova was about seventeen she was infatuated with Vladimir Golenishchev-Kutuzov and for months wrote letters to her brother-in-law begging for a picture of her beloved. The extravagant note of thanks which she sent off when the picture finally arrived has in its several hints that tempt us to suppose that Golenishchev-Kutuzov could be the hero of the poem, "Evening." "In it," she says of the photograph, "he is exactly as I knew him, loved him, and so madly feared him: elegant and so indifferently cold, he looks at me with the tired, calm gaze of light short-sighted eyes." Yes, that could be Kutuzov...a promising candidate for "unlike an embrace/The touch of that hand." But perhaps when the violins say, "Give thanks, thanks to the Gods," she is instead with her first husband, Lev Gumilev. Akhmatova's love poetry was drawn from life, mostly hers, but it is not always possible to trace the connections.

However it was made and whomever it is about, "Evening" is an in-depth moment, spontaneous and perfectly realized. The oysters and the laughing eyes, the drifting smoke all draw us in. It is like reading jottings in an intimate diary, or like participating in a scene from *Anna Karenina*. It was Mandelstam who first emphasized Akhmatova's debt to the tradition of the nineteenth-century novel: "The roots of her poetry are in prose fiction...the concern for tangible realities, objects, and events."

Akhmatova once criticized someone else's poetry as having "not enough *zagodka*." *Zagodka*—puzzle or mystery. As she herself used simple language, exact rhythms, strict meters, and short sentences and Mandelstam praises her for her tangible realities, how does she achieve in her own pages the mystery she found missing in other people's work? It is a large subject and a puzzle in itself. But it is instructive to notice how inventive she is in the use of the details of her own history.

Perhaps she is most inventive in the use of details when she is consistently persistent about leaving them out. There is a fragmentary quality in these jottings, these scenes that make up an Akhmatova poem. Objects, events, and characters have been omitted. We feel their existence but can't find them on the page. The images that are there, however, have a strange aptness to this missing context. This way of constructing poems may owe something to Akhmatova's having been a member of the Poets' Guild, an association of Russian imagist poets. The Russian imagists (if we may call them that, and as there are such startling parallels in intention and practice I think perhaps we can) had a different world for their literary ideals. Their word was acmeism, from acme, meaning "point, prime, flower, edge." The explanation I like best is that the acmeist poem is supposed to be like the tip of an iceberg. Only one-ninth of its mass juts out of the water, but the submerged eight-ninths is also present. Akhmatova often writes this sort of iceberg poem in her pursuit of *zagodka*. She tells us what she wants to tell us, shedding only such light as will render, but at the same time conceal, enchant, and mystify.

In the lovely "Under the frozen roof..." the sense of some larger story is particularly strong:

> Under the frozen roof of this deserted house
> I stop counting the dead days.
> I read the Acts of the Apostles.
> I read the Singer of the Psalms.
>
> And the stars are blue, and the frost like feathers

And our meetings, miraculous
                    —and each more than the last

And in my Bible
A leaf from the red maple
Marks the Song of Songs.

(translated by Lenore Mayhew)

Here there is a deepening of mystery by the use of another technique—
choosing words that carry a double level of meaning. The poem, which has
throughout presented a puzzling and effective juxtaposition of eros and divinity, ends by calling up both simultaneously, with the four words, "the
Song of Songs."

In all her poetry juxtaposition of images is a productive technique. The diversity, the suddenness of particular details is often astonishing. She never
wrote poems with the "boring unity of surface" which Pound warns against.
Unity should be not at the surface but in the connections underneath: in
"Evening," for instance, where the ice under the oysters suggests possible
ironies in "I am your faithful friend."

Louis Simpson speaks of the "secret affinity of things." Mostly secret
affinities by their very nature cannot be traced. The secret remains and contributes to Akhmatova's beloved *zagodka*. But sometimes if we pry a little we
can guess at these affinities and uncover the source of power in a particular
image. The maple leaf in "Under the frozen roof..." in its autumnal quality
connects to "the dead days" and "the frost like feathers" and to "this deserted
house," and in its redness and in its possible implication in some incident un-
specified connects to "our meetings, miraculous," so that when we find it,
this maple leaf, marking the Song of Songs, it has the rightness of a thing
ordained.

The same unity in diversity which can be found in "Under the frozen
roof..." and other individual poems is also a quality in the connections of her
love poetry. In each collection there is an accumulation in the inter-related-
ness of events and images that gives an illusion of wholeness and of narrative
in spite of all that has been neither explained nor spoken about.

Akhmatova had an extraordinary gift for choosing or inventing apt details,
an enviable virtuosity in their use, and no doubt that understanding of "the
secret affinity of things" that Louis Simpson says makes a poet's images
alive.

"FLOWERS AND NON-LIVING THINGS"

Flowers and non-living things
Make pleasant odors in the house.
By the garden beds, multi-colored vegetables
Lie in piles on the black earth.

Cold still hangs in the air
But they take away the matting from the seed-beds.
Near here is a pond, a pond
Whose mud is like brocade.

And the boy says to me with fear,
Very excited and hushed,
"A big carp lives in there
With his great big carp wife."

translated by Lenore Mayhew

Alberta Turner

TRANSLATING THE TRANSLATIONS

I do not read Russian. In front of a printed Akhmatova poem, I neither hear its rhythm nor see its images; nor do my insect feelers sense its fla-vor. To have the poem at all, I must depend on translations.

At the moment I am reading and rereading an Akhmatova poem that I think I like very much, an untitled poem from *Rosary*, dated 1913, an "in Just-/spring" poem about a boy and a carp. I have before me three transla-tions, by Walter Arndt, Lyn Coffin, and Lenore Mayhew. Each contains the same early spring scene: inside a house flowers and other sweet-smelling things make pleasure; outside are orchards, dug vegetables, newly-opened hot beds and a pond. A boy tells "me," in some excitement, that a large carp and its female live in that pond. Here are the other two versions:

> By smells of blooming things and dead
> This home is pleasantly pervaded.
> All bright against each black-earth bed
> Heaped vegetables have been spaded.

The air still runs with veins of cool,
But hot-beds glint, no longer padded.
There is a pool, the kind of pool
Whose muddy slicknesses look plaided.

A boy had seen beneath its glass
And whispers to me in a sweat
That in there lives a giant bass
With his enormous bassinette.

(translated by Walter Arndt)

The smell of inanimate things and flowers
Is pleasant in this pleasant home.
In the orchard, by beds and bowers,
Mounds of bright vegetables lie on the loam.

The air's still cool but they weren't afraid,
They uncovered the hothouses yesterday.
There's a little pond, about which I'll say
Just that its slime looks like green brocade.

A little boy, frightened, as if on a dare,
Told me with an excitement that carried,
That a giant carp is living in there
Along with the lady carp he married.

(translated by Lyn Coffin)

These translations are so different from each other that I am only sure that if I feel delights, they may be unjustified, and if I have demurs, they may be undeserved. But I record them anyway, if only to record how many ways a reader may doubt when her only access to a poem is three other readers.

First, the facts: The pleasant house is essentially the same in all three translations, and in the garden the earth is black, but the vegetables are "bright" in Arndt and Coffin and "multi-colored" in Mayhew. And the pond has "muddy slicknesses [which] look plaided" in Arndt, "slime [that] looks like green brocade" in Coffin and "mud...like brocade" in Mayhew. I don't know whether to see a bare, wet rim, with some sort of pattern (pebbles, runlets?), or a pond slimed over with algae, as many Ohio ponds are in summer. A boy tells "me" about the carp, but I don't know whether he is Arndt's "a boy," Coffin's "little boy," or Mayhew's "the boy," only that he could not have been Akhmatova's own son, who was not born until 1912. Nor do I know whether Arndt's "whispers to me in a sweat" or Coffin's "frightened, as if on a dare,/Told me with an excitement that carried "or Mayhew's "with fear, /Very excited and hushed" are mostly real fear, mostly dare or mostly a boy's pleasurable titillation meant to scare me.

These are confusions of meaning which affect tone. But there are also great variations of tone where meaning is agreed, chiefly caused by variations of connotation and sound. The three terms the translators use for the female carp are especially·diverse (perverse?). Arndt, evidently considering the poem a light and witty one, and following a regular end-rhyme pattern, calls the carp a *bass* and his female a *bassinette*. Is the Russian word for female bass the same as the Russian word for baby basket? If not, the pun is merely gross in an English translation. Coffin calls the female "the lady carp he married." Is the child's emphasis so much on the social proprieties if he is really frightened? Mayhew comes closest to what one might expect from a frightened child. Her speaker's report of what the child said sounds as if she had really heard it from a child. The one word *wife* leaves most emphasis on the great bigness of the pair, as a Dane in *Beowulf* might point in a tense whisper to the pool where Grendel lived with his great big mother.

The needs of rhyme and meter make Coffin's translation seem labored and inconsistent. The triple gallop of "Mounds of bright vegetables lie on the loam" is a jolt from the first lines and does not suit the meaning. After all, the vegetables are as still as the flowers in their vases. The half line, "About which I'll say," in stanza two, sounds like a filler to extend the line and find a rhyme for *yesterday*. It adds nothing to the meaning. And "with an excitement that carried," in stanza three, is surely redundant, but it rhymes with *married*. This translation seems to struggle. One does not feel that the translator has been moved to enjoy either spring's pleasure or its threat.

Mayhew's translation has dropped exact rhyme, but most of the lines have four major stresses. The first stanza sets the ear for it. But the third line and the sixth can barely be squeezed into that rhythm. One wonders why, since line six wouldn't miss the *away* from "take away," and in line three "In the garden" could almost replace "By the garden beds," though I confess I can think of no single-accent word for *multi-colored* except the *bright* that Arndt and Coffin used. But the language in Mayhew's translation is as simple and timeless as English can be, and the sentences short and as little modified as possible. The tone is very close to the tone of the actual experience as it would happen to a child's senses: The house smells good. Outside are mounds of vegetables, open seed beds, black earth. It's cold. There's a pond. "Look, a big carp lives in there." Sensation with pleasure and fear, felt simultaneously by child and reader, with no interference from the translator.

Mayhew's translation is clearly my favorite—except for *multi-colored*. But where is Akhmatova while one ignorant reader and three translators (with others in the wings) construct their own poems from hers? Though I have selected bits of each, my struggles have not fused them. I'm not even sure that I have *had* her poem at all. I'm not even sure that I could have it all even if I had grown up in northern Russia. But I do have a poem, partly mine, partly Coffin's and Arndt's and Mayhew's and partly Akhmatova's. It is an experience of pleasant smells, mounds of bright turnips and potatoes dug from black earth, a pond rimmed with silky mud, and an excited child pointing and whispering, "A big carp lives in there/With his great big carp wife."

Akhmatova's speaker seems delighted, a bit amused, a touch scared. And I, scarved in three layers of translation, am delighted, amused, and a touch scared too.

"I DON'T SPEAK WITH ANYONE FOR A WEEK"

I don't speak with anyone for a week.
I just sit on a stone by the sea.
It pleases me that the green waves' spray
is salt like my tears.
Springs and winters passed, but somehow
I only remembered one spring.
The nights became warmer, the snow began to thaw.
I went out to look at the moon.
Meeting me alone in the young pines
a stranger asked me quietly:
'Are you the one I searched for everywhere,
for whom since my earliest days
I have been glad and grieved—as though for a dear sister?'
I answered the stranger, 'No!'
And when the light from the heavens shone on his face
I gave him my hands.
He gave me a secret ring
to guard me against love.
And he told me four landmarks
where we must meet again:
the sea, the curving bay, the high lighthouse,
and—most important—the wormwood . . .
Let my life end as it began,
I have told what I know: Amen!

translated by Richard McKane

Marcia Southwick

A SLAB OF CLAY, A HANDFUL OF DUST

The speaker opens the poem by *saying* that she doesn't speak. Somehow she's both inside and outside of the experience at once, and the double perspective is what keeps the poem from becoming overly personal or confessional. The tone, in any case, remains buoyant, almost casual, in spite of the darker emotions at stake.

The double perspective is furthered by a shift to the past tense: "Springs and winters passed, but somehow/I only remembered one spring." She could have said that she *remembers* one spring, but here the past tense makes the incident with the stranger seem like a memory of a memory. In spite of the distancing, however, the incident stays in focus, almost as though viewed from far away through binoculars. No intensity is lost. The lenses are bright and clean. The poet presents the intricate details of the stranger's conversation: " 'Are you the one I searched for everywhere,/for whom since my earliest days/I have been glad and grieved—as though for a dear sister?' " The answer is liberating—a breathing space that allows us to imagine other possibilities. What if the speaker had said, "Yes!"? The incident would have turned into a miracle.

Nadezhda Mandelstam, Akhmatova's close friend, spoke about miracles in her memoirs: "What are people left with in the fairy tales after their three wishes have come true? What becomes, in the morning, of the gold obtained in the night from the lame man? It turns into a slab of clay, or a handful of dust. The only good life is one in which there is no need for miracles." In Akhmatova's poems, miracles don't happen. Wishing for them is a useless activity. On an artistic level, the poet is also saying "no," along with the figure inside the poem who is remembering the story. But the poet, from a perspective outside of the events, is resisting impulses that might have led the narrative into the unreal world of fairytales.

The Acmeists didn't believe in unreal worlds. They thought that such visions were reserved for the Symbolists. According to Gumilyov, the Acmeists were seeking "a direction requiring a greater equilibrium of powers and a more exact knowledge of the relationship between subject and object than was the case in Symbolism." They wanted accurately expressed relationships between word and "thing." Osip Mandelstam said:

> Let us take for example the rose and the sun, a girl and a dove. There is nothing real or genuine here, only a terrible *contredanse* of "correspondences" nodding at each other.... Nothing wants to be itself anymore.... A man is no longer master in his own house.... The household utensils have gone on strike. The broom has ceased sweeping, the pot refuses to boil, and requires the householder to contemplate its absolute significance.

The "things" in Akhmatova's poem do not go on strike. The four landmarks are just that: four landmarks. If the poem is difficult to interpret in places, most likely the problems are caused by the nearly impossible task of translating Russian into English. The phrase "light from the heavens" is probably too other-worldly for an Acmeist. A Russian friend tells me that a literal translation would be: light from under the sky. And the last two lines of the poem are troublesome. Apparently, in the original, there is no pronoun "my," so perhaps the lines are referring not to the speaker's life, but to life in general. If so, the *stranger* could be saying, "Let life end as it began," and the speaker at the end of the poem could be describing her own reply: "And I said that I know: Amen."

What does Gumilyov's phrase "equilibrium of powers" mean? And how does it relate to a "knowledge of the relationship between subject and object"? Akhmatova's skill in balancing out opposing forces in the poem contributes to our sense that the speaker is able to perceive herself as other. She is both subject and object at the same time. She describes her own tears, and yet as if witnessing herself from the perspective of someone else, she notices the resemblance between her tears and the waves' spray. Also, there is tension between autobiography and invention. Where, exactly, is the boundary that separates fiction and fact? The life of the poet enters powerfully, if indirectly, affecting the mood and overall sense of loss in the poem. And the invented experience refers back to the life it ventures away from, calling to mind what we know about Akhmatova's personal life: her marriage ended in divorce a year after this poem was written. It seems right, given the situation, for the speaker to accept a "secret ring" that would protect or "guard" her "against love."

The poem is a haunting one, partly because of what we know, in retrospect, about the poet's future: she would suffer the execution of Gumilyov, and the imprisonment of her son. Nothing would guard her against history. Considering the tragic circumstances, wouldn't it have been natural to wish, at times, that life would "end as it began"—without love?

"TERROR, FINGERING THINGS IN THE DARK"

Terror, fingering things in the dark,
Leads the moonbeam to an ax.
Behind the wall there's an ominous knock—
What's there, a ghost, a thief, rats?

In the sweltering kitchen, water drips,
Counting the rickety floorboards.
Someone with a glossy black beard
Flashes by the attic window—

And becomes still. How cunning he is, and evil,
He hid the matches and blew out the candle.
How much better would be the gleam of the barrels
Of rifles leveled at my breast.

Better, in the grassy square,
To be flattened on the raw wood scaffold
And, amid cries of joy and moans,
Pour out my life's blood there.

I press the smooth cross to my heart:
God, restore peace to my soul.
The odor of decay, sickeningly sweet,
Rises from the clammy sheets.

> August 27-28, 1921
> Tsarskoye Selo

> *translated by Judith Hemschemeyer*

Judith Hemschemeyer

A POET AND HER COUNTRY

The years of World War I and the revolution and its aftermath were the years in which Anna Akhmatova divorced her first husband, Nikolay Gumilyov, traveled through the south of Russia with her dear friend, the critic Nikolay Nedobrovo, met and fell in love with the artist Boris

Anrep, and then fell under the spell of the scholar Vladimir Shileyko, whom she married in 1918. Akhmatova wrote very few poems in 1918, 1919 and 1920. Then came 1921, a watershed year for her. In August of that year, Alexander Blok, exhausted and embittered, died at the age of 41 and Nikolay Gumilyov was arrested and executed on charges of counter-revolutionary activity.

For Akhmatova, the Terror had begun and in answer, her voice rang out again. Here is a poem written, according to the most reliable dating, when Gumilyov was under arrest; it anticipates his execution.

> You are no longer among the living,
> You cannot rise from the snow.
> Twenty-eight bayonets,
> Five bullets.
>
> A bitter new shirt
> For my beloved I sewed.
> The Russian earth loves, loves
> Droplets of blood.

August 16, 1921

But what happened to this outcry? According to Amanda Haight, Akhmatova's biographer, Akhmatova deliberately altered the dating of this poem to 1914 when including it in her next volume, *Anno Domini MCMXXI*, published in Petrograd in 1922.

The reason is obvious. As a poem written in 1914, it could, by some stretch of the imagination, be a lament for a fallen Russian soldier by his understandably embittered wife or sweetheart. As a report of the truth of the events of August 1921, it is itself counter-revolutionary.

So it is not surprising to find Akhmatova, as the former wife of Gumilyov and the mother of his son Lev (b. 1912), resorting to ante-dating as a form of self-censorship. With her talent for prescience, Akhmatova felt that Gumilyov's death was the first of many, and that the comparative freedom for writers and intellectuals in the early Twenties would not last. Still, her need to tell the truth forced her to come back again to the subject of Gumilyov's death. "Terror, fingering things in the dark" was written a few days after his execution.

This poem was first published in a journal in 1921, but without stanza four. Because Akhmatova resorted to Aesopian language, a common device of Russian writers, the poem could, especially without the fourth stanza, be a sort of fairy tale about a lonely woman imagining the attack of a midnight assassin. But stanza four describes a public execution and, in the line "...amid cries of joy and moans," Akhmatova's ambivalence toward this practice; it is probably for this reason that the editors of the journal omitted it. The last stanza contains one of Akhmatova's most powerfully telescoped images. The "odor of decay," I think, refers to two corpses, that of Gumilyov, who had once shared her bed and would, indeed, already be rotting, and her own precariously alive, sweating body, which she fears will soon join his in the grave.

Because of Gumilyov's execution, Akhmatova was thrust into the turmoil of the Terror almost a decade before most of her fellow writers and artists. And despite the fact that she was publicly stifled in the Twenties and Thirties, placed under surveillance and subject to sporadic room searches, she continued to write poems bearing witness to her country's travail.

Why would anyone who didn't have to endure such pain choose to endure it? Why did Akhmatova, who had many opportunities to leave Russia with various friends, choose to remain? A reading of the poems shows, I think, that Akhmatova simply never considered leaving. She had what her friend Osip Mandelstam believed every true poet must have: faith in the sacramental character of poetry and a sense of responsibility for everything that happens in this world.

Akhmatova's patience and stamina are legendary. The best tribute to her that I have read comes from Nadezhda Mandelstam in her second book of memoirs, *Hope Abandoned*: "One way or another I expect I shall now live out my life to the end, spurred on by the memory of Akhmatova's Russian powers of endurance; it was her boast to have so exasperated the accusers who had denounced her and her poetry that they all died before her of heart attacks."

> *(Excerpt from an essay entitled,*
> *"A Poet and Her Country: Anna*
> *Akhmatova's Early Political Poems")*

Stephen Berg

MY DOOR

A face or leg
on the frieze under the green roof of the customs building
caught my eye
and I saw the striped, weather-beaten flag;
its frayed, leading edge was a rainbowy blue-black blur,
a halyard clanked on the pole.
The orange haze that drifts up off the river
in late spring, usually, still dimmed the streets.
The sky was a watery green, the flag kept heaving and snapping;
I was afraid, suspicious, and held my breath.
I remember, too,
seeing myself as a child at the seashore,
my bare feet cool, sliding around in cracked leather shoes,
my braided hair
coiled back in a tight, shiny, coal-hard knot.
No images of death.
I was running; whatever filled my head
I sang; I saw myself
looking out my door
at the plump, silvery, turnip-shaped domes of the Chersonese temple,
glowing above all the houses,
and I thought
not to have fame and happiness is a worse despair
than loving them, these vices, as much as I do.

I think of the gentleness of snow, I see us
stop and hold each other. Raw, night air.
The sting of blown snow. Hollowness. Guns.
A dream of being somewhere else,
in a leveled city, that feels when I wake
as if I will never be the same now
but can't explain why, can't get up,
and when I do, finally, in the sluggish, bleary dawn,
can't recognize at first, looking into
the mirror above the sink, who it is: that flag—
I still sense its agony—
and the face and leg
(what's left of a story

about heroes, wives, chariots, battle scenes)
connected to no one
up there in the blurred stone,
down here among us,

some happiness annihilating us, stealing our identity
as I stand here—belonging to the face that looks into my face—
saying this.

Deborah Digges

TRANSLATION AND THE EGG

> *"some happiness annihilating us,*
> *stealing our identity..."*

O f the six shapes in nature, three—the spiral, the meander, and the branching—are open forms, and three—the circle, the hexagon, and the egg—are closed. Of these six, no doubt the egg is the most enigmatic. Its oval-curved surface as it lies, for instance, in a nest, can withstand many, many times its weight without cracking. In fact you can perch at least five generations, quail, ducks, eagles, whatever, in a kind of high-wire pyramid, like the Great Wallendas, on an egg and it still will not break. It is simply the hardest shape in nature to violate.

On the other hand, the offspring inside, coming to the end of its gestation and having, therefore, begun to starve and suffocate, initiates a weak, sporadic struggle, its relatively soft beak tapping against the inner surface, which, surprisingly, gives easily. The shell may be fractured at only one or two points before the chick inhales, rolls out, and lies still a while. Then it gets up nonchalantly and walks away. The egg is also the most efficient form to escape.

Last spring, having studied for a time the six shapes in nature, I introduced them to my undergraduate poetry-writing students in our discussions of existing and free verse forms. It seemed to me that after Darwin, we must be fatally arrogant or ignorant if we believe that our own intuitions and impulses in seeking out a language and a context for that language did not singularly or in combination discover these. If we human beings must credit ourselves with an additional form, the square, we must understand that it is really only an "off-shoot," so to speak, a reshaping of the circle with the help of the hexagon. And according to non-Euclidian, or elliptical geometry, the surface of the sphere (or planet) precludes a straight line. Thus, if language is linear.... But I'm losing my point here.

As our poetry class discussions progressed, we looked for poems whose content pushed their forms toward open or closed language. Roethke's greenhouse poems and their literal branchings and blossomings led us to "The Lost Son" and finally, "The Far Field," extended works that meandered and turned and circled the recent and far past. Dickinson's sprung rhythms and half-rhymes took on cellular, hexagonal patterns. Bishop's "The Fish," "The Bight," "Invitation to Miss Marianne Moore," and others spiraled through a series of comparisons until the similes themselves, poem by poem, became a kind of parallel spine that branched and overlaid the literal text. The more we searched, the more we found that our very vocabulary, inside or out of such a discussion, incorporated the six natural shapes, just as, for instance, none of us could ever avoid incorporating musical terms—rhythm, cadence, caesura—or visually artistic terms—composition, texture, surface.

But the egg remained for us an enigma because of its inherent three-dimensional qualities and because of the powerful dynamics of its outside and inside. It occurred to me much later, after the semester was over, that the egg may be the shape by which we can come to understand and appreciate the difficulties and discoveries a taut and inspired translation offers us.

Maybe you've listened, like me, to the endless academic argument that there is no such thing as a good translation. Recently I took part in a conference in Fano, Italy, an exchange of American and Italian poetry. A teacher named Cosma Siani had generously translated a number of our American poems, and one morning we sat in a medieval church around a huge table, flanked with Northern Italian wildflowers, and combed Cosma's efforts. As we talked, the old academic argument loomed darkly. How, for instance, in one of William Matthews' poems, could the phrase "flat drinks" be translated precisely? The Italians could think of no comparable description that had the same efficient, off-hand, and perfectly cynical tone. The nature of their language with its many words so musically superceding one of ours seemed to prohibit an economical and accurate translation. Another passionate discussion arose—with much passing of the microphone—over Yusef Komunyakaa's poem entitled "Prisoners," from a forthcoming collection set in Vietnam. What *was* a *croakasack*, anyway? And later, what did one of us mean by "skin-the-cat"? Happily, my ten-year-old, Stephen, was along on the trip and demonstrated this little gymnastic for Cosma, but our translator still worried that his work, though perhaps capturing the meaning, violated the hammer-line diction of the term.

In the end, Cosma, with the help of the rest of us, Americans and Italians alike, did the best he could to our great satisfaction. Without qualification it seemed to us—especially those of us with little or no experience in translation—that there would inevitably be certain inaccuracies which violated ei-

ther the music or meaning of a line. Resonances and puns, subtle tonal qualities would be missed. After all, each language had its own particular, simultaneously evolving etymologies, its own slang, its own closure. But this was-
n't the point, was it? Or not the whole point. If it was, we had no business
being there. What we were after was something else, something that lay inside the hard surface of each language, inside, even, the words of the individual piece, the poem.

This may sound to some of you—especially those of you who are effi-
ciently bi- or tri-lingual—like a language-poor woman's rationalization. Admittedly, I read a little Italian, a little French. On the other hand, that our fluent English-speaking Italian translator's background was Oxford, not Ohio
or Louisiana or Missouri or California, only compounded the problem. Any
language is a trap insofar as we remain hopelessly literal-minded about it.
But there are other ways to leave a house than through the front door.

Not unlike a powerful persona, a powerful translation admits to its blurred
edges just as, it seems to me, a powerful poet admits, in one way or another,
to an inadequacy in relationship to his or her subjects. Such an admission can
become part of the authenticity of a text. For instance, I was taken, some
years back, by Stephen Berg's *With Akhmatova at the Black Gates*, a collection which Berg calls "variations" written out of Richard McKane's translations from the Russian of Akhmatova. "I think," writes Berg in his afterword,
"I believed dimly that I was being released from myself by these poems
when, in fact, I was merely discovering, hearing from a part of myself I did
not remember or yet know." As I quote Berg, I'm remembering Jarrell's
"Seele im Raum," Merwin's "Departure's Girlfriend," Pound's "The River
Merchant's Wife," all "variations" of one kind or another that risk the language and/or gender barrier to speak from human issues so pressing that, yes,
it's hard to know where the poet's voice ceases and the persona's begins and
vice-versa. Somehow one keeps making it possible for the other to go on.

In *With Akhmatova...* the layering of voices is perhaps more complicated
as we move from Akhmatova to McKane to Berg. "The mixture is infinite,"
he admits, "the many sources unclear." Near the end of the collection, a poem
entitled "My Door" seems to me to be a moving celebration of this blurring
of identities. "The striped, weather-beaten flag... The orange haze that drifts
up from the river... Hollowness. Guns...a leveled city..." are merely a stark,
anonymous and timeless arena in which the intimate act of writing becomes
suddenly, startlingly possible. In fact, the poem's faceless objects and imagery are at odds with the particular, the exposed privacy of the voice. "I was
afraid," says the poet (Akhmatova? McKane? Berg?), "suspicious, and held
my breath."

How like the problem presented to each of us through the act of writing
and translating is the subtext or secret subject of this poem:

the face or leg
on the frieze...
(what's left of a story
about heroes, wives, chariots, battle scenes)
connected to no one
up there in the blurred stone
down here among us...

The poem's rhetorical structure—simply a "then/now" situation—further illuminates the poet's confusion. The face that looks back from "the mirror above the sink" is at first glance unrecognizable, as disparate and as dream-like as the formal setting for the poem. But it is this confusion that gives way to the poem's emotional clarity and gravity:

...that flag—
I still sense its agony...

some happiness annihilating us, stealing our identity
as I stand here—belonging to the face that looks into my face—
saying this.

In "My Door," the escape from one language into another, and from one identity into another, actually relies on the indistinct, ambiguous nature of translation and inspiration. The poet, Berg, authenticates the discovery of the self inside a foreign, chaotic context—war and its aftermath—and inside a time beyond him by authenticating, simply, "the moment of change" inside his own experiences, memories, sense of aging, "that feels when I wake/as if I will never be the same now/but can't explain why, can't get up...." Thus, by the end of the poem, Akhmatova, McKane, and Berg have been so absorbed into the text that "My Door" has become, itself, a point of view. The speakers and the words are one, looking back now, in strange chorus, at the reader. The most valuable poetry we have, I think, in any language, is the work that makes new poems possible. Translation is no exception. Beneath its hard surface, we might find our own "highest thoughts" inside.

from NORTHERN ELEGIES

FOUR

Memories have three eras.
The first feels like yesterday.
A blessed dome of memories
Shades the soul, the body luxuriates.
Laughter hasn't died away, tears still flow,
The inkspot hasn't been wiped off the table yet—
And like an imprint on the heart, the kiss
Is singular, valedictory, unforgettable . . .
But this doesn't last long . . .
The dome's disappeared, instead
Somewhere in the godforsaken suburbs
There's a secluded house
Where it's cold in winter, hot in summer,
Where a spider lives, and dust covers everything,
Where passionate letters decay,
Portraits change on the sly,
Like people who visit graves
And come home to soap their hands
And shake a superficial teardrop
Off their tired eyelids, sighing heavily . . .
But the clock ticks, one spring replaces itself
With another, the sky turns pink,
Names of cities change,
And there's no one left who saw it,
No one to cry with, no one to remember with,
And the shadows we no longer summon
Walk slowly away from us
Because their return would be terrifying.
And once awake, we see we even forgot
The way to that secluded house,
And gasping with anger and shame,
We run there but (the way dreams go)
Everything's different: people, things, walls,
And no one knows us—we're strangers.
We ended up at the wrong place . . . My God!
And this is the worst part:
We recognize we can't fit that past
Into the border of our lives,

It's almost as alien to us
As to our next door neighbor,
And we wouldn't recognize the dead.
And those we had to part with
Got along splendidly without us—everything
Was for the best.

1953
translated by Liza Tucker

David Young

MENDING WHAT CAN'T BE MENDED

The "Northern Elegies" constitute some of the finest poetry of Anna Akhmatova's later years. The best translation of them, and as far as I know the only complete one, appeared in FIELD in 1978 (and also, in an unauthorized "pirating," in *Modern Poetry in Translation*). My preference here is biased, since I worked closely with the translator, Liza Tucker, then an Oberlin student, and helped her polish and measure the phrasings over a period of several months. I think she succeeded admirably in catching the tone and lilt of Akhmatova's verse, and I know she also had good help with the Russian from Nina Berberova, a woman who had known the poet. Taking on this difficult set of poems was and is a very remarkable accomplishment for an undergraduate, and FIELD was happy to be able to print the results, along with a brief essay by the translator and some notes.

The best known of these poems is the third, the one that compares the poet's life to a rechanneled river. A number of translators have attempted it. The fourth, the one I've chosen as the subject of this essay, is a good deal less well known, and I'm aware of only one other translation, that of D. M. Thomas, who uses a different numbering system and calls it the sixth Northern Elegy. His version can be found in *Way of All the Earth* (Ohio U. Press, 1979); it's serviceable, but on the wordy and prosy side. What Tucker renders as "Where passionate letters decay,/Portraits change on the sly," for example, Thomas translates as "Letters that were like flames have burnt to ash,/Portraits have been changing stealthily." Reasonably accurate, but just not very poetic.

The Northern Elegies as a group, as Tucker observed in her FIELD essay, are about the tragic effects of time. Writing in her fifties and sixties, Akhmatova could use all her retrospective knowledge from a life crowded with pain and incident to attempt a summary and a sorting out. The pressure of history and of her troubled life bear down here as presences that threaten to be overwhelming unless the poetry can salvage some meaning and beauty from them. We sense the risk and admire the dignity and courage of the enterprise.

Somewhere at the center of Akhmatova's character there was a sustaining strength, related to her identity as a poet, that carried her through all the traumatic situations of her life. Once in awhile she could glimpse that calm center, and now and then others could too. During the war, when Akhmatova was living in Tashkent, she went out of her way to show concern for the health of Nikolay Punin, who had been her third husband. He had treated her badly in the past and they had parted bitterly, but her compassion when she heard of his serious illness was instantaneous; she met his train and saw him off the next day for the continuation of his journey. Amanda Haight's biography recounts this incident and quotes the letter that Punin wrote her afterwards. He tells her that he thought of her when he was sure he was about to die, and was amazed to recognize her spiritual strength:

> And it seemed to me then that I knew of no other person whose life was so whole and therefore so perfect as yours, from your first childish poems (the left-hand glove) to the prophetic murmur, and at the same time, roar of the *Poema*. I thought then that this life was perfect not through will, but—and this seemed to me to be particularly precious—through its organic wholeness, that is, its inevitability, which seems somehow not to have anything to do with you.... In your life there is a fortress that seems carved of stone, all at one time, by a very practiced hand.

In his notion of "organic wholeness" and his image of a fortress, Punin is searching for a way to express his sense that Akhmatova's art gave her a kind of invulnerability to the vicissitudes of war and totalitarianism. She had an uncanny ability to rise up through the frantic layers of pain and fantasy that surrounded her, to make sense of the senseless, to mend what couldn't be mended. It deserted her from time to time, but it always came back.

So there is something exhilarating, even healing, in the bitter retrospection of the fourth Northern Elegy. You say the worst and then you go on. If memory has three stages of development, each more disorienting than the last, you make a fearless little song out of that, an acceptance. You are not resigning yourself; there is an element of protest in what you utter, a refusal to submit. Or say that resignation and protest are in a productive tension with each other, two faces of the same thing.

Akhmatova's directness and simplicity are famous. Here she gives us the poem's thesis and structure right up front. Each stage or epoch of memory is clearly delineated. The figures of speech shine separately and clearly.

Since the first stage is happy, it doesn't detain the poet long. Why comment on the obvious? Akhmatova's genius with the hidden affinities among images is evident in her collocation of the kiss and the inkspot, the one from the experience of love, the other from the experience of the writer. We are simultaneously in the presence of creative inspiration and the thrill of dawning love. Tears and laughter are the same thing. It's also as if we're being given a quick summary of Akhmatova's early life, her famous youth. But this is anybody's experience. When you are young and your memory span is short, everything is fresh, immediate, bearable.

In the second, disillusioning stage of memory, Akhmatova develops one of her favorite tropes, the house. The dome or vault of heaven is no longer friendly enough to shelter the soul. Reality replaces idealism. One needs a place to live. The house stands variously for the self, mind and body, for relationships, for the accomplishments of the artist, and for the imprisoning contingencies of history. A room of one's own was a most literal problem in Akhmatova's Russia. She had stayed on with Punin (and his first wife and child) much longer than she wanted to simply because she couldn't find another place to live. The search for housing and the sense of homelessness became a lifelong concern. But if the secluded house in the disappointing suburbs offers shelter, it is a place where inexorable change shows its hostility to human happiness. Its furnishings, especially the unreliable family portraits, achieve only the kind of superficial sympathy that unwilling mourners, behaving ritualistically, manage to summon up. Time's relentlessness is starting to make itself felt. The "pleasure dome" has become an all too real "bleak house," but at least it is still a place to stay.

In the third era, the level of terror rises higher. Now isolation sets in; we lose touch with the living and, perhaps even more important, with the dead. The way to the house is forgotten, and if we happen to reach it in nightmare, we find it is the wrong place and we are forgotten too. We have no home to go to except this one we don't recognize and where we aren't recognized. Now we become irrelevant to our own past and our new absence from it is finally not even a matter for anybody's regret.

The tension between protest and resignation that I cited earlier is especially apparent at the poem's close. The end is a shock, going furthest toward saying that loss and isolation are parts of some design we need to reconcile ourselves to. A more literal version of "those we had to part with" would be something like "God sent us separation from": Thomas has "those whom God parted/From us." Amanda Haight tells us that Akhmatova's friend Lidia Chukovskaya "found it impossible not to believe that Akhmatova was not being ironical" in saying that everything was for the best, but Haight objects: "And yet this poem, written sometime between 1943 and 1954, not only does not sound ironical now, but was read 'straight' by Akhmatova when she recorded it toward the end of her life" (*Anna Akhmatova: A Poetic Pilgrimage*, Oxford, 1976, pp. 139-140). Surely it is not a case of either/or. From one point of view the note of acceptance has to be bitterly ironic because it obliterates a life and the coherence of a self. From another, the measure of understanding that transcends the personal and accepts the large patterns of change that govern our lives as having meaning and purpose, it is "straight" and very moving. I think we must allow the poet to have it both ways at this crucial moment.

Indeed, this simultaneity of tones and meanings is a principle that informs all of the poem. Akhmatova is talking about her own specific experience but she is also generalizing the stages of human maturity and loss. She is characterizing life but she is also writing about art; her first collection, *Evening*, dealt in remembered moments, and she saw the selective process whereby art transforms experience as deeply dependent on the poet's ability to remember accurately.

One further simultaneity: If the stages of human experience with memory can be generalized, then they are ahistorical. But this is also a poem embedded in specific facts of history. When Akhmatova says "Names of cities change," she means that St. Petersburg became Petrograd and then Leningrad. When she tells us that there is a kind of growing betrayal involved in recollection, she is thinking of the way all of Russia lived within the fantasies of its rulers, and especially within the nightmarish world created by Stalin. History was altered freely. People vanished. Akhmatova became a non-person. She lost her first husband to a firing squad, her son and second husband to arrest by the secret police, her friend Mandelstam to exile and then death in the labor camps. There is no way that that knowledge can be suppressed from this poem, and from her meditation on memory. If time betrays memory, it may do so in a general way for everyone who goes from youthful idealism to age and disillusion, but there were very specific ways in which it had done that, and more, to Akhmatova and her generation.

The simultaneous references give this poem's images enormous resonance. They also help explain our sense of the complex tone. Many of Akhmatova's poems risk being maudlin, but there is usually a biting humor that helps distance them from self-indulgence. This began with her early love poems, where self-pity is countered by self-mockery, and it is present in her later poems in touches like the crescendo of exaggeration that runs from "And once awake" to "My God!" There's a curious sense of fun behind this somber poem. I connect it to that calm core of Akhmatova's being that the insanities of war and politics could not reach. Yeats had it, Tu Fu had it, Rilke had it, Emily Dickinson had it. Perhaps it is always associated with the finest poetry. I think it also inhabits this companion piece, another "house" poem, that Liza Tucker translated at the same time she did the Northern Elegies:

"IT WAS FRIGHTFUL . . ."

It was frightful, living in that house.
Nothing, not even the ancestral hearth,
My child's small cradle,
The fact that we were both young
And full of plans,
Lessened this feeling of terror.
And I learned to laugh at it
And I used to leave a droplet of wine
And a breadcrumb for the one
Who scratched like a dog at the door, at night,
Or glanced in the low little window,
Just when we'd grown silent
Trying not to notice what was going on
In the looking glass,
Where someone's leaden walk
Made the steps of the dark staircase squeal,
Begging for mercy.
And smiling oddly, you used to say:
"Who are 'they' lugging down the staircase?"

Now you're there, where they know everything.
        Tell me—
What lived in that house besides us?

                    1945

The "looking glass" was one of Akhmatova's terms for the strange enclosed
world of Soviet Russia. By connecting it to Lewis Carroll she reduced its terrible dimensions and "learned to laugh at it." That did not, of course, make it
any less destructive to human lives. But it implicitly celebrated the human
spirit's capacity to resist.

"IT'S NOT WITH A LOVER'S LYRE"

It's not with a lover's lyre, not at all,
That I go around attracting a crowd.
It's the rattle with which lepers crawl
That in my hands keeps singing aloud.

translated by Lyn Coffin

Marilyn Krysl

THE LEPER'S RATTLE

T he poem: for all the reasons it's wrong it's right.
It lacks, happily, the preciousness of the minimal. This poem is not
a gem, but resembles instead a stick of dynamite—small package,
whopping effect.

It's a chestnut, yes, didactic in intent, its program oversimplified—except
for its reverberations. From what appears to be simple—diction, form, statement—springs an elaborate discernment. The poem goes after the speaker's
detractors with a finely tuned spirit of revenge. Akhmatova aimed for truth,
and truth is its own naked force. "I don't understand these big words," she
once said, "poet, billiard."

It's got the mindless, singsong personality of a nursery rhyme, tossed off.
And tossed off, probably for the sake of the rhyme, that indulgence which defeats subtlety—except that at the same time this poem travels powered by
such rhyme. And who can ignore the passing of a diesel truck?

And isn't it histrionic, for her, a mature writer. As the generation of our
parents might say, "At her age!" Except that just such an unexpected turn, of
just that intensity, is characteristic of Akhmatova. Passion, after all, is her
way of life. "An element of howl," as Joseph Brodsky has pointed out, is one
of her hallmarks.

So we admire the poem's blatancy. The take it or leave it tone. The way it
goes about its business slamming doors, breaking china, shattering crystal
against the hearth. How it mocks subtlety. Daring to speak as she feels at that
moment, unguarded and utterly frank, flatfooted, bald, short to the point almost of crudity but right on target—to such daring how we're drawn. And
then the whack of the imagery. What nerve in a woman, writing, to set the
lover square against the leper in the poem. It suggests the easy dualism of
stereotype: virgin/whore, princess/monster. Except that Akhmatova does this

on purpose, to fling the dualism in our faces. She insists that we understand just how crude such oppositions are, how they mask reality. We respond to the audacity with which she seems to say, "They want good girls? Then I'll be bad." And its counterpart: "They want bad girls? Then I'll be BAD!"

The poem takes a quantum leap when we learn that the diction is literally autobiographical. It is true that Akhmatova's first books spoke the lingua franca of romantic love. What is also true is that critics' insistence that her significance was as a writer of love lyrics was part of the move to silence her politically, humanly. These pronouncements mirrored the state's censorship of her work between 1923 and 1940. Precisely because she did not restrict her work to the production of the obligatory and harmless, she suffered. Her first husband, Gumiliov, was executed, probably on direct order from Lenin. Her close friend Mandelstam died in a concentration camp. Her son Lev was imprisoned, and her third husband Punin died in prison. About these sorrows and the sorrow she felt for her country under Stalin's thumb she was forbidden to speak, her work was banned. Thus she became, as the poem states so flatly, a leper. In the state's official view she was persona non grata.

But the poem describes her triumph as an untouchable. It is when the speaker is most dangerous, when she is most infectious, that she draws crowds. Just so Akhmatova spoke for and thus drew to her all those who, like her, suffered at the hands of the state, paid for a tyrant's whims. That crowd was nearly all of Russia. So in the poem the leprous speaker becomes a spiritual leader. These lines are spoken by a charismatic voice. And it is the charisma of the survivor who not only survives but triumphs. It is also the charisma of the survivor who lifts an awful truth up from darkness. Love is and lovers are blind, remember. But lepers see, and what she sees is what the crowd also sees: that the Emperor has no clothes.

Thus the poem rings out across cultures and down through our present epoch. Akhmatova was and we are citizen residents of opposing "superpowers" which, in that superiority only brute power can confer, have come to resemble each other. All of us here who dissent are made to feel we go not just against the Reagan era but against the American grain. Just so Akhmatova was proclaimed traitorous not to Stalin (she was forced to sing his praises in order to secure her son's release from prison) but to the ideals of the Russian nation.

And yet in the poem, in the speaker's hands, the rattle sings aloud. The poem does what only the single quatrain can do so well. It falls progressively downward through the first three lines, then soars into and beyond the final line, astonishing us. Think for instance of Dickinson's version of that stanza:

> Because I could not stop for Death—
> He kindly stopped for me—
> The Carriage held but just Ourselves—
> And Immortality.

Because the third line of Akhmatova's poem ends with the image of the leper crawling—ends with the word *crawl*, that leprous word—and how much lower can we fall than to *crawl*—the final line's lifting off feels like an immense surge.

The imagery too ("that rattle with which lepers crawl") has the intensity of nursery rhyme. Think how, in the lines "ashes, ashes,/we all fall down" the word *ashes* resonates to our ear. That verse recreates the atmosphere of the Middle Ages and the Plague, which made everyone "fall down," the infection which required that the bodies be burned: ashes. Similarly, in Akhmatova's poem, the lyre is too delicate an instrument with which to capture the true character of her century. We live still in a time of war, of epidemic, of famine amidst plenty, of the wasting of the earth. Ours is a time of blunt events, reeling reactions, a time of fear and cowering. Of crawling. As Joseph Brodsky writes in the introduction to Lyn Coffin's selection and translation of Akhmatova, the poet's work, characterized by "the note of controlled terror," took Russian poetry into "the real, non-calendar twentieth century."

Not the lyre but the rattle. Its drama, its repetitive insistence, its foreboding whirr, like the sound of a rattlesnake's tail striking that note of controlled terror—the rattle is the proper instrument of our epoch. How fitting then that the rattle, monochromatic, is an instrument of one tone only. It conveys no melody. Rhythm is its business. It can only mark time. And yet in Akhmatova's hands, the music of lyric poetry is neither lost nor blunted. For her, the rattle "keeps singing aloud."

OSIP MANDELSTAM
(1891-1938)

Thanks partly to his widow Nadezhda's memoirs, Osip Mandelstam is today perhaps as well known for the tragic circumstances of his life as for his writing. During his lifetime his work was suppressed, and for some time afterward encountered official silence, but his stature as a leading Russian poet has now been firmly established. With his friend Anna Akhmatova, he filled a central role in the Acmeist movement, arguing for a classical precision and scrupulous diction in evoking emotional experience. Mandelstam's mature work alternates between deeply personal concerns and meditations on fatality, power, and eternity; mythological motifs and images from ancient history provide a context for speculation about his country's fate under Soviet political dictatorship. Always impulsive and irrepressible in spirit, he fell openly into conflict with the state when his satirical epigram about Stalin came to light in 1934. Sent into exile, he attempted suicide; briefly reprieved, he was later arrested again and sentenced to a labor camp, where he died of starvation in 1938. In his work's extraordinary economy and vividness, and in his moral authority on issues of integrity and self-expression, he remains a vital force in twentieth-century poetry.

BOOKS IN ENGLISH TRANSLATION: *Selected Poems*, trans. Clarence Brown and W. S. Merwin (1973); *The Prose of Osip Mandelstam*, trans. Brown (1967); *Selected Essays*, trans. Sidney Monas (1977); *Complete Critical Prose and Letters*, ed. Jane Gary Harris, trans. Harris and Constance Link (1979). See also Nadezhda Mandelstam, *Hope Against Hope* (1970) and *Hope Abandoned* (1974).

"TAKE FROM MY PALMS, TO SOOTHE YOUR HEART..."

Take from my palms, to soothe your heart,
a little honey, a little sun,
in obedience to Persephone's bees.

You can't untie a boat that was never moored,
nor hear a shadow in its furs,
nor move through thick life without fear.

For us, all that's left is kisses
tattered as the little bees
that die when they leave the hive.

Deep in the transparent night they're still humming,
at home in the dark wood on the mountain,
in the mint and lungwort and the past.

But lay to your heart my rough gift,
this unlovely dry necklace of dead bees
that once made a sun out of honey.

November 1920
translated by Clarence Brown and W. S. Merwin

Franz Wright

PERSEPHONE'S BEES: THOUGHTS ON MANDELSTAM

I am working here from the translation by W. S. Merwin and Clarence Brown and would like to begin by acknowledging the debt of gratitude I feel to this team and their accomplishment with Mandelstam. Two gifted translators have come together in this instance to create what I believe is a great poem in English. It deserves our faith and trust, and it should serve to remind us that so-called free verse has the very same musical and rhythmical resources at its command as so-called formal verse. Perhaps we cannot expect Joseph Brodsky to understand that fact, but for anyone who grew up speaking American English and reading American poetry, any assertion to the contrary sounds like willful ignorance.

For my own part, I find writing about Mandelstam extremely daunting. There is something that sets him apart, even from the company of an Eliot or a Rilke or a Celan. It lies partly in the fact that he knowingly wrote and signed his death sentence, assuring his descent by the composition of a single brief poem, one that would not even be noticed in our culture. His short poem satirizing Stalin, for which one of his friends turned him in, led to his arrest and eventually his death. So there is something uncanny about him, about the death-beckoning intensity of his convictions. More than Pasternak, even more than Akhmatova, he would not or could not compromise, as his wife's memoir makes clear. Other poets, such as Rilke, address the spirit of Orpheus, the spirit of Christ; Mandelstam came to embody that Christ-like or Orphic spirit. He did descend. Whether he consciously chose to or not is of little importance. Has anyone ever chosen to?

But these events were still far-off when he composed "Take from my palms...." The poem possesses, in its initial setting, a kind of pre-Edenic innocence. Its speaker is an Orpheus who has done nothing wrong, has not disobeyed even the most illogical of the god's commands and so has not lost all and been torn to pieces for his error. Instead he has retained, in a saddened and aging, yet real and corporeal form, the gift of poetic perception and the gift of love. These two things turn out to be one and the same.

Since he has kept faith with love and endured its seasons—Persephone's comings and goings rather than Eurydice's disappearance—and has patiently endured the fluctuations of inspiration's power to transform reality, mortality is not a curse but a cause for grave and sober celebration. Hence the gift, a humble offering that symbolizes the fragile gifts of love and poetry.

How lovely it is that Mandelstam chose to mention, with seeming offhandedness, the mint and lungwort. Perhaps they are the herbs visited by Persephone's bees. In any case, they are plants to which, traditionally, powers to aid clear breathing and memory are attributed, two vital functions to the citizens of the underworld who are invoked in so many of Mandelstam's poems of this period. And the herbs are two items in a list where the third element is the past two concrete objects linked with something invisible, all in one breath. With elegant simplicity, the poet reminds us of the awesome reality of the past: how much more of it there is, and how ghostly and threadbare our present brief opportunity to breathe under the sun is by comparison. That is not a call to despair so much as an invitation to savor our humble gift.

In *The Sheltering Sky*, writing the dark story of a long-time relationship between a man and a woman, Paul Bowles says:

> Love for [him] meant loving her—there was no question of anyone else. And for so long there had been no love, no possibility of it. But in spite of her willingness to become whatever he wanted her to become, she could not

change that much: the terror was always there inside her, ready to take command. It was useless to pretend otherwise. And just as she was unable to shake off the dread that was always with her, he was unable to break out of the cage into which he had shut himself...long ago to save himself from love.

What a remarkable image to end this passage with. To protect ourselves from something dangerous don't we usually place *it* inside the cage? But this brings to mind one of those little cells marine scientists lock themselves into far under the water in order to observe the behavior of the most mindlessly ferocious creatures down there, in *that* underworld. What is Bowles's character protecting himself from? What unspeakably menacing form has love taken on in his mind? Clearly it is a force capable of obliterating him, attacking and annihilating the self. We realize that what is actually going on here is his perception of love as a giving up, a sacrificing of the self. To take on complete emotional responsibility for the well-being of another soul would entail a concomitant loss of privacy, solitude and concentration. It would interrupt the spiritual state essential to his exploration of the self, always the self. And the beloved, once a door spontaneously and effortlessly standing open in the quest for inner illumination, would become a wall.

We sense none of this self-absorbed anxiety in Mandelstam's poem. Instead, there is the desire and the courage to renounce the seduction of the self, the catastrophe of living-for-the-self-alone. There is a willingness to enter the unknowable self of the beloved, the other which one seeks mysteriously to become one with, which one *desires* without expecting anything in return. A terrible risk is involved—the loss of the self. Char wrote, "May risk light your way." Mandelstam signifies the fearful decision to seek and regain the self through devoting it to another by means of the gift, the necklace. It is a gift of remembered and reminding things, the sacramental giving of a "ring"—the eternal symbol of our subject, a constantly resurrected Persephone. There is a turning toward the source of what the self has come to think of as its own light, a turning toward the companion who is, finally and perhaps for the first time, a self, no figment of his need but separate and real as he.

"Take from my palms..." is surrounded, in the particular period of Mandelstam's poetry in which it was composed, by evocations of death, oblivion and descent. It draws its imagery from the Greek mythology that he loved and that reflects his determination to compose a poetry purely classical by nature, a poetry that had little in common with romantic poetry's obsession with the self. In Mandelstam, as in other great modernist poets, we find an awed manipulation of the real objects of the world, objects that continue to express the individual's thoughts and feelings but that also help poems take on a more universal human expression. This poem possesses the unmistakable aura of being staged *in the world*, among its dear and commonplace mysteries. What we are witnessing is not romance but resurrection, love's resurrection. Resurrection is hard and unattractive, like birth. We are reminded of this when we consider another well-known myth, that of Lazarus. Think of the grave-wrappings stuck to his flesh: one might have trouble finding the stomach to unwind them from his face.

Mandelstam's poem is one of the few written by anyone in our century that manages to transcend literature, to the same degree that poetry can transcend prose. Rare poems such as this attain a power to emanate emotion and thought that approaches the supernatural. For me this term has no heavenly connotations. On the contrary, I apply it in a very earthly sense to refer to the awe experienced by human beings when the inner pressure of remembrance or an abrupt interruption in the distracting struggle for survival allows them to realize that they *have* feelings and memories and thoughts about the mystery of their universe that can compel them to utter sounds. These sounds are true poetry, the best of which has always embodied skilled upwellings of songlike structures, spells, prayers, lamentations, or a triumphant joy inexpressible by any other means. True poetry shows nature that we are capable of being just as enigmatic and beyond explanation as it is. By means of it we claim our right to participate in its strange workings and manifestations.

The technical expertise involved in works of literature is helpless to explain this spiritual experience. It involves a sense of language as not simply describing external reality, but rivaling it, a belief in the power of words—when spoken in a certain secret order known only to a few adepts—to change reality and influence important events. Our own tradition carries this special sense of the power of language in the Biblical events reported in *Genesis*, where God causes objects—water, light, and so forth—to come into being by *uttering* them, then assigns man the job of *naming* the animals into fuller existence, and in *The Book of John*, based on the concept of the *logos*, the word made flesh.

Some years ago it was fashionable to classify as "hermetic"—a term with undeniably arcane associations—the writings of supposedly difficult and secretive poets like Mandelstam. I'm suggesting, however, a constant in our experience that relates to the poetic outcome of human beings finding themselves up against the futility of logical thought and expression and then discovering that they have the power, through a concentrated and highly charged use of speech or song, to placate, ward off, heal or daringly *invite* internal forces (ones we would now discuss in psychological terms) beyond their comprehension or control to speak for them and through them. This is accomplished through the unique human power of saying, naming, voicing the things of the world: not so much to mirror them for practical purposes, but to secretly rearrange and change them for the instinctual sake of a survival more than physical and for the sake of helping the community to participate in the incessant creation of the Creation.

I believe there have been a few poets who have maintained a connection with the supernatural and superliterate dimensions of language; and if any in our century have borne the burden and glory of this connection, Osip Mandelstam is certainly to be counted among them. I hope no one will suppose that I am claiming that Mandelstam perceived himself in some shamanistic light. As a Russian poet he naturally attached a high sense of calling and dignity to his position. But a poet like Mandelstam can never be pinned down. Certainly he could be secretive and ritualistic when it came to his sources of inspiration. In her magnificent book, *Hope Against Hope*, his wife speaks touchingly, for example, of the surprise he might express when he realized that others did not experience the same overwhelming significance he perceived in the number of verses in a poem. At the same time, he was constantly and fiercely aware of himself as an artist, a master of his craft.

As previously noted, many of the 1920 poems draw their imagery from the ancient Greek visualization of the afterlife. Mandelstam was seeking ways of turning away from direct, philosophical expression of the inner life. He was interested in things—the necklace of dead bees—and, like Rilke, in myth's modern malleability and relevance. These are preoccupations that he shared, as I've indicated, with other modernists. Yet there is always something different and disturbing about his brand of modernism. It certainly derives partly from his fate. There is an element of Greek drama about what happened, so that we cannot read his poems touching on descent to the Greek or Dantean underworld without a pang of horror. We know what Mandelstam could not know when he wrote them, that in the course of his own life he would have to enter hell himself. The Greek version is a place of oblivion, very different from the cruel and insane Christian conception of a place of wide-awake torture that proceeds without end. Mandelstam's fate was to combine these two hells, or so we surmise from what we can piece together about his last days.

Is this why "Take from my palms...," while relatively early, written when the poet was around thirty, sometimes sounds as if it was spoken by a much older man, even by a ghost?

Love poems are usually associated with the euphoric, fairytale period of early love, when it is untouched by sorrow or discord. But from the first moment of this one, not least in the somewhat frightening and melancholy figure of Persephone, we receive the far more complex sensation that love has had and repeatedly will have its changes, its seasons, its deaths and dormancies, its reawakenings. Love's rebirths are miraculous and touching because they can be felt at every moment to be ephemeral. They are not only the spring but the memory of every spring, linking us to the first one when age and love's alterations were still inconceivable.

Mandelstam's poem commemorates enduring love and is at the same time haunted to some degree by a sense of resignation and loss. It remains the embodiment of love experience while taking on the coloration of time. Hence the revelation it expresses, by its existence and the necessity of its composition: the need to love is an infinitely greater desire than the need to be loved.

People can survive without being loved. But no matter how poor human beings become, how bereft of things or spirit, they must love. They must love someone or something beyond the self or *they cease to have a self at all*. And to love involves in part the need to give. Giving will find a way, even where there is nothing that begins to be commensurate with what one feels. In Mandelstam's case, the gift is the poem itself. It is certainly the most moving poem of love I am familiar with. It expresses the fact that in love we are infinitely poor. We have no thing, object or word of great enough value to equal what we are going through when we realize the value another soul has for us, and at the same time recognize the impossibility of penetrating the other with our soul, with what we feel. We have nothing but inadequate symbols.

Another of poetry's many origins may have to do with the wish to circumvent this agonizing dilemma. Skillfully employed and placed in the correct order, made into song or prayer, might there not be, we feel, a way of employing words that both expresses what the lover is feeling and approximates an ability to penetrate the soul of the beloved as no object or body ever can? The power of Mandelstam's poem resides in the fact that the lover is able to state, with astonishingly concentrated and various brilliance, by way of ravishing images of poverty, that the world, the sun, the universe itself, could they be bestowed, would not be enough. In any event, he has nothing to offer but these husks of bees—Persephone's bees—who once made a sun out of honey, as perhaps he himself has attempted to do. There is nothing to give but these words, these dead bees, this absent wax and honey and light. There is an enormous sadness in all this, but also a sense of happiness in the survival of rough, daily love. The lovers are not separated, lost to each other. The earth has survived, a whole world exists and endures in its humble, unexplainable seasons that faith knows will always return. It endures as a particle of a sun that once exploded and, at an unimaginable distance but still close enough to blind us, goes on exploding forever.

"WE SHALL MEET AGAIN, IN PETERSBURG..."

We shall meet again, in Petersburg,
as though we had buried the sun there,
and then we shall pronounce for the first time
the blessed word with no meaning.
In the Soviet night, in the velvet dark,
in the black velvet Void, the loved eyes
of blessed women are still singing,
flowers are blooming that will never die.

The capital hunches like a wild cat,
a patrol is stationed on the bridge,
a single car rushes past in the dark,
snarling, hooting like a cuckoo.
For this night I need no pass.
I'm not afraid of the sentries.
I will pray in the Soviet night
for the blessed word with no meaning.

A rustling, as in a theater,
and a girl suddenly crying out,
and the arms of Cypris are weighed down
with roses that will never fall.
For something to do we warm ourselves at a bonfire,
maybe the ages will die away
and the loved hands of blessed women
will brush the light ashes together.

Somewhere audiences of red flowers exist
and the fat sofas of the loges,
and a clockwork officer
looking down on the world.
Never mind if our candles go out
in the velvet, in the black Void. The bowed shoulders
of the blessed women are still singing.
You'll never notice the night's sun.

25 November 1920
translated by Clarence Brown and W. S. Merwin

Agha Shahid Ali

THE BLESSED WORD

"...while outside the storm, that is, the infinite, rages in vain."
—Roland Barthes

I cannot divorce Mandelstam's poetry from his life though I still am trained to look New Critically, stripping poems of biography. Osip Mandelstam and a few other poets—Nazim Hikmet, Faiz Ahmed Faiz, Garcia Lorca—compel me to ignore that training. No matter what Auden says about Yeats, the death of this Russian poet could not and cannot be kept from his poems. Nor could, nor can his exile. No one would dare.

Clarence Brown, in his introduction to Nadezhda Mandelstam's *Hope Against Hope*, narrates: "One May evening in 1965 the students of the Mechanical Mathematics Department of Moscow University had organized on their own initiative the first memorial evening of Mandelstam's poetry to be held in Russia. They invited Ilia Ehrenburg...to preside." At one point

> Ehrenburg mentioned rather hesitantly...that Nadezhda Yakovlevna was in the auditorium. He continued, "She lived through all the difficult years with Mandelstam, went into exile with him, saved all of his poems.... I hesitated whether I should say the poet's widow was at this first evening. I don't ask her to come down here...." But here his words were smothered under thunderous applause that lasted for a long time. Everyone stood. Finally, Nadezhda Yakovlevna herself stood and a hush fell upon the house. Turning to face the audience, she said, "Mandelstam wrote, 'I'm not accustomed yet to panegyrics....' Forget that I'm here. Thank you." And she sat down. But the applause would not die away for a long time.

Whenever I recall this passage, that is, almost each time I read Mandelstam, I find myself choked.

For this symposium I've focused on "We shall meet again, in Petersburg," a first line that announces heartbreak as the poem's craft. Mandelstam never returned to Petersburg, only to Leningrad—and then again there was exile, where he perhaps reinvented Petersburg. The poem speaks to me because of the condition of my homeland today, Kashmir, the Valley longing to be free, the Vale in which the Titans once sought refuge. My friends from there write, "When you leave home in the morning, you never know if you'll return." I want to reply, "We shall meet again, in Srinagar," but I'm afraid to, for a promise like that already holds its own breaking, made as it is against the backdrop of "the Soviet night, in the velvet dark,/in the black velvet Void." So in the diaspora one reinvents the past or invents the future to transform Moscow or Petersburg or Srinagar into imaginary homelands, filling them, closing them, shutting oneself in them.

Am I misreading? The reader may accuse me. But I'm really un-reading the poem, maybe de-reading it. As long as I, while seeming to take the poem away from Mandelstam, do not keep him from it, I'm not violating his words, nor his death and exile. The poem's very fabric gives me the permission, if not the authority, to depart from it so that I may then return to Mandelstam more fully. The poem adopts strategies that enable me to do so: it raises question after question, answering none. Underlying its each move is a "maybe-ness" whereby the reader unravels and decodes it, revealing the poem beneath the poem. How else to account for the blessed word with *no* meaning, the flowers that will *never* die, the roses that will *never* fall, and the night in which the poet is *not* afraid and needs *no* pass? How else to grapple with our *never* noticing the night's sun, preceded as it is by the imperative:

> Never mind if our candles go out
> in the velvet, in the black Void.

Never. That word again. Negative spaces for the reader to fill in, but in such a way that the poem, though not fully clear, is never misunderstood.

"We shall meet again, in Petersburg,": After such simplicity, the absolute clarity of that affirmation, we come up in the second line, a subordinate clause, with the impossibility of the certainty just expressed: "as though we had buried the sun there." Is Mandelstam implying that the sun, its corpse, will be dug up, the Son resurrected? (I'm aware the pun may not exist in the Russian and that Mandelstam was Jewish.) And in that impossible moment—will the blessed word with no meaning occur? That word has no meaning in the present age, Mandelstam's, which will maybe die away, but will it acquire meaning when the meeting takes place in Petersburg? There is a strange hope here, this impossible longing made possible in the Soviet night simply because "the blessed women are still singing." As is the poet. Are they singing the blessed word itself or singing of that work, their song a prayer? Something impossible is happening in the night—flowers are blooming that will never die.

In the second stanza the poet pronounces the night as Soviet. The sun, as we already know, is buried in it. Strangely, he needs no pass, he is not afraid. Why? Perhaps because he can "pray" for the blessed word with no meaning. But that word does have meaning—for him and for the singing women. It— the word, or the Word?—has been stripped of meaning in the Soviet night, in which a patrol is stationed on the bridge and a car hoots like a cuckoo. We are far, far away from meeting again in Petersburg though we continue to be pursued by that hope. When the "arms of Cypris" are weighed down with "roses that will never fall," is the implication that the Soviet night will be over once they fall? And yet their not falling allows him to speculate, with hope perhaps, that maybe "the ages will die away/and the loved hands of blessed women/will brush the light ashes together." The plaintive persistence of the women, in contrast to the sudden cry of the girl, leads (if not to hope) perhaps to an arrested despair.

And where do the audiences of red flowers exist? Are they the flowers that will never die of the first stanza and/or the roses of the third? One can't be sure. And one shouldn't be. Nor should one be sure why we won't notice the night's sun. It may be because it is dark with excessive bright, like Milton's God, and we are so blinded that only the black Void is visible. Or it may be that if hope does not abandon us, we may not regret the going out of the candles. Each line raises questions, but without causing confusion. I am absolutely clear that I must fill in these spaces; the poem insists I do. If Mandelstam will not allow himself, or us, any certainty, he also will not allow us a one-dimensional surrendering of hope. The tenuousness of the poem, its "maybe-ness," works in both ways. That is why the poet does not begin "Maybe we shall meet again, in Petersburg," though that unsaid "Maybe" pervades the poem.

And so, to depart from the poem again and perhaps return to it via Kashmir:

What of the night's sun there in Srinagar, the summer capital of Kashmir? There are of course the stars the guns shoot into the sky, night after night, the storm, the infinite, that rages on, it seems in vain. On Id-uz-Zuha, when people celebrate God's inability, for even God must melt sometimes, to let Ishmael (not Isaac, in Muslim legend) be executed by the hand of his father, many parts of Srinagar and of the entire Vale were under curfew. The identity card, that pass, may or may not have helped in the crackdown, if one were rounded up by the sentries of the Central Reserve Police. There was no celebration, for son after son was taken away. All this was seen by an audience of narcissi, roses, magnolias, and all the flowers of Kashmir.

And will the blessed women rub the ashes together? I recall a Kashmiri of the sixteenth century, Habba Khatun, the "most picturesque figure in the literary, musical and, one may say, human history of Kashmir," according to one historian. A peasant girl who became the queen, "she was so completely merged in the life of her people as to become anonymous, and her personality became embodied in a collection of deeply-moving songs which the people have sung and the hills re-echoed." When her husband was exiled from the Valley by the Mughal king Akbar, she "went among the people with her sorrow.... [Her] grief has been shared by every sensitive Kashmiri to this day; in her own time its expression roused quite a few into frenzied opposition to Mughal rule." Each fall the women of Kashmir gather the chinar leaves, singing songs, often hers, and by a rustic process create fuel for winter: they set fire to the leaves, sprinkle water on them as they burn, and thus turn them into fragile coals. But already the reports are true, and without song: India's security forces have gang-raped and mass-raped women in the villages and have torched entire neighborhoods. The people have been roused into frenzied opposition to Indian rule, fighting one of the largest armies of the world. Maybe the ages will die away, or so we will pray in the Soviet night, in the Indian-enforced night, "and the loved hands of blessed women/will brush the light ashes together."

And that blessed word with no meaning—who will utter it? Is it Freedom? Will the women pronounce it, as if for the first time, or for the last? Srinagar too hunches like a wild cat. Sentries are stationed, in bunkers, at the city's bridges while the Jhelum flows under them, sometimes with a dismembered body. On Zero Bridge the jeeps rush by. The candles go out in the velvet Void, or they go out as travellers, to light up that Void. One day perhaps the Kashmiris will pronounce—as perhaps will the Armenians, the Croatians, the Kurds, the Palestinians, the Slovenians—that word for the truly first time. And give it meaning.

"TO SOME, WINTER IS ARAK AND BLUE-EYED PUNCH..."

To some, winter is arak and blue-eyed punch,
To some it's wine perfumed with cinnamon,
To some the salty orders of cruel stars
To be carried back into smoky huts.

Chicken-shit here and there, still warm,
And the blundering warmth of sheep;
I'd give up everything to live—I need life so—
A lighted match would keep me warm.

Look, all I have in my hands is a clay bowl,
And the twitter of stars to tickle my frail ears,
But under this wretched feather-down you can't
Help loving the yellow grass and warm black earth.

To curry fur in silence and turn straw,
Starved as an apple tree wrapped up for winter,
Filled with a tenderness for witless creatures,
Groping in emptiness, trying to be patient.

Let the conspirators scuttle across the snow
Like sheep, and let the snow-crust squeak,
To some, winter is smoke and wormwood, a bivouac
To some, the heady salt of tragic injuries.

Oh, I'd like to hoist a lantern on a pole
And wander, led by my dog, under the salt stars,
To the fortune teller's yard, with a rooster for the pot.
But the white of the snow chews my eyes till they ache.

1922
translated by David Young

David Young

STARS VERSUS SALT

Reading Russian poets in translation, knowing you not only lack the language but the context of poetic and cultural traditions that make the poetry specific, glorious, energizing, can be a discouraging process. Perhaps one should give it up, but with writers as fascinating as Mandelstam, how to resist? It's like listening to a radio program despite a lot of static, knowing you need to hear as much of it as you can.

In the case of this particular poem, I know of four translations, by W. S. Merwin and Clarence Brown, by Bernard Meares, by James Greene and by David McDuff. Each has its merits, but I've listed them in my order of preference, with Merwin/Brown and Meares very close, and Greene and McDuff a distant third and fourth. I've learned from each of them and I've learned the most, of course, by careful comparing. My own version, in this case, is more a way to get as close as possible to the poem, exploiting the four versions and adding my own ideas and hunches. It isn't intended to replace the others but to supplement them. Merwin's versions, backed up with Brown's expertise on the language, the culture and the poet, are the ones I will always love most because they gave me my first glimpses of Mandelstam and because they shine with Merwin's gift for image and phrase. They turn out not always to be as accurate as one could wish and they sometimes lose the point of the images or phrases they try to capture in English. Meares stays closer to the original, and he reveals a good ear and eye for what will work in a poem, but he sometimes gets into trouble when he tries to rhyme. The other two translators have many moments of effectiveness, but are capable of clunkers that make you wish a good poet had helped them out. McDuff's is the only book that has the Russian on facing pages, which is a reason for owning it if you have a Russian-speaking friend who can help you fine-tune your sense of what you are looking at. A glance at the text of the poem I'm treating here, for example, shows that the same phrase, "To some," begins each of the first three lines. McDuff's is the only version that does in English, but it's interesting to know that the formal repetition is a part of the poet's design. I'm not saying all the translators should have faithfully reflected it, just that it's a useful bit of information. Translation is made up of thousands of small interlocking choices, and you simply can't dictate rules or formulas for its success; you have to allow the translator to go where she or he feels comfortable in the pursuit and partial capture of the original, not to mention the creation of a new poem in the second language. If Merwin/Brown is sometimes rather far from Mandelstam, what compensates is the fresh and deeply moving quality of their versions, poems that live in the memory and make us realize what all the fuss concerning this poet is based on.

"To some, winter..." is from Mandelstam's 1928 volume and marks a shift in his imagery from classically and mythically based characters and situations to a world recognizably Russian and historical, shot through with implications of folklore and politics. I can best introduce its subject and imagery by means of a shorter poem that preceded it by a year; here it is in the brilliant Merwin/Brown version:

> I was washing outside in the darkness,
> the sky burning with rough stars,
> and the starlight salt on an axe-blade.
> The cold overflows the barrel.
>
> The gate's locked,
> the land's grim as its conscience.
> I don't think they'll find the new weaving,
> finer than truth, anywhere.
>
> Star-salt is melting in the barrel,
> icy water is turning blacker,
> death's growing purer, misfortune saltier,
> the earth's moving closer to truth and to dread.

The imagery here is clear and, I think, marked by this poet's greatness. Mandelstam is characterizing his sense of the changed and changing world of the Russian revolution and the twentieth century with details drawn from peasant life, from the rugged Russian winter, from the star/salt collocation that gives us heaven and earth, the dailiness of life and its spiritual and fatal meanings. The speaker is most confident when reporting his experiences and sensations; as he turns to speculation he is less sure of himself and the language and meaning of the poem waver. The last two lines of the second and third stanzas present us with whatever difficulty the poem can be said to pose (and it's one of the poet's clearest and most straightforward performances). Here Meares's version may be helpful. He translates lines 7-8 as "Fresh canvas is a purer base for truth/Than you're likely to find elsewhere," and lines 10-12 as "The freezing water is blacker,/Death cleaner, misfortune more bitter,/And the earth, though grimmer, is just." James Greene, who omits the middle stanza, renders the final line as "The earth more veracious, more awful." The differences among the versions suggest not so much that one is right and the others wrong as that there's a good deal of ambiguity, a leeway, in the original. The speaker wants to affirm the changes in his world, despite its iciness and bitterness, and in line with its beautiful austerity, but he is unsure of himself as a prophet: Meares has decided that he shades toward the hopeful; Merwin and Brown have shaded him toward the pessimistic. Greene just doesn't manage to make his adjectives work, separately or together. But from the three versions we can, I suspect, get a pretty fair sense of the tone and meaning of this poem: the poet is finding beauty in the simple things of his world, starlight, rain-barrel, axe-blade, a chance to wash in uncomfortable but invigorating conditions, but he is also finding fear and uncertainty. Something terrible is ahead and he will be swept up into it, like it or not. He is already retrenching in anticipation of it, simplifying his life, his requirements, his images. We can't read this without our own consciousness of the Stalin epigram Mandelstam would write eleven years later, leading to his arrest and eventual death, just as we can't leave out that ossifying social system ("The yard gates are locked up tight/And the earth, in all conscience, is grim" is Meares's version of lines 5 and 6) that would lead to Stalin and the purges and terrors of the thirties. We know what the poet and speaker were only guessing at. But the poem is not disadvantaged by our historical distance; it continues to take one's breath away with its simplicity, brevity and beauty.

I think of "To some, winter..." as a companion piece. The poet has smuggled favorite images across from one poem to the next, as he loved to do, and he has greatly expanded the peasant setting, crossed with the meditation on change and the impending sense of terror. This is like a painting the other poem was a sketch for; it brims with life and goes all over the place, tonally. We start with the relativities of what winter means, according to your wealth and station. Meares's note tells us that "blue-eyed punch" refers to the flames on the surface of punch, a cozy image of winter pleasures. He also notes that "arak" is an anise-based spirit in wide use throughout the Levant. I've never quite understood how Merwin/Brown got "nut-stains" out of "arak," but Greene has "nuts" in his first line too (the whole of which reads "Winter—to some—is a blue sky of steaming wine and nuts," an unfortunate muddle of the original as far as I can see), so "arak" must have some undertone or association involving nuts or nut-stains, unless Greene just borrowed from Merwin and Brown. In any case, the sense of what winter means evolves from the pleasant associations of the first two lines to the separation of heaven and earth in the next two, the brutal orders that come down from the high, salty stars and must suffice in the smoky huts where peasants are trying to keep warm. This evolution, or devolution, brings us in the second stanza to the world of the speaker, who sounds as though he may once have known the world of flaming punch, cinnamon-scented wine, and arak, but who now is reduced to picking his way around a barnyard ("the warm droppings of a few hens" is Merwin/Brown's felicitous version of what I have made a little more colloquial and pungent) and finding his small consolations in the warmth of animals. The phrase that interrupts the last two lines of the second quatrain seems to be untranslatable; none of the versions (Meares: "my need for care's so great"; Greene: "for cares I need"; McDuff: "so much I need the care"; Merwin/Brown: "For life, for life and care") works very well in English, though the sense is fairly clear. I've dodged the issue somewhat by dropping the word "care," but I think my choice makes sense for the rest of the poem. The match image is what makes this stanza finish with a flourish. Merwin/Brown's "kitchen match" is mighty tempting, given the sound and clarity (you can feel it between your fingers), but "lighted" is apparently closer to the literal.

The speaker portrays himself almost as a kind of village idiot, a Gimpel the fool, with his empty bowl or pot and his ears attuned to the stars. Through the years when I had only the Merwin/Brown version to look at I didn't understand the second half of the third stanza. Theirs reads "I can't help loving through unfledged bird skin/the yellow of grass, warmth of the black earth." The image simply puzzled me and I passed on. I now think—maybe I'm simple-minded—that Mandelstam's speaker is talking about looking at the snow on the ground, associating it with downy feathers, and loving the grass and earth it is obscuring. If I am right, "unfledged bird skin" is not helpful, and "wretched feather-down" (Meares) or "pitiful plumage" (Greene), while none too felicitous, are better guides to what Mandelstam is up to, leaving McDuff's "pathetic haze" no help whatsoever. I may be wrong about the import of this image, but my version represents my sense of what works best and what fits in with the preceding and following images.

I won't continue to rehearse the differences among the translators, simply say that I think the fourth stanza reiterates the simple pleasures associated with farm work, a life close to the soil, affirming them as appropriate to a time of uncertainty about the future. We have pastoral here, if you like, and it is moving and effective. The fifth stanza reiterates the sense of wanting to be out of the world of political aspirations and goes back to its opening affirmation of hard times and what they mean. In both stanzas, widely divergent readings are possible, but the fundamental sense of each and of the poem's direction seems reasonably clear.

The last stanza seems to me the poem's particular triumph. The speaker imagines a romantic quest, a Diogenes-like journey cast in folklore images appropriate to the peasant world he has been occupying. He would like to set off on his adventures, following where his dog leads, and to arrive where prophecy is possible, his gift of a rooster to be bartered, presumably, for a clearer sense of the future, but he can only dream about setting out. Snow-blindness, a winter too brutal and prolonged, leaves him imagining his quest rather than undertaking it. Even this imagining, however, gives the poem a life and surge before it settles down into its woeful and resigned recognition. The tonal changes I cited earlier are very evident here, and I scarcely need to itemize them. The whole bucolic dream is lit with magic for a moment and then ruefully snuffed out. The reality of winter, which is the reality of the historical change the poet is struggling to survive in, is wryly acknowledged and the poem, for a moment, defies it and bests it. Winter is a season; you place it among the cycles of nature that include its opposite states. The snow melts. The cold goes away. Flowers bloom and the sheep are let out to pasture. All these meanings are deepened by what happened subsequently. The winter got worse, much worse, and then it began to relent. Some poems are left behind by history, others are enhanced by it. Events of heartening change are occurring daily in Mandelstam's Russia as I write this in August, 1991. The miracle of survival, not the poet but the poems, continues to enchant and mystify us.

THE AGE

My animal, my age, who will ever be able
to look into your eyes?
Who will ever glue back together the vertebrae
of two centuries with his blood?
Blood the maker gushes
from the throats of the things of earth.
Already the hanger-on is trembling
on the sills of days to come.

Blood the maker gushes
from the throats of the things of earth
and flings onto a beach like a burning fish
a hot sand of sea-bones,
and down from the high bird-net,
out of the wet blocks of sky
it pours, pours, heedlessly
over your death-wound.

Only a metal the flute has mended
will link up the strings of days
until a time is torn out of jail
and the world starts new.
The age is rocking the wave
with human grief
to a golden beat, and an adder
is breathing in time with it in the grass.

The buds will go on swelling,
the rush of green will explode,
but your spine has been shattered,
my splendid derelict, my age.
Cruel and feeble, you'll look back
with the smile of a half-wit:
an animal that could run once,
staring at his own tracks.

1923, 1936
translated by Clarence Brown and W. S. Merwin

Sylva Fischerová

THE TIME VS. THE AGE

According to Mandelstam's essay "Talking about Dante," the poet's journey from conceptualizing a poem to instilling it in language is like crossing a river on foot: "One has to run across the whole width of the river, jammed with mobile Chinese junks sailing in various directions. This is how the meaning of poetic speech is created. Its route cannot be reconstructed by interrogating the boatmen: they will not tell how and why we were leaping from junk to junk" (Brown/Hughes translation). The aim of investigating the poem, then, isn't to discover how the poet worked—we want only to catch what he saw in the moment of creation.

I've chosen this Mandelstam poem because it seems to me to be one of the best examples of his way of seeing, of reconstructing things, which is linked, I think, to his attack on the Symbolists and to "the rehabilitation of the teapot," of everyday life and ordinary things in his poetry. At the same time, it's important to recognize the dynamic, visionary character of the world he creates. Lamarck, biology, chemistry, physics, geology—these are the external milestones along Mandelstam's way. But if, reading his poems, we're sometimes reminded of an anatomy lesson, we shouldn't fail to notice that what takes place here isn't the usual dissection: we witness the vivisection of an organism that grows, matures, gets old, and dies in a single metaphor or series of metaphors. Some of Mandelstam's poems are simply synchronic holograms where time becomes history, where one state is the result of previous states and a function of future ones, but where the person playing this colorful drama is a man who tries to grasp the whole of time through the medium of natural history. The poem, then, isn't a story someone's telling us: the instruments of the poet's language weren't ready before he started his difficult tour—he had to invent them while making his way.

The central image of "The Age" is an animal "symbolizing" (a very imprecise term for this method of writing when one thing for a time in fact becomes another) the age, the time in history, but simultaneously it's a living creature passing through it. Surely "my age" was for Mandelstam the nineteenth century, the epoch of tzarism, but also of accustomed, generally accepted humanity of some range, when even political prisoners could learn German while confined in jail, and when a brother of the tzar's assassin was peacefully allowed to study at a university—something unthinkable under the regime of a new humanity called Stalinism. At the beginning of the thirties Mandelstam said to his wife Nadezhda, according to her memoirs: "If there ever was a golden age, it was in the nineteenth century. We just failed to notice it."

But in "The Age" we're still at the beginning of the twenties. Imagine a man like Mandelstam in those times, a highly cultivated intellectual turned, besides to the natural sciences, mostly to history, Greek and Roman classics, and Dante, a man that designated himself "the last Christian-Hellenistic poet of Russia," imagine such a man in his "Buddhist Moscow" where the great "Assyrian" Stalin rules, speaking about a hanger-on, a parasite "trembling/on the sills of days to come"! He must have felt himself not a champion of the humanity which is the only condition that can give the possibility of a real human life and fate (which he in fact was), but an anachronism, a living relic of the dead age, a member of an ancient, cultivated civilization among the crowd of barbarians whose challenge nevertheless bore the noble names of Revolution, Liberation, Freedom. Even after his first return from jail in 1936, Mandelstam said he wanted to be united with the majority, that he was afraid of remaining outside the revolution and of missing just because of short-sightedness those grand acts taking place before his eyes. "The decisive factor in the taming of Russian intellectuals," Nadezhda Mandelstam quotes her brother as saying, "was neither fear nor corruption—though both were present—but the fact that nobody wanted to abandon the word 'revolution.' "

Revolution meant a new world, new order, new, new—in fact this word was a magic formula of the time, a dangerous formula smelling of capital punishment and absolutism. Thanks to this word the age, when "touched, answered 'yes' and 'no'/as a child answers/'I'll give you the apple,' or 'I won't give you the apple,' " Mandelstam wrote in the 1923 poem "He Who Finds a Horseshoe." No other answers were possible. "New" was a blackmailer's word: either you go along or you're a living corpse.

We find it twice in "The Age" (though this is obscured in the Merwin/ Brown translation): "the sills of the new days" in the first stanza and "the new world" in the third. But there's nothing like the crucial "Yes" said to revolution in the 1918 poem that symptomatically begins "Let us praise the twilight of freedom, brothers,/the great year of twilight!": "But what can we lose if we try one/groaning, wide, ungainly sweep of the rudder?" In 1922 the helmsman's direction is already clear—he steers the ship directly to the altar where the theme of life is to be sacrificed. And in the last stanza from the version of 1923 (which became the second stanza when Mandelstam revised the poem in 1936 but fits better, I think, as the very end of the poem) "blood the maker...flings onto a beach...a hot sand of sea-bones." The final image is that of total destruction and indifference, the only results of the brave new age: nothing is left uncertain now. Everything is almost finished.

We meet Mandelstam's animal age once more in the poem that follows "The Age" chronologically, "He Who Finds a Horseshoe," but from a different point of view: "Children play jacks with bits of animals' backbones./The frail tally of our age is almost done./For what there was, thank you./For my part, I made mistakes, got lost,/I came out wrong. The age clanged like a golden ball,/hollow, seamless, held by no one."

In spite of the difference, something important still remains, something that enables Mandelstam to say: "What I'm saying now isn't said by me./It's dug out of the ground like grains of petrified wheat." We may believe him, but nevertheless we ask: Who is the man who can say this? How can he be sure? How can he do this? But no explanations are possible. With Mandelstam, we find ourselves in a building constructed from inside: nature and architecture become a jail, and the chief builder is then proclaimed the first prisoner. Answering our question would be the same as trying to express Heisenberg's principle of uncertainty from inside a system, which is a contradiction: this principle makes sense if and only if formulated by an observer located outside the system. This is pure objectivity, and nobody knows who or what objectified it before our eyes. The poet-architect forgot to be a god for awhile: he didn't even want to be one. And on the other side, the sky he sees from his position inside the future building lacks the emptiness, the abyss, which only a subject completely lost under the heavens could catch a glimpse of. Mandelstam's confidence in nature was too great: it was not Giordano Bruno who ought to be celebrated, but Gilgamesh and his long, long journey in search of the flower of immortality. But in such a case we could never see that animal, the living architecture of the age—what would remain in our hands would be only the strange, foreign smell of time.

BLACK EARTH

Manured, blackened, worked to a fine filth, combed
like a stallion's mane, stroked under the wide air,
all the loosened ridges cast up in a single choir,
the damp crumbs of my earth and my freedom!

In the first days of plowing it's so black it looks blue.
Here the labor without tools begins.
A thousand mounds of rumor plowed open—I see
the limits of this have no limits.

Yet the earth's a mistake, the back of an axe;
fall at her feet, she won't notice.
She pricks up our ears with her rotting flute,
freezes them with the wood-winds of her morning.

How good the fat earth feels on the plowshare.
How still the steppe, turned up to April.
Salutations, black earth. Courage. Keep the eye wide.
Be the dark speech of silence laboring.

Voronezh, April 1935
translated by Clarence Brown and W. S. Merwin

Martha Collins

THE SPEECH OF SILENCE LABORING

Long before speaking and not speaking became political issues for
Osip Mandelstam, a complex and sometimes paradoxical play of
sound and silence, speech and music informed his work.

From "Silentium," a poem in his first book: "May my lips find/primordial
muteness,/like a crystalline note." And: "word turn back into music."

From "The Word and Culture," a 1921 essay: "The poem lives through an
inner image, that ringing mold of form which anticipates the written poem.
There is not yet a single word, but the poem can already be heard. This is the
sound of the inner image, this is the poet's ear touching it."

From "He Who Finds a Horseshoe," a long poem of 1923:

> Where to start?
> Everything cracks and shakes.
> The air trembles with similes.
> No one word's better than another;
> the earth moans with metaphors....

The fifth stanza, where air is like water "with wheels moving in it, and horses shying,/And Neaera's damp black earth," concludes: "The air is as deeply mingled as the earth;/you can't get out of it, and it's hard to get in."

It's difficult to "get in" here, partly because it's a difficult time: the "age" has begun to clang "like a golden ball,/hollow, seamless, held by no one." That sound "is still ringing, though what caused it has gone"; similarly, though a stallion lies in the dust, "the tight arch of his neck recalls/the stretched legs racing," and "human lips/that have no more to say/keep the shape of the last word they said."

Twelve years later, Mandelstam was exiled for having said too much. The first of the three notebooks he was to fill with poems during his exile in Voronezh opens with "Black Earth."

It's possible to see, in the first stanza of "Black Earth," a condensed and vitalized version of some of the Horseshoe poem's "inner images." Here, though, the earth does not "moan" with metaphors but delivers them up, indeed becomes them: how the ploughed earth comes to embody horse and then choir is not a simple (or simply) metaphorical matter, but the motion implicit in one and the music explicit in the other suggest, even before the astonishing fourth line, an identification between poet and earth. *Astonishing* because, of course, "my earth" which is also "my freedom" is the land of Mandelstam's exile.

In the second stanza, language emerges from the ploughing, succeeding music. The "thousand mounds" of rumor/language/words are reminiscent of the earth's metaphors in the Horseshoe poem, except that here the excavated language frees rather than frustrates, allowing the poet to discover within his limits/bounds/surroundings something without limits. (I'm referring, here, to three translations; Brown and Merwin's, while the most poetically satisfying, is unique in using "rumor" for what Jane Gary Harris identifies as a neologism and translates as "ploughed-up words.")

There *were* of course limits, and poems written later the same month shrink the black earth of this poem to "my shoe-size in earth with bars around it" (#307) and locate in it the grave where the poet lies "with my lips moving" (#305). Even here the earth is, in the third stanza, "a mistake, the back of an axe"; it does not respond to the poet, whose posthumous voice may be suggested by the "rotting flute" which replaces the choir of the first stanza.

But the poet is very much alive in the last stanza of "Black Earth." If the ploughed earth gives up its music and then its speech in the first part of the poem, in the end it is the poet who offers language and encouragement to the earth. His address echoes the end of "The Twilight of Freedom" (1918), a poem which only partially resolves its ambivalent stance toward the Revolution with "Courage,/brothers. as the cleft sea falls back from our plow...." In "Black Earth," ambivalence, or at least complexity, is certainly apparent in the paradoxical "dark speech of silence laboring": in a poem written from exile, the line resonates beyond the fact of the earth's silence, beyond the intricacies of Mandelstam's aesthetics.

But those aesthetics aren't irrelevant here, for poet or for reader, and the necessity of reading in translation may have the accidental virtue of bringing us closer to "the ringing mold of form which anticipates the written poem" than the original might do. We can, of course, pay primary attention to the music as well as the words of Brown and Merwin (or Harris, or James Greene); we can read a translation as if it were a new poem. But it is also possible to read beneath the translated words, into the "black earth" of them, so to speak.

From "The Word and Culture" again: "Poetry is the plough that turns up time in such a way that the abyssal strata of time, its black earth, appear on the surface."

And from a 1937 Voronezh poem: "The people need poetry that will be their own secret/to keep them awake forever" (#355). Courage, reader. Keep the eye wide.

"I'M IN A LION'S TRENCH, PLUNGED IN A FORT..."

I'm in a lion's trench, plunged in a fort,
And sinking lower, lower, lower,
Under the yeast shower of these sounds:
More trenchant than lions, more potent than the Pentateuch.

How close your summons:
Keener than commandments of childbirth, firstlings—,
Like strings of pearls at the bottom of the sea
Or meek baskets borne by Gauguin's mistresses.

Motherland of chastening songs, approach,
With the declivities deepening in your voice!—O primal mother,
The shy-sweet icon-faces of *our* daughters
Are not worth your little finger.

My time is still unbounded.
And I have accompanied the rapture of the universe
As muted organ pipes
Accompany a woman's voice.

1937
translated by James Greene

Robert Bly

THE BEAUTY OF SOUND

I love this poem very much. It amounts to a balance of opposites, an arch grounded at both foundations, a bird with two long wings. How to say this? With the full force of masculine thought he dedicates the poem to female song. Flying up into the air, he points to the earth; making houses out of sawn boards he points to the space inside; adopting the high architectural disciplines of male culture, he encloses in it a vision of an utterly female universe.

He himself is a lion, sharp-clawed, authoritative as the first five books of the Hebrew Bible, but he feels all these sounds that make the bread rise coming down.

This love of sounds that shower down from the dome belongs to oral culture rather than the newer written culture. The speaker offers the sounds from the center of a community, aware as he speaks of all those around him or her, and has no particular "line" to follow. He is following the lines of the dome above him, and the people dome around him. It is a circle:

> Like strings of pearls at the bottom of the sea
> Or meek baskets borne by Gauguin's mistresses.

It isn't Russia, the motherland, that calls to him, but this impalpable, hearable, yin, ear-shaped motherland of sounds, whose magnificence makes our own lives, even when endangered by Fascism, seem unimportant by comparison.

> The shy-sweet icon-faces of *our* daughters
> Are not worth your little finger.

How beautiful it is when a man can hold, as Mandelstam did, Greece and Rome, and their history, in honor, hold the Pentateuch in honor, hold great Western painters such as Gauguin in honor, and then kneel to Sophia and Aphrodite, and give all of his work to the female harmony underlying all.

EUGENIO MONTALE
(1896-1981)

A warded the Nobel Prize in Literature in 1975, Eugenio Montale represents the persistence of the individual lyric voice through the dark days of World War I and the Fascist period of Italian history. Reacting against the monolithic nationalism of Mussolini's regime, Montale chose to write poetry that expresses more personal and immediate experience as filtered through memory and association. Because of this apolitical and often quite private perspective, his work has been called hermetic, though he himself resisted that label, emphasizing his commitment to an austere metaphysics and search for truth. Montale spent much of his childhood on the Ligurian coast of the Mediterranean, and the rough beauty of this landscape pervades much of his early work. After World War II he joined the staff of the Milan newspaper *Corriere della Serra*, and for the next quarter-century he wrote about literature, politics, and culture. Musical, intuitive, breathtakingly alert to the possibilities of images, his work reaches its culmination in the 1956 volume *The Storm and Other Poems*, a milestone comparable to Yeats's *The Tower* or Rilke's *Duino Elegies*. Generally considered the greatest Italian poet of the century, Montale explored the relation of the self to the world, the hesitations of everyday life to the forces of history, in elliptical but ultimately luminous ways.

BOOKS IN ENGLISH TRANSLATION: *The Storm and Other Poems*, trans. Charles Wright (1978); *Collected Poems 1920-1954*, trans. Jonathan Galassi (1998); *The Second Life of Art: Selected Essays*, trans. Galassi (1982).

IN THE GREENHOUSE

The lemon bushes overflowed
with the patter of mole paws,
the scythe shined
in its rosary of cautious water drops.

A dot, a ladybug,
ignited upon the quince berries
as the snort of a rearing pony broke through,
bored with his rub-down—then the dream took over.

Kidnapped, and weightless, I was drenched
with you, your outline
was my hidden breath, your face
merged with my face, and the dark

idea of God descended
upon the living few, amid heavenly
sounds, amid childish drums,
amid suspended globes of lightning

upon me, upon you, and over the lemons . . .

translated by Charles Wright

Sandra McPherson

ON "IN THE GREENHOUSE"

I do not "understand" Montale. But I've had a conversation going with one of his poems for three years. We've been talking about a greenhouse. I couldn't talk to Roethke about this particular greenhouse because in it were few flowers. Montale started right out with "The lemon bushes overflowed." I said to the gardener of this glasshouse atop the Chemistry Building in a Midwestern university, "It's nice to see a grapefruit this time of year." "Grapefruit?" he said, "Oh that's a Ponderosa Lemon." Montale mentioned a "rosary of cautious water drops." More of a Protestant, I too wanted to say something holy; visiting that greenhouse I'd admired from below for years, I felt, I said, that I ran up its stairs like a person who had been around before Creation but who had been ignored by God. Montale imagined a mole; I thought, for an animal, maybe the pitiful pine tree which wasn't doing so well was itself imagining an owl, was wishing the snow were an owl. For there was a blizzard descending onto the steamy glass. Montale saw a scythe; I wasn't thinking of death until I realized the snow could not survive in that greenhouse. I didn't think a greenhouse would make me feel sorry for the snow, but as the outsider I identified with the snow, with its limited partnerships—it could be partners with only a few temperatures, a few latitudes, a few months. And Montale spoke about a strange blizzard: "the snort of a rearing pony broke through." Maybe this is literal. But I think *he* is the pony "bored with his rub-down"; he rears up from passivity to become a lover. In the Chemistry Building greenhouse was a very sexy plant called a zamia. We whistled at the zamia. What followed was Montale's own business:

> Kidnapped, and weightless, I was drenched
> with you, your outline
> was my hidden breath, your face
> merged with my face...

A swooning kind of darkness descended "upon me, upon you, and over the lemons"—but you could see through it like smoked glass. It involved God, lightning, and "childish drums." Whatever, it was fulfilling and quite an inimitable sensation. Maybe could my pre-God greenhouse turn white, with that cotton plant opening and aiming back up at the snow? Would that be as hazing as darkness? I like the paradox of Montale highlighting "the living few"—what is a greenhouse if not the living many? In his dream just a few survive. He and the lover merge and survive in their likeness. In our winter greenhouse snow and cotton were doubles. I worried about their mutual survival should the wind force things.

Shared categories of association. But Montale shows—in so few lines and with next to no transitions—what all the most intense ones are: beauty, awe, life, sex, spirituality, and death. In a small frame there are plants, animals, people, and supernatural beings. When one reads back to the beginning, each object in the poem could be erotic, yet the literal level asserts itself too. The blurring between them is handled with an enthusiastic respect for mystery. I love Montale's stroboscopic lemon grove. And the repercussions of God at the end. My poem, on the other hand, may be one of those lemons.

THE CUSTOM-HOUSE

You don't remember the custom-house
on the cliff's rim above the reef:
it has been waiting, deserted, ever since
that evening when your thoughts swarmed in
and paused there, restlessly.

For years the southwest gales
have pummeled the aging walls
and your laugh no longer sounds glad:
the compass has gone haywire,
the dice keep coming up wrong.
You don't remember; other times distract
your memory; a thread ravels out.

I hold one end of it still; but the abandoned
house dwindles and its grimy weathercock
keeps up a pitiless spin.
I hold one end; but you remain alone,
your breath gone from this dark.

Oh retreating horizon where the riding light
of the tanker so rarely shows!
Can I cross here? (Breakers
still seethe on this crumbling coast. . .)
You don't remember the house, or this, my night,
nor do I know who goes
and who remains.

translated by Vinio Rossi and David Young

Jerome Mazzaro

"THE CUSTOM-HOUSE" AND "LEMONS"

Critics have argued the subtlety of Eugenio Montale's political voice.
They have pointed out that in *Le occasioni* (1939) Montale's favorite
animals are in opposition to or hiding from creatures representing de-
generation. They have also suggested that the poems "Verso Vienna" and

"Verso Capua" may be read as "Toward Anschluss" and "Toward Capitula-
tion." At times, as in "Incontro," they have argued affinity based on vocabulary, style, and imagery. A phrase like "l'aria persa" invites evocations of and
comparisons to Dante and his use of "perso" in the *Inferno* (5:89). Montale's
equally subtle use and evocations of myth, individuation, and pluralism have
received less notice. The lines, "un filo s'addipana.//Ne tengo ancora un
capo" (a thread ravels out.//I hold one end of it still), from "La case dei doganieri," for instance, strike me as clearly evoking Theseus, Ariadne, the
labyrinth, and an effort at individuation. Earlier, "I limoni" had defined the
thread as a kind of Gordian knot lodged at "the still point of the world"—"il
filo da disbrogliare che finalmente ci metta/nel mezzo di una verità" (the
thread to disentangle that would finally place one/at the center of a truth).
Labyrinths and knots are both connected with descents into underworlds,
memory, identity quests, and sin. Their successful resolutions promise special knowledge, wealth, individuation, and salvation. Their equivalents in the
poetry of Montale are the ongoing emotions and objects that, like us, speaker
after speaker must come to terms with.

The use of Ovid's tale of Theseus and the minotaur *(Metamorphoses*
8:169-82) in "La casa dei doganieri," to instance one encounter, is consistent
with Montale's use of Ovid's Clizia (4:20670) throughout *Le occasioni.* The
woman of the poem is "a young holidaymaker," who like Ariadne dies
young. Montale reports that "for the short period she lived, she probably
didn't even notice [his] existence." The "house" borders on wilds ("sul rialzo
a strapiombo sulla scogliera"), recalling the minotaur's dual man/beast nature. Facing the house means survival. Changes have relegated it, however, to
a labyrinth of memory. For years, the walls have been pounded by the southwest wind, and now neither technology nor divination work: "the compass
has gone haywire/and the dice keep coming up wrong." A thread guided him
before, and he expects the woman's memory to provide a thread out. Her fail-
ures recall St. Peter's three denials (Matthew 26:34, 75) and further isolate
him from both his object (the house) and his means of attaining it (her). In a
reversal of cockcrow, darkness—often associated with Clizia—arrives. Paro-
dying Ariadne's transformation, an oiltanker offers its rare light. Disoriented,
the speaker wonders if passage may lie here. The answer is a clash of waves
against an inaccessible cliff. The deserted house has anticipated his own de-
sertion which reverses that of Ovid's Ariadne. Reduced completely to sub-
jectivity, he can no longer distinguish who goes from who stays, and in the
midst of his inability to escape himself, myth provides what rescue from
emotion readers feel.

The question, "Il varco e qui?," has, in addition, Dantean echoes. Uses of
the verb "varcare" in the *Commedia* are numerous, but in the *Purgatorio,*
Dante specifically brands Mathilda "la belle donna che mi trasse al varco"
(the fair lady who drew me across the ford—32:28). Unlike the woman of

"La casa dei doganieri," she has aided individuation. She has made possible
Dante's reformation by taking him across the river Lethe and removing his
painful memories. The link reinforces Montale's earlier use of "varco" in
"Case sul mare": "Penso che per i più non sia salvezza,/ma taluno sovverta
ogni disegno,/passi il varco, qual volle si ritrovi" (I think that for the majority, there's no salvation,/but someone can subvert every design,/cross over,
and discover the self he would be). The vocabulary of "La casa dei doganieri" thus reinforces failed individuation coevally as it conveys something
softer, more provisional, and more exciting than the mythic method of T. S.
Eliot. Instead of "manipulating a continuous parallel between contemporane-
ity and antiquity," Montale plays upon memory's ability to work also by contrast, contiguity, and cause-and-effect. He concentrates on idea and its expression in incident and word. Broadly echoing these aspects, he allows
specifics to alter. In so doing, he seems to acknowledge that one can be redundant by asserting something totally contradictory as well as by reassert-
ing the same thing. Like William Carlos Williams, who once said that the
only way to be like Walt Whitman was not to write like him, Montale affirms
that only difference preserves equal status. It proliferates and captures in
reenactment the sincerity of the original.

This redundancy in myth has its rhetorical counterpart in the several
voices that emerge in poems like "I limoni" as more evidence of pluralism.

LEMONS

Listen, the poet laureates
move only among those plants
with special names: boxwood privet, acanthus.
Myself, I like the roads to grassy ditches
where urchins can reach into drying puddles
and catch a skinny eel;
the lanes along the banks
wind down through canebrakes
emerging in orchards, among the lemon trees.

It's better when the tumult of the birds
fades and is swallowed in the blue:
you can hear, more clearly, the rustle
of friendly branches in still air,
the trace of this earthbound fragrance,
and an uneasy sweetness
rains in your breast.
Here the war of distracting passions
comes to a marvelous truce,
here even we, the poor, hold
our share of the wealth:
the odor of the lemons.

In these silences, you see, where things
abandon themselves and seem on the verge
of revealing their ultimate secrets,
sometimes we hope
to discover an error in Nature
the world's dead spot, the ring that won't hold,
the thread whose untangling will finally take us
to the center of a truth.
The eye rummages in the landscape,
the mind inquires, arranges, dismantles
in the perfume that comes flooding
when the day has grown languid.
These are the silences in which one sees
in each estranging human shadow
some troubled God.

But the illusion fails and time recalls us
to noisy cities where the sky appears
only in snatches, beyond the cornices.
Rain wearies the earth; winter's
tedium thickens upon the houses,
light grows stingy, the soul goes bitter.
And then, one day, through a half-shut gate,
among the trees of a courtyard
the yellow lemons catch our eye
and the heart's frost thaws
while somewhere within us songs
begin to shower
from golden trumpets of sunlight.

translated by Vinio Rossi and David Young

The poem brings together the idyllic, elegiac, and contemplative wellsprings of Montale's vision into what one critic called a "dialectic of sentiments." In contrast to the "I" and "tu" of "La casa dei doganieri," the "we" who are permitted resurrection and the poem's revelation of Last Judgment ("golden trumpets of sunlight") appear to be a successful pairing. As in cubist art, truth lies at "the intersection of loci . . . where several sense experiences of differing sorts coincide" either in an existentialist "intersubjectivity" or in Matthew Arnold's being "true to one another." At the onset, the poem's speaker feels the addressee caught up more by "the poets laureate" than by him. Although "bossi," "ligustri," and "acanti" evoke both Ovid and Vergil, Renaissance and modern imitators of Vergil's Messianic Eclogue (IV) and its golden age are the likely competition. Lemon trees to which the speaker inclines were not known in classical times. They were introduced to Europe during the Crusades. Better than these poets, he, or even the birds, is the murmur of the trees' friendly branches and "the meaning of this scent" that, like

Ovid's transformed Clizia (4:267-70), "knows not how to free itself from earth." By this point in the second stanza, Montale has begun to include the addressee impersonally in verb ("si ascolta"), pronoun ("noi"), and adjective ("nostra"). By its address, the imperative "vedi" at the beginning of the third stanza, however, makes clear a continuing division.

Like that of "La casa dei doganieri," the poem's prose-like argument generates multiple reference systems. If a "burden of the past" exists, it does not unduly intimidate. Montale balances pronoun disjunction (you, I, they) with differences in poetic and prosaic traditions (lines 1-3 vs. 4-10) and idyllic and meditative approaches (stanza one vs. stanza two). These disjunctions extend through the impersonal relations of the third stanza ("si aspetta," "ci," and "si vede"), despite the eye's replacing the ear in the mind's probing, reconciling, disjoining, and recognizing "in each estranging human shadow/some troubled God." Only by such derangement can what is so natural as to go unnoticed be perceived and the knots which these perceptions disclose be untangled. With the opening line of the last stanza, Montale admits that the eye, too, fails. It perceives knots but cannot untangle them. As in "La casa dei doganieri," time (memory) is needed to bring the competing systems into meaning. Reverie turns the poem's idyllic and meditative approaches elegiac/prophetic and melds speaker and addressee into an us ("ci"). The "intersubjectivity" of this us ("in petto")—unlike the paralyzing isolation of "La casa dei doganieri"—validates the work's somewhat disappointing close. "The golden trumpets of the sun," as Olga Ragusa's translation renders the last line, acts as less a solution to a labyrinth and individuation than a passport to that greater labyrinth which W. B. Yeats called "the one great memory, the memory of Nature herself," of which individual memories comprise separate but conjoinable parts.

Given what Arnold saw as the collapse of religion, I find the pursuits of individuation in both poems enormously instructive. The value they put on personal experience suits democratic ideals at the same time the experience argues concrete universals of larger issues. Deviations from myth or poetic idiom posit sincerity by demonstrating that Montale "has used, and not been used by words." His linking sincerity to "intersubjectivity" keeps the poems from becoming sentimental. His belief in joint realization—the inability of one to be anything unless others recognize him as such—aids individuation by increasing the likelihood that events which become fixed in the mind survive both "the distortions of fantasy" and "the blank befogging of forgetfulness." Not especially involved in salvation, these events evoke an individuation that is threefold: it is personal in that it integrates unconscious and conscious elements into a "coming to self-hood" or "self-realization"; it is literary in that it integrates his poetry (unconscious) with that of others (conscious) in order to achieve his identity in a literary tradition; and finally, it is philosophical in that it shows human transience against a more durable Reality. Important in each instance, as critics of labyrinths will argue, is the credibility and seriousness of the minotaur. Without a credible and serious minotaur, labyrinths dwindle into amusements. In a pluralistic world, Montale's minotaur is the paralysis and confusion that equally attractive options generate. Movement, direction, will rely on miracle, chance, *élan vital* to break through what is often "the delusion of the world as representation."

TWO IN TWILIGHT

A watery brightness flows between you and me
here on the belvedere, distorting the profiles of the hill,
and distorting your face.
It plays across a flickering background, cuts off
from you your every gesture; comes on without a trace,
and leaves in a way that fills in every track, closing over your footsteps:
you here with me, inside this fallen air,
it seals up
the numbness of boulders.
                                          And I turn back
from this force which weighs down around us, give in
to the witchcraft of recognizing nothing
in me that is outside myself: if I raise
my arm even an inch, the act
makes me something I'm not, it shatters against glass, its memory
unknown and shadowed over, and the gesture
no longer belongs to me;
if I speak, I listen to an astonished voice
descending to its farthest range,
or wasted, now, in the unsustaining air.

Thus, to the point that it resists until the last
wasting away of the afternoon,
this bewilderment goes on; then a gust of wind
lifts up the valleys again in a frenzied
jerking, and a tinkling sound
drifts from the foliage which scatters
in a fast-running smoke, and the first lights
sketch in the quays.

                                          . . . the words
drop lightly between us. I look at you
in the quivering dusk. I'm not sure
that I know you; I *do* know that I was never so far apart
from you as now, in this late returning.
These few moments have burned away
everything for us: except for two faces, two masks
which carve on their surfaces, with difficulty,
two smiles.

                                   translated by Charles Wright

David St. John

EUGENIO MONTALE'S "TWO IN TWILIGHT"

I have always been reluctant to discuss in print the work of Eugenio Montale. This is not because of any ambivalence I feel about his poetry, but because it has, for many years, been for me a place of sanctuary, a world of privacy I find consoling. Montale's work has always existed for me in a realm beyond the daily literary clatter of my life as a poet and teacher. Still, I am pleased by the attention Montale's work has received in this country, just as I'm delighted that he has been translated with such brilliance, in his poetry by William Arrowsmith and Charles Wright, and in his prose by Jonathan Galassi. Yet, what matters to me most about Montale is my own quite private relationship with his work, the intimacy I feel it can call up within me, and the influence I know it exerts upon my own sense of the emotional music within my own poems. All this said, I would like to consider a poem of Montale's that holds for me that intimate and elliptical architecture familiar to the best of his work, a poem that is, like many of his poems, a love poem, in this case a failed-love poem. It will not take an especially perceptive reader to find in Montale's poem a tenor and dramatic situation I have tried to make use of myself, which perhaps helps explain my long-standing attraction to this particular poem.

"Two in Twilight" appears in Montale's *La Bufera e Altro* (in the book's third section, entitled *Intermezzo).* Though the poem was first published in 1943, G. Singh, in his critical work, *Eugenio Montale,* quotes Montale, from Montale's note on the poem, to the effect that "a rough draft already existed as early as September, 1926. I recopied it, giving it a title somewhat reminiscent of Browning's 'Two in the Campagna' and inserted a few words where there were blank spaces or erasures. I also removed two superfluous verses. Thus I did what I would have done a long time ago, had I known that the draft could one day interest me."[1]

This comes, in fact, as no surprise; the dramatic situation of "Two in Twilight" echoes similar love poems from Montale's previous book of poems, *Le Occasioni.* In fact, one can imagine "Two in Twilight" in its first draft state as a kind of rehearsal for the final staging of, for example, the familiar concerns of Montale's "Mottetti," the latter being a more complex and sophisticated articulation of a similarly intimate yet metaphysically rich landscape. The core and axis of "Two in Twilight," as in many of Montale's poems, is the profound sense of *the other,* the lover to whom he speaks, about whom he

---

[1] G. Singh, *Eugenio Montale: A Critical Study of His Poetry, Prose, and Criticism* (Yale University Press, 1973), 153.

meditates even while addressing. It is this intimate address in so many of the poems that allows us to be *held* to them, as if the poems themselves had reached out to their readers with a lover's immediate and casual intimacy.

In "Two in Twilight," the whole of the landscape (including the speaker and his companion) is caught in the distorting light of day's close. Like the waning day, the exhausted affair is at its end; the poem is in fact a coda to the relationship, a final meeting of the sort in which two people establish the un-spoken final terms upon which they will part for good. At the beginning of the poem, every motion, gesture, or movement by either the speaker or his companion is simply a gesture cut off from any meaning, any substance. The two are held in an irreal, almost hallucinatory light—an underwater light playing over their faces as if they were the drowned. In the oppressive at-mosphere of their meeting, they are sealed as within a bell jar. Yet, they are not only estranged from each other; the events implicit to the poem have oc-casioned a self-estrangement as well. The speaker's own voice sounds, even to himself, disembodied, wasted, and unsustainable. Then, confronted by the day's erasure, transfixed by his own spiritless and confused dissolution, the speaker is yanked back into the world by a sudden gust of wind in the valley below, and with this small cathartic frenzy (of wind, of spirit) to disrupt the stale and stilled atmosphere, he is once again able to regard *outward,* out of himself; he is able to notice again the particulars of the world, the first lights of evening sketching in the outlines of the piers in the harbor below. The final stanza, in William Arrowsmith's translation, reads:

> . . . the words fall lightly
> between us. I look at you in a soft
> quivering. I don't know
> whether I know you; I know that never have I
> been so divided from you as in this late
> returning. A few instants have scorched
> all of us: all but two faces, two
> masks which, with a struggle, carve themselves
> into a smile.[2]

Now the speaker knows how separate and distinct he and his companion are, and will remain; he knows how little he knows her, if at all. There is no hope of any reconciliation, no possibility, it seems, of even a literal recogni-tion, for *who is she, is she the someone I knew?* the poem is forced to ask. Their life or their time together has seared and scorched them in such a way that what was whole and complete about them as human beings has been re-duced to the mere semblance of a life, of a person, of a face: they are again,

---

[2] William Arrowsmith's translation of "Two In Twilight" can be found in *Antaeus*, vol. 40/41.

at the poem's conclusion, portrayed as partial beings, as simply masks. In the small play which has been acted out in the course of the poem, the players themselves have been slowly erased by a past as failing as the light. All that remains is the brief relief of their masks, upon which a cruel knife of light carves a final, mutual smile of resignation and departure. It is this concluding image, the ultimate carving of the human mask, which, for me, lifts the poem out of its pathos and into the realm of the exquisite.

I find Montale's constant meditative poise, linked with his urgent intimacy, unfailingly appealing and convincing. If Montale's layers of verbal seduction are to some readers obfuscating, they are to me enthralling. Eugenio Montale has always been for me one of the few poets—like Yeats, like Stevens—I can return to repeatedly as a source of imaginative replenishment, as a source of mysterious delight.

MOTTETTI XVII

The frog, first to try its chords again
from the pond enclosing reeds and mist,
the rustle of the interwoven
carob trees where a cold sun
is snuffing out its own
weak rays, the slow
drone of hornets in the flowers
where there's still a little sap—
the last sounds,
the bare life of the country.

One breath
and the hour is extinguished: a sky
the color of slate prepares for the explosion
of death-thin horses, of flaming hooves.

translated by Dana Gioia

Dana Gioia

FROM PASTORAL TO APOCALYPSE IN MID-SENTENCE

The most remarkable aspect of Eugenio Montale's poetry is impossible to discuss meaningfully in translation—his use of language. Montale's Italian is not only strong and strangely beautiful. It is also strikingly original. Reading his amazing first book, *Ossi de Seppia* (published when he was still in his twenties) in the context of the Italian poetry which preceded it is like discovering a copy of Wallace Stevens' *Harmonium* after reading shelves of Carl Sandburg. But while some of Montale's power vanishes in translation, what is left is still formidable, and some particular strengths can be seen even more clearly, since the reader is not dazzled by the splendor of the language. I would like to discuss one of these features—his ability to surprise the reader, not by any tricks, but by the overwhelming power of his vision. To make the discussion specific I have chosen a short section of his sequence, *The Motets*.

Motet XVII begins with a series of three images of the countryside, but they are not as they seem at first glance visual images. Rather they are auditory impressions—what the poet imagines there to be as he hears the croak of an unseen frog, the rustle of tangled trees, and the drone of hornets. Therefore, although the reader is probably not aware of it yet, this landscape is presented very subjectively. There is also a static quality to these images which Montale emphasizes by conveying them in incomplete grammatical units—apposite phrases with verbs only in dependent clauses. (Indeed, as it will turn out, the entire first stanza is one grammatically incomplete sentence.) This fragmentary syntax heightens both the immediacy of his description and the mysterious interdependency of the things he describes. The landscape surveyed is very meager. The setting sun is cold and weak. The flowers are at the end of their season; the hornets slow and hungry. The poet tries to summarize the landscape before him—"the last sounds,/the bare life of the country." One is tempted to pass over the first phrase quickly. It doesn't seem to bring much to the poem except a heightening of the mood, and yet on some subliminal level the reader probably puzzles over what the mysterious "last" is intended to imply. But the puzzlement, if it comes at all, is momentary as the next phrase brings this part of the poem to a satisfactory conclusion.

Up to now one has read an effective but unsurprising poem. The language is exact, the imagery well-chosen, the tone convincing, but there is nothing so far which distinguishes it from a hundred other modern poems about the sparse beauty of the Italian countryside. Now Montale suddenly works one of his characteristic surprises, taking the poem in a direction no one could have foreseen, although one notices afterwards how carefully he has prepared the reader in a number of subtle ways.

The next section of the poem opens with a statement which seems to bring the earlier images to an expected closure—"One breath/and the hour is extinguished." The tone of this statement is particularly authoritative in context, since it is the first grammatically complete sentence the reader has heard so far. But the closure is deceptive. Montale will allow neither the meaning nor the syntax to rest at so comfortable a conclusion. At this juncture he places a colon, which in Montale can usually be taken for an equal sign for all that has come before, the whole which inevitably turns out to be more than the sum of its parts. Now nature turns unnaturally ominous as the normally transparent air acquires a stone-like opacity—"a sky/the color of slate prepares...." "Prepares" seems an odd, unsettling word here, implying some conscious, ulterior motive to the sky. One wants to ask what is being prepared for, but there is no need. Quickly and unexpectedly comes the answer—"the explosion/of death-thin horses, of flaming hooves." "Explosion" is the right word for these overpowering images that transform the poem from pastoral to apocalypse in mid-sentence. What do they mean? Are they only metaphors for the sunset or an impending storm? Or do they represent something more—a vision of death or even the world's end? There is no time left to ask, and Montale offers no subsequent paraphrase or abstraction to limit the resonance of these images. All one is left with are the images themselves—violent, inhuman, and mysterious.

What I admire most about this and the other *Motets* is the feeling of mystery and awe they leave me with each time I reread them. Over the years I have come up with various explanations for what is going on in them, but no explication adequately accounts for the depth of my response. Serious critics will consider it unpardonably impressionistic of me to say so, but I value Montale for staying just beyond the range of my comprehension, for speaking to my senses and emotions in ways I can experience but not fully understand. His work has become part of my world, not merely another commentary on it.

MOTTETTI VII

The black-white swooping
of the martins from telegraph pole to the sea
does not comfort your anguish on the pier,
nor bring you back where you no longer are.

Already the thick wild elderberry
perfumes the air; the drizzle thins.
If this clearing is a truce,
your dear threat consumes it.

translated by Irma Brandeis

Il saliscendi bianco e nero dei
balestrucci dal palo
del telegrafo al mare
non conforta i tuoi crucci su lo scalo
né ti riporta dove più non sei.

Già profuma il sambuco fitto su
lo sterrato; il piovasco si dilegua.
Se il chiarore è una tregua,
la tua care minaccia la consuma.

James Merrill

ON "MOTTETTI VII"

A beloved already half angel, all the somnambulist gloamings and bric-a-brac of the nineties, Montale shakes to alertness in his "Mottetti." Where smoke clears on scattered if not disintegrated sound effects ("sambuco" to "consuma" is more anagram than assonance), three or four hendecasyllabic columns have been left standing. It's the morning after an earthquake: old vistas sparkle in sun, redeemed by crisis.

IRIS

When suddenly St. Martin's[1] summer topples
its embers and shakes them down low in
Ontario's dark hearth—
snapping of green pine cones in the cinders
or the fumes of steeped poppies
and the bloody Face on the shroud
that separates me from you:
                              this and little else (if very
little is in fact your sign, a nod, in the struggle
goading me into the charnel house, my back
to the wall, where the sapphires of heaven
and palm leaves and one-legged storks don't shut out
the brutal sight from the wretched
strayed Nestorian);
                              this is how much of you gets here
from the wreck of my people, and yours,
now that the fires of frost remind me of your
land which you've not seen; and I have
no other rosary to finger, no other flame
has assailed you, if it's not this,
of berries and resin.

The hearts of others are nothing like yours,
the lynx not like the striped tabby, beautiful,
stalking the hummingbird above the laurel;
but do you believe them the same breed, when you
venture outside the sycamore's shade
or maybe that mask on the white cloth
has guided you, that image in crimson?

So that your work (a form born of
His) might bloom under new suns
Iris of Canaan, you were gone
in that nimbus of mistletoe and thornbush
ushering your heart through the world's
nighttime, past the mirage
of desert flowers, your first kin.

---

[1] Indian summer.

If you turn up, here's where you'd bring me, the arbor
of stripped vines, next to our river's
pier—and the ferry does not come back again,
St. Martin's sun is blacked out.
But it won't be you should you return, your earthly
story has changed, you don't wait for
the prow at the crossing,

you have eyes for nothing, and have no
yesterdays no tomorrows;

because His work (which translates
into yours) *must be kept going.*

translated by Sonia Raiziss and Alfredo de Palchi

Sonia Raiziss

MONTALE'S "DREAM" POEM

Montale's poetry is on the whole so consistent in its reflection of the "real" world and the other real world of the interior self that one cannot readily choose an exemplar of his meditative manner. As a matter of fact, I elected to talk about a poem that while conveying his style shows certain divergent aspects. It is at moments more dazzling, if one dare use such a word in the context of this dark, moody, controlled, and often hermetic poetry. Montale, of course, has shorter pieces (e.g. the sequence of *Mottetti*) and those done in a lighter vein or displaying a bemused wit. But the sound of much of his work is "northern," deep and reverberant like the sea he appeals to again and again for lessons in wisdom. The strong personal voice takes up the intense music of impersonal nature in its more rugged phases.

The shadowed seasons of the spirit as it is acted upon and reacts to the natural seasons; the intricate probing of a human relationship often in a one-sided dialog, are frequent characteristics of his method. They are evident in "Iris," representative of his subtilized molding of plastic lines with deliberate care into a sinuous entity. He works by quiet moves alternating (or rather surprising us) with abrupt gestures signaled by dashes or line breaks or stanzaic irregularities. Half lights and changing placements collaborate to establish his meaning—not easily accessible. I think of the painter Morandi, setting

the same or similar vases and urns to catch a different light, or still another
sharp shading in a series of chromatic effects.

However true it is to Montale's stylistic modalities and thrusts of thought,
"Iris" suggests a passionate aspect of his poetry. That's what I read into it.
The feelings are somehow more voluble, the language plunging as a heard
cataract behind a hill or a sullen stand of trees. The poet permits himself a
rush of suffering in the effort to understand another being. Or maybe in translating it, I experienced a headlong hurry of words and sensed an unexpected
breaking away from the more usual reticence of emotion and psychological
modulations. Rare too are references to religious symbols in a poetry that
strikes me as largely and profoundly pantheistic in its inherent and metaphoric leanings.

Even more curious is the fact that, according to Montale, this is the only
"oneiric" poem in the corpus of his work. He noted that "I dreamed and then
translated [the poem] from a nonexistent tongue. I am perhaps then more its
medium than author." The personage Iris (in the series *Finisterre,* included in
La Bufera e Altro, 1956) returns under the name of Clizia in "La primavera
hitleriana"—that "ulcerated" spring which will end in death before a tomorrow dawns without terror. And again scattered religious images occur. "Iris"
nevertheless unmistakably belongs to the poet, for all the mystic ambiguities
of the dream life, and how we live it and how it lives us. We have here a vivid,
intimate experience.

He describes a woman in a setting of Indian summer. The vehement start
of the poem is a caught breath:

> When suddenly St. Martin's summer topples
> its embers...
>
> snapping of green pine cones in the cinders
> ...
> and the bloody Face on the shroud...

It continues with a richness, an ordeal of the senses, exposing the less familiar side of Montale's idiom:

> ...in the struggle
> goading me into the charnel house, my back
> to the wall...

Precipitate details follow, some pungent, some lovely: "fires of frost"; "the
lynx not like the striped tabby, beautiful,/stalking the hummingbird..."—but
none of these will "shut out/the brutal sight from the wretched/strayed
Nestorian...." Bewilderment and a troubled yearning propel the particulars
and implicit questions toward the absent partner.

> Iris of Canaan, you were gone
> in the nimbus of mistletoe and thornbush
> ushering your heart through the world's
> nighttime...

The poem moves on to the resolution (without remedy) in a more contemplative temper, but with a noticeably despairing if accepting tone. The figure of the woman is mysterious against a backdrop of stormy light—as I see it—with a finger of intermittent lightning pointing: is she there, will she come again. It seems to be an actual "you" (not a rhetorical address to the reader nor the dream presence he acknowledges), a persona who appears variously in a number of his poems: "The Storm," "Dora Markus"...

> St. Martin's sun is blacked out.
> But it won't be you, should you return, your earthly
> story has changed, you don't wait for
> the prow at the crossing.

It is a moderately long poem. But it has a syntactical beat and gasp reminiscent of "Arsenio" and especially "The Eel," the latter one of Montale's most celebrated poems, written to be read without full punctuation stops, in a single accelerated exhalation, a tour de force all Montale translators have tried. "Iris" is of course rather more paced and resigned, and the hope here is not of regeneration as for the eel writhing through mud, across dry brooks, and swimming back from the Baltic to its spawning place, but of human duty to a life's work, another kind of regeneration: a measured persistence, one key to the poet's own career of a compact but singularly important output, and an essential of his work.

What then drew me to this poem was his idiosyncratic "Montalian" approach to nature, people, places—philosophical, internalized, at moments metaphysical—but in this instance somehow strangely urgent. There is poignancy in the straining toward woman as (Dantean?) idea...withheld by distance, time and ultimate withdrawal.

The deep-pitched and resonant timbre of most of his poetry is like his own withdrawn demeanor and his own baritone voice which we heard on tapes[2] brought for a New York reading of translations in 1961 at The Poetry Center and which I had the privilege of hearing personally in Milan years later. There was the same muted but attentive plainspoken quality evocative of his lines that yet allows the echoic crackling of his intellect and impassioned seriousness to touch the reader, the listener.

---

[2] The taping was arranged in Milan by my co-translator at the suggestion of Robert Lowell, who introduced the reading and gave several of his Montale "Imitations."

The poem is thus illustrative not so much of another facet of Montale as of one variation of the visionary sternness, both of material and style—elusive, far-reaching, at the same time closely watchful and concentrated. Two of the major stresses that underscore the power of his work run dark and light through "Iris": recollection and renewal, their exaltation tinged with pessimism. Loss by separation or alienation, fervently told in this poem, is apparently to be endured with disciplined patience. The compensation is surviving still faithful to oneself—as he was to his own nature in a sort of self-contained exile in Florence through World War II, vis-à-vis the Fascists. He lived his dignified way in a modestly full life, apart, and observing steadfastly the natural or human happenings that fell under his intelligent gaze. The resulting unaffected but nuanced diction can be dense, sometimes harsh when the scene is dour; the meaning oblique or doubling back on itself; the mood, as here, often fatalistic, existential.

NEWS FROM MOUNT AMIATA

Bad weather's fireworks become
the beehives' murmur at the other end
of evening. The room has wormy beams
and the smell of melons
floats up through the planks. Delicate
smoke signals, rising from a valley
of gnomes and mushrooms toward the summit's
diaphanous cone, cloud up the pane,
and I write you from here, from this distant
table, from the honeycomb cell
of a sphere hurtling through space—
and the hooded cages, the fireplace
where chestnuts explode, the veins
of mold and saltpeter, are the frame
into which you'll soon burst. The life
that stories you is still too short
if it contains you! The gleaming background
highlights your icon. Outside it rains.

                    * * *

If only you could have followed
the brittle architecture,
blackened by time and coalsmoke,
the square courtyards, centered
on almost bottomless wells; could have followed
the muffled passage of nightflying
birds, and in the deep ravine,
the mirrored glitter of the galaxy,
dressing for almost any wound...
But the step that echoes through the dark
belongs to the solitary one, who sees
only this crumbling of arches, shadows, folds.
The stars are quilted too subtly,
the campanile's eye is stuck
at two o'clock, even the creepers make
a tangle of climbing shadows,
their fragrance bitter with loss.
Come back, north wind, come colder tomorrow,
shatter the sandstone's ancient hands,

scatter the books of hours in the attics,
make everything a tranquil lens,
little dominion, prison of a sense
free of despair! Return,
cold wind, endear our chains to us,
and seal the spores of the possible!
The streets are too narrow, black donkeys
clattering single file, strike sparks,
magnesium flares on hidden peaks reply.

Oh the trickle that drips, so slowly,
from dark houses, time become water,
the long conversation with the meager dead,
the ashes, the long, delaying wind,
and death, the living death!

> * * *

This Christian brawl with its
shadowy words, its mere lament,
what does it bring you from me? Less
than the millstream, that burrows softly
in its concrete sluice, tears away.
A millwheel, an old log: the world's
last boundaries. A heap of straw
breaks up: and coming late
to wed my vigil to your deep
sleep that greets them, the porcupines
drink from a thread of pity.

translated by David Young and Vinio Rossi

David Young

THE POEM THAT TOOK THE PLACE OF A MOUNTAIN

A good poem is a little world. Some we enter and are immediately at home in; it's as if, however we may come and go, some part of us always belongs to that world. I had such a response to "Notizie dall' Amiata" in the early nineteen-sixties, and in order to make it more homey I translated it, so that I could see it in the mirror of my own language. When the New Directions *Selected Poems* appeared, I had two more mirrors, by Irma Brandeis and Robert Lowell, and, when a friend gave me George Kay's book of Montale translations (published in Edinburgh and later to be the Penguin edition), yet another. I naturally prefer my own version to the others, and will discuss the poem in terms of it, but an interested reader will want to consult the other versions too, on the ground that four mirrors are better than one.

Montale's strategy, again and again, is to be precise about detail and vague about situation and character. His little worlds combine great immediacy with unanswerable questions. They gravely mime our lives, brimming with sense data but troubled about direction, ultimate meaning. The resultant combination of pleasing and troubling is a modernist flavor that doesn't suit every appetite. For my part, as I say, it was love at first sight.

Precise detail, vague situation. To whom is the speaker writing? He is in a room in the mountains where he is conscious of all sorts of impressions—weather, time of day, rustic architecture, the odor of melons from the cellar, chestnuts on the hearth—but he does not tell us enough about the "you" he is addressing to enable us to decide whether the poem is an ironic prayer, a hopeless love letter, or a very strange way for a poet to address a reader. I think we are meant to settle for some combination of these possibilities, each reader coming up with a slightly different compound. Some major clues: the "you" is someone the speaker can write to, though the emphasis is on their separation and the resulting melancholy; the "you" has an icon (which could of course just be a snapshot on the writing table) and is a fabulous subject for life (the word I have translated as "stories" is "affàbula," rendered as "enfables" by Irma Brandeis, as "legendary" by Lowell, and as "fables" by George Kay); if the "Christian brawl" is a struggle to believe, then the prayer elements of the poem are brought to the foreground; if it is history, one's own time and what it does and doesn't have to offer, then the more secular possibility, the love letter, comes up stronger. What seems most accurate to claim is that the poem takes off from two rhetorical models, prayer and letter, because it wants to combine possibilities of both. Add to this that a poem is always in some sense addressed to its readers, so that the reader can assume the role of "you" (or "thou"; the poem is in second person familiar), and you have a fascinating triad of possibilities.

The poem's structure is triadic too; it consists of three related landscapes or little worlds. The first is attractive and mysterious, coherent enough to be a "frame" and inspire a prayer or a letter. It draws us in and opens our imaginations by its range of scale, from melons and mushrooms to the earth as a sphere hurtling—"lanciata," rendered also as "launched" (Brandeis), "rocketed" (Lowell), and "hurled" (Kay)—through space. The excitement includes the possibility of direct encounter with "you" but then trails off into more doubtful assertions and another observation about the weather: the fire-works have gone, the rain remains.

The second section is larger in scope and more affected by change and decay. It holds out no hope of "you" arriving on the scene, but only wistfully reviews what kind of meaning might have been achieved by "your" presence. The tense is a kind of past subjunctive—other translators have "Could you but see" (Brandeis) and "And would it were you who followed" (Kay), while Lowell just gives up on this little refinement—and the sense of resignation modulates to an apocalyptic despair, a call for the destruction of hope and possibility. I suppose this section can be accused of melodrama, but it has good company: Eliot, Jeffers, Yeats. I also hear echoes of Shakespeare: Mac-beth's "Even till destruction sicken," Lear's "Crack nature's molds, all ger-mains spill at once," Northumberland in *2 Henry IV*:

> And let this world no longer be a stage
> To feed contention in a lingering act;
> But let one spirit of the first-born Cain
> Reign in all bosoms, that, each heart being set
> On bloody courses, the rude scene may end,
> And darkness be the burier of the dead.

More to the point, I think, is this section's development of the poem as an ef-fective night-piece, a spreading out of the world of the first section that takes in perspectives, urban and rural, where human solitude and loss can be effec-tively evoked and framed. The sense of trying to find one's way in meta-phoric and literal dark is richly evoked here, and the specificity of the poem's world is what holds our attention and captures our emotions.

The third section combines qualities of the first two, both tonally and in its images. It attempts a summary but is distracted, apparently, by more details. Its movement completes a kind of sonata structure, an *andante*, perhaps, to follow the *allegro* of the first section and the *largo* of the second. The rain of the opening section and the trickle, "time become water," of the middle movement are here transformed into the millstream and "thread of pity" at which the nocturnal porcupines quench their thirst. The oddly hopeful note struck in this section comes not from any better contact between the speaker and "you," but from the ambiguous animal vigor of those porcupines. They survive the brawl and the "mere lament," and they somehow marry the con-cern of the speaker and the apparent indifference of the "you," the necessary opposites of anxious vigil and healing sleep. The porcupines don't mind darkness and solitude. Life, their life at least, goes on. It seems to me almost indubitable that these night-visitors are the source of the similarly treated skunks in Lowell's "Skunk Hour." He may have had his problems translating this poem, but he took its splendid closure and made it over for one of his own best poems.

As I look back over the poem as a whole, I am struck by one more thing about it: its effectiveness as a nocturne is based in great part on its handling of light, the "flashes and dedications," to borrow from another Montale title, that light its dark night of the soul with brief but heartening gleams and glimmers. The distant lightning of the opening, along with the glow of the hearth, is answered in the second section by the "mirrored glitter of the galaxy," the sparks struck by the donkeys' hooves, and the mysterious flares from "hidden peaks." We seem to move from late dusk to deep night, and the third section, with only the speaker awake and almost no light at all, still has enough illumination to allow one to make out the debris and the porcupines as they arrive to drink. Is it my imagination that makes that thread of pity glitter in the starlight, or allows me to imagine the gradual arrival of dawn on this scene? Perhaps, but Montale clearly invites this kind of participation and speculation. That is one secret of his success.

And finally, this: in the summer of 1979, when I had an opportunity to visit Italy, an ad for an Italian farmhouse in an obscure part of Tuscany caught my eye because it mentioned "vicinity of Mt. Amiata." That was enough; I had an opportunity to visit a favorite poem, or one of its sources, as one can visit Tintern Abbey or East Coker or Macchu Picchu. I wasn't disappointed. The mountains are refreshing and remote. Chestnut forests are everywhere, and they have mushrooms if not gnomes. The architecture of the little towns—Montelaterone—and modest cities—Arcidosso—does indeed feature brittle architecture, wells with courtyards, and narrow streets that become details of the poem. Even the great wine made in that area, Brunello, seemed to me to have the dark, rich flavor I associate with this poem. All of this is not to say that verification of detail is necessary or even useful to a poem like this. It is rather to illustrate how art invades life and enhances it. Loving the poem led me to a translation, to other poems, to other translations, and finally to the landscape that partly inspired it. I have had rich rewards from my long love affair with "Notizie dall'Amiata." This is by way of a modest attempt at repayment.

DORA MARKUS

1.

It was where the wooden pier
at Porto Corsini juts into open sea
and one or two men, all but motionless, cast out
or haul in their nets. With a wave
of the hand you signaled toward the other shore,
invisible, your true country.
Then we followed the canal far as the docks
of a city glittering soot,
there in marshflats, where an inert springtime
sank out of memory.

And here where an ancient life
stipples with pleasant uncertainties
brought from the East
your words prismed color like scales
on a mullet, stranded and dying.

Your restlessness reminds me of migrant birds
who hurl against lighthouses
during evening gales—stormy as even your sweetness
eddied with hidden swirls. And your calms,
rarer than those of the sea.

How you hold out, day to day
utterly spent, within a heart
like a lake of indifference
I do not know. Saved
perhaps by some amulet
kept next to your lipstick,
eye-shadow nail-file: a white mouse
of ivory. Making it that way!

2.

Home by now in your Carinthia
of the flowering myrtle and ponds
you lean from the bank
to study the timid nibbling of carp

or among branching lime trees, thick pinnacles,
follow dusk catching fire
in the flare of waterfront awnings
and budget hotels, flashing off water.

As twilight lengthens through harbor mist
mixing with engine-chug, it carries nothing
but goose-squabbles and an interior
snow-white with china speaks into the dark
tarnish of a mirror that saw you
once very differently
a tale of mistakes, of wanderings
unshaken, and inscribes it
where no erasure can reach.

Your legend, Dora! But already written
in those sidewhiskered men looking haughty
and feeble from their grand portraits
gilt-edged and echoing
within every chord uttered
by the cracked keyboard as the hour
darkens and latens.

It's written there. The evergreen
laurel leaves used in the kitchen
persist like a voice,
Ravenna's a long way off, within a brute credo
poison gathers. What's it want from you?
There's no giving up a voice
or legend, or destiny. . .
But it grows late. Always later.

translated by Reg Saner

Reg Saner

MONTALE AND THE OUTSIDER

Years back, studying Italian, I arrived at Montale and modern poetry simultaneously: a congruence. Having reached his style through anthology-centuries of Petrarchan diction, I understood Montale's program for punishing the audience, his perverse equation of poetry with sewers: his anti-poetic. Understanding the bracing effects of a hard-nosed approach is one thing; genuinely to enjoy it, another. Like lashing yourself with birch twigs and bathing in snow—you mean to sample those virtues,...someday, maybe.

"Dora Markus," compared with the few other Montale pieces I then knew seemed less Spartan. A woman, a story line. Not so theoretically admirable as much else in Montale, but far more emotionally accessible than "Chrysalis," say, or "Eastbourne," or "Hitlerian Spring."

On first readings I was tantalized, wanting to learn more about Dora Markus. Who was she "in real life"? What happened to her? Biographers said Montale never met the woman, knew her only as a pair of legs in a photo, wrote the first part as a challenge, added part two a full thirteen years later. Disillusioning...if you believe facts equal the truth.

To this day I remain impressed by Montale's economy of means in the poem. Part one tells us nothing of Dora's body or face or hair. Her single gesture consists of "a wave/of the hand" signaling toward somewhere unseen. Part two continues this obliquity, which, through physical setting, implies not only Dora's past but her future. The restlessness, nervous exhaustion, pathetic reliance on a bit of charmed ivory, likeness to self-destructive birds—all reinforce our guess-work about a woman on the edge, cut off from an invisible elsewhere, her "true country."

Each succeeding stanza of part one is dominated by an image significant as the signaling hand. In the second stanza Montale's glance at Ravenna's late-Roman mosaics "where an ancient life/stipples with pleasant uncertainties/brought from the East" is traduced by the aggressively anti-romantic colorations on a dying fish. From the next stanza's birds we pass to a detail famous as any in Italian poetry—the white mouse, symbol of Dora's vulnerability.

This brilliant indirection of part one tricks us into mistaking two or three meager hints for some middle-European sophisticate whom Montale "must've really known."

Part two continues the water imagery of part one, but with a crepuscular mood more like Gozzano than Montale. Yet its placid dusk effectively sets off the poem's ominous closure. How cunningly the second stanza modulates!—from innocuous "goose-squabbles" and "an interior/snow-white with china" to a mirror whose tarnish accords with Dora's own change: "a tale of mistakes, of wanderings/unshaken." Our hunch that the errant Dora Markus is being almost subliminally associated with wanderings of the Jewish race receives support from stanzas three and four. Dora's "legend," it may be, is both personal and racial—a character and heritage pre-figured in "grand portraits/gilt-edged," looking down as variations of one face, theirs and hers.

"It's written there." What, exactly, is written? And whose voice is it that "there's no giving up"? Why does it matter "Ravenna's a long way off"? In time, thus in safety from the "brute credo" where "poison gathers"?

True Europeans of 1939 would hardly have felt the answers to be veiled in Delphic obscurity. After all, didn't Montale himself lose a job at the Gabinetto Vieusseux, in Florence, through not being a fascist? Within the poem, however, specific sources of threat matter less than the deepening, postponeless fatality. More important still, Montale in an untypical poem has, typically, told us far less than we know about Dora Markus. Has told us more, through her, of himself. Which is to say the "outsider" Dora is an aspect of Montale. One thinks of "Non chiederci la parola," which ends with the famous "Today this is all we can tell you,/Who we are *not*, what we *don't* want"; of the poet who supposes that "perhaps one morning," turning round, he'll catch sight of a miracle,—the void felt daily at his back. Recalling Dora's gesture toward an unseen shore, her "true country," one thinks of "Casa sul Mare," in which the speaker stands "where travels end," at the sea's edge speculating that perhaps for some there is a beyond to cross over to, and enter. "And maybe you could, who knows, not me." Adding that although for him the road ends where we see it end, at the water's edge, maybe others can go further. To their scant chances he offers his "niggardly hope."

But the closure of "Dora Markus" virtually guarantees Dora's marginality. And for the marginal person of such a Europe, "the trip ends here." Yet Montale's greatness arises from his astonishing faith in his own marginality, his very estrangement. As if, with a certain American poet, he "knew the eccentric to be the base of design."

"Even tomorrow," Montale commented, "the important voices will be those of the artists who, through their voice of isolated people, will let [the world] hear an echo of the fatal isolation of every one of us. In this sense, only those who are isolated speak; the others—the people of mass communication—repeat, echo, vulgarize, the poets' words, which are today not words of faith but may someday perhaps be so."

VISIT TO FADIN

Past Madonna dell'Orto, then under the galleries which run through the center of town, I turned at last up the ramp which led to the hospital, arriving soon afterward where the patient had not been expecting to see me: on the balcony with the incurables, taking the sun. He caught sight of me immediately, and didn't seem at all surprised. He still had his hair cut short, recently barbered; the face, however, was hollower, flushing red at the cheekbones; the eyes, as beautiful as before, were beginning to blear into a deeper halo. I had come without warning, and on a bad day: not even his Carlina, 'the angelic musician,' had been able to be there.

The sea, below, was empty, and scattered along the coast were the marzipan architectures of the newly rich.

Last stop of the voyage: many of your occasional companions (workmen, clerks, hairdressers) had already gone down ahead of you, noiselessly, vanishing from their beds. You had brought many books with you, and had put them in the place you used to reserve for your battered knapsack: old books no longer in style; except for one small volume of poetry that I had taken once and that now will remain with me, as we had then guessed without saying so.

Of the conversation I remember nothing. Certainly he didn't need to bring up any of the deeper matters, the universal ones, he who had always lived in a human way; that is to say, simply and silently. Exit Fadin. And to say now that you are no longer here is to say only that you have entered a different order of things, in that the one we move in here, we latecomers, as insane as it is, seems to our way of thinking the only one in which "god" can spread out all of his possibilities, become known and recognized within the framework of an assumption whose significance we do not understand. (Even he, then, would have need of us? If that's a blasphemy, well, it's certainly not our worst.)

Always to be among the first, and to *know*, this is what counts, even if the *why* of the play escapes us. He who has had from you this great lesson of *daily decency* (the most difficult of virtues) can wait without haste for the book of your relics. Your word, perhaps, was not among those that are written down.

translated by Charles Wright

Charles Wright

IMPROVISATIONS ON MONTALE

I

"Visit to Fadin," stylistically, is very atypical Montale. In his "normal" range he is Dantescan, shifting belief over to the realm of the image, the simple message over into complex metaphor. By this shift in emphasis, language becomes religious and "god" becomes a possibility; we begin to try to approximate the divine through language. That this is not happening in "Fadin" points out its "normal" occurrence elsewhere in Montale's canon. For it does become canonical, in its way and structure.

Most of Montale's poems are wise imagistically. "Visit to Fadin" is wise expositionally. The exposition is the object. It also contains one of my favorite Montale sentences: *Exit Fadin.* Precise verbal definition. Everything in the poem is exact.

Fadin and the speaker both enter a "different order of things." Fadin's is of ivory, Montale's regret. Both become assimilated, but in different intensities and at different layers.

"Of the conversation I remember nothing." And then proceeds to tell us about their many conversations over the years. Which is what he (Montale) has to tell us—that being decent people is what counts. Poems don't count (unless they help us to be that way), fame doesn't count (unless it helps to further that cause among us), "nothing matters but the quality of the affection." The greatest words we speak, perhaps, are the words we speak to the air and the sunlight.

"Simply and silently." How better to live than that? You don't talk about the universal virtues, you live them and keep your mouth shut. And then follows the most complicated syntactical movement in the poem, saying this world is not our home, "god" may be elsewhere as well, waiting to take us back in and forget the past.

Fadin leaves Montale's "real" world, the one with the sense of time as a steady destroyer, the one where existence, for all its delights, is entropy, an inevitable process of decay, to enter another one. If we are "latecomers" to this one, are we lateleavers from the other?

We read poems to implicate ourselves. It's easy to do that here, as we walk on both sides of the line, eternity on one side and a daily landscape on the other. Which is how we live, as he points out to us so elegantly.

No matter how well a poem is written, it always comes down to the same thing: is it a telegram or is it a recipe? Is it something I didn't know, or does it tell me what I do know in a different combination? Both are appealing, but only the first is truly revelatory.

Is "Visit to Fadin" prose or poetry? Given the assumption that "prose should be at least as well written as poetry" these days, it does have a certain cast of eye, a certain tone of voice that takes it up a step from the ordinary ride of straight prose. It has a certain condensation of story line and enlargement of character and situation that set it apart. It has a willingness for serious gesture, and takes a step back from itself. It limits itself to essentials and essences. It has the earmarks, if not the eyemarks, of poetry. And even if it is "mere" prose, it's wonderfully written, which is often more than enough.

I have always liked the way the pronouns shift without warning, and so skillfully, throughout the poem. The first paragraph is in third person singular, the second is the narrator's observation, the third is in second person singular, the fourth is half and half, second and third person, and the last paragraph is in the second person. He talks of him and to him and you sense that he (Fadin) is still very much with us in the life of the poem, and will always be alive to Montale as long as he can speak "to" him. The gear changes are so fluid, and the shifts seem so natural, that never is one put off by what, in lesser hands, would seem a gimmick. It is a man speaking to another man because of the exemplary way he lived his life.

To "know," to be among the "knowers" of this world, *coloro che sanno* as Dante had it in a slightly different context, is to be among the content, the blessed. The stillness that exists at the center of self-realization, holding fast in the middle. Know yourself and you will know everything. It is not written down that you should know "why." To exist truly and wisely is to regain splendor...

II

La Bufera, the context for "Visit to Fadin," is Montale's book about his "Donna," his Lady, the *donna salutifera* "who heals and redeems" about her (I. B.) and Her (Clizia, Love, Light). Like all great books, it is ultimately religious and, more often than not, Manichean: love of light is love of life (in whatever form). To make my point—that Montale is a religious poet of a unique sort—let me go on to glance at four other poems.

In "Syria," from the *Flashes and Dedications* section of *La Bufera*, this comes out clearly, if idiosyncratically. "The ancients said that poetry/is a stairway to God." Some of us still say that. I do. (I think Montale does.) The poem is elusive and aphoristic. Allusive. The way we think of real things, the poet as pick-pocket and pilgrim. "Maybe it isn't so/if you read me." False modesty. Courtly belittling. "But I knew it the day/I found the voice for you again..." When the voice is found, then the right words are in the right order, the ladder descends and the steps are there.

SYRIA

The ancients said that poetry
is a stairway to God. Maybe it isn't so
if you read me. But I knew it the day
that I found the voice for you again, loosed
in a flock of clouds and goats
bursting out of a ravine to browse the slaver
of thorn and bulrush; the lean faces
of the moon and sun became one face,
the car was broken down and an arrow
of blood on a boulder pointed
the way to Aleppo.

The voice here comes from the wilderness, the lights come together and are one light, they become one face, today is broken down and useless and the blood of history, the blood of the way things are, becomes directional and points to The City....

THE EEL

The eel, siren
of the cold seas, who leaves her Baltic playground
for our warm waters, our estuaries,
our rivers, who cuts through their deepest soundings,
against their angry tides, from branch to branch,
from stem to stem as they thin,
farther and farther inward, snaking
into the heart of the rocky landscape, worming
through the arteries of slime until one day
a blaze, struck from the chestnut blossoms,
flares her tracks through the pools of dead water,
in the ruts cut out of the cliffs
which fall away from the Apennines to the Romagna;
the eel, whiplash, twisting torch,
love's arrow on earth, which only
our gullies and dried-out, burned-out streams
can lead to the paradises of fecundity;
green spirit that hunts for life

only there, where drought and desolation gnaw,
a spark that says everything starts
where everything is charred, stumps buried;
vanishing rainbow, twin sister
to her you set behind your own eyelids
and let shine out over the sons of men, on us
up to our hairlines in your breathing mud...
and *you* can't call her sister?

Perhaps his most famous poem, and arguably among the handful of his very best. La Donna as temptress, Passion, Plato's mirror flipped over to silver and Aristotle. If "she" throughout the book is I. B., as I am assuming she is, and if I. B. comes from Canada, as I assume she does, then she is a "siren/of cold seas" (Baltic becomes geographic/metaphoric). The speaker becomes the landscape she invades, and worms to the heart of until Love strikes (always in flash and fire). Then we know who she is, "love's arrow on earth"—a fairly unusual reversal—who can be led to fruition—again an unusual reversal—and fulfillment only through the aridity and otherness of his own being. The eel brings renewal, the eel brings a transubstantiation from "other" to "you." Always the conductor of electricity. Always the shaping force. This time she's feminine. This time she's come to stay.

****

DORA MARKUS

1.

It was there, where the wooden pier
sticks out over the high tide at Porto Corsini
and a few men, almost without moving, drop
and pull up their nets. With a stab
of your finger, you pointed out the invisible landfall
across the water, your true country.
Then we followed the canal back to the city dock,
shiny with soot,
in a lowland where a catatonic April
was sinking, flushed of all memory.

And here where an ancient way of life
is speckled with a sweet,
oriental anxiety,
your words became iridescent, like the scales
of a beached mullet.

Your fidgeting makes me think of
those birds of passage who crash against the lighthouse lamp
on stormy nights.
Your sweetness is also a storm

whirling unnoticed,
and its calms become rarer and rarer.
I don't know how you resist, exhausted
in this lake
of indifference that is your heart; maybe
some charm protects you that you keep
near your lipstick pencil,
your powder-puff or nail-file: an ivory mouse;
and thus you survive.

2.

Now in your own Carinthia
of flowering myrtle and small ponds,
you look down over the edge to watch
the carp lazily open and close their mouths,
or follow under the lindens, through their bristly
cupolas, the slow assumption
of twilight, and in the water a flare
of awnings from the quay stalls and small hotels.

The evening that's stretched out
over the humid inlet
brings only, along with the hum of motors,
the whistles of geese, and an interior
of snow-colored Majolican porcelain
spells out in the blackened mirror that sees you
altered a story of unwavering mistakes,
and cuts it in acid
where the sponge can't reach.

Your legend, Dora!
But it's already written in those stares
the men have, with their weak sideburns
and weak mouths, in the great
gold-framed portraits, and it returns
in each chord the broken harmonica
declares in the twilight's bruise,
always later and later.

It's written there. The evergreen
laurel in the kitchen
survives, the voice doesn't change,
Ravenna is far away, distilled
poison a fierce faith.
What does it want from you? Don't give up
your voice, your legend or your destiny...
But it's late, always later and later.

A new translation, with one or two additions. It should speak for itself.

****

FIESOLE WINDOW

Here where the unrelenting cricket bores
through silk clothes,
and the odor of camphor fails to rout
the moths that turn to dust in the books,
a bird, in spirals, swings
up to the elm tree where the sun
is trapped among darkened foliage.
Another light that does not brim,
other flashes, O my scarlet ivies.

For years my favorite Montale poem, and I haven't the slightest idea of its literal meaning after the seventh line. And, of course, it's the last two lines that brush in the final ideogram, the abstract one, the one that pulls the observation over into meaning. Is abstraction worth only what you bring to it? Possibly. Phenomenology? Perhaps. More likely the sudden conjunction of the human with the divine (hypostasis), matter with spirit, light with dark. The light can't get through the impediments of the physical world, even though that world is green and fructive. One more light that doesn't flow over, a reminder of the "other flashes" that go on in the true place of light. It's addressed to his fading vicinities, woman, place, object, the human condition—always, like Dante, the human condition....

ROBERT FRANCIS
(1901-87)

R obert Francis was born in Pennsylvania and educated at Harvard, but he lived virtually the rest of his life in Amherst, Massachusetts, mostly in a small house he called Fort Juniper. On a tiny income derived from writing and occasional teaching, he survived with remarkable frugality, and this quality seems also to have been reflected in the economy, modesty, and harmony of his writing. Francis's work is characterized by wit, precision, a keenly observant eye, and a remarkably intelligent curiosity about nature and the commonplace. Through all of his work in poetry, short essays, and autobiography, a resilient honesty, a formidable facing up to the facts of experience shines forth. He was, as he says in *The Trouble with Francis*, at bottom deeply pessimistic, but his poems shine with an exuberant love of language and its possibilities. His attentiveness to the passing of the seasons, to the ordinary processes of life in rural New England, leads to extraordinarily vivid and exact observations. His command of form is unerring, his diction exacting and lucid. Despite being relatively little-known through most of his life, Francis was deeply admired by those poets who knew his work; as a craftsman, a word-enchanter, an artist utterly devoted to the necessity of exploring the world through language, his achievement is immense.

BOOKS: *Collected Poems: 1936-1976* (1976); *Late Fire, Late Snow: New and Uncollected Poems* (1992); *The Trouble with Francis: An Autobiography* (1971).

BLUE JAY

So bandit-eyed, so undovelike a bird
to be my pastoral father's favorite—
skulker and blusterer
whose every arrival is a raid.

Love made the bird no gentler
nor him who loved less gentle.
Still, still the wild blue feather
brings my mild father.

David Young

ROBERT FRANCIS AND THE BLUEJAY

It is a troublesome fact that Robert Francis, at the age of 80, is still so little known. His modest and retired life near Amherst, Massachusetts, may
partly explain his obscurity, along with a relatively slow development—
most of his best poems were written after he turned fifty—and a number of
years spent in the shadow of his friend and mentor Robert Frost. Then too, it
must be noted that his poems are modest in scale and scope, and that in a
time when it has been fashionable for poets to stress angst and anguish, their
own and that of others, Francis has made a serious exploration of pleasure
and delight. He is, as he says in his autobiography, *The Trouble With Francis*,
a deeply pessimistic man, but his poems, while they occasionally reflect that
outlook, mostly search out the properties of the natural world and of language that can act to offset or qualify the pessimism.

The short, precise, exquisitely balanced poems that Francis writes find the
same kinds of things to celebrate in nature and in language: effects of doubling, rhyming, compounding, punning and echoing. The flow of experience
reveals curious and chancy links between objects and among words, and the
poet catches them on the wing. Francis does not so much create metaphors
and forge likenesses as he does find them, discover them, in natural things—
toads, cypresses, waxwings, weather—and in words that rhyme, pun, wed in
compounds, or reveal sudden family resemblances based on etymology, consonance, or similarity of meaning. For years cypresses (in the poem titled for
them) have been "teaching birds/In little schools, by little skills,/How to be
shadows." The shading of "schools" into "skills" is partly an effect of rhym-

ing and punning, partly an observation of the world. Similarly, the two riders in "Boy Riding Forward Backward" are like "Swallows that weave and wave and sweep/And skim and swoop and skitter until/The last trees take them." This is both a celebration of the way swallows behave and of the language's capacity for verbs. When good likenesses appear between the words themselves and the things they name or imitate, a special pleasure is created from simultaneous matching in nature and language, the two realities of world and word. That the process can involve tension and paradox as well as pleasure is superbly illustrated by Francis' eight-line poem, "Blue Jay," which first appeared in *The Orb Weaver* (1960).

The whole poem can be seen as a series of odd pairings—of bird and father, stanza and stanza, word and word. All these pairs combine likeness and difference. "Bandit-eyed" and "undovelike" are compounds created by different means. "Pastoral" becomes a kind of pair by being a pun: Francis' father was countrified, a lover of nature, and a minister of the church. "Skulker" and "blusterer" suggest two very different kinds of activities that immediately develop a psychological kinship when put together. Even "arrival" and "raid" manage to become a duo by virtue of a syntax that turns one into the other. "Raid" also pairs up with "bird" to close the stanza on an off-rhyme that foreshadows the brilliant one that will close the poem.

In the second stanza, the pairings occur between lines, an effect of expansion, and they take comparative form ("gentle" and "gentler" or, more precisely, "no gentler" and "nor...less gentle") before becoming the full internal rhyme of "wild" and "mild" and the off-rhyme that seems to sum up and concentrate in itself the entire poem, "feather" and "father." The unlikely way in which things associate for us, declaring their likenesses and differences at the same time, is the implicit subject of that whole last sentence, with its repetition of "Still" (yet another kind of pair, and again mimetic of the experience, this time of recurrence) and the slight disruption of perfect symmetry created by "blue." If you imagine taking out "blue" or balancing it with a color word or punning effect in the last line, you see how much Francis has gained by keeping the poem slightly asymmetrical even as he is locking its final surge of meaning into place. The accomplishment is the more impressive for its economy and concentration. The whole poem is paradoxical by virtue of those qualities too: a short, small thing that weighs more, means more, requires more attention, than we thought likely.

When one has pointed out the technical mastery of a Francis poem, one has only partly accounted for its effectiveness. There's a mysterious something beyond technique in his best poems. In "Blue Jay," it's tied up with the way I connect my own experience—with bluejays, with my own father, with words—to the poem. That's the last and most important pairing, for without it the poem would be something to admire for its craft and little more. But its

ending has always had a strong emotional punch for me, a release of feeling
and a summoning of diverse emotions and experiences, that makes me go
back to it and want to share it with others. Different readers will no doubt
have different degrees of involvement with this particular poem, but the delights and recognitions that lie in wait for readers of Robert Francis are manifold. In Japan major artists are sometimes designated as national treasures or
national resources while still alive. If our culture had the good sense to do
that, one of my first nominations would be Robert Francis of Amherst, Massachusetts.

HIS RUNNING MY RUNNING

Mid-autumn late autumn
At dayfall in leaf-fall
A runner comes running.

How easy his striding
How light his footfall
His bare legs gleaming.

Alone he emerges
Emerges and passes
Alone, sufficient.

When autumn was early
Two runners came running
Striding together

Shoulder to shoulder
Pacing each other
A perfect pairing.

Out of leaves falling
Over leaves fallen
A runner comes running

Aware of no watcher
His loneness my loneness
His running my running.

Donald Hall

ON "HIS RUNNING MY RUNNING"

The rhythm does it. The rhythm fixes it, as the acid bath fixes the photograph. The most common line is c/cc/c, for which there is doubtless a Greek name in Saintsbury—irrelevant because Francis's lines are variant and nonquantitative. Two loud noises a line, that does not vary; usually two unaccented syllables mid-line; *always*—and this is the most important item of description—the falling rhythm's soft final syllable, so that the rhythmic signature, no matter whether the line begins loud or soft, remains its gentle falling-off at the end.

Yet prosodic description though accurate may give the lie. This meter was never counted out on fingers; it is a short enough line that the poet's ear could never deceive itself into irregularity; instead this ear or this tapping foot *improvises* metric integrity. It is not making free verse, but it finds a variety of procedures for arriving at the same arithmetic sum and rhythmic resolution.

The sound compels. As for the sense? Well, Robert Francis (one could have said the "I of the poem," if one were given to such things, and if there were an I in the poem; even "my" waits for the last two lines) or the eye of the poem sees a jogger in autumn twilight, remembers that earlier it had watched two joggers together, and returns to the observant present by feeling itself into the runner outside.

(Paraphrase reminds me of Public Television.)

The poem is its rhythm. If it is also an enactment of loneliness, and a cure for loneliness, it is reticent about its purposes. There is something attractive about those "bare legs gleaming"; the watcher's furtiveness comments on the attractiveness. The watcher's memory of two joggers, which is literal enough, makes reference to past companionship *outside* which must refer to past companionship or lost companionship *inside*—or behind the glass; as Whitman's lament for the widowed bird is his lament for everything lost. The loss lessens itself by empathy, the power of the eye to imagine, as watcher becomes runner and therefore companion. Eye met two runners; eye lost a runner; eye joins a runner.

So it is with the repetitions or rhythm, which establish, depart, and reestablish.

EXCELLENCE

Excellence is millimeters and not miles.
From poor to good is great. From good to best is small.
From almost best to best sometimes not measurable.
The man who leaps the highest leaps perhaps an inch
Above the runner-up. How glorious that inch
And that split-second longer in the air before the fall.

Robert Wallace

THE EXCELLENCE OF "EXCELLENCE"

In an era of the Avant-Avant-Garde, Robert Francis, who can be passionate without being puffy, is a poet daringly Horatian. *Ars celare artem.* The art is to hide the art. Like Herbert or Herrick a technician, a metrical Swiss-watchmaker, fond of the chime and the golden cogs, he happily relishes versing. His poems wound us cleanly by their diminutive and lovely precisions.

Consider, because it has so much to say on the matter, his poem "Excellence." Little seems at first to astonish. The words are plain, the syntax easy. The meaning seems a truth so common we need hardly acknowledge it. The athletic metaphor earns its force by being obvious. But the poem sticks in the mind and its phrases come to hand. "From poor to good is great. From good to best is small." The simplicity of the elements makes the precision, when at last we attend, surprising.

Not many poets are worth scanning, and only a few, a very few, make it delightful. Here's how it might go for "Excellence":

(x)Éx|cĕllénce| ĭs míl|lĭmé|tĕrs ǎnd| nŏt míles.

Frŏm póor| tŏ góod| ĭs gréat.| Frŏm góod| tŏ bést| ĭs smáll.

Frŏm ál|mŏst bést| tŏ bést| sŏmetímes| nŏt méas|ŭrá|blĕ.

Thĕ mán| whŏ léaps| thĕ high|ĕst léaps| pĕrháps| ǎn ínch

Ăbóve| thĕ rún|nĕr-úp.| Hów glór|ĭoús thát ínch

Ănd thát| split-séc|ŏnd lóng|ĕr ín| thĕ áir| bĕfóre| thĕ fáll.

The first surprise is that the poet has chosen hexameters for a poem about legerity. The headless first line—[(x)]Éx|cĕllĕnce—at first disguises the choice. Perhaps the line, with its alliteration, gave Francis the meter. Having said that to himself, or written it down, he had at least to consider writing the poem in hexameters. He might have changed to "Excellence is inches and not miles" for a lighter, pentameter line. (As he uses "inch" later in the poem, it wouldn't have been out of place.) But the poem, we realize, is less about the jumper's ease than about his difficulty, the long training, the extra effort that earns excellence, that buys "that split-second longer in the air." Possibly because hexameter feels as though it goes a little beyond the pentameter norm of English—seems to have to somehow push its way to its end—it was a perfect choice.

Having made that choice, the poet exploits it beautifully, especially in the last line where, after we have become accustomed to lines of six feet, he pushes yet a little farther and ends with a heptameter. We don't see that extra length because the words are shorter; but we hear it. The line lasts in the ear just a split-second longer than the others.

Once we begin noticing, the poem grows richer and richer in meaning. It isn't only the handy alliteration that makes "millimeters and not miles" so exact and contrasting, but the short "i" of "mil-" and the long "i" of "miles." In line 2, the unrelenting monosyllables and the caesura suggest the distance between "poor" and "best," a distance that can only be crossed by such a dogged pace as the line itself has. In line 3, the almost completely unaccented secondary accent of the word "measurable," followed by the unaccented feminine syllable, blurs the beat so much that we almost have to force the voice to record it. (We can't bring ourselves to say "MÉAS-ŭr-Áblĕ.") And so, coming after the nearly level accents of "bést| sómetímes| nŏt méas-," the line's end mimes the meaning of "not measurable." Even the slight temptation to hear an off-rhyme of "-ble" with "miles" and "small"—and so to displace the accent falsely onto that syllable—reinforces the effect. The run-on from line 4 to line 5, the poem's first, marks the effort, the spring. The more static second run-on, from line 5 to line 6, and the clustering of accents in the first half of the sentence fragment, followed by the light accent of "[(ˊ)]in| thĕ áir," give the final line its appropriate rhythm.

Robert Francis' poems are filled with such minor, hidden exactnesses that bring the poems alive to the ear and so to the attentive mind. The wonderfully elusive syntax of "The Base Stealer" is such an effect, or that poem's gaily metered last line, which leans backward until the very end and forces us to scan it "Délĭcătĕ,|délĭcătĕ,|délĭcătĕ,|délĭcătĕ—|[(x)]nów!" Or the knuckleball off-rhyming of "Pitcher," which keeps us unsure the poem's couplets are being rhymed until the final

Not to, yet still, still to communicate
Making the batter understand too late.

Or the dazzlingly unlikely "rhyme" words of "Hallelujah: A Sestina": *Hallelujah, boy, hair, praise, father,* and *Ebenezer*, which Francis turns and returns with apparent ease.

A reader may well feel, perhaps due to the word "meters" buried in "millimeters," that "Excellence" is also, intentionally, about poetry. Several of Francis' poems about sports suggest a similar resonance. In "Catch," for instance: "Two boys uncoached are tossing a poem together,/Overhand, underhand, backhand, sleight of hand, every hand,/...to outwit the prosy." "Pitcher," "The Base Stealer," "High Diver," and "Sailboat, Your Secret" offer tempting symbols of the poet's craft and methods, as do "Skier" ("He swings down like the flourish of a pen") and of course "Apple Peeler" (the spiral of peel is "Like a trick sonnet in one long, versatile sentence"). They make a delicious cluster.

Small though Francis' poems mostly are, and unpretentious, they are magical. Not the least of the magic is the almost unnoticed "formality and formal ease" by means of which the poet so slyly and surely gets the rabbits into the hat.

SILENT POEM

backroad   leafmold   stonewall   chipmunk
underbrush   grapevine   woodchuck   shadblow

woodsmoke   cowbarn   honeysuckle   woodpile
sawhorse   bucksaw   outhouse   wellsweep

backdoor   flagstone   bulkhead   buttermilk
candlestick   ragrug   firedog   brownbread

hilltop   outcrop   cowbell   buttercup
whetstone   thunderstorm   pitchfork   steeplebush

gristmill   millstone   cornmeal   waterwheel
watercress   buckwheat   firefly   jewelweed

gravestone   groundpine   windbreak   bedrock
weathercock   snowfall   starlight   cockcrow

Alberta Turner

PERMITTING CRAFT

Enough of Robert Francis, Craftsman. He *is* a craftsman, one of the best, but if the grain were flawed, craft could only emphasize the flaw. I should rather examine the grain, a perception both wry and straightforward, complex and complete.

"Silent Poem" was invited before it was made. Francis says that he became "fond of the strong character of solid compounds." These were chiefly paired single-syllable words for concrete things. He "made a list purely for pleasure," set them in clumps of four to a line, two lines to a clump, then let their juxtaposition of concrete objects suggest meanings considerably more various and contradictory than they could have been if they were embedded in sentences that explicitly made some connections and excluded others.

The poem contains forty-eight words. The first eight are details perceivable only to a slow walker along a backroad so narrow and overgrown and silent that the walker would identify the names of weed shrubs and vines, such as shadblow and wild grape, see unafraid rodents, such as chipmunk and woodchuck, and examine the leafmold below the undergrowth and notice the stone wall, which in Francis country marches through undergrowth to mark the boundaries of abandoned pastures. He would see that man has made a life in this country, persisted for a time, and at least partially withdrawn.

The second eight words describe the farm that the road leads to, a farm made by hand from the woods and still surviving by hand, possibly by a succession of single pairs of hands, which saw, pile and burn the wood; build and repair the cowbarn, wellsweep and outhouse; and now, from age or weariness, give some of it back to honeysuckle.

The third eight words show the entrance and inside of the farm house. Here is the same work of hands in ragrug and brownbread, the same dependence on the hands' transformation of wood, tallow and buttermilk to heat, light and nourishment, the same lack of pretense or waste, in entering over the flagstone and under the bulkhead through the back door.

The fourth group of eight words inspects the land that makes this life possible and necessary: the steep land only partly covered with soil; the sparse, weedy pasture where cattle must be belled because they wander out of sight; the sharp, grinding nature of both the land and the manual task of living on it. The fifth group continues the list of tools that grind both the man and his food (gristmill, millstone) and contrasts it with things that exert no effort (waterwheel, watercress, firefly and jewelweed). Line ten is composed entirely of those effortless things, which have been anticipated by grapevine, shadblow, chipmunk and woodchuck in group one and by honeysuckle, buttermilk and buttercup in groups two, three and four. This contrast between the easy grace and sure survival of natural species (man's weeds and pests) and the man's own hard, marginal subsistence could make the poem a statement of human futility, but the last eight words bring back the achievement and dignity of flagstone and candlestick; ragrug, firedog and brownbread. This man takes his very precise and permanent place in the *nature* of *things*—upon the bedrock. Under the gravestone, the groundpine, the snowfall and the starlight, he awaits the cockcrow. He has *made* his place. The woodchuck, firefly and jewelweed have merely *occurred* in theirs.

Francis calls this poem silent, but its silence is like the spaces in a peal of bells—just enough to hear reverberations. The perception which can lace these things by sound, rhythm and position to each other's meanings; that observes the psychological accuracy of joining *gristmill* to *millstone*, that gradually dissipates effort by the sequence of *cornmeal* to *waterwheel* to *watercress* to *jewelweed*; the humor that visualizes *sawhorse* next to *bucksaw*; the twisting of the pastoral clichés *cowbell* and *buttercup* to signify hard rather than easy grazing; the very recognition and manipulation of the irony built into a word like *jewelweed*; the near-rhyming of the first and last words of the poem, *backroad* and *cockcrow*, to describe without pity the whole physical, local, social and spiritual human journey from ground to galaxy and be-yond—these are the insights that make Francis' craftsmanship possible. Craft alone could not have kept this poem from becoming a Currier and Ives calendar towel if a particularly honest perception had not gathered wood and weed, pitchfork and thunder, man and rock and clanged them together.

SHEEP

From where I stand the sheep stand still
As stones against the stony hill.

The stones are gray
And so are they.

And both are weatherworn and round,
Leading the eye back to the ground.

Two mingled flocks—
The sheep, the rocks.

And still no sheep stirs from its place
Or lifts its Babylonian face.

Richard Wilbur

ON ROBERT FRANCIS' "SHEEP"

I think that I have known this poem since my undergraduate days at Amherst, and I remain grateful for its perfection.

It is, if you look for tricks, a very artful poem indeed. Two motionless constellations of things—sheep and rocks—are being likened, and this is formally expressed by the linked twoness of tetrameter couplets, and of tetrameter broken in two to make dimeter couplets. By the time you get to the second line of the fourth couplet, a line which simply juxtaposes "The sheep, the rocks," there are two mirroring monometers within the dimeter measure.

The first line of the poem is the only one, to my ear, which remotely threatens to run over into the next; elsewhere, pauses and punctuation give an even balancing movement to each couplet, and so enforce the idea of parallelism. There is balance or mirroring, too, in the words and sounds of the poem, most obviously in the *stand/stand* and *stones/stony* of the first couplet, more subtly in the way the first line's *still* reappears all the way down in the last line but one.

Each of the couplets ends with a full stop, and the effect of these repeated arrests is to keep the idea of movement from getting started, to stress the idea of fixity.

All of this formal appropriateness (so pleasing to experience, so dry to hear about) is there in the poem, and yet in fact the poem does not seem tricky. Why not? For one thing, the language and word-order are so plain and natural that the sheep and rocks seem almost unmediated. The reader has scarcely any sense of a poet standing between him and the scene, brandishing a rhetoric and offering clever interpretations. Because the poet thus effaces himself, because he writes so transparently, his formal felicities—though they have their effect—are not felt as part of a performance. The poem's first line—"From where I stand the sheep stand still"—very firmly begins this minimization of the poet's presence: it focuses the poem not on "I" but on the sheep, and it presents the poet not as a sensibility but as a mere locus or vantage-point.

A final effect of that line, of course, is to convey a sense of a fixed scene fixedly viewed. The witness doesn't move any more than the stones or sheep do. However, the mind of the poet shapes and moves the poem far more than his plain manner lets on. Each of the first four couplets states some resemblance between the sheep and the rocks: their stillness, their grayness, their rondure and texture, their flocklike arrangement. These statements have a cumulative force, but it also strikes me that, beginning with the modest simile of the first couplet, they grow progressively stronger in nature, until stones and sheep are "mingled flocks," and the mirroring elements of the poem approach a state of fusion.

Fusion occurs in the word "Babylonian." In this poem, what a word! "Sheep" begins with ten successive monosyllables, but here at the end we meet a grand five-syllable word with a capital letter, a word which suddenly flies off beyond the poem's preserve toward something far and ancient, a word with none of the plainness of what has gone before it, a word in which the poem drops all pretense that it is not a product of imagination. The effect is explosive, and then there is an immediate doubletake as the reader sees that "Babylonian" is after all quite at home in this accurate poem, by reason of its evocative accuracy. The word asks us first and most importantly to combine sheep and stone by recalling Babylonian and Assyrian sculpture—in particular, I should think, those famous Assyrian bas-reliefs which represent men and animals in profile, and have a stylization of the hirsute which renders the sheep an ideal and frequent subject. The line "Leading the eye back to the ground" compels us, by the way, to see Francis' sheep in a side view, as if they were posing for a relief.

The faces of sheep do, in fact, suggest the physiognomies of Mesopotamia and the Near East, and I remember Umberto Saba's poem in which he describes *una capra dal viso semita*, a goat with a Semitic face. Finally, I believe, the poem asks us to think of how long—in the lands which the Bible mentions, and in others, and in unrecorded times and places—the sheep have been with us. At the end of Robert Francis' poem, the stillness of a New England scene partakes of the timelessness of art and of things unchanged.

REMIND ME OF APPLES

When the cicada celebrates the heat,
Intoning that tomorrow and today
Are only yesterday with the same dust
To dust on plantain and on roadside yarrow—
Remind me, someone, of the apples coming,
Cold in the dew of deep October grass,
A prophecy of snow in their white flesh.

In the long haze of dog days, or by night
When thunder growls and prowls but will not go
Or come, I lose the memory of apples.
Name me the names, the goldens, russets, sweets,
Pippin and blue pearmain and seek-no-further
And the lost apples on forgotten farms
And the wild pasture apples of no name.

David Walker

FRANCIS READING AND READING FRANCIS

T he first time I heard Robert Francis read his poems seemed a miraculous occasion. Never had I experienced such rapport between a writer and his listeners: we were in the hands of a master who could do no wrong. Every lifted eyebrow, every shifting nuance, every puzzled repetition—"Could I have meant that? Yes, I suppose I did..."— was caught and savored by the audience. The poems themselves emerged as small treasures, perfectly ordered, paced, and delivered. Amazingly, the whole performance seemed entirely artless, spontaneous, generated by the occasion itself. Afterwards, I remember walking in the woods (this all took place, incredibly, in a narrow valley in the Kentucky hills), slightly dazed, sure I'd participated in something unique.

Two years later I heard Francis read again, this time in a lecture hall in Ohio. Almost immediately my scalp began to tingle: it was happening again. The courtly, gentle poet—part Thoreau, part Edward Everett Horton—was casting the same spell. And only because I'd heard him before did I realize how deliberately, how *carefully* he was doing it. What had seemed artless, even innocent, now emerged as fully considered and orchestrated. Again, near the end he confessed that he wasn't really reading, that he was reciting and only used the books as props, and again individually we prided ourselves on having noticed several minutes before that his eyes wandered from the page as he "read," and again (of course) he had intended us to notice. Both readings were deeply memorable, but it was the second—in which I fully recognized his skill as a *performer*—that, in Dickinson's phrase, took the top of my head off.

I shouldn't have been surprised. The principle that makes a Francis reading such an event—apparent spontaneity and modesty supported by an extraordinary measure of craft and calculation—is precisely what renders his best poems so attractive. As he says in that much-anthologized poem, "Pitcher":

> His art is eccentricity, his aim
> How not to hit the mark he seems to aim at,
>
> His passion how to avoid the obvious,
> His technique how to vary the avoidance.

Or, in a formulation from "The Black Hood":

> I marry freedom to fastidious form.
> I trust the spirit in the arms of sense.
> I can contrive a calm from any storm.
> My art, my business is ambivalence.
> In every poem by me on my shelf
> Confidentially yours I hide myself.

It's hard to choose a favorite Francis poem, but "Remind Me of Apples" demonstrates most of the virtues I admire in his work. It makes no extravagant gestures, and its limits at first seem narrow, but it marshals its resources so skillfully as to produce a haunting, powerful small masterpiece.

Francis' title is perhaps a slightly flattened version of the Biblical injunction to "comfort me with apples," and the difference between comfort and reminder—the latter with its stronger implication of self-reliance—suggests the complex mood he is aiming to evoke. The poem is built on a foundation of seasonal opposition, but its further subject is the psychological need for balance, and the ability of imagination and memory to save us from extremities. The first four lines are a perfect example of an apparently straightforward statement that is in fact exquisitely modulated and arranged for complicated effects: the tonal shift from "celebrates" to the darker "intoning," the faint echo in lines 2-3 of Macbeth's "Tomorrow, and tomorrow, and tomorrow.../And all our yesterdays have lighted fools/The way to dusty death," the line break that keeps "dust/To dust" from sounding too heavily. The whole clause is heavy, vaguely Biblical in its diction and rhythms—which are appropriately broken by the intrusion of the autumn vision, with its crisper metrics (compare "apples coming" to "roadside yarrow") and simpler syntax.

Time shifts and blurs: the vision of apples is not simply memory, since these are future apples, apples *coming*, though they can be glimpsed only through knowledge of the past. The vision will save the speaker from the heat and dust of summer, and from the sort of death that it evokes, though paradoxically there are in turn intimations of mortality in their "prophecy of snow," in their "white flesh." ("My art, my business is ambivalence....")

The second stanza repeats the pattern of summer followed by fall, but in a different key. The emphatic rhymes ("haze" and "daze," "growls and prowls") and especially the way in which "dog days" is literalized into the image of canine thunder lighten the tone considerably—as if the mention of apples in the first stanza has already begun to soothe the speaker's imagination. By this point the future tense of "Remind me, someone" has modulated into the suspended present: "I lose the memory." Another paradox here: the rest of the poem proves that the memory is anything but lost. Providing for his future need, the speaker stores up apples by naming them. This is another favorite Francis tactic: the list that gains resonance and mystery as it proceeds, in this case from the familiar ("the goldens, russets, sweets") to the exotic ("blue pearmain and seek-no-further") to the near-mythic: "And the lost apples on forgotten farms/And the wild pasture apples of no name." To my ear this is both exultant and melancholy, vital and autumnal, sweet and tart at the same time, this artless, artful harvest of nature and of language.

PABLO NERUDA
(1904-73)

One of the great South American poets of the century, the prodigious Pablo Neruda published over 40 books of poetry while simultaneously pursuing his calling as a political activist. A long career in the Chilean diplomatic service took him to various posts in the Far East, Argentina, and Spain. Although Neruda's early work focused on personal themes (*Twenty Love Poems and a Song of Despair*, published when he was twenty, remains his most widely read book), his experience of the Spanish Civil War, in which he witnessed widespread violence and the imprisonment of friends, deeply affected him. His Communist sympathies led him to organize support for the Spanish Republicans; he also began to write epic political poems exploring the relation between contemporary social questions, nature, and history. Perhaps his greatest achievement is *The Heights of Macchu Picchu* (1948), in which the majestic Inca ruins evoke a profound meditation on individual death and the fate of civilizations. Neruda's late poems, often returning to more personal and elemental subjects, demonstrate remarkable richness and variety. He was awarded the Nobel Prize in Literature in 1971.

BOOKS IN ENGLISH TRANSLATION: *Twenty Love Poems and a Song of Despair*, trans. W. S. Merwin (1993); *Canto General*, trans. Jack Schmitt (1991); *The Book of Questions*, trans. William O'Daly (1991); *Selected Odes of Pablo Neruda*, trans. Margaret Sayers Peden (1990); *Odes to Common Things*, trans. O'Daly (1994). See also John Felstiner, *Translating Neruda: The Way to Macchu Picchu* (1980).

MELANCHOLY INSIDE FAMILIES

I keep a blue bottle.
Inside it an ear and a portrait.
When the night dominates
the feathers of the owl,
when the hoarse cherry tree
rips out its lips and makes menacing gestures
with rinds which the ocean wind often perforates—
then I know that there are immense expanses hidden from us,
quartz in slugs,
ooze,
blue waters for a battle,
much silence, many ore-veins
of withdrawals and camphor,
fallen things, medallions, kindnesses,
parachutes, kisses.

It is only the passage from one day to another,
a single bottle moving over the seas,
and a dining room where roses arrive,
a dining room deserted
as a fish-bone; I am speaking of
a smashed cup, a curtain, at the end
of a deserted room through which a river passes
dragging along the stones. It is a house
set on the foundations of the rain,
a house of two floors with the required number of windows,
and climbing vines faithful in every particular.

I walk through afternoons, I arrive
full of mud and death,
dragging along the earth and its roots,
and its indistinct stomach in which corpses
are sleeping with wheat,
metals, and pushed-over elephants.

But above all there is a terrifying,
a terrifying deserted dining room,
with its broken olive oil cruets,
and vinegar running under its chairs,
one ray of moonlight tied down,
something dark, and I look

for a comparison inside myself:
perhaps it is a grocery store surrounded by the sea
and torn clothing from which sea water is dripping.

It is only a deserted dining room,
and around it there are expanses,
sunken factories, pieces of timber
which I alone know,
because I am sad, and because I travel,
and I know the earth, and I am sad.

translated by Robert Bly
and James Wright

Marianne Boruch

THE SHAPE OF HIS MELANCHOLY

" I keep a blue bottle," Neruda begins, then stops. Or rather *Conservo un fransco azul*, he says, idling on the line break a half breath or two. So we're launched with a simplicity that is misleading, into "Melancholy Inside Families," this great odd piece that reduces nothing, a thing more like a sponge than a poem. Unlike the English first line which Bly and Wright end-stop calmly and dramatically with a period, Neruda's line is only the beginning of one long sentence that will thread itself down the stanza, bit by rushing bit, to bring us the darkened owl or the cherry tree's "menacing gestures," on and on, a roaring jumble of detail and circumstance. Roaring as in Whitman. Jumble as in dream, though slowed mid-chant by a whisper— "there are immense expanses hidden from us." So these piecemeal things, cast in melancholy and wildly out of context, suggest larger, stranger shapes.

One reason it's impossible to get tired of Neruda has to do with this outrageous reach, grotesque and lovely by turns, earthy and weird and exact. One stanza in, and already we're deep in slugs and ooze, deranged cherry trees, withdrawals, kisses. The other reason is that hard against this unruly, welcoming passion is humility, a quieter thing and far more surprising. The world is seriously weighted by that. One *hears* this double vision; it's in the sound, the pace really, even in translation. The rangy sentence turns early to litany, a shifting, spinning backdrop that both belies and shores up the stopped, elegant statement buried in it, that "so much is hidden from us." Past lyric, in a near-visionary descent, the speeding imagery, the sudden idea, mime both ecstasy and revelation, and beyond that a point where we are speechless and everything empties again.

I think Neruda most loved that point. The rest of the piece grows right out of it. It's in the human scale of his beginning again, in stanza two, with another modest statement. It's in the second bottle there, this one "moving over the seas," thus animating the poem, turning it to journey. Such loss triggers the central image of the poem, giving rise to the abandoned dining room, its decay of romantic even mythic proportions, an example of what Neruda himself called his "funereal imagination."

Spooky probably isn't the right word here. *Nightmare* is closer, though there is jewel-like comfort in the vines the poet includes, and even in the fact that it is a dining room that haunts, once a place of warmth and reassurance. Neruda's camera work gives grandeur to the desolate scene, great intimacy too, as it underscores the unearthly feel and multiplies longing. First the flash of sea, made endless by its plural form, and then the sudden room itself, zoom lens within to bare detail—smashed cup and curtain—the place flooded with water and stone, rain and more rain unto the very foundation. Then the wide pan out and up to take the whole house, two floors of it, and the final rest on windows and vines, undisturbed.

No one lives here, of course. So there is heartbreak. Solitude and melancholy, already the most intricate embroidery in the poem, deepen color to a stain. One cannot lift one's eyes from the sea-drugged dining room. It fascinates the way ruins always do—the richly *made* thing broken down by the repeated violence of storm and water and wind, shapes which may well suggest but finally overwhelm any human wish or focus. Thus the dazed quiet of another stanza break, and the leap to a more chilling litany, nothing like quartz and kindnesses, this time earth itself pulled out by the roots, elephants cut down, corpses, the speaker himself "full of mud and death."

Maybe it's never possible to know what poems cost. Neruda wrote this piece sometime in his late twenties toward the end of his various government assignments in the Far East where he felt profoundly isolated from the resident cultures. Years later, remembering those places, the poet saw himself young, wandering about miserably alone, neither understanding much nor understood. But biographical fact is mere shadow on the page. Not much is narrative here; all is too interior. That's perhaps what keeps us reading Neruda, his direct way to what is felt but barely knowable, past the need for exposition or summary. Still there is no clarity like his, disembodied imagery notwithstanding. No sorrow like his dirge-like, haunted repetitions of detail, no innocence darker than the questions he has the sweetness to ask, ones that pierce the heart and take us back to the reasons that led us to poetry in the first place.

The penultimate stanza is to me the major movement of the poem, a great strange wheel coming round again. It's a replay on the dining room, the same "terrifying deserted dining room," but its weight here is as large as its new particulars are small and beautifully detailed. We see the broken cruets now, vinegar making a river under the chairs. And then, out of nowhere, "one ray of moonlight tied down." (I love the milky Spanish too: *un rayo detenido de la luna*.) "Something dark," he adds. And finally, the defining point for this poet—perhaps for all poetry worth the name—"I look for a comparison inside myself...."

One can't make too much of this astonishing turn inward. It's not simply Neruda's metaphor as he reaches twice, both times brilliantly, for some image to explain himself to himself—the "grocery store surrounded by the sea," or the amazing "torn clothing dripping with sea water." It's the gesture itself that stuns, Neruda's willingness to step back and *not know* how any of this equals or adds up—shattered glass, vinegar and moonlight, all this gorgeous misery not something *other* to be taken in and thus understood, but something already there darkening the mind, probably never to be untangled. And the moment is subterranean and moving in another way. Rhetoric's polish and finish dropped, we are witness to the actual making in such a phrase, that humble and often frightening split-second of nowhere and nothing where all one has is the looking. *A comparison inside myself*—as if we could ever know, but where else does great poetry come from?

There is music like this, composers who work a frail, brave moment against some overpowering sweep of sound, Neruda's expanse now that takes every broken thing out to sea and sadness, "sunken factories, pieces of timber." Out that far, one hears it—the human heartbeat, tentative, remarkable.

ODE TO THE TABLE

I work out my odes
on a four-legged table,
laying before me bread and wine
and roast meat
(that black boat
of our dreams).
Sometimes I set out scissors, cups and nails,
hammers and carnations.

Tables are trustworthy:
titanic quadrupeds,
they sustain
our hopes and our daily life.

The rich man's table,
scrolled and shining,
is
a fabulous ship
bearing bunches of fruit.
Gluttony's table is a wonder,
piled high with Gothic lobsters,
and there is also a lonesome
table in our aunt's dining room,
in summer. They've closed
the curtains,
and a single ray of summer light
strikes like a sword
upon this table sitting in the dark
and greets the plums' transparent peace.
And there is a faraway table, a humble table,
where they're weaving
a wreath
for
a dead miner.
That table gives off the chilling odor
of a man's wasted pain.
There's a table
in a shadowy room nearby
that love sets ablaze with its flames.
A woman's glove was left behind there,
trembling like a husk of fire.

The world
is a table
engulfed in honey and smoke,
smothered by apples and blood.
The table is already set,
and we know the truth
as soon as we are called:
whether we're called to war or to dinner
we will have to choose sides,
have to know
how we'll dress
to sit
at the long table,
whether we'll wear the pants of hate
or the shirt of love, freshly laundered.
It's time to decide,
they're calling:
boys and girls,
let's eat!

translated by Ken Krabbenhoft

David Young

THE WAVE THAT DOES NOT DIE

Pablo Neruda is one of those titanic figures of twentieth-century poetry, like Akhmatova and Montale and Williams, who lived long lives, faced a variety of difficulties, both personal and historical, and emerged triumphant by means of patience, accumulating wisdom, and sustained creativity. We may know that we want to think mainly of the work, not the life, when contemplating a poet's achievement, but how in the world do you separate these things when you consider someone like Neruda? His life and art weave in and out of each constantly, in ways that are both negative and positive. Neither can be understood on its own, and the life, as a narrative that shapes and illuminates the work, is eventually going to make itself felt fully in the work.

I write this in a summer during which, every time I turn around, I see yet another review of Elizabeth Bishop's letters. Is there any newspaper or magazine that hasn't run a review of that volume? Part of me is slightly exasperated by this: if Bishop is so important, it is because she is a fine poet, yet one does not see reviews of the many excellent volumes of poetry published each year, nor did one see extensive reviews of Bishop's poetry during or after her lifetime. Now, suddenly, there are some letters and everyone gets into the act.

Another part of me accepts this, however: Bishop's excellence as a writer is to be found in her letters as well as her poems. They are more accessible for most readers. Reviewers are human and probably more confident judging and praising letters than poems. And so it goes. My point here is a link to the question of Neruda's life and work. Consider how much the growing appreciation of Bishop is based on the way we are learning, through letters and biographies and critical studies, what her life was like. If it sometimes feels like gossip or prurient interest, distracting readers from the art and craft and effort behind the poems, that is a price we must probably pay for a larger sense, especially a popular sense, of the meaning of the poet's work.

All this is partly by way of saying that Neruda is still coming into view for his readers, who may, if they are like me, know very little about his life. At the moment, what is making Neruda more real and more vivid to his readers is not his letters and people's reminiscences—we haven't reached the Bishop stage with him yet—much less anything like a full biography, but the work, which is still being translated, still being discovered. To read it is to begin to know the man and the life because Neruda's celebratory, candid and direct responses to experience were so naturally drawn from his life and the historical events he lived through.

I am very heartened by the number of translations of Neruda's work that have appeared recently. In British bookstores, browsing around, I could find almost nothing in the way of Neruda translations. In this country, to our credit, it's a different story:

1. There are the remarkable translations of the late poems, by William O'Daly, published in several short volumes by Copper Canyon Press. James Nolan has done a book in that series too.
2. There is the large *Canto General*, translated by Jack Schmitt and published by California; I find the translations a bit uneven, but the book as a whole is a wonderful addition to any library. California has also published a selection of the Elemental Odes, translated by Margaret Sayers Peden.
3. Any Neruda fan should have read John Felstiner's *Translating Neruda: The Way to Macchu Picchu*.
4. There is New Directions' volume of *The Captain's Verses,* translated by Donald D. Walsh, a remarkable sequence of love poems that Neruda first published anonymously.
5. There is Dennis Maloney's translation of *The Stones of Chile*, another fine sequence, published by White Pine Press.

6. There is Milkweed's lovely edition of the prose poems, *The House in the Sand*, translated by Dennis Maloney and Clark Zlotchew.
7. Texas has published, in its Pan American Series, a handsome illustrated edition of Neruda's 1966 volume, *Art of Birds*, translated by Jack Schmitt, and Stephen Tapscott's translation of *One Hundred Love Sonnets*.
8. And there is the brand new book from which I have chosen my exemplary Neruda text, *Odes to Common Things*, translated by Ken Krabbenhoft, illustrated by Ferris Cook, and handsomely presented by Bulfinch Press, an imprint of Little, Brown.

Since poetry books so seldom get reviewed, I mention all these titles and publishers for the benefit of readers who may not know one or more of them. They certainly do credit to our small press scene and our ability to produce gifted translators. In New York, where they think they live in the real world, publishing success consists of things like huge piles of Oprah Winfrey's diet book. They are wrong. Reality and achievement in publishing are represented by the list above.

My list is not exhaustive, but it's indicative of the steady current of Neruda translations that are bringing this major figure into view for us. My advice: don't wait for letters and biographies and critical studies. Jump in and discover this master where he is at his best, in his poems, as mediated through his increasingly capable translators.

****

Odes appeal to the kind of poetic temperament that is celebratory, generous, ecstatic. Neruda, when he had grown too ideological and didactic, too ornate and gorgeous, too adept at performing surrealist somersaults, deliberately remade himself as a poet of simplicity and directness. He developed a short line, a limpid style and a voice of great confidence and sincerity. It all feels perfectly natural when you read it, but there was immense effort and concentration involved in making it seem so spontaneous.

Neruda's odes are to be found all over the place in his later work, sometimes designated that way, over two hundred of them, sometimes just reflecting that character. The *Odas Elementales* belong to the nineteen-fifties and I can remember having glimpses of them in the rather erratic versions of Ben Belitt and in the sometimes riveting versions of James Wright and Robert Bly. What I find especially gratifying about the Krabbenhoft/Cook volume by Bulfinch is the way that the odes have been presented, in Spanish and English, with drawings that feel altogether appropriate to their spirit and style. "Ode to the table" comes second in the collection and has a slightly ornate dining room table with folding leaves above the italicized Spanish text and a simple solid work-

table above the English text. Elsewhere in the book there are especially capti-
vating drawings of bowls and plates, spoons, scissors, dictionaries, onions,
tomatoes, dogs, cats, oranges, guitars, beds, violins, apples, a pair of socks
and, on the cover, a salt shaker that positively shimmers with that same combination of the ordinary and the magical that Neruda sought for his poems.

"Ode to the table," in its four stanzas, makes moves that are quite characteristic of the genre as Neruda developed it. He begins with himself, writing
these odes at a table, this ode's subject, and he puts on his poet's worktable
an assortment of objects, thus nesting other odes and ode subjects within this
one, emphasizing the communal spirit that pervades the ode collections and
that leads the reader easily from one ode to the next.

The parenthetical phrase after "roast meat" shows us the Neruda who is always willing to dip into the expressionist/surrealist grab-bag to enhance the
reader's sense of mystery. Because roast meat can be the "black boat of our
dreams," "*la nave negra/de los sueños*," we understand instantly and by inference that bread and wine, scissors, cup and nail, hammers and carnations
(oh what a felicitous pairing!) have their inherent magic too.

The second stanza opens out to generalizations of two kinds: a linking of
the organic and the inorganic, again with implications that are childlike and
mythic, and a simple statement about the broad relation between the object
and some large concepts—hope and life—that we use to chart our existences.
A more literal version of this stanza would run something like "The faithful
table/sustains/dream and life,/titanic quadruped." While his choice of the
passive risks loss of energy, Krabbenhoft's solution achieves the naturalness
of voice that Neruda cultivates in the odes.

The expansive gesture of this stanza is very characteristic. In a companion
piece, "Ode to the plate," Neruda similarly opens the poem up, both spatially
and temporally. The plate is the "*disco central/del mundo*," and inhabits a
world where "at noon, when/the sun, itself a plate of fire,/crowns/the/
height/of day/your stars/appear, plate,/upon/the tables of the world." A few
moments later this cosmic reach is matched by the plate's ancient genealogy:
"you were spawned by a spring on a stone."

After the short second stanza, Neruda moves into a kind of social catalogue of tables. The speaker seems not to want to bother judging the rich man
or the glutton, simply to note how variously tables can be used. But by
putting these lesser figures early in the catalogue, he produces a crescendo of
emotional depth that is associated first with family and memory—that ray of
light, coming swordlike through the shut dining room to strike the bowl of
plums in the aunt's summer-darkened house, is far more memorable than the
bunches of fruit or the Gothic lobsters—and then with human poverty and
suffering. We assent to this deepening and to the upsurge of human emotion
it provokes partly because we feel that the speaker is beyond simplistic political judgments and ideological agendas; abandoning his overt Marxism,

Neruda has found a way to be more profoundly and powerfully "political" than in any of his heavy poems about Spain or Stalingrad. One might quibble about whether Krabbenhoft's "the chilling odor/of a man's wasted pain" quite captures the full sense of "*el frio aroma/del último dolor desbaratado,*" which seems to me to translate to something more like "the cold smell of the last corrupting pain."

The stanza ends, also characteristically for Neruda, with another great human passion. Sex is not an answer to the anguish of memory and the burden of suffering, of course, but it is the other great mystery, the second wing of the angel, and Neruda handles it here with a defter touch than he had sometimes used in previous work. The abandoned glove speaks volumes but leaves much to our imaginations. As with the politics, this making space for the reader to feel, judge, respond and narrate, seems like a powerful, if by now obvious, way to go.

In the final stanza, the poet embarks on his grand summing-up. He is now ready, because we are, to understand that "The world/is a table/engulfed in honey and smoke,/smothered by apples and blood." And existence itself becomes a matter of being summoned to a meal with others, a summoning that involves crucial choices and necessary alliances. That "freshly laundered" shirt of love wins me over. My appetite quickens and I am a child again, being summoned by my mother to another mundane and magical meal with my family.

The last line is certainly difficult to translate. It means, of course, "let's eat," Krabbenhoft's choice, and it also means "Come to dinner" or "Soup's on" or "Come and get it," or whatever signal was used in your household to summon you, even a gong. But of course it is in Spanish a phrase that by its simplicity—*a la mesa!*—sums up the whole poem, putting the key word at the end as if to confirm Neruda's belief that words themselves are somehow magical, mythic, inherently mysterious and powerful. And since "mesa" also has a landscape connotation, the parameters and features of our existence are more emphatically evoked by it than by any such phrase as "let's eat." Still, I think Krabbenhoft has chosen sensibly; it's simply that to like the English is to go on through and love the Spanish. Say the last few lines in Spanish—"*pero hay que hacerlo pronto,/están llamando:/muchachas y muchachos,/a la mesa!*"— and you have in your mouth that flavor of simplicity and goodness that ordinary speech can carry. You are at your table and at Neruda's table too. There is honey and smoke, there are apples and blood. The roast is a boat of dreams, the plums are a transparent peace. Maybe a pair of scissors lies there too, maybe a glove. You wear the freshly laundered shirt of love and it's time to decide: who you are, where you belong, what your allegiances are.

****

Neruda's last phase, when he knew he was dying, was very remarkable. We are told that eight finished books lay on his desk the day he died. Among them was the wonderful sequence on Easter Island, *La rosa separada,* a kind of companion piece to *Heights of Macchu Picchu*; there was the beautiful book of poems composed entirely of questions, *El libro de las preguntas*; and there was *Àun,* which William O'Daly has translated as *Still Another Day.* Eight finished manuscripts, an astonishing burst of creativity and a masterly summing-up that seems to have stemmed in part from a confidence Neruda felt about what he had managed to accomplish in poems and sequences like the Odes. The last three poems of *Àun* say it with tremendous and moving simplicity. Here is the last of them, in O'Daly's fine version:

> So long, visitor.
> Good day.
> My poem happened
> for you, for nobody,
> for everyone.
>
> I beg you: leave me restless.
> I live with the impossible ocean
> and silence bleeds me dry.
>
> I die with each wave each day.
> I die with each day in each wave.
> But the day does not die—
> not ever.
> It does not die.
> And the wave?
> It does not die.
>
> Gracias.

It takes one's breath away in its simplicity and conviction. And it is a more fitting tribute than the Nobel Prize or any other, more complicated, form of recognition. Probably the best response is simply silence.

WALKING AROUND

As it happens I am tired of being a man.
As it happens I go into tailors' shops and movies
all shrivelled up, impenetrable, like a felt swan
navigating on a water of origin and ash.

The smell of barber shops makes me sob out loud.
I want nothing but the repose either of stones or of wool,
I want to see no more establishments, no more gardens,
nor merchandise, nor eyeglasses, nor elevators.

As it happens I am tired of my feet and my nails
and my hair and my shadow.
As it happens I am tired of being a man.

Just the same it would be delicious
to scare a notary with a cut lily
or knock a nun stone dead with one blow of an ear.
It would be beautiful
to go through the streets with a green knife
shouting until I died of cold.

I do not want to go on being a root in the dark,
hesitating, stretched out, shivering with dreams,
downwards, in the wet tripe of the earth,
soaking it up and thinking, eating every day.

I do not want to be the inheritor of so many misfortunes.
I do not want to continue as a root and as a tomb,
as a solitary tunnel, as a cellar full of corpses,
stiff with cold, dying with pain.

For this reason Monday burns like oil
at the sight of me arriving with my jail-face,
and it howls in passing like a wounded wheel,
and walks like hot blood toward nightfall.

And it shoves me along to certain corners, to certain damp houses,
to hospitals where the bones stick out of the windows,
to certain cobblers' shops smelling of vinegar,
to streets horrendous as crevices.

There are birds the color of sulfur, and horrible intestines
hanging from the doors of the houses which I hate,
there are forgotten sets of teeth in a coffee-pot,
there are mirrors
which should have wept with shame and horror,
there are umbrellas all over the place, and poisons, and navels.

I stride along with calm, with eyes, with shoes,
with fury, with forgetfulness,
I pass, I cross offices and stores full of orthopedic appliances,
and courtyards hung with clothes hanging from a wire:
underpants, towels and shirts which weep
slow dirty tears.

translated by W. S. Merwin

David St. John

PABLO NERUDA'S "WALKING AROUND"

"Walking Around" was the very first poem of Pablo Neruda's I was lucky enough to encounter. Though I've told the story of this first discovery of his work before (in an essay entitled "Neruda's Wings"), I think it bears retelling in order to situate my responses to and my prejudices (I think it's one of Neruda's truly great works, from his strongest period) about the poem.

It was the spring of 1968, an astonishing time for those of us caught up in the delirium of what seemed to be the promise of great changes and even greater freedoms ahead. At times during those glorious spring afternoons, my poetry class—that is, the class of which I was a member—would meet outdoors, especially if our leader felt like it, and that spring Philip Levine often did feel like taking us out of our dreary modular classroom at Fresno State College and into the leering air.

I could have said "electric" air, or "revolutionary" air (especially given the time), but at eighteen years old I felt everything that spring was terribly sexy and leering. It was a rich, ripe, and often oppressively fecund world that seemed to be exploding all around me. It was, of course, also the dark, morose and somewhat embittered world of any eighteen-year-old, though whatever chip was on my shoulder seemed to me just to make my walk (swagger?) that much more memorable, yet I doubt anybody else felt that way. And that spring, my friends and I seemed to be doing a lot of walking around. Except for Larry Levis, who rode his very cool black motorcycle. While quoting Whitman. I'm not lying.

On one of those spring afternoons Levine, as he often would in class, read to us a few of his favorite poems, perhaps one or two that he'd recently come across in magazines and just-published books, or others that were some of the poems he cared for most in the world, something from Wyatt or Shakespeare or Thomas Hardy or Elizabeth Bishop. That day he read to us Neruda's great poem, "Walking Around."

One could feel the whole class collectively holding its breath. I'd never heard anything like this poem. It embodied what I would soon discover were Neruda's many astonishing virtues: the understated, inevitable and almost "natural" surrealism; the explosive image-making; the often deceptive calm of the tone; the richness of presence; the tremendous generosity and expansiveness of both poem and poet, their embrace of the world with all of its gorgeous paradoxes; the sensuality, sexuality and whiff of true magic; and finally, that sense of the world's own defiant resonance and inexhaustibility.

The opening of "Walking Around" continues to be haunting to me. The fatigue and irony, the flat, world-weary fierceness of "As it happens I am tired of being a man..." and its repetition (at the end of stanza three) still startle me with each rereading. And I would guess that many poets of my generation can remember the moment they first saw or heard the phrase, one of Neruda's most famous, "like a felt swan/navigating on a water of origin and ash." It is a phrase that not only embodies the sense of passage through a life the poem wants to echo, it also slaps us in the face with the child-like memory of the felt swan pressed to the child's play board, collapsible and two-dimensional, fleeting as a hand-shadow on a bedroom wall, flat as a soft black mirror of the broken adult self.

It's this opening, with its catalogue of discouragement, that gives us first that kaleidoscopic experience of passage. The speaker's weary walk leads him into the tailors' shops and movies ("all shrivelled up, impenetrable"), until the huge dimension of his fatigue arrives: "The smell of barber shops makes me sob out loud." Already on our way, as we walk hand in hand with the poem's speaker, the world seems a place too much for us, too overwhelming; its ordinariness and its bald pathos seem, simultaneously, impossible to accept. The speaker wants only the stillness of a kind of death ("I want nothing but the repose of either stones or of wool"), a stasis, a final *stop* to this moving around, this endless walking around of our pathetic lives.

And it is at this very moment, at the opening of the fourth stanza, where the lips of the speaker curl with the taste of revenge: "Just the same it would be delicious/to scare a notary with a cut lily/or knock a nun stone dead with

one blow of an ear." One can see how these images of blows against propri-
ety and official culture (and the culture of death the notary represents) remain
so appealing to the adolescent within us all. It's no accident that the poem
then spends its next two stanzas stating the speaker's defiance of that fate, the
living death in which he finds himself, the streets of which he continually
finds unrolling beneath his slowly shuffling feet.

It is the terror of this possibility, of this *being* the speaker's fate, that drives
him on through his city, its shops and avenues appearing to him like images
from a familiar *Inferno* ("There are birds the color of sulfur, and horrible in-
testines/hanging from the doors of the houses I hate..."). It is a landscape in
which "there are mirrors/which should have wept in shame and horror,"
given what they've been forced to witness and reflect, as well as a world of
"orthopedic appliances/and courtyards hung with clothes hanging from a
wire:/underpants, towels and shirts which weep/slow dirty tears." This is a
world in which even the intimate and ordinary clothes of men and women
have reason to weep, and even those tears are fouled by the filth, pollution
and waste they have been touched by. And perhaps the most violently lonely,
most wickedly solitary image of this poem: "there are forgotten sets of teeth
in a coffee-pot," an image that rivals anything in the young Eliot's highly celebrated annals of disaffection.

In looking back upon this poem, I think too that the poem's brilliant enactment of the *walk*, of its movement and passage, is a model that has held
tremendous power for me throughout the years. Here, Neruda's (or the
speaker's) restless, world-weary fatigue seems to me to be both Odyssean
and Dantescan, yet startlingly personal, undeniably universal.

Whether at eighteen or at forty, I think most readers will feel as I do, that
"Walking Around" is one of those rare poems that feels fresh, new, just written. It is a poem that, like its author, remains for me still an inexhaustible resource.

Robert Bly

WALKING AROUND WITH PABLO NERUDA

Neruda provided the title himself in English. He recognized how sweet
the phrase "walking around" was with its circular movement from
alk to ound. And so he writes a circular poem, not advancing into
some unknown place like the hero's poem going up into the upper atmosphere around some Himalayan peak; but on the contrary, he writes a dog's
poem, a dog that wanders around the neighborhood, sniffing in improper

places, having no urge to save the world, just exploring. As William Stafford, another poet who disliked the hero, said, "I'd rather slime along than be heroic."

It's an old tradition that the hero, despite his extravagant maleness, is really a servant of the mother, grandstanding for her. In another poem, Stafford said, "Our mother knew our worth—not much." Neruda begins by saying, "It so happens I am sick of being a man." To me, it's an astonishing line. One of the jobs of the poet is to find out what sensations human beings are feeling; some sensations are so contrary to the norm that the very people who feel them can't recognize them. The norm throughout the eighteenth century was Pope's "The proper study of mankind is man." Ortega says that people in the nineteenth century felt they had arrived at a height which earlier generations had only hoped for: "That psychological state of feeling lord and master of oneself and equal to anybody else was felt in Europe and America, since the eighteenth century, as the natural state of things." People would argue against a certain policy as being "unworthy of the advanced times."

> This is the plenitude of the time, the full ripening of historic life. And, in fact, thirty years ago, the European believed that human life had come to be what it ought to be, what for generations previous it had been desiring to be, what it was henceforward always bound to be.

The Revolt of the Masses was published in 1930, so Ortega is saying that even in 1900 people had this view of the heroic heights to which European civilization had reached: "This was the feeling with regard to their own time held by our fathers and all their century." Now we'll notice what Neruda says in 1933:

> It so happens I am sick of being a man.
> It so happens that I walk into tailor shops and movie houses
> dried up, waterproof, like a swan made of felt
> steering my way in a water of wombs and ashes.
>
> The smell of barbershops makes me break into hoarse sobs.
> The only thing I want is to lie still like stones or wool.
> The only thing I want is to see no more stores, no gardens,
> no more goods, no spectacles, no elevators.

Neruda was by ancestry Basque, so we can say that the European body that has found in its cells the glory of Pascal, the deep friendliness of Montaigne, the high vibrations of Mozart and Bach, now finds in its body cells as it walks down the street a disgust for human beings. This disgust, Neruda implies, is neither right nor wrong, it's simply there; and the dog's nose found it. Is he smelling his own anus? David Ignatow would probably say so. Freud held his nose a little as he strolled among Viennese sexual garbage, but his prose was impeccable, heroic, filled with the longing to honor earlier writers of great prose. Neruda lays out one sniff after the other, one sniff per line. What could have intervened between Pope and Neruda? Let's look at Ortega once more:

> The fact is this: from the time European history begins in the VIth century up to the year 1800—that is, through the course of twelve centuries—Europe does not succeed in reaching a total population greater than 180 million inhabitants. Now, from 1800 to 1914—little more than a century—the population of Europe mounts 180 to 460 millions! I take it that the contrast between these figures leaves no doubt as to the prolific qualities of the last century. In three generations it produces a gigantic mass of humanity which, launched like a torrent over the historic area, has inundated it. This fact, I repeat, should suffice to make us realize the triumph of the masses and all that is implied and announced by it. Furthermore, it should be added as the most concrete item to that rising of the level of existence which I have already indicated.

So the disgust has to do with the increasing numbers of people. Neruda senses that:

> It so happens that I am sick of my feet and my nails
> and my hair and my shadow.
> It so happens I am sick of being a man.

It's now 60 years since that poem was written. No one has expressed this disgust more clearly than Neruda did in 1933, and yet millions of people now feel that disgust. And Neruda clearly indicates that it's a disgust of the malls. We feel it, and yet the greed increases to fantastic levels, and some people live in the malls for days at a time. Underneath, we all want "no more goods, no spectacles, no elevators."

This disgust deepens. As Alexander Mitscherlich said, "We are aware of millions of siblings like us all over the globe." And there's nothing we can do about that. Our brothers and sisters in Czechoslovakia and China are just as greedy as those in Maryland. More malls are being built every day. The new mall in Minneapolis has a statue of Snoopy taller than any statue of Jesus in the city. The trouble with this disgust is that it can shade off into despair, a feeling that the whole culture is on a slide downhill, that everything is getting worse, that nothing can be done to stop it, that more NAFTAs will be passed by corrupt legislators, that more GATTs will be imagined by rotten economists. The suicidal desperation of many young musicians testifies to the reality of this sense of helplessness.

But that turn is not the turn that Neruda takes in the poem. He feels behind him all the fierce energy of the French surrealists, the satiric intensity of Quevedo and Goya, the grounded laughter of Villon, and the delicate sensibility of Lorca. Neruda says:

> Still it would be marvelous
> to terrify a law clerk with a cut lily,
> or kill a nun with a blow on the ear.
> It would be great
> to go through the streets with a green knife
> letting out yells until I died of the cold.

Great literature cannot be sustained through giving in to the victim emotions, self-pity, passivity, blaming, claims for exemption, requests for a grant on the grounds that I am worse off than you are. Great literature asks us to keep our defiance and our laughter. It's not politically correct to categorize all law clerks as people who would be terrified by a cut lily, but so what? Martin Prechtel mentions that the Mayans in Guatemala say there are only two things to look forward to: jokes and death.

We began by talking of what Neruda was sensing with his dog's nose in the cells of his body, sniffing here and there, barking at hubcaps and postmen. This is what he senses in his cells:

> I don't want to go on being a root in the dark,
> insecure, stretched out, shivering with sleep,
> going on down, into the moist guts of the earth,
> taking in and thinking, eating every day.

That's a bitter detail at the end there: Neruda puts thinking in along with eating as activities that make us all still more disgusted. He'll describe now what it feels like not to be in the plenitude of the time, not be self-satisfied, not be on the heights.

> I don't want so much misery.
> I don't want to go on as a root and a tomb,
> alone under the ground, a warehouse with corpses,
> half frozen, dying of grief.

We're a long way from the hero now on the top of Mt. Everest, in some cold, icy, fiery tower of spirit, far from Milton writing of joy and melancholy with Italian names. This disgust is utterly modern, and it can't be described without words like "gasoline" or "tire" or "carburetor." To feel the full disgust, we have to remember how many brilliant inventors have succeeded in the last hundred years in inventing more cars, more baby seats, more pacifiers, more BMWs, more ski runs, more yachts, more prisons, more electric chairs, more attack rifles, more machetes, more kidney machines. Even in the face of all that we need exuberance:

> That's why Monday, when it sees me coming
> with my convict face, blazes up like gasoline,
> and it howls on its way like a wounded wheel,

and leaves tracks full of warm blood leading toward the night.

And it pushes me into certain corners, into some moist houses,
into hospitals where the bones fly out the window,
into shoeshops that smell like vinegar,
and certain streets hideous as cracks in the skin.

We're going to see now how far you can carry political uncorrectness.
Human beings are such that they hate certain people without knowing why.
It's a part of their dog nature, their unheroic sloppiness, their inability to tell
their mother from a Swedish whore, the way aggression bubbles out of people as if it were under pressure. Only heroes can set heroic standards for
other people. Neruda admits he not only hates certain people, but he hates the
doors behind which they live:

There are sulphur-colored birds, and hideous intestines
hanging over the doors of houses that I hate,
and there are false teeth forgotten in a coffeepot,
there are mirrors
that ought to have wept from shame and terror,
there are umbrellas everywhere, and venoms, and umbilical cords.

Donald Hall has spoken of the McPoem that we see more and more coming
out of the poetry workshops, bland food the same in all states, "no surprises
in the sandwich": the sandwich includes a good-hearted grandfather, a dog
that liked you, a mother who tried as hard as she could, an aunt who died of
cancer at the appropriate time—just before the deadline for my M.A. creative
thesis. Stafford quoted poetry as being "a certain attention to language," and
in language particularly attention to surprise. Neruda's rebuking of certain
mirrors because they don't weep enough from shame and terror is a lovely
surprise. And rather than going from the umbrellas to raincoats to aquariums,
he goes from umbrellas to venoms, and from venoms—watch out—to umbilical cords.

I haven't been able to describe in these pages the amazing artistry in sound
that "Walking Around" exhibits, because the artistry inheres in his Spanish;
the English version—my own—staggers along getting the main idea but
without the grace.

Neruda is nearly ready to end the poem now. He and T. S. Eliot, one of his
old ideological enemies, were brother geniuses in feeling the disgust. Eliot at
the end wasn't quite as honest. He imagined heroic English women going out
into the tropics to be eaten by ants when the natives got irritated with them.
And he imagined exhausted Europeans ignoring Ortega and talking about it
at cocktail parties. Neruda knows that the ones really suffering in this sliding
downward from the heights are those in apartments with washing hanging
from the line. They feel disgust for their own children. None of them can be

heroic. In the housing projects, everyone has to be a dog. Neruda then, still keeping his defiant and spirited Goya-like intensity, lets compassion come through for those human beings that cannot live on the heights, for whom Monday doesn't get excited at all when it sees them coming:

> I stroll along serenely, with my eyes, my shoes,
> my rage, forgetting everything,
> I walk by, going through office buildings and orthopedic shops,
> and courtyards with washing hanging from the line:
> underwear, towels and shirts from which slow
> dirty tears are falling.

BIRD

An elegant bird,
slender feet, endless tail,
comes
close to me, to see what animal I am.

It happens in the spring,
in Condé-sur-Iton, in Normandy.
It has a star or drop
of quartz, flour or snow
on its tiny forehead
and two blue stripes run
from the neck to the tail,
two turquoise lines of stars.

It takes small hops
watching me surrounded
by green pasture and sky,
and they are two question marks
those nervous eyes waiting in ambush
like two pins,
two black points, thin rays of light
that stop me in my tracks and ask
if I fly and where to.
Fearless, dressed
like a flower in fiery feathers,
direct, determined
facing my tall threatening frame,
suddenly it discovers a grain or a worm
and hopping away on thin wire feet
it abandons the mystery
of this giant who remains alone,
apart from its small, fleeting life.[1]

translated by William O'Daly

---

[1] Pablo Neruda, trans. William O'Daly, *Winter Garden* (Copper Canyon Press, 1986), 29.

William O'Daly

TO THE EARTH AND ITS WINTER

I imagine that by now Pablo Neruda would be thoroughly enjoying himself, after wrestling with the initial discomfort of being the center of our attention. The poet would ultimately have enjoyed the idea of this symposium in his honor, this assemblage of interested writers and readers gathered to discuss his poetry. I imagine him settling in among us and before long offering to concoct some bizarre cocktail, or to pour any takers a glass of deep red wine from the Maipo valley—if only to revitalize the ancient camaraderie of the symposium. From the discussion, from charting the distances and intersections among themselves, the guests would end the evening having sketched an unfinished, temporal image of Pablo Neruda and his poetry. Readers will take that image or map of the poet and find their way to places in his work that we have not charted. In this way, the journey of discovery and renewal continues for the reader and for the poet's work.

> I am here while from sky to sky
> the shiver of migrating birds
> leaves me sunk in myself and in my flesh
> as in a deep well of perpetuity
> dug by a motionless spiral.[2]

Though Neruda died before I had a chance to meet him, I spent a number of years translating six books from his late and posthumous work. I wanted to publish those particular books in a particular order because I believe the result best represents the poet's conscious, truehearted recapitulation of his lifelong themes. The books also represent the poet's coming to terms with his imminent death. Because they were composed with the urgent care of a dying master, I've found living inside them as a translator no casual matter. Translating them has immeasurably altered and enriched my intellectual, emotional, and spiritual lives. Having spent many years engaged in such conversation with Neruda's work, I now find it impossible even to jerryrig a traditional exegesis of his poetry.

> On my violin that sings out of tune
> my violin declares,
> I love you, I love you my double bass . . .[3]

---

[2] *Winter Garden*, 57.
[3] Pablo Neruda, trans. William O'Daly, *The Yellow Heart* (Copper Canyon Press, 1990), 65.

While it's possible that my critical faculties may finally have slipped regarding Pablo Neruda, I am able to offer a few thoughts on what makes him one of the most widely translated poets of the century. Having participated as a translator in the beloved poet's recapitulations and reckonings, I feel I know something of who he is beyond the words, beyond the public figure and the political icon. I've often imagined arriving at his door in Isla Negra, being ushered inside by his wife Matilde, and within moments being greeted warmly by don Pablo. He has been navigating since early morning in his study, so the interruption though unexpected is welcomed. He and I retire to the rowboat in his backyard. Settled into the rowboat, bow pointed toward the Pacific and distant Rapa Nui, we sip tri-colored concoctions and let the conversation find the current.

> I can only say: I am here,
> no, that didn't happen and this happens:
> meanwhile the ocean's algae constantly
> rises and falls, tuned
> to the wave,
> and everything has its reason:
> across every reason a movement
> like a seabird that takes flight . . . [4]

But I really have no idea what the poet and I would say to each other, or if we would have much to say. Most of our collaboration has been non-verbal, surrounded by a silence similar to the silence surrounding the communication in the opening poem between the poet and the small bird of mystery. What can and cannot be translated between separate existences occurs in the white space, in the interval or musical rest, where we spend the greater part of our lives. The poet's breath as well as his strategies are interpreted by the translator's ear and eye—heart and mind—and recreated according to the translator's guided breath.

> and they are two question marks
> those nervous eyes waiting in ambush
> like two pins,
> two black points, thin rays of light
> that stop me in my tracks and ask
> if I fly and where to.[5]

Perhaps the poet and this translator would be content to sail our delicate craft in silence, past indomitable stone statues staring out to sea and past multina-

---

[4] Pablo Neruda, trans. William O'Daly, *The Sea and the Bells* (Copper Canyon Press, 1988), 61.

[5] *Winter Garden*, 29.

tional conquistadors in their filthy feathered hats. Underlying all 3000-plus pages of my companion's collected poetry, the most compelling preoccupation is the liberation of the heart and mind from whatever he perceived as tyrannical. Whether the tyranny was political or linguistic, or simply pervasive in people's lives, Neruda rallied against it with his words and with direct political action. Later in life, he came to repudiate certain mistakes in this regard, but he also came to embrace his humanity—the paradox and mystery of being—and even the sometimes quixotic pursuit of his ideals. Neruda discovered a sense of community in his struggle to see clearly, whether discussing and reading poems with his friends Lorca and Alberti in his "house of flowers" or later finding himself a part of the political and cultural destiny of the Chilean people. The poet and I might have nothing to say as we rolled in the wake of illustrious ships running tourists and minerals, or as we sailed past the sad houses of the Mapuche and the icy purity of the Bío Bío.

> Pardon me, if when I want
> to tell the story of my life
> it's the land I talk about.
> This is the land.
> It grows in your blood
> and you grow.
> It if dies in your blood
> you die out.[6]

Neruda translated Shakespeare and Baudelaire, among others. Yet, like most poets who translate, he seems to have spent little time bothering to distinguish between his roles as poet and as translator. This is probably because he thought of himself as a translator of experience, as a translator of "the earth and its winter." Whether writing a poem or translating one, the poet thought of the process as being an exploration of experience to determine cycle, textures, sounds, truths, and lies. The experience of *that* animated and guided the composition or translation of a poem; it guided the journey of his soul as translator, a shrouded poet who ferries experience from one body to another. The only meaningful difference between the roles may be that the translator responds first and foremost to his experience of an original poem, or the "visible" text, as Borges liked to say.

> Tell me, is the rose naked
> or is that her only dress?[7]
> . . .

---

[6] Pablo Neruda, trans. William O'Daly, *Still Another Day* (Copper Canyon Press, 1984), 23.

[7] Pablo Neruda, trans. William O'Daly, *The Book of Questions* (Copper Canyon Press, 1991), 3.

> Who was she who made love to you
> in your dream, while you slept?[8]

No sane (or experienced) translator ever promised to deliver an identical rose in another language. Yet translators still encounter the argument that we are by definition failed "copyists," mostly in my experience from individuals who sound somewhat embittered when they profess the ultimate impossibility of the existence of a successful translation of a poem. That disillusionment must be a painful thing to carry around, especially for those who love to read poetry. On the other hand, I can see my companion rolling his large eyes at the idea of a reader feeling betrayed because the translation process falls short of creating clones of originals. The inescapable fact is, a poem in a new body is a new poem; its soul cannot be an identical copy of an original soul. Perhaps people resist because this truth balances more toward multiplicity, or multiple versions of experience, than toward the more comforting theory of the *definitive text*. As a young poet, I too struggled against Borges' declaration: "The concept of a definitive text pertains either to fatigue or religion." Don Pablo and now I, as a more "mature" poet, are not alone. Poets/translators/readers could fare worse than having to settle for some manner of new poem in translation, especially when the translation's body and soul exist at all points in intimate dialog with the original (experience).

> And this time among seductions
> I was afraid to touch the sand, the sparkle
> of this wounded and scattered sea,
> but accepting of my unjust acts,
> my decision fell with the sound
> of a glass fruit that shatters
> and in this resounding blow I glimpsed life,
> the earth wrapped in shadows and sparks
> and the cup of the sea below my lips.[9]

The poet's face brightens when he spots another small boat coming toward us in the mist. He recognizes certain passengers—Manuel Puig, Guillermo Cabrera Infante, Severo Sarduy—who are being ferried across by Suzanne Jill Levine, translator of Latin American novels. I too am delighted. I've long admired their converging perspectives on creation as a cyclic gift the artist participates in—a view which pervades the content and structure of their novels. I also have been a long-time fan of Ms. Levine's essay, "From 'Little Painted Lips' to *Heartbreak Tango*." In speaking of the three novelists' work,

---

[8] *The Book of Questions*, 43.
[9] *Winter Garden*, 41.

Ms. Levine writes: "Their originals are already proposed as translations of texts, traditions, realities, touching upon the gaps between word and sense. The 'author' has been dethroned in their writing, and as self-translators they are self-subverters." She continues: "...an effective translation is often a '(sub)version,' a latent version, 'underneath,' implied in the original, which becomes explicit."

> I am a book of snow,
> a spacious hand, an open meadow,
> a circle that waits,
> I belong to the earth and its winter.[10]

All present agree. We are quite content to think of ourselves as "subversive scribes," whenever the use of subvert is close to its original Latin root meaning of "sub" and "vetere," meaning "to turn" from underneath: to till. Neruda himself says, "Poetry is rebellion. The poet is not offended if he is called subversive. Life is more important than societal structures, and there are new regulations for the soul."

> Nothing is gained by flying
> to escape this globe
> that trapped you at birth.
> And we need to confess our hope
> that understanding and love
> come from below, climb
> and grow inside us
> like onions, like oak trees,
> like tortoises or flowers,
> like countries, like races,
> like roads and destinations.[11]

Neruda's autumnal years were his most lucid, his vision the least tainted by the questionable assumptions and outright lies we live with daily. Those years were springtime of the seer, translator of experience, who betrays an original to make an *other*, another suitable home for a soul. From the *Elemental Odes* and *Extravagaria*, through the impeccably crafted late and posthumous books, Neruda wrote with what he called "guided spontaneity." In his final decade, the poet's method moved ever closer to casting the spoken to capture what cannot be spoken. The poem or translation, that transcreation of experience, was a musical construct in intimate collaboration with an other. It was an improvisational score written by the established and

---

[10] *Winter Garden*, 33.
[11] *The Yellow Heart*, 53.

the ever-changing, shaped to withstand harsh weather, corrosive air, and for
at least a brief moment, time.

> Well, that day that contains that hour
> will arrive and leave everything changed:
> we won't know whether yesterday has passed
> or if what returns is what never happened.
> . . .
> And we will possess a satanic power:
> to turn back or speed up the hours:
> to arrive at birth or at death
> like an engine stolen from the infinite.[12]

The separation between life and death, the dead's sudden and perpetual re-
moval from the living, was the first rip in the fabric for the very young
Neruda. Whether it was his true mother passing away in his first month, or
the lamb separated from its blood at family celebrations, the young Neftalí
Ricardo Reyes Basoalto was no stranger to death. But where some turn to religion or dogma to repair that rip in their soul, the apprentice poet turned almost immediately to love, particularly to love in poetry. Shakespeare's stories of love (and war) stirred the young poet's heart and moved him later in
life to translate *Romeo and Juliet*. Love was his *religio*, his binding force.
After an earthquake nearly destroys his and Matilde's home in Valparaiso, he
beseeches his *Romeo and Juliet* to rise from the floor:

> Come on, love poem, get up from the broken glass, the time to sing has
> come.
>
> Help me, love poem, to make things whole again, to sing in spite of
> pain.
>
> It's true that the world does not cleanse itself of wars, does not wash off
> the blood, does not get over its hate. It's true.
>
> Yet it is equally true that we are moving toward a realization: the vio-
> lent ones are reflected in the mirror of the world, and their faces are not
> pleasant to look at, not even to themselves.
>
> And I go on believing in the possibility of love. I am convinced that
> there will be mutual understanding among human beings, achieved in spite
> of all the suffering, the blood, the broken glass.[13]

At the heart of all issues of translation is a person's fundamental understanding of what is meant by "original." Originality is one topic, however, that

---

[12] *The Yellow Heart*, 91.

[13] Pablo Neruda, *Memoirs*, trans. Hardie St. Martin (Farrar, Straus and Giroux, 1977), 275.

probably wouldn't come up between don Pablo and me. Weariness of it would be one reason. "I don't believe in originality," he says in *Memoirs*. "It is just one more fetish made up in our time...an electoral fraud." This, from one of the most prolific poets of all time, whose wide-ranging work carries a sensibility and tone universally recognizable as the many Nerudas who compose a single Neruda. Instead he believed in origins that have origins. To adore originality is to miss or ignore the connection between what has existed and what is brought into being. We lose the current when we exalt something as being visionary when its true strength, for instance, is its compelling eccentricity. Neruda believed in personality, in keeping his own personal tone. But he warns of losing the connection to the roots that bind the present to the past, particularly when the roots are lost in a misplaced pursuit of origins that claim no origins. The poet had a natural suspicion of origins that come from nowhere, of the One that came before the Many. Neruda was interested in multiplicity and paradox. He endowed his brand of dialectical materialism with intense humanity and with humility in the face of mystery.

> our lives come and go, dying, making love:
> here on Easter Island where everything is altar,
> where everything is a workroom for the unknown,
> a woman nurses her newborn
> upon the same steps that her gods tread.[14]

Long before I began translating *The Separate Rose*, the source of this excerpt, I was familiar with my companion's sense of his responsibilities as a poet (much more a fetish of his than originality). I had thought of those responsibilities, however, as primarily literary and political in nature. Translating those late poems of wind, carved stone, blue water, and the Unknown caused me to redefine the relatively narrow understanding I previously held of Neruda's sense of his investiture as a poet. I reconsidered his words: "Poetry is a deep inner calling in man; from it came liturgy, the psalms, and also the content of religions. The poet confronted nature's phenomena and in the early ages called himself a priest, to safeguard his vocation. In the same way, to defend his poetry, the poet of the modern age accepts the investiture earned in the street, among the masses. Today's social poet is still a member of the earliest order of priests. In the old days he made his pact with the darkness, and now he must interpret the light."

> Someone will ask later, sometimes
> searching for a name, his own or someone else's
> why I neglected his sadness or his love
> or his reason or his delirium or his hardships:

---

[14] Pablo Neruda, trans. William O'Daly, *The Separate Rose* (Copper Canyon Press, 1985), 35.

and he'll be right: it was my duty to name you,
you, someone far away and someone close by . . .[15]

I began to widen my view of the younger poet in *The Heights of Macchu Picchu,* who reaches his hand into the earth hoping to trans-create a lost culture, accepting from the start that he is doomed to failure. In the gesture, he has done all he can do with his poem. He has not done enough, he cannot go on as a poet failing to raise the dead with his song, and so he goes on.

> Why is it so hard, the sweetness
> of the heart of the cherry?
>
> Is it because it must die
> or because it must carry on?[16]

Early in the process of translating *The Separate Rose,* the second book in the series, I spent the summer in Eugene, Oregon. Every morning I would bicycle through the drizzle to the university. I had grown accustomed to working in the library's reference area, at a cubicle close to their fine collection of Spanish dictionaries, each cheerfully representing a different major dialect. Just before reaching the library, I would pass through the old graveyard adjacent to it. I usually stopped to read the thick headstones, leaning one way or another, worn nearly smooth by a hundred years of a hundred kinds of rain. Some mornings I discovered new stones; other mornings I read the same stones I always did. I would stand before each stone long enough to imagine moments in the life of the daughter or son, mother or father, buried there. I imagined homesteaders, frozen in motion, arriving from the east to plow this damp land, and then others arriving to bury the homesteaders. One elderly gentleman was pruning his grapevine; an elderly woman was carrying a bucket of water. Some family plots were fenced off by knee-high, wrought-iron railings. At one of those plots, I saw a family sitting motionless at a table set for supper, somehow caught in a perpetual prayer of thanks. When I stopped at one young woman's stone, she was holding a coral hairbrush and staring into the dull surface of her bureau. Her name was British, yet she had large hands like the women in the drawings of Colombian artist Enrique Grau.

> I am not going to the sea in this long summer
> covered with heat, I'm not going any farther
> than the walls, the doors and the cracks
> that surround other lives and my life.[17]

---

[15] *Winter Garden,* 19.

[16] *The Book of Questions,* 25.

[17] *Winter Garden,* 25.

The images in the graveyard were mostly of difficult lives, or of lives experiencing a single moment of glory. A dry goods merchant is elected mayor; a child is born to a widow of San Juan Hill. Then there were "The Newlyweds," a young couple traveling from British Columbia to California, who died when their hotel room caught fire, and whose perpetual lovemaking provided the only motion, aside from the soft rain and the swaying of high branches. I'd never been in a graveyard so verdant, with exuberant moss among the cracked stepping stones, tangled blackberry vines, and evergreens that broke ground centuries before the first citizen arrived and was buried there.

> In which distance, facing what window,
> in which train station
> did I leave the sea forgotten, and there we were left,
> I turning my back on those things I love
> while there the struggle went on and on
> of white and green and stone and glimmer.[18]

At some point, my imagination would travel farther south. I would find myself in the damp forests of southern Chile. I never had to wait too long. From the hinterlands of Tierra del Fuego and past the volcanoes, the poet Pablo Neruda would come walking. He would enter quietly from the opposite end of the graveyard, most often appearing as a hefty man in his mid-sixties. He wore a dark gray suit and hat, rumpled from the long journey. Walking stick in hand, he stopped to visit every grave. He would read each weathered stone without missing a single one. He stopped just long enough to confabulate a suitable ending to the story the deceased himself may not have had the time to finish. Then he would move to the next headstone, to lay his hands upon yet another life. Once, as he drew closer, I saw him as a younger man, an exile, fleeing across the *cordillera* to escape President Videla's assassins. Standing beside his horse, the poet was awestruck at the prodigious root of a fallen tree which blocked the rugged Andean trail. He would not be allowed to return to Chile for several years.

> So it went, at least that's the way it seems:
> lives change, and he who has begun to die
> doesn't know that that side of life,
> that major chord, that abundance
> of rage and splendor were left in the distance
> they were blindly sliced away from you.[19]

---

[18] Ibid.

[19] Ibid.

Sometimes I saw him as a boy, wandering alone through the forests surrounding the frontier town of Temuco. Young Neftalí liked to examine all
manner of natural objects and to fill his pockets with colorful leaves, small
cones, and the occasional cricket. Throughout that summer, I never had occasion to feel that he wasn't there in the graveyard with me. I think some mornings I failed to recognize him. Those were mornings of confusion, filled with
prickly questions about what I was doing translating the untranslatable
Neruda. I struggled to understand what my role should be. Other mornings I
was confused about why I loved the work. Not Neruda's poetry, but why I, a
fledgling poet who had taken up translation primarily "to practice" the craft,
continued to focus on translating another poet. After all, my own poetry lay
unfinished and waiting in a drawer. On those mornings especially, I found
myself calling his name aloud—"Neruda, Pablo Neruda"—in long, slow ex-
halations.

> Or maybe it was the strain of the city, of time,
> the cold heart of the clocks
> that beat interrupting my measure,
> something happened, I didn't decipher it,
> I couldn't grasp each and every meaning:
> I ask forgiveness from anyone not here:
> it was my duty to understand everybody, becoming delirious,
> weak, unyielding, compromised, heroic, vile,
> loving until I wept, and sometimes an ingrate,
> a savior entangled in his own chains,
> all dressed in black, toasting to joy.[20]

Strange as calling his name was, my pretense was not meant as a summons.
El poeta del pueblo never comes when you call him; he prefers to appear unexpectedly and unannounced, when he knows you need him the most. On
those mornings, it was clear that I felt the need to reckon the distance from
my companion, just as the small bird does, before I continued with my work.
I needed to understand my role, to determine whether I participated in the
dark or in the light. I felt the need to reckon my responsibility to the dead and
to the Mystery, and to translate the unknown into fragile terms of the material world. I felt the need to give it all back again.

> I'm not going to the sea this summer: I am
> shut in, buried, and inside the length
> of the tunnel that holds me prisoner
> I faintly hear the green thunder,
> a cataclysm of broken bottles,
> a whisper of salt and of agony.

---

[20] *Winter Garden,* 19.

The liberator lives. It is the ocean,
far away, there, in my motherland, that awaits me.[21]

Whenever I walked through that graveyard in the rainy Willamette Valley, I was walking to return what I had been given. I was returning to the earth the Pablo Neruda his poems had given to me to others who would read the poems and who might allow the struggles within the poems to participate in transmuting their personal struggles. I was also beginning to see that our deaths, and the poet's own death, are part of what gives his poetry purpose. I wasn't beginning to understand it only because we all share that death, the Mask of Mystery. It was because Neruda's late poetry's greatest gift to readers is the acceptance of the struggle of being human, of living consciously in a fragile state of not-knowing. It was because Neruda's late work is an affirmation of life, of the day and the wave, of that which dies to become an integral part of that which never dies.

My hands reach into the earth
mornings when the faces of my dead
smolder like embers and their wildflowers
blossom up that windless hillside again.
Say I, who am alive, burn in the word.
Say my hand cramps to write this poem.[22]

We are the People, and everybody not here is the People, who invest Neruda with his role as *poeta del pueblo*, whiskey priest of the Word in the crowded street. As the People, we say *gracias* with all our hearts and our indifference, with our lives and our deaths. As translators or as observers we all trans-create the poem, each in our own imaginations, as we encounter its words and silences. We give life to the poet, the mountains and the waves, the statues and the bells, and ourselves every day. Translation is breathing; it is the tilling of the earth and the sea, of the expanse that *is* poetry. Yet I sometimes find myself asking why I translated six books by this poet whose home was so distant from my own. Having answered that question many times over the years, I only regret never having had a chance to meet him. I still ask my companion, as we sail on our long journey, a question he sometimes asks me:

Why describe your truths
if I lived with them,
I am everybody and every time,
I always call myself by your name.[23]

---

[21] *Winter Garden*, 25.

[22] William O'Daly, *The Whale in the Web* (Copper Canyon Press, 1979), 15.

[23] *Winter Garden*, 19.

THEODORE ROETHKE
(1908-63)

T heodore Roethke was one of the most daring and adventurous of the generation of poets who matured in mid-twentieth-century America. The experiments he undertook in verbal music, in highly stylized diction, in subject matter, all led to often brilliantly expressive results. His work shares affinities with a wide range of poets he studied and admired, including John Clare, Wordsworth, Blake, Whitman, Yeats, and Dylan Thomas, yet his voice is utterly distinctive. Roethke's poems develop through several clearly delineated styles, from precisely controlled formal lyrics through nonsense verse to the long, intuitive metaphysical sequences of his last volume, *The Far Field* (1964). Always a Romantic at heart, he explored the nature of the self—its private journeys from despair to ecstasy, its unconscious ties to the natural world, its struggle to achieve transcendent understanding—in language that is at once deeply personal and hauntingly sensuous. A Midwesterner, Roethke taught at various colleges around the country before settling at the University of Washington. His periodic experiences of mental illness clearly influenced his writing, but at its best his work exhibits an almost preternatural clarity and control.

BOOKS: *Collected Poems* (1966); *On the Poet and His Craft: Selected Prose of Theodore Roethke*, ed. Ralph J. Mills, Jr. (1965); *Selected Letters*, ed. Mills (1968); *Straw for the Fire: Selections from Theodore Roethke's Notebooks 1943-63*, ed. David Wagoner (1972).

FRAU BAUMAN, FRAU SCHMIDT, AND FRAU SCHWARTZE

Gone the three ancient ladies
Who creaked on the greenhouse ladders,
Reaching up white strings
To wind, to wind
The sweet-pea tendrils, the smilax,
Nasturtiums, the climbing
Roses, to straighten
Carnations, red
Chrysanthemums; the stiff
Stems, jointed like corn,
They tied and tucked,—
These nurses of nobody else.
Quicker than birds, they dipped
Up and sifted the dirt;
They sprinkled and shook;
They stood astride pipes,
Their skirts billowing out wide into tents,
Their hands twinkling with wet;
Like witches they flew along rows
Keeping creation at ease;
With a tendril for needle
They sewed up the air with a stem;
They teased out the seed that the cold kept asleep,—
All the coils, loops, and whorls.
They trellised the sun; they plotted for more than themselves.

I remember how they picked me up, a spindly kid,
Pinching and poking my thin ribs
Till I lay in their laps, laughing,
Weak as a whiffet;
Now, when I'm alone and cold in my bed,
They still hover over me,
These ancient leathery crones,
With their bandannas stiffened with sweat,
And their thorn-bitten wrists,
And their snuff-laden breath blowing lightly over me in my first sleep.

Marianne Boruch

THREE SPIRITS

About twenty years ago, I heard a story. And whether it's the true or should-be-true variety may not matter. But Robert Lowell had thrown a party; Roethke was his houseguest. Later, all the revelers having gone home to bed, Lowell was holding forth on this one and that one, the usual party post-mortem, stopping particularly to point out someone—who it was I can't recall—as his "best friend." To which Roethke, large and sad and half-lost by that hour to good drink, is said to have said quietly to Lowell: you're my best friend.

I'm still inordinately touched by this anecdote. Roethke's sweetness, his lack of self-consciousness and embarrassment, works wonderfully against the way the elegant Lowell must have surely felt awkward all of a sudden. But other things are carried too—Roethke's edge of self-pity, for instance, disconcertingly near the easy, the sentimental, an apt illustration of his much loved and suspect line, "We think by feeling,/What is there to know?" I knew something turned in me nonetheless, and won me over. Irony has its pleasures when you're 25. But Roethke—he was downright corny in such a moment, putting himself out there anyway.

I like that *anyway* about him. In this he's one of the most American of our century's poets: expansive, passionately accurate about detail, especially natural detail; secret, sometimes sloppy, reverent, maybe too close for his own good to the heart. He is also one of our most daring (his probably the best ear going), risking not merely ornamental change but real change, from the abstract verities of his first book though the amazing grounding of his second—with the so-called "greenhouse poems"—past that into a disturbing near-wacko ranging toward sing-song rhythms and childish diction, into, finally, the long meditative poems, true wonders of human discovery. Stroked as he was for his first book, *Open House*, he could have easily paid in full and bought that farm—its formal, distant grace—and farmed it for a lifetime. He didn't.

What's forever interesting to me is *how* he didn't, how—because of what?—his second book, *The Lost Son*, arrived. Here's where Michigan comes in, his what must have been, in fact, a rather difficult childhood, son of stolid no-nonsense immigrants (as in "My mother's countenance/Could not unfrown itself"). Still, it was "a wonderful place for a child to grow up," he has written as though in cahoots with the region's PR people, going on to count specific treasures—twenty-five acres under glass, and farther out, the last stand of virgin timber in the Saginaw Valley, its herons, muskrats, frogs. And the famous greenhouses of that book? "They were to me, I realize now," he told the BBC, "both heaven and hell, a kind of tropics created in the savage climate of Michigan, where austere German-Americans turned their love of order and their terrifying efficiency into something truly beautiful."

Poems, of course, are built of heaven and hell, the earth *as is*, and under glass, Roethke's world forever in that greenhouse shadow, decay there, and danger, certainly death though beauty—it's the thing beyond all doubt. His major life-luck was probably finding that his own odd place and time made directly for poems, beauty large and close as an ordinary or awful day of childhood. And so he takes us straight to that place. He shows us something.

Memorable poetry has this way of orbiting the beginning of things to bring on darkness, and thus one's first awareness—of pattern, ancient cycle, universal turn. "Frau Bauman, Frau Schmidt, and Frau Schwartze" ends the first section of *The Lost Son*, and on the face of it, the poem is pure elegy, three old greenhouse workers of his father's whom Roethke returns to life, and so praises them. We witness, it seems, everything they ever did or imagined doing—their winding the sweet-pea tendrils, straightening carnations, tying and tucking, dipping, sifting, sprinkling, sewing, teasing out "the seed that the cold kept asleep." The whole first stanza is a busy, lush assemblage of unending duties, the intricate clockwork of the greenhouse in wild motion before us, quickened by the shortened lines, enjambment making turns both urgent and graceful. Roethke's eye for the right detail brings an almost surreal focus on many things, stems "jointed like corn" or the way these women draw out their silent charges, using "a tendril for needle," sewing up the air. It's the view of a child really, a child amazed as an adult might be, looking up the greenhouse ladders to their superhuman handiwork, their "skirts billowing out wide tents." Finally, by the stanza's end, one's nearly squinting to see up there. "They trellised the sun," the poet tells us. And of their generosity, "they plotted for more than themselves."

Roethke liked to say, quoting Yeats, that "we go from exhaustion to exhaustion." In life, and perhaps in any writing too. But immortal now by elegy, these women never tire. The second, final stanza goes abruptly another way. Out of the very public sweep of stanza one, everything goes private, Roethke's favorite way of moving. These focused, workaday women poke and tickle the "spindly kid" the speaker dreams he was. And he laughs too much, "weak as a whiffet." I love this layer, its release against the solid bramble above of so much work, the previous climbing, tying, sprinkling, tucking. This other, warmer side is play, and spirit—three spirits, to be exact. Next line or two, they are invoked like that. They hover now; all's gone hushed, interior. They guard the speaker, who's grown and haunted by what's least romantic in them, these "leathery crones," their "bandannas stiffened with sweat," their "thorn-bitten wrists." Yet even these bits of fact are cherished; they bring if not peace, at least a curious consolation. I like to say that fierce, three-stressed phrase, *thorn-bitten wrists*, and know the zoom-lens closeness of that hand, moved by the history of pain and labor in the scratches. Dark and light, heaven and hell in some hopeless mix. The poet honors the essence of those women when he honors that, as well as something larger.

After I heard that story of Roethke and Lowell, which is to say, when I first read Roethke, I was living in a place where sometimes at night, driving home, we'd pass four or five greenhouses way off the road in a distant field. They glowed that eerie green they glow, in winter, in summer, it didn't matter. I can't say that every time I thought of Roethke. But I always thought the world stranger and more dear, such moments.

from **THE LOST SON**

1. *The Flight*

At Woodlawn I heard the dead cry:
I was lulled by the slamming of iron,
A slow drip over stones,
Toads brooding wells.
All the leaves stuck out their tongues;
I shook the softening chalk of my bones,
Saying,
Snail, snail, glister me forward,
Bird, soft-sigh me home,
Worm, be with me.
This is my hard time.

Fished in an old wound,
The soft pond of repose;
Nothing nibbled my line,
Not even the minnows came.

Sat in an empty house
Watching shadows crawl,
Scratching.
There was one fly.

Voice, come out of the silence.
Say something.
Appear in the form of a spider
Or a moth beating the curtain.

Tell me:
Which is the way I take;
Out of what door do I go,
Where and to whom?

> Dark hollows said, lee to the wind,
> The moon said, back of an eel,
> The salt said, look by the sea,
> Your tears are not enough praise,
> You will find no comfort here,
> In the kingdom of bang and blab.

Running lightly over spongy ground,
Past the pasture of flat stones,
The three elms,
The sheep strewn on a field,
Over a rickety bridge
Toward the quick-water, wrinkling and rippling.

Hunting along the river,
Down among the rubbish, the bug-riddled foliage,
By the muddy pond-edge, by the bog-holes,
By the shrunken lake, hunting, in the heat of summer.

The shape of a rat?
        It's bigger than that.
        It's less than a leg
        And more than a nose,
        Just under the water
        It usually goes.

Is it soft like a mouse?
Can it wrinkle its nose?
Could it come in the house
On the tips of its toes?

        Take the skin of a cat
        And the back of an eel,
        Then roll them in grease,—
        That's the way it would feel.

        It's sleek as an otter
        With wide webby toes
        Just under the water
        It usually goes.

Thomas Lux

THE SECRET JOINERY OF SONG

What I have always loved about this poem is its tremendous *physicality*. Even though it is a poem that evokes great emotional/spiritual pain (and some resolution thereof) it is the physical energy of the poem, manifested in its rhythms and onomatopoeic reverberations, that makes it so palpable, so alive.

I can think of no greater leap in growth between a poet's first and second books than that of Roethke's *Open House* and *The Lost Son and other poems,* published in 1941 and 1948, respectively. *Open House* was a solid book of traditional, somewhat metaphysical lyrics. *The Lost Son* (and particularly its title poem and companion pieces "Give Way, Ye Gates," "The Long Alley," "The Shape of the Fire," etc.) is completely different: looser (though still exquisitely crafted), wilder, more intuitive than intellectual, intense, disturbing, playful, and utterly original. These longish poems seem almost surreal at times, but on closer reading are much less arbitrary than most surrealist verse. Their verbal energy is closer to Joyce than anything else. Another admitted influence is Mother Goose. Those two are an interesting combination of influences. Roethke also read widely, though not systematically, in eastern philosophies and religions.

"The Lost Son" and several other poems in the volume were written after Roethke returned to his home town of Saginaw, Michigan, in early 1946 to recuperate from his second major manic-depressive episode. There had been a gestation period for these poems, several years, in fact, and he had already written many of the so-called "greenhouse poems" before working on these even more innovative poems. His father, who died when Roethke was thirteen, was a greenhouse owner and operator. "The Lost Son" is a "father" poem and a poem filled with the things of the greenhouse and its surrounding properties. The poem itself is not so much *about* manic-depression (I'm not even sure it was called manic-depression then) as it is—in its rhythms, its mood swings, its heights and depths—a literary equivalent. Highly controlled, of course, distilled, its chaos yielding insight rather than obscuring it. In a letter to William Carlos Williams in May of 1946 he writes of "The Lost Son": "It's written, as you'll see right away, for the ear, not the eye. It's written to be heard. And if you don't think it's got the accent of native American speech, your name ain't W. C. Williams, I say belligerently." And, a little later in the same letter, he says he is trying to get "the mood or the action on the page, not talked about, not the meditative T. S. Eliot kind of thing." In an essay called "Open Letter" Roethke says of the "Lost Son" poems in general (before going on to offer a useful gloss of the specific poem): "But believe me: you will have no trouble if you approach these poems as a child would, naively, with your whole being awake, your faculties loose and alert. *Listen* to them, for they are written to be heard, with the themes coming alternately, as in music, and usually a partial resolution at the end."

"The Lost Son" is a difficult poem from which to excerpt because so much of its power depends on the *movement* of the poem, on the contrast between sections, or the contrast within sections, or even the contrasts in individual *lines* (see the longer-lined parts of section 3, "The Gibber") but it might be useful to discuss the first stanza because it sets the mood, the central themes, and the *modus operandi* of the whole poem:

> 1. *The Flight*
>
> At Woodlawn I heard the dead cry:
> I was lulled by the slamming of iron,
> A slow drip over stones,
> Toads brooding wells.
> All the leaves stuck out their tongues;
> I shook the softening chalk of my bones,
> Saying,
> Snail, snail, glister me forward,
> Bird, soft-sigh me home,
> Worm, be with me.
> This is my hard time.

The poem begins with an evocation of the dead. The central death in the poem, the heart of its heart, is the death of the speaker's father. The music, the oxymoronic and onomatopoeic quality, of the second line is wonderful—the "l" consonance sets us up for something soft, mellifluous, but what we get is the opposite, something harsh, aurally painful. We are pulled both ways, at the same time. The speaker is lulled by what would not normally be lulling: the slamming of iron: coffins, crypts, cemetery gates? He is lulled by this loss? Sometimes yes, sometimes not, for the struggle with the father, alive and dead, is a difficult struggle. The next line has three open evocative "o" sounds and is heavily stressed, giving a visual/tactile quality to time, making concrete what is normally abstract. The next line contains a typo that I believe Roethke consciously chose not to correct in later printings. The line was intended to be "toads brooding *in* wells," which is grammatically correct, but without the preposition "brooding" becomes more associative, making it more likely for the reader to also hear the word "breeding." This line too (particularly without the "in") is heavily stressed: *bang, bang, bang*, the dolorous tone hammered slowly into the reader's ear, heart. Robert Frost said the best way to the reader's heart/mind (he used the words synonymously) was through the reader's ear. Roethke knew this was true and is establishing it very early and very deliberately, in the poem. The childlike serio-comic paranoia of the next line is important because it prepares us for other similar things that happen in the poem and it "lulls" us momentarily before the more serious next line, a line that suggests the breakdown of the body, perhaps even as a symbol for impotence, either physical and/or emotional. Something is going on, there is action, reverberation, every rift in every line loaded with ore, nothing wasted or in excess, nothing lazy or prosy! The last four lines of this stanza announce many of the strategies of the poem (addressing an animal or an inanimate object, for example, almost as one would address a deity) while at the same time containing a powerful evocation of a human condition. The rhythm is again heavily stressed and descending, a lot of spondees and trochees. This combination of imagery, metaphor, and music never fails to shoot me into the rest of this poem, fully arresting my attention and firing my pulse, despite having read and taught this poem hundreds of times. "Glister" is a brilliant word choice here, normally a noun (and archaic) but here a verb and a command making us concentrate on the shiny trail of slime the snail leaves behind as it ekes forward, a brilliant metaphor for the emotional and psychological struggle this poem illuminates.

I heard someone say once that there is a lesson in good poetry writing in every line Theodore Roethke wrote. This is true. And also true, always true, is the incredible integrity of imagination, the wide open singing, the whole heart, the gift of this splendid poet.

THE WAKING

I wake to sleep, and take my waking slow.
I feel my fate in what I cannot fear.
I learn by going where I have to go.

We think by feeling. What is there to know?
I hear my being dance from ear to ear.
I wake to sleep, and take my waking slow.

Of those so close beside me, which are you?
God bless the Ground! I shall walk softly there,
And learn by going where I have to go.

Light takes the Tree; but who can tell us how?
The lowly worm climbs up a winding stair;
I wake to sleep, and take my waking slow.

Great Nature has another thing to do
To you and me; so take the lively air,
And, lovely, learn by going where to go.

This shaking keeps me steady. I should know.
What falls away is always. And is near.
I wake to sleep, and take my waking slow.
I learn by going where I have to go.

Alberta Turner

A SECOND READING

It is an axiom among contemporary poets that a fine poem cannot be para-
phrased, and though I have for many years felt instant pleasure from
Roethke's "The Waking," I tremble when anyone asks, "What does he
mean by 'I wake to sleep'? Has he a snooze alarm on his clock? Is he trying
to sleep off a hangover? Is there something he has to do this morning that he
doesn't want to do? What does he mean by 'I feel my fate in what I cannot
fear'?" To all such questions I should have to answer, "What do you think?"
or "Ask the poet." One widely published poet of my acquaintance said of his
own poem, in effect, "Don't analyse my poem. Float on it." Others have said,

"It just came to me." Others have handed me their worksheets. For years I
have floated on the pleasures of "The Waking." Now it is time to re-examine
those lines and decide, if possible, why and how they have created my pleasure.

The villanelle is a difficult form to write. It consists of four tercets and a
final four-line stanza, and it uses only two end rhymes. The first and last line
of the first tercet should each be repeated exactly as the last line in alternate
tercets, and the final stanza should conclude with both the first and last lines
of the four tercets, thus making eight of the poem's nineteen lines refrains.
The success of the villanelle depends upon the poet's finding two lines that
he can bear to repeat four times each. The poet's genius lies in being able to
vary these two key lines just enough to keep their refrain quality while allowing the meaning of the poem to grow. Roethke wrote just one villanelle
with such flexible key lines. I find only one other villanelle in the *Collected
Poems*: "The Right Thing," part of "Sequence, Sometimes Metaphysical," in
The Far Field. This villanelle uses as its key lines, "Let others probe the mystery if they can" and "The right thing happens to the happy man." The resulting villanelle reads almost like a parody of "The Waking" or a failed first
draft, although it was published in a later book.

The first tercet of "The Waking" immediately creates mystery by using
paradox. Waking to sleep suggests both a need to evade reality and a new reality altogether, a need to let go of mind, to stop using conscious effort and
trust dream or perhaps intuition instead. He feels that his fate (destiny) will
lie in something familiar or so insignificant that whatever it does will be a
surprise, good or bad or perhaps insignificant. There is threat in this line.
Roethke was not a man who relished insignificance. The third line may suggest to him complacence or despair or an acknowledgment of the power of
death.

The first line of the second tercet is not a repetition of the opening line of
the poem, but it is, in fact, a restatement and amplification of that line's idea.
Feeling is the sleep that frees the spirit to drift and dream. Roethke doubts
that any other kind of knowing is possible or important. In the next line his
mind is dancing in his head between his ears. Is the dancer trying to get out,
or is the slumbering mind dreaming of dancing, a dream that an active, sensual man might have? In the last line he is still asleep, still waking slowly
into this new kind of perception.

The first line of tercet three appears to move still farther from the first line
of the poem. It seems to throw Roethke back into the waking world that he
had drifted from, but actually he has drifted farther into his sleep world. He
seems to see another person and speak to him. But is the creature he speaks
to a person? Is the creature he sees beside him perhaps a feathered or a furred
one or perhaps something very small and very precious that he must not step
on? The refrain line at the end of this tercet is part of the preceding sentence,

in which Roethke asks God to bless the ground. He is not wholly asleep now. Slowly, he is waking into kindness.

In the fourth tercet Roethke continues to observe and enjoy the creatures and the landscape in his dream country: he sees a tree as if by new light. He notices a worm, a "lowly worm," inching up a "winding stair." Literally it is a worm, but the words *lowly* and *winding stair* suggest an abject self starting to climb toward self-respect in a devious, tortuous manner.

Tercet five deifies "Great Nature," not as Mother, but as a god who commands. Roethke's mood by this time is idyllic, a mood reinforced by the l's of *lively, lovely,* and *learn.* Nature's sleep has brought him to a state of playful bliss.

The final four-line stanza of the poem wakes Roethke finally out of that bliss. He speaks of his "shaking" and recognizes what it means. I read "shaking" as a reference to the confusion that caused him to "wake to sleep," a doubt about his identity that makes him want to see himself from a different perspective. The metaphor of shaking works well here: shaking can return balance to a wobbling cup or to a pair of human legs that stagger from weakness. Cold can cause shaking and fear. Roethke knew all the inner shakings of fear: fear for his sanity, fear for his self-respect, and especially fear for his life, without which none of the other fears could be cured. "What falls away is always" is a literal statement, not a pun or an adjective but a synonym for *forever.* He suspected that death was near, and it was. He died at fifty-five.

"The Waking" may not be an orthodox villanelle, since it does not repeat the first and last line of each tercet exactly, but his variations make a static form into a lively narrative and permit a progression of tones from wonder to bliss to dread.

A second reading of Roethke goes far to persuade me that his work is not as profound as Rilke's nor as subtle as Stafford's nor as quirky as Simic's nor as mysterious as Merwin's early work. But his humility and music and courage are very appealing qualities in the confused 1990s. I myself often walk in his dark woods, and for pure pleasure I reread "The Waking."

Martha Collins

WORD-WORK

When I want an example of language doing its damnedest, its very best, its nothing-else-can-do-it work, I often think of one of the repeated lines of Theodore Roethke's villanelle "The Waking": "I learn by going where I have to go." It's the *have* that does it: is it the *have* of necessity, the one we sometimes pronounce "haff," the one we learn to protest against as children (Oh Mom, do I *have* to?)? Or is it the *have* of possession, of opportunity (Look what I have!)? I can hold that *have* in my hand, I can have that *have*, and it's precisely its indeterminacy that makes it so solid.

I could have gotten it from another utterance, and indeed the "lesson" carries over: "This is what I have to do," I sometimes remind myself. But it's of course the line, and ultimately the poem itself, that give Roethke's word its power. The line contains a life, and summarizes endless debate about free will and determinism too: do we have to go where we go, or is "where" to some extent up to us? Death, our ultimate "have to," is there as well, of course, so abundantly that it's possible to read the poem with little else in mind. But such a reading is precisely what the language keeps pushing against. Though the infinitive in "I have to go" echoes the infinitive in the poem's other repeated line, "I wake to sleep, and take my waking slow," there's a tense play in both lines between gerund and infinitive, between process and arrival. If the poem allows us to balance freedom and necessity, to have both in a single word, it also allows us, through an intricate play of language, to balance death and life, ending and going on.

"I wake to sleep" has its own tense power: is "sleep" indeed part of an infinitive, as in "I wake in order to sleep," or is it a noun, as in "I wake to a new day," or "I wake to the sound of your voice"? The phrase is so odd, so insistently backwards, that it's difficult not to hear "I go to sleep" in it, too. That suggests the end of it; but the "and" that follows implies either concurrence or sequence, and then voilà, there's the waking again. As in take it easy, enjoy it while you can—or even as in take a nap or take a cure, a prescription for happy living. More hauntingly, "waking" may be experienced not only as a grammatical object, but also as a personified one. There's a curious change of grammatical partners here: the speaker wakes to the presence of "sleep" in the first part of the line, but then takes "waking" in the last part, as a man might take a woman, for instance. If this seems farfetched, consider the other lines where "take" appears: in the fourth stanza, "Light takes the Tree"; in the fifth, the reader (or someone) is told to "take the lively air"—another prescription, maybe, or maybe more. "Who can embrace the body of his fate?" Roethke asks in "Four for Sir John Davies."

Several characteristics of "The Waking" recur in Roethke's other published villanelle, "The Right Thing": one of the repeated lines of the later poem plays a similar game of repetition ("The right thing happens to the happy man"); "God bless the roots!" is about as direct an echo as one can imagine of "The Waking"'s "God bless the Ground!"; and what's "learned" in the two poems is certainly similar. But "The Right Thing" is a lonely poem; it has no one to talk to but itself, whereas "The Waking" is haunted by other presences.

Five of the poem's first six lines begin with "I," and the interruption in the fourth line ("We think by feeling. What is there to know?") is inconspicuous, marking an easy shift to a universal *we*. A similar statement and question universalize the beginning of the fourth stanza ("Light takes the Tree; but who can tell us how?"), and even the "you and me" of the fifth stanza seems to reach out to a universal reader.

Or would seem to, if it weren't for the line that opens the third stanza with its suggestive internal rhyme: "Of those so close beside me, which are you?" Which, indeed? *Which* itself hovers: which of many, or which of a few, or even (as *beside* may suggest) of two? The poem doesn't tell us, but the line creates a presence that carries over into the fifth stanza:

> Great Nature has another thing to do
> To you and me; so take the lively air,
> And, lovely, learn by going where to go.

Here "having to" and "having" confront each other directly: Nature is given the power of possession in the first half of the stanza, carrying with it the poem's most unequivocal reference to death; but *you* are advised to take charge in the last half, where, for the first time, the powerful *have* disappears altogether from the repeated line.

And who is *you*? All of us, surely, and those of us who read this poem, in particular: this is the kind of imperative we're apt to take personally. But "which are you?" hovers in the background, and when "lively" transforms itself into "lovely," we're certainly near the language of love poetry. Which is not to suggest that this is a love poem: there's a carpe diem sentiment in this stanza, but it points away from the speaker, and the question of who is taking whom, or what, is after all a mighty shifty business.

One of the formal lessons Roethke has to teach in this villanelle is that a form laden with repetition can be enhanced by even more repetition: thus the two additional *takes*, as well as the *waking/wake* and *going/go* of the repeated lines. Another end rhyme gets repeated when the second stanza's "What is there to know?" is echoed in the sixth ("I should know"); but here it's *there* that acts up most, wanting to contain the thereness of place ("What is *there* to know?") as well as the absence of meaning that its expletive function implies (What is there to know, after all?).

But is there a there there? When *there* gets repeated in "God bless the Ground! I shall walk softly there," it carries the echo of "waking slow," and once again resonates with apparently conflicting possibilities. Is the ground of the line the one we walk on now, in contrast to the transcendent light and air of the next two stanzas? Or is it, as the future tense suggests, the ground we end up *in*? If it's the latter, "I shall walk softly there" makes a little joke about the grave, nodding toward the sleeping dead and considering, in the next line, a destination beyond it.

The beginning of the poem's last stanza seems both to sum up its process ("This shaking keeps me steady") and to illustrate it once again (Where do we put the stress on "I should know"?). But then there's a final turn of language, before the two repeated lines assert themselves quietly one last time. "What falls away is always" makes the adverb a noun, but this reification is part of a lively process: the word both appears and disappears, becoming something, then falling away. When the line continues, *always* finds its partner in *near* and returns to something more like its usual function. The poem lets us have *always*, even as it's taking it away. That the sound of the language once again helps this happen is part of the magic of the line: one can hear the sounds of *always* in "falls away," so that the falling away inevitably produced by "going where I have to go" leaves something linguistically dynamic in its place.

"The word outleaps the world," Roethke says in "Four for Sir John Davies," suggesting dance, suggesting play. But it's more than word-play. It's word-work, doing what only language can do, taking us—or helping us go—where only language can take us.

THE CHUMS

Some are in prison; some are dead;
   And none has read my books,
And yet my thought turns back to them,
   And I remember looks

Their sisters gave me, once or twice;
   But when I slowed my feet,
They taught me not to be too nice
   The way I tipped my hat.

And when I slipped upon the ice,
They saw that I fell more than twice.
   I'm grateful for that.

Gerald Stern

MORE MAJOR

When I think of the Roethke poems I love the most, "Meadow Mouse," "The Thing," "Otto," "The Storm," "Dolor," "Frau Bauman," "Slug," "The Geranium," "All Morning," "Moss Gathering," "Child on Top of a Greenhouse," "My Papa's Waltz"—to name what comes to me first—I realize how non-political, how non-social, they are, how they are concerned with the helpless victim, with the good thing ruined, with the anguish and wonder of the small and ignored, with the soul besieged, and that the main emotion is pity or fear or terror. There is a little social commentary in "The Geranium"—the "snuffling cretin of a maid" is after all "sacked" for throwing the plant out (pot and all) and that shows something of "socio-economic dynamics," including, I am ashamed to say, the arrogance and cruelty of the employer, as well as female-bashing—but the poem truly centers on the pathetic and almost wise flower, the plant as female companion and the desperate loneliness of the poet, those other issues being subsidiary. And "Otto." Though that beautiful poem is not political, it contains, like a novel, a whole world of information about culture, character, gestures, dreams and lost dreams, ambitions and passions, and it therefore reflects social conditions and moral imperatives. This in forty-two lines, three stanzas of eleven lines and a fourth of nine. Or "Dolor" and "Academic." These can be seen perhaps as poems of social commentary, the soul lost to institutional horror: "...dust from the walls of institutions,/Finer than flour, alive, more dangerous than silica" . . . "Glazing the pale hair, the duplicate grey standard faces." Though that poem is more Kafka than it is Rexroth or Shapiro, as the second one, "Academic," is more Pope than anything else—or Swift—a rage against (and a contempt for) the unmanly, blustering, stylized, theoretical fool.

Maybe "The Chums," of all his poems, is the most politically conscious. It is one of his few where the action points *out* instead of *in*, where the world, as world, is considered in preference to the one victim, the one sufferer, or the other. The speaker is the poet, it is the poet most literally, and he is acted upon and different, indeed he is pushed down "more than once" upon the ice, but Roethke changes the note, and the speaker, instead of being helpless and subject to unbearable forces and cruel uncontrollable pressures—and thereby driven into a state of terror or horror—is subject, as far as the poet is concerned, to a more or less reasonable and unsurprising assault, considering the circumstances. After all, the poet left the confines of that restricted world and "made good," and even when he was still one of the "chums" he had a slightly different head upon his shoulders. He was a semi-outsider; he tipped his hat. Roethke has no anger, no resentment; he got what he deserved. He knows that.

I love the first two lines:

> Some are in prison; some are dead;
> And none has read my books.

There is affection for those friends, and a kind of pity, as if for the dead. And enormous separation, psychically and temporally. There is almost a kind of loyalty to them—and their code. And in a fit of genius he expresses his "gratitude" for their judgment, for the punishment.

I feel a whole world in eleven lines. The economy is amazing, and the delicacy; and the balances, pauses, rhythmic repetitions and rhymes. It is a poem that comes out of a certain culture at a certain period of time. The word choices are unerring, and the symbolic action is so perfect that we forget it is just that, and take it for mere narrative. But what I love most about it is the sanity, the wisdom and the moral tone. We are not here in the world of lost childhood, abominable *or* beautiful, we are not about to be assaulted and perhaps destroyed by irrational forces not to our understanding and control. We are—he is—an actor in a familiar social situation who understands, and even thinks appropriate, the judgment and force used against him, and who looks at his judges with love and calls them "chums." It is a little bit of rural America from the late twenties and early thirties. It is an experience that almost every one of us who moved out of his or her first culture has experienced. And it is rife with knowledge of that culture and a gentle approval of its severe egalitarian ethos.

Roethke was not a crazy tortured victim out of some internal or external madhouse; he was sophisticated, educated and cunning. He chose a certain subject matter over another. He was obsessed with certain things. He was *not* innocent and helpless, any more than the rest of us are. He broke down from time to time because he had an ailment. He was obsessed with isolation, helplessness and the terrible onslaught. In a way, it was the subject of his times. "Chums" shows a slightly different way he could have gone. The way of responsibility, irony, social connection. He did go that way, to one degree or another, in many others of his poems. That quality only makes him more complete, as it makes him more complicated. It makes him more major.

THE TREE, THE BIRD

Uprose, uprose, the stony fields uprose,
And every snail dipped toward me its pure horn.
The sweet light met me as I walked toward
A small voice calling from a drifting cloud.
I was a finger pointing at the moon,
At ease with joy, a self-enchanted man.
Yet when I sighed, I stood outside my life,
A leaf unaltered by the midnight scene
Part of a tree still dark, still, deathly still,
Riding the air, a willow with its kind,
Bearing its life and more, a double sound,
Kin to the wind, and the bleak whistling rain.

The willow with its bird grew loud, grew louder still.
I could not bear its song, that altering
With every shift of air, those beating wings,
The lonely buzz behind my midnight eyes;—
How deep the mother-root of that still cry!

The present falls, the present falls away;
How pure the motion of the rising day,
The white sea widening on a farther shore.
The bird, the beating bird, extending wings—.
Thus I endure this last pure stretch of joy,
The dire dimension of a final thing.

Beckian Fritz Goldberg

THE CASE OF "THE TREE, THE BIRD"

Chapter I

It was a still, hot day, the kind that makes your ears ring and your eyelids sweat. I was tired, bone tired, from a late night working up a list of oral imagery in Donne and Marvell. I leaned back in my chair. The truth was I just didn't want to get started on the case. Previous investigators had called it open and shut, written it off as a simple allegory. A misdemeanor at worst.

But the poetry detective must have a criminal mind, get inside the perp's head, understand his motives, his habits, reconstruct the crime.

In the case of "The Tree, the Bird," I had few clues. But it struck me it bore a mysterious resemblance to a case I handled years back, the case of the "Night Crow." It paid, in my profession, to keep up one's ornithological knowledge because nine times out of ten you could bet where there's a poem there's a bird involved somewhere. In the "Night Crow" case I was dealing with duplicity, the kind of mind that seemed to be in two places at once. I'd been hired to find out *what does the bird symbolize* by the author of a text-book on poetry. That was a tough one.

So was this. What I had was one Theodore Roethke, vanished. One bird, one tree. And a whole lot of questions: Why was the poem so little discussed by critics, relegated to an "also ran," a Roethkean et cetera in his *Sequence, Sometimes Metaphysical*? Why the sigh in the seventh line, considering the speaker seemed to be in a fine mood until then? Why the return to formalism after the expansive free verse of the *North American Sequence*? Was the speaker journeying toward true mystical transcendence or returning to the sense of exaltation which characterized the manic phase of his manic-depressive cycle? And what could I make of the cryptic clue that the deceased had "discovered the secret of Nijinsky"?

I popped open a Snapple. I leaned forward in my chair.

Chapter II

I decided to begin by reviewing my earlier case. Like the man often said, "You must go backward to go forward." Maybe I could find a connection. I dug up my file on "Night Crow" in which Roethke's conjunctive tree-bird image first occurs.

> When I saw that clumsy crow
> Flap from a wasted tree,
> A shape in my mind rose up:
> Over the gulfs of dream
> Flew a tremendous bird
> Further and further away
> Into a moonless black,
> Deep in the brain, far back.

It is an image that haunts the closing sequence of *The Far Field*. In "The Sequel," the lines "A shape called up out of my natural mind;/I heard a bird stir in its true confine" can't help but recall "Night Crow" as well as fore-shadow "The Tree, the Bird." In "The Decision," Roethke writes, "A bird kept haunting me when I was young—/The phoebe's slow retreating from its song,/Nor could I put that song out of my mind,/The sleepy sound of leaves in a light wind."

Obsession is the mother of craft. There aren't too many hard and fast rules in this business, but that's one I try to stick by. Because no image is ever complete, a poet may return to the same image again and again. What does the bird symbolize? my client wanted to know.

It was a question that begged the question. Which bird? The crow flapping from the tree or the "tremendous bird" rising in the speaker's mind? Either way it was a question that mistakenly isolated thing from process—the journey of the bird is followed through space "further and further away" and, simultaneously "far back," not away from the speaker but toward some netherhorizon in him. The transient image (bird taking flight) reaches a different duration in the mind.

I set down the Snapple and let it sweat on my notes. Maybe I was on the wooly edge of some epiphany, maybe not. But it seemed the initial mirroring in "Night Crow" between bird and bird, outward space and inward, distance and intimacy, brevity and duration, is finally rendered in "The Tree, the Bird" in a language and form that physically embody and enact it, yoking the obsessive image to mature craft.

While much critical discussion of the *Sequence, Sometimes Metaphysical* debates the "success" of Roethke's return to formalism and whether or not his language convincingly renders a mystical transcendence of the self, "The Tree, the Bird," with its archetypal landscape and highly orchestrated use of language, dramatizes the duality of the sensory and the spiritual through its "double sound." I wasn't so sure the issue here was transcendence as much as it was a conscious experiment in craft to use formal elements—doubling, repetition, echo—to evoke "oneness." The poem looked likely to reveal much about the demands Roethke made on language. I'd studied his m.o. and was ready to sift the evidence.

Chapter III

It was about midnight, still still and still hot. I was thinking to myself, Either the amount of repetition of single words contained in such a short lyric points to a failure of language, a lapse into mannerism, or it serves as part of form following function, a language in which the word repeated is part of the larger correspondence of the poem. In "The Tree, the Bird," *still* occurs five times, *pure* three times, *joy, midnight, beating, wings* each occur twice. And then there's *bird*, of course, three times. There is, as well, a pattern that goes from *bearing* to *bear* to *endure* and from *unaltered* to *altering* to *shift*, reflecting the poem's tension between form and transformation.

A solid lead, but I'd need more to crack the case. I knew that much; I'd attended Lit Crit basic training regularly, until I was kicked out for refusing to translate metaphors. A misdemeanor at worst. But my training in surveillance was proving more relevant now. On a stakeout, 90% of the time you're looking at patterns—what time X or Y comes or goes, when he eats, when he sleeps. X is the poem.

Each stanza contains a line wherein part of the same phrase is repeated, yet the meaning shifts. In the opening stanza, "part of a tree still dark, still, deathly still" is not only rhythmically effective, a rocking motion that prepares us for "Riding the air" in the next line, it shifts our sense of the word *still* from time, as in "it's still dark out," through the second *still* which at once emphasizes time/duration and yet evokes also our sense of motionlessness, to "deathly still" which clearly evokes the motionless while the modifier *deathly* gives a sense of finality to the element of time.

Similarly, "grew loud, grew louder still" in the second stanza does not use the word *still* merely to emphasize the increasing loudness of the bird. For the speaker, "grew louder still" means "grew louder" in its stillness. It recalls the line from "Infirmity"—"My ears still hear the bird when all is still." The loudness-in-stillness of the stanza's opening "rhymes" with its closing in which the speaker refers to "that still cry."

I was beginning to wonder how much the poem had to do with listening. And calling. I made a note to follow up. Scrawled on the opposite page in my notebook was an earlier note I'd left myself. It said, "Present tense."

The third stanza opens with another twinning within the line, "The present falls, the present falls away." Again, Roethke uses echoing phrases to yoke altered meanings: "the present falls" quite literally in the poem as it shifts with this stanza into the present tense, and then "the present falls away" as the speaker shifts into an experience of the eternal present.

A good night's work. I tumbled into bed and dreamt I was in a hall of mirrors. Each time I went forward toward one mirror, my image receded backward into it. Down the hall a cloud drifted. Nested atop it was a giant talking raven named Otto.

Chapter IV

One of the entries in Roethke's *Notebooks* says, "Yes, it's possible to create a true natural order simply by putting things down repeatedly." But the pattern of repetition in "The Tree, the Bird" is only part of Roethke's "double sound." The poem's initial reverie creates an animated landscape where *uprose* in the first line, *dipped* in the second, the contrasting motions of being met and walking toward, in the third, create a dance-like movement which continues as the speaker is drawn toward the voice calling from a cloud and then describes himself "pointing at the moon." Within this excitation of opposite motions, one auditory image—"the small voice calling"—initiates an antiphonal structure in the poem which embodies another thematic element.

I was on the track of the sigh.

The pattern of calling to and from the self, listening and reply, begins in that fourth line as the speaker walks toward the voice calling to him from a cloud. The response is the "I sighed" of the seventh line. In terms of the speaker's description of being "at ease with joy" and "self-enchanted," the reader isn't led to expect a sigh except perhaps of supreme contentment. But clearly, since the sigh initiates imagery of darkness, "midnight," "bleak whistling rain," it is not an expression of enchantment but a response to a call outside it, the call to "stand outside" the self. Roethke's "self-enchanted" here means quite literally its etymological roots, *in* + *cantare*, the self in chant, the self in song.

I wondered if Heidegger was anywhere in Roethke's library or if coincidence was just coincidence. The calling to and from seemed to resonate with Heidegger's notion that "language speaks" and that the poem is a calling of *world* and *things* into a onefold intimacy in their being "toward one another." The calling toward this dimension of the onefold is the "double-stilling" and the calling from it, "the peal of stillness."

Additionally, the stillness Heidegger speaks of "stills by carrying out, *bearing* and *enduring* world and things in their presence" (my italics). At the end of the first stanza, the speaker becomes part of a tree which he describes as "bearing its life and more, a double sound." The double sound becomes again a calling and response in the next stanza where the speaker cannot "bear" the bird's song, a song louder in its stillness. The response is the "lonely buzz behind my midnight eyes." The listening to the song sets off a vibration in him and produces the recognition which closes the stanza, "How deep the mother-root of that still cry!" No longer standing outside the self, the speaker re-calls the self, its original being, its natural childhood relation to the world. Like the man says, "You must go backward to go forward."

In Roethke's work, the connection between communion and communication goes far back. It is manifested in *The Lost Son*, according to Kenneth Burke, through a rhetorical strategy of using "whenever there is no specific verb required" some word "in the general category of *communication*" to effectively suggest "a world of natural objects in vigorous communication with one another" or, at least, their "mystic participation." The embodiment of communication in the images of tree and bird seems a natural extension of this process.

Roethke's transformation of the speaker into part of the tree is coupled with an awareness it is "bearing its life and more." The double sound is at once the voice outside and within the self, and the bird then appears not only as an allegorical figure for "spirit" but as a muse figure in the pattern of calling and reply that runs through the first two stanzas as the speaker approaches the jump from one plateau, "at ease with joy," to another, "enduring" the "last pure stretch of joy."

Now that I had the bird in hand, so to speak, I still wasn't out of the woods. I still had some questions—oneness or transcendence, mystic or manic, Apollonian or Dionysian? An acceptance of death or premonition of death by water? Was the tree really part of the "secret of Nijinsky"? This was another entry in Roethke's *Notebooks*: "Drink, coffee, cigar. Or cigar, coffee, drink. Or cigar, drink, coffee—or—?"

Chapter V

I emerged from Roethke's psychic landscape into the glare. The thermometer had hit 121°. The kind of day that made you want to haul off and smack it if only personification worked. I decided to go back in.

The poem's journey, whether toward self-transcendence and acceptance of death or toward the oneness and exaltation that characterized Roethke's experience during an early manic episode, also traces a "more homely but related form of exaltation: creativity itself." In "On 'Identity,'" Roethke describes the metaphysical poet as one who "thinks with his body." Such poets "jump more frequently from one plateau to another." The creation of the poem, for Roethke, is "one of the ways man at least approaches the divine."

These remarks immediately follow his description of writing "The Dance" during which he felt aided by an "actual Presence." Finishing, he "wept for joy. At last I was somebody again." This sense of being entered by, or entering into, a presence outside the self and then being returned, somehow, to a more magnified—exalted—sense of identity parallels his description of "writing the really good poem."

Roethke mentions a line from "The Dance" in a description of his manic episode among the interviews for *In a Dark Time* (cited by Neal Bowers in *Theodore Roethke: The Journey from I to Otherwise*). "I tried to fling my shadow at the moon"—which resembles "The Tree, the Bird"'s "I was a finger pointing at the moon"—was, according to Roethke, an attempt to capture the "dance that accompanies exaltation." An earlier comment on the episode, that he'd had a "mystical experience with a tree" and "discovered the secret of Nijinsky," led biographer Alan Seager to cite a passage in Nijinsky's *Diary* relating a similar experience of ecstatic identification with a tree as a possible explanation of the "secret," thus equating the tree image with the secret of Nijinsky. Yet Roethke's 1935 breakdown occurred the year before the *Diary* appeared and it is a "copy of Nijinsky's life" (the 1934 biography) that Roethke seems to have requested in the sanitarium. He had clearly already connected his experience with Nijinsky because of his experience of "the dance." And what could be closer than dance to "thinking with the body" that, for Roethke, was the process of poetry, his approach to the divine?

In the eternal present of the closing stanza, the movements contrast with the opening stanza's series of opposite motions. The speaker observes the "pure" motion of "the rising day," of the "white sea widening" and the bird "extending." The corresponding movement of the speaker is indicated with the word *thus* in the penultimate line, "Thus I endure this last pure stretch of joy." He is, like the rest of creation, rising to that new plateau, and yet the word *stretch* not only suggests distance as well as enlargement; it also suggests "stretch of time." The speaker may be enduring a difficult expansion of the spirit beyond the body, but as a poet in dialogue with the spirit, he is also enduring that what is "present" in the creative act's approach of the divine "falls away" and the poem becomes the "dire dimension" he fills only briefly until it is finished, "a final thing."

No doubt there was a sexual metaphor in there somewhere, but I'd get my fill of those soon enough. I'd gotten a desperate call from a victim of Dickinson burn-out about her poem number 1395, a.k.a., "After all Birds have been investigated and laid aside."

ELIZABETH BISHOP
(1911-79)

B orn in Nova Scotia and raised in Boston, Elizabeth Bishop spent a great deal of her life traveling: the landscapes of eastern Canada, New England, New York, Paris, Key West, Mexico, and Brazil all figure prominently in her work. Though fascinated by geography, she never uses the foreign simply as material for travelogue; rather, the exploration of unknown territory and customs always gains metaphorical, and frequently metaphysical, significance. For Bishop the world is stubbornly resistant to our understanding: enchanting and often delighting us, it equally frustrates our attempts to map it, leaving us dislocated and unsettled. As in the work of her friend Marianne Moore, the brilliant surface of a Bishop poem often appears cool and impersonal; like Moore, she is such a meticulous and attentive observer that the object of her scrutiny seems to occupy all our attention. Yet careful reading reveals an extraordinary emotional force and acuity: in her considered, carefully oblique way, she is one of our bravest explorers of the tangled nature of identity. Unfailingly modest and graceful, unerringly musical, her poems chart the mind's attempt to maintain stability and balance in a mysterious, always challenging world. Her quiet, bemused, stunningly perceptive voice is one of the most distinctive in modern letters.

BOOKS: *Complete Poems 1927-79* (1983); *Collected Prose*, ed. Robert Giroux (1984).

THE ARMADILLO

for Robert Lowell

This is the time of year
when almost every night
the frail, illegal fire balloons appear.
Climbing the mountain height,

rising toward a saint
still honored in these parts,
the paper chambers flush and fill with light
that comes and goes, like hearts.

Once up against the sky it's hard
to tell them from the stars—
planets, that is—the tinted ones:
Venus going down, or Mars,

or the pale green one. With a wind,
they flare and falter, wobble and toss;
but if it's still they steer between
the kite sticks of the Southern Cross,

receding, dwindling, solemnly
and steadily forsaking us,
or, in the downdraft from a peak,
suddenly turning dangerous.

Last night another big one fell.
It splattered like an egg of fire
against the cliff behind the house.
The flame ran down. We saw the pair

of owls who nest there flying up
and up, their whirling black-and-white
stained bright pink underneath, until
they shrieked up out of sight.

The ancient owls' nest must have burned.
Hastily, all alone,
a glistening armadillo left the scene,
rose-flecked, head down, tail down,

and then a baby rabbit jumped out,
short-eared, to our surprise.
So soft!—a handful of intangible ash
with fixed, ignited eyes.

Too pretty, dreamlike mimicry!
O falling fire and piercing cry
and panic, and a weak mailed fist
clenched ignorant against the sky!

Sandra McPherson

"THE ARMADILLO": A COMMENTARY

I don't know if there will be Elizabeth Bishop scholars making their living writing exegesis-after-theoretical-analysis of her poems. Because those poems seem supremely self-sufficient. Nonetheless, every year some student says, "I bought the Bishop like you said; sometime could you tell me what's so great about her?" Then I try to think back to before I knew her, so my judgment will not be colored by personal loyalty. At age 21 or 22, I felt that I needed to read EB to learn how to use *anything* as the subject of the poem or as an object in the poem. Her work said, if you like things enough they'll stay alive even in a poem, whatever their nature. And another thing: her work *didn't* say "I am a poet." In fact, the I was omitted from her work for pages on end, the better to show her affection for her subjects.

One can't add to "The Armadillo." It happens to be the Fourth of July and we can hear illegal noises of shock and delight. I have never seen fire balloons, though. For six stanzas we watch her guide us through them, before we come to the animals. The poem is 60% balloon, 13% owl, 13% rabbit, 13% armadillo—a strange proportion. One of her trademarks is taking time to notice details and to state them in the slowed-down wording of musing: the third through fifth lines of this passage, for instance—

Once up against the sky it's hard
to tell them from the stars—
planets, that is—the tinted ones;
Venus going down, or Mars,

or the pale green one.

We're glad she didn't know the name of "the pale green one." That wording

makes her an observer, not an expert in an observatory. Again, when "a baby
rabbit jumped out,/*short*-eared, to our surprise," she is not so startled by the
flashier fire balloons that she can't save a line for both the short ears and her
surprise.

In this poem she's skillful at both slow and quick portraiture. The patient
portrayal of the balloons through eighteen applicable verbs; the quickly-real-
ized sketch of the "glistening armadillo.../rose-flecked, head down, tail
down/...and a weak mailed fist/clenched ignorant against the sky."

The last stanza is something I wouldn't have predicted from Miss Bishop.
An outcry in italics. Every emotion (beauty, mockery, fear, panic, anger, frustration, bafflement) is highlighted and exclamation-marked. This is the conclusion to her patient lines. She began saying this was the time of year such
events happen. I like this poem partly because this is the time of *life* they happen. And I fear the poem because this is the century, the administration, in
which they happen to those whose armor is weakest.

4 July 1983

FILLING STATION

Oh, but it is dirty!
—this little filling station,
oil-soaked, oil permeated
to a disturbing, over-all
black translucency.
Be careful with that match!

Father wears a dirty,
oil-soaked monkey suit
that cuts him under the arms,
and several quick and saucy
and greasy sons assist him
(it's a family filling station),
all quite thoroughly dirty.

Do they live in the station?
It has a cement porch
behind the pumps, and on it
a set of crushed and grease-
impregnated wickerwork;
on the wicker sofa
a dirty dog, quite comfy.

Some comic books provide
the only note of color—
of certain color. They lie
upon a big dim doily
draping a taboret
(part of the set), beside
a big hirsute begonia.

Why the extraneous plant?
Why the taboret?
Why, oh why, the doily?
(Embroidered in daisy stitch
with marguerites, I think,
and heavy with gray crochet.)

Somebody embroidered the doily.
Somebody waters the plant,
or oils it, maybe. Somebody

arranges the rows of cans
so that they softly say:
ESSO—SO—SO—SO
to high-strung automobiles.
Somebody loves us all.

David Walker

ELIZABETH BISHOP AND THE ORDINARY

To read through Elizabeth Bishop's poems, now collected under one elegant roof, is to re-experience all those qualities for which she is celebrated, not least her skills as guide to the marvelous and the arcane. As the titles of her individual volumes suggest, Bishop was fascinated by the experience of travel, the extremes of geography and the varieties of human experience. Her precise and penetrating sense of observation allows us to visit landscapes from Cape Breton to Key West, from Paris to Mexico and her tapestried, extravagant Brazil. Her taste for the extraordinary also produced poems displaced into the strange worlds of history ("Brazil, January 1, 1502"), myth ("The Gentleman of Shalott," "The Prodigal"), and literature ("Crusoe in England"). What keeps these poems from representing mere exotica or a tourist's souvenirs is that Bishop herself always remains present as a kind of balancing or qualifying element, never content simply to accept the glittering surface as given, always probing for the echo of something richer and more resonant beneath. The details of Bishop's poems are always compelling, but they are never the whole point, even in those apparently most purely "descriptive." The true subject of the travel poems is the mysterious act of perception by means of which we learn to distinguish ourselves from the peculiar landscape and the bizarre artifact, and also to discover what binds us to them.

Perhaps less often recognized is Bishop's interest in the plainly and even stubbornly ordinary. Her curiosity extends to the mundane and the banal, the universal emotion and the domestic scene, and here the process of perception is equally crucial: it is the fierce intelligence and affectionate accuracy with which such subjects are evoked that makes them seem so fully worthy of our attention. In a poem like "Filling Station," the ordinary becomes mysterious, revelatory, unique.

The first line demonstrates the sort of ambiguities from which the poem is constructed, immediately raising questions of situation, voice, and tone. (I've sometimes thought "Filling Station" would make a good exercise for acting students, given the number of different ways the first line—and much of the rest—might be stressed.) Is the opening exclamation solemn and childlike, or prissy and fastidious, or enthusiastic? All we can identify with certainty, I think, is the quality of fascination, the intent gaze on the filling station's pure oiliness. Nor is the scale on which the observation takes place very clear. Filling stations can, after all, be pretty dirty places, and yet there's something peculiar about an oiliness so deep that it turns the whole place translucent, almost into the essence of oil itself. And just how "little" is this place, anyway? Try to imagine Bishop standing across the street observing, and it doesn't work: the quizzical tone seems to miniaturize the filling station and divorce it from any context, as though its designer were Mother Goose or Walt Disney. (Or, more appropriately, Joseph Cornell, a favorite of Bishop's, and who with Edward Hopper seems to have had a hand in the poem's origins.) The sense of the miniature and the fabulatory is developed in the second stanza, where the human element is introduced in the form of a generic Father and his generic saucy sons, all cut from the same oily cloth—though the cheeriness of this is characteristically qualified if we notice that Father's costume doesn't fit, or that Mother seems to be absent from the scene.

In the third stanza, the accumulation of details is matched by an increasing involvement on the part of the speaker. Curiosity ("Do they live in the station?") overtakes description, as she tries to probe beyond the flat, drab, objectified surface to the human meaning beneath. By this point the oiliness has become so pervasive that the "set of crushed and grease-/impregnated wickerwork" may seem like appropriate designer decor, and the "quite comfy" dirty dog sounds the detached, parodic note even more strongly. But in the next stanza the camera bores in more relentlessly, almost obsessively listing the dumb details, qualifying and repeating ("the only note of color—/of certain color," "a big doily...a big hirsute begonia") until it's clear that the perceiver has somehow become implicated in the scene. And the mask of detachment is shaken by the pressure of questions breaking through:

> Why the extraneous plant?
> Why the taboret?
> Why, oh why, the doily?

Clearly, much is at stake here. I'm reminded of Frost's poem "Design," which also seeks to discover a meaningful pattern in apparently random details, but whereas that poem points uncomfortably toward a sinister architecture in the world of nature, here the speaker seeks to understand a goofy "extraneous" beauty, a concern for harmony at the heart of this oil-soaked darkness. Her answer comes—and here the poem is at its most mysterious—in the final stanza, a vision of domestic attention anonymously embodied. It's a measure of the poem's richness that it's difficult to tell metaphysical or even theological implications here from a parody of them. The tone is quiet and delicate, but also bemused ("Somebody waters the plant,/or oils it, maybe"), and we're left facing the irony that the poem's final proof of "love" is a row of Esso cans. What I find most remarkable is that all these opposing elements are held in perfect balance. On repeated readings the mystery deepens rather than resolving itself: I think no other poet of Bishop's generation could manage such poignancy and wit simultaneously.

AT THE FISHHOUSES

Although it is a cold evening,
down by one of the fishhouses
an old man sits netting,
his net, in the gloaming almost invisible
a dark purple-brown,
and his shuttle worn and polished.
The air smells so strong of codfish
it makes one's nose run and one's eyes water.
The five fishhouses have steeply peaked roofs
and narrow, cleated gangplanks slant up
to storerooms in the gables
for the wheelbarrows to be pushed up and down on.
All is silver: the heavy surface of the sea,
swelling slowly as if considering spilling over,
is opaque, but the silver of the benches,
the lobster pots, and masts, scattered
among the wild jagged rocks,
is of an apparent translucence
like the small old buildings with an emerald moss
growing on their shoreward walls.
The big fish tubs are completely lined
with layers of beautiful herring scales
and the wheelbarrows are similarly plastered
with creamy iridescent coats of mail,
with small iridescent flies crawling on them.
Up on the little slope behind the houses,
set in the sparse bright sprinkle of grass,
is an ancient wooden capstan,
cracked, with two long bleached handles
and some melancholy stains, like dried blood,
where the ironwork has rusted.
The old man accepts a Lucky Strike.
He was a friend of my grandfather.
We talk of the decline in the population
and of codfish and herring
while he waits for a herring boat to come in.
There are sequins on his vest and on his thumb.
He has scraped the scales, the principal beauty,
from unnumbered fish with that black old knife,
the blade of which is almost worn away.

Down at the water's edge, at the place
where they haul up the boats, up the long ramp
descending into the water, thin silver
tree trunks are laid horizontally
across the gray stones, down and down
at intervals of four or five feet.

Cold dark deep and absolutely clear,
element bearable to no mortal,
to fish and to seals . . . One seal particularly
I have seen here evening after evening.
He was curious about me. He was interested in music;
like me a believer in total immersion,
so I used to sing him Baptist hymns.
I also sang "A Mighty Fortress Is Our God."
He stood up in the water and regarded me
steadily, moving his head a little.
Then he would disappear, then suddenly emerge
almost in the same spot, with a sort of shrug
as if it were against his better judgment.
Cold dark deep and absolutely clear,
the clear gray icy water . . . Back, behind us,
the dignified tall firs begin.
Bluish, associating with their shadows,
a million Christmas trees stand
waiting for Christmas. The water seems suspended
above the rounded gray and blue-gray stones.
I have seen it over and over, the same sea, the same,
slightly, indifferently swinging above the stones,
icily free above the stones,
above the stones and then the world.
If you should dip your hand in,
your wrist would ache immediately,
your bones would begin to ache and your hand would burn
as if the water were a transmutation of fire
that feeds on stones and burns with a dark gray flame.
If you tasted it, it would first taste bitter,
then briny, then surely burn your tongue.
It is like what we imagine knowledge to be:
dark, salt, clear, moving, utterly free,
drawn from the cold hard mouth
of the world, derived from the rocky breasts
forever, flowing and drawn, and since
our knowledge is historical, flowing, and flown.

Elizabeth Spires

QUESTIONS OF KNOWLEDGE

"At the Fishhouses" by Elizabeth Bishop is a meditation on empirical knowledge vs. absolute truth, the human problem of "netting" or knowing anything with any degree of certainty in a physically ever-changing world. As the poem opens, Bishop details a darkening Nova Scotian landscape in literal and metaphorical decline. Early on, the poet introduces the means by which the scene is to be mediated, the five senses represented by the five fishhouses, the senses mediating between the mind ("storerooms in the gables") and the external world. All five senses come strongly into play as the poem progresses. Land and water are seen as distinctly opposed entities with the poem's stanzaic structure reinforcing this opposition. The descriptive focus of the first stanza centers on land whose silver surfaces at dusk are of "an apparent translucence." In contrast, the sea is opaque and apparently conscious, described as "swelling slowly as if considering spilling over," its silver surface hiding a quite different kind of knowledge, one not necessarily apprehended by the senses. And yet, the word "apparent" qualifies the land's seeming translucence, hinting at illusion or disguise and suggesting limits on what can be known or apprehended even as we stand on solid ground.

The emphasis then in the dense descriptive lines of the first stanza is on the *appearance* of things. The old man, both Time personified and in time himself, links the invisible past of the poet's dead grandfather with the immediate present:

> There are sequins on his vest and on his thumb.
> He has scraped the scales, the principal beauty,
> from unnumbered fish with that black old knife,
> the blade of which is almost worn away.

The repetitive physical action described parallels the eroding action of time itself and places an implicit value on surface appearance: the fish scales, likened to sequins, are, importantly, "the principal beauty," the flies crawling on the fish tubs "iridescent." The old man's knife is talismanic, an earlier incarnation, we can guess, of Crusoe's knife in "Crusoe in England."

Up to this point, a kind of impersonal visual esthetics has predominated. The short middle stanza serves as a mediating passage between the disparate elements of land and water. Poetically self-referential, the lines, "...thin silver/tree trunks are laid horizontally/across the gray stones, down and down/ at intervals of four or five feet," describe the actual construction of the poem, the horizontal laying down of the lines and the descent at (musical and temporal) intervals of four or five (poetic) feet into a sea of knowledge.

It is at this point, with the opening of the third stanza, that the poem lifts with rhetorical grandeur into Bishop's "high style" even as it makes its descent into the "Cold dark deep" of the sea. The sea, as a representation of absolute knowledge, of knowledge out of time, is an "element bearable to no mortal," in stark opposition to the half-truths and "apparent" perceptions of ordinary human existence. The gravity of the statement is counterbalanced by the seemingly playful scene with the seal. The seal's presence is crucial. Without it, the sea would be utterly inhuman and non-relational. The creature is presented as a skeptical, yet kindred intelligence, like the poet, "a believer in total immersion." The seal's bemused and curious reaction to the singing of "A Mighty Fortress Is Our God" raises the question as to the spirit in which the speaker sings the hymn. Seriously? Playfully? Presumably the latter, given the tone of the scene.

The haunting echo-effect of repeating the line "Cold dark deep and absolutely clear" moves the poem toward a powerful and sweeping conclusion. Behind the speaker and seal, temporally as well as spatially, "a million Christmas trees stand waiting for Christmas." The Christmas trees seem both hopeful and wistful projections, signifying perhaps the poet's yearning for the lost innocence of an earlier time. The value of repeated sensory experience is emphasized over the nostalgic or sentimental with the line, "I have seen it over and over," as if the senses were a means to at least a partial apprehension of a higher order of knowledge. The poet's desire for absolute knowledge, some contact with omniscience, through secular or poetic epiphany takes the form of an invitation to the reader to participate in a painful baptism:

> If you should dip your hand in,
> your wrist would ache immediately,
> your bones would begin to ache and your hand would burn
> as if the water were a transmutation of fire
> that feeds on stones and burns with a dark gray flame.

The utter physicality of the action is a comment on the limitations of the corporeal state as well as being a metaphoric statement: the body a metaphor for the spirit or soul, and one's ability to suffer or accept physical pain a metaphor for the soul's growth.

The idea of knowledge as an outgrowth of pain or adversity is developed further by the startling image of "the cold hard mouth" and "rocky breasts" of the world. The world, as posited by Bishop, is a harsh mother, neither nurturing nor protective. Considering the poem was written in an historically dark period (1945 or 1946), one must read "At the Fishhouses" as a poem allusive not only to private pain but to the pain of history. The complex and highly paradoxical nature of knowledge is both "dark" and "clear," a necessary contradiction, like the formed formlessness of the sea, and "moving" not only in the sense of fluidity but in the sense of being able to arouse emotion. (A handwritten early draft rendered the attributes more positively: "beautiful, clear, dark, utterly free.") The bitter briny "taste" of knowledge is also the taste of tears, related to the tears alluded to at the beginning of the poem:

> The air smells so strong of codfish
> it makes one's nose run and one's eyes water.

By the poem's end, these are no longer the simple tears of sensation. They have become the tears of a feeling intelligence in a shifting world of appearance.

"At the Fishhouses" insists that what little we know to be true keeps changing. The stance is both heroic and tragic. And yet we can trust that for Elizabeth Bishop, "a believer in total immersion," the pursuit of knowledge, however evanescent, extended much farther than dipping only a wrist in truth's cold dark deep element.

THE END OF MARCH

For John Malcolm Brinnin and Bill Read: Duxbury

It was cold and windy, scarcely the day
to take a walk on that long beach.
Everything was withdrawn as far as possible,
indrawn: the tide far out, the ocean shrunken,
seabirds in ones or twos.
The rackety, icy, offshore wind
numbed our faces on one side;
disrupted the formation
of a lone flight of Canada geese;
and blew back the low, inaudible rollers
in upright, steely mist.

The sky was darker than the water
—*it* was the color of mutton-fat jade.
Along the wet sand, in rubber boots, we followed
a track of big dog-prints (so big
they were more like lion-prints). Then we came on
lengths and lengths, endless, of wet white string,
looping up to the tide-line, down to the water,
over and over. Finally, they did end:
a thick white snarl, man-size, awash,
rising on every wave, a sodden ghost,
falling back, sodden, giving up the ghost . . . .
A kite string?—But no kite.

I wanted to get as far as my proto-dream-house,
my crypto-dream-house, that crooked box
set up on pilings, shingled green,
a sort of artichoke of a house, but greener
(boiled with bicarbonate of soda?),
protected from spring tides by a palisade
of—are they railroad ties?
(Many things about this place are dubious.)
I'd like to retire there and do *nothing*,
or nothing much, forever, in two bare rooms:
look through binoculars, read boring books,
old, long, long books, and write down useless notes,
talk to myself, and, foggy days,
watch the droplets slipping, heavy with light.

At night, a *grog à l'américaine*.
I'd blaze it with a kitchen match
and lovely diaphanous blue flame
would waver, doubled in the window.
There must be a stove; there *is* a chimney,
askew, but braced with wires,
and electricity, possibly
—at least, at the back another wire
limply leashes the whole affair
to something off behind the dunes.
A light to read by—perfect! But—impossible.
And that day the wind was much too cold
even to get that far,
and of course the house was boarded up.

On the way back our faces froze on the other side.
The sun came out for just a minute.
For just a minute, set in their bezels of sand,
the drab, damp, scattered stones
were multi-colored,
and all those high enough threw out long shadows,
individual shadows, then pulled them in again.
They could have been teasing the lion sun,
except that now he was behind them
—a sun who'd walked the beach the last low tide,
making those big, majestic paw-prints,
who perhaps had batted a kite out of the sky to play with.

Marianne Boruch

ORIGINAL SHELL

"The End of March," like so much of Elizabeth Bishop, travels well. The poem appeared in the *New Yorker* in 1975. I cut it out, and after her death, took it with me to Taiwan for a couple of years: a map, a kind of message scrawled suddenly, sadly, and kept. Only one walk I took ever resembled it at all, but I gladly took that one glaring morning. After stretches of hot machine-and-concrete gutted land, my husband and I crossed a small bridge, entered a bamboo thicket. Deep shade, its hazy quiet. Relief enough. But nothing prepared us for the real treasure: the cabin of split bamboo, the tiny porch, chickens in idle happiness, fruit in a wooden bowl. What a bare and hospitable place. We peered in every window. Absolutely empty! Abandoned? Impossible. Every inch spoke, suggested, sang. We hurried off, feeling marvelous and guilty, savoring each detail of the place as though it were possible to us, lived in for years, loved.

Possible. Even when it is not in front of me, no longer tied to words on a page, "The End of March" keeps intact its kernel of sense and solitude, coming forward in the mind physically and imaginatively through that strange "artichoke of a house." Here power increases by careful timing. Two stanzas of annoyances precede it: foul weather, the inexplicable string and footprints, the prosaic stop-start web of italics, parenthesis, comparison, complaint. Not a pretty landscape. What it is, is interesting, withholding more than it offers—inscrutable in spite of any human rush for meaning or loveliness. What it is, most of all, is possible. This sense of possibility—a lack of the inevitable, finally, of ego—is pure Bishop; we enter so many of her poems on that offhand silk. "It was cold and windy, scarcely the day/to take a walk on that long beach." Consider yourself warned, I read. So we are reckoned with, not assumed or condescended to in the odd invitation. And of course the house, where these two meandering, hard-working stanzas are headed, is not the house beautiful retreat of the writer, but "dubious," "a crooked box," in short—possible. At once it is ours too: something longing creates, the eccentric dream.

What delights is that eccentricity. "I wanted to get as far as my proto-dream-house,/my crypto-dream-house...." In the half-frozen muddy stupor of the walk, that voice—joking, matter-of-fact—wakes us. Yet what a pathetic, lovely, cartoonish place it points to: shingled greener than the artichoke "(boiled with bicarbonate of soda?)," makeshift, shielded by railroad ties, a chimney, "askew...braced with wires." A gem of flotsam set adrift against murky seascape. And how careful Bishop is to know it, in busy proprietorship, assuming stove, electricity from a few feeble wires, finding its pilings for us, imagining spring tides. But more, right before our eyes, she has moved in, joyously and for good, her days and nights already planned, or rather, quite rescued from plan. *Nothing,* she emphasizes, to do nothing, "or nothing much, forever, in two bare rooms."

Of course Bishop's "nothing" brims with life and humor: books to read, but of a specific nature—old, long and boring; things to write, but just "useless notes"; conversations, but only the kind of consoling, ranting banter one practices alone. After dark, the splendid moment arrives, lit double against the window, when the final drink is readied, its flame "lovely diaphanous blue." So the house—this unlikely wreck propped up against confusing shoreline—becomes, in the deepest sense, inhabited, and in the most authentic way, renewing.

Maybe all poems, in one way or another, redefine shelter. One enters such places and notices things. More simply, one enters and closes the door. It was Gaston Bachelard's notion in his *Portraits of Space* that *the house* as image and fact, began and ended here: to shield the dreamer, to allow one "to dream in peace," to return us, be the structure palatial or primitive, to that immediate sure sense of "the original shell" and so into well-being, into memory and thought. Solitude surrounds these rooms; however fanciful Bishop's "nothing," her boredom clears the place for private truth. Risk in her poem—the long and difficult trek down the unseasonable beach—is stalking something of crucial value: safety.

Safety. How safe are we? She could have turned up a collar, buttoned a higher button, holding forth feverishly on the cutting wind. So goes another poetic opportunity. Instead, with sharp flourish, we are plucked out of the weather into warmth and grace and light—enough "to read by" anyway— maybe. Now when I take up this poem, I read for this stanza, hope for its rescue. Here are the confusions of the world. We pass through them. And here, in the shoddy lean-to, is sense. They are a separate music, each quite indifferently drowning out the other. Bishop is no idealist; we are where we are. There is little reason for it, only forbearance before it, or gratitude.

Maybe things go harder, more complex than this. Characteristically, Bishop refuses to leave us glad and alone in our elation, and gently, reasonably leads us, where? Simply *back*. "...—perfect! But—impossible." The fact remains that no place exists—not on that day at least—and never, in spite of Bishop's sweet invention, either day or night spent there. The wind, "too cold," the house no doubt "boarded up," the return's small comfort is that now the *other* side of the face is freezing. Yet in anything by Elizabeth Bishop, such a deprecating remark should make us suspect.

In fact, something happens. This is a journey; we hold the map in our hands and it is changed as it is traveled. In a moment, "the drab, damp, scattered stones" assume color and movement into shadow. In a moment, resolution, almost too fantastic—but of course Bishop knows this—takes a playful leap. At once, the artifacts—footprints, string—of an earlier bedevilment are cleared. Suddenly no return is possible. No going back. Wherever that odd artichoke of a house continues—its single wire bolted so wryly, reluctantly to the world—I know one goes there to begin.

Sherod Santos

A CONNOISSEUR OF LONELINESS

On the dust jacket of Elizabeth Bishop's *The Complete Poems*, Robert Lowell observes that "when we read her, we enter the classical serenity of a new country." If we hear our own doubts in that description (ours is an age not easily characterized by the classical or the serene), then we also hear the hope which is the treatment for our convention. If we enter a new country when we read her, then a new country enters us as well. For of all the poets of her generation, Bishop most nearly approaches (hence most nearly restores to us) the idea and the ideal of the perfectable poem. In a sonnet from *History* Lowell hints at the extraordinary restraint which made that approach possible:

> *...Do*
> you still hang your words in air, ten years unfinished,
> glued to your notice board, with gaps or empties for the
> unimaginable phrase—unerring Muse who makes the
> casual perfect?

Given the strict demands of that "unerring Muse," it comes as no surprise that Bishop produced such a remarkably small number of poems (over a writing career which spanned nearly forty-five years, she published fewer than ninety poems), a reserve that carried over into her private life as well. She avoided, for the most part, public readings and interviews; she dissociated herself from "schools" and literary movements; and she served only a few short stints teaching in colleges and universities. If it didn't suggest something anachronistic, one could say that there's a touch of the spiritual solitaire in her. She can be painfully reclusive, yet she can also evoke a disarmingly intimate (if decidedly disembodied) sense of herself through her poems: the "I" conceding its primary dramatic role to the interplay of the perceptive, on the one hand, and the evocative, on the other.

Because of that, the relation of the parts to the whole is of utmost importance in a Bishop poem. With an alertness that proves divinely unflagging, the poems offer up a series of diminutive yet inclusive worlds, worlds which, by the vigilant care of their construction, appear to have left nothing out. And yet, as if composed by a slightly melancholy god, a god unsettled to find herself "all alone above an extinct world" ("Objects and Apparitions"), they also recognize the pointlessness of hurrying to conclusions. That now-famous method which Marianne Moore called "enumerative description" remains the most widely-celebrated aspect of her work, and I won't pretend to add to that discussion. What I'd like to focus on instead is a quality without which that method can all too easily become, in less mindful or less capable hands, either superfluous or ornamental or journalistic.

The quality I refer to is *patience*, a radical and indefatigable patience born of a Stevensesque (death-is-the-mother-of-beauty) realization that, in the world of appearances, reality lasts only "as long as this phrase lasts" ("Objects and Apparitions"). I say radical because Bishop arrived at a time when the ruling orthodoxies in poetry were urging a very different, if not altogether opposite approach. To take one prominent example: Ezra Pound's early imagist dictum was simple and unequivocal—*condensare*—condense, compact, concentrate, trim. A principle of physics establishes that when matter is compressed it becomes more volatile, and a similar principle governs Pound's theory of the image. Subjected to a process of intense concentration, the particular acquires a heightened energy, what Pound called *luminosity*. In terms of time, that concentration occurs by contracting or foreshortening the act of perception, by snaring one's subject on the wing: the emotional complex caught in an *instant* of time. And regardless of what poets have felt about Pound or Imagism since, that single principle of composition has held enormous sway over this century.

But then, one might say, along came Elizabeth Bishop. And along came poems like "The Map," "A Cold Spring," "The Bight," "At the Fishhouses," "Questions of Travel," "The Armadillo," and "Under the Window: Ouro Preto." And something very different started to happen. The method, it seemed, was in the *waiting*, in allowing the eye to *linger,* in the feeling that the imagination—like the grandparents' voices in "The Moose"—can *take its time* "uninterruptedly/talking, in Eternity." It was a new cognitive music altogether, a new way of hearing the mind, and it was a music inseparable from the poem's ostensible subject. The poet's intuitive responses to the world became, not the uniquely entitled subject of the poet, but yet another set of things within that world. Bishop's poems remind us that attention—that faculty which, as Simone Weil observed, "is the very substance of prayer"—is yet another term for the imagination.

That reminder brings with it a feeling for the humdrum, everyday wonders which attention releases from the chain of fact, a feeling with roots in what Emerson called "the joy of the beholding and jubilant soul." To put it another way, that persistent transaction between object, eye and mind becomes an ultimate dramatic concern, a theater within which the mind plays out the visionary's call "to see what it was I saw."

This makes a reader feel awfully lucky to be hanging around when Bishop is doing fairly ordinary things, as she is in "The End of March," one of what I'm inclined to call "the late masterpieces" from *Geography III*. The poem, you'll remember, recounts a walk the poet takes ("in rubber boots" no less!) along the seashore in Duxbury, one of the rare poems in which Bishop actu-

ally appears as a "character." (That may slightly overstate the case: the following passage, for example, is as close to self-portraiture as we ever get.)
But it's also revealing in another way, for it points up the poet's disinclina-
tion to hasten the poem toward its end. Consider this: a woman is hurrying
down the street to the post office, but in order to remember exactly what it
was she said in her letter, she slows to a snail's pace, as if that slower pace
were somehow essential to the thought itself. It's that same sense of an essential slowness one feels when, mid-poem, Bishop pauses to refine her first
perception, or to ask herself a question, or to issue a private aside:

> ...that crooked box
> set up on pilings, shingled green,
> a sort of artichoke of a house, but greener
> (boiled with bicarbonate of soda?)
> protected from spring tides by a palisade
> of—are they railroad ties?
> (Many things about this place are dubious.)
> I'd like to retire there and do *nothing*,
> or nothing much, forever, in two bare rooms:
> look through binoculars, read boring books,
> old, long, long books, and write down useless notes...

(Those are, one suspects, the notes from which her poems are made.) By exposing, as she does, the inner workings of the poem—like the magician who,
while performing his illusions, keeps telling the audience how the illusions
are made—Bishop confers on her readers the impression (or the fact?) that if
we paid attention we might see the same things she does. In that context I'd
like to consider one of the least eventful passages in the poem:

> On the way back our faces froze on the other side.
> The sun came out for just a minute.
> For just a minute, set in their bezels of sand,
> the drab, damp, scattered stones
> were multi-colored,
> and all those high enough threw out long shadows,
> individual shadows, then pulled them in again.

John Hollander has referred to the "almost infernal particularity" of these
lines, though it's a somewhat different music I hear, a music more finely attuned to her characteristic instinct for self-effacement. One notices how refined an instinct that is in the ease with which the "poet" is eclipsed by these
lines, not only by appearing to take so little credit for her discoveries—what
are they, she seems to say, but mental notes of the type that memory ordinar-
ily keeps?—but also, and more importantly, by refusing to make the image
appear more "magical" than it actually is. A lesser, or at least a different poet
might have condensed this all to a tidy quatrain:

> Set in their bezels of sand,
> the multi-colored stones
> threw out long shadows
> then pulled them in again.

In this condensed version the image appears more mysterious, or more "poetic"—or, to use Pound's term, more luminous—than in Bishop's. In any case, it clearly appears more "made." To that degree, the poet's presence is accentuated, the poet's facility (no mere mental notation) occupies a larger space on the stage. Like the magician pretending to his supernatural powers, the poet becomes the imaginative source of the image—the conjurer's gift, not the collapsible hat, receives our rapt applause. In Bishop's version, as though the hat were acknowledged as the source all along, we're provided with the process by which that image arrived quite naturally from a complex of forces within the world. And the accumulation of fairly predictable adjectives—"drab," "damp," "scattered," "multi-colored," "long," "individual"— only serves to make the poem less a specialized utterance of the Poet than a careful gathering of perceptions drawn from the provenance of our daily lives.

In one very fundamental sense, Bishop has managed, and managed by example, to demystify the role of the poet; and, by doing that, she has awakened her readers to the possibilities of poetry within the world. Ruskin saw this as the highest calling of the artist, perhaps even of humankind; as he wrote in *Modern Painters* (in a passage, by the way, which Marianne Moore recorded in her notebooks), "The greatest thing a human soul ever does in this world is to see something, and tell what it saw in a plain way. Hundreds of people can talk for one who can think, but thousands can think for one who can see."

Of course, Bishop's method should not be confused with the artless or the haphazard; nor should it be construed as yet another form of twentieth-century nihilism. Howard Moss, one of Bishop's early and lifelong admirers, has written revealingly about the sophisticated operations, and the secret ethos, of her deceptively simple style: "We test an image by its reality, and by its reality we test the truthfulness of the writer. It is by what one chooses to see and *how* one chooses to see it that this underground proving takes place. Not only does the image lead us to comparisons and therefore to thought, but those eyes, in a second, put both the viewed and the viewer onto the scale."

Kafka was said to have tacked a piece of paper above his writing table, and on that paper was written the single word *Warten* (the German for "Wait"). To read Bishop's poems is to learn, among other things, the far-reaching aesthetic and ethical implications of that profoundly difficult lesson.

ONE ART

The art of losing isn't hard to master;
so many things seem filled with the intent
to be lost that their loss is no disaster.

Lose something every day. Accept the fluster
of lost door keys, the hour badly spent.
The art of losing isn't hard to master.

Then practice losing farther, losing faster:
places, and names, and where it was you meant
to travel. None of these will bring disaster.

I lost my mother's watch. And look! my last, or
next-to-last, of three loved houses went.
The art of losing isn't hard to master.

I lost two cities, lovely ones. And, vaster,
some realms I owned, two rivers, a continent.
I miss them, but it wasn't a disaster.

—Even losing you (the joking voice, a gesture
I love) I shan't have lied. It's evident
the art of losing's not too hard to master
though it may look like (*Write* it!) like disaster.

J. D. McClatchy

SOME NOTES ON "ONE ART"

*The forms themselves seem to invite [some little departure from tradition], in
our age of "breakthroughs." Take the villanelle, which didn't really change
from "Your eyen two wol slay me sodenly" until, say, 1950. With Empson's
famous ones rigor mortis had set in, for any purposes beyond those of vers de
société. Still, there were tiny signs. People began repunctuating the key lines
so that, each time they recurred, the meaning would be slightly different. Was
that just an extension of certain cute effects in Austin Dobson? In any case,
"sodenly" Elizabeth's ravishing "One Art" came along, where the key lines
seem merely to approximate themselves, and the form, awakened by a kiss,*

simply toddles off to a new stage in its life, under the proud eye of Mother, or the Muse.

—James Merrill

It is the poems you have lost, the ills
From missing dates, at which the heart expires.
Slowly the poison the whole blood stream fills.
The waste remains, the waste remains and kills.

—William Empson

****

Bishop was not often attracted to formal patterns. The key words in various titles show her preference for the bracing leads of rhetorical conventions (exercise, anaphora, argument, conversation, letter, dream, a view) or for occasional premises (visits, arrival, going, wading, sleeping). Twenty years separate her two sestinas; her double-sonnet "The Prodigal Son" appeared in 1951, her ballad "The Burglar of Babylon" in 1964, her last poem "Sonnet" in 1979. When she did write by formula, her line stiffened toward the regularity of the pattern's grid, her tone of voice gave over its intimacy. At the same time, of course, her way with the line and her tone transfigured each of the forms she worked in—none more so, as Merrill notes, than the villanelle.

A poet's debt is her starting-point; her interest cancels it. Bishop's debt to Empson's "Missing Dates" is clear. His variations on "the consequence a life requires" are a study in slow poison. No less than Bishop's imperatives, his series of denials and definitions ("It is not ...," "It is...") serves as an instruction. And his contradictory rhyme *fill/kill* sets up Bishop's similar (but, because feminine, more difficult) *master/disaster*.

****

Villanelles are inventions like triangles and their
use is to cause "nature" to find its form only if it can
do so in arbitrary human terms.

—A. R. Ammons

The art of life is passing losses on.

—Robert Frost

Sweet salt embalms me and my head is wet,
everything streams and tells me this is right;
my life's fever is soaking in night sweat—
one life, one writing! But the downward glide
and bias of existing wrings us dry—

—Robert Lowell

****

The exemplary poems are the grand Wordsworthian encounters—"At the Fishhouses," "The End of March"—that find their moral in their own slow pace. But I remain fascinated by those few poems—uncharacteristic, one might say, except that they are as central to an understanding of her work as anything else—that are *private* (or seem so), that defy decoding, are mysterious in their references and effect. The end of "Roosters" is such a moment, but I am thinking of whole poems that are short, their obliquity (is threatened love the lurking shape?) wrought up to a pitch of extreme lyricism. I am thinking of "Insomnia," "The Shampoo," "Varick Street," "Conversation," "Rain Towards Morning," and "O Breath." "One Art" is in this mode too. (And it looks more like a short poem as it's now printed, on one page, in *The Complete Poems* than it did, padded over two, in *Geography III.*) It is directly, even painfully autobiographical (or seems so), yet more accessible than the earlier poems. It *shares* its subject with the person who reads and not just with the person written about. Perhaps it seems more accessible because of the quality of resignation that dominates. Or perhaps it is because of the form, that does not mask the experience but strips it of the merely personal. That is to say, the form characterizes the autobiography; in the arbitrary is discovered the essential. The villanelle serves as a field to explore the self's history, but also as a vantage point above it.

It is a familiar advantage in Bishop's poems, achieved by tone rather than by form: "awful but cheerful." Over the poems in *Geography III* could hang, sampler-like, the more dire motto of "The End of March": "perfect! but impossible." The nine poems in the book all exemplify that strain in Bishop—the strain native to Frost and Stevens as well—of dark knowing. "Cold is our element and winter's air/Brings voices as of lions coming down," says Stevens in "The Sun This March." That same element, the element bearable to no mortal, is where Bishop hears her voices. In its own way, "One Art" is their after-echo, the lyrical form a defense against extremes, against both perfection and impossibility.

Her title I take to mean "one art among others," as defense is the obverse of access. And I take "art" to mean "skill," but I want to come back to "art" in its other—primary? secondary?—meaning. What stays to puzzle is that the

celebrated skill (a word we associate with *acquiring*) is for *losing*. The peculiar resonance of the phrase "the art of losing" is that the word has two meanings, transitive and intransitive. It can mean to mislay, or to fail. We hear the
second meaning in the poem's first line, and the ghost of it throughout.
"Lose" has other overtones: to elude, to stray, to remove, to be deprived. And
etymologically (its root is to cut, loosen, divide) it's linked with pairs of
terms that define the poem's emotional borders: analyze and solve, forlorn
and resolve.

The catalogue of losses, from keys to continent, is a masterful sequence.
The key starts a chain of being, objects to ideas, the course of a life. Much is
named without being specified. When I read "Then practice losing farther,
losing faster," I hear—because of the mother's watch in the next stanza—
"losing *father*." Then, the watch as an emblem of time is joined with the
houses' containment of space. If the cities stand for society, then the rivers
and continent stand in for nature.

****

> *Years foll'wing Years, steal something ev'ry day,*
> *At last they steal us from our selves away;*
> *This subtle Thief of Life, this paltry Time,*
> *What will it leave me, if it snatch my Rhime?*

> —Alexander Pope

> *Love hath my name ystrike out his sclat,*
> *And he is strike out of my bokes clene*
> *For evermo; ther is no other mene.*

> —Geoffrey Chaucer

****

Before the terrible estrangement both recorded and enacted in the final
stanza, there is an odd moment just ahead that cues it:

> I lost two cities, lovely ones. And, vaster,
> some realms I owned, two rivers, a continent.
> I miss them, but it wasn't a disaster.

The rhythm is exact, low-keyed, but the diction is queer. "Vaster" strikes a
discordant note, not just because it is a forced rhyme-word, but because it is
the first of three "literary" words (a usage Bishop avoided). The others are
"realms" and "shan't," not including the "*Write* it!" that caps the sequence.

They are words that seem out of place unless accounted for by some less obvious motive. I mean a reader's, not necessarily the poet's motive: the need to interpret, to allow the poem to make sharp departures from itself, and add layers of meaning. Any poet—any reader—so surprises himself, and form, that psychopomp, leads by its exigencies.

But "realms," secure in mid-line, is a deliberate choice. Is it a deliberate allusion? Brazil *was* a kingdom—but that's not it. "Realm" is a word from books, old books, and one use of it springs immediately to mind: "Much have I travelled in the realms of gold/And many goodly states and kingdoms seen." Keats's sonnet is about acquiring—a poem, a planet; a continent, an ocean; a *power*—in much the same way (and in roughly the same locale) Bishop's Brazilian poems are, and she may be alluding to having abjured the more exotic style of poetry she wrote during her Brazilian years in favor of the sparer style of her later poetry. But "realms" is a royal trope not just for style but for poetry itself, in Keats's and (perhaps? surely!) in Bishop's reckoning here. This being so, could the poem—one of its layered meanings, that is—be about the loss of poetic power, the failure of mastery? If that were the case, then the "you" addressed in the last stanza (and no wonder her "voice" is singled out) is akin to Apollo in Keats's sonnet—say, the enabling god, or familiar muse. That the poem traces its diminishments in so rigorously lyrical, even keening, a pattern; that it must force itself at the end to do what the poet no longer can do, to *Write*—there is the poignancy of this dejection ode.

But to say these days that a poem is "about writing" is both a critical cliché and a method to dismiss. Besides, the "you" of this stanza—her "joking voice" that mocks both mastery and disaster—has all the specific gravity (and general levity) of a real person. The loss of love here is not over and thereby mastered, but threatened: a possibility brooded on, or an act being endured. How Bishop dramatizes this threatened loss is uncanny. "I shan't have lied," she claims. Under such intense emotional pressure, she shifts to the decorous "shan't," as if the better to distance and control her response to this loss, the newest and last. And again, my mind's ear often substitutes "died" for "lied." In self-defense, lying makes a moral issue out of the heart's existential dilemma; a way of speaking is a habit of being. The real moral force of the stanza comes—and this is true in many other Bishop poems—from her adverbs: *even* losing you; not *too* hard to master. These shades of emphasis are so carefully composed, so lightly sketched in, that their true dramatic power is missed by some readers.

And then that theatrical last line—how severely, how knowingly and helplessly qualified! It reminds me of that extraordinary line in "At the Fishhouses," at three removes from itself: "It is like what we imagine knowledge to be." The line here begins with a qualification ("though"), goes on to a suggestion rather than the assertion we might expect of a last line ("it may look"), then to a comparison that's doubled, stuttering ("like...like"), interrupted by a parenthetical injunction that is at once confession and compulsion, so that when "disaster" finally comes it sounds with a shocking finality.

The whole stanza is in danger of breaking apart, and breaking down. In this last line the poet's voice literally cracks. The villanelle—that strictest and most intractable of verse forms—can barely control the grief, yet helps the poet keep her balance. The balance of form and content, of "perfect! but impossible."

FIRST DEATH IN NOVA SCOTIA

In the cold, cold parlor
my mother laid out Arthur
beneath the chromographs:
Edward, Prince of Wales,
with Princess Alexandra,
and King George with Queen Mary.
Below them on the table
stood a stuffed loon
shot and stuffed by Uncle
Arthur, Arthur's father.

Since Uncle Arthur fired
a bullet into him,
he hadn't said a word.
He kept his own counsel
on his white, frozen lake,
the marble-topped table.
His breast was deep and white,
cold and caressable;
his eyes were red glass,
much to be desired.

"Come," said my mother,
"Come and say good-bye
to your little cousin Arthur."
I was lifted up and given
one lily of the valley
to put in Arthur's hand.
Arthur's coffin was
a little frosted cake,
and the red-eyed loon eyed it
from his white, frozen lake.

Arthur was very small.
He was all white, like a doll
that hadn't been painted yet.
Jack Frost had started to paint him
the way he always painted
the Maple Leaf (Forever).
He had just begun on his hair,
a few red strokes, and then

Jack Frost had dropped the brush
and left him white, forever.

The gracious royal couples
were warm in red and ermine;
their feet were well wrapped up
in the ladies' ermine trains.
They invited Arthur to be
the smallest page at court.
But how could Arthur go,
clutching his tiny lily,
with his eyes shut up so tight
and the roads deep in snow?

Alberta Turner

On "First Death in Nova Scotia"

Why do I love this poem? Because it is funny and appalling and accurate. The humor draws me in, the contrast between the adult's and the child's perception of death appalls me, and the accuracy strips me.

When a child asks questions, he assumes there are answers, and he faces soup, death, or a stranger on the porch with the same implacable stare. The child in "First Death" stares at the dead loon and the dead cousin as if both deaths meant the same thing: an achievement of permanent worth. The loon has achieved a white marble lake all his own and red glass eyes the envy of every other loon or child. Arthur has acquired a coffin like a frosted cake and has been chosen to be a page, the youngest page, at the court of St. James. The only difference is that the loon's honor is complete, Arthur still has to complete his. The details of transportation still have to be worked out. For the child there is no sting in either death, just practical details to be worked out.

Both the humor that attracts and the irony that appalls are created by the child's point of view. She is quite a small child and has to be lifted to see into the coffin. She observes in a child's sequence of additions rather than an adult's weaving of causes and qualifiers, and she speaks in a rhythm almost as simple as a nursery rhyme: short, three-accent lines, often end-rhymed, with each line containing a single segment of thought or syntax or breath. She sees things her elders are too familiar with to mention, such as the loon's glass eyes, the pictures and names of the royal family, the coldness of the best parlor (which in Victorian houses was almost never used and so was kept unheated in winter; warmth was in the kitchen). She uses adult phrases she has heard and only partly understood, such as "keep his own counsel" or "much to be desired," and phrases which are normally used in other adult contexts, such as "the Maple Leaf (Forever)" from the Canadian national anthem; and she borrows phrases from other childhood contexts: "He was all white, like a doll," and "eyes shut up tight."

But the skill of the adult who is steering the child's thoughts and writing the poem chooses images for her to notice that will appall the reader beyond the child's understanding of them—the white of the marble table, the white of Arthur's body, the white of the roads outside; the red of the loon's eyes, the red of Arthur's hair, the red of the royal family's robes; and the stillness and cold that pervade both them and the child herself.

The last four lines climax the poem's mounting horror. Without a body how shall we "go"? We shan't, not for any hope, prayer, or evasion. But this *is* the way we go, the way *it goes, I* go! The child's question has stripped me accurately to the one fact that won't dissolve. Elizabeth Bishop has stripped me of my defenses. I guess I love this poem because I want to be stripped.

SONNET

Caught—the bubble
in the spirit-level,
a creature divided;
and the compass needle
wobbling and wavering,
undecided.
Freed—the broken
thermometer's mercury
running away;
and the rainbow-bird
from the narrow bevel
of the empty mirror,
flying wherever
it feels like, gay!

1979

Jean Valentine

ON "SONNET"

I want to emphasize two impressions that I have of Elizabeth Bishop's
work. The first is that her vision was always, right from the start, historical and moral: the vision of a friendly, and removed, prophet, sitting
down with us and standing back from us, both at the same time. I saw where
a reviewer said that her work had the air of an amnesiac, but it seems to me
just the opposite.

The second quality of her life's work that I'd like to take notice of is the increasing daring of her poetry; its opening out, particularly from *Questions of
Travel* on to the end of her life, into a freely accepted authority.

This short poem, "Sonnet," was to be the last poem she would write: one
of her most purely joyful poems about "the size of our abidance"; a redemptive poem for any particular guests on this earth who start out "caught" and
hope to end up "freed." In a published manuscript draft, Bishop tries the first
line as "Oh brain, bubble"; in the finished poem, the bubble itself is freed to
be more than brain, to be "creature." At the end, the mirror is empty, and the
creature is not only freed, but lives to tell the story.

ROBERT HAYDEN
(1913-80)

T he work of a consummate craftsman, Robert Hayden's poetry balances meticulous attention to detail with a passionate, sensuous vision. A deeply private individual, he nonetheless found ways to bring the human truth of history, particularly African-American history, richly and movingly to life. Though he wrote lovingly about landscapes and works of art, his imagination seems to have been engaged most deeply by human dramas: he was fundamentally a storyteller, and wrote extraordinary poems about such figures as Harriet Tubman, Sojourner Truth, Phillis Wheatley, Nat Turner, and Frederick Douglass, often assuming his subjects' voices as he explored their experiences. His poems about nineteenth-century history, assembled in a collage of fragments and voices, bring into focus a remarkably immediate and often harrowing sense of the human cost of slavery. Despite the centrality in his work of African-American themes, Hayden explicitly rejected a narrowly ethnocentric outlook, arguing that black poets should be judged by the same criteria as other writers. Born in Detroit, educated at the University of Michigan, he became a professor at Fisk and Michigan, and Poetry Consultant to the Library of Congress. A self-described "romantic realist," Hayden was one of our most compassionate and eloquent poets.

BOOKS: *Angle Of Ascent: New and Selected Poems* (1975); *American Journal* (1978); *Collected Prose* (1984); *Collected Poems* (1985).

THOSE WINTER SUNDAYS

Sundays too my father got up early
and put his clothes on in the blueblack cold,
then with cracked hands that ached
from labor in the weekday weather made
banked fires blaze. No one ever thanked him.

I'd wake and hear the cold splintering, breaking.
When the rooms were warm, he'd call,
and slowly I would rise and dress,
fearing the chronic angers of that house,

Speaking indifferently to him,
who had driven out the cold
and polished my good shoes as well.
What did I know, what did I know
of love's austere and lonely offices?

Alberta Turner

ON "THOSE WINTER SUNDAYS"

I ask myself why "Those Winter Sundays" is my favorite Hayden poem. Partly, I think, because it is already a part of my life. I remember the sounds of my father banking the furnace at night, shaking down the ashes, shoveling on fresh coal; and I remember the quick dive from under the covers in the morning to the warm dining room, the warm bathrobe, and the hot Wheatena with cream, all this taken for granted, with no thanks given or expected.

It is also my favorite because it is not angry, in a politically orthodox way. It might have been written for any father, anywhere, for whom love is habitual.

The poem is my favorite too because it draws so little attention to itself, as if it were unpremeditated art. It is a poem that happens to one. The poet uses slant rhyme in every line and repeats a serious reproach in exactly the same words in the next-to-last, but he so subordinates these devices that they seem to be a natural part of his spoken voice. And he restrains his judgment until the end, where he implies it, chiefly in two words, *austere* and *lonely*.

This poem's power is such that one sits silent after reading it, slowly absorbing what has happened, as I have just done, slowly realizing that my father's morning and evening furnace chores were not merely habit, but love, that love is an austere master, not soft or kind, that shined shoes are not just "keeping up with the Joneses," but a form of worship, that loving is lonely because it is its own reward, that most domestic nagging is superficial, and, finally, that love is dailiness, as all grown-ups know, and now, at long last, I know too.

I cannot think of any poem more certain or any that I am more profoundly thankful to have known.

FREE FANTASIA: TIGER FLOWERS

(For Michael)

The sporting people
along St. Antoine—
that scufflers'
paradise of ironies—
        bet salty money
on his righteous
        hook and jab.

I was a boy then, running
(unbeknownst to Pa)
errands for Miss Jackie
and Stack-o'-Diamonds' Eula Mae.
. . . Their perfumes,
rouged Egyptian faces.
        Their pianolas jazzing.

O Creole babies,
Dixie odalisques,
speeding through cutglass
dark to see the macho angel
        trick you'd never
turn, his bluesteel prowess
        in the ring.

Hardshell believers
amen'd the wreck
as God A'mighty's
will. I'd thought
        such gaiety could not
die. Nor could our
        elegant avenger.

The Virgin Forest
by Rousseau—
its psychedelic flowers
towering, its deathless
        dark dream figure
death the leopard

claws—I choose it
now as elegy
for Tiger Flowers.

Niccolò N. Donzella

ELEGY FOR AN AMERICAN

Becoming an American is not as easy as it looks. We have known for a long time that being born here does not dispose of the matter. Generally, it requires some degree of acceptance by the "natives" before the applicant will be able to believe it himself. Some triumph over origin also is required, some breaking of old bonds, even if the origin we are talking about is one's neighborhood. Put another way, there is something of the harlequin in every American, a reconciliation of warring elements—colors, especially—in one integrated whole. The essential tension is provided by the pull of where we are from as against who we are trying to become.

Robert Hayden was singularly effective in documenting this process of becoming American. This seems a curious inquiry and, to be sure, many if not most American writers begin from the premise that the appellation comes with the territory. But Hayden hails from a people for whom becoming American has been a difficult and bitter experience, and so it is not surprising that Hayden, like Ralph Ellison, has given the matter much thought. Like Ellison, Hayden believed that the definition of what it is to be an American is still open and evolving. Despite appearances to the contrary, we are still trying to reach some larger consensus, and that consensus must revolve around the core of American experience—to transcend our individual and collective histories without betraying them, to make of the nation, as well as of ourselves, a whole that is more than the sum of its parts.

As a boy growing up in the Detroit slum known as Paradise Valley, Hayden saw posters advertising the bouts of Tiger Flowers, who became the first black middleweight champion in 1926. It is easy to see why the name attracted Hayden. Like the other harlequins who inhabit his poems—the quadroon mermaids, the cannibal mockingbird, the part Seminole Gypsy confidante, and the Tattooed Man—Tiger Flowers proffers the quintessential American profile: the artful reconciliation of personal and ethnic origins in one new and powerful whole.

Men do not climb into boxing rings with other men out of an inability to decide among more desirable options. Nor do they climb into the ring alone.

422   POETS READING

Instead, they carry the anger and hope of those who look and feel and live like them. So it was with Tiger Flowers, "elegant avenger" of St. Antoine, "scuffler's paradise of ironies," champion of "sporting people," "Dixie odalisques," "hardshell believers," and errand boys.

The fighter's name suggests the tension between personal and racial origins that Hayden, former errand boy and spy in his own country, must have felt all along. It combines the lushness of African landscape with the Detroit savvy of an urban nickname. In its marriage of animal and vegetable, there is reference both to the natural balance of an unretrievable past and the mocking denial of an inhospitable present with its violent and tragic end. Finally, there is the suggestion of beauty that must be admired from a distance, that protects itself from intruders, including gamblers and envious whores.

The reconciliation of these origins, however, does not come to the eyes of the errand boy, but to those of the man. Presumably, it is years later in the future Pa envisioned, far away from the influences of Miss Jackie and Eula Mae. In Rousseau's *The Virgin Forest*, painted by a self-taught "primitive" like Hayden's avenger, Hayden finds a scene that plays out the fighter's name on canvas. The dead fighter, "dark dream figure," is at peace among the bright dream flowers. He has fought the good fight. Like Rousseau, like Hayden of Paradise Valley, he has transcended his origins without betrayal or loss. He has accomplished the task of becoming American.

MIDDLE PASSAGE

I

Jesús, Estrella, Esperanza, Mercy:

Sails flashing to the wind like weapons,
sharks following the moans the fever and the dying;
horror the corposant and compass rose.

Middle Passage:
            voyage through death,
                        to life upon these shores.

"10 April 1800—
Blacks rebellious. Crew uneasy. Our linguist says
their moaning is a prayer for death,
ours and their own. Some try to starve themselves.
Lost three this morning leaped with crazy laughter
to the waiting sharks, sang as they went under."

Desire, Adventure, Tartar, Ann:

Standing to America, bringing home
black gold, black ivory, black seed.

> *Deep in the festering hold thy father lies,*
> *of his bones New England pews are made,*
> *those are altar lights that were his eyes.*

Jesus   Saviour   Pilot   Me
Over   Life's   Tempestuous   Sea

We pray that Thou wilt grant, O Lord,
safe passage to our vessels bringing
heathen souls unto Thy chastening.

Jesus   Saviour

"8 bells. I cannot sleep, for I am sick
with fear, but writing eases fear a little
since still my eyes can see these words take shape
upon the page & so I write, as one

would turn to exorcism. 4 days scudding,
but now the sea is calm again. Misfortune
follows in our wake like sharks (our grinning
tutelary gods). Which one of us
has killed an albatross? A plague among
our blacks—Ophthalmia: blindness—& we
have jettisoned the blind to no avail.
It spreads, the terrifying sickness spreads.
Its claws have scratched sight from the Capt.'s eyes
& there is blindness in the fo'c'sle
& we must sail 3 weeks before we come
to port."

> *What port awaits us, Davy Jones'*
> *or home? I've heard of slavers drifting, drifting,*
> *playthings of wind and storm and chance, their crews*
> *gone blind, the jungle hatred*
> *crawling up on deck.*

Thou   Who   Walked   On   Galilee

"Deponent further sayeth *The Bella J*
left the Guinea Coast
with cargo of five hundred blacks and odd
for the barracoons of Florida:

"That there was hardly room 'tween-decks for half
the sweltering cattle stowed spoon-fashion there;
that some went mad of thirst and tore their flesh
and sucked the blood:

"That Crew and Captain lusted with the comeliest
of the savage girls kept naked in the cabins;
that there was one they called The Guinea Rose
and they cast lots and fought to lie with her:

"That when the Bo's'n piped all hands, the flames
spreading from starboard already were beyond
control, the negroes howling and their chains
entangled with the flames:

"That the burning blacks could not be reached,
that the Crew abandoned ship,

leaving their shrieking negresses behind,
that the Captain perished drunken with the wenches:

"Further Deponent sayeth not."

Pilot   Oh   Pilot   Me

II

Aye, lad, and I have seen those factories,
Gambia, Rio Pongo, Calabar;
have watched the artful mongos baiting traps
of war wherein the victor and the vanquished

Were caught as prizes for our barracoons.
Have seen the nigger kings whose vanity
and greed turned wild black hides of Fellatah,
Mandingo, Ibo, Kru to gold for us.

And there was one—King Anthracite we named him—
fetish face beneath French parasols
of brass and orange velvet, impudent mouth
whose cups were carven skulls of enemies:

He'd honor us with drum and feast and conjo
and palm-oil-glistening wenches deft in love,
and for tin crowns that shone with paste,
red calico and German-silver trinkets

Would have the drums talk war and send
his warriors to burn the sleeping villages
and kill the sick and old and lead the young
in coffles to our factories.

Twenty years a trader, twenty years,
for there was wealth aplenty to be harvested
from those black fields, and I'd be trading still
but for the fevers melting down my bones.

III

Shuttles in the rocking loom of history,
the dark ships move, the dark ships move,

their bright ironical names
like jests of kindness on a murderer's mouth;
plough through thrashing glister toward
fata morgana's lucent melting shore,
weave toward New World littorals that are
mirage and myth and actual shore.

Voyage through death,
                              voyage whose chartings are unlove.
A charnel stench, effluvium of living death
spreads outward from the hold,
where the living and the dead, the horribly dying,
lie interlocked, lie foul with blood and excrement.

> *Deep in the festering hold thy father lies,*
> *the corpse of mercy rots with him,*
> *rats eat love's rotten gelid eyes.*
>
> *But, oh, the living look at you*
> *with human eyes whose suffering accuses you,*
> *whose hatred reaches through the swill of dark*
> *to strike you like a leper's claw.*
>
> *You cannot stare that hatred down*
> *or chain the fear that stalks the watches*
> *and breathes on you its fetid scorching breath;*
> *cannot kill the deep immortal human wish,*
> *the timeless will.*

> "But for the storm that flung up barriers
> of wind and wave, *The Amistad*, señores,
> would have reached the port of Principe in two,
> three days at most; but for the storm we should
> have been prepared for what befell.
> Swift as the puma's leap it came. There was
> that interval of moonless calm filled only
> with the water's and the rigging's usual sounds,
> then sudden movement, blows and snarling cries
> and they had fallen on us with machete
> and marlinspike. It was as though the very
> air, the night itself were striking us.
> Exhausted by the rigors of the storm,

we were no match for them. Our men went down
before the murderous Africans. Our loyal
Celestino ran from below with gun
and lantern and I saw, before the cane-
knife's wounding flash, Cinquez,
that surly brute who calls himself a prince,
directing, urging on the ghastly work.
He hacked the poor mulatto down, and then
he turned on me. The decks were slippery
when daylight finally came. It sickens me
to think of what I saw, of how these apes
threw overboard the butchered bodies of
our men, true Christians all, like so much jetsam.
Enough, enough. The rest is quickly told:
Cinquez was forced to spare the two of us
you see to steer the ship to Africa,
and we like phantoms doomed to rove the sea
voyaged east by day and west by night,
deceiving them, hoping for rescue,
prisoners on our own vessel, till
at length we drifted to the shores of this
your land, America, where we were freed
from our unspeakable misery. Now we
demand, good sirs, the extradition of
Cinquez and his accomplices to La
Havana. And it distresses us to know
there are so many here who seem inclined
to justify the mutiny of these blacks.
We find it paradoxical indeed
that you whose wealth, whose tree of liberty
are rooted in the labor of your slaves
should suffer the august John Quincy Adams
to speak with so much passion of the right
of chattel slaves to kill their lawful masters
and with his Roman rhetoric weave a hero's
garland for Cinquez. I tell you that
we are determined to return to Cuba
with our slaves and there see justice done. Cinquez
—or let us say 'the Prince'—Cinquez shall die."

The deep immortal human wish,
the timeless will:

Cinquez its deathless primaveral image,
life that transfigures many lives.

Voyage through death
                    to life upon these shores.

W. D. Snodgrass

ROBERT HAYDEN: THE MAN IN THE MIDDLE

R obert Hayden's mother, a glamorous woman of mixed race, appeared
   to be white; his father, Asa Sheffey, was a black laborer. That marriage failed and, at eighteen months, Robert was given to be raised
by Sue Ellen and William Hayden. At that time he was rechristened; some
question arose whether he had been legally adopted. A long and damaging
struggle for his custody and loyalty ensued. Late in life, he considered
changing his name back to Asa Bundy Sheffey.

The Hayden household was, moreover, troubled with poverty and its own
internal struggles. Robert's foster-father, another black laborer, was sternly
patriarchal; his wife had previously been married, probably to a white. According to Hayden's biographer, the wife "could never forget [her first hus-
band] and, unfortunately, never let William Hayden forget him either." In any
case, Robert had ample cause to be aware of race and racial mixtures; he
himself said that he was nearly as light-skinned as Italian or Jewish play-
mates in their mixed neighborhood.

Not only in matters of race did he find himself between stools. Like many
intellectuals at that time, he felt a sympathy for Marxist theory and politics,
but quickly became disillusioned with the Communist party. Raised a strict
Baptist, he later converted to Baha'i, a faith that recognizes the viability of
all the major religions. Though he was a devoted husband and father, he
wrote of the torments of his bisexual condition. His literary allegiances were
similarly divided. He never lost his early love for the black poets Paul Lawrence Dunbar, Countee Cullen, Langston Hughes; in time, however, he came
also to admire, and learn from, Keats, Auden, Yeats, Eliot.

Most of this information comes from Pontheolla Williams' admirable
study, *Robert Hayden: A Critical Analysis of His Poetry*. Prof. Williams
notes that though he often felt torn between antagonistic races, competing
families, religions, political groups, artistic traditions, such a position has,
for an artist, peculiar advantages. We might recall Isaiah Berlin's recognition
that we all make our decisions, define our lives, under the influence of com-

peting systems of value. Just as Hayden's familial division caused him life-long pain, he must often have longed for an exclusive racial, political or philosophical commitment—to be a hedgehog, not a fox. Yet that would have meant suppressing some part of his background, so of himself. In a lesser person, this might have led to a desperate clutching at some narrow code of allegiance and self-definition. For a man of Hayden's compassion and honesty, it led to a recognition of his pivotal position as an American, himself the "melting pot" of multiple demands, influences and traditions. To his work, it brought the kind of "negative capability" so much admired by Keats—a willingness to see the many sides, the complex relativity of our situation, a freedom from any "irritable reaching" after some comforting dogma.

I shall aim, here, to take this aspect of Prof. Williams' argument and to demonstrate, in greater detail than she could spare, how this broader humanism informs three of Hayden's best known and most admired poems.

"Those Winter Sundays," deservedly famous, describes William Hayden, the foster-father with whom Robert did not always get along. Yet, despite the family's grinding poverty and his own lack of education, he made it possible for Robert to continue his schooling at Detroit City College (now Wayne State University) and the University of Michigan. It remained a matter of constant self-reproach to Robert that he had never adequately shown the gratitude he felt.

The poem displays an almost uncanny skill in handling its subject. In its very first line, a wealth of meaning lurks in the simple word "too"—an awareness that each and every day, the father rose early to a cold house and either went off to work or, worse, to seek work. The following five lines are linked by a beautifully crafted chain of echoes underlining the hardship of the father's life: "clothes...blueblack cold...cracked...ached...weekday weather...banked...blaze...thanked...wake...breaking." Only in the second stanza, once the cold abates and the boy rises to dress, is this pattern dissolved into the comforting sounds of "warm," "call" and "slowly."

It is the third stanza, though, to which I would draw particular attention for its tact and generosity. To have "driven out the cold" might seem enough; to have "polished my good shoes as well" reaches, without losing credibility, toward a higher goodness. If we changed this line to read something like "and ironed my Sunday clothes as well," the poem would evaporate. Not only does polishing his foster-son's shoes show a deep humility (especially when blacks have often been reduced to such menial tasks for whites), but it carries the suggestion, however slight, of Jesus washing his disciples' feet. So the father lowers himself to an almost priestly, if not saintly, height. This alone justifies the suddenly elevated language of the last line, crediting the father with "love's austere and lonely offices"—those duties or ceremonial acts which, in themselves, constitute a religious observance.

Yet despite these literary excellences, it is another quality—one related to the overall argument of the paper—which most attracts me. That is the willingness to say, "I was wrong"—to be shocked at one's own insensitivity. What could more acutely bespeak guilt than "No one ever thanked him" or, more personally, "I would rise.../Speaking indifferently to him" and again, "What did I know, what did I know...?" We need not draw attention to the myriads of accusatory and self-justifying poems one sees almost daily— poems meant to prove that "I am right to hate whom I hate"—to recognize this poem's humane warmth and a humility comparable to the father's. It is this, I think—or dare to hope—that has made it Hayden's best-known poem.

One might argue, however, that Hayden's broad humanism and awareness of other existences, other viewpoints than his own, while informing the subject matter and attitude of this poem, do not express themselves through its technique. There is little in its style or structure idiosyncratic to Hayden—in these qualities it seems not unlike certain poems by Thomas Hardy, William Stafford or, more recently, Len Roberts. Something quite different happens in such a poem as "Night, Death, Mississippi."

The first of the poem's two sections presents a rural white Southerner who overhears a lynching in the woods near his house and regrets that he cannot be there with "Boy"—probably his son. Two voices are heard, the narrator and the old man, though neither punctuation nor typography distinguishes them. Some of the lines describing the old man's thoughts or recollections—

> A quavering cry.
>
> White robes like moonlight
> In the Sweetgum dark

—seem too literate for a man who refers to his son merely as "Boy." Such lines, I think, represent the old man's perceptions as filtered through the narrator's richer consciousness.

No doubt, some of those who attacked Hayden's work would find it offensive that he devotes such vivid realization to this violent and ugly old man, not to a condemnation of lynching or to a contrastingly admirable figure, probably black. Yet, though the poem may appear detached and objective, at no point do we doubt Hayden's opinion or values. From the first, the narrator has established a disgust for the old man's crudity:

> The old man in his reek
> and gauntness laughs—

Later, we find much the same tone:

> He hawks and spits,
> fevered as by groinfire.

That word, of course, openly defines the subject's driving sadism. But we have heard that even more clearly in the man's own words:

> Unbucked that one then
> and him squealing bloody Jesus
> as we cut it off.

When a man has so clearly damned himself from his own mouth, any commentary could only weaken the portrait's force by suggesting some element of self-interest in the writer.

The second section creates a musical construct based on the material of the first, but as seen from different perspectives. Prof. Williams sees the three primary stanzas as comprising a single scene, contiguous with the first section: the first two being "Boy's" tale when he comes back from the lynching; the third spoken by a woman, probably the old man's daughter, telling the children to bring water so "Paw" can wash the blood off "Boy." At the same time, if one read the third stanza to mean that "Paw" should wash the blood off himself, one could take these stanzas as pertaining to other lynchings, other characters. In either case, a horrifying irony is created by the contrast between the family's solicitude for a family member and the virulent exultation shown over the victims of his savage violence.

These stanzas are interrupted and balanced, however, by three separate lines given in italics much as a refrain might be. These lines both associate the victim with Jesus' crucifixion and identify the crucial darkness as neither that of the night, nor of the Negroes' skin, but as that of the lynchers' souls. The tone here is of lyrical lamentation; the antiphonal effect is comparable to a church service where the choir interrupts and punctuates the preacher's text with a series of sung refrains.

Yet there is an important difference: one assumes that the choir and preacher are ultimately in harmony, saying the same thing; here the narrative and the lyrical interjections stand in sharp contrast and opposition. To find a comparable musical effect one would have to turn, I think, to classical music—to something like the first chorus from Bach's "St. Matthew Passion" where the doubts and questionings of the main choir are balanced against the pure faith and certainty of the boys' choir. Or to the slow movement of Beethoven's Fourth Piano Concerto where the angry assertions of the lower strings are balanced and finally soothed away by the calm and tender rejoinders of the soloist. Such a comparison may, at first, seem strained; I do not think Hayden would have found it so. Had his eyesight been stronger, he might have become a violinist; an early poem is devoted to "Beethoven." In any case, he would have been aware of the principles of opposition between themes upon which all sonata forms are built.

Only by such an example can I indicate the kind of musical construct Hayden is creating. Above all, he is preserving opposed and various parts of his awareness, counterposing them in a structure that does justice to the variousness of experience and imagination. At the same time, he never obscures his own sense of values, of confronting a positive and horrifying evil.

This technique of juxtaposing fragments of scenes and the voices of differing points of view reaches its fullest realization in such poems as "Runagate, Runagate" and most especially in "Middle Passage." The method owes much to Eliot's *The Waste Land*, yet its purpose is, finally, completely different. All the voices one hears in *The Waste Land* are, finally, aspects of one mind, memories retained by, or emotions discovered in, a single personality. The various scenes in "Middle Passage" would not all have been experienced by any one character; the various voices one hears belong to a multiplicity of characters, each having a disparate and independent existence. Not only do they not speak for Hayden or his narrator, several are allowed, once again, to damn themselves from their own mouths. *The Waste Land*'s final aim is to concretize and explore the sensibility of its speaker and his sense of meaninglessness which rises from an affectional and sexual loss. The purpose of "Middle Passage," even though we have some interest in the narrator's meditations, is not to render a state of mind, but rather to let the reader partake of an experience in the outside world, the horror of the slave trade, then to join in celebrating Cinquez who fought against it.

To do so, Hayden has collected, during a long period of research, a great variety of materials. His weaving of these into the three sections of the poem is masterful. In part I, the first group, six stanzas, present and comment on the general scene of the slave ships. First we encounter a simple list of ships' names, names which would translate, Jesus, Star (with a suggestion of Fate), Hope, Mercy. Immediately the narrator's imagery, "Sails flashing...like weapons/sharks following.../horror the corposant and compass rose," underlines the irony of those pious names and establishes, once and for all, the poem's attitude.

The narrator continues:

> Middle Passage:
>   voyage through death
>   to life upon these shores

lines which will be repeated as the last lines of the poem. This is succeeded by a dated entry from a ship's log, recording and concretizing the misery inflicted upon the blacks, another list of ships, the narrator's statement of destination:

> Standing to America, bringing home
> black gold, black ivory, black seed.

This mention of seed reminds the speaker that his own ancestors were brought here by just such ships:

Deep in the festering hold thy father lies,
of his bones New England pews are made,
those are altar lights which were his eyes.

The mention of pews and altar lights brings the poem into a new grouping of stanzas, another scene—a New England church where the congregation sings a hymn befitting mariners:

Jesus   Saviour   Pilot   Me
Over   Life's   Tempestuous   Sea

We continue with the smarmy hypocrisy of the sermon and a repetition of the hymn's opening, "Jesus Saviour." This time, however, the hymn may be taken also as the narrator's prayer as he imagines the sufferings of the cargo blacks.

The ensuing pair of stanzas takes us back aboard ship. "8 bells. I cannot sleep, for I am sick/ with fear..." might well come from that same sailor who wrote the earlier log entry. This much more personal passage, however, must come from a diary or letter he is writing. His fear is not only of a potential re- volt of the imprisoned blacks but also of the illness—"Ophthalmia: blind- ness"—which has spread from the slaves to the crew and captain. The ship is still 3 weeks from port "& there is blindness in the fo'c'sle." "Which one of us/has killed an albatross?" he asks, so witnessing his own moral blindness to the crimes of his mates and himself.

The following deeply indented and italicized lines, beginning "*What port awaits us, Davy Jones'/ or home?...*," render the narrator's effort to identify with such a sailor. This particular passage, with its fear of aimlessly drifting with "the jungle hatred crawling up on deck," also serves as a plant for the poem's ending where Cinquez and the slaves rebel and take command of the *Amistad.*

Another portion from the earlier hymn, "Thou Who Walked On Galilee," brings us to a third scene: the courtroom where we hear the deposition of a sailor who escaped the burning and sinking of the *Bella J*. This was appar- ently caused by the carelessness of the drunken captain and his sexually ra- pacious crew who either fled or perished leaving the blacks to be burned with the ship. A particular irony is created, however, by the contrast between the formal courtroom language and the horrors depicted:

"Deponent further sayeth...

"That there was hardly room 'tween-decks for half
the sweltering cattle stowed spoon-fashion there;
that some went mad of thirst and tore their flesh
and sucked the blood:

"That Crew and Captain lusted with the comeliest
of the savage girls kept naked in the cabins;...

"Further Deponent sayeth not."

A final recollection of the hymn, "Pilot Oh Pilot Me," closes the section.

I have treated part I in considerable detail because its somewhat difficult materials must be fully grasped if we are to realize the overall structure of the poem, but also because this seems to me one of the most remarkable structures in American poetry. Read aloud, with the appropriate parts sung (as, incidentally, portions of *The Waste Land* should be) it has an almost overwhelming effect.

Part II embodies a single voice; its comparative simplicity is rather like the slow movement of a symphony or other musical composition containing several contrasting parts. The single voice is that of an old slave-trader recounting his exotic adventures to a younger man or boy. Several passages—

Twenty years a trader, twenty years...
...and I'd be trading still
but for the fevers melting down my bones

—are reminiscent of the old would-be lyncher of "Night, Death, Mississippi":

Be there with Boy and the rest
if I was well again.
Time was. Time was.

...fevered as by groinfire.

Part III returns to the juxtapositions of part I but is altogether simpler in construction. It opens with the narrator's brief summation of the significance of the slave trade, then goes to a passage, again indented and italicized, in which he turns to a deeper meditation. This, again, includes the attempt to feel his way into the mind of one of the sailors, a man not devoid of pity or guilt:

But, oh, the living look at you
with human eyes whose suffering accuses you,
whose hatred reaches ...

The climax of this last section, however, lies in the long speech by a Spanish sailor who survived the mutiny aboard the *Amistad*—and who asks now that the mutineers, "Cinquez and his accomplices," be sent to Havana for execution. His speech has its eloquence, yet its effect on the reader is tempered by the inclusion of his plea that the court should not heed the words of John Quincy Adams who, indeed, actually defended the *Amistad* mutineers. The Spaniard's complaint is that Adams would "with his Roman rhetoric weave a hero's/garland for Cinquez." Though intending sarcasm, these lines begin the open celebration of Cinquez as a hero who brings his people, unlike those aboard the *Bella J*, out of captivity.

Where part I had ended in the tragic and grisly burning of the *Bella J*, part III closes in a moment of triumph. This triumph, however, summarizes and collects much material which went before and subjects it to important ironies. Above all, the fact that this Spanish sailor had served as the blacks' steersman, or pilot, misleading and finally bringing them to America, projects crucial questions backward toward the earlier hymn, "Jesus, Savior, Pilot Me." The blacks, fresh from Africa, cannot serve as their own steersmen, yet Jesus—at least that Jesus imagined by the white New England congregation or by the Spanish sailor—cannot save them, may even mislead them into death and slavery. This questioning of Christian guidance must be closely related to Hayden's conversion to the Baha'i faith.

The poem *does* end, however, on a note of triumph, picking up two lines on the will to freedom from earlier in this section, applying them directly to Cinquez:

> The deep immortal human wish,
> the timeless will:
> Cinquez its deathless primaveral image,
> life that transfigures many lives.

On this tribute, the poem closes, incorporating two lines from the poem's very beginning to serve as summation and coda:

> Voyage through death
>   to life upon these shores.

Now, however, this line has added ironies since it is clear that, for many, "life upon these shores" will not be much better than death at sea. Yet some will indeed survive and, especially with such examples as Cinquez's love of freedom, may yet build a better life there.

As might be expected, this did not satisfy many of the extremists. Some criticized Hayden for using his "best" irony to depict the Spanish cause. Yet it is hard to believe that any intelligent or sensitive person could read this passage and think it favored the Spanish side.

That "negative capability" for which Keats so honored Shakespeare is, of course, the breadth of his sympathy, the near-universality of his empathy. The honor we bestow upon our greatest poet, Walt Whitman, is again because of that inclusive humanity—that he can identify not only with the victim, with the wounded slave, but also with the overseer and the patroller.

It may be that the only good poet is a dead poet. It would seem that Robert Hayden has now been dead long enough that we might pay him some part of the respect and honor which he so painfully and patiently earned.

RUNAGATE RUNAGATE

I.

Runs falls rises stumbles on from darkness into darkness
and the darkness thicketed with shapes of terror
and the hunters pursuing and the hounds pursuing
and the night cold and the night long and the river
to cross and the jack-muh-lanterns beckoning beckoning
and blackness ahead and when shall I reach that somewhere
morning and keep on going and never turn back and keep on going
                Runagate
                          Runagate
                              Runagate

Many thousands rise and go
many thousands crossing over

                              O mythic North
                      O star-shaped yonder Bible city

Some go weeping and some rejoicing
some in coffins and some in carriages
some in silks and some in shackles

                Rise and go or fare you well

No more auction block for me
no more driver's lash for me

      If you see my Pompey, 30 yrs of age,
      new breeches, plain stockings, negro shoes;
      if you see my Anna, likely young mulatto
      branded E on the right cheek, R on the left,
      catch them if you can and notify subscriber.
      Catch them if you can, but it won't be easy.
      They'll dart underground when you try to catch them,
      plunge into quicksand, whirlpools, mazes,
      turn into scorpions when you try to catch them.

And before I'll be a slave
I'll be buried in my grave

North star and bonanza gold
I'm bound for the freedom, freedom-bound
and oh Susyanna don't you cry for me

        Runagate

          Runagate

  II.

Rises from their anguish and their power,

        Harriet Tubman,

        woman of earth, whipscarred,
        a summoning, a shining

        Mean to be free

And this was the way of it, brethren brethren,
way we journeyed from Can't to Can.
Moon so bright and no place to hide,
the cry up and the patterollers riding,
hound dogs belling in bladed air.
And fear starts a-murbling, Never make it,
we'll never make it. *Hush that now,*
and she's turned upon us, levelled pistol
glinting in the moonlight:
Dead folks can't jaybird-talk, she says;
you keep on going now or die, she says.

Wanted   Harriet Tubman   alias The General
alias Moses   Stealer of Slaves

In league with Garrison   Alcott   Emerson
Garrett   Douglas   Thoreau   John Brown

Armed and known to be Dangerous

Wanted   Reward   Dead or alive

Tell me, Ezekiel, oh tell me do you see
mailed Jehovah coming to deliver me?

Hoot-owl calling in the ghosted air,
five times calling to the hants in the air.
Shadow of a face in the scary leaves,
shadow of a voice in the talking leaves:

Come ride-a my train

Oh that train, ghost-story train
through swamp and savanna movering movering,
over trestles of dew, through caves of the wish,
Midnight Special on a sabre track movering movering,
first stop Mercy and the last Hallelujah.

Come ride-a my train

Mean mean mean to be free.

Calvin Hernton

SHINING

For two hundred fifty years one of the main actions of resistance and survival for slaves was the action of flight. Even after slavery, flight from injustice and violence continued into the present century as an incumbent feature of being black in the United States.

Consistent with the African cultural heritage where art is not only a reflection of but an integral part of everyday life, flight became a dominant theme in the New World expressions of African-American people. The theme first appears in the "primitive" sorrow-and-hope songs, which are the sacred spirituals and secular blues created by the unlettered black masses. Later on, flight occupies a major place in the "classical" works of the learned, self-conscious Negro artists. Robert Hayden's "Runagate Runagate" is one of the most highly polished examples.

During the mid-1930s, Hayden was employed in one of the Federal Writers Projects where he researched Negro history and culture. Eventually a number of significant works came out of this research. "Runagate Runagate" is one of them. In the first stanza Hayden captures the danger and terror of Negro flight by weaving a tapestry of common words without the interruption of punctuation, words that reach out and engage if not engulf the reader. The matrix of words running on for seven rather long lines creates a forest of language that conjures the thick danger of the chase. The rush of words suggests both the relentless drive of black vernacular expression and the indefatigable determination to "keep on going and never turn back and keep on going...." It is more than interesting, more than coincidental, that as an adjective Webster's New World Dictionary defines "vernacular" as belonging to homeborn slaves.

From the beginning slaveholders were plagued by the "disease" that infected their slaves with the alien desire to run away. By 1793 many states began passing laws providing for the capture and punishment of slaves, often stipulating handsome rewards for their return. During the nineteenth century, after the Atlantic Trade was outlawed, the flight of slaves became a serious threat to the entire plantation system in the South which was now dependent on an internal trade, buttressed largely by plantations, and even whole states, that bred and grew their own slaves. "Runaways," "fugitives," "escapees," "maroons," and "contraband" were terms that put fear and anger in every slaveholder's heart, and initiated freelance "patterollers," hunters and catchers of Negroes. From about 1830 until the end of the Civil War, an unbroken stream of slaves escaped from the South via what had come to be known as the Underground Railroad. The metaphor was inspired by the labyrinthine sundry routes, along which many acts of ingenuity, bravery and sacrifice were transformed into legendary feats of mythological proportions:

> Some go weeping and some rejoicing
> some in coffins and some in carriages
> some in silks and some in shackles.

Ellen Craft was light enough to pass for white; she dressed as a white master and escorted her dark-complexioned husband out of the deep South in clear view of everybody. Henry "Box" Brown acquired his nickname by having himself sealed in a box and shipped aboard a steamer to a northern port. A mother with babe in arms got trapped on a bridge between catchers on either side; rather than be captured she leaped to death in the ice-cold waters. The first play written by a black person, *Leap to Freedom*, was based on the legend that grew out of the incident. "Many Thousand Gone" became a familiar phrase in black cultural lore, and various plays, songs, novels, essays, and even paintings have been entitled with it. During the height of Underground Railroad activity, Congress passed the infamous Fugitive Slave Law of 1850, to little avail. "Catch them if you can, but it won't be easy./They'll dart underground...,/plunge into quicksand, whirlpools, mazes,/turn into scorpions when you try to catch them."

The facts, circumstances, and incidents of the Underground Railroad movement, and the mythology, form a vast reservoir of collective memory which—through word of mouth, tales, rhymes, and songs—is passed on from generation to generation. Hayden's research took him into that great experiential resource of black folk culture which Richard Wright labeled "The Form of Things Unknown." The entire first part of the poem is composed of words, phrases, song titles, expressions, wanted posters, escaped slave advertisements, all taken from the African-American experiential heritage. "No more auction block for me/no more driver's lash for me.../And before I'll be a slave/I'll be buried in my grave" are lines from one of the songs that whites banned the blacks from singing. Hayden is working with the most rudimentary forms and elements of the African-American poetic tradition, which includes call and response, improvisations, polyrhythmic sounds, runs and syncopations, with "bassing" ("Runagate Runagate") as the leitmotif. This tradition is collective rather than individual. There is only one "I" in the entire first part of the poem, and it is a communal "I." The narrative voice is omnipotent and omniscient because it belongs to everybody, to the many thousands who rise and go, who are crossing over. To where—and to what?

> O mythic North
> O star-shaped yonder Bible city

The flight that informs "Runagate Runagate" is not cowardly running away. The "fugitives" are not fleeing from justice because of heinous acts they have committed. The flight of the runagate is anointed by the call of an unimpeachable quest, the quest for Zion—"star-shaped yonder Bible city"—which is North, which is at once reality, symbol, and metaphor (as North represents freedom and South represents slavery). Both the theme and the phenomenon of flight demand of and imbue the fugitives and those who aid them with the grit and valor of the heroic. The above couplet, as well as the lines "before I'll be a slave/I'll be buried in my grave," are heroic. The price of the quest may very well mean death, but the prize is "the" freedom: "the" signifying an already existing quality of life into which one may enter, if only one can reach that "somewhere morning."

Thus, in the final stanza of part I of the poem, "North Star" represents another symbol and metaphor for the reality and mythology of Underground Railroad activity. In 1848 Frederick Douglass named his anti-slavery newspaper *The North Star*. The Ghanian shipping line is named after the North Star. Marcus Garvey's back-to-Africa fleet, as well as many more Negro and African enterprises, were named in honor of the North Star. Equated with bonanza gold, the North Star is the compass star by which the runaways steered the train to keep on track. The powerfully understated irony of the line from the Negro song, "oh Susyanna don't you cry for me," is not that they are going to Louisiana with a banjo on their knees, but that the runagates are bound for the freedom, "freedom-bound." The hyphenation of "freedom-bound" puts an unbreakable seal on the fugitive's commitment to the quest for freedom, which is precious and valued more than bonanza gold:

> North star and bonanza gold
> I'm bound for the freedom, freedom-bound
> and oh Susyanna don't you cry for me
> > Runagate
> > > Runagate

When we come to the second part of Hayden's poem, we realize that the first part is a rather elaborate exposition, a portrayal of the collective experience in a general context. It relies on and emphasizes the communal voice and lore, wherein, along with their collective secular and sacred heritage of signs, symbols, songs, idioms, Biblical allusions, and double meanings, the heroic is the folk, and the will and deeds of the collective slave Underground Railroad community constitute the hero.

Swiftly progressing from the general to the specific, the second part of the poem moves from the anonymity of mass folk experience to the singling out of a particular individual. Now the individual becomes the hero and her deeds are the heroic. In 1829 a bounty was placed on the life of David Walker for publishing his incendiary anti-slavery pamphlet, the *Appeal*. His "mysterious" death quickly followed. The next most dangerous person to the slave system was declared to be Harriet Tubman, with rewards ranging from ten to forty thousand dollars, which would be millions today. In the second part of "Runagate," Harriet Tubman is named, her credentials are cited, and she is placed at the center of the Underground Railroad movement. As in real life, in the poem she is larger than life, she is "General," "Moses," "Armed," and "Dangerous." She is "Wanted...Dead or Alive."

Again as in real life, Harriet Tubman does not drop out of the sky, she does not descend from Mount Olympus. Rather, she "rises from their anguish and their power." Whose anguish, whose power? The collective anguish and power of the masses of slaves who numbered four million at the onset of the war. Nor was Harriet Tubman a house servant slave, she was a field slave with whip scars on her back, a woman of earth who received a "summoning" from God and became herself a "shining," a visionary and soldier. Though only about five feet in stature, she braved the journey back and forth, in and out of the South dozens of times, freeing hundreds of slaves. Her leitmotif is "mean to be free," signifying unfaltering determination and courage. In the scenario that begins with "and this was the way of it," we witness The General "stealing" slaves, leveling her pistol "glinting in the moonlight"; we see and hear her admonish a discouraged runaway, "Dead folks can't jaybird-talk.../you keep on going now or die." Suddenly we get the sensation of the heroic aura of Harriet Tubman retroactively empowering the first part of the poem "Runs falls rises stumbles on from darkness into darkness/and keep on going and never turn back and keep on going...."

> Come ride-a my train

Hayden was assailed (by others) with the trick question of whether he was a poet or a Negro poet. This is the albatross around the neck of every African-American writer who has ever lived, as if there is some inherent antipathy between poet and Negro poet. Obviously Hayden did not recognize or feel any such antipathy. He refused to be limited or ghettoized by others on account of his race; rather, he explored, improvised and expanded the artificial boundaries that both white racism and narrow black nationalism would impose on him and his work. He meticulously worked with the matter and the elements of his heritage, bringing the labor, instinct, skill, talent and dedication of an incredibly hard-working poet to bear on every page he wrote. That is to say, there is nothing new or original in "Runagate Runagate," except the genius of Robert Hayden and the genius he recognized in the experiences and aesthetic tradition of African-American people. Lines such as "hound dogs belling in bladed air," "over trestles of dew, through caves of the wish," and "tell me Ezekiel, oh tell me do you see/mailed Jehovah coming to deliver me?" are wrought from exquisitely controlled feelings of poetic passion. Consider the first half of each of the four lines beginning with "Hoot-owl calling in ghosted air":

> Hoot-owl calling to...
> five times calling to...
> Shadow of a face in...
> shadow of a voice in...

Now the second half of these same lines:

> the ghosted air,
> the hants in the air.
> the scary leaves,
> the talking leaves.

Then the five lines in italics that are connected to and by the bass (conductor's call) lines before and after, rather like the cars of a train with an engine at the front and one at the rear:

> Come ride-a my train
>
> *Oh that train, ghost-story train*
> *through swamp and savanna movering movering,*
> *over trestles of dew, through caves of the wish,*
> *Midnight Special on a sabre track movering movering,*
> *first stop Mercy and the last Hallelujah.*
>
> Come ride-a my train

Hayden does what Ellison does in *Invisible Man*. He employs the tools and modes of the African-American oral tradition, right along with the Western intellectual tradition, to create an incredibly rich and moving matrix of meanings. Robert Hayden was a big man, well over six feet with big bone structure and big hands. He was the kindest man I have known, courteous and charitable, and exuded a warmth that only humility can convey. Much like a diamond cutter hovering over his desk with magnifying glass in his eye, he turns uncut stones into icons and signs of precision. From carefully selected words and their structure on the page, he gives us a jewel of precious perfection. But "Runagate Runagate" is more than a mechanical work of art. Brimming with people, places, incidents, bits of songs, lore, and tales, the poem is a living, moving organism. From the first word, "Runs," to the last word, "free," Harriet Tubman's heroic motif is the triple-powered driving force behind the unalterable quest:

> mean mean mean to be free.

MONET'S WATERLILIES

Today as the news from Selma and Saigon
poisons the air like fallout,
      I come again to see
the serene great picture that I love.

Here space and time exist in light
the eye like the eye of faith believes.
      The seen, the known
dissolve in iridescence, become
illusive flesh of light
      that was not, was, forever is.

O light beheld as through refracting tears.
Here is the aura of that world
      each of us has lost.
Here is the shadow of its joy.

Anthony Walton

THE EYE OF FAITH

The current perception of Hayden's achievement manifests itself in the inability of many critics and tastemakers to look at all of his poems, to let him out of a ghetto, as it were, of "black" poetry, or more accurately, of a being a black who wrote very well. As Hayden is increasingly included in anthologies, the poems are too often the same four or five "Black History Month" poems which convey only a sliver of Hayden's wide-ranging skills and interests.

His own words are helpful here: "There's a tendency today—more than a tendency, it's almost a conspiracy—to delimit poets, to restrict them to the politically and the socially or racially conscious. To me, this indicates gross ignorance of the poet's true function as well as of the true function and value of art.... I resist whatever would force me into a role as politician, sociologist, or yea-sayer to current ideologies. I know who I am, and pretty much what I want to say."

In the spirit of the foregoing, I have chosen to look at Robert Hayden's poem "Monet's Waterlilies." To my mind, "Waterlilies" is a "raceless" poem, if such a thing is possible. On its most obvious level, it is a testament from one artist to another. It's interesting that Hayden, a child of the inner city, thought that this painting of a bygone French countryside carried him to some restorative past. Monet fought his entire artistic life for a certain kind of light, what he called the "light that pervades everything," and Hayden found spiritual, psychological and emotional sustenance in the products of those efforts.

Hilton Kramer describes the painting: "...a world in which sky and clouds and mists and water-lilies and river grass and willows and underwater flora all converge, unhampered and undivided by horizon lines or by spatial demarcations derived from fixed perspectives. All elements are consumed in their own reflection and counter-reflection on the pond's surface and by their own proliferating refraction in the air above and the water below. As these convergences become more and more intricate, the surfaces of the pictures lose their details.... To define this order we must go beyond these proliferations of light and shade, object and atmosphere, to the vaster subject which pervades these paintings...nothing less than the fluidity of experience itself" (*The Age of the Avant-Garde*).

Correlating the citations of "Selma" and "Saigon," we can infer that the "today" of the poem is somewhere in the first half of March, 1965. In the preceding three months, the Selma, Alabama, campaign of the civil rights movement had raged through the national media, featuring photos and news footage of a silver-helmeted Sheriff Jim Clark of Selma and his deputies brutalizing black women and children, throwing Martin Luther King in jail, Malcolm X (who would be assassinated two weeks later) making speeches, and badly wounded NBC reporter Richard Valeriani broadcasting his report from a hospital bed.

On March 7, Alabama State Police attacked marchers on the Edmund Pettus Bridge. NBC broke into regular programming to broadcast the carnage. On March 9, white minister James Reeb was killed. That's some of the news from Selma that Hayden was thinking about. The news from Saigon wasn't any more comforting. By that March, the Vietnam conflict had been escalating for several months. In late 1964, the Viet Cong had attacked Bien Hoa, killing five and wounding 76 Americans. In February there was a VC massacre at Pleiku, and a bombing at Qui Nhon which killed 23 young soldiers. At this time, the United States was not an active, or stated, participant in the civil war, and in March 1965, at the same time Selma was in chaos, the VC bombed the American Embassy in downtown Saigon, killing 20, Marines landed at Da Nang, Operation Rolling Thunder—the saturation bombing of North Vietnam—commenced, and theater commander William Westmoreland requested 300,000 combat troops.

These were the public events Robert Hayden carried in his mind as he walked into the Museum of Modern Art; we'll assume it was a brisk, clear late winter afternoon. Hayden is explicit about the turmoil events thousands of miles away were causing him. His choice of the word "fallout" drags in the third public crisis of that time, the constant possibility of nuclear conflict. In two clear and deceptively offhand lines, Hayden has positioned the poem squarely at the center of the three consuming moral dilemmas of the day.

Hayden was a member of the Baha'i faith, which emerged in the mid-19th century in Iran. Its adherents are non-violent and believe that humanity is "young," slowly maturing toward an egalitarian world order built on the elimination of prejudice and superstition. Baha'is strive to "see" clearly; sight, vision and, most importantly, light, are the constant metaphors of their religious texts. It can be argued that looking at this "serene great picture" was a religious experience for Hayden. Monet's work became a shrine of art and light into which he could retreat. Human evil, for him, was the result of mis-understanding the continuum of space, time and light, the seamless universe that all humans are equally a part of. He believed in one ultimate light, a light that was explained by physics as composed of all the colors of the spectrum, for him an appealing metaphor. Looking at Monet's painting, Hayden was able to view this light with his "eye of faith" and be restored. He describes this transformation explicitly in the second stanza. "Iridescence," strictly de-fined, is the partial reflection of white light. Hayden was able to stand in front of Monet's painting and be carried, emotionally, from the painting itself and from his psychic distress, through "flesh of light" (in a beautiful phrase) to a timeless state, the original state, Eden.

And there we find Hayden in the final stanza, grieving and miles from Eden:

> O light beheld as through refracting tears.
> Here is the aura of that world
>   each of us has lost.
> Here is the shadow of its joy.

The "lost world" of the poem can be childhood, worldly innocence, or sim-ply good memories, but it is a place that "time" has carried us through "space" away from, irrevocably. For a moment, in the presence of great and redemptive art, a "shadow of its joy" can be revisited and reclaimed.

Read in this fashion, "Monet's Waterlilies" stands as a statement of lyric feeling in the tradition of "Lines Composed Above Tintern Abbey" and "Dover Beach," a romantic mixture of idealization and lament. It belongs equally to the American tradition of Whitman and Stevens, blending human-itarian concerns with metaphysical explorations. And it suggests the larger context in which Hayden's work must be viewed if his achievement is to be fully understood and appreciated.

(AMERICAN JOURNAL)

here among them   the americans   this baffling
multi people   extremes and variegations   their
noise   restlessness   their almost frightening
energy   how best describe these aliens in my
reports to The Counselors

disguise myself in order to study them unobserved
adapting their varied pigmentations   white black
red brown yellow   the imprecise and strangering
distinctions by which they live   by which they
justify their cruelties to one another

charming savages   enlightened primitives   brash
new comers lately sprung up in our galaxy   how
describe them   do they indeed know what or who
they are   do not seem to   yet no other beings
in the universe make more extravagant claims
for their importance and identity

like us they have created a veritable populace
of machines that serve and soothe and pamper
and entertain   we have seen their flags and
foot prints on the moon   also the intricate
rubbish left behind   a wastefully ingenious
people   many it appears worship the Unknowable
Essence   the same for them as for us   but are
more faithful to their machine-made gods
technologists their shamans

oceans deserts mountains grain fields canyons
forests   variousness of landscapes weathers
sun light moon light as at home   much here is
beautiful   dream like vistas reminding me of
home   item   have seen the rock place known
as garden of the gods and sacred to the first
indigenes   red monoliths of home   despite
the tensions i breathe in i am attracted to
the vigorous americans   disturbing sensuous
appeal of so many   never to be admitted

something they call the american dream   sure
we still believe in it i guess   an earth man
in the tavern said   irregardless of the some
times night mare facts we always try to double
talk our way around   and its okay the dreams
okay and means whats good could be a damn sight
better   means every body in the good old u s a
should have the chance to get ahead or at least
should have three squares a day   as for myself
i do okay   not crying hunger with a loaf of
bread tucked under my arm you understand   i
fear one does not clearly follow i replied
notice you got a funny accent pal   like where
you from he asked   far from here i mumbled
he stared hard   i left

must be more careful   item   learn to use okay
their pass word   okay

crowds gathering in the streets today for some
reason obscure to me   noise and violent motion
repulsive physical contact   sentinels   pigs
i heard them called   with flailing clubs   rage
and bleeding and frenzy and screaming   machines
wailing   unbearable decibels   i fled lest
vibrations of the brutal scene do further harm
to my metabolism already over taxed

The Counselors would never permit such barbarous
confusion   they know what is best for our sereni
ty   we are an ancient race and have outgrown
illusions cherished here   item   their vaunted
liberty   no body pushes me around i have heard
them say   land of the free they sing   what do
they fear mistrust betray more than the freedom
they boast of in their ignorant pride   have seen
the squalid ghettoes in their violent cities
paradox on paradox   how have the americans
managed to survive

parades fireworks displays video spectacles

much grandiloquence much buying and selling
they are celebrating their history   earth men
in antique uniforms play at the carnage whereby
the americans achieved identity   we too recall
that struggle as enterprise of suffering and
faith uniquely theirs   blonde miss teen age
america waving from a red white and blue flower
float as the goddess of liberty   a divided
people seeking reassurance from a past few under
stand and any scorn   why should we sanction
old hypocrisies   thus dissenters   The Counse
lors would silence them

a decadent people The Counselors believe   i
do not find them decadent   a refutation not
permitted me   but for all their knowledge
power and inventiveness not yet more than raw
crude neophytes like earthlings everywhere

though i have easily passed for an american   in
bankers grey afro and dashiki long hair and jeans
hard hat yarmulke mini skirt   describe in some
detail for the amusement of The Counselors   and
though my skill in mimicry is impeccable   as
indeed The Counselors are aware   some thing
eludes me   some constant amid the variables
defies analysis and imitation   will i be judged
incompetent

america   as much a problem in metaphysics as
it is a nation earthly entity an iota in our
galaxy   an organism that changes even as i
examine it   fact and fantasy never twice the
same   so many variables

exert greater caution   twice have aroused
suspicion   returned to the ship until rumors
of humanoids from outer space   so their scoff
ing media voices termed us   had been laughed
away   my crew and i laughed too of course

confess i am curiously drawn   unmentionable   to
the americans   doubt i could exist among them for

> long however   psychic demands far too severe
> much violence   much that repels   i am attracted
> none the less   their variousness their ingenuity
> their élan vital   and that some thing   essence
> quiddity   i cannot penetrate or name

Yusef Komunyakaa

JOURNEY INTO "(AMERICAN JOURNAL)"

In 1975, after years of admiring such poems as "The Ballad of Sue Ellen Westerfield," "Night, Death, Mississippi," and "Homage to the Empress of the Blues," I was fortunate to meet the formidable Robert Hayden. After his Friday-night reading at Colorado College in Colorado Springs, we made plans to meet Saturday afternoon.

I had no idea what I'd say to him. A barrage of elusive questions plagued me throughout the night. The next day I phoned Alex Blackburn, the founding editor of *Writers Forum*, and asked him if he wished to meet Hayden. Alex was elated, and I got off the hook. That afternoon we visited the Garden of the Gods.

Of course, years later, when Michael S. Harper gave me a copy of Hayden's *American Journal* in early 1981, I was surprised by the title poem. I remember how it rekindled sensations and images of that Colorado afternoon; I read the poem repeatedly, each time feeling Hayden's presence intensifying. The man had a penetrating, indecorous eloquence—so does his poetry. I felt linked to this poem personally. "(American Journal)" taught me how language and imagination can transform a physical landscape into a spiritual one. We had talked about how the Garden of the Gods parallels a moonscape, something otherworldly. It was from there that Hayden began to orbit his imaginative tableau. Where many of us would have written a realistic narrative to recreate that day as we gazed out at the rocky formations called Kissing Camels and Balanced Rock, as myriads of birds flashed in the high reddish crevices, Hayden's poem took a leap into the fantastic—a risk. It is a voyage from the known to an approximated unknown that resonates with an almost-observed realism. It seems as if the narrator is on a spiritual quest, that this voyage into the brutal frontier of the American experience is a confrontation with his own alienation. He is transported through the power of reflection (the mind as spacecraft) in order to arrive at the scary truth of his species.

The poem's syntax suggests that everything is fused by a stream of consciousness—people, situations, ideas. Its satire is enhanced because numerous contradictions coexist, a tabulation of positives and negatives that insinuate: "new comers lately sprung up in our galaxy.../...yet no other beings/in the universe make more extravagant claims/for their importance and identity." The crude, egotistical Americans are attractive and repulsive; they are redeemable only if they can name their crimes and insanities, or if someone can speak on their behalf—a seer, a poet, or a Christ-like sympathizer. The poem's fractured syntax also highlights the narrator's alienation, as if spoken by a foreigner striving to grasp the structure and nuances of a new language.

Indeed, the "humanoid" amongst us narrates as might an early Western anthropologist, descending into the wilds of his galaxy to do fieldwork. He uses outdated jargon—"charming savages" and "enlightened primitives"—to describe us. Of course, this is the same ethnocentric lingo used by early anthropologists to dehumanize various peoples throughout the world. The narrator, however, employs the oxymorons in a satirical, almost cynical way, to articulate the supreme contradiction of our culture, the American Dream.

After interviewing an "earth man" at a tavern, who maintains he still believes in the dream, "irregardless of the some/times night mare facts we always try to double/talk our way around," the narrator, after further investigation of our society, records the American Dream as a great lie—a cultural materialism based on illusions and paradoxes. The idea that "every body in the good old u s a/should have the chance to get ahead.../...three squares a day" pales under the narrator's witnessing of "the squalid ghettoes in their violent cities." Like a mortified anthropologist, the narrator renames our dream as "vaunted liberty," and typically compares America with the more evolved society from which he travelled: "we are an ancient race and have outgrown/ illusions cherished here."

As an outsider himself, he is able to ridicule this illusion, orchestrated by our mythmakers, because he, a "humanoid," like others who are physically or culturally "different," are not welcomed into American society, let alone given access to the means of attaining the Dream. The narrator can only exist in the American context if he prostitutes his individuality through "mimicry" and assimilation: "though i have easily passed for an american.../exert greater caution   twice have aroused/suspicion   returned to the ship." The speaker is raceless, without gender or genus, but knows this fearful sense of otherness that had driven most Americans into the psychological melting pot.

The narrator speaks as an insider/outsider, a freak in an elastic limbo, whose sensitivity is violated by "unbearable decibels." This investigator knows the impending tragedy programmed by America's love of technology—its machine-oriented existence: "more faithful to their machine-made gods/technologists their shamans." Similarly, he records the cultivated national ignorance that protects and facilitates America's collective ego: "earth men/in antique uniforms play at the carnage whereby/the americans achieved identity."

Is the poet an anthropologist also? Are we responsible for what we witness? Perhaps the speaker is also an artist, one who must not only record the patterns of the universe one finds oneself in, but decode, translate and critique them also. In any case, for me, this poem gains more and more authority and significance as the last piece in Hayden's *Collected Poems*. It is a perfect summation and coda to his career as a poet. He always saw himself and his work as totally *American*. Yet, I believe he identifies with the displaced speaker in "(American Journal)"—the outsider.

RANDALL JARRELL
(1914-65)

R andall Jarrell played a central role in the development of modern American literary culture: he was a prolific essayist and reviewer, and his enthusiasm for particular writers—Frost, Williams, Moore, Bishop, and Lowell, among others—helped establish them in the modern canon and continues to influence the way we read them. Nonetheless, his most lasting interest as a writer lies in his poetry. In a late sequence called "The Lost World," Jarrell writes about living with his grandparents in Hollywood, and in a sense he remained all his life that precocious, volatile child fascinated by the film industry. His persistent theme is the disparity between reality and illusion: central to his work is a passionate, even desperate desire for transformation. Jarrell's interest in the psychology of the child led naturally to German fairy tales and Freud, and through them to an interest in German culture generally; throughout, his work locates itself in the world of innocence threatened by experience. Many of his early poems derive from his experience of the Second World War, capturing with heartbreaking intensity the psychological damage inflicted on all sides. His later poems are often dramatic monologues, expressing, like the persona of "The Woman at the Washington Zoo," an agonizing longing for transcendence: "You know what I was,/You see what I am: change me, change me!" Dazzlingly intelligent and sophisticated in his criticism, he chose to cultivate a more innocent voice in his poems, in order to uncover issues at the heart of everyday lives.

BOOKS: *Complete Poems* (1969); *Poetry and the Age* (1953); *A Sad Heart at the Supermarket* (1962); *The Third Book of Criticism* (1969); *Kipling, Auden, & Co.* (1980); *Randall Jarrell's Letters*, ed. Mary Jarrell (1985).

THE BAD MUSIC

I sit, sit listening; my lashes droop
And the years come close around me like a crowd
Of the strangers I knew once; and they say nothing,
And I see at last that they were never mine.
The breast opening for me, the breaths gasped
From the mouth pressed helplessly against my wrist
Were lies you too believed; but what you wanted
And possessed was, really, nothing but yourself:
A joy private as a grave, the song of death.

. . . These are lies, too? I sit here like a fool
And think half-tenderly, as my lips curve:
What do you know? How can you say it?
You were something, you loved something—
And where have they gone? What are you now?
There is no answer. I don't cry now,
So I don't cry; and I don't laugh—
What's happening to all of us is in its way
Laughable—why don't I laugh? Why don't we laugh?

It's bad music; but it's what we hear. . . .
It's night here; outside my big windows
The students come home from carolling, the candles
Wink out and on and out, like mixed-up stars.
I sit here like a mixed-up star:
Where can I shine? What use is it to shine?
I say; and see, all the miles north inside my head,
You looking down across the city, puzzling.
You always cried. And now are you trying

Instead, to be lucky? To be happy, really,
Where your small light is seen and shining
High over the millions who breathe and wait and sparkle
With the rain's globes, the worlds that roll like laughs
To the dark stream and its immediate sea?
Of those millions how many know or love at all
You, Anna? A few; so few. Enough.
This world holds more than we can see or say,
And it stuffs us like a goose before it kills us.

Laura Jensen

POTENTIAL FOR WHOLE TOTEM

The vanity plate read MY GUY, in the back window a hollow flocked dog and a placard declaring I WILL NEVER GROW UP, in the side window rocking on a spring a foot that read I'M A SONICS FAN. As I looked down from the bus window I told myself I had been confronted with too ridiculous a sight, now I could never understand Randall Jarrell, because the question I kept asking myself was, "Why does Randall Jarrell have such an unendingly serious world view?" It is not a rhetorical stance, it is too complete and convincing. It is also forgiving: through Jarrell's eyes I began to see the car decorations differently—the driver thinks the news is like a feather inside doing brain surgery, or the rat race makes her long to display madness, or she feels a car cannot be made more ridiculous than it is in fact—too much motor and metal and glass to drive one person to work, a person who needs a quiet place with trees and grass.

In Jarrell's letters another side of the man emerges, humorous and playful. Jarrell might have been delighted with the car, he shared the car enthusiasm and might have used a vanity plate himself. (He owned a Mercedes vacuum cleaner for his car—so maybe EUREKA.) He wrote a novel he called a comedy. He acted the lively and delighted man who loved to joke, whose conversations with friends could make him inebriated with happiness.

But Louise Bogan reviewed his work as solemn. In a 1952 *New Yorker*, she considers four books which "illustrate the methods...by which the modern imagination tries to project feelings of mystery and awe." She calls the books Gothic and Jarrell's characters "too young to have known life or too baffled to act. These creatures revolve in a limbo of pain and fear."[1] Jarrell saw poetry as the sphere for truths from many frames of reference, truths which could be dreadful because human life has winter, death, and visits with the afterlife—and life is always within the context of life-and-death matters.

In an essay on criticism Jarrell wrote: "Everyone speaks of the negative capability of the artist, of his ability to lose what self he has in the many selves, the great self of the world. Such a quality is, surely, the first that a critic should have; yet who speaks of the negative capability of the critic? how often are we able to observe it ?"[2] In asking for negative capability he opens the door for truth which can be difficult and for devoting the energy

---

[1] Louise Bogan, "Verse," review of *The Seven League Crutches, The New Yorker* (16 Feb. 1952): 107-08.

[2] Randall Jarrell, "Poets, Critics, and Readers," in his *A Sad Heart at the Supermarket* (New York: Atheneum, 1962), 98-99.

and concentration of poetry to essays and criticism. And according to his letters, Jarrell's treatment of critics, especially his own, could be biting; so
could his criticism of others.

I found I had not known Jarrell after studying his poems at the University
of Iowa, but my education was far less rote than writing. I knew his name as
I knew shrubs in my vocabulary; a shrub I might recognize if the leaf or
flower was obvious. I would recognize some Jarrell poems. I read through
the *Collected Poems* for words that explained or defined the serious world
view, and found these in "The Bad Music."

Understanding "The Bad Music" might require some knowledge of Jarrell's life. Anna is Jarrell's mother, but is the description in stanza one Anna
nurturing the child or someone else? After her divorce, Jarrell and his brother
and mother visited his grandmother, whom he called Mama; he called his
great-grandmother Dandeen. "The Bad Music" was written before 1940,
probably during the time he was suffering a disappointment in love, and was
included in his first book *Blood for a Stranger*. In the poem a young poet approaches uncertainty and doubt, determined that there will be transcendence.

I see Jarrell saying I am a fool, embarrassed, a goose. "What's happening
to all of us is in its way/Laughable—why don't I laugh?" "I sit here like a
mixed-up star." Has Jarrell seemed to himself for a moment as incongruous
to his world view as the car of my first paragraph—ridiculous and pointless?

But Jarrell finds his potentially laughable situation to be universal and his
spirit and forgiveness include himself. The ambiguity at the sixth line of the
last stanza increases the encompassing universality. Anna comes to represent
a great deal—all of those who told Jarrell he was loved, and Jarrell himself,
and all the young who live their foolish lives as statesmen indulge in rhetoric,
as Hitler marches through Europe. His world view remains real—"goose"
does not stay a word meaning in slang a fool. The goose is in real pain as it is
being stuffed for pate, and it is also a real goose, with a potential for the full
totem of the free wild goose—beautiful. All beings in Jarrell's world maintain an intrinsic potential for full totem—whole owl, whole bat, whole goose,
whole human being.

Jarrell declares an expansive freedom which flowers in the later poems
that expand into narrative. "This world holds more than we can see or say."
When Jarrell sees with delight and detail a nose like three strawberries, a lion
once an MGM movie star, these have comic potential, but are never only
comic. They are wonderful. Their forces explain that they are made of the
metal of the gods, too beautiful or threatened in potential to be comic.

During the precarious McCarthy era, throughout the 1950s, Jarrell poured
out creative work, especially essays and criticism, and he was influential in
his teaching and positions of responsibility. Early in the 50s his essay defining a class—"The Intellectual in America"—won him substantial praise. Despite a question raised about his background by a committee, which he an-

swered with a letter, he was appointed Poetry Consultant to the Library of Congress in 1956. He can be called formative in the poetry we know today.

In a review Beth Bentley writes of Jarrell, "He was in some sense androgynous. His sympathy and identification with women are striking."[3] Many of his poems were written in the persona of a woman. For instance, in "The Woman at the Washington Zoo," the woman may long for release from her caged life, but it is important that she is caged in her human life, and only happens to be a woman, that Jarrell is free to use a woman or a man as a persona. Jarrell was loved by women, and maintained long friendships with both men and women. If androgyny's definition includes causes, if Jarrell's fate was formed by women, he seems to have developed this to a symbiotic structure, to have reached a success in nature that includes the ideal of mutual benefits. Jarrell's work may have helped some women see themselves and accept themselves through his writing and acceptance, allowed them to enter the world of the 60s and 70s determined and taught.

Was I in some ways one of these? Jarrell became depressed in 1965 because of illness and other reasons; in spring he attempted suicide, one act in a life of creativity. In autumn, at a hospital for treatments to his hand, he was walking by a roadside and struck by a car and killed. This was found to be an accidental death. I found myself wishing I could read Jarrell's response to the popular movements of the late 60s, and to the 70s. But his work has taught me some things. The spine of my paperback suggests I read Jarrell carefully, but I found only one note—"The Chicago Art Institute" at the end of "A Ghost, A Real Ghost." This returned me to an unpublished poem from my Iowa thesis. The poem was about something I remembered as seeing in the Art Institute in a Hogan exhibit. The poem's character returned in a long story or novella I wrote a few years later. The lines from Jarrell had defined for me what I had seen:

> —Am I dead? A ghost, a real ghost
> Has no need to die: what is he except
> A being without access to the universe
> That he has not yet managed to forget?

Jarrell has guided my vision and helped me define myself. To rephrase Bogan's words, we were too young to have known life as students, even today we can be too baffled to act. But Jarrell's world view sees us and knows lives are wonderful, have potential for the full human totem.

---

[3] Beth Bentley, "The Feminine Mystique in Randall Jarrell's Poetry," review of *The Lost World, Northwest Review of Books* (Spring 1986): 22.

THE DEATH OF THE BALL TURRET GUNNER

From my mother's sleep I fell into the State,
And I hunched in its belly till my wet fur froze.
Six miles from earth, loosed from its dream of life,
I woke to black flak and the nightmare fighters.
When I died they washed me out of the turret with a hose.

Bruce Weigl

AN AUTOBIOGRAPHY OF NIGHTMARE

"The abnormal is not courage...."
Jack Gilbert

Among the many fine critical responses to what is arguably one of Jarrell's best and most widely recognized poems there is a predominantly common thread in the form of a strict metaphorical exegesis of the poem. Most significantly these metaphors are seen in the fetus-like description of the gunner trapped in the womb-gloom of his turret, and in the poem's coldly distanced and impersonal final line in which the fetus/gunner is washed out or aborted from the turret/womb by a steam hose. It's clear that Jarrell himself had at least one of these metaphors in mind. In an extensive note on the poem included in *The Complete Poems*, the poet wrote that "hunched upside-down in his little sphere, he [the gunner] looked like the foetus in the womb." In addition to these specific metaphors, there occurs throughout the poem a great deal of highly suggestive, allusive, and even ambiguous imagery which leads naturally to a figurative reading. Although any fair and careful consideration of the poem must surely address itself to these insistent metaphorical tendencies, the poem is most powerfully felt when the reader pursues its literal layer as well. Indeed, Jarrell is careful to point the reader in that direction when he writes in the same note that "a ball turret was a plexiglass sphere set into the belly of a B-17 or B-24, and inhabited by two .50 caliber machine-guns and one man, a short small man.... The fighters which attacked him were armed with cannon firing explosive shells. The hose was a steam hose," thus emphasizing the importance of our literal appreciation and understanding of the poem. However adroitly we may argue for the metaphors' significance, especially for the way they provide a manageable form for this particularly horrible experience, even the most powerful metaphors pale in the face of the layer of literal consciousness upon which the figurative structure is constructed. One is reminded here of Neruda's "the blood of the children ran in the streets like the blood of children...." Through an intense compression of language (the poem is only five lines long, roughly five beats per line depending on your scansion), and a powerfully ironic understatement, the gunner is figuratively born into his death. Yet what should and does resonate long after we've put the poem down is the literalness of the almost completely unadorned presentation of that death, what Douglas Dunn has called "the indignation of acceptance."

With this poem and with other, similar war poems Jarrell echoes Wilfred Owen's regard for soldiers as objects of our pity, and, in spite of the so-called popularity of his war, Jarrell also reveals the empty and mocking offices of patriotism as well. The speaker, a dead man, is alive enough to speak to us of his death but too dead in spirit to evoke anything more than a stripped-down version of his brief existence and his eventual confrontation with the "black flak" of life. Like the speakers of Jarrell's "Losses" and "Eighth Air Force," the gunner stands as a symbol for combat's relentless squashing of innocence.

The poem's first line precisely sets the post-lapsarian point of view: there has been a fall from grace, a descent from the idyllic peace and safety of "mother's sleep" into the cold arms of the State. The gunner is of course a grown man at least of the age for conscription, but in terms of understanding just what exactly the State has in mind for him, he is an innocent and naive recruit, a newborn. The State replaces the mother in line two in one of many skillful and dramatic transformations which Jarrell manages through a precise telescoping of time. Once within the State, which becomes more specifically the turret, the gunner assumes a fetal position necessitated by the close-quartered design of the turret. From this position the speaker presents himself as a kind of *ur*-man whose "wet fur froze," a primal being dehumanized by the demands of warfare. When the gunner wakes to the brutal realities of war he no longer resembles the boy who fell from his mother's sleep. This waking does in fact represent one of two murders in the poem: first the *boy* is murdered through the exact dismantling of his innocence, and then the *man* is murdered by the exploding cannon fire. But what allows this *ur*-man metaphor to exist at all is the literal reality of the gunner in his Army Air Force issue fur-lined jacket, his perspiration freezing in the cold air of 35,000 feet.

Line three sweeps us away from the earth's dream of life to the vacuum-like and emotionless world "six miles" above. So much happens so quickly here that the patient and passionate reader may suffer the same disembodiment of spirit as the gunner. The earth has been torn loose from his feet and he is suspended in an ironic reversal of the apollonian perspective, forced to hover above his life so that he may now see it as it actually is: only a dream. Once removed from the physical constraints of earth, the gunner realizes too late the lie of the State's promise of an after-life. The irony of the poem's sleep imagery is also most fully realized in line three, when we come to see that life for the gunner was and is only a fiction, a fantasy, and that the only reality he will ever know is death in the form of the "nightmare fighters." Between this line and line four there occurs another of the poem's transformations: in this case the gunner's waking becomes the dark vision of the enemy coldly poised for the kill.

Line four is perhaps the most direct and unadorned line of the poem, qualities which emphasize the irrevocable and inevitable fate of boys in combat, including those who physically "survive," and the literalness of the line, the plainly presented *said* quality offers no escape from the huge facts which loom up and dominate in the form of those strangely superior fighters. As in the Greek way, all critical action with regard to the gunner's actual death happens off stage. In the brief moment between lines four and five the exploding shells have reduced the gunner to something that now must be washed out of the turret with a steam hose. The final line, like the previous one, is flat and unequivocal. Because the gunner (like the fetus) has never been allowed to fully achieve an independent life, moving as he did from one womb to another, his observations of even his own horrible death read more like reportage than lyric poetry. Though this ghost may speak a literal truth: "When I died they washed me out of the turret with a hose," because he has been robbed of his innocence he is no longer able to render an imaginative and therefore a hopeful or redeeming vision of the world which had only provided a "dream of life" in the first place. What this final line most significantly reveals, however, is that the poem's essential form takes the shape of an inevitable movement through a series of unconscious conflicts which can never be resolved, only repeated again and again, and the gunner's death is reduced to one more grim statistic of war, hopelessly announcing itself.

C. D. Wright

MISSION OF THE SURVIVING GUNNER

Death is not my subject. And it is among the balder assertions of French feminist Christine Rochfort that while literature has no sex, death is a specifically male obsession. She has a point. However, having once taken a bed in death's adjoining room and moved around among its furnishings after the room was absented, I do not view it, even on nightly news, as an abstraction. Of those inexorable endings to dread, the most dreadful to me, most aberrant, if you will, are the violent, especially those institutionally directed, namely capital punishment and warfare. Thus in war poem heaped upon war poem, beginning with "...The Ball Turret Gunner" and never again with such dexterous compression and plain eloquence, Jarrell blames the villainy of the world not on Germans (whose literature he would wholly adopt), nor on Japanese, but on the one neutrally destructive force, the State.

Yet Jarrell's war poems are not politically resolute. He was not a pacifist, after all, but a participant. Too much the poet to be a patriot. Too much of a traditionalist, a Southerner, to resist. To avoid killing when the State gives the order is a rebellious act, a punishing but also a stirringly lonely act. Something in the makeup of Stafford and Lowell, born the same year as he, that was not in Jarrell's. And the world was far and gone for romanticism. Jarrell's entry into the war, as into poetry, would be on the side of realism. Because the experience of war had been pivotal his mission would become that of the survivor. It was to express what he felt, which could touch a chord in any civilian or combatant who survived, being so close to what others felt. A war, even one widely perceived as just, even given our tremendous capacity to absorb our destructability, alters the old borders of the self more surely than those of nations, which are not after all living organisms. In the poem "Terms" the amputated pensioner "...looks at the leaf, as he looks at things/ With mixed feelings—/And says, 'I've changed.'" Part of his mission then was to impress upon us that we could not and would not be the same once we have tasted our own blood. No less haunting than killing is outliving. Jarrell took the charge upon himself—talking through, on behalf of, and directly to the inarticulate, the fallen: "You are something there are millions of..../Surely your one theory, to live/Is nonsense to the practice of the centuries./What is demanded in the trade of States/But lives, your lives?—the one commodity" (from "The Sick Nought").

I am in rare agreement with Robert Bly when he prefaced *Forty Poems Touching On Recent American History* saying "...the poet's main job is to penetrate that husk around the American psyche, and since that psyche is inside *him*[1] too, the writing of political poetry is like the writing of personal poetry, a sudden drive by the poet inward.... Once inside the psyche he can speak of inward and political things with the same assurance." Jarrell resolves nothing, but in five virtually monosyllabic lines he does conclude this much: we are of the earth's issue, woman born, delivered onto death by the indifferent instruments of the State. In "The Death of the Ball Turret Gunner" the metaphor is that conclusive, that exacting: from his mother's sleep, the gunner falls—whether from her anesthetized birthing or post-partum drift—their separation is involuntary. The newborn seeks shelter in the belly of the

---

[1]Pronoun and emphasis Bly's.

beast. His wet lanugo transformed to furlined flight gear—which freezes to him. The beast becomes the State, and the hostile womb it creates a B-24. Suspended upside down in his plexiglass sac his animate darkness is shattered by the perpetually inanimate dark. In the final line, with a rhetorical gesture clearly derivative of Wilfred Owen, the poet shifts the bomber's voice from a limited first to the omniscient first person, thus commanding the grisly perspective of the newly-born dead, who watches the womb evacuated of his own remains.

"I feel just like an Angel," Jarrell was quoted as saying astride a pair of skis before he ever brought the mercy of his vision to bear on the onus of war. And "May I die on the day the world ends" prays an old woman on a bus, a providential passenger in one of his last poems, re-positing his one theory—to live.

MOVING

Some of the sky is grey and some of it is white.
The leaves have lost their heads
And are dancing round the tree in circles, dead;
The cat is in it.
A smeared, banged, tow-headed
Girl in a flowered, flour-sack print
Sniffles and holds up her last bite
Of bread and butter and brown sugar to the wind.

Butter the cat's paws
And bread the wind. We are moving.
I shall never again sing
Good morning, Dear Teacher, to my own dear teacher.
Never again
Will Augusta be the capital of Maine.
The dew has rusted the catch of the strap of my satchel
And the sun has fallen from the place where it was chained
With a blue construction-paper chain. . . .
Someone else must draw the bow
And the blunderbuss, the great gobbler
Upside-down under the stone arrow
In the black, bell-brimmed hat—
And the cattycornered bat.
The witch on the blackboard
Says: "Put the Plough into the Wagon
Before it turns into a Bear and sleeps all winter
In your play-house under the catalpa."
Never again will Orion
Fall on my speller through the star
Taped on the broken window by my cot.
My knee is ridged like corn
And the scab peels off it.

We are going to live in a new pumpkin
Under a gold star.

There is not much else.
The wind blows somewhere else.
The brass bed bobs to the van.
The broody hen
Squawks upside-down—her eggs are boiled;

The cat is dragged from the limb.
The little girl
Looks over the shoulders of the moving-men
At her own street;
And, yard by lot, it changes.
Never again.
But she feels her tea-set with her elbow
And inches closer to her mother;
Then she shuts her eyes, and sits there, and squashed red
Circles and leaves like colored chalk
Come on in her dark head
And are darkened, and float farther
And farther and farther from the stretched-out hands
That float out from her in her broody trance:
She hears her own heart and her cat's heart beating.

She holds the cat so close to her he pants.

Fred Chappell

THE LONGING TO BELONG

It is the dread question the interviewer never fails to ask: "Why did you become a writer?" The author sweats and stammers. He doesn't know why he became a writer. If he knew that he would know perhaps more than is good for him, certainly more than is good for his work.

But the novelist Jose Luis Donoso has a telling answer. Why is he a writer? "Because," he says, "l wasn't invited to the party."

His explanation is incomplete, of course, but it is neat, lacks self-aggrandizement, and encapsulates much of the theme of *Tonio Kröger*. And it points up the fact that the sense of detachment, even of alienation, which is indispensable for a writer is often established in childhood and that the memory of this alienation may remain powerful throughout a long literary career.

The child as outsider is an important theme in the poetry of Randall Jarrell, one that he returns to again and again. In fact, when we number those stages or conditions of our lives when we haplessly find ourselves social outsiders—as travelers, as invalids, as students or soldiers or refugees or elderly—we can note that Jarrell has treated of most of them with fine sensitivity. While some writers have welcomed and celebrated their status as outsiders—Shelley, for example, and Lermontov and Poe and Rimbaud—

Jarrell has emphasized instead the loneliness and bewilderment and the feeling of abandonment.

There is in Jarrell's poetry the longing to belong to some settled, established, and humane order of existence. There is at the same time a painful recognition that this sort of order does not, and probably cannot, exist in the world that we know. Yet still it ought to exist somewhere; it is a necessary Ideal, just beyond the fringe of the terrible Actual.

Jarrell would like to posit childhood as one part of this ideal order. He would like to describe childhood in the words with which Hölderlin describes it in his novel, *Hyperion*:

> Yes, divine is the being of the child, so long as it has not been dipped in the chameleon colors of men.
> The child is wholly what it is, and that is why it is so beautiful.
> The pressure of Law and Fate touches it not; only in the child is freedom.
> In the child is peace; it has not yet come to be at odds with itself. Wealth is in the child; it knows not its heart nor the inadequacy of life. It is immortal, for it has not heard of death.

He would like to think of childhood in these terms, but he cannot do so. Children in the twentieth century are familiarly conversant with death, and they are a long way from being immortal, and Jarrell dramatizes the true state of things in poems like "Protocols," "The State," and "The Truth." In "Come to the Stone..." the war victim child has imagined his epitaph: *"Come to the stone and tell me why I died."* But no one can give him any better answer than his own terrified earlier question which he has formulated in a child's terms of the consequences of bad behavior. "The people are punishing the people—why?"

His fiction is another matter, but in Jarrell's poetry there is not, so far as I can find, a single portrait of a genuinely happy child. All the children in his poems—and there are a great many of them—are under attack by a world intent on robbing them of the experience of what the poet regards as a true childhood. Losing comfort, security, certainty, these children look toward their future lives—when they are to have any—with bewilderment and sorrow and sometimes with a skeptical weariness. In some near direction or other lies Childhood, but they have been barred from it.

A solid example of this kind of subject matter is the poem called "Moving." It is one of the simpler and quieter examples, and is perhaps the more effective because of these qualities. "Moving" consists of five stanzas of fairly regularly iambic in irregular line lengths, irregularly rhymed. The three outer stanzas (the final one is a single line) are spoken by a sympathetic outside observer; the inner two stanzas are the interior monologue of a little farm girl, probably of a poor family ("A smeared, banged, tow-headed/Girl in a flowered, flour-sack print"), who watches as their belongings are loaded into a van when the family has to move to a new address. It is a disturbing experience for the child, and it is the only experience the poem deals with. The poem's economy is a necessary part of its pathos.

The time is autumn, between Halloween and Thanksgiving (an irony not insisted upon); the girl sits outside, watching her cat play in the windblown fallen leaves. Her weeping has been pacified with a homely sweet, and now she only "Sniffles and holds up her last bite/Of bread and butter and brown sugar to the wind." She holds the sugared bread up as a ritual offering, rather like a libation, trying to gain some sense of security with rituals both traditional and private. "Butter the cat's paws/And bread the wind. We are moving." There is probably an ironic echo here of Ecclesiastes: "Cast thy bread upon the waters: for thou shalt find it after many days."

The child in "Moving" is an exceptional little girl, and what she most regrets leaving is her grammar school. It used to be common for sharecropper or poor farm children to have the education they enjoyed and desired so often interrupted and disjointed that it amounted to no education at all. Novelists like Faulkner and Elizabeth Madox Roberts have written touchingly of the experience. Seven lines exhibit the girl's feeling of accomplishment and belonging and her sense of loss:

> I shall never again sing
> Good morning, Dear Teacher, to my own dear teacher.
> Never again
> Will Augusta be the capital of Maine.
> The dew has rusted the catch of the strap of my satchel
> And the sun has fallen from the place where it was chained
> With a blue construction-paper chain....

The latter two lines introduce the strain of imagery of the wallboard pin-up display in the classroom, the imagery that characterizes her feeling of established order breaking down, of things coming apart. She will not be present to help finish the Thanksgiving display with its turkey and pilgrims and Indians. In a sudden brief flight of fancy, she identifies the paper cut-outs pinned to the wallboard with the constellations which look as if they were pinned to the night sky:

> The witch on the blackboard
> Says: "Put the Plough into the Wagon
> Before it turns into a Bear and sleeps all winter
> In your play-house under the catalpa."

Part of the poet's purpose here is to indicate the boundaries of the girl's universe, which is both enormous and minuscule at the same time; it encompasses the earth and the stars, but only in terms that are homely and familiar. The apocalyptic collision of the constellations, "the Plough into the Wagon," disorders her universe; but she would have observed a real plow loaded into a real wagon anytime that a new field was ready to be plowed. The natural order of things is so intimate to her that she has used one constellation as a reading lamp: "Never again will Orion/Fall on my speller through the star/ Taped on the broken window by my cot." The natural order she has depended upon is smashed. These lines echo the poignant earlier lines which emphasize the fact that order has disappeared: "Never again/Will Augusta be the capital of Maine."

The conclusion of the child's train of thought brings in another of Jarrell's favorite themes, that of transformation or metamorphosis. In order to prepare for her new life elsewhere, she must shed her old life, as a snake sheds its skin. "My knee is ridged like corn/And the scab peels off it." The tactile association of the scab with seed corn on the cob, new seed to be planted in a new field, is a daring one and maybe a little strained—but it is muted. Jarrell, always a tactful poet, no more insists upon his subtler ironies than upon his more obvious ones.

The little girl's final thought is hopeful, or rather, wishful, and wraps up the three separate thematic elements—astronomy, her classroom and scholarly accomplishment, and transformation—in a single couplet alluding to the story of Cinderella. "We are going to live in a new pumpkin/Under a gold star."

Perhaps there will be a happy ending; perhaps this moving to a new place signals her family's magical transformation into a secure and happy one.... At any rate, she is mollified, she has found a fantasy that enables her to accept the hard facts of the real world.

The comfort she finds is almost certainly illusory. "One makes a solitude and calls it peace," Jarrell says in his poem, "Conversation with the Devil," and that is what the little girl has done. But for the moment, for her, this comfort is sufficient.

The third part of the poem, however, with its shift to an objective outside observer shatters the warm tone of the girl's thoughts with an abrupt monosyllabic line: "There is not much else." It is an ambiguous line, pointing forward and backward at once: "there is little alternative in the way she *can* think," and, "there is not much left to report."

Jarrell then gives a series of literal details which in their disorder mirror the earlier phantasmagoria of the child's fancies:

> The brass bed bobs to the van.
> The broody hen
> Squawks upside-down—her eggs are boiled;
> The cat is dragged from the limb.

These events are reported in passive mood so that there seems no human agency responsible for them. The bed is not carried, but on its own "bobs" to the van. No one is holding the broody hen by her legs, she simply "Squawks upside-down," and her eggs, which were to be the beginning of a flock, have been boiled. The Halloween cat is dragged from the tree as if being unpinned and taken down from the classroom wallboard. The details are perfectly realistic, but, in passive mood and after the child's confused thoughts, take on an eerie unreal quality. The outer world of fact has become the unfactual world of her inner vision.

This is the real transformation, the true metamorphosis—very unlike the one in the Cinderella story—and the girl now recognizes it. The comfort of her momentary fantasy deserts her. She looks round her at the place she is leaving. "And, yard by lot, it changes./Never again." She has lost belief in her fairy tale, "And inches closer to her mother." Now she makes one final desperate attempt to look into her future.

> Then she shuts her eyes, and sits there, and squashed red
> Circles and leaves like colored chalk
> Come on in her dark head
> And are darkened, and float farther
> And farther and farther from the stretched-out hands
> That float out from her in her broody trance:
> She hears her own heart and her cat's heart beating.

The young girl makes an unlikely oracle; she cannot foresee the future. She resembles a little the unsuccessful oracles in *The Waste Land*, but Jarrell's reference here is to Gerard Manley Hopkins' sonnet, "Spelt from Sybil's Leaves," and the mood is just as dark as in that poem. But again it is a muted reference; the image of the girl amid falling leaves both real and imaginary is effective whether Hopkins comes to the reader's mind or not. Yet the contrast between Hopkins' great dark figure at the end of her world and Jarrell's wistful heartsick farm girl at the end of hers adds an unexpected ironic overtone.

Her visionary attempt fails. For comfort and security the child has to return to the real things that surround her in present time. "She holds the cat so close to her he pants."

Now the direction in which Childhood lies is, for this little girl at least, entirely clear: it lies behind. "Never again." And it is as much a geographical place as it is a state of mind or a temporary condition of life. For in Jarrell's poems Childhood exists apart from the children: it is a sort of utopia from which they have been barred.

Exile is the theme of "Moving," just as surely as it is the theme of Jarrell's poems about refugees, displaced persons, and prisoners. And just as it is the theme of some of the poems about aging, like "Next Day." The Marschallin, "die alte Frau," of *Der Rosenkavalier* is a very different person indeed from the little farm girl; yet it seems inevitable that in her future life she will utter the same words that the Marschallin does in "The Face":

> This is what happens to everyone.
> At first you get bigger, you know more,
> Then something goes wrong.
> You are, and you say I am—
> And you were . . . I've been too long.

SEELE IM RAUM

It sat between my husband and my children.
A place was set for it—a plate of greens.
It had been there: I had seen it
But not somehow—but this was like a dream—
Not seen it so that I knew I saw it.
It was as if I could not know I saw it
Because I had never once in all my life
Not seen it. It was an eland.
An eland! *That* is why the children
Would ask my husband, for a joke, at Christmas:
"Father, is it Donner?" He would say, "No, Blitzen."
It had been there always. Now we put silver
At its place at meals, fed it the same food
We ourselves ate, and said nothing. Many times
When it breathed heavily (when it had tried
A long useless time to speak) and reached to me
So that I touched it—of a different size
And order of being, like the live hard side
Of a horse's neck when you pat the horse—
And looked with its great melting tearless eyes
Fringed with a few coarse wire-like lashes
Into my eyes, and whispered to me
So that my eyes turned backward in their sockets
And they said nothing—
                                    many times
I have known, when they said nothing,
That it did not exist. If they had heard
They *could* not have been silent. And yet they heard;
Heard many times what I have spoken
When it could no longer speak, but only breathe—
When I could no longer speak, but only breathe.

And, after some years, the others came
And took it from me—it was ill, they told me—
 And cured it, they wrote me: my whole city
Sent me cards like lilac-branches, mourning
As I had mourned—
                                    and I was standing
By a grave in flowers, by dyed rolls of turf,
And a canvas marquee the last brown of earth.

It is over.
It is over so long that I begin to think
That it did not exist, that I have never—
And my son says, one morning, from the paper:
"An eland. Look, an eland!"
                                        —It was so.

Today, in a German dictionary, I saw *eland*
And the heart in my breast turned over, it was—

It was a word one translates *wretched.*

It is as if someone remembered saying:
"This is an antimacassar that I grew from seed,"
And this were true.
                          And, truly,
One could not wish for anything more strange—
For anything more. And yet it wasn't *interesting* . . .
—It was worse than impossible, it was a joke.

And yet when it was, I *was* —
Even to think that I once thought
That I could see it is to feel the sweat
Like needles at my hair-roots, I am blind

—It was not even a joke, not even a joke.

Yet how can I believe it? Or believe that I
Owned it, a husband, children? Is my voice the voice
Of that skin of being—of what owns, is owned
In honor or dishonor, that is borne and bears—
Or of that raw thing, the being inside it
That has neither a wife, a husband, nor a child
But goes at last as naked from this world
As it was born into it —

And the eland comes and grazes on its grave.

                          This is senseless?
Shall I make sense or shall I tell the truth?
Choose either—I cannot do both.

I tell myself that. And yet it is not so,
And what I say afterwards will not be so:
To be at all is to be wrong.
                                    Being is being old
And saying, almost comfortably, across a table
From—
            from what I don't know—
                                    in a voice
Rich with a kind of longing satisfaction:
"To own an eland! That's what I call life!"

David St. John

RANDALL JARRELL'S "SEELE IM RAUM"

One of the most fascinating aspects of Randall Jarrell's stunning dramatic monologue "Seele im Raum" is the way we can see so many of Jarrell's lifelong concerns embodied in the poem: his deep love of fable and folk tale; his knowledge of psychology and his close reading of Freud; his constant empathy with the isolate sensibility, so often a woman at odds with her world; his devotion to Rilke, two of whose poems form the underpinning of "Seele im Raum"; and his love of the German language itself, which provides the serious and motivating pun upon which the poem revolves.

****

In the notes to his *Selected Poems*, Jarrell explains, "*Seele im Raum* is the title of one of Rilke's poems; 'Soul in Space' sounded so glib that I couldn't use it instead." In Rilke's poem, the speaking "soul in space" considers both the body it has just left and the question of whether it will ever again enter such a worldly, flesh-bound "body" of constraint. It is a voice that echoes the same raw nakedness as the voice in Jarrell's "Seele im Raum." Yet there is another Rilke poem that stands even more wholly behind "Seele im Raum," a poem Jarrell had translated. The fourth sonnet in the second part of Rilke's *Sonnets to Orpheus*, based upon the famous tapestry "The Lady and the Unicorn," reads, in Jarrell's version:

This is the animal that never existed.
None of them ever knew one; but just the same

They loved the way it moved, the way it stood
Looking at them, in pure tranquillity.

Of course there wasn't any. But because they loved it
One became an animal. They always left a space.
And in the space they had hollowed for it, lightly
It would lift its head, and hardly need

To exist. They nourished it, not with grain
But only, always, with the possibility
It might be. And this gave so much strength to it

That out of its forehead grew a horn. One horn.
Up to a virgin, silverily, it came
And there within her, there within her glass, it was.

M. Herter Norton's more literal rendering of the final line tells us that the Unicorn "was in the silver-mirror and her." In the second part of *Sonnets to Orpheus*, the fourth sonnet follows Rilke's previous meditations about "space," both exterior and interior space, and about the reflective (reflected) "image" (self) and the nothingness of space within mirrors. It is no accident that Jarrell had linked these two poems of Rilke's in his mind, nor that he chose to braid their concerns into the new fabric of "Seele im Raum." In the tapestry, the Lady holds a mirror, showing the Unicorn its own reflection. It is this same conjunction of self and Other, of self and the mirrored nothingness, that Jarrell exploits in his echoing of the Rilke poems.

****

The woman in "Seele im Raum" has, of course, her own attendant Unicorn—an eland that only she can see, the embodiment and reflection of her own unhappiness. In those same notes to his *Selected Poems*, Jarrell describes an eland as "the largest sort of African antelope—the males are as big as a horse, and you often see people gazing at them, at the zoo, in uneasy wonder." "Uneasy wonder" is a good way to describe how the speaker's family, and we, view her eland as well, as it becomes clear that the animal is an emblem of her soul's trapped, breathless terror. In her own self-doubt, in the erosion of her identity, the woman in "Seele im Raum" has posited an eland to stand for her soul, an objectified and palpable (if only to her) manifestation of her soul's distress. Hers too is a soul in space, solitary and remote.

After her eland has been "taken" from her, after she has been "cured," the woman stumbles upon the unconscious link that language has forged for her; she discovers the unwitting proclamation her eland has been: "Today, in a German dictionary, I saw *eland*/And the heart in my breast turned over, it was—//It was a word one translates *wretched*." She goes on to express her

tremendous ambivalence about this discovery, and about her companion of
the past.

> And, truly,
> One could not wish for anything more strange—
> For anything more. And yet it wasn't *interesting* . . .
> —It was worse than impossible, it was a joke.

> And yet when it was, I *was*—

It's wonderful to now recall Rilke's own comment about his Unicorn,
quoted from a letter: "In the Unicorn no accompanying parallel with Christ is
meant; only all love for the not-proved, the not-tangible, all belief in the
worth and reality of that which our spirit has through the centuries created
and exalted for itself, may be praised in it."

****

In the whole of the second half of "Seele im Raum" the speaker considers
exactly what the "worth and reality" of her spirit's creation, the eland, has
been for her as she reflects upon her present "healthy" state. Her recognition
that the raw, pure being—her soul's naked self/creation—is dead is absolutely harrowing. In the culmination of her meditation, she wonders:

> Yet how can I believe it? Or believe that I
> Owned it, a husband, children? Is my voice the voice
> Of that skin of being—of what owns, is owned
> In honor or dishonor, that is borne and bears—
> Or of that raw thing, the being inside it
> That has neither a wife, a husband, nor a child
> But goes at last as naked from this world
> As it was born into it—

> And the eland comes and grazes on its grave.

> This is senseless?
> Shall I make sense or shall I tell the truth?
> Choose either—I cannot do both.

The profound conflict in this passage, between her own emotional truths
and with "making sense," creates one of the most poignant moments in all of
Jarrell's poetry. Yet there remains something indomitable about her, something valiant, wise, and defiant.

> I tell myself that. And yet it is not so,
> And what I say afterwards will not be so:
> To be at all is to be wrong.

                              Being is being old
And saying, almost comfortably, across a table
From—
            from what I don't know—
                                      in a voice
Rich with a kind of longing satisfaction:
"To own an eland! That's what I call life!"

                         ****

   It is this unravelling of emotional self-truths, the baring of such searing
pain, that always startles me when I read "Seele im Raum." The dualism that
both Jarrell and Rilke saw as a necessary and vital aspect of life is, for most
of us, an unresolvable tension. Perhaps the lesson is simply that one needs
great courage if one is to try living like the panther of Norman Dubie's poem
"For Randall Jarrell," leaping, and "Making it, which could mean,/Into this
world or some other. And between." Certainly the woman of "Seele im
Raum" is living in the held breath of that leap.

THE TRUTH

When I was four my father went to Scotland.
They *said* he went to Scotland.

When I woke up I think I thought that I was dreaming—
I was so little then that I thought dreams
Are in the room with you, like the cinema.
That's why you don't dream when it's still light—
They pull the shades down when it is, so you can sleep.
I thought that then, but that's not right.
Really it's in your head.

And it was light then—light at *night*.
I heard Stalky bark outside.
But really it was Mother crying—
She coughed so hard she cried.
She kept shaking Sister,
She shook her and shook her.
I thought Sister had had her nightmare.
But he wasn't barking, he had died.
There was dirt all over Sister.
It was all streaks, like mud. I cried.
She didn't, but she was older.
                              I thought she didn't
Because she was older, I thought Stalky had just gone.
I got *everything* wrong.
I didn't get one single thing right.
It seems to me that I'd have thought
It didn't happen, like a dream,
Except that it was light. At night.
They burnt our house down, they burnt down London.
Next day my mother cried all day, and after that
She said to me when she would come to see me:
"Your father has gone away to Scotland.
He will be back after the war."

The war then was different from the war now.
The war now is *nothing*.

I used to live in London till they burnt it.
What was it like? It was just like here.
No, that's the truth.

My mother would come here, some, but she would cry.
She said to Miss Elise, "He's not himself";
She said, "Don't you love me any more at all?"
I was *my*self.
Finally she wouldn't come at all.
She never said one thing my father said, or Sister.
Sometimes she did,
Sometimes she was the same, but that was when I dreamed it.
I could tell I was dreaming, she was just the same.

That Christmas she bought me a toy dog.

I asked her what was its name, and when she didn't know
I asked her over, and when she didn't know
I said, "You're not my mother, you're not my mother.
She *hasn't* gone to Scotland, she is dead!"
And she said, "Yes, he's dead, he's dead!"
And cried and cried; she *was* my mother,
She put her arms around me and we cried.

Ralph Burns

THE PLAIN TRUTH IN "THE TRUTH"

Thirty years ago, in an essay that begins, "Why are we two?," James Dickey complained that Randall Jarrell's poems lack verbal intensity, that "the unstated and insistent principle underlying the later poems is 'The situation is enough.'" One poem upon which Dickey focuses in his dialogue between Reader A and Reader B is "The Truth." Reader A reads the poem aloud in a "slow, grave, choking voice," then pouts, "It takes *courage* to be sentimental nowadays." Reader B devilishly advocates "Collingwood's definition" of craft, which is "just sophisticated journalism...working up a predictable emotion"; and says that the writer behind "The Truth" lacks "the power, or the genius, or the talent, or the inclination, or whatever, to make experience rise to its own most intense, concentrated, and meaningful level, a level impossible without that poet's having caught it in *those* words."

I disagree. Jarrell's care in creating such a difficult speaker rescues "The Truth" from sentimentality. He attends to the rhetorical powers in choosing *that* character to speak, inevitably, "*those* words" in *that* way. The words are plain, and they must be. They are spoken by a child who has no choice but to go over and over his situation. Jarrell steals the poem from its situation through his attention to the rhetorical possibilities of choosing an expressively limited speaker, one whose available vocabulary works with and against obsessive internal and end rhyme, word repetition, tactical line breaks, parallel sentence-structures, and a few well-placed grammatical mistakes that leap out like passion marks on a Baptist.

In his introduction to the *Selected Poems*, Jarrell informs the reader (needlessly, I think) that "the little boy in 'The Truth' has had his father, his sister, and his dog killed in one of the early air-raids on London, and has been taken to the country, to a sort of mental institution." From the beginning the boy questions the reality of his situation, suggested chiefly through two of Jarrell's most distinctive devices—sestina-like repetition of end words and the repetition of sounds, words, and phrases in close juxtaposition. In a poem of fifty-four lines, four rhymes or repeated end words—*dreams, light, night, cried*—ride the poem loosely to its close. The child speaker, traumatized by the death of his father, sister and dog and his own physical and emotional dislocation, yearns for any repeatable pattern.

Early in the poem Jarrell uses the dash, particularizing the tentative, contradictory and complex nature of the boy's getting at the truth of where his father and sister are; who his mother is; how dream and reality remain discrete (if they do) and what they are. In the first two-line stanza the boy repeats as end phrases "went to Scotland," underscoring his helplessness in "locating" his father; and points accusingly to an amorphous "They," presumably the clinicians at the mental hospital and his mother, who kept him from "The Truth." In the first line of the second stanza he numbly repeats the pronoun "I" four times, combining them with three closely positioned, tongued-thickening "th" sounds. Each successive line qualifies both the boy's and our own understanding of the truth of his situation, whether "dreams/Are in the room with you, like the cinema," that imitation of dream and life that was often, as Jarrell's war children understood it, a means of escape; whether by way of Goethe, the truth will set him free; or whether he can escape from the present through dreaming a selective past: "Sometimes she was the same, but that was when I dreamed it./I could tell I was dreaming, she was just the same."

Jarrell's syntax is usually straightforward, and the sentence types in "The Truth" are harrowingly alike and simple. In fact, the values that inform "The Truth," that plain language and syntax are fit for a poem spoken by a plain child after a plain ugly air-raid, also say that the best arrangement for the poem is predominantly syntactical line breaks which work with and against a number of disquietingly deadpan parallel sentence-structures:

They pull the shades down when it is, so you can sleep.

I thought that then, but that's not right.

But it was light then—light at *night*.

But he wasn't barking, he had died.

They burnt our house down, they burnt down London.

Moving down the poem, the reader becomes increasingly aware of an enervating, almost hypertensive sameness, a nausea of recurrence, the absurdity, the dread that claims, "The war now is *nothing*." And that revealed absence is echoed and prepared for by a lack of descriptive particulars, hardly any informative adjectives and adverbs, only three metaphors, none elaborately drawn—

> I thought dreams
> Are in the room with you, like the cinema.

It was all streaks, like mud.

It didn't happen, like a dream.

Further, the referents for "they" in the first and sixth stanza and the immediate referent for the "it" of "Really it's in your head..." are ambiguous and prepare for two crucial confusions of person—the switch from Sister to Stalky back to Sister in the boy's grappling with the truth of his sister's death, and later, in the last stanza, when he begins to accept his father's death through a strategic "wrong" pronoun:

> I said, "You're not my mother, you're not my mother.
> She *hasn't* gone to Scotland, she is dead!"
> And she said, "Yes, he's dead, he's dead!"
> And cried and cried; she *was* my mother,
> She put her arms around me and we cried.

The audacity of the last line is in its predictable, yet engagingly courageous and emancipating sob, its faith that the real unreality of war and personal trauma can, by simply being what it is, serve paradoxically as its own most imaginative emblem. I can think of no other modern dramatic poet who, more than Jarrell, speaks plainly without being flat or who sees more piercingly by seeing what is there. Toward the end of "The Obscurity of the Poet," an essay written a few years before Dickey's, in the late forties, Jarrell says:

> Art matters not merely because it is the most magnificent ornament and the most nearly unfailing occupation of our lives, but because it is life itself. From Christ to Freud we have believed that, if we know the truth, the truth will set us free: art is indispensable because so much of this truth can be learned through works of art and through works of art alone.

NESTUS GURLEY

Sometimes waking, sometimes sleeping,
Late in the afternoon, or early
In the morning, I hear on the lawn,
On the walk, on the lawn, the soft quick step,
The sound half song, half breath: a note or two
That with a note or two would be a tune.
It is Nestus Gurley.

It is an old
Catch or snatch or tune
In the Dorian mode: the mode of the horses
That stand all night in the fields asleep
Or awake, the mode of the cold
Hunter, Orion, wheeling upside-down,
All space and stars, in cater-cornered Heaven.
When, somewhere under the east,
The great march begins, with birds and silence;
When, in the day's first triumph, dawn
Rides over the houses, Nestus Gurley
Delivers to me my lot.

As the sun sets, I hear my daughter say:
"He has four routes and makes a hundred dollars."
Sometimes he comes with dogs, sometimes with children,
Sometimes with dogs and children.
He collects, today.
I hear my daughter say:
"Today Nestus has got on his derby."
And he says, after a little: "It's two-eighty."
"How could it be two-eighty?"
"Because this month there're five Sundays: it's two-eighty."

He collects, delivers. Before the first, least star
Is lost in the paling east; at evening
While the soft, side-lit gold-leafed day
Lingers to see the stars, the boy Nestus
Delivers to me the Morning Star, the Evening Star
—Ah no, only the Morning *News*, the Evening *Record*
Of what I have done and what I have not done
Set down and held against me in the Book
Of Death, on paper yellowing

Already, with one morning's sun, one evening's sun.

Sometimes I only dream him. He brings then
News of a different morning, a judgment not of men.
The bombers have turned back over the Pole,
Having met a star. . . . I look at that new year
And, waking, think of our Moravian Star
Not lit yet, and the pure beeswax candle
With its red flame-proofed paper pompom
Not lit yet, and the sweetened
Bun we brought home from the love-feast, still not eaten,
And the song the children sang: *O Morning Star*—

And at this hour, to the dew-hushed drums
Of the morning, Nestus Gurley
Marches to me over the lawn; and the cat Elfie,
Furred like a musk-ox, coon-tailed, gold-leaf-eyed,
Looks at the paper boy without alarm
But yawns, and stretches, and walks placidly
Across the lawn to his ladder, climbs it, and begins to purr.
I let him in,
Go out and pick up from the grass the paper hat
Nestus has folded: this tricorne fit for a Napoleon
Of our days and institutions, weaving
Baskets, being bathed, receiving
Electric shocks, Rauwolfia. . . . I put it on
—Ah no, only unfold it.
There is dawn inside; and I say to no one
About—
             it is a note or two
That with a note or two would—
                                                say to no one
About nothing: "He delivers dawn."

When I lie coldly
—Lie, that is, neither with coldness nor with warmth—
In the darkness that is not lit by anything,
In the grave that is not lit by anything
Except our hope: the hope
That is not proofed against anything, but pure
And shining as the first, least star
That is lost in the east on the morning of Judgment—
May I say, recognizing the step

Or tune or breath. . . .
                                        recognizing the breath,
May I say, "It is Nestus Gurley."

David Young

DAY FOR NIGHT

About one-third of the way through Randall Jarrell's *The Woman at the Washington Zoo* (1960), his next-to-last collection, comes "Nestus Gurley," a poem about a paperboy, or, more accurately, about a man's mythologizing of his paperboy. A hushed, ecstatic piece, full of verbal music and appreciative side-glances, it is not very characteristic of the tones and subjects of its collection. Most of the book is more somber, and even the more lighthearted pieces, like "Deutsch Durch Freud" and "Charles Dodgson's Song" are cross-cultural and historical in subject. "Nestus Gurley" is emphatically local, domestic, of its own place and time, like the book's title poem and like many of the poems in the final collection, *The Lost World* (1965). While it is not spoken by Randall Jarrell in Greensboro, North Carolina, its speaker is a very similar person in an even more similar place.

Place matters in this case, I think. The poem is about the mythologizing of the everyday, and the everyday here is the one that the poet lived and worked in. Jarrell has put aside his fruitful preoccupation with European, especially German, culture and imagination. The effect is even more striking when one considers that the poem is followed in the volume by twelve translations from the German. I'm not claiming that the organization of *Zoo* is ideal, just that the poem tends to stand out in its context in Jarrell's canon.

Is "Nestus Gurley" too long? I don't think so. Jarrell is experimenting, here as elsewhere, with a garrulous style, with a somewhat compulsive speaker. It's risky, but I think he gets away with it. Once inside the poem's circle of invention and precarious enchantment, we don't want it to end. Seventy-eight lines on this curious subject don't seem excessive, even though the poem doesn't advance rapidly from one insight to another but slowly wraps its subject in a dreamy web of meanings and associations, standing back, as it were, between stanzas to admire its handiwork.

The first thing we are apt to notice about the poem's style is its extensive use of balance. Waking and sleeping, day and night, morning and afternoon, cold and warm, birdsong and silence, collecting and delivering, dark and light: the speaker could strike us as indecisive with all his qualifying if what seems at first to be hesitation didn't turn out to be precision:

> Sometimes waking, sometimes sleeping,
> Late in the afternoon, or early
> In the morning, I hear on the lawn,
> On the walk, on the lawn, the soft quick step....

It's not either/or, it's both, and the sense of magic, the ground for the poem's eventual metaphysical (and mock-metaphysical) reach, comes from the paperboy's apparent freedom from normal space and time. He comes and goes as angels and deities do.

The qualifyings and overlappings of the style also give rise to incantatory effects of repetition. Rhymes are infrequent in this poem but they occur here (isn't the very same word in some sense the purest form of rhyme?) in the form of single and double repetitions:

> Sometimes he comes with dogs, sometimes with children,
> Sometimes with dogs and children...
>
> And he says, after a little: "It's two-eighty."
> "How could it be two-eighty?"
> "Because this month there're two Sundays: it's two-eighty..."
>
> In the darkness that is not lit by anything,
> In the grave that is not lit by anything...

Mornings return, seasons return. Words recur, circulating in a slow, hypnotic dance.

The paperboy's magic is a wonderful compound of familiar and unfamiliar possibilities. His "half song, half breath" is in "the Dorian mode." It is also "the mode of the horses" in the field at night and of the constellation Orion, a mixture of wondrous vastness and comical indignity, "wheeling upside-down,/All space and stars, in cater-cornered Heaven." And Nestus's times are special too, the thresholds when light is mythic—"at evening/While the soft, side-lit, gold-leafed day/Lingers to see the stars"—and when transformations affect even housecats—"Elfie,/Furred like a musk-ox, coon-tailed, gold-leaf-eyed." Morning rhymes with evening; the cat's eyes rhyme with the "side-lit" part of the day.

At some point in the exploration of this poem our attention shifts from Nestus Gurley to the unnamed speaker, whose half-conscious self-portrait the poem really is. He has a daughter (which helps us distinguish him from Jarrell). He is very literate. He is wry and tender and observant. He can catch himself waxing too poetic—"Ah no"—and his heroic mode tends to deflate gently into mock-heroic, as in "When, in the day's first triumph, dawn/Rides over the houses" and "to the dew-hushed drums/Of the morning." His consciousness can just barely keep at arm's length the sorrows contained in the daily papers Nestus Gurley brings. An irony lurks in the fact that the newsboy both makes the world *new* by providing structure, freshness and magic, and brings the *news* that kills the sense of wonder and renewal. Twice the outside world, the world of the newspaper, encroaches dangerously, first in the form of anxiety about nuclear war (treated as ludicrously fanciful "news" in "The bombers have turned back over the Pole,/Having met a star..."), and again in the image of the modern world as a madhouse with a Napoleon in a paper hat as its only appropriate ruler, a role the speaker starts to accept ("I put it on/—Ah no, only unfold it") before rejecting it. He seems to know quite a lot about how mental illness is treated. If he has had episodes of his own, he now seems to have found a balance that allows fantasy a crucial role in life ("There is dawn inside") without assuming too much for it. Whether we see his peace as precarious or firm, we sense that it is hard-won. Our enthusiasm shifts from Nestus to his most appreciative customer.

The shy comedy of the final stanza has several marvelous touches. There is the suspended syntax that does not tell us what tense we are in from "When I lie coldly" to the first "May I say" eight lines later. There are the line breaks between first and second, fourth and fifth, lines. There is the recycling of images—e.g. star, candle, dawn, Judgment Day—from the rest of the poem. There is the repetition of "Recognizing the breath."

What does that last repetition *mean?* Better to ask what it suggests. The speaker imagines himself after death, waiting in the grave for a possible Day of Judgment. He imagines the newsboy coming to announce it and asks that he be able to recognize this herald and name him. That act would turn him back to an ordinary paperboy and the Day of Judgment to just another "dew-hushed" morning, the worldly and the otherworldly, the diurnal and the eternal, twinning, interacting, rhyming. The emphasis on breath will evoke the Holy Ghost for some, the idea of inspiration for others. Gods are sometimes recognized in classical epics by their step. Angels may be known by their music, their "tune." Breath seems so mortal, so quintessentially human, that it both evokes the old myth of bodily resurrection and returns us to the everyday, where the poem began and must end, since the speaker is only fantasizing a death and resurrection in which he hopes his paperboy might figure. How strange! How American! Could any other culture have produced it? Jarrell's thoughtful study of Frost and Williams probably contributed to this poem; his increasing sympathy for Stevens too. And the result is queer, comical, touching.

Jarrell was an enthusiast, but deeply melancholy for all his wonder and energy. Most of his best poems are tinged with terror and loss as well as with joy. "Nestus Gurley" is a little different in having so much celebration and so little sorrow. Perhaps that makes it a lesser piece. But who would want to change it?

BATS

A bat is born
Naked and blind and pale.
His mother makes a pocket of her tail
And catches him. He clings to her long fur
By his thumbs and toes and teeth.
And then the mother dances through the night
Doubling and looping, soaring, somersaulting—
Her baby hangs on underneath.
All night, in happiness, she hunts and flies.
Her high sharp cries
Like shining needlepoints of sound
Go out into the night and, echoing back,
Tell her what they have touched.
She hears how far it is, how big it is,
Which way it's going:
She lives by hearing.
The mother eats the moths and gnats she catches
In full flight; in full flight
The mother drinks the water of the pond
She skims across. Her baby hangs on tight.
Her baby drinks the milk she makes him
In moonlight or starlight, in mid-air.
Their single shadow, printed on the moon
Or fluttering across the stars,
Whirls on all night; at daybreak
The tired mother flaps home to her rafter.
The others all are there.
They hang themselves up by their toes,
They wrap themselves in their brown wings.
Bunched upside-down, they sleep in air.
Their sharp ears, their sharp teeth, their quick sharp faces
Are dull and slow and mild.
All the bright day, as the mother sleeps,
She folds her wings about her sleeping child.

Nancy Willard

RADIANT FACTS

> My grandmother, like other grandmothers,
> used to tell me fairy tales; when she was
> tired she would just reminisce. I used to say,
> when I couldn't get a story: "Nanny, tell me
> some Facts."
>
> *Pictures from an Institution*

If all the existing copies of Randall Jarrell's books for children were to vanish from the earth, the one I would miss most is *The Bat-Poet*, with *The Animal Family* a close second. How could I describe my loss to those who hadn't read them? I could say *"The Bat-Poet* is the story of a brown bat who differs from the rest of his species: he stays awake during the day and makes up poems." But I have given away only the plot, the shape of *what happens next*—a question very few readers are likely to ask.

Jarrell himself described *The Bat-Poet* as "half for children and half for grown-ups." Probably Jarrell knew that children would outgrow his first book for children, *The Gingerbread Rabbit*. "I enjoyed it," he told an interviewer for WBAI, "but it wasn't a real book." He had turned to children's books at a time when he found himself unable to write poems. When he started *The Bat-Poet*, it absorbed him as deeply as any poem.

> You know how it is...you work on it all the time. You stay awake at night...you wake up in the middle of the night.... I did it just like a grown-up book. By good luck, we had some bats on our porch and so I imagined a bat who would not write poems, but anyway make them up. And so, I had to make up poems for him. And a couple of the poems were pretty much like grown-up poems. Anyway the *New Yorker* printed them....[1]

"Once upon a time there was a bat—a little light brown bat, the color of coffee with cream in it." Though Jarrell uses the traditional fairy tale beginning, *The Bat-Poet* is no fairy tale; there are unpleasant characters but no evil ones, there are animals that talk but no transformations. Neither is it a fable, for all its beasts. The bat is not a stand-in for an idea; ideas do not hang upside down from the roof of one's porch. "He was a kind of cafe-au-lait brown and I made him the Bat-Poet." The cardinal and chipmunk took sunflower seeds at Jarrell's back yard feeder long before they took their places in his story.

---

[1] All the direct quotations from Randall Jarrell are taken from the interview with Aaron Kramer, excerpts of which are printed on the jacket of Caedmon recording TC 1364, *The Bat-Poet*, read by the author.

Only the mockingbird, the self-centered, territorial genius, would be at home in one of Aesop's tales. There he would get his just deserts. Here he merely offends and dazzles the animals with whom he reluctantly shares his world. "Mockingbirds are not only more like artists than other birds, they're more like people, too," Jarrell observed. His wife was more specific. "In life, Frost and Cal were Mockingbirds; Michael di Capua and I were Chipmunks, of sorts; and Bob Watson and Randall were bats."[2]

We are given the bat's poems but not the mockingbird's; the paradox of how the mockingbird creates is sufficient reason for including him in the book. And it's the bat, not the bird, who sees the paradox clearly:

> Now, in the moonlight, he sits here and sings.
> A thrush is singing, then a thrasher, then a jay—
> Then, all at once, a cat begins meowing.
> A mockingbird can sound like anything.
> He imitates the world he drove away
> So well that for a minute, in the moonlight,
> Which one's the mockingbird? which one's the world?[3]

The progress of the bat-poet is less paradoxical. Starting with the slow awakening of the senses, it unfolds along more familiar roads: groping for the right image, overcoming writer's block ("I can't make up a poem about the cardinal.... I watch him and he's just beautiful, he'd make a beautiful poem; but I can't think of anything" [p. 25]), and finding an audience ("The trouble isn't making poems, the trouble's finding somebody that will listen to them" [p. 15]). The philosopher who crept out of Plato's cave was not more dazzled than the bat-poet, nor more in need of a new language to tell what he saw. "Shadows are black," exclaim the other bats, "how can a shadow be bright?" "What's green-and-gold-and-blue? When you say things like that we don't know what you mean." "And it's just not real.... When the sun rises the world goes to sleep" (p. 6).

While the mockingbird turns away from the world he imitates, the bat-poet turns toward it and makes "portraits in verse." He and William Carlos Williams would have understood each other, though the bat-poet's portraits, metered and rhymed, are a far cry from the gallery of Williams' old women, flowers, and still lifes. If Jarrell's bat were a painter instead of a poet, he would paint his portraits with the inspired realism of a Van Eyck; he would show us every feather on the angel's wing. And his faithful audience, the

---

[2] Mrs. Randall Jarrell, "The Group of Two," *Randall Jarrell 1914-1965*, ed. Robert Lowell (New York: Farrar, Straus, Giroux, 1967), 290. All quotations from Mrs. Jarrell are taken from this essay, and page numbers noted in the text.

[3] *The Bat-Poet* (New York: Macmillan, 1964), 28. For all other quotations from this book the page numbers will be noted in the text.

chipmunk, would respond to a painting of himself as he does to the poem: "You put in the seeds and the hole and everything.... I didn't think you could" (p. 22).

When at last the bat-poet composes a poem for the other bats, he has learned how to build poems out of facts. But these are radiant facts; images, verbs, music, and story have worked on them:

> A bat is born
> Naked and blind and pale.
> His mother makes a pocket of her tail
> And catches him. He clings to her long fur
> By his thumbs and toes and teeth.
> And then the mother dances through the night
> Doubling and looping, soaring, somersaulting—
> Her baby hangs on underneath.
> All night, in happiness, she hunts and flies.
> Her high sharp cries
> Like shining needlepoints of sound
> Go out into the night and, echoing back,
> Tell her what they have touched.
> She hears how far it is, how big it is,
> Which way it's going.
> She lives by hearing.

In their best moments, poets do not choose their material; their material chooses them. Both *The Bat-Poet* and *The Animal Family* chose Jarrell, "took hold of him," as his wife put it. In *The Animal Family*, a man left alone on the coast where he has lived all his life finds himself a family by letting himself be found—by a mermaid, a bear, a lynx, and a boy. A fantastic story, yet like *The Bat-Poet* it is built on the observable details of Jarrell's life. His own family watched with astonishment the transformation of the familiar into the stuff of story:

> Daily, like a small glacier, it gathered up objects such as deerskin rugs from Salzburg, the new window seat we'd added, the Gucci hunting horn over our brick hearth.... Into this setting Randall put a bearded hunter and a mermaid, the lynx from the Washington Zoo, the seals from Laguna days, and finally he gave them a boy who wanted to be adopted by *The Animal Family*.
> ("The Group of Two," pp. 296-297)

Very likely the wise women who told their tales to the brothers Grimm gathered the stuff of *their* surroundings when they set forth a new story; spinning wheels and miller's daughters were common as pennies once upon a time. Jarrell is both the wise woman telling the story and the amazed writer respectfully setting it down. "Sometimes you feel you have good luck with a book.... Things *come* to you. And I feel that...*The Bat-Poet*, for what it is, is done right."

FIELD AND FOREST

When you look down from the airplane you see lines,
Roads, ruts, braided into a net or web—
Where people go, what people do: the ways of life.

Heaven says to the farmer: "What's your field?"
And he answers: "Farming," with a field,
Or: "Dairy-farming," with a herd of cows.
They seem a boy's toy cows, seen from this high.

Seen from this high,
The fields have a terrible monotony.

But between the lighter patches there are dark ones.
A farmer is separated from a farmer
By what farmers have in common: forests,
Those dark things—what the fields were to begin with.
At night a fox comes out of the forest, eats his chickens.
At night the deer come out of the forest, eat his crops.

If he could he'd make farm out of all the forest,
But it isn't worth it: some of it's marsh, some rocks,
There are things there you couldn't get rid of
With a bulldozer, even—not with dynamite.
Besides, he likes it. He had a cave there, as a boy;
He hunts there now. It's a waste of land,
But it would be a waste of time, a waste of money,
To make it into anything but what it is.

At night, from the airplane, all you see is lights,
A few lights, the lights of houses, headlights,
And darkness. Somewhere below, beside a light,
The farmer, naked, takes out his false teeth:
He doesn't eat now. Takes off his spectacles:
He doesn't see now. Shuts his eyes.
If he were able to he'd shut his ears,
And as it is, he doesn't hear with them.
Plainly, he's taken out his tongue: he doesn't talk.
His arms and legs: at least, he doesn't move them.
They are knotted together, curled up, like a child's.
And after he has taken off the thoughts
It has taken him his life to learn,

He takes off, last of all, the world.

When you take off everything what's left? A wish,
A blind wish; and yet the wish isn't blind,
What the wish wants to see, it sees.

There in the middle of the forest is the cave
And there, curled up inside it, is the fox.

He stands looking at it.
Around him the fields are sleeping: the fields dream.
At night there are no more farmers, no more farms.
At night the fields dream, the fields *are* the forest.
The boy stands looking at the fox
As if, if he looked long enough—
                                            he looks at it.
Or is it the fox that's looking at the boy?
The trees can't tell the two of them apart.

Marianne Boruch

RHETORIC AND MYSTERY

Some poems are profoundly, willfully plain. Like efficient but passionate hosts bored by the party, they usher us out, past the church, past the large showy houses that look like cakes, into the blank countryside of a listless month, November maybe. Little is said really, and what's said is repeated, moving with reserve and overlap toward the secret of the trip. No digression, that brief glad accident against purpose. Nothing ornate, airy, playful. Wonder is carefully distilled into weight, not a gift but a given. When all stops, just above treeline, we are nodded to the old quarry abandoned for years, spread out before us like some heroic aftermath, cliffs that startle by color, size, but mainly now by a massive repetitive uselessness. This presence, kept, is what the poem exhausts itself to know, this private thing which has no reason but being, that lovely fierce mystery. I'm imagining Randall Jarrell writing "Field and Forest," and I imagine it caught him off-guard. In spite of his rhetorical current and rise, something unpredictable swamps the journey by the end, something mute and close as joy—or terror. Jarrell, with a kind of spent courage, lets it take over, lets the poem steer itself.

    All begins coolly enough, in an airplane, higher than we normally conceive of things. That the country below keeps to its "terrible monotony" or reminds us of something it never is close up—roads become webs and nets, cows "toy cows"—is more than a visual trick; it settles us into our seats, makes us believe we are, in fact, in air. From this distance, seeing the whole thing—what appears to be the whole thing—we can judge, dismember, calculate, condescend with impunity. After all, no one's watching us. We are oddly alone here, though technology—the airplane itself with its humming complex order, or this initial perspective that abstractly gathers in groups, thinks "ways of life," thinks people and their "fields"—is public not private realization. Immediately, seemingly irreversibly, we are in the grip of Jarrell's familiar rhetoric: his automatic assumption of audience, his authority, his careful definition: all trademarks—consciously so, I suspect—and lovingly nurtured through years. As usual then, we are sitting back, waiting for Jarrell's offhand intellectual delight or anguish, waiting, that is, until the jolt. One word—"but"—opens the heavy door swiftly. "But," the poet warns, "between the lighter patches there are dark ones."

Returning, reconsidering, reopening the seamless world, delivering us out of completion by the gift of doubt: the line is a second look. Though we still feel that guarded rhetorical momentum, there *is* darkness now—thank god—amid the "lighter patches," and cleverly Jarrell tells us that "a farmer is separated from a farmer/By what farmers have in common: forests"—a cleverness which turns on itself as Frost's sometimes does, in deadpan deliberate measure. What I love next is the undercut—abrupt and childlike—a fresh way of definition in the poem, spoken right now. "Forests," Jarrell declares, "those dark things—what the fields were to begin with." One hears earnest, young impatience in the voice. "Those dark things...." *You* know. And then, with reverie, belied by an encyclopedic calm, come the dangerous facts of such woods: foxes emerge and eat chickens; deer move out and destroy crops. Always "at night," of course, that universe without distinction or control, reason or safety, that absolute and inhuman substance.

By now we are deeply, helplessly descending, launched from the plane completely, inventing an owner, a farmer and his lifetime of sweat and silence in these fields. The farmer thinks like a farmer, with practicality; he is not romanticized. Jarrell is too realistic a poet for that. Sure the guy would like to farm all this knotty worthless woods. Ways exist; they don't work. "There are things there you couldn't get rid of/With a bulldozer, even—not with dynamite," we hear, or overhear, for this is the sort of remark that comes drifting above the spring seed bins in hardware stores, this wonderful injunction that layers like a virus, hitting the body by degrees, in various calculations of meaning. We know by its weight that here is some major artery of the poem, some forecast, some gleaming shard heralding a buried city. Still, Jarrell is offhand, staging, still in-character. "Besides," the poet tells us of the farmer, "he likes it. He had a cave there, as a boy," as if apology were needed at this image that cuts back to our primitive longing for shelter and solitude, for a place before history or manners, ambition or definition. It would be a waste, the poet-farmer voice continues with purposeful bravado, purposefully beside the point, a waste of land, time, money to make it "anything but what it is." *What it is.* We are suddenly arrived at the primal kernel of something. What is it? One feels the chill, the suspension at the edge: the possibility of embarrassment or vision. The idea at hand is that large.

Instead, Jarrell's off target, not ready. He shifts back, barely, breaking stanza—back to observation, description, to the high concise confines of the plane in a brief seizure of routine and reason. He chants the hard details. Up here, one sees "lights,/a few lights, the lights of houses, headlights,/And darkness." Mostly, of course, darkness. Which is to say, one sees nothing at all. This is dream. We are aloft over fields that may or may not be fields anymore. We lose hold of proof. There is memory certainly, and Jarrell loves its earnest, if inexact, digressions, like those of the eye to explain and continue. Darkness, however, is indifferent; it levels and forgets, and one feels the poet stalling in these few lines, a swimmer coming up in a passion for common air, lulled by the plane's bright efficiency, gearing up—for what? Does he even know? Before, invention took us as far as the cave, the farmer disguising his need with such reasonable reasons. How willing is Jarrell now to let imagination fall as darkness falls, as a seed falls windward, complete and inert; how willing is this rational poet to disappear at his high fluorescent window? If he is stalling—I sense he must be—then some dangerous turn is imminent, some impossible possibility. "Somewhere below," the poet gropes, "beside a light"—of course, he enters in secret, his eye at the keyhole—"the farmer, naked, takes out his false teeth." Not any farmer, *the* farmer—of the cave, of the ominous orderly tangle of field and forest. In a second, all is aging. The farmer's instantly old, alone for years. And the listing that follows, echo of grandparent after grandparent witnessing to ailments like a serious collector at his stamps, buries us with stilling detail: tooth and eye, ear and tongue, all diminished. "...he doesn't move them." Arms and legs. "They are knotted together, curled up, like a child's."

Envision this room then, and the gradual, almost matter-of-fact reduction of body. The poet, however, cuts further, *faces* further—to experience, to human memory itself. "And after he has taken off the thoughts/It has taken him his life to learn,/He takes off, last of all, the world." Jarrell ends the stanza with extraordinary poise: one word again—the world—which takes a lifetime to enter. But beyond exhaustion now, beyond gratitude even, one slips out of it easily, in a minute, the way at bedside, one slips out of a shirt too big, too worn, too familiar. In turn, a stanza break stalls us, just when we need it, silent here, witness to the full dark expanse within the farmer, which seeps past this hour back to middle age, to youth, to boyhood like a rich black greed. We are down in this descent to "what's left," to the final living nub, this thing that can't be altered in us. "A wish," Jarrell insists, that is blind and not so blind, for what it "wants to see, it sees." Desire then, past will, which is to say, past human invention or relish or courage, as if our lot is to endure desire, its ravages and gifts, as if this alone defines us.

At this point, though, Jarrell is past philosophy too, narrowing like some heat-sensitive device toward the heart of the vision, off abstraction at last, off its surgical distillation onto pure image. There is the forest, and there inside it, like hidden wealth, is the cave. Smaller, like some folktale riddle, the next secret waits in these rich dim layers: the fox of course, curled up in the cave, fetal and complete. "He," Jarrell tells us simply, "stands looking at it." *He*— the farmer, with his one wish, returning merely to witness what beauty and danger he kept from harm, to look as long as it takes to be there. The poet pulls back, to backdrop and foreground telling us everything's near this knowledge: "the fields dream," he tells us. More, "At night...the fields are the forest." Then, in a similar transfer, more remarkable, it's "the boy" looking at the fox, as if what light there is—light of wish, of desire—springs this single sudden flight back to pure attention. "As if," the poet manages, "if he looked long enough—" As if, as if.... The poet is, unbelievably out of words—out of metaphor, explanation, out of meaning.

Jarrell—does he have a choice?—waits here, poised in the near-empty length of line. One recovers from mystery slowly, no doubt more slowly than this, but now the speaker is not asking to know anything at all. What began in this poem, this need to contain, to classify, to distance and simplify, has ended—was anything less predictable?—in this extraordinary moment of speechlessness: night and its dreaming field taken mutely into the body like some ancient elixir to cleanse and merge. The boy or the fox? Who's looking at whom, Jarrell asks. But even as he asks, he's beyond us, long past this calculation, this concern, throwing such small confining dazzlements elsewhere, to trees even.

THE HOUSE IN THE WOOD

At the back of the houses there is the wood.
While there is a leaf of summer left, the wood

Makes sounds I can put somewhere in my song,
Has paths I can walk, when I wake, to good

Or evil: to the cage, to the oven, to the House
In the Wood. It is a part of life, or of the story

We make of life. But after the last leaf,
The last light—for each year is leafless,

Each day lightless, at the last—the wood begins
Its serious existence: it has no path,

No house, no story; it resists comparison . . .
One clear, repeated, lapping gurgle, like a spoon

Or a glass breathing, is the brook,
The wood's fouled midnight water. If I walk into the wood

As far as I can walk, I come to my own door,
The door of the House in the Wood. It opens silently:

On the bed is something covered, something humped
Asleep there, awake there—but what? I do not know.

I look, I lie there, and yet I do not know.
How far out my great echoing clumsy limbs

Stretch, surrounded only by space! For time has struck,
All the clocks are stuck now, for how many lives,

On the same second. Numbed, wooden, motionless,
We are far under the surface of the night.

Nothing comes down so deep but sound: a car, freight cars,
A high soft droning, drawn out like a wire

Forever and ever—is this the sound that Bunyan heard
So that he thought his bowels would burst within him?—

Drift on, on, into nothing. Then someone screams
A scream like an old knife sharpened into nothing.

It is only a nightmare. No one wakes up, nothing happens,
Except there is gooseflesh over my whole body—

And that too, after a little while, is gone.
I lie here like a cut-off limb, the stump the limb has left . . .

Here at the bottom of the world, what was before the world
And will be after, holds me to its black

Breasts and rocks me: the oven is cold, the cage is empty,
In the House in the Wood, the witch and her child sleep.

David Walker

THE SHAPE ON THE BED

If Randall Jarrell was, as Robert Lowell claimed, the most heartbreaking poet of his generation, surely one crucial reason was his treatment of childhood. In many of his poems, of course, we hear children speaking: from the longing for the unknown in "A Sick Child" through the somber, spectral duet of "Protocols" to the lyric memoir of a boyhood in Hollywood, that irrecoverable Eden, in "The Lost World," Jarrell's work is pervaded by children, most of them isolated and unhappy. Indeed, these lines from "Childhood" (adapted from Rilke), might well stand as emblematic: "O loneliness, O leaden waiting-out of time....//O knowledge ever harder to hold fast to,/O dread, O burden." And yet these poems are not unremittingly gloomy; their voices, never flatly melancholy, tend rather to be precise, solemn, poignantly innocent—in fact, much like that of the careful, precocious, alert boy I imagine the young Jarrell to have been. It is the way in which the poems' profound sadness is tempered by the vitality of their observations and language—the way, in short, the children are made authentic rather than simply emblematic—that gives them their richly distinctive tonality.

I find it particularly interesting how often these same tonalities emerge in the voices of Jarrell's adult speakers, how often—whether through the shock of warfare or through the ordinary traumas of loss and aging—they seem stunned into simply *registering* the facts of their lives in a characteristically childlike way. Many of Jarrell's adults are perpetually moving from inno-

cence to experience, viewing their lives as an endless rite of passage. The result, particularly in the late poems, is that the distinction between childhood
and adulthood dissolves, both as a dramatic element in the poem and in the
reading experience. We might notice, for instance, that "A Hunt in the Black
Forest," in Jarrell's last volume, is apparently a reworking of the briefer and
much earlier "The Prince." Both are poems of considerable compression and
power. But while "The Prince" resolves itself fairly easily as a narrative of a
child's nightmare about his dead father, it is never clear whether the
"dreamer" of the later poem is child or adult, or indeed whether the poem's
events are dreamed or actually experienced. The pathos of "The Prince" develops when we recognize that its speaker is a child who understands less
about his experience than we can. "The Hunt in the Black Forest" is considerably more tangled and phantasmagoric; although its murky narrative of
hunter, mute, and dwarf draws on the child's world of folktale and magic adventure, there seems to be no way for either "dreamer" or reader to get outside it, to attain the "adult" perspective that would allow us to account for it
more easily. To read the poem is to claim that world as our own.

"The House in the Wood," a companion poem, is equally mysterious and
multilayered, and to my mind even more effective. Its title implies that the
poem may center on a fairly conventional narrative, and a certain rationality
may be suggested, at least subliminally, by the regular appearance of couplets on the page. But these early expectations are soon subverted: the poem
is in fact deeply intuitive, irrational, and unpredictable. Jarrell had earlier
written poems grounded in traditional folktales ("The Black Swan," "The
Sleeping Beauty: Variation of the Prince," "Cinderella"), and the story of
Hansel and Gretel clearly underlies "The House in the Wood." But only very
superficially: to recognize the model is merely to see how radically Jarrell
departs from it. Plot, character, symbol, narrative perspective—all are subor-
dinated to the play of images on the edge of consciousness, to the drift of
dream-discovery. Hansel and Gretel are collapsed into a single subject who
somehow seems to speak universally ("It is a part of life, or of the story/We
make of life"), and whose voice plays in the uncertain territory between child
and adult. What at first may seem the characteristically innocent precision of
Jarrell's children ("At the back of the houses there is the wood") soon begins
to reflect a more mature, reflective sensibility ("each year is leafless,/Each
day lightless, at the last"), and we recognize that it may simply represent the
flat, uncritical voice in which we narrate our dreams.

But such a simple formulation is finally false to the poem. The experience
of reading "The House in the Wood" does not easily allow the sort of distance that is necessary to talk critically about it. Like the wood, the poem itself "has no path,/No house, no story; it resists comparison...." To read it an-
alytically according to the codes of Freud or Jung would be no more effective
than Hansel's trail of breadcrumbs. From the point when the speaker leaves

civilization behind and plunges into darkness, we are forced to make our own dream-discoveries, and I suspect every reader's will be different. We become the landscape, the landscape becomes a mirror, and the house I find in the wood belongs not to the witch but to me. This is only one of the poem's manifold surprises, and it is followed by an even greater one:

> On the bed is something covered, something humped
> Asleep there, awake there—but what? I do not know.
>
> I look, I lie there, and yet I do not know.
> How far out my great echoing clumsy limbs
>
> Stretch, surrounded only by space! For time has struck,
> All the clocks are stuck now, for how many lives,
>
> On the same second. Numbed, wooden, motionless,
> We are far under the surface of the night.

At this point the Hansel-and-Gretel narrative has been left far behind, and the metamorphosis becomes dazzlingly circular: the hidden, sinister object on the bed becomes oneself asleep there, dreaming the object. The solipsistic implications of the disappearance of character and plot from the narrative come relentlessly and terrifyingly into focus. The excursion "as far as I can walk" into the wood leads inevitably to "nothing," and the triple repetition of the word within three lines gives it its necessary weight. The recognition that "it is only a nightmare" provides no comfort at all, easing as it does the passage to utter passivity, unconsciousness, silence: "No one wakes up, nothing happens,/Except there is gooseflesh over my whole body—//And that too, after a little while, is gone."

The poem's ending unfolds a series of quite wonderful surprises:

> Here at the bottom of the world, what was before the world
> And will be after, holds me to its black
>
> Breasts and rocks me; the oven is cold, the cage is empty,
> In the House in the Wood, the witch and her child sleep.

The first couplet seems to take us deeper into the abstract, almost purely metaphysical limbo of space and time that was promised us earlier: we appear to have entered an absence that is both prehistoric and post-holocaust. And yet there is something peculiar about the syntax: it may take a moment to realize that what "holds me" is in fact that absence, that limbo that existed before the world. And as we cross the line break—surely one of the most powerfully dislocating line breaks I know—and the blackness suddenly becomes "breasts," absence becomes presence and narrative boldly reenters the poem, but radically transformed. There *is* a witch, there *is* an oven, but here they are far from simply fearful. The other presence that has finally entered the poem is nurturing, calming, rocking us as the poem's rhythms have begun to. The simplicity of the final clause, suspending the identities of witch and child until the last possible moment, is the ultimate measure of Jarrell's control. All the predictable distinctions—time and space, day and night, good and evil, past and future, witch and mother, adult and child—are erased in a vision of profound emotional ambivalence. As in "A Hunt in the Black Forest," this vision is so compelling, so elemental, as to make rational critical distance virtually impossible. "We are all children to the past," Jarrell says in "The Memoirs of Glückel of Hameln"; here with extraordinary power he makes us all that child, rocked and sleeping.

WILLIAM STAFFORD
(1914-93)

W illiam Stafford seems an almost quintessentially American poet: born and raised in Kansas, an inhabitant of the Pacific Northwest from 1948 until his death, his experience is deeply rooted in the American heartland and pioneer traditions. What is most striking about his work is the way that openness to experience transforms itself into wisdom, so that the processes of seeing and knowing become one. The characteristic sensibility in his poems is so quietly neutral, so far removed from rhetorical effects, that it sometimes seems a sort of universal spirit, speaking from the center of experience itself. Yet it would be a mistake to take Stafford's plain-spokenness and deliberate receptivity for naiveté: the calm voice of his poems is that of a canny, clear-eyed individual who simply chooses not to impose his will unduly on the world, but to listen patiently and good-humoredly for what it will reveal. Stafford's sustained attention to places, to landscapes, to animals frequently uncovers the profound moral or metaphysical questions that underlie them. He was a remarkably prolific poet, willing to risk the trivial and the overly passive in quest of the genuine revelation; at his best he was a writer of indispensible vision, truly one of our most valuable.

BOOKS: *Stories That Could Be True: New and Collected Poems* (1977); *The Way It Is: New and Selected Poems* (1998); *Writing the Australian Crawl: Views on the Writer's Vocation* (1978); *You Must Revise Your Life* (1986); *Crossing Unmarked Snow: Further Views on the Writer's Vocation*, ed. Paul Merchant and Vincent Wixon (1998).

AT THE BOMB TESTING SITE

At noon in the desert a panting lizard
waited for history, its elbows tense,
watching the curve of a particular road
as if something might happen.

It was looking at something farther off
than people could see, an important scene
acted in stone for little selves
at the flute-end of consequence.

There was just a continent without much on it,
under a sky that never cared less.
Ready for a change, the elbows waited.
The hands gripped hard on the desert.

Charles Simic

ON "AT THE BOMB TESTING SITE"

A political poem in which not a single political statement is made, what Stafford himself calls more "nonapparently political than apparently political."

Let me quote Nietzsche here: "The consequence of reverie which would borrow from intelligence the means to force upon the world its folly.... We are a race committed to the test of the act, hence pledged to the bloodiest fate."

In poetry a choice is made about the part that will represent the whole. Form, in its deepest sense, is selection. True form is the product of an extraordinary vision.

There's a lizard at the bomb testing site. The poem is an attempt to measure everything according to the duration and intensity of that little life.

A "weasel-worded" poem.

The naked world. The innocent lizard. A most primitive form of life. Ugly. Expendable—like those laboratory animals stuck inside a maze under the bright lights.

One assumes they're afraid too.

"How pure and great must be the cause for which so much blood is spilled," says Aleksandar Wat.

For now, just the timeless moment. Just the lizard, the desert. He's panting, trembling a little. Think of Elizabeth Bishop's "Armadillo," the fire raining on him.... That will come later.
History is marching.... Or, History is a throw of the dice....

The poem is an attempt to convey certain old premonitions. The first lizard knew the world will end some day.
And at the heart of it—Incomprehension! Bewilderment!

Out there, perhaps, scratched in stone, there's the matchstick figure of the Indian humpbacked flute player. He is surrounded by other match-stick figures. They are enacting a scene, a sacred dance....

The sphinx is watching. An American sphinx waiting for history. The hands grip hard, so we are on the very verge. It is the instant in which all past and all future wait suspended.

One should speak of Stafford's disappearing acts. As in "Traveling Through the Dark," he leaves us at the most crucial moments. At the end of his great poems we are always alone, their fateful acts and their consequences now our own to consider.
Solitude as an absolute, the only one.

The heavens above couldn't care less. The poet asks the philosopher in us to consider the world in its baffling presence.

An American sphinx in the desert of our spirit. Let us keep asking her questions.

In the meantime, we can say with Heidegger that poems such as this one open the largest view of the earth, sky, mortals and their true and false gods.

THINKING FOR BERKY

In the late night listening from bed
I have joined the ambulance or the patrol
screaming toward some drama, the kind of end
that Berky must have some day, if she isn't dead.

The wildest of all, her father and mother cruel,
farming out there beyond the old stone quarry
where highschool lovers parked their lurching cars,
Berky learned to love in that dark school.

Early her face was turned away from home
toward any hardworking place; but still her soul,
with terrible things to do, was alive, looking out
for the rescue that—surely, some day—would have to come.

Windiest nights, Berky, I have thought for you,
and no matter how lucky I've been I've touched wood.
There are things not solved in our town though tomorrow came:
there are things time passing can never make come true.

We live in an occupied country, misunderstood;
justice will take us millions of intricate moves.
Sirens will hunt down Berky, you survivors in your beds
listening through the night, so far and good.

Henry Taylor

MILLIONS OF INTRICATE MOVES

I

In "Thinking for Berky," many of the qualities that make Stafford's poetry
what it is are at their best. The meter, strictly speaking, is unstable; some
of the lines are iambic pentameter, and others stray from that toward
fourteen syllables, yet the rhythmical rightness of each line is firmly there,
not to be quarreled with. Similarly, the rhyme is the very opposite of insistent; though the rhymes between the first and fourth lines of each stanza are
solid and true, there is enough between the rhymes to keep them from being

more than a gentle and mysterious reminder that this is utterance weighed and wrought. Within this delicate scheme, the sentences move easily from immediate description to generalization and back again, the tone never modulating beyond the conversational. And yet there is something close to bravura in the calm statements of large truths: "there are things time passing can never make come true," "justice will take us millions of intricate moves."

Certain qualities of calmness and unpretentious gravity may create the impression that this voice is not easily modulated, or inclusive of various tones. But many of the qualities evident in "Thinking for Berky"—discursiveness, directness, delicacy of meter, specificity of description, definitiveness of general statement—are to be found in "Adults Only," a recollection of an evening at the state fair, in the tent reserved for the strip-tease act. The poem begins with a general statement: "Animals own a fur world;/people own worlds that are variously, pleasingly, bare." The rest of the stanza recalls how those worlds came clear to "us kids" the night they found themselves in that tent. The poem ends:

> Better women exist, no doubt, than that one,
> and occasions more edifying, too, I suppose.
> But we have to witness for ourselves what comes for us
> nor be distracted by barkers of irrelevant ware;
> and a pretty good world, I say, arrived that night
> when that woman came farming right out of her clothes,
> by God,
>
> At the state fair.[1]

Certain lines in this stanza—the first two, the last four—are quite clearly different from anything in "Thinking for Berky"; they are looser, more conversational. But only a few of the words—"pretty good," for example—are foreign to the diction of the other poem. The use of the word *farming* in each poem is indicative of Stafford's unusual sensitivity to context: in "Thinking for Berky" the word has a hard and desperate sound, as if the parents farmed mostly with sickles and whips. In "Adults Only" the word is quirky but exact: the woman comes rolling out of her clothes like a combine out of a wheat field.

Along the spectrum from pure conversation to elaborate oratory, Stafford's poems occupy a relatively narrow range. But his acquaintance with that zone, and his sense of what context can yield, seem to have been, from the beginning, more than sufficient to the creation of explosions which many other poets would expend far more energy to bring about.

---

[1] William Stafford, *Stories that Could Be True: New and Collected Poems* (New York: Harper & Row, 1977), 93. Subsequent citations of this book will be made in the text, to *Stories* and a page number; quotations from other collections, all published by Harper & Row, will be identified in the text and followed by a page number.

Stafford's first collection, *West of Your City* (1960), was published in an elegant limited edition by a small press; except for a few poems which have been widely anthologized, and fourteen which were reprinted in *The Rescued Year*, the work in it was unavailable for several years, until the appearance of *Stories That Could Be True: New and Collected Poems* (1977), which reprints Stafford's first two books, and three others: *The Rescued Year* (1966), *Allegiances* (1970), and *Someday, Maybe* (1973). *West of Your City* turns out to be a first book of great maturity, distinctiveness, and understated power; Stafford, it seems, is among those rare poets who do not publish a book before they have hit their stride. We are in danger now of taking Stafford's particular stride for granted, but it must have been earned courageously; most of the noisier proponents of this or that way of writing poems in the 1950s would have been reluctant to embrace these quiet, durable poems. In meters that are never too insistent, yet never out of control, the poems in *West of Your City* record the observations of a questing spirit— evoking the past, revealing in the present many small but significant signs of where we are, and heading westward, into the future. The tone is discursive, the diction conversational, but everywhere in these poems shines Stafford's amazing gift for arranging ordinary words into resonant truth and mystery: "Wherever we looked the land would hold us up."

Though *West of Your City* was out of print before it came to wide attention, *Traveling Through the Dark* (1962) immediately established Stafford as a poet of rare gifts and unusual productivity. As the citation of the poetry judges for the National Book Award put it, "William Stafford's poems are clean, direct and whole. They are both tough and gentle; their music knows the value of silence." True enough; and one is then awe-struck to realize that these splendid poems—seventy-six of them, enough for two collections— were published only two years after *West of Your City*. As James Dickey once said, poetry appears not only to be the best way for Stafford to say what he wants to say, but also to be the easiest. This may be an exaggeration, but it is true that even in the most casual of circumstances, Stafford's utterances can have the distinctive and memorable flavor of his poetry, as when he closes a letter, "So long—I look toward seeing you everywhere."

In *Traveling Through the Dark*, the major advance over the first book is in breadth of tone. Looking at the ways in which his poems can break into humor, I begin to think that Stafford has a talent, never quite indulged, for self-parody. He is attuned to the effects he can create, and so sensitive to various modes of surprise, that even within a restricted range of word choices, he can be haunting, wistful, or slyly humorous.

In *The Rescued Year*, there are many poems which surprise only because they did not exist before; they are otherwise very much like Stafford's earlier work. As he says at the end of "Believer,"

> You don't hear me yell to test the quiet or try to shake
> the wall, for I understand that the wrong sound weakens
> what no sound could ever save, and I am the one
> to live by the hum that shivers till the world can sing:—
> May my voice hover and wait for fate,
>   when the right note shakes everything. (*Stories*, p. 123)

But if the poems continue to sound exactly like the poems his earlier work led us to expect, there are among the subjects of these poems a few matters which Stafford had not previously staked out as his kind of territory. The title poem, longer and more leisurely than most of Stafford's earlier poems, is a fine evocation of a year of happiness lived in his youth, when his father had a job in another town, and moved the family there. In "Following the *Markings* of Dag Hammarskjöld: A Gathering of Poems in the Spirit of His Life and Writings," Stafford fashions a moving long sequence of related poems, the more valuable because they do not depend too heavily on the inspiration acknowledged in the title. And in "The Animal That Drank Up Sound," he creates a myth of remarkable freshness, which has yet the flavor of folklore that makes it sound ancient. The first part of the poem tells how the animal came down and swallowed the sounds of the earth, until at last all sound was gone, and he starved. In the second section, a cricket, who had been hiding when the animal came by, awoke to a heavy stillness, and with one tentative sound, brought everything back:

> It all returned, our precious world with its life and sound,
> where sometimes loud over the hill the moon,
> wild again, looks for its animal to roam, still,
> down out of the hills, any time.
> But somewhere a cricket waits.
>
> It listens now, and practices at night. (*Stories*, p. 147)

The boldness of this poem and others in *The Rescued Year* is carried forward into *Allegiances* and *Someday, Maybe*. The strain of odd metaphor against discursive diction is rewardingly increased: "He talked like an old gun killing buffalo,/and in what he said a giant was trying to get out."

As always, any observation might start a poem, but in *Allegiances* Stafford seems freer to let the observation go either as far as necessary, or to let it stop when it should. Several of these poems are tiny, fragmentary, but complete, like "Note":

> straw, feathers, dust—
> little things
>
> but if they all go one way,
> that's the way the wind goes. (*Stories*, p. 181)

Sometimes these small observations are gathered in bunches under one title, like "Brevities" or "Religion Back Home." In these clusters of short poems, the tension between their disparateness, and their being gathered under one title, reminds us of Stafford's sense of his vocation: "The world speaks everything to us./It is our only friend."

More and more often in *Allegiances* and *Someday, Maybe*, Stafford evokes the spirits of those whose ancestors lived here before white people came. "People of the South Wind," for example, is a mythic explanation of where a person's breath goes after he dies; the tone is radically conversational, even for Stafford, but the effect is, magically, dignified. And the title poem of *Someday, Maybe*, "The Eskimo National Anthem," recalls a song, "Al-eena, Al-wona," that echoes often through the speaker's daily life. The phrase is translated as "Someday, Maybe." (A small misfortune has befallen the version of the poem in *Stories*: "Someday" is misprinted as "Somebody.") The poem ends with the observation that the song might be to blame if the speaker's life never amounts to anything, though it is a comforting keepsake. The paradox is gracefully concealed; it is hardly possible, in the poetic world of William Stafford, to notice so much, and still live a life that amounts to nothing.

The gathering of previously uncollected poems, *Stories That Could Be True*, extends the range of Stafford's apparently boundless empathy. Many of the speakers in these poems are not the observer, but the thing observed—wind, seeds, trees, ducks—and they speak of how things are with them, in a voice that is of course truly Stafford's, but which is profoundly convincing; it is a lively extension of the myth-making tendency that began to be displayed in *The Rescued Year*. It is also noteworthy that in these more recent poems, Stafford often permits himself a strictness of meter and rhyme that is rare in his earlier work. He has usually preferred to suggest a form rather than commit himself fully to it; but there are poems here whose simplicity, memorability, and charm are like the verses people who speak English have had in their heads from childhood. It takes a lifetime of thoughtful and wide-ranging work to arrive at the stage where one can write a miniature masterpiece like "At the Playground," which in its way can speak for what Stafford has been up to all along, and for what he has been looking for in the books he has published since:

> Away down deep and away up high,
> a swing drops you into the sky.
> Back, it draws you away down deep,
> forth, it flings you in a sweep
> all the way to the stars and back
> —Goodby, Jill; Goodby, Jack:
> shuddering climb wild and steep,
> away up high, away down deep. (*Stories*, p. 11)

II

In the past few years, Stafford has published a number of prose pieces about how his poems come to be. Many of these have been collected in *Writing the Australian Crawl* (1978) and *You Must Revise Your Life* (1986), both published in the University of Michigan's Poets on Poetry series. It is widely recognized by now that Stafford presents himself as a poet for whom the process is in many ways more important than the product. He wants an openness to any possibility during the initial stages of—I almost said *composition*. He is therefore suspicious of technique, especially if it is used for its own sake, or used to force a poem in a preconceived direction. His rhetorical stance toward these matters is exemplified in "Some Notes on Writing," a prose statement at the beginning of his most recent collection of poems, *An Oregon Message* (1987):

> My poems are organically grown, and it is my habit to allow language its own freedom and confidence. The results will sometimes bewilder conservative readers and hearers, especially those who try to control all emergent elements in discourse for the service of predetermined ends.
> Each poem is a miracle that has been invited to happen. But these words, after they come, you look at what's there. Why these? Why not some calculated careful contenders? Because these chosen ones must survive as they were made, by the reckless impulse of a fallible but susceptible person. I must be willingly fallible in order to deserve a place in the realm where miracles happen.
> Writing poems is living in that realm. Each poem is a gift, a surprise that emerges as itself and is only later subjected to order and evaluation. (p. 10)

As direct as these paragraphs seem, there are certain questions which they do not quite answer. Is Stafford describing a process like automatic writing? Language must have "its own freedom and confidence," and "after they come," by "reckless impulse," the words "must survive as they were made." This is certainly suggestive of a method which involves little in the way of revision. On the other hand, the poems are "later subjected to order and evaluation," whatever "order" might mean here.

In "A Way of Writing," one of the essays collected in *Writing the Australian Crawl*, Stafford notes that others "talk about 'skills' in writing." He goes on to explain his difficulty with the concept:

> Without denying that I do have experience, wide reading, automatic orthodoxies and maneuvers of various kinds, I still must insist that I am often baffled about what "skill" has to do with the precious little area of confusion when I do not know what I am going to say and then I find out what I am going to say. That precious interval I am unable to bridge by skill.... Skill? If so, it is a skill we all have, something we learned before the age of three or four. (p. 19)

It is statements like that last one, taken out of context—sometimes, admittedly, by Stafford himself—which have recently given rise to the notions that Stafford wants all poems to be equally valued, that writing teachers should not evaluate student work, and that a kind of open basking in possibility is more important than any talk of how to make a poem better than it is. "Well," we hear the teacher saying, "this might show us something important. Next?" I ponder the Zen of workshopping, the guru as wise ignoramus.

Again. In an interview with Cynthia Lofsness (*Writing the Australian Crawl*) Stafford speaks suspiciously of technique:

> It's not a technique, it's a kind of stance to take toward experience, or an attitude to take toward immediate feelings and thoughts while you're writing. That seems important to me, but technique is something I believe I would like to avoid. (p. 98)

In conversation on various occasions since that interview, which was first published in 1972, Stafford has said similar things; but in those contexts, the interviewer's definition of technique, included in her question, has not always been present as a background: "I would define technique as a belief on the part of the poet that there are certain rules or forms into which his ideas must be channeled for proper expression. A belief that there is a proper 'framework,' into which he must fit his specific feelings...."

It is instructive to note the extremism of the positions Stafford opposes when he talks about these things. In one case, we have the desire to control absolutely every impulse, to work everything toward a predetermined effect or end; in another, we have a belief in rules, in a proper framework. The first method is obsessive, the second oversimplified and ignorant. Of course these ways of trying to write poems are doomed; and of course it is better to be ready for surprises. More conservative voices than Stafford's have been heard to say, for example, that a poem glides on its own melting, like a piece of ice on a hot stove, or that poetry should come as naturally as leaves to a tree.

Perhaps Stafford is increasingly concerned to address the notion that all one needs to be a poet is to learn the things that are taught in writing classes. It may be that his own extraordinarily prolific output has often brought him questioners who want to know exactly how he does it. It is certain that he falls rather easily into moods that inspire him to easily misunderstood pronouncements; he says what he means, most of the time, but the most audible part of what he says is the more radical part. In the passage about "skill" above, for example, he is careful to establish that he has "experience, wide reading, automatic orthodoxies and maneuvers of various kinds."

In a couple of passages from *You Must Revise Your Life* there are useful examples, first of the haste with which Stafford can sometimes say things which his poems contradict, and second, of the ease and friendliness with which he can discuss matters of great technical importance. In a short piece about a short poem, "Where 'Yellow Cars' Comes From," there are these sentences about sound:

> As for sound, I live in one great bell of sound when doing a poem; and I like how the syllables do-si-do along. I am not after rhyme—so limited, so mechanical. No, I want all the syllables to be in there like a school of fish flashing, relating to other syllables in other words (even words not in this poem, of course), fluently carrying the reader by subliminal felicities all the way to the limber last line. (p. 44)

The paragraph begins with the general and modulates toward the specific poem, but the dismissal of rhyme sounds general.

A few pages later, in another essay about the same poem, he writes:

> And line breaks, too, happen along. By now, in my writing, many considerations occur to me in jotting down even first hints of a poem. I like to feel patterns—number of stresses, multi-unstressed or few-unstressed sound units, lines that carry over and make a reader reach a bit, pauses in the line that come at varying, helpful places: early in the line, middle of the line, later in the line. But I make the lines be the way they are by welcoming opportunities that come to me, not by having a pattern in mind. (p. 47)

If we think of technique, not as some rigid belief in proper frameworks and rules, but as a partial and growing understanding of an enormous array of verbal effects and opportunities, some of them traditional and some of them more nearly unprecedented, then it becomes harder to entertain the idea that Stafford cares much less about it than Richard Wilbur does.

III

In the light of these remarks, it is useful to look more closely at "Thinking for Berky," and at one or two poems from Stafford's most recent collections. A sense of Stafford's skill, or technique, or outrageous good fortune, is barely suggested in the brief metrical description at the beginning of this essay.

For some readers, the metrical question will be difficult; for even more doctrinaire readers, it will be easy, or nonexistent. There are respectable people, in the school of J. V. Cunningham, who believe that lines either exemplify a strict meter, or that they do not, and that a mixture of both kinds of line in one poem is some sort of default on the contract. But Stafford has arrived at the contract, if any, with nearly evasive tact: the meter of the first three lines is so far from firmly established that it is purely a matter of opinion where to place stresses among the syllables "must have some" in the fourth. Yet, even veering as they do between nine and twelve syllables, and between four and six stresses, the first four lines arrive satisfyingly at their ends, and at the rhyme. Much of the satisfaction emerges almost unnoticed from rhymes and echoes elsewhere than at the ends of lines: *joined-kind-end, screaming-drama*, the march of four *l* sounds proceeding from beginning to end of words in the first two lines.

This kind of local sonic richness continues throughout the poem, even as a larger net is also being cast, to make connections among stanzas by means of end-words not included in the "official" rhyme scheme (*patrol-soul*, both connecting with the second stanza's rhymes; *come-came, wood-misunderstood*), and over the whole poem by the echo between *bed* and *beds*, and the repetition of listening and night in the first and final lines.[2] Meanwhile, another aspect of the poem's rhythmical balance is maintained by the tension between lengthening lines and shortening sentences.

Stafford's prose remarks seem intended to forestall the conclusion that these kinds of things are always calculated. Very inexperienced readers often want to know how many of a poem's effects could have been planned, and most practitioners know that many are not. But most practitioners also know that thinking about such matters, in one's own poems and in others', is a useful way to deepen acquaintance with them, and to grow toward recognizing them when an unpressurized knowledge, disguised as good luck, brings them into the lines we are writing.

The convergence of impulses—from the tradition and from the individual train of thought—can even result in a sonnet. The discovery that a sonnet is under way is usually made before all the rhymes are in place, so some searching and rephrasing must usually be done. During that process, I imagine, Stafford might constantly weigh the effects of either staying with tradition, or noticeably departing from it, perhaps to the point that strict readers might decide that the result is not a sonnet. Here, for example, is "Seeing and Perceiving," from *A Glass Face in the Rain* (1982):

> You learn to like the scene that everything
> in passing loans to you—a crooked tree
> syncopated upward branch by pre-
> established branch, its pattern suddening
> as you study it; or a piece of string
> forwarding itself, that straight knot so free
> you puzzle slowly at its form (you see
> intricate but fail at simple); or a wing,
> the lost birds trailing home.
> These random pieces begin to dance at night
> or when you look away. You cling to them
> for form, the only way that it will come
> to the fallible: little bits of light
> reflected by the sympathy of sight. (p. 46)

---

[2] For a while in the early 1970s, Stafford read this poem aloud, and authorized reprinting it, with a slightly different last line: "While in the night you lie, so far and good " It has admirable qualities, but Stafford had reverted to the original ending by the time he assembled *Stories That Could Be True*.

I believe it is possible to be drawn into this poem, to follow its sentences with enough absorption not to notice rhyme until the final couplet. It is unusual to find a sonnet, or near-sonnet, in which the form itself does not seem to constitute much in the way of a statement; these days, to elect the sonnet form is usually to make a gesture with something behind it. Here, the form seems gradually to evolve, as it might "come/to the fallible," so that the short ninth line has a rightness that outweighs its failure to meet rigid expectation.

Rhyme is infrequent in Stafford's most recent collection, *An Oregon Message* (1987). One of its more obtrusive manifestations is in "Brother," a mysterious poem which defies literal paraphrase:

> Somebody came to the door that night.
> "Where is your son, the one with the scar?"
> No moon has ever shone so bright.
>
> A bridge, a dark figure, and then the train—
> "My son went away. I can't help you."
> Many a clear night since then. And rain.
>
> I was the younger, the one with the blood.
> "You better tell Lefty what his brother done."
> They went off cursing down the road.
>
> A boy in the loft watching a star.
> "Son, your big brother has saved your life."
> He never came back, the one with the scar. (p. 98)

The difficulty of assembling the details into coherence is emphasized by the self-contained lines, each of which is resonant with possibility. There is reference to what sounds like a threatening encounter, and possibly some catastrophe; but the details hang in the memory as they might in the mind of a traumatized victim of imperfect recall. Because it borders on the incomprehensible, in most prose senses of the term, the poem benefits immeasurably from the added mystery of regular rhyme. A line such as the fourth, with its assortment of three images which could add up in several ways concluding in departure, death, or rescue, becomes one of twelve beads on a string, attractive in itself; the same is true of the seventh, in which the phrase "the one with the blood" could suggest several paraphrases. The poem is reminiscent of certain ballads, like "Sir Patrick Spens," from which such usual narrative elements as motivation are absent, so that the events take on a stark necessity.

Some readers have called Stafford's poetry "simple," as if it had failed to comprehend our civilization's great variety and complexity. But the simplicity exemplified in "Brother" is exactly the kind that makes for complexity in contemporary life. None of us knows enough, it seems. William Stafford's many ways of reminding us of that, and of offering consolation, constitute one of the most secure and solid of recent poetic achievements.

WITH KIT, AGE 7, AT THE BEACH

We would climb the highest dune,
from there to gaze and come down:
the ocean was performing;
we contributed our climb.

Waves leapfrogged and came
straight out of the storm.
What should our gaze mean?
Kit waited for me to decide.

Stand on such a hill,
what would you tell your child?
That was an absolute vista.
Those waves raced, far and cold.

"How far could you swim, Daddy,
in such a storm?"
"As far as was needed," I said,
and as I talked, I swam.

Jonathan Holden

ON "WITH KIT, AGE 7, AT THE BEACH"

It was 1964 when I first encountered Stafford's little lyric "With Kit, Age 7, at the Beach," and I immediately liked it, especially the turn which its last line takes; but it wasn't until years later, rereading Martin Heidegger's *Introduction to Metaphysics*, that I could say that I had grasped the gist of the poem's argument, an argument built into the poem's very structure. The last time I saw Bill Stafford himself—at the Port Townsend Writers conference in July 1987, where we were both on the staff—I asked him if he had read the Heidegger. He said he hadn't, and this pleased me, because it meant that Stafford and Heidegger had independently discovered the same metaphysical ground. Or, put it more precisely: they had discovered, on their own, strikingly similar metaphors by which to illuminate the same ontological vantage point, structures subtle enough to convince me that, as with mathematics, there are certain kinds of subject matter which can be accurately named (or "measured") *only* by means of certain metaphors. It is impossible, for example, to make certain kinds of scientific measurements—say to describe accurately, or even *to define the meaning of* the rate of acceleration of a particle—without a differential equation. It is similarly impossible to dramatize certain kinds of experience—say ontological intuitions—without utilizing the imagery and the structure of lyric.

What was especially pleasing about this "accidental" similarity between the Heidegger and the Stafford texts was that it constituted evidence that metaphysical intuition (and the metaphors to express it) is *not*, as it might sometimes appear to be, entirely subjective. Poetic metaphor, like the calculus, like Chemistry, constitutes a body of knowledge.

The fundamental issue Heidegger grapples with in his *Introduction* he sets forth as follows:

> Why are there essents...? Why, that is to say, on what ground? from what source does the essent derive? on what ground does it stand? ...The question aims at the ground of what is insofar as it is. To seek the ground is to try to get at the bottom.

A little later, Heidegger approaches this book's main question phenomenologically, by means of imagery:

> How does it stand with being? ...We hear the flying bird, even though strictly speaking we should say a grouse is nothing audible, it is no manner of tone that fits into a scale. And so it is with the other senses. We touch velvet, silk; we see them directly as this or that kind of essent, the one different from the other. Wherein lies and wherein consists being? ...Is it situated anywhere at all?

Heidegger's quest for "being," like all religious quests, is for the Absolute, and with this word—"the Absolute"—in mind we are equipped to read Stafford's "With Kit...."

The first two stanzas set the scene of a dramatic lyric—father and son climb a dune, to get a vantage point from which to observe the world—and they end in a question, "What should our gaze mean?" In the third stanza, with "*such* [my italics] a hill," the poem takes on allegorical overtones, and there is posed the word "absolute," on which the poem turns—a word which retroactively is going to be, in the context of the poem's final word, "swam," radically enriched. The "vista" spread out before the viewers, a vista not unlike the 18th-century Sublime, is so grand, so menacing, dwarfs the viewers so totally that it might as well be an absolute vista, be mistaken for The Absolute. But the word "absolute" is double. Its Latin origins, *ab* (from) + *solvere* (to set free), suggest that the "absolute" is never out there in a vista like the ocean seen from a dune. It is "set free" from any boundaries. We are swimming in it *now*. We *are* it. In fact, the very literal ground on which we are standing—"such a hill"—in order to survey the world, no matter how

"high," is inherently unstable: it is a "dune." Terry Eagleton, in his paraphrase of Heidegger's *Being and Time*, writes:

> The world is not an object 'out there' to be rationally analyzed, set over
> against a contemplative subject: it is never something we can get outside of
> and stand over against. We emerge as subjects from inside a reality which
> we can never fully objectify, which encompasses both 'subject' and 'ob-
> ject', quite as much as we constitute it.

This is superb paraphrase. But it is only paraphrase. It lacks the agonized
sense that we find in Heidegger of the philosophic mind in the very process
of attempting to clarify. It lacks the concreteness, the drama, the sense of realization (through structural discovery) that we find in Stafford's poem. If we
compare the lucidity of Stafford's poem to the turgidness of Heidegger, or
compare the narrative vision of Wordsworth's *The Prelude* to the psycholin-
guistic jargon of Jacques Lacan (who deals with the same issues which
Wordsworth does), we are tempted to conclude that, when it comes to exis-
tential/phenomenological inquiry or psycho-linguistic inquiry, achieved poetry is probably a mode of discourse that is conspicuously superior to that of
systematic philosophy.

WAKING AT 3 A.M.

Even in the cave of the night when you
wake and are free and lonely,
neglected by others, discarded, loved only
by what doesn't matter—even in that
big room no one can see,
you push with your eyes till forever
comes in its twisted figure eight
and lies down in your head.

You think water in the river;
you think slower than the tide in
the grain of the wood; you become
a secret storehouse that saves the country,
so open and foolish and empty.

You look over all that the darkness
ripples across. More than has ever
been found comforts you. You open your
eyes in a vault that unlocks as fast
and as far as your thought can run.
A great snug wall goes around everything,
has always been there, will always
remain. It is a good world to be
lost in. It comforts you. It is
all right. And you sleep.

Margaret Atwood

ON "WAKING AT 3 A.M."

Many of William Stafford's poems seem to me to be devotional in nature. But devotional in a muted, late-twentieth century mode. When you listen to a Stafford poem spoken (and Stafford's is a poetry for the speaking voice, as distinct from the chanting voice or the singing voice), you hear, among other things, the other, earlier voices that may be shining through from behind it. What I hear behind this poem is Protestant, even Puritan, in tonality; a plainsong. There is something of the Henry Vaughan of "Eternity," matter-of-factly seen as "a great ring of pure and endless light"; the Blake of the "Songs"; George Herbert, with his metaphors for religious experience drawn from commonplace objects; but all of these with the central object of the devotional poem removed to a greater distance, made more problematic, and shorn of its name, and the mode transmuted from the ecstatic to the stoic.

The voice is serious, though personal and informal, like a New England Puritan's spiritual journal—again, transposed to our new sadder, less certain century. The speaker's notes to himself about how one remains alive; about the small affirmations that can be wrung from the too-large, too-cold, too-remote universe that surrounds us and in which we feel ourselves cut adrift, "free and lonely": a pairing familiar to us. Such small comforts will have to do, because they are the best thing available under the circumstances; and they may add up to a good deal, after all. Not salvation, exactly. But more than might be expected.

If "Waking at 3 A.M." were a piece of music, it would be (formally speaking) a congregational hymn, though sung by one voice; if a building, it would be a white wooden meeting house. But to say that a thing has a plainness and simplicity of line is not to say it lacks complexity or mystery. Often the simplest form is also the most enigmatic. Take the egg.

Like many of Emily Dickinson's poems—which spring from the same unornamented Protestant tradition—"Waking at 3 A.M." proceeds by a series of riddles. These however are not so obviously riddles, and not so obviously answered.

The poem begins comprehensibly enough, with four lines about the experience of being awake and alone in the middle of the night. Fair enough, although we may pause to ask what sort of loving things belong in the category of "what doesn't matter." The "big room no one can see" is any child's room at night, but also the same as the "cave of night"; both are darkness, which encloses without offering a limit to the eye. Darkness can be as big as a room or as big as the sky, or as big as the impenetrably dark universe. Although it is big, this darkness is claustrophobic rather than comforting. It is the opposite of cosy.

But what are we to make of the next three lines?

> ...you push with your eyes till forever
> comes in its twisted figure eight
> and lies down in your head.

Pushing with the eyes captures exactly the feeling of what we do, with our eyes, in the dark. But what is this strange "twisted figure eight," and why is it the shape taken by "forever"?

A figure eight is the shape the Magician juggles with, in the Tarot Pack, and is supposed in some interpretations to be a symbol of Eternity. It is also the shape of the Mobius Strip, that conundrum you can make by twisting a strip of paper once and glueing the ends together, the property of which is that it has only one side. Students are usually asked to prove this by running a finger along it; they find that their end is in their beginning. It is the Celtic snake with its tail in its mouth. "Twisted"? It does not exist in two planes, but in three; it's an eight taken by top and bottom half and twisted so that it separates at the intersection of the halves and becomes a single line which runs through three dimensions. It is imagined not as a static shape but as a dynamic one—it is "forever" because it *runs on* forever, around and around the line of the figure eight.

The next two images are suggested naturally by this flowing "forever": the water flowing in the river, and the "tide" in the grain of the wood. (Trees have tides, as their sap travels up in spring and down in fall.) Through contemplating this flowing motion, the meditator becomes a kind of space—not a "cave" or a "big room," but a "storehouse." But what about this "secret storehouse that saves the country,/so open and foolish and empty"? How can a storehouse with nothing in it, not even wisdom—for it is "foolish"—save anything? And yet, we are told, the "country" is saved. Someone other than the meditator is saved; or something, because "country" can mean both a collectivity of nationals and an expanse of land.

Perhaps the storehouse (which is also the speaker) has the power to save because it is open; "foolish" (from the worldly point of view) because it has given all away; empty, because what was once in it has gone for the general welfare. "Secret," because its gifts were given in silence, and because they were held back until all other resources had been used up. Perhaps in the background of this paradoxical image are Pharoah's storehouses in the Biblical story of Joseph in Egypt, which held supplies stored up against famine, and were opened and emptied in time of extreme need.

So the flowing figure eight of "forever" and the flow of river and tree move into a vision of another kind of flow—the flow of giving, which always moves out and away from the giver. The night meditator feels the flow of eternity moving through him, outward, towards the world. He becomes a vehicle—an empty space, because emptied; and empty also because one must be empty in order to receive such a flow, spiritual emptiness being a precondition for the reception of the mystical experience, as mystics from all faiths have testified.

In the third stanza the meditator experiences the result of his spiritual openness. "More than has ever/been found" arrives, to replace his initial feeling of being lost; the immensity of the universe, its inexhaustibility, its unnameability—it is just "more"—become a source of comfort rather than a trigger for Cartesian fears. The closed "cave" and "room" images, having transmuted themselves into the "secret storehouse," transform again, into an ever-expanding "vault that unlocks as fast/and as far as your thought can run."

As soon as this space has opened, it becomes closed again, although in a very different way. It is now "snug," and the loneliness and abandonment of the opening lines have been changed to a sense of security and comfort. "It is/a good world to be/lost in," partly because the speaker is not truly lost but cradled within a "great snug wall," which is apprehended as permanent.

The speaker is no longer orphaned, unloved, but parented by the universe, as the end of the poem makes clear. The last three lines have the simplicity and trust of a child's bedtime prayer. "It comforts you" and "It is/all right"— the second being what every mother says, more or less, after a child's nightmare—render the enclosing universe maternal and tender. The childlikeness of the speaker, both as the initial orphan and as the protected child of the last lines, is reinforced by the scarcity of adjectives, and the choice of very plain ones: big, secret, great, snug, good.

Incidentally, there are only two lines that don't rhyme (or off-rhyme) with other lines in the poem, the ones terminating with "head" and "sleep," and of these, "head" is a concealed off-rhyme with "tide in." So the last line of the poem does not connect back to any of the previous lines, and does not complete a sound pattern. Instead it seems to point to something unfinished, beyond the poem—to some other rhyme that will come later.

This poem is both an account of meditation and an object of meditation itself. It does not merely lay out the result of the experience, it forces the reader to undergo the process by attempting to solve the riddles it poses. As with a New England meeting house, it presents us with basic materials, elegantly put together. And what you see, at first, is by no means all you get.

ASK ME

Some time when the river is ice ask me
mistakes I have made. Ask me whether
what I have done is my life. Others
have come in their slow way into
my thought, and some have tried to help
or to hurt: ask me what difference
their strongest love or hate has made.

I will listen to what you say.
You and I can turn and look
at the silent river and wait. We know
the current is there, hidden; and there
are comings and goings from miles away
that hold the stillness exactly before us.
What the river says, that is what I say.

Linda Pastan

ON "ASK ME"

Writing about poems is not something that I am comfortable doing, so I have chosen Bill's poem "Ask Me" because it seems to give me permission to be almost silent, to stand with him a moment quietly at the edge of the frozen river and to just wait.

In a way, this is something that I have been doing with him for years. In the mornings, alone in my study, when the blank page seems to stare malevolently up at me demanding a new poem, I have so often turned to his work, almost any page of it in any of his books. And I always find myself listening to a voice seemingly simple, addressing simply the most urgent of matters. ("Ask me whether/what I have done is my life.") Miraculously, and over and over again, I find myself wanting to engage with that voice, to talk back to it, to put something down on the empty page because he makes it seem at once so natural and so necessary to do so.

I do not mean to analyze "Ask Me" or to speculate on the answers to its several unanswerable questions. But I do want to say that this is a quintessentially Stafford poem and that the reader need go no further than the title itself to be invited in. "Ask Me," the writer says, and how can we fail to do so?

From time to time I meet someone who speaks of Stafford's poetry as kindly, benign, and full of homilies, and I am always mystified. Are we talking about the same poetry? In this particular poem we stand at the edge of a frozen place and are asked to contemplate some of the most devastating of possibilities. The mistakes hinted at here are clearly not typing errors. The acknowledgment that we may reach a place in our own lives where the strongest love or hate, where human intention, may not make any difference is one of the hardest things we have to think about, one of the most terrifying. This is only partly mitigated here, after a stanza break, by the possible comfort of shared conversation, by the possibility of some kind of eventual thaw.

American literature and landscape are full of rivers, and William Stafford is a very American poet. I won't speculate on whether these rivers are meant to stand for time or for the continuum of human life—analyze a river and you are in danger of ending up with hydrogen, oxygen, and assorted proteins. But I think it would be fair to say that much of the characterization of the river in this poem could also be a prescription for what a poem should be, what a Stafford poem so often is: a simple surface with hidden currents underneath, with comings and goings from miles away, and there right on the page, the stillness *exactly* before us, and the italics here are mine. "What the river says, that is what I say," the poet tells us.

I am deeply grateful to William Stafford not only because he himself will always listen to what you have to say but because he has rescued me time after time not only from the silence of the empty page but, with his wisdom and support, from the far more serious silence of desperation. What difference has his love made? My answer is that for me at least it has often made all the difference.

KNOWING

To know the other world you turn
your hand the way a bird finds angles
of the wind: what the wing feels
pours off your hand. Things invisible
come true, and you can tell. But are
there shy realities we cannot prove?
Your hand can make the sign—but begs for
more than can be told: even the world
can't dive fast enough to know that other world.

Tom Andrews

GLIMPSES INTO SOMETHING EVER LARGER

Anyone writing about William Stafford's poems has Stafford's uncanny example to aspire to. He has been so straightforward about his
work, has said so many useful things (especially in the two University of Michigan Press books, *Writing the Australian Crawl* and *You Must
Revise Your Life*), that I almost wonder if we shouldn't ask him to engage the
poems celebrated in this symposium. He has also made it clear what he
thinks about the practice of criticism—it's "like boiling a watch to find out
what makes it tick." And, in a characteristic turn, he has offered a shrewd
analysis of praise:

> You need to watch out, or a follower will
> praise you, and the stumbles you need for your life
> will be harder to take.

Still, I suspect Stafford wouldn't want his comments to get in the way of a
"reckless encounter" with one of his poems; at least I'll assume that as I try
to clarify what I find so valuable about "Knowing."

The story goes that when Kurt Gödel was a child his insatiable curiosity
prompted his parents to nickname him "Mr. Why." When I ran across that
anecdote recently in a biography of Gödel, I thought: Stafford! Who else
among contemporary American poets has been as nakedly curious in poem
after poem about the variousness of the world and the processes by which we
discover it? I say "nakedly" because he seems able to approach the poem
without anticipating in the least what he'll find there. It is this spirit of open-

ness, this receptivity to whatever comes along, that quickens me as I read him. And perhaps Stafford is able to make such good use of whatever comes along because his curiosity is so tenacious.

One of the things I love about "Knowing" is how that curiosity keeps turning on itself. The poem questions itself as it asserts itself; in Alberta Turner's phrase, Stafford "seems to assert but really invites." A precise prose rendering of "Knowing" is beyond me, and would seem to be contrary to the spirit of the poem. But I'm fascinated by the way the poem mimics a gesture of certainty—How do you know the other world? Well, "you turn/your hand..."—and, after the speaker's alert, respectful intelligence thoroughly interrogates that gesture, establishes a difficult rhythm of doubt, intuition, and affirmation.

"Knowing" is a model of efficiency. It says the needful and clears out. Again it's fascinating to watch Stafford take such a potentially "poetic" (or "Poetic") conceit as the opening lines and unfold from it a poem without the least bit of decoration or filigree. Each word is essential. A good example is the word "feels" in the third line. A hasty reader might dismiss the word outright as flat or unimaginative, but the careful echo of "angles" in the previous line combined with the torque and pull of the following word "pours" gives "feels," to my ear at least, an unlikely solidity and presence.

Where does a poem like "Knowing" come from? It seems to come from a quiet center. Robert Hass has suggested that sensibility, finally, is the triumph of James Wright's poems, and I think that's true also of Stafford's work. A typical Stafford poem has the stamp, like a thumbprint, of sensibility—that shrewd, gentle, quizzical, ironic, playfully metaphysical yet firmly grounded quality of attention that gives him the sense that "everything is telling one big story." It may be that Stafford's most helpful contribution to our poetry and to other poets (if that's not too grand a phrase) is the example of this sensibility, its inner generosity. Analogously, in a review of Louis Simpson's *At the End of the Open Road*, published in *Poetry* in 1964, Stafford wrote that

> the poems...lead again and again to an implied big story; the reader has a sense of living in a sustained pattern which works along behind the poems and makes of them a succession of glimpses into something ever larger.... In our time, this implied story is never embodied in a complete work—a *Paradise Lost* or a *Divine Comedy*—and apparently such an established story cannot be at this time convincingly delivered to us. But some writers do entertain hints that back of the shifting present there impends a meaning.

Stafford is such a writer, and he gives in his investigation of Simpson's poems an important insight into his own.

I said earlier that a precise prose rendering is at odds with the spirit of "Knowing." Reading the poem, and thinking of the ironic relation between the poem and the title, brings to mind a passage from the *Tao Te Ching* which may be emblematic: "He who thinks he knows, doesn't know. He who knows that he doesn't know, knows." But even that implies a measure of certainty that "Knowing" doesn't presume. The slippery world of a Stafford poem embodies, and provokes, a sense of alertness rather than assurance; as the speaker of "Knowing" puts it, "Your hand can make the sign—but begs for/more than can be told...." "Knowing" is a prime example of a poem in which Stafford's sensibility takes things—"the shifting present" as well as the "glimpses into something ever larger"—as he finds them, leaving their mystery intact:

> even the world
> can't dive fast enough to know that other world.

THINGS I LEARNED LAST WEEK

Ants, when they meet each other,
usually pass on the right.

Sometimes you can open a sticky
door with your elbow.

A man in Boston has dedicated himself
to telling about injustice.
For three thousand dollars he will
come to your town and tell you about it.

Schopenhauer was a pessimist but
he played the flute.

Yeats, Pound, and Eliot saw art as
growing from other art. They studied that.

If I ever die, I'd like it to be
in the evening. That way, I'll have
all the dark to go with me, and no one
will see how I begin to hobble along.

In The Pentagon one person's job is to
take pins out of towns, hills, and fields,
and then save the pins for later.

Alberta Turner

ON "THINGS I LEARNED LAST WEEK"

When people have asked me why William Stafford is my favorite poet, I have heard myself say, "Because he is so comfortable inside his own skin." Yet just now, looking for a poem that epitomizes what I mean, I realize how misleading that statement can be. "In a Corner" shows a moment of despair; "Confessions of an Individual" shows self-reproach; "A Glass Face in the Rain" anticipates a bleak self-dissolution; "Epitaph Ending in And" shows an unassuageable anger; "When You Go

Anywhere," a self-conscious selflessness; and "Why I Am Happy," a happiness so far and secret it is almost a brash defiance, as he "laugh[s] and crie[s] for every turn of the world, its terrible cold, innocent spin." These make "comfortable inside his own skin" sound insipid and untrue. Yet it is true. His comfort comes from his acute awareness of paradox and his faith that the world can be endured, even enjoyed, with all its paradoxes flying.

One of the poems that shows Stafford's awareness of paradox most clearly is "Things I Learned Last Week." Four of the seven stanzas are self-contained couplets, unusual for one who uses so much enjambment. None of the seven are linked by subject or syntax, and none, even the last one, interprets itself or any of the others or suggests a synthesis of tone or meaning for the whole poem. So we read this one with suspicion, our geiger counters clicking: (1) Ants passing on the right: Solid-state brains, creatures of habit? Creatures of courtesy? How dull, how safe, how frightening. (2) Sticky doors that elbows might open: Problems more easily solved by improvising? Serious problems made light of? Trifles made much of? (3) A man in Boston selling what everyone already knows: Funny? Not funny? (4) A pessimist playing the flute: to cheer himself up? A realist? An optimist fooling himself? (5) Yeats, Pound and Eliot studying art as the source of art: Discovering where art really comes from? Elaborating the obvious? Making themselves important? (6) "If I ever die": Pretending death's O.K.? Selfless? Selfish? (7) The Pentagon preparing for the next war: Caring pins for it? Not caring pins for it?

When readers finish the poem, they dutifully ask what it adds up to. They try one answer after another but still have trouble fitting all the separate items under one theme. Nor does the order of the sequence seem climactic or inevitable. So—we have to suspect (I say *suspect* because I think Stafford doesn't want us to come to a single stateable conclusion), that he wants us to bound on each separate statement as on a spring that will twang us off into a thicket of paradoxes, all harmless, all terrifying, most somehow amusing, and none cancelling its apparent opposites.

The thing I like about this poem, Bill, is that it lets me admit that self-reproach is self-indulgence and that selves are quite as inept as they are cruel, and are often wonderfully funny. To lift the terrible *ought* off a quivering self is a generous boon. Thank you.

1940

It is August. Your father is walking you
to the train for camp and then the War
and out of his life, but you don't know.

Little lights along the path glow under their hoods
and your shoes go brown, brown in the brightness
till the next interval, when they disappear in the shadow.

You know they are down there, by the crunch of stone
and a rustle when they touch a fern. Somewhere above,
cicadas arch their gauze of sound all over town.

Shivers of summer wind follow across the park
and then turn back. You walk on toward
September, the depot, the dark, the light, the dark.

David Young

SHIVERS OF SUMMER WIND

Lots of our best poets since World War II have been heavy breathers, characters with high energy, wild language, hectic lives and spectacular brands of individualism. One thinks of Roethke and Lowell, Berryman and Dickey, Plath and Sexton, Ginsberg and Bly. We wouldn't want to be without any of them, but we need a counter-tradition. Our culture is too easily infatuated by hyperbole and hucksterism, even in the arts. We need poets who pick up on the possibilities of plainness and understatement, who take us into little-noticed areas of rich simplicity and calm delight. Many of FIELD's symposia have reflected this need by celebrating the likes of Robert Francis, Randall Jarrell, and Elizabeth Bishop. It's a tradition in our own poetry that goes back through Williams and Frost to Dickinson, but it is reflected in many other areas of life, in the Shakers and Quakers, in much of our music and humor, our architecture and food.

But when I think of William Stafford, I don't just associate him with Emily Dickinson and Shaker furniture. I also think of Wallace Stevens and of jazz. That is because I think a big part of his success lies in his willingness to improvise, to play, even to fail deliberately at one moment in order to survive, artistically and psychologically, for the next. No poet can wholly escape being a rhetorician, a craftsman and manipulator, but every poet needs to find a way to forget craft, to wring the neck of rhetoric, to slip through the confines of his or her own style. Stafford has proved to be a master at eluding the stiffening effects of success and of infatuation with his own rhetorical accomplishments. A pinheaded critic can always prove to you that every move you come up with is just another bit of art, of craft, of rhetoric. To make yourself forget what you know about form and technique is, of course, just another way to arrive at them. But the argument is sophomoric and tedious, like the ones about relativity and determinism and Zeno's paradox. Experience refutes the traps of logic, and art goes wild and free.

How clearly I remember the summer afternoon two years ago when I read through *An Oregon Message*, Stafford's newest collection, then in galley proofs. By the end of my reading I was breathless with emotion and gratitude. I felt refreshed and confident about this country, about poetry, about my own life and its commitments. I wondered how it was that I could slip periodically into taking for granted things I ought to be daily praising and acknowledging: small things and large things all around my life, and the modest, deep-reaching poems of William Stafford.

But that taking for granted seems almost a part of Stafford's aesthetic. He wants to invoke rhythms of recognition and obliviousness. He has a larger public and a better claim to being our pre-eminent living poet than anyone else I can think of, but he is also deliberately self-effacing and offhand about what he does. His poems imply that poetry needs no special language. His persona and person and career seem to argue that the poet needs no special identity to justify a place among us. And he lives his life and writes his poems with remarkable and lovable consistency.

Going back to *An Oregon Message* now to select a poem to represent my delight of that day (as well as before and since), I find myself in a mild difficulty. Which poem to select? It was the entirety of the collection that moved and refreshed me. No single poem sums up that experience, partly because Stafford, in his playful and improvisatory aesthetic, his deep suspicion of final answers and summary statements, never allows a poem to carry the burden of saying and being everything, pretending to wholeness or permanence or authority or closure. One poem leads to the next, and as that happens you move along gradually, reading Stafford, into a spiritual affluence and openness to existence that you can't paraphrase and that no single poem need exemplify.

So I face a number of intriguing choices. Why not choose as exemplary a poem that fails in some respects, as for example I think this intriguingly titled piece does:

OWLS AT THE SHAKESPEARE FESTIVAL

How do owls find each other
in the world? They fly the forest
calling, "Darling, Darling."

Each time the sun goes out a world
comes true again, for owls:
trees flame their best color—dark.

At Shakespeare once, in Ashland,
when Lear cried out two owls
flared past the floodlights:

On my desk I keep a feather
for those far places thought
fluttered when I began to know.

I love the wit and rapidity of this, its juxtapositions, and I may well be
scorched by Stafford fans for calling it a failure, but I find the last stanza disappointing. The next-to-last stanza gives us a moment that might provoke a
flood of insight, but the speaker turns away from it, despite the colon that
seems to signal its arrival. He is left at his desk, with his token feather and his
somewhat lamely phrased thoughts about far places and beginning to know.
The poem fizzles out, abandoning its promise.

My point is not to show that Stafford is bad, but to indicate that there is
something exemplary and endearing about his less successful moments. In
this poem the distrust of big statements and the instinct for self-effacement
take over: this speaker isn't going to tangle with owls and Shakespeare as a
teller of truth. He's going to let us know about his respect for mysteries, his
knowing how little he knows. And he ducks out of the poem, clutching his
feather, leaving us with the task of making more sense of it than he has. This
strategy, if that is the right word for it, is in a sense what allows Stafford to
survive. No ovens, no jumping off bridges, no mental institutions for this fellow. He can shrug and cut his losses right in front of us, without embarrassment, without betraying his rhetoric or his persona. His modesty protects
him like an invisible armor. "Owls" is not a bad poem—it has great charm
and imagination—but the limitations of its ending might be used to illustrate
Stafford's peculiar strengths.

Another poem I might have picked is the sly and funny piece called
"Thinking About Being Called Simple by a Critic":

I wanted the plums, but I waited.
The sun went down. The fire
went out. With no lights on
I waited. From the night again—

those words: how stupid I was.
And I closed my eyes to listen.
The words all sank down, deep
and rich. I felt their truth
and began to live them. They were mine
to enjoy. Who but a friend
could give so sternly what the sky
feels for everyone but few learn to
cherish? In the dark with the truth
I began the sentence of my life
and found it was so simple there was no way
back into qualifying my thoughts
with irony or anything like that.
I went to the fridge and opened it—
sure enough the light was on.
I reached in and got the plums.

Just how ironic is the forswearing of irony here? The speaker is a kind of sim-pleton who sits in the dark and tries to use clichés about friends and enemies, light and dark, falsehood and truth, to talk himself out of the depression that comes from unjust criticism. He is more or less William Stafford, maybe re-acting to having someone like Paul Zweig accuse him of "strained simplicity" and "deliberate naïveté."[1] But he's also the sly character who thought of a poem that would allude, by way of defending itself and its author, to a nursery rhyme (little Jack Horner), a celebrated poem of extreme simplicity by an-other William ("This is Just to Say"), and maybe to an old joke about a moron and the light in the refrigerator. The poem is funniest at the end, when the mo-ment of illumination comes from the fridge and the deferred grats of fame and praise take the form of a midnight snack. It's all so open and self-deprecating that we are totally on Stafford's side, and Zweig or whoever is completely re-futed. Simplicity shines forth as the great thing it is. Yet it is nearly impossible to tell where the irony begins and leaves off. How do you read the statement, "They were mine/to enjoy"? No irony there? Okay, and the same for "Who but a friend" and "I began the sentence of my life" and "anything like that"? I'm with you, whatever you choose. I don't even know if there's irony built into the design and structure of the poem, though I have to suspect it. Under-staters are famous for this, but Stafford is wonderfully elusive, and we wouldn't have him any other way. Still, I suppose this poem seems a little friv-olous and specialized to stand for the excellences of a whole collection.

A better candidate would be the poem "Surrounded by Mountains." In its evocation of experience, its sense of wonder, and its diffidence about provid-ing answers, it is quintessentially Staffordian:

---

[1] Zweig's review appeared in *Partisan Review* in 1974. It is cited by Judith Kitchen in *Under-standing William Stafford* (U. of South Carolina, 1989). Kitchen also discusses "1940," 121-23.

Digging potatoes east of Sapporo
we would listen at noon to world news.

The little radio was in one of the furrows,
propped against a lunch bucket.

We didn't make any judgments. Our fields
were wide, slanting from wooded foothills.

    Religious leaders called for
    a revival of spirit in the world.

    Certain statesmen from important
    nations were considering a summit meeting.

Old Mrs. Osaka, permanently
bent over, stirred the clods beside her.

Rice fields, yellow as sunflowers,
marked off kilometers below us.

The shrine where the crows lived
had a bell that told us when rest was over.

Goodby, old friends, I remember the Prime Minister
talking, and the water jar in the shade.

The speaker could be Stafford, but he needn't be. His anonymity matches his technique of juxtaposing things, immediate and far, small world and big one, radio and furrow, without commenting on their significance to each other or in themselves. He represents a community that apparently preferred not to "make any judgments." If there's irony in the big world's representative, the little radio, being dwarfed by the furrows around it, he prefers to leave that inference to us. If statesmen and religious leaders and prime ministers dwindle before the reality of Mrs. Osaka and a simple water jar, that's not something he cares to insist upon. The poem's openness is its source of attraction. We can mine values from it, but would we be able to tell the difference between what we found and what we brought? Stafford the artist has again and again disavowed total control, and his speakers follow suit, leaving readers a great deal of room to evaluate, interpret and participate.

He has disavowed preoccupation with technique as well. It seems almost tactless to point out how well the choice of the couplet serves this poem, how neatly he pairs words and phrases that sound off each other—potatoes/Sapporo, bucket/judgment, sunflowers/kilometers, remember/Prime Minister/water jar—in a kind of offhand form of internal rhyme that is clearly more important than the end-of-line effects (e.g. six lines ending with S sounds, four with R sounds). Stafford doesn't have to measure and calculate such things. They are part of his working habit when he's attentive to words and sounds and sights. The little couplet about the shrine with the crows and bell has a kind of pun—told/tolled—but it's so lightly placed that you can't assume it's deliberate. Besides, what difference would that make? Stafford has offered you a quick-sketch pastoral, a chance to join, or rejoin, a peasant culture that will alter your perspective on history and power. You take it, and you trust him to get out of the way as much as possible. And he does.

So why did I finally chose "1940" over "Surrounded by Mountains"? In order to cite one more poem I liked? Partly, and partly because I think finally it has greater impact. I think it shows Stafford operating with all the same values and preferences that the other poems reveal, but reaching just a little farther and a little deeper. Perhaps comparisons are odious with this poet, but they necessarily surface when one is picking a poem to discuss and praise. I like "1940" because it plays a risky game with time, the second biggest mystery we live next to, and it can be heart-shaking if you let yourself be open to it.

If we could go back in time, what might we learn? What might it mean? Another powerful Stafford poem, "The Rescued Year," plays out that hypothesis too. Here the moment returned to is one of parting. As in "Surrounded by Mountains," history coexists with personal experience, but the parting of father and son, a final one, is what truly matters. If you could go back to that, the poem surmises, you would know so much more. And yet you would still know nothing, really. By saying "but you don't know" the poem makes you divide your consciousness between knowing and not-knowing. And you walk forward. Again as in "Surrounded by Mountains," particulars are all you have, are most of what you can know: cicadas, stones crunching, the little lights, your shoes. The distance of some forty-five years is also a distance from your observing eyes to your sometimes invisible feet as well as up to the overarching canopy of trees and cicadas. Ahead of you lies the partly known, the years you have lived since, and the unknown that even the wind turns back from, your mortality and the explanation, if there is any, of these rhythms of light and dark, knowing and not-knowing, the awesome movement of time.

Stafford handles all this in lightly rhymed triplets. He uses the second person to distance himself from his own experience and to offer it to us, in time, out of time. He uses the first and last stanza for panoramic shots and the two middle stanzas for closeups. One hundred and ten simple words. Lots of repetitions. Anticipations of the final line, with its repetitions and alterations, in effects like "you don't know.... You know" and "your shoes go brown, brown in the brightness." And again it feels a little bit beside the point to insist too much on the technique because Stafford himself would pooh-pooh it, refusing to take credit for the artful design of the experience, encouraging us to focus instead on the uncalculated, unmanageable life of the thing and its potential for touching our own lives.

Think what the poet has left out here! There is no mention of emotion, of the webs of experience that led Stafford to choose to be a conscientious objector during World War II, of when and how his father died. The choice is made to concentrate on the walk in the mysterious summer dark (I think of the middle section of "Ode to a Nightingale") in order to find out what meaning and illumination little things—fern, cicada, shiver of summer wind—will yield. The poet has gone back in time, defying its erasures and destructions, like Orpheus going down into hell. But he has refused to ask it to yield anything more than itself, the succession of moments by which we know and inhabit it. There is great mystery and depth of feeling here, and one can't help but admire the success of the poem's simple design and understated presentation. They make the walk from August to September a little easier. We step a little more lightly. Here they come: the depot, the dark, the light, the dark.

I reached for one plum and took four. Every time I opened the fridge the light was on. A reassuring experience. And I remember again my first, captivated reading of this book. I don't recall seeing any reviews of *An Oregon Message*. Not even ones that grumbled about "deliberate naïveté." But I may have missed them. Whether this essay constitutes a review or a salute, it will have served its purpose if it tempts some readers to put a few hours aside for that collection and be rewarded as I was.

MIROSLAV HOLUB
(1923-98)

M iroslav Holub was an anomaly among contemporary world literary figures: one of Czechoslovakia's most original and prolific poets, he was also a world-famous immunologist with more than 150 published scientific papers to his credit. The scientist and the poet in Holub are never very far apart: his poetry has a gimlet-eyed precision, a sophisticated detachment that allows him to explore historical and existential questions without a shred of sentimentality. The poet Seamus Heaney praised him as a poet who could lay things bare, "not so much the skull beneath the skin, more the brain beneath the skull." Holub's poetry, he wrote, is "too compassionate to be vindictive, too skeptical to be entranced." Shortly after the Prague Spring of 1968, he became a "nonperson" in his homeland, forbidden to publish or to be publicly discussed. In underground poetry, and then openly as he was gradually "rehabilitated" after the fall of Communism, he brought a sardonic and mordant humor to questions of totalitarianism and oppression. Astringent, absurdist, often employing scientific metaphors, Holub investigated the world's ironies with enormous intelligence and courage.

BOOKS IN ENGLISH TRANSLATION: *Selected Poems*, trans. Ian Milner and George Theiner (1967); *Sagittal Section*, trans. Stuart Friebert and Dana Hábová (1980); *Interferon, or On Theater*, trans. David Young and Hábová (1982); *Vanishing Lung Syndrome*, trans. Young and Hábová (1990); *Intensive Care: Selected and New Poems* (1996); *The Rampage*, trans. Young et al. (1997); *The Dimension of the Present Moment*, trans. Young (1990); *Shedding Life: Disease, Politics, and Other Human Conditions*, trans. Young (1997).

IN THE MICROSCOPE

Here too are dreaming landscapes,
lunar, derelict.
Here too are the masses,
tillers of the soil.
And cells, fighters
who lay down their lives
for a song.

Here too are cemeteries,
fame and snow.
And I hear murmuring,
the revolt of immense estates.

translated by Ian Milner

Edward Hirsch

SURVEYOR OF WORLDS

Reversing two traditional stereotypes, Vladimir Nabokov once said that his ideal was to bring together the passion of the scientist and the precision of the poet—and that is what Miroslav Holub has done in his probing, improvisational, investigative poems. Each of Holub's lyrics is an organic experiment in language, a testing of the limits of metaphor, not so much a rendering as an extension of experience. His work displays both a way of thinking and a method of inquiry, enacting what it is about: the condensation of disparate meanings, the transmutation of energy.

"What I basically like is novelty," Holub has said, "knowing by experiment, trial and error." He has shown a persistent interest in the continuum of living forms, the unceasing metamorphosis of shapes—hence his ongoing attraction to the biomorphic surrealism of Miró. His first characteristic strategy (the "before" section of *Before and After*: a rapid progression of near-surreal and quasi-objective images that move on the legs of a lucid Williams-like free verse) is evident in the early poem, "In the Microscope." Here the research immunologist peering into the lens of a microscope becomes a modern-day Prospero, a dispassionate surveyor of worlds. What he discovers is a universe analogous or parallel to our own, the human estate in miniature.

"In the Microscope" consists of five sentences—images—divided into two parts, uneven stanzas. How much is implied in this short poem by the rhetorical structure of "Here too"—how little about the social and political realms (Czechoslovakia in 1958) is stated directly; all is inferred. The poem begins with a striking image of estrangement, a world, like our own, suddenly defamiliarized. The evocation of the broken countryside, of "dreaming landscapes" (moon-like, outside the pale) is followed by a playful, Marxist-inspired image (the idea of a playful Marxism may be an oxymoron) in which biological organisms take on the character of rural proletarians. And this is followed by an image of cells which like their human counterparts die heroically for an ideal, a song.

The poem concludes with a contrasting pair of assertions: a death-ridden image, a life-giving music. More fully entering into the microscopic countryside, the vigilant day-dreamer envisions burial grounds for the dead cells. The invocation of a human-centered term, an almost classical notion of "fame" (the means by which soldiers become known for their deeds after death), is juxtaposed with the image of a snow-covered world (snow which covers up, obscures or obliterates). Underneath the snow, the poet (for by now he has become a poet) hears "murmuring," the faint stirrings of life, "the revolt of immense estates." The political intonations of this final phrase are inevitable, I think: the sense of protesting cells—the claim of citizens with distinct rights (the Estates of the Realm)—gathering to rebel or mutiny. What initially appeared to be a silent or uninhabited universe laid out on a glass slide for inspection has turned out to be a rich countryside teeming with rebellious life.

"In the Microscope" is a quick take, an act of attention. It implies the anthropomorphic even as it resists anthropomorphizing. It is the uncanny work of a poet who is both a keen observer—cool, anti-literary, watchful—and a wary visionary, a scientist who discovers the world—to borrow Blake's words—"Within a Moment: a Pulsation of the Artery."

MEETING EZRA POUND

I don't know what came first, poets or festivals.

Nevertheless, it was a festival that caused me to meet Ezra Pound.

They seated him in a chair on a square in Spoleto and pushed me towards him. He took the hand I extended and looked with those light blue eyes right through my head, way off into the distance. That was all. He didn't move after that. He didn't let go of my hand, he forgot the eyes. It was a lasting grip, like a gesture of a statue. His hand was icy and stony. It was impossible to get away.

I said something. The sparrows chirruped. A spider was crawling on the wall, tasting the stone with its forelegs. A spider understanding the language of a stone.

A freight train was passing through the tunnel of my head. A flagman in blue overalls waved gloomily from the last car.

It is interesting how long it takes for a freight train like that to pass by.

Then they parted us.

My hand was cold too, as if I'd touched the Milky Way.

So that a freight train without a schedule exists. So that a spider on a stone exists. So that a hand alone and a hand per se exists. So that a meeting without meeting exists and a person without a person. So that a tunnel exists—a whole network of tunnels, empty and dark, interconnecting the living matter which is called poetry at festivals.

So that I may have met Ezra Pound, only I sort of did not exist in that moment.

translated by Dana Hábová and Stuart Friebert

Larry Levis

So That: On Holub's "Meeting Ezra Pound"

Time is a violation, someone once remarked in a lecture hall, and then went on to say that the time in which one is born is a violation, that time itself is a violation committed against everyone alive. It makes us finite, and therefore the violation is always personal: its final form is both banal and intimate, for it is simply one's death, but finally all of us get the idea, an idea which is actually the absence of any idea, and, therefore, unimaginable. About as close as one can get to a statement of it is: "The meaning of life is that it stops." And there it is: the empty, white, blank, un-blinking center of it all.

It was an elaborately lovely way of saying the most obvious thing of all, and the pleasure was in the elaboration, and that, I think now, was the whole point of doing it, saying it there, in the first place, the pleasure of reformulating it.

Holub's poem is, among other things, an elegy, and maybe the remembrance above isn't inappropriate, especially because one theme Pound introduces and repeats in his *Cantos* is this one: "Time is the evil." And Holub, if we attend to the precision of what is supposedly a vague phrase, and isn't, concurs: "only I sort of did not exist in that moment." For "sort of" is precise, at least in the American idiom of the translation. It means that condition, common to all of us, just beneath all possible explanation of that "moment," *that* violation.

****

But what first fascinated me about Holub's poem had nothing to do with any of this. What I first noticed was a little riff, an echo, a variation, or so I thought. But it wasn't an echo nor any real variation. It was repetition. It was two notes from someone else's music, the two notes repeated no less than *six* times toward the close of Holub's prose poem. As if in answer to something. But to what? To this, I think:

> Cypri munimenta sortita est, mirthful, orichalchi, with golden
> Girdles and breast bands, thou with dark eyelids
> Bearing the golden bough of Argicida. So that:

> Ezra Pound, *Canto I*

So that what? I still wonder. In Pound's odd finale to his opening *Canto*, those two notes, that spondee, are not closure at all. The phrase leaves us looking off into space, at the cliff's edge, with only a colon as a guardrail. Pound violates, as in fact he has already interrupted, his translation of Book XI of *The Odyssey* from a Renaissance Latin source, itself a translation, so that.... But that's just the trouble with it. "So that:" is just *left* there, staving off closure on the way to Hell so that everything might continue, so that:

> So that a freight train without a schedule exists. So that a spider on a stone exists. So that a hand alone and a hand per se exist. So that a meeting without meeting exists and a person without a person. So that a tunnel exists, a whole network of tunnels, empty and dark, interconnecting the living matter which is called poetry at festivals.
> So that I may have met Ezra Pound, only I sort of did not exist in that moment.

But does every poet go to Hell, just because Homer, Virgil, Dante, Milton and Pound have? Is Holub going there? Or is that just Holub's problem, and, in a way, our own, that it isn't possible for us to get there anymore, that Hell has become the sound of chalk screeching on a blackboard in an auditorium, someone else's paradigm, bundle of connections, history's abandoned spiderweb with its cockeyed embroidery you can look right through? Look through to what?

****

The riptides and gnarly surf that *The Cantos* are so famous for, all the discontinuities of the polyvocal, spatial, juxtaposed, referential form, conceal the larger quest of the poem, which is passionately involved in a dream of continuity, not its opposite. And critical terms, like those above, try to protect us from a poem that is, therefore, passionately involved in its own failure. Pound said of it, at the end, "It won't...cohere" and "I botched it." And certainly what moves us in *The Pisan Cantos* is the poet's awareness of just how wrong he has been, what moves us is how the poet endures the tragedy of his name.

Holub arrives at the scene, intent here on restoring what continuity he can to the meeting, and yet ends up in a place at once too similar to Pound's, and too different, a place that becomes space: "So that I may have met...."

So that. If we take the occasion of the poem seriously, it's impossible not to hear that insistent repetition as anything less than an answer, even though it is an answer that fails.

****

O.K., so what happens? Holub takes Pound's hand. But then Pound won't let go of his hand. Or isn't able to let go of it. Or forgets to. Pretty soon Holub is holding hands, not with Pound, not with anyone, but with space itself, which has a surprisingly tight, light grip.

"How is it far if I think it?" was the question Pound asked in *The Cantos*. For Pound, for the Modernists generally, it was never far. But in this curious scene, Holub is by now holding hands with the Milky Way. Pound is dying and his death is inevitable. He is alive and he is not alive and Holub is with him and not with him in this moment.

Holub brilliantly avoids the kitsch of a delusional *ars poetica* here, for it might be consoling to think that "living matter" is, categorically, poetry. But Holub is too tough for a kind of thinking which overrates all things. His qualification is searing: "the living matter which is called poetry at festivals."

At festivals.

One need only to compare a literary festival with an ancient one to note, with Holub and Pound, what has been lost, or what we all assume has been lost. After all, we have little way of knowing what those festivals were like, and so we invest them with a vanished vitality. Who knows? Maybe the dancers on Crete were bored out of their minds like adolescents in a catechism class. Since we can never know, we speculate, we "invest" in the ancient ritual, and invest it with significance. How could we do otherwise?

World War II destroyed the Modernists' paradigms, their systems, mythical methods, their luxuriant organic forms. Time is a violation. "It's a faster game now, and a ruder one," said Ransom at the dawn of our era. If one wants to see the difference in sharp relief, he should listen to first lines on tapes Harvard has produced, first to Wallace Stevens: "This is where the serpent lives, the bodiless"; and then to John Berryman: "Life, friends, is boring." The idiom travels a long way between the two.

****

What typifies the era, the one we live in now?

For Pound, it was never far if he could think it. For us, what is near is often far away from us, what is far off remains remote even when we erase the distance between it and us, Heidegger thought. Heidegger thought our anxiety about the atom bomb was strange considering that "the terrible has already happened." It isn't that we can't get "there" from here; we can. What is terrible is that we simply can no longer get *here* from here.

And this I think is why Holub and his translators, who are brilliantly comic, absent, and relentless in this elegy, have chosen to represent the age in all its paucity, its frailty, the neutral modesty and honesty of the concluding figure in which "sort of" is given its full range at last, the idiom reminding me of those in wet suits, surfing off Capitola, spinning out just as the gray wall of rock looms up suddenly in front of them.

"Sort of" isn't glory. "Sort of" isn't tragedy. And that is the point. That is also the trouble. Holub's imagination, which does typify our time, seems to move at the speed of light. It delivers us from history, so that, in this way, Holub's elegy becomes a kind of birth. Everything comes rushing back into his poem but it's all without history: a train, a tunnel, a hand *per se* and a hand alone. And even though it is a birth in a world that is now a vast orphanage, there's something familiar about it, "homey" even, for it's *our* vast orphanage. What would we do without it, and the irony of its ceaseless catcalls and whistles? I like to think that the poet who will write its epitaph is three hours old at this moment, only I sort of doubt it.

HALF A HEDGEHOG

The rear half was run over,
leaving the head, thorax,
and two front hedgehog legs intact.

A scream, cramping the mouth
open: the scream of mutes,
more horrible than the silence after a flood,
when even black swans
swim belly up.

And even if a hedgehog doctor
could be found in a hollow stump,
under leaves in a stand of oaks,
it would be no help
to a mere half, here on Route E 12.

In the name of logic,
in the name of teachings on pain,
in the name of hedgehog god the father,
the son and the holy ghost amen,
in the name of children's games and unripe berries,
in the name of fast creeks of love,
always different and always bloody,
in the name of roots that grow
over the stillborn baby's head,
in the name of satanic beauty,
in the name of fresh-dressed human skin,
in the name of all halves
and double helices, purines
and pyrimidines

we tried to run over
the hedgehog's head with the front wheel.

This was like operating
a lunar module from a planetary distance,
from a control center seized
by a cataleptic sleep.

And the mission failed. I got out
and found a heavy piece of brick.

Half a hedgehog cried on. And now
the crying became speech

repeated from the ceilings of our graves:

And then comes death
and he will have your eyes.

translated by Dana Hábová and David Young

Dennis Schmitz

DISTANCING

Humor may seem to distract and irony offer emotional distance when a topic hurts; in the exchange between author and reader, the author acknowledges that possibility and hurts both of them anyway, using irony instead to intensify the emotional content.

One of my favorite illustrations of ironic perception in Miroslav Holub's work is the passage in stanzas six through eight of "Half a Hedgehog." Having accidentally run over the animal, destroying the lower body, the driver(s)—notice that the speaker says "we" in stanza six to maintain intellectual distance and indirectly disengage from responsibility—must kill the screaming hedgehog. Intentionally driving the car over the other half of the animal is impossible.

The driver tries, but the mechanics of the process require moral and physical coordination beyond human abilities. Also, the car seems to insulate one further from the deed. How difficult to run the wheel of a car, whose actual position the driver can only guess, over something as small as the head of a hedgehog. Ironically, it was easy to run over the lower half of the animal— what does that say about conscious control as a characteristically human feature?

Note the change from the safety of "we" to the "I" who must take responsibility and, through the crude instrumentality of the brick, kill the suffering hedgehog. A "lunar module" is, on the contrary, technologically sophisticated. There is "planetary" distancing—separation of instrument from directing mind—does scale change responsibility? Is the hedgehog an even smaller life because of the human technology of the car? The hedgehog, dumpy and inconsequential in human terms, lives on the fringes of human habitat. The car extends human influence but also separates the two realms by providing protective metal and larger-than-human-or-hedgehog size. Scale is acknowledged distance.

"And the mission failed. I got out..."—the extended comparison ends as a transition. Puck-ata, puck-ata: one cannot continue as Walter Mitty or the hero of an astronaut newsreel. Projection is evasion. The suggestion may be that substitution, or even the kind of substitution and distance that metaphor and simile provide, will be inadequate. The poignancy in "Half a Hedgehog" comes from the acknowledgment that the driver cannot totally lose guilt nor proficiently kill—he must soil his hands and his human feelings (a different approach to a similar situation in roadkill poems by Gerald Stern).

In coming to the hedgehog's level, the speaker acknowledges kinship. We knew that kinship from the start. The development of the poem has prepared us for surrendering to that recognition. That's why the last stanza's twist works. In the Cesare Pavese poem ("Death Will Come with Your Eyes") which seems to be quoted here, one looks into a mirror to see death. There is an ambiguity in the original Italian poem: one could translate the line "death will come *wearing* [or *using*] your eyes." Before a mirror we can't equivocate, using what we think we look like—death is the way in which we are mirrored, conjoined image and self, the point at which illusion cannot distort vision.

The first stanza gives us a picture to look at, a summary of parts, an inventory to show what constitutes a hedgehog which has just encountered the human—one term of the hedgehog/human comparison. An establishing shot. The delivery of the poem changes from stanza one's orienting description, feeling for a mode because the event is too horrifying on the flesh-and-blood level and too trivial on the human scale. Stanza two reaches for tragic parallels. Is stanza three's tension relieved by folktale references, the sort of Disney whimsy of giving animals human characteristics? No, one is more disoriented. After an accident, one behaves erratically, searching for a true, personal response, or an excuse. This reaction is manic.

All the listing of the interpretive arguments in stanza four, the human wish to mythologize, even through the scientific terminology which seems factual in that it recognizes the make-up of matter itself, remains a retreat or distancing from hedgehog flesh. All these interpretations still leave a human at the steering wheel.

If irony is distancing, it is also a way of looking at both sides of a proposition at the same time and not a way to avoid responding. Is the observer's distance in a Holub poem ever great enough not to be able to feel? Later in *Interferon, or On Theater*, the volume in which "Half a Hedgehog" appears, a "lousy egghead" is caught under a streetcar much as the hedgehog is crushed by a car. "Collision" is one of Holub's most powerful poems. But there is an interesting reversal: the street-car driver won't move the streetcar because he won't assume responsibility—he wants to be "directed" to move by an official who will absolve him, free him before the driver will free his victim. The "lousy egghead"—actually, a scientist friend of Holub's, his mentor—coincidentally dies because the streetcar isn't moved.

The situation in "Collision" parallels stanzas six through eight in "Half a Hedgehog." Ironically, the "lousy egghead" dies apologizing, ashamed for forgetting the traffic rules though he "almost/understood the approximate universe." His dying is a pattern in the universe like the "loneliness of the first genes/accumulating amino acids/in shallow primeval puddles..." or the process followed by the "mortal migrations of birds/obeying the sun's inclination/and the roar of sexual hormones...," the girl in the leukemia ward who keeps sliding into the toilet as she uses her hands to show what a mustache her doctor has. The list itself does not distance us from the "lousy egghead" or from our self-consideration, but the changing scale, the diversity of patterns in kind and urgency, the delay in storyline—all these notions make the effect greater when we return to the dying professor, now called "lousy egghead" rather than "he," as he had been earlier in the poem. There is pain for the speaker in using what might've been the streetcar driver's term, "lousy egghead." The list accumulates power as it comes to focus on the leukemia patient just before the dying professor comes back into the poem. The streetcar driver's attitude is the other side of the professor's humility, the perceptions of both are askew. And the driver would be horrified at the idea of using a brick to finish the professor.

Animals are different enough from human beings but close enough in certain qualities that Holub can use them as human substitutes, gaining perspective because of the effect of distance. His animals are not exotic. What is the destiny of the fish in "Brief Reflection on the Butchering of Carp"? Is destiny purpose? Meaning? Can the carp intend anything? The poem suggests a human also stretches out, waiting for the mallet blow. The mallet appropriately indicates the completion of a commercial transaction, the matter-of-fact conclusion to an ordinary life. More seemly than using a brick.

Holub's flies are flies, and if the dogs suffer, long for companionship and are victims of doggy angst, they are still dogs in spite of human parallels and the ironies that shadow them—the way humans may enact higher dramas of which they are not aware in their own dogginess. "On the Dog Angel" is the apotheosis of roadkill dog, comic and rueful. This poem prepares us for the later poem "The Dog That Wanted to Return"—both poems are from *Sagittal Section* (1980).

"The Dog Who Wanted to Return" is a longer prose poem about a universal innocent, a lab animal the storyteller traces through episodes of dog-life so close to human routine that the storyteller (the use of point-of-view is important here) doesn't have to forsake distance. As a lab animal, the dog finds solace in the communality of lab-dog fate. When by chance he escapes, the experience is not transcendent—he becomes a "dog-as-such," a reduction to dog-essence. He can't find a way to belong to the life outside his former kept-dog experience, nor can he have the freedom that not belonging should bring.

The dog returns to the pens in the first of several cycles of dog-confusion, but "such is the natural disposition of things: it's impossible to reenter one's destiny." He can't get back into the "cage" that was his. The distance here is alienation. "His flight became a circular pilgrimage from the non-existence of freedom to the indubitable existence of the cage." He's an "experimental dog"—as all life is testing—and cannot go back, "for such is the natural disposition of things: even though it's impossible to go back, it's imperative to keep going back."

At night the dog stays under the rabbit hutch, the closest he can get to his original condition, his eyes radiating "the red, reflected light of lamps and planets and the canine supernatural life" until, in the cycle of his pilgrimage, he is hit by a car, becoming an "experimental dog angel." His experiment is a testing of what living is. The poem has a development and complexity that "On the Dog Angel" can't have because of its size. The poem also has a philosophical distance that "Half a Hedgehog" can't have because the poem concerns existence as such.

"The Dog That Wanted to Return" is poignant because of the bemused tone in which the storyteller dramatizes "Everydog," distancing himself through the conventions of the point-of-view—a different approach but as effective in its way as the involvement of the narrator-driver in "Half a Hedgehog," who gives up distance, puts himself inside the mirror by coming close.

Holub is a master poet in every respect. His background as a research scientist gives him a vocabulary and philosophical inclination unique among poets. His precision, his economy of expression, makes other poets seem windy and self-indulgent. No other poet can startle in the same way with metaphor and console with wisdom. Who could not love his work and humbly salute him? Happy Birthday, Miroslav.

SEEING

A child encounters a mirror and looks.
The child grins and waves.
The child droops the corners of its mouth
and hunches its back.
The child pulls down its eyelids
and sticks out its tongue.

It plays the fool
and the sad sack and
it plays Jack-in-the-box.
Not yet, says the child.
It's not me yet.

Cronus the gravedigger used to get drunk after funerals and sleep it off in the morgue. Kids threw old wreaths at him through the broken windows: Good-bye Forever, Rest in Peace, and We Shall Remember You. The gravedigger tried chasing the kids for a while, then went back to his digging. At last he crawled into the grave and looked at the walls. He grinned and pulled down his eyelids. Not yet, he said. One day he went instead on his bike to get another bottle, fell down and broke his cranial bone. He was lying on the asphalt, his blue eyes wide open and his face sandy and rigid: he made no faces. Any more.

Mirrors come in October
and stroll through the city. The images
of images enliven November.

Pedestrians pass each other.
Wait, says mother,
Santa Claus won't find you.

The child is happy, because Santa Claus
prickles. The child mistakes him
for a hedgehog. But it can see him.

Once in the highlands, on a dry, grassy hill, I met a blind horse at dawn. The horse began to follow me, taking quiet, regular steps. A huge owl sat on a bush and turned its head. We went down to the valley. When we reached the road, I sat on a stone and waited, wondering what one could do with a blind horse from the highlands. The horse stood humbly behind me for a long time.

Then it turned back and walked uphill until it disappeared in the skies. The
sun was high and a rawboned wind began to blow.

> We are passing a suffocated pond.
> I don't want my gloves, says
> the child, and searches with its little hand
> resembling a tame finch
> for my hand.
>
> I observe
> the meeting of hands
> in the glassy December light.
> I guess it's not me yet.

translated by Dana Hábová and David Young

Sylva Fischerová

A GAME WITH FACES

Where to begin? No one word is better than any other, says Mandelstam. Let me begin from a seeing—from a vision: When I was a
child I once saw, on Christmas Eve, a golden piglet. It ran across
the roof of a house opposite ours, gleaming brightly. There's an old belief in
Bohemia: if you fast all Christmas Day, you'll see a golden piglet in the
evening. I fasted, and I saw it. But how did I know what it would look like?
What information could I have had about Christmas piglets? This summer,
having returned to my parents' flat for a few days, I found the answer: way in
the back of the desk I found an image of a golden piglet, in profile, stuck on
the side of an old box of Christmas cakes. And that's it, that's it—images of
images enliven November. And December. And.... What we can see and recognize are only images of images; we're imprisoned in them, and they don't
belong to us.

The image of Santa Claus lived in a small basket on the wardrobe and
prickled. It's interesting that images can prickle. But Santa Claus isn't a
Santa Claus for Czech children, he's little Jesus—"Jezisek." Which reminds
one, of course, of a hedge-hog—*"jezek." Jezisek* and *jezek*. But the basket in
which little Jesus lived was so small that I was afraid, every Christmas, that
he wouldn't be able to carry enough presents for me. If there weren't enough,
maybe it wouldn't be me, then.

Miroslav Holub writes extremely beautiful and strange poems about children. Speaking for myself, I prefer them to his strictly biological and medical ones, and to his historical poems that set up parallels, explicit or implicit, based on an analogy. Analogy presents us—as spectators, readers, auditors—with a world of correspondences, maybe complicated and sophisticated, a world bound together with incredible and wonderful ties that is nevertheless clear and understandable in its principles. In short, a world that is calculable. "In analogy there sleeps a fiend," an old saying maintains. It is the fiend of our eagerness for simplicity, smoothness, order. Naturally, Miroslav knows all this. In his poems analogy usually cracks, breaks, and falls like a dead leaf, like a weak tea that is of no use to those of us who need different drugs, different explanations, different images.

But the gravedigger Cronus constitutes no analogy at all. He is just you and me, any and all of us who unceasingly, morning to night, are buried with old wreaths by the others, our beautiful friends and non-friends. Rest in peace. We shall remember you. Or: Are you fine? Are you okay?

But we won't rest in peace, we say. We aren't fine and okay. No, we prefer to go for another bottle of wine or of eternity, and to break our cranial bone. Having such choice, we'd prefer to make no faces after all, as a newborn baby does. Maybe then, under no face, it'll be us in the end.

In Kundera's *Immortality* the hero Agnes hopes that after death there will be no faces. Not anymore. Her question comes to: "What does this game with faces mean? Where does my individuality really lie? How to shape it, how to escape it?" Miroslav Holub's guides in this game are very often children, who play it not because they must, as adults do, but because they want to. They want to play mommy and daddy, a doctor, a death. They know that after awhile they can stand up and go get a sandwich. Look: the oldest passion play....

But soul has no face. You can't play a soul. Confronted by the soul's game, the children's stops. Images of images are silent. Suddenly, they are nothing at all. From this point on you're like the blind horse from the highlands, looking for its guide, at dawn, in the rawboned wind. But no guides are available now. Maybe the word, the poetry, stops here too. Maybe the word is like the face. Maybe not. And we are or we aren't companions of the Muses. Holub's poems, even when they contain nostalgia, give us a sudden hope and strength and hidden energy, that which we need most. And in any case, the rest doesn't belong to us. As Miroslav wrote some thirty years ago:

> Go and open the door.
>   Maybe outside there's
>   a tree, or a wood,
>   a garden,
>   or a magic city . . .
>   Maybe you'll see a face,

or an eye,
or the picture
                    of a picture . . .

    Even if there's only
    the hollow wind,
    even if
                    nothing
                                    is there,
go and open the door.

At least
there'll be
a draught.

               translated by Ian Milner

HEMOPHILIA/LOS ANGELES

And so it circulates
from the San Bernardino Freeway
to the Santa Monica Freeway and
down to the San Diego Freeway and
up to the Golden Gate Freeway,

and so it circulates
in the vessels of the marine creature,
transparent creature,
unbelievable creature in the light
of the southern moon
like the footprint
of the last foot in the world,

and so it circulates
as if there were no other music
except Perpetual Motion,
as if there were no conductor
directing an orchestra of black angels
without a full score:

out of the grand piano floats
a pink C-sharp in the upper octave,
out of the violin
blood may trickle at any time,
and in the joints of the trombone
there swells a fear of the tiniest staccato,

as if there were no Dante
in a wheelchair,
holding a ball of cotton to his mouth,
afraid to speak a line
lest he perforate the meaning,

as if there were no genes
except the gene for defects
and emergency telephone calls,

and so it circulates
with the full, velvet hum of the disease,
circulates all hours of the day,

circulates all hours of the night
to the praise of non-clotting,

each blood cell carrying
four molecules of hope
that it might all be something
totally different
from what it is.

translated by Dana Hábová and David Young

Tom Andrews

LIVES OF A CELL

"Considering how common illness is," Virginia Woolf wrote in "On Being Ill,"

> ...it [is] strange indeed that illness has not taken its place with love and battle and jealousy among the prime themes of literature. Novels, one would have thought, would have been devoted to influenza; epic poems to typhoid; odes to pneumonia; lyrics to toothache. But no; ...literature does its best to maintain that its concern is with the mind; that the body is a sheet of plain glass through which the soul looks straight and clear, and, save for one or two passions such as desire and greed, is null, and negligible and non-existent. On the contrary, the very opposite is true. All day, all night, the body intervenes.

Of this "daily drama of the body," Woolf went on, "there is no record."

Miroslav Holub's work contradicts that last assertion. For forty years now Holub has contributed, as a poet and as a research immunologist, to the "record" of the body's "daily drama." Surely Holub knows as well as any poet alive the extent to which "All day, all night, the body intervenes." And while "Hemophilia/Los Angeles" exists somewhere in the interregnum between "epic poems to typhoid" and "lyrics to toothache" (though who better to write such epics and lyrics than the author of "Interferon" and "Teeth"?), it, like many Holub poems, serves as a lens into the unexpected richness of the body's interventions.

I should acknowledge at the outset that "Hemophilia/Los Angeles," as the title's slash mark suggests, can be read from two distinct angles. From one angle it is a poem about the fractured city at the end of the Open Road: hemophilia as emblem of cultural and social hemorrhaging. From another angle it is a poem about the "hum" of hemophilia: Los Angeles—or at least its freeway system—as emblem of the disease's complexity and turbulence. The "LA poem" and the "hemophilia poem" interweave in important ways, of course, but I have emphasized the latter, for reasons I hope will be clear. It's worth noting in this context that the poem's first publication was in an English translation—in FIELD in 1985—and that the original title was simply "Hemophilia." According to the translators, "Los Angeles" was later added to the first Czech publication, to help Czech readers place the freeways mentioned.

The language of "Hemophilia/Los Angeles" is densely metaphorical. This raises a vexed issue—vexed, that is, in the wake of Susan Sontag's masterly *Illness as Metaphor*, in which Sontag discloses the dangers of using metaphorical language to speak about diseases. Hemophilia, one would think, could easily provoke what Sontag calls "punitive or sentimental" metaphors: metaphors that use a disease as a commentary on a patient's psychology or character. Two prejudicing metaphors associated with hemophilia, for example, are that a hemophiliac's character must be effete—one isn't sufficiently "hot-blooded"—and that hemophiliacs must be of royal ancestry (which is related to the notion of effete character). But "Hemophilia/Los Angeles," while certainly embodying metaphor and metaphorical thinking, does not give in to this prejudicing impulse. The poem uses metaphor not as a comment on the patient but as a means of articulating the disease itself, its idiosyncrasies, its strangely autonomous life. Holub does not address the patient except briefly in the fifth stanza (a stanza I'll return to). Holub's decision to approach hemophilia "clinically," from the cellular and vascular level, gives the poem a remarkable imaginative freedom.

The poem begins—to state the obvious—by establishing its central metaphor of the bloodstream as a stream of traffic on the Los Angeles freeway system. The whole poem, appropriately, moves with a heavily-trafficked breathlessness. It consists of one sentence: four images of "circulation" interrupted by an extended digression (beginning "as if there were no other music"), which contains within it several further digressions. Acceleration is crucial. The first stanza accelerates from 0 to 60 mph, as it were; it has the dizzying "fast-forward" quality of certain sequences in Godfrey Reggio's film *Koyaanisqatsi*. In *Koyaanisqatsi*, Reggio offers the reversal, a negative, of Holub's image: cars slipping through the LA freeway system, filmed over hours and then viewed in fast forward, look like nothing so much as blood cells slipping through capillaries. One half expects to hear Philip Glass's mercurial soundtrack while reading "Hemophilia/Los Angeles." But where Reggio and Glass offer a hymn to "Perpetual Motion," Holub offers an anti-hymn.

I say "interrupted by an extended digression" matter-of-factly, as if I weren't astonished by the strange and confident metamorphoses the poem undergoes! Like other Holub poems, "Hemophilia/Los Angeles" views its subject through a microscope and, paradoxically, finds within that circumscription of vision the scale necessary to perceive otherwise hidden affinities and transformations, to take the long view. And yet the poem is anything but dry or coldly intellectual. The images are by turns comic or irreverent ("an orchestra of black angels/without a full score"), straightforwardly serious ("no genes/except the gene for defects/and emergency telephone calls"), or even, in its most characteristic moments, both irreverent *and* serious:

> out of the violin
> blood may trickle at any time,
> and in the joints of the trombone
> there swells a fear of the tiniest staccato,
>
> as if there were no Dante
> in a wheelchair,
> holding a ball of cotton to his mouth,
> afraid to speak a line
> lest he perforate the meaning...

The unusual mix here of antic invention and profound human sympathy is Holub's signature, and brilliant. Moreover, these lines are exacting in their description of the experience of hemophilia. A moderate to severe hemophiliac may not know what instigates a bleed: one is indeed watchful for "the tiniest staccato" which may break a blood vessel in a joint. (Such fears usually center on the joints, the most persistent problem area for many hemophiliacs.) Some bleeds, in fact, begin "spontaneously," without any visible cause. It is not surreal hyperbole, then, to note that "blood may trickle at any time." For all the poem's antic invention, which I love, it is quite realistic about the phenomenon of hemorrhaging.

I want to linger a moment over the fifth stanza, the stanza beginning "as if there were no Dante...." Underlying these lines, or informing them, is a striking and resonant pun. A joint is said to be "articulate" when it has available its full range of motion. A hemorrhage inside a joint fills the joint with blood, first diminishing and finally occluding the range of motion. In other words, a bleed makes a joint "inarticulate." But the body—let alone the hemophiliac—desires articulation. It works to break down and absorb the blood in a joint, engaging in "a raid on the inarticulate" (to quote Eliot in "East Coker"). The hemophiliac's role in this process is "Dantesque," fraught with purgatorial uncertainties and terrors: if he (hemophilia occurs almost exclusively in males) tries too hard or too soon to articulate a joint, he can start another bleed. So he waits, "afraid to speak [articulate] a line/lest he perforate the meaning." That Holub is able to address this event so deftly, with such intricacy of design and yet with such a light touch, is another occasion for astonishment.

The word "perforate" is a microcosm of this intricacy and precision. It is a word I see often in the literature on hemophilia. It suggests seeping, penetrating, boring through. Blood perforates a joint; if not stopped, it can perforate cartilage, permanently obstructing full articulation. Holub's integration of the word into his ingenious and experimental (in all senses of the word) context is so satisfying that I wondered if it was the result of inspired translation or if the Czech original was similar in sound and meaning. Given the opportunity, I asked Holub about the word, and he confirmed both the precision I suspected and his good fortune with translators. He wrote: "The Czech word for perforate...is almost the same as in English, *perforace*. David Young's translations are very accurate even in sound."

Granted, my experience with hemophilia makes me a conspicuously interested, rather than disinterested, reader of the poem. Perhaps I take Holub's felicity to the particulars of the disease too far. There is the poem's rich play of invention, its wonderfully outlandish side. But it is the poem's balance between play of invention and scientific exactitude, as well as its compassion, that I find so unique. Wallace Stevens's idea that "The real is only the base, but it is the base" has rarely found more convincing embodiment.

The poem's ending gives further evidence of that embodiment, that balance. True to form, those "four molecules of hope" can be read as both the four globin chains each red blood cell carries *and* as a typical number of commuters in a car on the freeway. To say that each blood cell hopes that "it"—non-clotting, endless circulation and perpetuation of the disease— "might all be something/totally different/from what it is" is not to commit the pathetic fallacy, as some readers I've shown the poem to have suggested. Or rather, it is to commit the pathetic fallacy but not in the sentimental way we might think on a hasty reading. The lines get at another of the body's interventions. Hemophiliacs, even those severely affected, have *some* percentage of factor VIII, the factor responsible for clotting, in the bloodstream. Just as the body "desires" joint articulation, the bloodstream desires or "hopes" to clot in the event of a trauma. Mild to moderate hemophiliacs, in fact, can be treated with desmopressin acetate (DDAVP), a synthetic drug which capitalizes on the blood's "hope" of clotting by stimulating what active factor VIII the bloodstream carries. Each blood cell is an unregenerate overachiever; each refuses to be lulled by "the full, velvet hum of the disease." But without a certain amount of factor VIII, or without help from a stimulant, such cellular "hope" remains frustrated. Once again Holub is able to incorporate complex clinical information—which a less resourceful poet might rule out as aggressively unpoetic—with remarkable agility and energy.

The mind at work in "Hemophilia/Los Angeles" is supple, daring, humane, exacting. What Seamus Heaney said of *Sagittal Section*, Holub's first collection to be published in the United States, is true also of "Hemophilia/Los Angeles": "It is a very nimble and very serious anatomy of the world, too compassionate to be vindictive, too sceptical to be entranced, a poetry in which intelligence and irony make their presence felt without displacing delight and the less acerbic wisdoms." It is a sensibility of which many of us could use repeated infusions.

W. S. MERWIN
(b. 1927)

W. S. Merwin has served as a presiding spirit over the whole history of American poetry in the second half of the twentieth century. One of the most prolific poets of his generation, he has also published acclaimed translations, memoirs, critical essays, fiction, and plays. His deeply multifaceted work might be seen as a sustained meditation on the evanescence of the natural world, and the ethical and existential dilemmas inherent in the process of living within it. Beginning as a traditionally formal poet (his first book, *A Masque for Janus*, won the Yale Younger Poets prize in 1952), Merwin then began to forge a more transparent, intuitive style as his work became more personal. *The Lice* (1967) was perhaps the most urgently significant volume of its period, bringing ecological, cultural, and political concerns to a blazing pitch of expression, and at the same time linking those concerns to wider epistemological and spiritual questions. Merwin is fundamentally a poet of liminality, exploring the territory between different states of being, between the conscious and the unconscious, between life and death. While his vision of the modern condition is often marked by anger and despair, he also celebrates sustained moments of reconciliation, grace, and luminous vision. Having lived abroad much of his life, he now makes his home in Hawaii.

BOOKS: *The First Four Books of Poems* (1975); *The Second Four Books of Poems* (1993); *The Miner's Pale Children* (1970); *The Compass Flower* (1977); *Houses and Travellers* (1977); *Finding the Islands* (1982); *Opening the Hand* (1983); *The Rain in the Trees* (1988); *Selected Poems* (1988); *Travels* (1993); *The Vixen* (1996); *Selected Translations 1948-1968* (1968); *Selected Translations 1968-1978* (1979); *Unframed Originals* (1982); *Regions of Memory: Uncollected Prose* (1987).

SOME LAST QUESTIONS

What is the head
    A. Ash
What are the eyes
    A. The wells have fallen in and have
    Inhabitants
What are the feet
    A. Thumbs left after the auction
No what are the feet
    A. Under them the impossible road is moving
    Down which the broken necked mice push
    Balls of blood with their noses
What is the tongue
    A. The black coat that fell off the wall
    With sleeves trying to say something
What are the hands
    A. Paid
No what are the hands
    A. Climbing back down the museum wall
    To their ancestors the extinct shrews that will
    Have left a message
What is the silence
    A. As though it had a right to more
Who are the compatriots
    A. They make the stars of bone

Bruce Beasley

THE ANTI-CATECHISM OF W. S. MERWIN

All week I've been reading catechisms and rereading W. S. Merwin. What a juxtaposition: the catechists' unironic faith in reasoned and pious inquiry, against the jeremiad-like voice of *The Lice*, a voice so aware of its own complicity in the lies of language and reason that it barely dares to speak. A catechism by Calvin particularly fascinates me: how smoothly the child's memorized responses (recited, sabbath by sabbath, to the minister) fill up the vast mysteries the questions carve out in time: What is the principal and chief end of man's life? To know God. What is man's chief felicity? The same, to know God. As the sabbaths proceed, the questions become more theologically sophisticated, more cutting: "But it appeareth not that any profit cometh unto us by this, that Christ hath won the victory over death, seeing that we notwithstanding cease not to die?" And the child is made to answer: "That doth not hinder; for the death of the faithful is now nothing else, but a ready passage unto a better life."

It's that kind of epistemological confidence, that simplicity, in the child's forced confession of faith that Merwin lambasts so bitterly in his famous anti-catechism, "Some Last Questions." Like the catechisms, Merwin's "last" questions are eschatological investigations, questions about ultimate things (the last things in human time, the first things in transhuman significance). The title seems at first disarmingly casual: just a few more final questions to tie up loose ends before you go. But these are "last questions," more darkly, in that the questioner has become exhausted with the futility of tethering question to answer. "Some Last Questions" borrows the form of the catechism, but sets out to radically undermine the linkage of rational question to rational answer, or of insuperable questions to piously surrendered answer. Merwin here, as in so many of his poems in the '60s and '70s, critiques the whole notion that language can begin to contain any intelligible or meaningful response to "last questions," questions that "last" or endure precisely because they can't be satisfactorily answered, can't be walled-in by reasoned words and their attendant metaphysical certainties. The poem, appearing near the beginning of *The Lice* in 1967, announces a shorting-out of the wires of logic and coherence, philosophical and theological inquiry; question and answer repel each other like magnets of the same charge, and the poem makes a mess of any of our attempts to set it right.

"That doth not hinder," the child is made to retort in catechism. But in Merwin's poem, every question hinders, and every answer hinders all the more. Merwin conducts a kind of verbal dissection of a body—autopsying the head, eyes, feet, tongue, hands—leaving us to wonder who or what has died, and what fatal agent the inquest has discovered.

Imagine a satisfactory answer to the deceptively straightforward question with which the poem begins: "What is the head." The seat of the brain, of the face, of the eyes and ears and mouth and nose, we might say; center of all human sensing and cognition. But in Merwin's anti-catechism, the answer is blunt and terminal: "Ash." We hardly know what to do with such an abrupt and impatient beginning: ashes to ashes, dust to dust; the seat of reason, imagination, emotion, and sense is ash in the sense of being mortal; ash meaning that it has been exterminated, as in a crematorium (Plath's "Ash, ash—/You poke and sting./Flesh, bone, there is nothing there—"). Well, then, the interrogator continues, "What are the eyes"? Not, certainly, mirrors of the soul; the response here is a blunt statement that at first has no discernible relationship to the question: "The wells have fallen in and have/Inhabitants." What are the "inhabitants" of the eyes but light, vision, the entire phenomenal world? The world is trapped in the bottomless, sinking well of our flawed perception, secreted, inaccessible, dying.

And so on through the post-apocalyptic landscape of the head: ashes, collapsed wells, signs of desolation and catastrophe. And on through the body: feet, tongue, hands: Merwin defines the extremities and instruments of sense and speech through grotesquely disconnected metaphors, vehicle so far from tenor they can barely hear each other's shouts. Everything's immobilized, falling down, dehumanized: the hands are left as a preserved cultural artifact "on the museum wall"; the feet are "left after the auction." The hands, "Climbing back down the museum wall/To their ancestors the extinct shrews that will/Have left a message," attempt to reconnect with the prophets of their own extinction. But the message of extinction, though "left," is never heeded, and Merwin becomes a kind of 20th-century Cassandra, tearing down the certainties and the terrible logic that has brought us, technologically, to where we are.

Asked why her stories of redemption were always so violent and grotesque, Flannery O'Connor said you have to shout when speaking to the hard-of-hearing; in a secularized and complacent culture, you've got to shock an audience into coming to terms with issues of ultimate significance. In his own way, Merwin does the same thing here. The feet, in a grotesque substitution, are "thumbs" (our categories of differentiation—feet vs. hands, toes vs. thumbs—disintegrate into nonsense). And not just thumbs but thumbs "left after the auction." We can't quite make sense of that in any way we're used to making sense, and so we're forced to shudder and go on, bringing with us a vague sense of violation and displacement and loss (auctions, after all, are often conducted to dispose of the belongings of the dead). Something is wrong with the language here, with the whole divorce of response from question. (It's as though, in the liturgy, when the priest proclaimed "Lift up your hearts," the congregation should answer, not "We lift them up to the Lord" but something violent, incongruous, antisensical, like "Spears in the pierced side.") Merwin won't tell us what's wrong; it's the very sense of wrongness, of violation, the breakdown of our traditional ways of making sense of the world around us, of feeling at *home* here, that provides the only hope. For Merwin's world of the 1960s is one in which human logic and common sense and order have led to unthinkable horrors of destruction and extinction (animal and potentially human) we've managed not to let ourselves even see. "What are the eyes/A. The wells have fallen in and have/Inhabitants."

Part of the terrifying structure of "Some Last Questions" is that, just as soon as we've rehabituated ourselves into a new kind of poem (and logic) where questions and their answers are futilely cast-apart, the poem resists such comfort (like bacteria that immunize themselves to whatever antibiotics bombard them). Refusing to allow us the comforting complacency and passiveness of surrealistic nonsense (nothing makes sense so we might as well sit back and enjoy the ride), the poem seems to insist that there are, after all, wrong or unacceptable answers, meaning the catechistic responses aren't arbitrary and meaningless after all. It's unsettling, because it forces us to look back at the answers and questions, try harder to discover in what sense the answers have, all along, been *right*. "What are the hands"? "Paid" won't do as the answer: the commercial vision of the hands as receivers of funds, of the self as earner of its own material keep, isn't what the interrogator means to get. "No," the interrogation insists, "what are the hands." And the second answer links them, much more tellingly, instead to the extinction of other species, to the hands' own status as a kind of grotesque stuffed trophy mounted in a museum. What we have done to others will be done to us. Similarly, the feet aren't going to remain "thumbs left after the auction," disturbing and violent as that is. Instead, they are made motionless, passive, helpless, while the road beneath them moves and mice, "broken-necked" from mousetraps, keep moving as irrepressible reminders of human violence. Like the trained mice of laboratory experiments, like the trained seal performing at Sea World, the hideous spectacle goes on (the mice pushing their own dried blood), and the feet suffer its going.

And so on throughout the poem. The tongue, instrument of speech, suffers a sea-change into something strange, but hardly rich: "the black coat that fell off the wall/With sleeves trying to say something." As the feet are stilled over the "impossible road," so the tongue is inanimate, incapable of speech, impotently "trying to say something." And what it is trying to say, we'll never be told.

Perhaps the saddest question and answer exchange is the enervated "What is the silence/A. As though it had a right to more." The answer refuses to respond to the question; takes silence as natural, as deserved, as only appropriate: speech, poetry, any language don't deserve to exist because of the poverty of their content and the violence of the dream of reason that underwrites them. The poem wells up out of silence long enough to declare its own lack of right to exist, the hopelessness of its own utterance.

Nevertheless, the poem goes on, to one *last* last question: "Who are the compatriots." The saying that comes in reaction—"They make the stars of bone"—is a slippery one. They transform the bone into stars ("Of his bones are coral made"): that is, the bodily is remade, transfigured into the heavenly. Or its converse: the stars themselves are made of bone, are celestial signs of the mortality of all they shine upon. "Compatriots" is, of course, a highly charged word in the political landscape of *The Lice*: the patriots have armed themselves with instruments of ultimate destruction, the patriots are napalming the jungles of Vietnam. To make, then, the "stars of bone" suggests, on one level, to elevate—through abstractions like heroism and love of freedom—Death into a transcendental ideal, to stellify something hideous and unthinkable, to make death our very fate.

Merwin's despairing catechism instructs, like any catechism, in the ways of talking about things that are, by definition, beyond language's power to speak. (Augustine, the story goes, compared his effort to write a treatise on the Trinity, and thus contain the nature of godhead in human language, to a child trying to pour the sea, bucket by bucket, into a tiny hole he'd dug in the sand.) But "Some Last Questions" suggests, darkly, that it is the very logic of question and answer, the Socratic method and all of its reverberations, that has led us inexorably to the last times, times where any day, any question, could be the last. In the years just after the Cuban missile crisis, during massive escalation of the Vietnam War, Merwin's catechist declares the human head "ash" and the stars above us "bone"; the voice breaks through silence long enough to sever the sinister logic of human progress and to suggest the human race doesn't deserve more than silence, for our reason and our rationalizations and our patriotic rhetoric have brought us to catastrophe not prefigured but self-made. It's one of the most seethingly angry poems I've ever read, and yet thrilling in its comic savagery and its implicit hope that its critique of Western logic and transcendental idealism can sever the terrible certainties of progress that have brought us where we are.

I LIVE UP HERE

I live up here
And a little bit to the left
And I go down only

For the accidents and then
Never a moment too soon

Just the same it's a life it's plenty

The stairs the petals she loves me
Every time
Nothing has changed

Oh down there down there
Every time
The glass knights lie by their gloves of blood

In the pans of the scales the helmets
Brim over with water
It's perfectly fair

The pavements are dealt out the dice
Every moment arrive somewhere

You can hear the hearses getting lost in lungs
Their bells stalling
And then silence comes with the plate and I
Give what I can

Feeling *It's worth it*

For I see
What my votes the mice are accomplishing
And I know I'm free

This is how I live
Up here and simply

Others do otherwise
Maybe

David Walker

W. S. Merwin as Dramatist

The *Lice* (1967) is a dreambook, a mirror, a chamber of horrors, a scathing political critique, an eschatology, a survival manual. For members of my generation who were in college in the late 60s and early 70s, the book was a totem we carried around and memorized, a talisman we used to help us define the world we lived in and the poems we longed to write. Many of its individual lines came to have the inevitability of familiar aphorisms:

> Of all the beasts to man alone death brings justice
> (50)

> On the door it says what to do to survive
> But we were not born to survive
> Only to live
> (33)

> What you do not have you find everywhere
> (55)

> If I were not human I would not be ashamed of anything
> (71)

The poems' distinctive vision exemplified something both contemporary and timeless, both strikingly original and hauntingly universalized. Indeed, much of the volume's power seemed to lie in its emphasis on paradox, its ability to balance—or, better, to hold in suspension—apparently opposing and even mutually exclusive impulses: a landscape at once pastoral and apocalyptic, a perspective both private and prophetic. One of the most familiar ways of describing this quality, this ability to establish a double consciousness by highlighting the fluidity of boundaries, is to call the poems "mythic."

In talking about Merwin's work as mythic, critics seem to refer to at least three related qualities: its displacement from the immediate circumstances of time and place, so that even the most mundane of objects and events imply something beyond themselves; its air of philosophical detachment, whereby even moods of terrible shame and suffering are coolly, objectively rendered; and its rhetorical strategies, imbuing his subjects with a riddling, sybilline sense of mystery. All of these tendencies, of course, reflect a certain degree of distancing, and while there is ample testimony to the power it has on many readers, for others it raises thorny questions. For poets like Robert Pinsky and Alan Williamson, as characterized with evident approval by Marjorie Perloff, it represents "a thinly disguised evasiveness, a turning of one's back on the real world" (141). James Atlas calls Merwin's poems of this period "monotonous, interminable, self-imitative," and laments their detached perspective: "excessive transmutation of our 'modern dilemmas' has caused us to misinterpret them; what there should be more of at this time are critiques, poems that situate us in the world, or elaborate on real conditions" (78-79). And Charles Molesworth finds the results dispiritingly formulaic: "I feel he has trapped himself in a mythic and psychological cul-de-sac which makes his language increasingly flavorless, like the exhaustion of an irony that has hung on too long.... Merwin asks too much of the lyric poem since he asks it to perform many of the functions of myth but without an anthropological love of detail and locale, and without the obsessive sense of release and containment we associate with ritual" (156-57). What links all these critics is their objection to what Atlas calls Merwin's "disembodied voice," which they characterize as abstract, overgeneralized, and ungrounded.

Returning to *The Lice* on its thirtieth anniversary, though, I find myself struck by the degree to which its mythmaking is countered by a delicate and evocative dramaturgy. I use these terms in response to Molesworth, who continues his critique of Merwin by contrasting him with Beckett:

> His vision has some affinities with Beckett's, and his language has similar barrenness. But Beckett's dramaturgy, his sense of scene and narrative, give his minimalist language a richness that is further strengthened by an irreducible lyricism lurking beneath the corrosive irony.... Merwin's mythography doesn't fully realize just what Beckett's dramaturgy provides: a sense of an audience, a dialogue, even a dialectic, between despair and renewal, comedy and tragedy. (156)

But in fact I find considerable evidence in *The Lice* of exactly this "dramaturgical" quality, this effort to balance the timeless reach of myth with the immediate richness of scene and narrative. It is not well known that in his early career Merwin thought of himself as at least as much a playwright as a poet, with several plays produced in this country and in England. And while he seems gradually to have abandoned that ambition, I believe its traces may be seen in many of the poems' explorations of character, psychology, and dramatic situation. The tendency to criticize Merwin's work as unremittingly self-enclosed results, I believe, from a fundamentally Romantic bias, a perhaps unconscious assumption that the "I" of the poems represents the poet's own perspective and experience. I'd like to challenge that perspective by suggesting that Merwin does *not* lack "a sense of an audience," that the speaker is often a deliberately staged construction designed to infuse the poem's experience with irony and wry humor. "I Live Up Here" is a useful example.

The crux of the issue is of course in how one hears the voice of the poem. Is the "I" a "disembodied voice," simply a device Merwin can use for projecting certain abstract notions? On the contrary, for me the interest of this poem is in its persona's quirky individuality, the intricate nuances of his self-perception, the surprises with which the particular circumstances of his life and world swim momentarily into focus. This happens in quite a minimalist way, of course: "I Live Up Here" is anything but histrionic, and indeed it is the very absence of dramatic gestures that defines the pathos of the speaker's existence:

> I live up here
> And a little bit to the left
> And I go down only
>
> For the accidents and then
> Never a moment too soon
>
> Just the same it's a life it's plenty
>
> The stairs the petals she loves me
> Every time
> Nothing has changed

His is a Prufrockian life: isolated, lived on the margins, voyeuristic ("I go down only/For the accidents"), sadly self-deluded ("she loves me/Every time"). The speaker attempts to persuade us of the advantage of his elevated position—he never has to risk being involved in an accident because he's only around for the aftermath—but succeeds only in revealing the stasis in which he's trapped. This mood is enhanced by the plainspoken, self-effacing diction and the Beckettian rhythm of hesitation imposed by line breaks and stanza divisions.

In the central section, as the speaker turns his attention to the life he imagines taking place in the streets below, his language tellingly becomes richer and more metaphorical. A world which has been urban and contemporary now is inflected through icons of heraldry:

> Oh down there down there
> Every time
> The glass knights lie by their gloves of blood
>
> In the pans of the scales the helmets
> Brim over with water
> It's perfectly fair

Read as disembodied mythography, these images are apt to support the criticism of Merwin's work as generic and formulaic: if we ask in the abstract why the knights are glass or precisely what the brimming helmets represent, we're likely to reach fairly arbitrary (and therefore formulaic) conclusions. If, on the other hand, we read these images as projections of the speaker's overdeter-

mined imagination, forcing his ambivalence to the surface, they seem much
more emotionally persuasive. Reminiscent of tomb effigies, the glass knights
lying next to their gloves of blood evoke both violent death and heroic transcendence, both of which seem to repel and attract the speaker. Unlike the static precision of his life, the world of the streets is ruled by chance and change
("The pavements are dealt out the dice/Every moment arrive somewhere"),
and it's striking that he can describe this process without being able to express
his feelings about it. He strains to maintain a sense of equanimity in the face
of his uncertainty: in that sense "It's perfectly fair" has the same self-justifying weight as the earlier "Just the same it's a life it's plenty."

And then, in the poem's most expressive moment, he conflates the external
and interior worlds as a way of extricating himself from both:

> You can hear the hearses getting lost in lungs
> Their bells stalling
> And then silence comes with the plate and I
> Give what I can
>
> Feeling *It's worth it*

The hearses echo the earlier references to accidents, blood, and mortality;
significantly, his elevated position "up here" means that he can only hear, not
see, them, but the lungs in which they become lost may well represent the
depths of his own body, from which he seems equally detached. The ensuing
silence is figured as an usher with a collection plate, we are now presumably
at the funeral service itself, but significantly the speaker seems to be the only
mourner. "I/Give what I can," he says (the line break is a perfect hesitation),
and we suspect that what he can give—money, blood, love—is very little.
"Feeling *It's worth it*": that smugly self-congratulatory moment of *feeling*,
the only one in the poem, is perhaps its saddest.

The ending struggles to maintain the note of bland satisfaction. The
speaker affirms his belief in democracy ("I see/What my votes the mice are
accomplishing") and freedom, though in his self-imposed isolation these
concepts must by definition lose any real meaning. By this point his voice is
so attenuated and bleached of feeling that it rings deeply hollow: at the end
he is reduced to the most elemental sort of self-definition:

> This is how I live
> Up here and simply
>
> Others do otherwise
> Maybe

His "simple" existence is of course anything but simple; the fact that he can
only hypothesize about the possibility of other options signals the degree of

his denial. The multiplicity of the poem's irony, as revealed through the speaker's gradual self-revelation, depends crucially on a dramaturgical strategy. Certainly not all the poems in *The Lice* are built so fundamentally on the model of the dramatic monologue; many seem to draw much more directly from the poet's own consciousness. My point is that the book's voices are far more various and complex than the totalizing "mythological" analysis would allow; the collection is designed in a way that forces readers constantly to renegotiate their easy assumptions about the monolithic nature of the self.

WORKS CITED

Atlas, James. "Diminishing Returns: The Writings of W. S. Merwin," in Robert Shaw, ed., *American Poetry Since 1960: Some Critical Perspectives.* Carcanet Press, 1973.

Molesworth, Charles. "W. S. Merwin: Style, Vision, Influence," in Cary Nelson and Ed Folsom, eds., *W.S. Merwin: Essays on the Poetry.* Univ. of Illinois Press, 1987.

Perloff, Marjorie. "Apocalypse Then: Merwin and the Sorrows of Literary History," in Nelson and Folsom.

THE BRIDGES

Nothing but me is moving
on these bridges
as I always knew it would be
see moving on each of the bridges
only me

and everything that we have known
even the friends
lined up in the silent iron railings
back and forth
I pass like a stick on palings

the echo rises from the marbled river
the light from the blank clocks crackles
like an empty film
where
are we living now
on which side which side
and will you be there

C. D. Wright

ECHO RISING

B egin with Nothing, remote starting point, the area of darkest color. Begin with Nothing which is yourself, Eternal Stranger, the poem which always acts alone. The poem supplies its references from its own surround. Sounds its own memory. The mind of the poem passes along interior surfaces. One does not contact the poem's ground without feeling bound to its secrecy. Its bridges reach in both directions; they appear as tangible lengths across an opening. They attach to neither side. They duplicate themselves. And you, who are Nothing, are duplicated on them. Moving. Dizzy with motion and altitude, but unafraid; "see," it is just as you imagined it would be. And Everything we have known, which is Nothing, lines up, as do our friends, who are immanent in the lustrous element of the bridges themselves. And we who are Nothing, along with Everything we have known, which is Nothing, have learned to listen so deeply, we have learned to "say it with silence our native tongue," with a fluency which distributes both sound and light just so, until there is no *horror vaccui* left in us. The un-fathomable emptiness, negation, loss, absence have themselves become fill-ing if not fulfilling.

The poem is not given to nattering punctuation; the coextensive conjunc-tion *and* admits its only grammatical transport. The river is *marbled*, which, in an adjective, supplies the multidirectional vein and opaque luminosity the entire envisions. Rhyme causes *railings* to ring on *palings; be* to *see.* Asso-nance narrows the circumference of physical tonal values: *lined...in silent iron railings.* Consonance intensifies the psychic distance: *stick...echo... clock...crackles.* Outright repetition of words appears strangely less obtru-sive, yet simultaneously more insistent: *moving* is *moving, bridges* are *bridges,* and *on which side which side* reverberates back through the poem's dependent architecture. The Source, which may or may not be *logos,* is an imperatively ambiguous realm.

Explicit delineation is eschewed. Friends are present, but remain faceless and silent. A clock (likewise faceless) is positioned in space, but not in time. The poem's voice assumes a body only as a likening to a stick passed over palings. Our immanent separation appears not as material self-interest, but as common feeling which gives meaning and shape to the obsessions that sim-ple being provokes. Herein the forebrain shuts up. The Spirit, which only or may not be *logos,* is barely written. The poem has direction but not Destiny. These bridges, which are Thresholds, will, without a doubt, indifferently leave us hanging. Chuang Tze said it, "Perfect joy is to be without joy."

The marbled river, the blank clock, the empty film, the unanswered echo will not affirm us, but unerringly confirm our intense, spectral presence stretching into forever. Perhaps Glenn Gould was right, "The purpose of art is not the momentary ejection of adrenaline but the lifelong construction of a state of wonder and serenity." If this precept is not unsound, W. S. Merwin is the quintessential exemplar.

THE PIPER

It is twenty years
since I first looked for words
for me now
whose wisdom or something would stay me
I chose to
trouble myself about the onset
of this
it was remote it was grievous
it is true I was still a child

I was older then
than I hope ever to be again
that summer sweating in the attic
in the foreign country
high above the piper but hearing him
once
and never moving from my book
and the narrow
house full of pregnant women
floor above floor
waiting
in that city
where the sun was the one bell

It has taken me till now
to be able to say
even this
it has taken me this long
to know what I cannot say
where it begins
like the names of the hungry

Beginning
I am here
please
be ready to teach me
I am almost ready to learn

James Baker Hall

IF THERE IS A PLACE WHERE THIS IS THE LANGUAGE

I read W. S. Merwin's poems for twenty years, by way of 'keeping up,' before my life opened me to their influence. During the late 70s and on into the early 80s, beginning when I was in my mid-forties, one and then another of them helped me to straighten my spine (dramatically) and to commence looking this way and that over my shoulders, wondering where I was, and doing what, and for what reasons, and who were all these other people, especially those looking to me for poetry—what was I supposed to say? His work has ripened in the twenty years since, and my appreciation of it has ripened, but that's not the story I want to tell.

I had been older than I hope ever to be again, as the voice of "The Piper" put it, and for too long, and I was almost ready to learn. That word "almost" thrilled me, I thought I knew why it was there, I had a hunch about what it must have taken to know to put it there. I was having "a long look at some-one/Alone like a key in a lock/Without what it takes to turn," nearing the end of reading to keep up, and of other commotions in the world of reading to keep up. I was in the middle of transferring my allegiance from one part of my mind to another, a piece of work that took years.

HABITS

Even in the middle of the night
they go on handing me around
but it's dark and they drop more of me
and for longer

then they hang on to my memory
thinking it's theirs

even when I'm asleep they take
one or two of my eyes for their sockets
and they look around believing
that the place is home

when I wake and can feel the black lungs
flying deeper into the century
carrying me
even then they borrow
most of my tongues to tell me
that they're me
and they lend me most of my ears to hear them

This was the voice of the night mind, many of the poems had it, addressing broad daylight, putting certain things on notice, common sense and the ego foremost, enlarging the world exponentially, saying it too played only by its own rules, saw through what it chose to see through, especially abstraction. For years I'd been involved with poetry, deeply, as a writer and teacher, but I hadn't heard words with such a charge in a long time, not since the beginning, with Eliot, who taught me I was on a journey, and would encounter guides.

"Habits" and "The Piper" were two of a number of such poems, they struck a sound I'd never heard before. They created a realm, "in the high barrens/where the light loved us," that I could visit, where "at last the juggler [was] led out under the stars," that often I could hang out in. It was "a long way/to the first/anything/come even so," where the language took me, within hearing of psychic boxcars coupling and uncoupling farther on up the draw. Remoteness was a god in those poems, sitting at the right hand of freedom, acerbity to the left, and when I was worthy they would invite me to the many wonders they presided over. Mostly I listened to the voices of the unborn, to the rumbles of competing lords, to the snap of whips loud and not so loud, and most of all to cries "frozen in another age." Those poems afforded me insight and great succor and replenished energy, provided the key stuck in my lock the wherewithal to turn; and their realm, with "only the nameless hunger/watching us out of the stars," made awe and reverence possible for me again, in a rush. Passage upon passage took the darkness of my mind in a flash. This from "Something I've Not Done":

> Every morning
> it's drunk up part of my breath for the day
> and knows which way
> I'm going
> and already it's not done there

This from "Glass":

> One day you look at the mirror and it's open
> and inside the place where the eyes were
> is a long road gray as water
> and on it someone is running away
> a little figure in a long pale coat
> and you can't move you can't call
> it's too late for that
> who was it you ask

This from "Lemuel's Blessing," addressed to the wolf:

> You that know the way,
> Spirit,
> I bless your ears which are like cypruses on a mountain
> With their roots in wisdom. Let me approach.

> I bless your paws and their twenty nails which tell their own prayer
> And are like dice in command of their own combinations.
> Let me not be lost.
> I bless your eyes for which I know no comparison.
> Run with me like the horizon, for without you
> I am nothing but a dog lost and hungry,
> Ill-natured, untrustworthy, useless.

This from "The Saint of the Uplands":

> I took a single twig from the tree of my ignorance
> And divined the living streams under
> Their very houses. I showed them
> The same tree growing in their dooryards.
> You have ignorance of your own, I said.
> They have ignorance of their own.

This from "Teachers":

> what I live for I can seldom believe in
> who I love I cannot go to
> what I hope is always divided
>
> but I say to myself you are not a child now
> if the night is long remember your unimportance
> sleep

The language of these poems had been slept on, had acquired the dream. Sometimes I would be up off my seat, slapping the wall with the book, or down on my hips, dancing, or down further, bowing. They spoke not to or about the unnamable, they spoke from it, as they were talking to the names. My soul cried—dared I say it—of joy and sorrow.

Holed up for a school year in two rooms in downtown Lexington, the only tenant on the block, I was sleeping in a bag on a floor mattress, worn copies of *Writings to an Unfinished Accompaniment* and *The Moving Target* within reach, over there with a table lamp, my smokes and bourbon. *The Carrier of Ladders* was there sometimes and sometimes *The Lice* or *The Compass Flower,* though three was too many—I wanted things kept simple over there.

Without looking I'd reach out, occasionally during the day, always at night before I went to sleep, pick up one of those volumes, and open it at random, very rarely reading more than two or three poems, sometimes only one. Or I would reach for the book on the passenger seat, pull off into a rest area, with a flashlight once, as if it were a road map. There coming up off the page would be "The Child" or "The Nails" or "Mist" or "Search" or "Lemuel's Blessing," teachings that seemed, often, directed straight at me. Many poems from these books seemed to have been everywhere I'd been, and understood a lot more, and others seemed to be out mapping, with princely bravado, territory I'd only heard about. "The Place of Backs" began:

> When what has helped us has helped us enough
> it moves off and sits down
> not looking our way
>
> after that every time we call it
> it takes away one of the answers it has given us

With a box of kitchen matches I'd fire up a Winston, my back to the pillowed wall, and a passage like that one would dance out of its cold fire into my mind, in that thrilling way only poetry can. Great poetry, I should say— encountered in time of change. The world as I had always known it was being set aside, not looking my way any longer, and the language of those poems was one of my principal guides, the principal one. What a life would be like, that knew what it knew, knew what "Lemuel's Blessing" knew, or "'Mist,'" well, certain poems sang that song, quite a few sang it. "Here the nuthatch blows his horn/leading a thin procession of white wind//past the black trees/through the world," a world far more vivid and deeply experienced than the one I was fighting free of. The imagined experience of "A long line of ghosts waiting at a well/laughing/in the evening/and I am standing among them/the line runs through me/I feel it/a procession of dry clouds" was a good deal more real to me than most of what was going on in my actual life. You didn't seem to have to be simply bewildered so much of the time, after all, and paralyzed—shame was not the only condition of the soul.

BREAD AND BUTTER

> I keep finding this letter
> To the gods of abandon,
> Tearing it up: Sirs,
> Having lived in your shrines
> I know what I owe you—
>
> I don't, did I ever? With both hands
> I've forgotten, I keep
> Having forgotten. I'll have no such shrines here.
> I will not bow in the middle of the room
> To the statue of nothing
> With the flies turning around it.
> On these four walls I am the writing.
>
> Why would I start such a letter?
> Think of today, think of tomorrow.
> Today on the tip of my tongue,
> Today with my eyes,

Tomorrow the vision,
Tomorrow

In the broken window
The broken boats will come in,
The life boats
Waving their severed hands,

And I will love as I ought to
Since the beginning.

It was the poet's voice, as unmistakably and irresistibly as that of Rilke, or of
Eliot, Stevens, Hopkins, language from the other side of the mind, from within the deep channel, full of legendary private urgency and the dream. Saying
listen, listen, you lived by your ear in poetry's realm. The voice that brought
nature poems and love poems and political poems and story poems and
satires and on, all out in the same unmistakable signature. The poet's voice
was his root sound, what words could and couldn't do its brooding subject.

A beginning-of-the-morning "dog barking at its echoes in the mountains"
was one of his many totem creatures, another the wolf who knew the consequences of having "hidden at wrong times for wrong reasons," another the
spirit of poetry, that wanted to reclaim the undivided attention of the original
ear, and the silence of sounds. Comfort had no place in the endeavor, "that
lay in ambush for joy."

That call to the ear, for devotion, was poetry's first sound, and its last, and
in these poems, the source of their pride and their fierceness—they sent the
night mind to open the door, not the cop; the ear, not the intellect. "The
crown turns/and the eye/drilled clear through his head/turns/it is north every-
where/come out he says." Until you'd heard the dream and responded, this
language was leading me to understand, poetry was likely to be stuck in your
head, along with the rest of your life. You might just have to choose between
studying and being studied, working on and being worked upon—the notion
that you could have poetry both ways, back and forth, that might be just a
school talk. "Not part of the country/part of the horizon," that was the way
poetry sounded, talking of itself.

"How do you think up all the surprising turns one finds in your poems," he
was asked when he read on campus.

"I don't think things up," was his answer. "I hear them."

BEGINNING

Long before spring
king of the black cranes
rises one day
from the black
needle's eye

on the white plain
under the white sky

the crown turns
and the eye
drilled clear through his head
turns
it is north everywhere
come out he says

come out then
the light is not yet
divided
it is a long way
to the first
anything
come even so
we will start
bring your nights with you

In the presence of this language I knew . . . that you ought not begin a sentence this way unless you can finish it, without apology. Knew the sound of a poem when a sword was being drawn from between the lines, when essential nature was the aim. Knew that all the muddles of the workplace had the same domestic stamp, underneath the bureaucratic one; and many of my private life muddles as well, oh for sure, marked by fear. Knew that "Today seventy tongues/are hiding in the trees" for those whose ears weren't in hock. In poem after poem the journey was into a crisis with abstraction, salvation in avoiding it, staying within the light "not yet divided," or trying to get there.

Among the several shocks and challenges of "Habits" was this, I could hear that voice, through my students' ears and my own—"even in the middle of the night/they go on handing me around"—as poetry itself talking about its life in the academy. Conceptualizations were dropping more of it each year, it seemed, and for longer, taking away far too many of the answers it had given us. Leaving the would-be poets confused and sometimes bent out of shape, often suspicious of what was offered to them in the name of literary studies, sometimes hostile.

I remember D. especially, who after years of studying and writing poetry papers heard the poet for the first time in "The Piper," and asked me to read it to him, and I asked him to read it back. You had to give up wanting to have anything to say when the words got white, it was static on the line, that was my experience, and his experience. "Listen to this," he said without preamble when I picked up the phone one morning. He was a lineman for Bell South, calling from the top of a pole, "a white note nailed there in a can/with white words," to recite his latest favorite from *The Moving Target*.

We listened a lot to Louise Glück too, and C. K. Williams, Lucille Clifton,

Emily Dickinson, wherever the poet's voice was being heard. Ai, Gerald
Stern, Kinnell, Ginsberg, Rich, St. John Perse in English. "Listen to this," I
said every chance I got at school, and then went home and said it some more
to Mary Ann or over the phone, without preamble, or someone would say it
to me, and then read a poem, maybe a second, and that would be the call,
mostly, from the top of the pole.

THE PORT

The river is slow
and I knew I was late arriving but had no idea
how late
in the splintery fishing port silence
was waving from the nails
dry long since
the windows though rattling
were fixed in time and space
in a way that I am not nor ever was
and the boats were out of sight

all but one
by the wharf
full of water
with my rotted sea-clothes lashed to a piling
at its head
and a white note nailed there in a can
with white words
I was too late to read

when what I came to say is I have learned who we are
when what I came to say was
consider consider
our voices
the salt

they waken in heads
in the deaths themselves

that was part of it
when what I came to say was
it is true that in
our language deaths are to be heard
at any moment through the talk
pacing their wooden rooms jarring
the dried flowers
but they have forgotten who they are
and our voices in their heads waken
childhood in other tongues

> but the whole town has gone to sea without a word
> taking my voice

There were the things imagined, the charms you wore along the way, and there was the imagination, the guide. The way this mind moved through a scene or a drama or an idea, its "impetuous prudence," well, there was a body yoga for the witness that went with the mental and spiritual one, a classical shiver and rearrangement, an astonishing intimacy, a string without pulled from within. Another of its favorite gestures was to buckle and unbuckle. "Do I? Did I ever?/With both hands/I've forgotten, I keep/Having forgotten." "Maybe he does not even have to exist/to exist in departures." Even at its most concrete the language of those poems was a wand, and each thing or moment or situation it touched opened up, could be seen through, became part of other goings-on that were seen through, inside time and outside simultaneously, "two seasons." When it had a visage, the visage was divided up and down, almost two of them, and the eyes not the same—and like everything else in that realm, they beheld you in a one-way transaction. For all the sensual delight with which those words took up the things of this world, they did it the way a dancer took up the next gesture, and for all the sense the form of the poem made of its accumulated gestures, it did it the way a button slipped out of a buttonhole. Or a knot was untied, or revealed to be no knot at all, just another first step on the long noway to anything. D. and I wondered if maybe ballet didn't have a term for the upward evaporation that so often occurred at the end of those poems, where Time was a string that got pulled, and you felt it in parts of yourself otherwise remote, even secret.

Dance, choreography, the language of those poems invited such comparisons, so palpably was the deepest beat kinetic and sensual, not intellectual, the razzle of ideas and metaphysics notwithstanding; its deepest knowledge in movement, in performance. It proposed always to see the thing through, that was its specific gravity—"Born once/born forever"—a promise and the presence of fierce honor, great intelligence. Words afforded the stage, attitude the setting, the poet's mind the drama, flashing through them like lightning, the bandit's whip, come to tell us we were not who we thought we were, and never had been. In the "clear night" of his words, I saw for myself "fish/jumping at stars." The intelligence in this language could get from a dead standstill to a modern dance of profiles as quickly as zen calligraphy, and maintain it with such ease, it was a princeliness not just of style but of character, of essence. A poise in angular and wondrous action, of fearlessness, engagement, panache—teaching much deeper than thought.

The urgency that always accompanied his words came not just from the subject at hand, and what he had to say about it, but from the work the words were doing—he was writing for his life, not about it.

THE COLD BEFORE THE MOONRISE

It is too simple to turn to the sound
Of frost stirring among its
Stars like an animal asleep
In the winter night
And say I was born far from home
If there is a place where this is the language may
It be my country

THE WEIGHT OF SLEEP

At the very mention of it there is one kind of person who laughs or looks away. You know at once where he is—in his life, in the story of the species, in the adventure of the planet. For the weight of sleep cannot be measured. By definition, some might say, though has it ever been defined? At least it cannot be measured by any scale known to the perspectives of waking. Presumably it might be measured one day if machines were contrived that resembled us so closely that they slept. And required sleep. But there again, can we tell how they would differ from us? How their sleep would differ from ours? There again one reaches for definitions and touches darkness.

And yet the weight of sleep is one of the only things that we know. We have been aware of it since we knew anything, since the first moment after conception. It grew with us, it grows along with us, it draws us on. Its relation to the gravity of the planet is merely one of analogy. The weight of sleep draws us back inexorably toward a unity that is entirely ours but that we cannot possess, that resembles the sky itself as much as it does the centers of the heavenly bodies.

When did it begin? With life itself? Long before? Or a little time after, when consciousness, the whole of consciousness, scarcely begun, suddenly became aware of itself like a caught breath, and was seized with panic and longing and the knowledge of travail? Yes, it was then that the weight of sleep came to it, the black angel full of promises. With different forms for each life. Different dances.

For the planet itself it was simpler. To the whole of the globe's first life as it became conscious of itself, everything seemed to have stopped in the terrible light. Everything stood in the grip of the single command: Weariness. Forever and ever. Then came the black angel.

For the planet his shape can be pictured as that of a driving wheel of a locomotive. The rim is darkness; he is always present. The spokes are darkness. They divide the light, though they disappear as they turn. They meet at the center. The hub is darkness. Across one side is a segment of solid black. There is the weight of sleep, properly speaking: its throne. There the wheel's mass preserves its motion. There its stillness dreams of falling. There what it is dreams of what it is.

David Young

CAUGHT BREATH

We encounter strange reversals when we enter Merwin's world. The substantial grows ghostly, while the invisible becomes more and more distinct and unmistakable. Processes that had seemed to have only one direction backtrack and undo themselves. The careful segmentations of time and history coil up and writhe like anacondas. Familiarity recedes into strangeness and the wildest possibilities turn matter-of-fact.

In his poems, these transformations have often occurred beforehand and the poem's utterance is likely to be mysterious to us until we have fully comprehended the irreality, or heightened reality, which it presupposes. Thus, in "Caesar" (*The Lice*), we had to understand how the thug on duty could call "night out of the teeth," and do it "one by one," before we can fully understand what it means for the speaker to be "Wheeling the president past banks of flowers/Past the feet of empty stairs/Hoping he's dead." The poem feels languid, but its effects are extremely concentrated and carefully measured. When we have made the right alignments, then Kennedy's assassination is also Caesar's, and Roman anomie is American anomie. There's a shiver of horror, recognition, delight (at the gothic gesture and at having someone speak forbidden thoughts) and quiet anger, all at once.

Acclimating ourselves to these dreamy, photo-negative worlds is part of the pleasure and challenge we face with Merwin, and the unerring rightness of a poem can withhold itself until we have stepped fully into its implications. The prose poems, by contrast, often teach us how to step and step again, feeling our way, tracing a process. By borrowing the procedures of the essay and parable, flirting with the discursive, the objective, and the systematic designs of allegory, they are less apparently subversive than the poems, but finally equally so, wolves in sheepskins, more lupine when they finally reveal themselves behind their apparently reasonable rhetoric.

"The Weight of Sleep" is a case in point. With this title and concept, Merwin already, in a sense, has his poem. The idea instantly invites metaphoric elaboration and speculation. It's a poem-kit. One sees this frequently in Merwin's work, as for instance in "For the Anniversary of My Death" (*The Lice*). There the idea that we all have an unknown death-day to match a known birthday is so intriguing that the point of the poem seems almost fully realized in its title. In that particular instance, Merwin quickly sketches out the implications and then moves to an image that looks beyond his own insecure knowledge and time-entrapment: "As today writing after three days of rain/Hearing the wren sing and the falling cease/And bowing not knowing to what."

In "The Weight of Sleep," there's more opportunity, given the scope and leisure of the prose poem, for play, for hide-and-seek, for doubling back. By risking the prosaic as an extension of a poetic subject and concept, Merwin keeps the enterprise aloft for longer than we thought he could, a sleight-of-hand virtuoso turn.

His models here are primarily French—the piece has affinities with Ponge, Follain, Michaux—and he is adapting them to his distinctively American idiom and outlook. That should serve to remind us that Merwin has read widely and translated extensively, extending our literary horizons and demonstrating an eclectic taste that has helped keep American postmodernist literature from becoming too parochial or monochromatic.

****

The poem's first move is to engage the world of quantifying and digitalizing. The speaker's air of certainty—"one kind of person," "you know at once"—seems to mark him as very much at home in the mindset where measurement is a confident means of dispelling mystery. But his logic—machines that would resemble us closely and even require sleep—constrains him to admit that differences would continue to trouble the idea of any accurate measurement. His conclusion—"one reaches for definitions and touches darkness"—opens the topic up for narrative, for analogy, for a celebration of mystery. It's not the poem's fault that reason and quantification have failed to address the subject successfully; it's their own limitations that we have stumbled upon.

The second paragraph confronts us directly. We "know" the immeasurable weight of sleep because each of us experiences it bodily, regularly. The meaning of "knowledge" has shifted now from mere information to deep intimacy. The stakes are higher. This is not something to quantify; this is what you and I experienced last night, drifting off, and again this morning, waking up.

The speaker drives home the point of our necessary familiarity. He dismisses gravity as "merely" analogous, not an explanation. And he uses gravity as a springboard for the paradoxes of his final sentence. The weight of sleep recalls a unity, moving forward toward it and backward as well. It is ours but we can't possess it. It has to do with the earth and gravity, but it has as much to do with sky and deep space.

The poem could conceivably stop here, leaving the reader pondering. Instead, it goes on to consider origins. And it answers its own question. Sleep, with its weight, is the dark twin of consciousness. It responds to our experiences of panic and longing, Adam's double curse of labor and self-awareness. It is the alternative to life and consciousness, somehow, made up of the chthonic, of metaphysical origins and endings, of obliterated consciousness and oblivion itself.

The canny trope, "like a caught breath," stands right in the middle of this middle paragraph, an emblem for life and consciousness that combines the momentary and the prolonged in a way that affects the reader physically. Involvement in this poem is piercingly kinetic; it embraces the whole body and all its dim memories, its sleeping and waking and breathing, the intricate interplay of life and death, conscious and unconscious. Different dances, as the poem puts it. Each life a shape and rhythm all its own.

****

One would think that the black angel of sleep-weight, having been revealed or created in this middle paragraph, might go on to dominate the poem's final phase. That he both does and does not shows, I think, Merwin's tricky subtlety, his willingness to shift his ground and keep us off balance.

The poem's next move is away from the human and toward the simpler version of activity and rest, as conceived by the life forms of the whole planet, the biosphere. As soon as life existed, the need for rest would be apparent. We now have the origin of the angel, who predates the dilemmas of human self-awareness and is more simply associated with rhythms of work and rest, activity and stasis.

But he is not exactly an angel. He becomes, by being likened to it, the drive wheel of a locomotive, the one way he can be successfully pictured. I believe this is the most brilliant stroke of the poem. Sleep is now associated not so much with rest as with motion, with power and industry, and, for Americans, with what Leo Marx has described as the machine in the garden, the technological imposition on our landscape about which we feel an endless ambivalence. It means power and progress, but it also means death and oblivion. Walt Whitman and Emily Dickinson's locomotives hover in the background here, contributing to the strength of this image. William Carlos Williams's ("Overture to a Dance of Locomotives") too, not to mention the folksongs and folklore associated with trains, loneliness, night whistles, hoboes, and the huge size of this country, spanned by thin tracks and long freights.

Merwin does not need to invoke all this. He can instead stay with the specificity of how the angel can be sleep-weight and be a wheel, "for the planet." His imagery and rhythms are unerring:

> The rim is darkness; he is always present. The spokes are darkness. They divide the light, though they disappear as they turn. They meet at the center. The hub is darkness. Across one side is a segment of solid black. There is the weight of sleep, properly speaking, its throne. There the wheel's mass preserves its motion. There its stillness dreams of falling. There what it is dreams of what it is.

This is a straightforward description of a locomotive wheel, including that solid segment that is flat on one side and curved to the shape of the wheel on the other. A friend of mine who knew the poem thought that Merwin was being metaphorical in this image, but these segments show up on drive wheels, as real as everything, and they are there, I take it, to balance the wheel with a counterweight to the driving rods and side rods and eccentric cranks attached to the wheels (terminology courtesy of the wonderful locomotive diagram in my venerable Webster's Second Unabridged). The reader can of course "translate" all this into information about how rest, sleep, dreams and their weight counterbalance the rhythms and energies of our waking lives, but there is scarcely any need. Pondering that wheel, where stillness dreams of falling, is somehow enough.

****

The last sentence is the oddest of all, in a way, and might be thought by some readers a sort of blemish, less compelling rhythmically than what precedes it and awkward conceptually as well. But the twinning of dreaming and waking, the way the self acts out its daylight life in the world of dreams, is the final and most necessary piece of information in this poem. It is more precise in its way than any attempts at measurement or quantification could hope to be. The world of quantities is invaded again by the world of mirrors, or analogies and likenesses, the slants and approximations by which the spirit feels its way forward in darkness toward light.

Merwin's name is almost like an anagram of *mirror*. He is one of those masters of likeness and twinning whom we can trust to lead us deeper into the labyrinth. He will not lead us out or give us answers, but he will teach us how to be at home there, at peace with the strangeness and infinite wonder of our existence.

It seems important to insist on these qualities, and on their distinctiveness just now. I admit that Merwin can be mawkish at times, sentimental, overly romantic, a bit Victorian in his outlook and diction. But he stands for a quality of spirit and imagination that I do not want my fellow poets to lose sight of.

To test my attempt at identifying this value, try for a moment to imagine attributing this text I have just been discussing to W. H. Auden or to Robert Lowell. By acknowledging that neither could have written it, you can perhaps glimpse an aspect of poetry's best possibilities that is sometimes dismissed or overlooked in the current discussion. Auden was too grounded in his certitudes, early and late, to adventure in this way. Lowell was too convinced of the distinctiveness of self and history, his own in particular. Both of them hewed to an English sense of poetic tradition that associated them too closely, for me, with T. S. Eliot and his narrow, patrician perspectives. I know this is heresy to some ears.

If, on the other hand, I propose to myself that Elizabeth Bishop could have authored "The Weight of Sleep," or Wallace Stevens, those more plausible suggestions help me see why Merwin's willingness to ask the largest questions and to journey into mystery are significant to my own attempts to identify my values as a reader and writer. I might also have said Charles Simic, and, possibly, John Ashbery. It's not a matter of religious beliefs or of geographical location, or even of subject matter. It's a quality of openness that I value in Rilke, in Neruda (at his best, anyway), in Montale, and that I find too often absent in the poetry of my own contemporaries.

The Miner's Pale Children appeared in 1970. It's extremely rich in material of the kind I've discussed here, and yet it is seldom mentioned or anthologized these days. *Models of the Universe*, the anthology of prose poems I co-edited with Stuart Friebert, is the exception. But Merwin's prose poems should not just be encountered in rare anthologies of the genre. They should come back in many contexts, to teach and delight us, and they should continue to remind us of how gravity and legerity can combine to make prose that is more poetic than we could have thought possible.

SEARCH PARTY

By now I know most of the faces
that will appear beside me as
long as there are still images
I know at last what I would choose
the next time if there ever was
a time again I know the days
that open in the dark like this
I do not know where Maoli is

I know the summer surfaces
of bodies and the tips of voices
like stars out of their distances
and where the music turns to noise
I know the bargains in the news
rules whole languages formulas
wisdom that I will never use
I do not know where Maoli is

I know whatever one may lose
somebody will be there who says
what it will be all right to miss
and what is verging on excess
I know the shadows of the house
routes that lead out to no traces
many of his empty places
I do not know where Maoli is

You that see now with your own eyes
all that there is as you suppose
though I could stare through broken glass
and show you where the morning goes
though I could follow to their close
the sparks of an exploding species
and see where the world ends in ice
I would not know where Maoli is

Christopher Merrill

IN SEARCH OF THE GENUINE

W. S. Merwin once remarked that "a real poem comes out of what you don't know. You write it with what you know, but finally its source is what you don't know." The poet's tools—rhythm and rhyme, image and idea, the warp and woof of language—are thus useful only insofar as they serve to plumb the depths of that which is ultimately unknowable. The mysterious light given off by memorable poetry, like the phosphorescent flaring of fish in the night tides, derives from its contact with a larger order—the source, illuminated in flashes and starts, which shapes a poet's vision. An ancient presence, Merwin calls it, which is never far from an authentic poem, of which he has written considerably more than most poets. Indeed, his is an exemplary search for the genuine in poetry—and in life.

Surely a measure of his genius resides in his willingness, at crucial moments throughout his distinguished career, to abandon subjects and forms which have become familiar in favor of exploring the unknown; his vitality, in a number of genres, is a function of his desires to reinvent himself. He is not the sort of artist who traps himself in one style or vision but rather discovers a seemingly infinite variety of ways to apprehend the world, listening for what he calls "the vibrancy of life"—in nature, in his attention to detail, in the various poetries that he translates into English. At the age of seventy, Merwin continues to teach himself—and his readers—how to hear and see anew, because for all his technical mastery and experience he retains what he describes as "an indelible awareness of [poetry's] parentage with that biblical waif, ill at ease in time, the spirit. No one has any claims on it, no one deserves it, no one knows where it goes." Fortunately, it has left its tracks all over Merwin's books.

A recent poem, "Search Party," from *Travels* (1992), juxtaposes the known and unknowable with such force that it is difficult not to read it as an artistic credo. The poem was inspired by a real event: a beloved chow chow was kidnapped, and during the long search for him up and down the island of Maui the poet began to chant, "I do not know where Maoli is"—a line which, among other things, happened to fall into iambic tetrameter. It became the refrain of "Search Party," part of the sturdy metrical underpinnings and rigorous rhyme scheme crucial to the poem, which in other hands might well have succumbed to bathos. That there are no traces of sentimentality in Merwin's record of his search for a lost dog is a testament to his dependence on traditional poetic elements.

An odd thing to say of a poet widely credited with helping to usher in the free verse revolution in American poetry. In fact, *Travels* is a highly formal affair; and I would argue that its regular stanzas and rhymes represent not so much a return to the traditional glories on display in *A Mask for Janus, The Dancing Bears, Green with Beasts* and *The Drunk in the Furnace*, as a breakthrough on the order of *The Moving Target*, the book in which Merwin announced his departure from the studied elegances of his earlier work. It is as if he finds new energy in that which is no longer familiar; like a painter trained as an Abstract Expressionist—William Bailey, say—who treats recognizable figures with an abstract sense of design, Merwin brings to his ballade all that he has learned from thirty years of working in open forms, rescuing a form which by the end of the last century had become a cliché.

Here, then, are four octaves in eight-syllable lines (which in all but two cases are iambic), with the same rhyme throughout, now true, now slant: a rich musical experience. Back of the poem lies François Villon's "*Ballade des Vérités*," and it is well to remember what Merwin has said about the French poet: "For years I have had a recurring dream of finding, as it were in an attic, poems of my own that were as lyrically formal, but as limpid and essentially unliterary, as those of Villon." At least part of that dream has come true in "The Search Party," which considers *la vérité* in a contemporary light, through the prism of a dog's name—Maoli, a Maori word whose meanings include *native, indigenous, aboriginal, true, real, actual, genuine,* all of which apply to this poem.

What luck to have named his dog so well—and then to recover him! What remains is a poem in which a domestic tragedy takes on universal significance. Apart from his inability to find a certain chow chow, Merwin is haunted by the limitations of knowledge, more than a dozen categories of which he catalogues—memory, intuition, sight, touch, hearing, aesthetics, pragmatism, law, linguistics, mathematics, ethics, geography, ecology, eschatology. His is the quintessential modern dilemma: not knowing where to look for the truth. It is a candid admission from a poet who has devoted much of his life to careful observation of his surroundings, in the hope of discovering meaning. As he said of *Unframed Originals*, his book of reminiscences: "I felt if I could take any detail, any moment, anything I could clearly see, and pay enough attention to it, it would act like a kind of hologram. I'd be able to see the whole story in that single detail—just the way, if you could really pay attention to a dream, the dream would probably tell you everything you needed to know for that time and place."

But Merwin's concern for aboriginal wisdom, which he celebrates in his writings, honors in his studies of native Hawaiian lore, and works to preserve through his translations and environmental activism, makes him ever more wary of human arrogance, the certainty which leads men, for example, to sanction the destruction of indigenous peoples, wild places, and precious sources of knowledge. What the poet offers instead is a hymn to the actual, in all its glorious complexity, the starting point of which is the realization that he can grasp only part of the whole. "Search Party" thus magnifies the tension between what he knows and what will always lie beyond him by linking sounds: the rhymes on *is* marry the known to the unknown and the refrain darkly counterpoints the speaker's certainties, creating a ceremony, by turns magical and sobering, in which Merwin discovers the genuine.

COMPLETION

Seen from afterward the time appears to have been
   all of a piece which is of course how it was but how seldom
it seemed that way when it was still happening and was
   the air through which I saw it as I went on thinking
of somewhere else in some other time whether gone
   or never to arrive and so it was divided
however long I was living in it and I was where
   it kept coming together and where it kept moving apart
while home was a knowledge that did not suit every occasion
   but remained familiar and foreign as the untitled days
and what I knew better than to expect followed me
   into the garden and I would stand with friends among
the summer oaks and be a city in a different
   age and the dread news arrived on the morning when the plum trees
opened into silent flower and I could not let go
   of what I longed to be gone from and it would be that way
without end I thought unfinished and divided
   by nature and then a voice would call from the field
in the evening or the fox would bark in the cold night
   and that instant with each of its stars just where it was
in its unreturning course would appear even then
   entire and itself the way it all looks from afterward

William Matthews

LAYERED VISION

The passage of time has always been Merwin's central, goading subject. You can't see it—breath, spirit, ghost. Invisible itself, its effects are almost everything we see: the roiling leaves, the taxi's blue plume of exhaust, the scroll of clouds across the brightening and then the darkening sky. Like Merwin's 1992 prose book, *The Lost Upland,* his recent (1996) book of poems, *The Vixen*, is set in southwestern France and driven by a kind of layered vision.

Do you remember the biology books in which there were transparent overlays—one depicted the skeleton, one the musculature, one the circulatory system, and so on? When the student peered down through all the layers, a whole human anatomy was visible. Everything seemed more jumbled to-

gether and confusing than the subway system under Columbus Circle, but
something complete had been made knowable from its easier-to-look-at
components.

In *The Vixen* we see time most readily by its fragments, and seldom whole.
These few lines from "Old Sound" provide another example:

> many lives had begun and ended inside there
>   and had passed over the stone doorsill and looked from the windows
> to see faces arriving under trees that are not
>   there any more with the sky white behind them and doorways
> had been sealed up inside the squared stones of their frames.

The poems in *The Vixen* abound in temporal disjunctions like the one in
which "...faces arriving under trees that are not/there any more with the sky
sky white behind them..." both unites two distinct times and insists on their
absolute separation. The poem ends, a few lines later, still thinking about the
palimpsest of times the house is:

> now its age is made of almost no time a sound
>   that you have to get far away from before you can hear it.

Here's the beginning of "Bodies of Water."

> In the long stone basin under the apple tree
>   at the end of one spring in the garden I saw the faces
> of all the masons who had built there on the edge
>   of the rock overlooking the valley their reflections
> smiled out from the still surface into the speechless
>   daylight each of them for the moment the only one

It takes a steady sentry to see these moments of completion, for, as the one of
the poems in *The Vixen* ends, "something keeps going without looking back."

The book is full of memorable, summary last lines. Here's a bou-
quet of them:

> Most of the stories have to do with vanishing.

***

> it went as it came and the fragile green survived it

***

> if any of this remains it will not be me

***

> each of them coming from what was already gone

The interiors of the poems in this book are frequently rehearsals of the ways we experience time in fragments and think by shifting from fragment to fragment. Consider the last three lines of "Completion":

> and that instant with each of its stars just where it was
> in its unreturning course would appear even then
> entire and itself the way it all looks from afterward

It was after translating Jean Follain's unpunctuated poems (that book appeared in 1969) that Merwin followed suit. The rich ambiguities of the three lines quoted above can perhaps best be savored by following the pronoun "it" on its shapeshifting way through all three lines. It appears five times: (1) possessive form, meaning "the instant's stars"; (2) the instant; (3) the instant has an unreturning course because time goes one way only, although the stars that instant contains make us think of orbits, or returning courses, even though stars are suns and have no courses but are still while their planets circle them; (4) the instant itself, again; (5) this last "it" now means something vast, like a vista from which the instant and its place in a larger scheme can all be seen.

To punctuate those three lines would be to reduce their ambiguity and wrongly to housebreak them.

In those three final lines "Completion" shows us in microcosm the extraordinary accomplishment of these poems: over and over they enlist us in partial experiences and understandings of time and then lead us from that choreographed disjunction to the austere clarities of the book's many aphoristic final lines.

THE RED

It was summer a bright day in summer and the path kept
    narrowing as it led in under the oaks
which grew larger than those I was used to in that country
    darker and mossed like keepers it seemed to me
of an age earlier than anything I could know
    underfoot the ground became damp and water appeared
in long scarves on the trail between overhanging
    ferns and bushes and reflected the sky through the leaves
the birds were silent at that hour and I went on
    through the cool air listening and came to a corner
of ruined wall where the way emerged into
    a bare place in the woods with paths coming together
the remains of walls going on under trees and the roofless
    shoulders of stone buildings standing hunched among heavy
boughs all in shade the mud tracks of animals led
    past a tall stone in the center darker than the stone
of that country and with polished faces and red
    lines across them which when I came close I saw
were names cut deep into the stone and beside each one
    a birth date with each letter and numeral painted
that fresh crimson I read without counting to the foot
    of one side and the date of death and the account
of how it had come to them one day in summer when they
    were brought out of those buildings where they had lived
old people most of them as the dates indicated
    men and women and with them children they had been
ordered in German to that spot where they were
    shot then the Germans set fire to the buildings
with the animals inside and when they had finished
    they went off down the lane and the fires burned on
and the smoke filled the summer twilight and then the warm night

Carol Muske

THE TRANSPARENT MASK

As epigraph for my first book of poems I borrowed a celebrated line from W. S. Merwin: "...unless I go in a mask, how shall I know myself among my faces?" This choice was more than a reinforcement of theme (my book was entitled *Camouflage*)—it was an acknowledgment of my timid admiration for an esthetic stance. The idea of the "mask," through which the poet's consciousness could radiate, unimpeded by the self (which I had always understood as a tenuous construct at best), seemed to me an enormously liberating proposition. This liberation, this lightfooted traveling through the world, was what drew me (and continues to draw me) to Merwin's poems.

He had, he once said, learned the same song at the feet of many masters: that Song inherent in the natural world, which the many masks divined. Merwin's range, from formal to a kind of visionary free verse, dramatized this variety, as did his translations of the Poems of the Cid, Chanson de Roland, Euripides, Neruda, Mandelstam, the Vietnamese. His poems seemed a charged field of possibility. To sing without impediment, he seemed to be saying, the poet must shake off the expectations of identity, go in a disguise, cloaked, humble, attentive. The epigraph line that I freely appropriated, for a first book published in 1975, when masks were being stripped away indiscriminately as symbols of deception or hypocrisy—was the merest *breath* of resistance. I cloaked myself in a master's words, uncertain. Perhaps *truth*, or its approximation, might still elude us, even in defiant nakedness, stripped of our masks, bristling with the facts of our lives?

It is ironic, thinking of masks, that here we have, with "The Red"—a "political" poem. It is a poem about a specific historical event, with a point of view. The reader understands, from the beginning, that the poem's unfolding, if not strictly sequential, is moving forward by momentum (or gathering momentousness) toward a dreadful event from the past made manifest in the present. The event is a brutal atrocity, a massacre of innocents. This poem could be about My Lai or Guernica or Rwanda, except for one detail. The poet identifies "the Germans"—and with that single reference, gives us a probable time, a probable place. World War II, an occupied country—"that country" he says, with a grieving irony—so that we understand the universality of this country, the reason for its anonymity. (Maybe it is France, where Merwin lived for years, maybe it is Poland, maybe Slovakia.)

What Merwin has done is to give us the much-vaunted poem of "witness," without the self. To be sure, there is an "I" in the poem. The narrator "I" is invisible, breath-colored, a transparent mask frequently donned by Merwin: I as eye. He obliterates any expectation of self-important testimony. The speaker's voice is disembodied, yet it remains our guide—the voice (perhaps) of a wanderer, ghost among ghosts—yet it is in no way objective. It is the poet's voice, unmediated by ego, and we trust its self-effacing authority, its long breathless lines, pushing each other onward.

The *act* of witness itself is what this poem is about; the *act* speaks to us through the poet. His shrewd introduction of "Germans" triggers a series of conditioned responses, he shows us what facts do—and the rhetoric of facts—they provide immediate context. No other evidence of a historical period is given, but now the word "Germans" echoes, reduced to a kind of mindless *sign*, banal as Hannah Arendt's definition of evil, collected and dismissed. The "Germans" could be Pharoah's legions or the destroyers of the Temple, seen as smoke curling upward by Jeremiah, they could be the priests of the Inquisition. But the poem's other *signs*: names, dates, "accounts," wounds in stone—struggle against this collectiveness; the individual epitaphs are struck in red, fresh as an opened vein. Whoever chose to grimly testify to, to *record*, this horror, chose the earth itself as page, as headstone, then carved symbols, painted the unforgiving color into stone. Because of that red (clearly renewed by new generations), the wound will stay immediate, raw, the terrible fire will never go out, smoldering near the "keepers," the most ancient witnesses: the trees, silent citizens of "an age earlier than anything I could know."

The limitations of the "I" of human intellect and memory, the harking back to an age free of human arrogance and mayhem, are familiar themes in Merwin's poetry. The point of view in the poem is not a facile indictment of Nazi slaughter—rather it is an ominous hymn to Nature's memory, as well as the human, animal and inanimate apocrypha, "with paths coming together"—like the word *legend* from the Latin "legenda," *to be read*. The read words (red) of the fire coaxed from stone: paths, legends, poems.

His images rivet: the crimson slashed stones standing like sentinels, the ruined wall, the dark mossy "keeper" trees. The point of view is unwavering indictment of amnesia, a refusal to forget, and thus it also makes its powerful argument for art. Merwin has always maintained that poetry pre-dates identity, that humility wears a mask made not of deception but illumination, that witness belongs to the earth, as well as the earth's warring inhabitants, its selves and claimants. My admiration for this poem is total—like so many Merwin poems, it seems to me miraculous in its capacity for lyric understatement, for rejuvenation of awe, for honor paid to the origins, the legends, the masks that help us to see (witness?) ourselves.

NOTES ON CONTRIBUTORS

Agha Shahid Ali's seven collections of poetry include, most recently, *A Nostalgist's Map of America* and *The Country without a Post Office*.

Tom Andrews teaches at Purdue University. His books include *The Hemophiliac's Motorcycle* (poems), *Codeine Diary* (memoir), and *The Point Where All Things Meet: Essays on Charles Wright*.

Margaret Atwood is author of more than twenty-five books of fiction, poetry, and nonfiction. Her most recent books include the novel *Alias Grace* and the poetry collection *Morning in the Burned House*.

Bruce Beasley is the author of *Spirituals* (Wesleyan), *The Creation* (winner of the 1993 Ohio State University Press/*Journal* Award), and *Summer Mystagogia* (winner of the 1996 Colorado Prize). He teaches at Western Washington University.

Marvin Bell has published sixteen books of poetry and essays, the latest being *Ardor* (vol. 2 of *The Book of the Dead Man*), the illustrated *Poetry for a Midsummer's Night*, and an Irish release titled *Wednesday*. He has taught at the U. of Iowa Writers' Workshop for many years.

Robert Bly's most recent book of poems is *Morning Poems* (HarperCollins, 1996). His *Eating the Honey of Words: New and Selected Poems* will be published in 1999.

Philip Booth's *Lifelines: Selected Poems 1950-1999* has just been published by Viking.

Marianne Boruch is the author of four books of poems, including *Moss Burning* and *A Stick That Breaks and Breaks* (both from Oberlin), and a collection of essays. She teaches in the MFA program at Purdue University.

Ralph Burns's last book, *Swamp Candles*, won the 1995 Iowa Poetry Prize. He edits *Crazyhorse* and teaches at the University of Arkansas at Little Rock.

Fred Chappell's latest book of criticism is *A Way of Happening: Observations of Contemporary Poetry* (Picador, 1997). His new novel will appear in 1999.

Martha Collins has published four books of poems, most recently *Some Things Words Can Do* (Sheep Meadow, 1998), and translated *The Women Carry River Water: Poems by Nguyen Quang Thieu* (Massachusetts, 1997). Since 1997 she has been Director of the Creative Writing Program at Oberlin College and an editor of *FIELD*.

Deborah Digges's most recent collection of poems, *Rough Music*, won the Kingsley Tufts Prize from the Claremont Colleges.

Niccolò N. Donzella is an attorney practicing in Baltimore. A graduate of the writing program at Brown, he has received a poetry fellowship from the NEA, and his work has appeared in *Poetry*, *The New York Quarterly*, and *The Village Voice*.

Norman Dubie is the author of numerous collections of poetry, including *Groom Falconer* (1989) and *Radio Sky* (1991). He is a professor of English at Arizona State University.

Sylva Fischerová teaches at the Charles University in Prague and has published several volumes of poems. *The Tremor of Racehorses* (Bloodaxe) is a selection of her work in English.

Dana Gioia's many books include *The Gods of Winter* (poems) and *Can Poetry Matter?* (essays). His translation of Eugenio Montale's *Mottetti* appeared in 1990 from Graywolf Press.

Albert Goldbarth is the author of numerous collections of poetry, including *Heaven and Earth*, for which he won the National Book Critics Circle Award, and *Troubled Lovers in History*. He lives in Wichita.

Beckian Fritz Goldberg is the author of *Body Betrayer* (1991), *In the Badlands of Desire* (1993), and *Never Be the Horse* (1999). She teaches creative writing at Arizona State University.

Donald Hall has published a dozen books of poetry, most recently *Without*, and five books of critical essays about poetry.

James Baker Hall is the author of five books of poems and two novels. Winner of an NEA grant, a Pushcart Prize, and an O. Henry Award, he teaches at the University of Kentucky.

Judith Hemschemeyer's translation of *The Complete Poems of Anna*

Akhmatova was published by Zephyr Press in 1990 in a bilingual, two-volume edition. An English-only paperback edition is now in its third printing.

Calvin Hernton, one of the country's pioneers in African American scholarship, recently retired as Professor of African American Studies at Oberlin College.

Edward Hirsch has published five books of poems, most recently *On Love* (Knopf). He teaches at the University of Houston.

Jonathan Holden is University Distinguished Professor and Poet-in-Residence at Kansas State University. His most recent book is *Guns and Boyhood in America: A Memoir of Growing Up in the Fifties*, in the University of Michigan's Poets on Poetry Series (1997).

Miroslav Holub is featured in the symposium that begins on page 535.

Laura Jensen's full-length books are *Bad Boats* (1977), *Memory* (1982), and *Shelter* (1985). From 1994 through 1996 she organized readings with the Distinguished Poet Series and co-edited and co-designed 28 broadsides compiled into a limited-edition book, with the support of the Lila Wallace Reader's Digest Fund.

Donald Justice is the author of seven books of poetry, most recently *New and Selected Poems* (Knopf, 1995), as well as a collection of critical essays, *Oblivion* (Story Line, 1998). He has received the Pulitzer Prize, the Bollingen Prize, and a Lannan Literary Award.

Shirley Kaufman, American-Israeli poet and translator, has published seven volumes of her own poems, and books of translations from the Hebrew of Amir Gilboa and Abba Kovner, and from the Dutch of Judith Herzberg. Her *Selected Poems*, translated into Hebrew by Aharon Shabtai, was published in Jerusalem where she now lives.

Yusef Komunyakaa is the author of ten books of poems, most recently *Thieves of Paradise*, and co-edited *The Jazz Poetry Anthology* and *Second Set*. In 1998 he received the Morton Dauwen Zabel Award from the American Academy of Arts and Letters and *Poetry* magazine's The Union League Civic and Arts Poetry Prize. He teaches at Princeton University.

Marilyn Krysl's *Warscape with Lovers* won the Cleveland State University Poetry Center Prize in 1996. Her third book of stories, *How to Accommodate Men*, is published by Coffee House Press.

Maxine Kumin's *Selected Poems: 1960-1990* was published by Norton in cloth in 1997 and in paper in 1999.

James Laughlin (1914-1997) was the greatest American publisher of the twentieth century. The founder and head of New Directions, he published many of the most consequential and revolutionary writers of his time.

Larry Levis published five collections of poems before his untimely death in 1996, including *The Widening Spell of the Leaves* (Pittsburgh, 1991), as well as a collection of stories. His posthumous collection, *Elegy*, was published by Pittsburgh in 1997.

Thomas Lux's most recent book is *New and Selected Poems 1975-1995* (Houghton Mifflin). He teaches at Sarah Lawrence College.

Paul Mariani has published biographies of William Carlos Williams, John Berryman, Robert Lowell, and, this year, *The Broken Tower: The Life of Hart Crane* (Norton). His most recent books of poetry are *Salvage Operations* and *The Great Wheel*. He is Distinguished University Professor at the University of Massachusetts in Amherst.

William Matthews, before his sudden death in 1997, wrote over a dozen books of poetry and translations, including *Time & Money* (Houghton Mifflin, 1995), for which he received the National Book Critics' Circle Award, and *After All*, published posthumously. In 1997 he was awarded the Ruth Lilly Poetry Prize.

Lenore Mayhew is the co-translator, with William McNaughton, of Anna Akhmatova's *Poem without a Hero and Selected Poems* (Oberlin, 1989).

Jerome Mazzaro's books include *The Caves of Love* (poetry) and *The Figure of Dante: An Essay on the "Vita Nuova"* (criticism).

J. D. McClatchy is the author of four collections of poems, most recently *Ten Commandments* (Knopf, 1998), and two collections of essays, *White Paper* (1989) and *Twenty Questions* (1998). He is editor of *The Yale Review*.

Lynne McMahon's third book of poems, *All Quail to the Wallowing*, appears from David R. Godine this spring. She has received an Ingram Merrill Award and a Guggenheim.

Sandra McPherson is the author of eight book-length collections of poetry, most recently *Edge Effect* and *The Spaces Between Birds* (both Wesleyan/

UPNE, 1996), and several smaller books. She is Professor of English at the University of California at Davis.

Christopher Merrill is the author of a dozen books, including *Watch Fire* (poetry) and *The Old Bridge: The Third Balkan War and the Age of the Refugee*. He teaches at the College of the Holy Cross.

James Merrill died in 1995. His *Collected Poems* is forthcoming from Knopf.

Barbara Molloy-Olund is the author of *In Favor of Lightning* (Wesleyan, 1987).

Carol Muske is Professor of English and Creative Writing at USC. Her new and selected poems, *An Octave Above Thunder*, was published in 1997 by Penguin, and a collection of her reviews and essays, *Women and Poetry: Truth, Autobiography, and the Shape of Self*, was published in the University of Michigan's Poets on Poetry Series (1997).

William O'Daly has published six volumes of his translations of Pablo Neruda's late and posthumous poetry with Copper Canyon Press. He has also published poems, essays, and reviews in numerous journals, and is at work on a manuscript of poems and a historical novel based on the Chinese Cultural Revolution.

Linda Pastan's tenth book of poetry, *Carnival Evening: New and Selected Poems 1968-1998*, was recently published by Norton.

Stanley Plumly is a Distinguished University Professor at the University of Maryland. His most recent book of poems, *The Marriage in the Trees*, appeared in paperback last year.

Sonia Raiziss was a translator, editor, poet, and critic until her death in 1994. Her books include *Bucks County Blues* (poems, 1977) and *Metaphysical Passion* (criticism).

David St. John's most recent collections are *The Red Leaves of Night* (HarperCollins) and *In the Pines: Lost Poems, 1972-1997. Study for the World's Body: New and Selected Poems* (HarperCollins, 1994) was nominated for the National Book Award in Poetry.

Reg Saner's interest in Montale began as a Fulbright student at the Università di Firenze. His own poetry exists in several prize-winning collections drawing on nature in the American West, as do his books of nonfiction. For the past several decades he has taught at the University of Colorado in Boulder.

Sherod Santos's fourth book of poems, *The Pilot Star Elegies*, is published by Norton this spring. He teaches at the University of Missouri—Columbia.

Dennis Schmitz has received several awards, including NEA and Guggenheim grants and the Shelley Memorial Award. He is the author of a half-dozen collections of poetry, most recently *About Night: Selected and New Poems* (Oberlin, 1993).

Charles Simic has published numerous books, among them *Jackstraws* (Harcourt Brace, 1999), *The World Doesn't End: Prose Poems* (1990), for which he received the Pulitzer Prize for Poetry, and *Selected Poems: 1963-1983* (1990). He has also published many translations of French, Serbian, Croatian, Macedonian, and Slovenian poetry, and four books of essays, most recently *Orphan Factory* (Michigan, 1998).

W. D. Snodgrass's most recent book is *Selected Translations* from BOA, who will also publish *After-Images*, a book of autobiographical sketches, this year.

Marcia Southwick's books include *Why the River Disappears* (Carnegie-Mellon) and *The Night Won't Save Anyone* (Georgia). Her third book, *A Saturday Night at the Flying Dog and Other Poems*, winner of the 1988 Field Poetry Prize, is published by Oberlin College Press this year.

Elizabeth Spires is the author of four collections of poetry: *Globe, Swan's Island, Annonciade*, and *Worldling*. A Guggenheim and Whiting Fellow, she holds the Chair for Distinguished Achievement at Goucher College.

William Stafford is featured in the symposium that begins on page 501.

Gerald Stern's newest book is *This Time: New and Selected Poems* (Norton). He won the National Book Award for 1998.

Pamela Stewart lives and works in Hawley, Massachusetts. Her most recent book is *The Red Window* (Georgia, 1997).

Henry Taylor is Professor of Literature and co-director of the graduate program in creative writing at American University. His books of poems include *The Flying Change* (Pulitzer Prize, 1986) and *Understanding Fiction: Poems 1986-1996*.

Alberta Turner's five collections of poems include *Beginning with And: New and Selected Poems* (1994). She is Emerita Professor of English at Cleveland State University and an editor of *FIELD*.

Lee Upton is the author of three books of poetry and three of criticism, most recently *Approximate Darling* and *The Muse of Abandonment*. She teaches at Lafayette College.

Jean Valentine has published seven books of poetry, most recently *Growing Darkness, Growing Light*. Her next book, *The Cradle of the Real Life*, will be published by Wesleyan. She lives and works in New York City.

David Walker is Professor of English at Oberlin College and an editor of *FIELD*. He is the author of *The Transparent Lyric*, a study of the poetry of Wallace Stevens and William Carlos Williams, and edited the revised edition of *A FIELD Guide to Contemporary Poetry and Poetics* (Oberlin, 1997).

Robert Wallace's next book will be a collection of essays, *Free Verse and the Orbit of Meter*.

Anthony Walton is the author of *Mississippi: An American Journey* (Vintage). He is Writer-in-Residence at Bowdoin College.

Bruce Weigl has two books of poetry out this spring: *Archeology of the Circle: New and Selected Poems* (Grove/Atlantic) and *After the Others* (TriQuarterly Books/Northwestern U. Press).

Richard Wilbur's *New and Collected Poems* (1987) won him a second Pulitzer Prize. He continues to work on translations of Molière's verse plays, and expects to bring out a new book of poems, *A Wall in the Woods*, later this year.

Nancy Willard's recent publications include *Swimming Lessons: New and Selected Poems* (Knopf) and an anthology, *Step Lightly: Poems for the Journey* (Harcourt Brace).

C. D. Wright has published ten collections of poetry, most recently *Deepstep Come Shining* (Copper Canyon, 1998). She is co-editor of Lost Roads Publishers and teaches at Brown University.

Charles Wright's latest book of poems is *Appalachia* (Farrar Straus). His many honors include the National Book Award, the National Book Critics Circle Award, the Ruth Lilly Poetry Prize, and the Pulitzer Prize. He teaches at the University of Virginia.

Franz Wright is the recipient of many awards and fellowships, including Guggenheim, Whiting, and NEA awards, for his poetry and translation. His most recent book is *Ill Lit: Selected & New Poems* (Oberlin, 1998).

David Young is Longman Professor of English and Creative Writing at Oberlin College and an editor of *FIELD*. He has published eight books of poems, including *The Planet on the Table: Selected and New Poems 1960-1990* (Wesleyan, 1991) and *Night Thoughts and Henry Vaughan* (Ohio State, 1994), as well as many volumes of translation and criticism. His most recent book is *Seasoning: A Poet's Year* (Ohio State, 1999).

ACKNOWLEDGMENTS

Anna Akhmatova: "Evening" and "Flowers and non-living things..." from *Poem without a Hero and Selected Poems*, trans. Lenore Mayhew and William McNaughton, copyright © 1989, reprinted by permission of Oberlin College Press. "The smell of inanimate things and flowers..." and "It's not with a lover's lyre, not at all..." from *Poems* by Anna Akhmatova, trans. Lyn Coffin. Translation copyright © 1983 by Lyn Coffin. Reprinted by permission of W. W. Norton & Company, Inc. "By smells of blooming things...," trans. Walter Arndt, from Anna Akhmatova, *Selected Poems*, copyright © 1976. "I don't speak with anyone for a week," trans. Richard McKane, from Anna Akhmatova, *Selected Poems*, copyright © 1969. "Terror, fingering things in the dark...," trans. Judith Hemschemeyer, from Anna Akhmatova, *Complete Poems*, copyright © 1976, reprinted by permission. "Four" from *Northern Elegies* and "It was frightful...," trans. Liza Tucker, first appeared in FIELD #18 (Spring 1978), reprinted by permission.

Agha Shahid Ali: "The Blessed Word" first appeared in FIELD #45 (Fall 1991). Reprinted by permission of the author.

Tom Andrews: "Glimpses into Something Ever Larger" first appeared in FIELD #41 (Fall 1989). "Lives of a Cell" first appeared in FIELD #49 (Fall 1993). Both selections reprinted by permission of the author.

Margaret Atwood: "On 'Waking at 3 A.M.'" first appeared in FIELD #41 (Fall 1989). Reprinted by permission of the author.

Bruce Beasley: "The Anti-Catechism of W. S. Merwin" first appeared in FIELD #57 (Fall 1997). Reprinted by permission of the author.

Marvin Bell: "On 'Arrival at the Waldorf'" first appeared in FIELD #21 (Fall 1979). "Williams and 'Dedication...'" first appeared in FIELD #29 (Fall 1983). Both selections reprinted by permission of the author.

Stephen Berg: "My Door" from *With Akhmatova at the Black Gates*, copyright 1981 by Stephen Berg. Used with the permission of the University of Illinois Press.

Elizabeth Bishop: "The Armadillo," "At the Fishhouses," "The End of March," "Filling Station," "First Death in Nova Scotia," "One Art," and "Sonnet" from *The Complete Poems 1927-1979* by Elizabeth Bishop. Copyright © 1979, 1983 by Alice Helen Methfessel. Reprinted by permission of Farrar, Straus & Giroux, Inc.

Robert Bly: "The Beauty of Sound" first appeared in FIELD #45 (Fall 1991). "Walking Around with Pablo Neruda" first appeared in FIELD #51 (Fall 1994). Both selections reprinted by permission of the author.

Philip Booth: "On 'Domination of Black'" first appeared in FIELD #21 (Fall 1979). Reprinted by permission of the author.

Marianne Boruch: "Original Shell" first appeared in FIELD #31 (Fall 1984). "Rhetoric and Mystery" first appeared in FIELD #35 (Fall 1986). "Becoming 'Epithalamion'" first appeared in FIELD #43 (Fall 1990). "The Shape of His Melancholy" first appeared in FIELD #51 (Fall 1994). "Three Spirits" first appeared in FIELD #53 (Fall 1995). All selections reprinted by permission of the author.

Ralph Burns: "The Plain Truth in 'The Truth'" first appeared in FIELD #35 (Fall 1986). Reprinted by permission of the author.

Fred Chappell: "The Longing to Belong" first appeared in FIELD #35 (Fall 1986). Reprinted
by permission of the author.

Martha Collins: "The Speech of Silence Laboring" first appeared in FIELD #45 (Fall 1991).
"Word-Work" first appeared in FIELD #53 (Fall 1995). "The Outer from the Inner" first appeared in FIELD #55 (Fall 1996). All selections reprinted by permission of the author.

Emily Dickinson: Poems reprinted by permission of the publishers and the Trustees of
Amherst College from *The Poems of Emily Dickinson*, Thomas H. Johnson, ed., Cam-
bridge, Mass.: The Belknap Press of Harvard University Press, copyright © 1951, 1955,
1979, 1983 by the President and Fellows of Harvard College.

Deborah Digges: "Translation and the Egg" first appeared in FIELD #39 (Fall 1988).
Reprinted by permission of the author.

Niccolò N. Donzella: "Elegy for an American" first appeared in FIELD #47 (Fall 1992).
Reprinted by permission of the author.

Norman Dubie: "Some Notes: Into the Sere and Yellow" first appeared in FIELD #33 (Fall
1985). Reprinted by permission of the author.

Sylva Fischerová: "The Time vs. the Age" first appeared in FIELD #45 (Fall 1991). "A Game
with Faces" first appeared in FIELD #49 (Fall 1993).

Robert Francis: "Blue Jay" reprinted from *The Orb Weaver* © 1960 by Robert Francis, Wesleyan University Press by permission of University Press of New England. "Sheep," "Excellence," "Remind Me of Apples," "His Running My Running," and "Silent Poem" ©
1938, 1944, 1974 by Robert Francis. Reprinted from *Robert Francis: Collected Poems,
1936-1976* (Amherst: University of Massachusetts Press, 1976) by permission of the publisher.

Dana Gioia: "From Pastoral to Apocalypse in Mid-Sentence" first appeared in FIELD #29
(Fall 1982). Reprinted by permission of the author.

Albert Goldbarth: "On 'The Glass of Water' " first appeared in FIELD #21 (Fall 1979).
Reprinted by permission of the author.

Beckian Fritz Goldberg: "The Case of 'The Tree, the Bird' " first appeared in FIELD #53 (Fall
1995). Reprinted by permission of the author.

Donald Hall: "Robert Francis: 'His Running My Running' " first appeared in FIELD #25 (Fall
1981), and subsequently in his *The Weather for Poetry: Essays, Reviews, and Notes on Poetry, 1977-81*, copyright © 1982 by the University of Michigan. "William Carlos Williams
and the Visual" first appeared in FIELD #29 (Fall 1983), and "Pound's Sounds" first appeared in FIELD #33 (Fall 1985); both were reprinted in *Poetry and Ambition: Essays,
1982-88*, copyright © 1988 by the University of Michigan. Reprinted by permission of the
author.

James Baker Hall: "If There Is a Place Where This Is the Language" first appeared in FIELD
#57 (Fall 1997). Reprinted by permission of the author.

Robert Hayden: "Middle Passage," "Those Winter Sundays," "Runagate Runagate," "Monet's
'Waterlilies,' " "Free Fantasia: Tiger Flowers," and "(American Journal)" copyright © 1962,
1966, 1970, 1975, 1978, 1982 by Robert Hayden. From *Collected Poems of Robert Hayden*
by Frederick Glaysher, editor. Reprinted by permission of Liveright Publishing Corporation.

Judith Hemschemeyer: "A Poet and Her Country" first appeared in FIELD #39 (Fall 1988).
Reprinted by permission of the author.

Calvin Hernton: "Shining" first appeared in FIELD #47 (Fall 1992). Reprinted by permission
of the author.

Edward Hirsch: "Surveyor of Worlds" first appeared in FIELD #49 (Fall 1993). Reprinted by permission of the author.

Jonathan Holden: "On 'With Kit, Age 7, at the Beach'" first appeared in FIELD #41 (Fall 1989). Reprinted by permission of the author.

Miroslav Holub: "Seeing" from *Interferon, or On Theater*, trans. David Young and Dana Hábová, copyright © 1982, reprinted by permission of Oberlin College Press. Other poems from *Intensive Care: Selected and New Poems*, copyright © 1996, reprinted by permission of Oberlin College Press. "W. C. Williams on Death" first appeared in FIELD #29 (Fall 1983).

Randall Jarrell: "The Bad Music," "Bats," "The Death of the Ball Turret Gunner," "Field and Forest," "The House in the Wood," "Moving," "Nestus Gurley," "Seele im Raum," and "The Truth" from *The Complete Poems* by Randall Jarrell. Copyright © 1969 and copyright renewed © 1997 by Mary von S. Jarrell. Reprinted by permission of Farrar, Straus & Giroux, Inc.

Laura Jensen: "Why I Like 'The Snow Man'" first appeared in FIELD #21 (Fall 1979). "Potential for Whole Totem" first appeared in FIELD #35 (Fall 1986). Both selections reprinted by permission of the author.

Donald Justice: "On Purity of Style" first appeared in FIELD #29 (Fall 1983) and subsequently in *Oblivion* (Story Line Press, 1998). Reprinted by permission of the author.

Shirley Kaufman: "On 'A Rabbit as King of the Ghosts'" first appeared in FIELD #21 (Fall 1979). Reprinted by permission of the author.

Yusef Komunyakaa: "Journey into '(American Journal)'" first appeared in FIELD #47 (Fall 1992). Reprinted by permission of the author.

Marilyn Krysl: "The Leper's Battle" first appeared in FIELD #39 (Fall 1988). Reprinted by permission of the author.

Maxine Kumin: "On 'A Postcard from the Volcano'" first appeared in FIELD #21 (Fall 1979). Reprinted by permission of the author.

James Laughlin: "Rambling Around Pound's Propertius" first appeared in FIELD #33 (Fall 1985). Reprinted by permission of New Directions Publishing Corp., agents for the Estate of James Laughlin.

Larry Levis: "So That: On Holub's 'Meeting Ezra Pound'" first appeared in FIELD #49 (Fall 1993).

Thomas Lux: "The Secret Joinery of Song" first appeared in FIELD #53 (Fall 1995). Reprinted by permission of the author.

Osip Mandelstam: "Take from my palms...," "We shall meet again...," "The Age," and "Black Earth" reprinted with the permission of Scribner, a division of Simon & Schuster, from *Osip Mandelstam: Selected Poems*, trans. Clarence Brown and W. S. Merwin. English translation copyright © 1973 Clarence Brown and W. S. Merwin. "I'm in a lion's trench..." reprinted by arrangement with Shambhala Publications, Inc., Boston, from *Osip Mandelstam* trans. James Greene © 1977. "To some, winter...," trans. David Young, first appeared in FIELD #45 (Fall 1991), reprinted by permission of the translator.

Paul Mariani: "An April of Small Waves" first appeared in FIELD #29 (Fall 1983). Reprinted by permission of the author.

William Matthews: "Young Ezra" first appeared in FIELD #33 (Fall 1985). "Layered Vision" first appeared in FIELD #57 (Fall 1997).

Lenore Mayhew: "Images from a Life" first appeared in FIELD #39 (Fall 1988). Reprinted by permission of the author.

Jerome Mazzaro: "'The Custom-House' and 'Lemons'" first appeared in FIELD #27 (Fall 1982).

J. D. McClatchy: "Some Notes on 'One Art'" first appeared in FIELD #31 (Fall 1984). Reprinted by permission of the author.

Lynne McMahon: "On 'The Steeple-Jack'" first appeared in FIELD #37 (Fall 1987). Reprinted by permission of the author.

Sandra McPherson: "On 'In the Greenhouse'" first appeared in FIELD #29 (Fall 1982). "'The Armadillo': A Commentary" first appeared in FIELD #31 (Fall 1984). Both selections reprinted by permission of the author.

Christopher Merrill: "In Search of the Genuine" first appeared in FIELD #57 (Fall 1997). Reprinted by permission of the author.

James Merrill: "On 'Mottetti VII'" first appeared in FIELD #29 (Fall 1982). Reprinted by permission of the Literary Estate of James Merrill at Washington University.

W. S. Merwin: "Some Last Questions," "I Live Up Here," "The Bridges," "The Piper," "Habits," "Bread and Butter," "Beginning," "The Port," and "The Cold Before the Moonrise" from *The Second Four Books of Poems*; "The Weight of Sleep" from *The Miner's Pale Children*; "Search Party" from *Travels*; "Completion" and "The Red" from *The Vixen*. All poems copyright by W. S. Merwin and reprinted with his permission.

Barbara Molloy-Olund: "Man—Sea—Silence" first appeared in FIELD #37 (Fall 1987).

Eugenio Montale: "In the Greenhouse," "Two in Twilight," "Visit to Fadin," "Syria," "The Eel," "Dora Markus," and "Fiesole Window," trans. Charles Wright, reprinted by permission of Oberlin College Press from Eugenio Montale, *The Storm and Other Poems*, copyright © 1978 by Oberlin College. "The Custom-House," "Lemons," and "News from Mount Amiata," trans. Vinio Rossi and David Young, reprinted by permission of the translators. "Mottetti XVII," trans. Dana Gioia, first appeared in FIELD #27 (Fall 1982), reprinted by permission of the translator. "Dora Markus," trans. Reg Saner, first appeared in FIELD #27 (Fall 1982), reprinted by permission of the translator.

Marianne Moore: "The Steeple-Jack" (46-line version) and "By Disposition of Angels" reprinted with the permission of Simon & Schuster from *The Collected Poems of Marianne Moore*. Copyright 1951 by Marianne Moore; copyright renewed © 1979 by Lawrence B. Brinn and Louise Crane. "A Grave," "Silence," "Nine Nectarines and Other Porcelain," and "The Frigate Pelican" reprinted with the permission of Simon & Schuster from *Selected Poems of Marianne Moore*. Copyright 1935 by Marianne Moore; copyright renewed © 1963 by Marianne Moore and T. S. Eliot.

Carol Muske: "Alba LXXIX" first appeared in FIELD #33 (Fall 1985). "The Transparent Mask" first appeared in FIELD #57 (Fall 1997). Both selections reprinted by permission of the author.

Pablo Neruda: "Melancholy Inside Families," trans. Robert Bly and James Wright, reprinted from *Neruda and Vallejo: Selected Poems*, ed. Robert Bly (Beacon Press, 1993). Copyright © 1967 by Robert Bly, reprinted with his permission. "Ode to the Table," trans. Ken Krabbenhoft, copyright © 1994, reprinted with his permission. "Walking Around," trans. W. S. Merwin, copyright © 1970, reprinted with his permission. All poems translated by William O'Daly first published as credited in his essay and reprinted with his permission.

William O'Daly: "To the Earth and Its Winter" first appeared in FIELD #51 (Fall 1994). Reprinted by permission of the author.

Linda Pastan: "On 'Ask Me'" first appeared in FIELD #41 (Fall 1989). Reprinted by permission of the author.

Stanley Plumly: "'The Glass of Water': A Footnote" first appeared in FIELD #21 (Fall 1979). "Reading Williams" first appeared in FIELD #29 (Fall 1983). "Pound's Garden" first appeared in FIELD #33 (Fall 1985). "Absent Things" first appeared in FIELD #37 (Fall 1987). "Hear What I Do" first appeared in FIELD #43 (Fall 1990). "Doors Ajar" first appeared in FIELD #55 (Fall 1996). All selections reprinted by permission of the author.

Ezra Pound: Poetry from *Personae* and *The Cantos* copyright 1928 by Ezra Pound. Copyright © 1971 by Ezra Pound. Copyright © 1971 by the Trustees of the Ezra Pound Literary Property Trust. Used by permission of New Directions Publishing Corporation.

Sonia Raiziss: "Montale's 'Dream' Poem" first appeared in FIELD #29 (Fall 1982).

Theodore Roethke: "The Lost Son," "Frau Bauman, Frau Schmidt and Frau Schwartze," "The Waking," copyright 1947, 1952, 1953 by Theodore Roethke. "The Tree, the Bird" and "The Chums" copyright © 1961, 1963 by Beatrice Roethke, Administratrix of the Estate of Theodore Roethke. From *The Collected Poems of Theodore Roethke*. Used by permission of Doubleday, a division of Bantam Doubleday Dell Publishing Group, Inc.

David St. John: "Eugenio Montale's 'Two in Twilight'" first appeared in FIELD #27 (Fall 1982). "Randall Jarrell's 'Seele im Raum'" first appeared in FIELD #35 (Fall 1986). "Pablo Neruda's 'Walking Around'" first appeared in FIELD #51 (Fall 1994). These essays subsequently appeared in *Where the Angels Come Toward Us: Selected Essays, Reviews and Interviews* (White Pine Press, 1995), © 1995 by David St. John. All selections reprinted by permission of the author.

Reg Saner: "Montale and the Outsider: 'Dora Markus'" first appeared in FIELD #27 (Fall 1982). Reprinted by permission of the author.

Sherod Santos: "A Connoisseur of Loneliness" first appeared in FIELD #31 (Fall 1984). Reprinted by permission of the author.

Dennis Schmitz: "On 'Peter Quince at the Clavier'" first appeared in FIELD #21 (Fall 1979). "On 'Carrion Comfort'" first appeared in FIELD #43 (Fall 1990). "Distancing" first appeared in FIELD #49 (Fall 1993). All selections reprinted by permission of the author.

Charles Simic: "Streets Strewn with Garbage" first appeared in FIELD #29 (Fall 1983), and subsequently in his *The Uncertain Certainty: Interviews, Essays, and Notes on Poetry*, copyright © 1985 by the University of Michigan. "On 'At the Bomb Testing Site'" first appeared in FIELD #41 (Fall 1989), and subsequently in his *Wonderful Words, Silent Truth: Essays on Poetry and a Memoir*, copyright © 1990 by the University of Michigan. "Ambiguity's Wedding" first appeared in FIELD #55 (Fall 1996), and will appear in *Jackstraws* (Harcourt Brace, 1999). Reprinted by permission of the author.

W. D. Snodgrass: "Robert Hayden: The Man in the Middle" first appeared in FIELD #47 (Fall 1992). Reprinted by permission of the author.

Marcia Southwick: "On 'Dedication for a Plot of Ground'" first appeared in FIELD #29 (Fall 1983). "A Slab of Clay, a Handful of Dust" first appeared in FIELD #39 (Fall 1988). Both selections reprinted by permission of the author.

Elizabeth Spires: "Questions of Knowledge" first appeared in FIELD #31 (Fall 1984). Reprinted by permission of the author.

William Stafford: "Seeing and Perceiving" and "Knowing" © 1982 from *Glass Face in the Rain* (Harper & Row); "Owls at the Shakespeare Festival" and "Brother" © 1987 from *Oregon Message* (Harper & Row); these selections reprinted by permission of the Estate of William Stafford. "At the Bomb Testing Site," "Thinking for Berky," "Note," "At the Playground," "With Kit, Age 7, at the Beach," "Waking at 3 A.M.," "Ask Me," "Things I Learned Last Week," "1940," "Thinking about Being Called Simple by a Critic," and "Sur-

C. D. Wright: "Mission of the Surviving Gunner" first appeared in FIELD #35 (Fall 1986). "Echo Rising" first appeared in FIELD #57 (Fall 1997). Both selections reprinted by permission of the author.

Charles Wright: "Improvisations on Montale" first appeared in FIELD #29 (Fall 1982). "Improvisations on Pound" first appeared in FIELD #33 (Fall 1985). "Improvisations: With Father Hopkins on Lake Como" first appeared in FIELD #43 (Fall 1990). All selections reprinted by permission of the author.

Franz Wright: "Persephone's Bees: Thoughts on Mandelstam" first appeared in FIELD #45 (Fall 1991). Reprinted by permission of the author.

David Young: "Gaiety of Language" first appeared in FIELD #21 (Fall 1979). "Robert Francis and the Bluejay" first appeared in FIELD #25 (Fall 1981). "The Poem that Took the Place of a Mountain" first appeared in FIELD #27 (Fall 1982). "Day for Night" first appeared in FIELD #35 (Fall 1986). "Clipped Wings" first appeared in FIELD #37 (Fall 1987). "Mending What Can't Be Mended" first appeared in FIELD #39 (Fall 1988). "Shivers of Summer Wind" first appeared in FIELD #41 (Fall 1989). "Surprised by Grief" first appeared in FIELD #43 (Fall 1990). "Stars Versus Salt" first appeared in FIELD #45 (Fall 1991). "The Wave That Does Not Die" first appeared in FIELD #51 (Fall 1994). "Electric Moccasins" first appeared in FIELD #55 (Fall 1996). "Caught Breath" first appeared in FIELD #57 (Fall 1997). All selections reprinted by permission of the author.

Every effort has been made to locate all rights holders and to clear reprint permissions. This process has been complicated, and if any required acknowledgments have been omitted, or any rights overlooked, it is unintentional and forgiveness is requested.

INDEX

Akhmatova, Anna: 213-40

Ali, Agha Shahid: on Osip Mandelstam, 248-52

Andrews, Tom: on Miroslav Holub, 551-56; on William Stafford, 523-25

Atwood, Margaret: on William Stafford, 517-20

Beasley, Bruce: on W. S. Merwin, 558-62

Bell, Marvin: on Wallace Stevens, 88-90; on William Carlos Williams, 100-103

Bishop, Elizabeth: 385-415

Bly, Robert: on Osip Mandelstam, 266-67; on Pablo Neruda, 340-45

Booth, Philip: on Wallace Stevens, 66-68

Boruch, Marianne: on Elizabeth Bishop, 398-401; on Gerard Manley Hopkins, 56-59; on Randall Jarrell, 491-95; on Pablo Neruda, 326-29; on Theodore Roethke, 360-63

Burns, Ralph: on Randall Jarrell, 478-81

Chappell, Fred: on Randall Jarrell, 465-71

Collins, Martha: on Emily Dickinson, 17-19; on Osip Mandelstam, 263-65; on Theodore Roethke, 371-74

Dickinson, Emily: 1-26

Digges, Deborah: on Anna Akhmatova, 227-31

Donzella, Niccolò N.: on Robert Hayden, 420-22

Dubie, Norman: on Ezra Pound, 154-60

Fischerová, Sylva: on Miroslav Holub, 547-50; on Osip Mandelstam, 259-62

Francis, Robert: 307-23

Gioia, Dana: on Eugenio Montale, 282-84

Goldbarth, Albert: on Wallace Stevens, 83-84

Goldberg, Beckian Fritz: on Theodore Roethke, 378-84

Hall, Donald: on Robert Francis, 311-12; on Ezra Pound, 134-37; on William Carlos Williams, 106-10

Hall, James Baker: on W. S. Merwin, 571-80

Hayden, Robert: 417-53

Hemschemeyer, Judith: on Anna Akhmatova, 224-26

Hernton, Calvin: on Robert Hayden, 437-44

Hirsch, Edward: on Miroslav Holub, 536-37

Holden, Jonathan: on William Stafford, 514-16

Holub, Miroslav: 535-56; on William Carlos Williams, 113-17

Hopkins, Gerard Manley: 27-59

Jarrell, Randall: 455-500

Jensen, Laura: on Randall Jarrell, 456-59; on Wallace Stevens, 73

Justice, Donald: on William Carlos Williams, 96-99

Kaufman, Shirley: on Wallace Stevens, 79-80

Komunyakaa, Yusef: on Robert Hayden, 448-53

Krysl, Marilyn: on Anna Akhmatova, 238-40

Kumin, Maxine: on Wallace Stevens, 74-75

Laughlin, James: on Ezra Pound, 144-53

Levis, Larry: on Miroslav Holub, 538-41

Lux, Thomas: on Theodore Roethke, 364-68

Mandelstam, Osip: 241-67

Mariani, Paul: on William Carlos Williams, 126-31

Matthews, William: on W. S. Merwin, 591-93; on Ezra Pound, 138-41

Mayhew, Lenore: on Anna Akhmatova, 214-16

Mazzaro, Jerome: on Eugenio Montale, 272-77

McClatchy, J. D.: on Elizabeth Bishop, 406-11

McMahon, Lynne: on Marianne Moore, 182-85

McPherson, Sandra: on Elizabeth Bishop, 386-88; on Eugenio Montale, 270-71

Merrill, Christopher: on W. S. Merwin, 587-90

Merrill, James: on Eugenio Montale, 285

Merwin, W. S.: 557-96

Molloy-Olund, Barbara: on Marianne Moore, 193-97

Montale, Eugenio: 269-306

Moore, Marianne: 181-211

Muske, Carol: on W. S. Merwin, 594-96; on Ezra Pound, 161-71

Neruda, Pablo: 325-57

O'Daly, William: on Pablo Neruda, 346-57

Pastan, Linda: on William Stafford, 521-22

Plumly, Stanley: on Emily Dickinson, 11-16; on Gerard Manley Hopkins, 51-56; on Marianne Moore, 198-200; on Ezra Pound, 141-43;

on Wallace Stevens, 84-85; on William Carlos Williams, 123-25

Pound, Ezra: 133-79

Raiziss, Sonia: on Eugenio Montale, 286-90

Roethke, Theodore: 359-84

Saner, Reg: on Eugenio Montale, 296-99

Santos, Sherod: on Elizabeth Bishop, 402-405

Schmitz, Dennis: on Gerard Manley Hopkins, 47-50; on Miroslav Holub, 542-46; on Wallace Stevens, 62-65

Simic, Charles: on Emily Dickinson, 5; on William Stafford, 502-503; on William Carlos Williams, 118-19

Snodgrass, W. D.: on Robert Hayden, 423-36

Southwick, Marcia: on Anna Akhmatova, 221-23; on William Carlos Williams, 104-105

Spires, Elizabeth: on Elizabeth Bishop, 393-97

St. John, David: on Randall Jarrell, 472-77; on Eugenio Montale, 278-81; on Pablo Neruda, 337-40

Stafford, William: 501-34; on Wallace Stevens, 81-82

Stern, Gerald: on Gerard Manley Hopkins, 35-37; on Theodore Roethke, 375-77; on William Carlos Williams, 120-22

Stevens, Wallace: 61-93

Stewart, Pamela: on Wallace Stevens, 86-87

Taylor, Henry: on William Stafford, 504-13

Turner, Alberta: on Anna Akhmatova, 217-20; on Elizabeth Bishop, 412-14; on Robert Francis, 316-

18; on Robert Hayden, 418-19; on
Theodore Roethke, 369-71; on
William Stafford, 526-27; on Wal-
lace Stevens, 69-72

Upton, Lee: on Gerard Manley Hopkins, 44-46; on Marianne Moore,
201-203

Valentine, Jean: on Elizabeth Bishop,
415

Walker, David: on Elizabeth Bishop,
389-92; on Emily Dickinson, 6-
10; on Robert Francis, 321-23; on
Randall Jarrell, 496-500; on W. S.
Merwin, 563-68; on Marianne
Moore, 186-92; on Wallace
Stevens, 91-93; on William Carlos
Williams, 111-12

Wallace, Robert: on Robert Francis,
313-15

Walton, Anthony: on Robert Hayden,
445-47

Weigl, Bruce: on Randall Jarrell, 460-
62

Wilbur, Richard: on Robert Francis,
319-20

Willard, Nancy: on Emily Dickinson,
2-4; on Randall Jarrell, 487-90

Williams, William Carlos: 95-131

Wright, C. D.: on Randall Jarrell, 462-
64; on W. S. Merwin, 569-70

Wright, Charles: on Gerard Manley
Hopkins, 28-34; on Eugenio
Montale, 300-306; on Ezra
Pound, 172-79

Wright, Franz: on Osip Mandelstam,
242-47

Young, David: on Anna Akhmatova,
232-37; on Emily Dickinson, 20-
26; on Robert Francis, 308-10; on
Gerard Manley Hopkins, 38-43;
on Randall Jarrell, 482-86; on
Osip Mandelstam, 253-58; on W.
S. Merwin, 581-86; on Eugenio
Montale, 291-95; on Marianne
Moore, 204-211; on Pablo
Neruda, 330-36; on William
Stafford, 528-34; on Wallace
Stevens, 76-78